A
DICTIONARY OF
DIFFICULT
WORDS

SIGNET Books for Your Reference Shelf

A
DICTIONARY OF
DIFFICULT
WORDS

Compiled by
ROBERT H. HILL

A SIGNET BOOK
NEW AMERICAN LIBRARY
TIMES MIRROR

PREFACE

THE only aspects of this Dictionary requiring comment or explanation are those concerned with the arrangement of entries and the pronunciation system.

The arrangement is, of course, alphabetical; but in certain cases where it is convenient or where the alphabetical order is not unduly departed from by doing so, a system of grouping for compounds and derivatives has been adopted. The entry that heads the group is either the first word in the group from the alphabetical standpoint, or the most familiar word of the group; the remaining entries of the group comprise different "endings" to the same stem as that of the main entry. By means of such grouping reference is facilitated, and the number of entries which it is possible to include in a book of this size is greatly increased.

Foreign words and phrases are not relegated to a separate vocabulary, but are included in the body of the book in their alphabetical order.

As regards pronunciation, the simplest method consistent with accuracy has been adopted. The ordinary alphabet, with the addition of only six phonetic symbols, has been used. Vowels are clearly distinguished; short vowels are printed with no modification, and long vowels bear the conventional sign of length (–) above them. Consonants are printed as ordinarily pronounced. The six symbols referred to are: ə, representing the vowel murmur; dh, representing the voiced *th* sound; zh, representing the sound of *s* in *pleasure*; and ṅ, ü and k̇, representing the French nasal and fronted *u*, and the Scottish guttural *ch* respectively. At the foot of each pair of facing pages there is a key to the pronunciation, and the system is more fully explained on page 8.

It should be emphasised, since this is one of the departures from common practice in this Dictionary, that the pronunciations given are those occurring in ordinary speech, particularly as it is spoken *at the usual speed* by a fluent speaker, and do not represent the pedantic exactitude that insists on the clear and full value being given to every vowel and consonant.

Extremely precise pronunciations, though of course correct, are too often merely the sign of ignorance; one who is thoroughly familiar with a word does not say it as if he were reading it syllable by syllable from a pronouncing dictionary. For this reason the difficult words in this work are given the pronunciations with which they are spoken by those who habitually use them; the aim is to show how a word *is* pronounced by the majority of educated persons rather than how it *should be* pronounced.

R. H. H.

ABBREVIATIONS
USED IN THIS WORK

abbr.—abbreviation, abbreviated as.
adj.—adjective.
adv.—adverb.
agric., *Agric.*—agricultural, agriculture.
Amer.—American, America.
anat., *Anat.*—anatomical, anatomy.
anct.—ancient.
app.—applied.
Arab.—Arabic, Arabian.
arch., *Arch.*—archaic; archæological, archæology.
archit., *Archit.*—architectural, architecture.
arith., *Arith.*—arithmetical, arithmetic.
astrol., *Astrol.*—astrological, astrology.
astron., *Astron.*—astronomical, astronomy.
Austral.—Australian, Australia.
biol., *Biol.*—biological, biology.
bot., *Bot.*—botanical, botany.
bp.—bishop.
Brit.—British.
c.—circa (about).
Can.—Canadian, Canada.
cent.—century.
Cent.—Central.
chem., *Chem.*—chemical, chemistry.
Chin.—Chinese, China.
comm.—commercial, commerce.
dept.—department.
dial.—dialect, dialectal.
E.—East.
eccl., *Eccl.*—ecclesiastical.
e.g.—for example.
elec., *Elec.*—electrical, electricit
erron.—erroneous(ly).
espec.—especially.
etc.— and other things.
Eur.—Europe, European.
excl.—exclamation.
fem.—feminine.
Fr.—French, France.
gen.—generally.
geog., *Geog.*—geographical, geography.
geol., *Geol.*—geological, geology.
geom., *Geom.*—geometrical, geometry
Ger.—German, Germany.
govt.—government.
Gr.—Greek.
gram., *Gram.*—grammatical, grammar.
Gt. Brit.—Great Britain.
her., *Her.*—heraldic, heraldry.
Hind.—Hindu, Hindi, Hindustani.
Hung.—Hungarian.
i.—intransitive.
i.e.—that is.
Ind.—India, Indian; Indies.
instr.—instrument.
Ir.—Irish, Ireland.
It.—Italian, Italy.
Jap.—Japanese, Japan.
lat.—latitude.
Lat.—Latin.
lit., *Lit.*—literally; literary, literature.

log., *Log.*—logical, logic.
long.—longitude.
mag., *Mag.*—magnetic, magnetism.
manuf.—manufacture.
Matt.—Matthew (Gospel).
mech., *Mech.*—mechanical, mechanics or machinery.
med., *Med.*—medical, medicine.
metall., *Metall.*—metallurgical, metallurgy.
meteor., *Meteor.*—meteorological, meteorology.
Mex.—Mexican, Mexico.
mil., *Mil.*—military (affairs).
mod.—modern.
Moham.—Mohammedan.
MS(S).—manuscript(s).
mt., Mt.—mountain.
mus., *Mus.*—musical, music.
myth., *Myth.*—mythical, mythology.
n.—noun.
n.pl.—plural noun.
N.—North.
N.Z.—New Zealand.
obs.—obsolete.
opp.—opposite.
orig.—originally.
ornith., *Ornith.*—ornithological, ornithology.
parl., *Parl.*—parliamentary, parliament.
pert.—pertaining.
phil., *Phil.*—philosophical, philosophy.
philol., *Philol.*—philological, philology.
phon., *Phon.*—phonetic, phonetics.
photog., *Photog.*—photographical, photography.
phys., *Phys.*—physical, physics.
pl.—plural.
pop.—popularly.
Port.—Portugal, Portuguese.
psych., *Psych.*—psychological, psychology.
rad., *Rad.*—radio.
R.C.—Roman Catholic.
relig.—religious, religion.
respec.—respectively.
rhet., *Rhet.*—rhetorical, rhetoric.
Rom.—Roman.
Russ.—Russian, Russia.
S.—South.
Scot.—Scottish, Scotland.
sev.—several.
sing.—singular.
sl.—slang.
Sp.—Spanish, Spain.
surg., *Surg.*—surgical, surgery.
t.—transitive.
theol., *Theol.*—theological, theology.
Turk.—Turkish, Turkey.
v.—verb.
v.i.—intransitive verb.
v.t.—transitive verb.
W.—West.
Yid.—Yiddish.
zoo., *Zoo.*—zoological, zoology.

Note.—In order to save space the word that forms the main entry of a group of derivatives and compounds is often abbreviated to its initial letter when it occurs again in the group. E.g., under aberration occur the entries chromatic a. and spherical a., meaning "chromatic aberration" and "spherical aberration" respectively.

PRONUNCIATION

a	=*a* in *fat*.	ōō	=*oo* in *fool*.
ah	=*a* in *father*.	ōōr	=*oor* in *moor*.
ā	=*a* in *fate*.	ow	=*ou* in *foul*.
ār	=*are* in *fare*.	u	=*u* in *hull*.
aw	=*a* in *fall*.	ū	=*u* in *tune*.
e	=*e* in *fell*.	ūr	=*ure* in *cure*.
ē	=*e* in *feel*.		
ēr	=*ear* in *fear*.	th	=*th* in *think*.
ə	=*er* in *father*.	dh	=*th* in *there*.
əi	=*ur* in *furl*.	zh	=*s* in *leisure*.
i	=*i* in *fill*.	ṅ	=Fr. nasal :
ī	=*i* in *file*.		
īr	=*ire* in *fire*.	ahṅ	=*ant* in *gant*.
o	=*o* in *fond*.	awṅ	=*on* in *bon*.
ō	=*oa* in *foal*.	aṅ	=*ain* in *pain*.
ōr	=*ore* in *fore*.	uṅ	=*un* in *lundi*.
oo	=*u* in *full*.	ü	=Fr. fronted *u*, as in *tue*.
		k̇	=*ch* in Scottish *loch*.

Note.—Pronunciations of Latin phrases follow the "old" or "English" style, which is still more common in everyday usage than the so-called "neo-Classical" style.

A DICTIONARY
OF DIFFICULT WORDS

A

aardvark (ahd′vahk), *n.* long-snouted, ant-eating, burrowing mammal of S. Africa.

aardwolf (ahd′woolf), *n.* hyena-like, burrowing mammal of S. Africa.

aasvogel (ahs′fōgl), S. African *n.* vulture.

aba (ah′bə), *n.* coarse, striped, camel-hair or goat-hair fabric of Arabia ; loose Arab coat.

abaca (ab′əkə), *n.* Philippine Is. plant, yielding fibre for Manila hemp.

abaction (abak′shn), *n.* cattle-stealing.

abacist (ab′əsist), *n.* person using abacus ; calculator.

abaculus (abak′ūləs), *n.* small tile for mosaic.

abacus (ab′əkəs), *n.* frame with beads for calculation ; *Archit.*, uppermost member of capital of column.

abalone (abəlō′ni), *n.* ear-shaped marine shell-fish, yielding mother-of-pearl ; ear-shell.

abandonment (aban′dənmənt), *n. Comm.*, giving over by owner to underwriters of ship or cargo damaged beyond recovery. **-nee** (abandənē′), *n.* underwriter to whom such ship or cargo is abandoned.

abapical (abap′ikl), *adj.* at lowest point.

abarticular (abahtik′ūlə), *adj.* not connected with joint. **-lation**, *n.* diarthrosis.

à bas (ah bah′), *Fr.*, "down with."

abasia (abā′zhiə), *n.* inability to control muscles in walking. **-sic** (-sic), *adj.*

abatement (abāt′mənt), *n. Law*, statement of cause why civil action should be abandoned ; interposition of stranger between death and entry of heir on a seisin ; *Her.*, mark on arms to indicate bastardy.

abatis, -ttis (ab′ətis), *n.* barricade of fallen trees.

abatjour (abazhūr′), *Fr. n.* skylight ; device at window to throw light downwards.

abat-sons (abasawn′), *Fr. n.* device for directing sound downwards.

abattoir (ab′atwah), *n.* slaughter-house.

abat-vent (abavahn′). *Fr. n.* sloping slats to break force of wind.

abat-voix (abavwah′), Fr. *n.* sounding-board.

abaxial, -ile (abaks′iəl, -īl), *adj.* distant, or turned away, from axis.

abb (ab), *n.* yarn for warp ; part of fleece.

abba (ab′ə), Aramaic *n.* father ; bishop in Syriac and Coptic churches.

abbozzo (abot′sō), *n.* rough, preliminary sketch.

abditive (ab′ditiv), *adj.* remote ; hidden. **-tory**, *n.* secret hiding-place.

abdominous (abdom′inəs), *adj.* having big belly.

abducent (abdūs′ənt), *adj.* carrying or turning away, *espec.* of nerve or muscle.

abecedary (ābēsē′dəri), *n.* book arranged in alphabetical order ; elementary text-book. **-rian** (-dār′iən), *n.* member of 16th-century German Anabaptist sect who refused to learn to read.

abele (abēl′), *n.* white poplar.

aberdevine (abədevīn′), *n.* siskin.

aberrant (aber′ənt), *adj.* wandering ; deviating, *espec.* from virtue ; abnormal. **-nce**, *n.*

aberration (abərā′shn), *n.* deviation ; momentary mental lapse ; *Astr.*, apparent deviation from heavenly body's true position due

---

hat, bah, hāte, hāre, crawl ; pen, ēve, hēre ; it, īce, fīre ; on, bōne, boil, bōre, howl ; foot, fōōd, bōōr, hull, tūbe, pūre. ə=*er* in *father* ; ə̄=*er* in *pert* ; th=*th* in *thin* ; dh=*th* in *then* ; zh=*s* in *pleasure* ; k=*ch* in *loch* ; ñ=Fr. nasal *n* ; ü=Fr. *u*.

to movement of observer. **chromatic a.**, focusing of light of different colours at different points. **spherical a.**, focusing at different points of rays passing through different parts of lens.

ab extra (ab eks'trah), *Lat.*, "from outside."

abietic (abiet'ik), *adj.* pert. to fir tree or resin.

ab initio (ab inish'iō), *Lat.*, "from the beginning."

abiochemistry (abiəkem'istri), *n.* inorganic chemistry.

abiogenesis (abiəjen'isis), *n.* generation of living from inanimate matter. **-netic** (-jinet'ik), *adj.* **-nist** (-oj'ənist), *n.* believer in that theory.

abiology (abiol'əji), *n.* study of inanimate things.

abiosis (abiō'sis), *n.* absence of life. **-otic** (-ot'ik), *adj.*

abiotrophy (abiot'rəfi), *n.* physical degeneration; loss of vitality. **-phic** (-of'ik), *adj.*

abirritate (abir'itāt), *v.t. Med.*, reduce irritation or sensitiveness. **-tant**, *n.* such drug. **-tation**, *n.* loss of sensitiveness in tissues; debility.

abkari (abkahr'i), Anglo-Ind. *n.* sale or manufacture of, or excise duty on, spirits.

ablactate (ablak'tāt), *v.t.* wean. **-tation**, *n.*

ablation (ablā'shn), *n.* removal; wearing away. **-titious**, *adj.* decreasing, *espec. Astron.*, app. to force decreasing gravitational pull between heavenly bodies.

ablative (ab'lətiv), *adj.* signifying agency; *n.* such gram. case. **a. absolute**, Lat. adverbial phrase formed by noun and adjunct (*espec.* participle), both in a.

ablaut (ab'lowt), *n.* special change or relation in vowel sound, as in vowels of "ring, rang, rung."

ablegate (ab'ligāt), *n.* special papal envoy.

ablepsia (ablep'siə), *n.* blindness. **-ptic**, *adj.*

abluent (ab'looənt), *n.* & *adj.* cleansing (substance).

ablution (ablōō'shn), *n.* act of washing; *pl.* washing the face and hands; washing place. **-ary**, *adj.*

abnegate (ab'nigāt), *v.t.* renounce. **-tion**, *n.*

aboma (abō'mə), *n.* S. Amer. snake; ringed boa.

abomasum (abomā'səm), *n.* fourth stomach of ruminants.

aboral (abōr'əl), *adj.* distant from, or opposite to, mouth.

aborigine (abərij'inē), *n.* inhabitant from earliest times. **-nal**, *adj.* indigenous; *n.* aborigine.

aboulia, **-bul-** (aboo'liə, -ū'-), *n.* loss of will power. **-ic**, *adj.* **-iomania**, *n.* form of insanity marked by a.

ab ovo (ab ō'vō), *Lat.*, "from the egg"; from the beginning. **a.o. usque ad mala**, "from the egg to the apples"; from the beginning to the end.

abrade (abrād'), *v.t.* rub off; scrape; cause injury thus.

abrasion (abrā'zhn), *n.* injury caused by, or act of, rubbing or scraping; graze. **-sive**, *adj.* causing or used in abrasion; *n.* such substance.

abreaction (abriak'shn), *n.* removal of psych. complex.

abreuvoir (abrā'vwah), *n.* gap between stones in masonry.

abrogate (ab'rəgāt), *v.t.* cancel; repeal. **-tion**, *n.*

abruption (abrup'shn), *n.* sudden stop; breaking in two.

abscind (absind'), *v.t.* cut off; pare.

abscissa (absis'ə), *n.* (*pl.* -ae), *Math.*, horizontal distance of point from fixed line.

abscission (absish'n), *n.* cutting off; separation, *espec.* of cells at base of leaf-stalk.

absconce (abskons'), *n. R.C.*, dark lantern used in night offices.

absentee (absentē'), *n.* one not present; worker absent from work; *adj.* app. to landlord not living in country from which he derives his rent. **-ism**, *n.* practice of such landlords; habitual absence from work.

absente reo (absen'ti rē'ō), *Lat. Law*, "the defendant being absent" (*abbr.* **abs. re.**).

absinth(e) (ab'sinth; Fr., absańt'), *n.* wormwood; liqueur flavoured with wormwood. **-thial**, *adj.* **-thism**, *n.* condition due to excessive consumption of a.

absit omen (ab'sit ō'men), *Lat.*, "may there be no evil omen"; may no harm result.

absolutism (ab'səlootizm), *n.* tyrannical government ; principle of autocracy.

absolutory (absol'ūtri), *adj.* absolving ; forgiving.

absorptiometer (absawptiom'itə), *n.* instrument measuring solubility of gases in liquid.

abstemious (abstē'miəs), *adj.* practising temperance ; teetotal.

absterge (abstəj'), *v.t.* wipe clean ; purify. **-nt,** *adj.* cleansing ; *n.* such substance. **-rsion,** *n.*

abstinent (ab'stinənt), *adj.* abstemious ; fasting. **-nce,** *n.*

abterminal (abtə'minəl), *adj.* from end inwards.

ab urbe condita (ab ə̄'bi kon'ditə), *Lat.,* "from the foundation of the city" (Rome), in c. 753 B.C. (*abbr.* **A.U.C.**).

abut (abut'), *v.i.* & *t.* be adjacent to ; lean upon. **-ment,** *n.* supporting part of arch, etc. ; part of bridge next to land. **-tal,** *n.* land or parish boundary. **-ter,** *n.* proprietor of premises adjacent.

aby(e) (abī'), *v.t.* pay penalty of ; atone for.

abyssal (abis'əl), *adj.* like or pert. to abyss ; *Biol.,* more than 300 fathoms below surface of sea.

academic (akədem'ik), *adj.* pert. to academy ; learned ; unpractical. **-al,** *adj.* pert. to university or other academy. **-als,** *n. pl.* university costume. **-ian** (akadəm ish'ən), *n.* member of academy, *espec.* of Arts. **-mism,** *n.* formalism. **-s,** *n.pl.* learned debate.

acajou (ak'əzhōō), Fr. *n.* cashew nut and tree ; mahogany tree and timber.

acaleph (ak'əlef), *n.* kind of stinging jellyfish.

acanaceous (akənā'shəs), *adj.* prickly.

acantha (akan'thə), *n.* prickle. **-ceous,** *adj.*

acanthion (akan'thiən), *n.* species of porcupine.

acanthus (akan'thəs), *n.* kind of prickly herbaceous plant, the bear's breech ; *Archit.,* leaf decoration used on Corinthian capital.

acariasis (akarī'əsis), *n.* infestation with mites or ticks ; the itch.

acaricide (akar'isīd), *n.* substance killing mites. **-dal,** *adj.*

acarpous (akah'pəs), *adj. Bot.,* not yielding fruit.

acatalectic (akatəlek'tik), *adj.* metrically complete ; *n.* such verse line.

acatalepsy (akat'əlepsi), *n.* state of being impossible to understand ; *Phil.,* Sceptic doctrine that knowledge cannot be certain ; *Med.,* uncertainty of diagnosis ; feeblemindedness. **-ptic** (-lep'tik), *adj.*

acaudate (akaw'dāt), *adj.* lacking tail.

accelerometer (akselərom'itə), *n.* instrument measuring acceleration.

accensor (aksen'sə), *n.* R.C., acolyte.

accentor (aksen'tə), *n.* hedgesparrow ; *Amer.,* water-thrush.

acceptance (aksep'təns), *n. Comm.,* agreement to pay bill of exchange when due. **a.-house,** merchant banker. **a. for honour,** taking up by person other than drawer of bill of exchange to protect honour of party to bill.

acceptilation (akseptilā'shn), *n.* free remission of liability or debt ; *Theol.,* God's acceptance of Christ's sufferings as complete atonement for man's sins.

accessit (akses'it), *n.* honourable mention of one who comes nearest to a prize.

acciaccatura (achakətūr'ə), *n. Mus.,* very short note played before a longer note ; short appoggiatura.

accidence (ak'sidəns), *n.* science of gram. inflexions.

accident (ak'sidənt), *n. Log.,* nonessential ; attribute not included in definition ; *Gram.,* change in form of word, *espec.* by inflexion.

accidental (aksiden'təl), *n. Mus.,* note made temporarily sharp, flat, or natural. **-ism,** *n. Med.,* system based on symptoms only.

accipiter (aksip'itə), *n.* bird of prey. **-tral, -trine,** *adj.* like such bird ; rapacious. **-trary,** *n.* falconer.

accismus (aksiz'məs), *n.* rhet. device of pretending to refuse.

acclinate (ak'lināt), *adj.* sloping upward.

acclivity (akliv'iti), *n.* slope upward. **-tous, -vous** (-li'vəs), *adj.*

accolade (ak'əlād), *n.* ceremony of knighting ; *Mus.,* vertical line coupling staves ; *Archit.,* curved moulding.

ə=*er* in *father* ; ə̄=*er* in *pert* ; th=*th* in *thin* ; dh=*th* in *then* ; zh=*s* in *pleasure* ; k=*ch* in *loch* ; ñ=Fr. nasal *n* ; ü=Fr. *u.*

accolent (ak'ələnt), *adj.* neighbouring.

accommodation (akomədā'shn), *n.* adjustment, *espec.* of eye muscles ; adaptation ; lodgings ; loan. **a. bill,** bill of exchange signed by person lending his name to another. **a. train,** *Amer.*, train stopping at all or most stations.

accouchement (akōōsh'mahn), *n.* childbirth. **-cheur, -cheuse** (-shȫr', -ȫz'), *n.* male and female midwife respec.

accoutre (akōōt'ə), *v.t.* equip ; clothe. **-ments,** *n.pl.* equipment.

accredit (akred'it), *v.t.* attribute ; gain belief for ; attach officially.

accrementition (akrimentish'n), *n.* growth by addition of similar matter.

accrescent (akres'ənt), *adj.* growing larger. **-nce, -ncy,** *n.*

accretion (akrē'shn), *n.* growth, *espec.* by addition from outside.

accubation (akūbā'shn), *n.* act or state of reclining ; *Med.*, accouchement.

accumbent (akum'bənt), *adj.* reclining. **-ency,** *n.*

accusative (akū'zətiv), *adj. Gram.*, objective ; *n.* such case in declension of nouns.

aceldama (asel'dəmə, ak-), *n.* field, or scene, of bloodshed.

aceology (asiol'əji), *n.* therapeutics.

acephalous (asef'ələs), *adj.* lacking a head or a leader. **-lus** (*pl.* **-li**), *n.* hexameter line commencing with short syllable ; headless monster.

acerate (as'ərāt), *adj.* needle-like.

acerbity (asȯ'biti), *n.* bitterness, *espec.* of feeling. **-bate** (as'-), *adj.*

aceric (aṣer'ik), *adj.* pert. to the maple.

acerose (as'ərōs), *adj.* like a needle ; like chaff.

acerous (as'ərəs), *adj.* without horns or antennae.

acervate (asȯ'vāt), *adj.* in heaps ; clustered. **-tim** (-vā'tim), Lat. *adv.* summarily. **-tion,** *n.* heaping up. **-tive,** *adj.* **-vuline,** *adj.* like little heaps.

acescent (ases'ənt), *adj.* becoming, or tending to be, sour. **-nce,** *n.*

acetarious (asitār'iəs), *adj.* app. to plants used in salads.

acetic (asē'tik, -set'-), *adj.* sour ; of vinegar. **a. acid,** acid of vinegar.

-tate (as'itat), *n.* salt of a. acid. **-tated,** *adj.* treated with a. acid.

acetify (asē'tifi), *v.i. & t.* turn or become sour ; make into vinegar. **-fiable,** *adj.* **-fication,** *n.*

acetimeter, -om- (asitim'itə, -om'-) ; *n.* instr. measuring strength of acetic acid or vinegar. **-try,** *n.*

acetone (as'itōn), *n.* liquid obtained from maize or wood spirit, used as solvent, in manuf. of chloroform, etc. **-tonaemia,** *n.* presence of a. in blood.

acetous, -ose (as'itəs, -ōs), *adj.* sour ; of vinegar.

acetyl (as'itil), *n.* the radical of acetic acid. **a.-salicylic acid,** aspirin.

achar (achah'), Anglo-Ind. *n.* kind of pickles.

a chara (akar'ə), *Ir.*, salutation, equiv. of *Dear Sir,* in Ireland.

achene (akēn'), *n.* small one-seeded fruit of plant ; naked seed.

à cheval (ah shəval'), *Fr.*, "on horseback" ; astride ; straddling.

Achilles (akil'ēz), *n.* anct. Gr. hero ; mighty soldier. **A.'s heel,** vulnerable spot. **A.'s spear,** anything curing injury made by itself. **A.'s tendon,** hamstring ; tendon between calf and heel.

achloropsia (aklōrop'siə), *n.* colourblindness, *espec.* towards green.

acholia (akō'liə), *n.* lack of bile. **-lic** (-ol'ik), **-lous** (ak'-), *adj.*

achor (ā'kaw), *n.* eruption on the scalp ; "scald-head."

achroma (akrō'mə), *n. Med.*, pallor. **-mic, -mous,** *adj.*

achromat(e) (ak'rəmat, -māt), *n.* achromatic lens ; colour-blind person. **-tic, -tous** (-ō'mətəs), *adj.* non-coloured ; free from chromatic aberration ; *Mus.*, having few accidentals. **-tin,** *n.* liquid plasmic substance in nucleus of cells resistant to staining agents. **-tise,** *v.t.* **-tism,** *n.*

achromatopsia, -sy (akrōmətop'siə, -si), *n.* colour-blindness. **-pe,** *n.* colour-blind person.

achrous (ak'rōəs), *adj.* colourless.

acicular (asik'ūlə), *adj.* needle-like. **-late** *adj.* having bristles or spines ; with scratched appearance.

acidaemia (asidē'miə), *n.* undue acidity of blood.

acidimeter, -om- (asidim'itə, -om'-), *n.* instrument for measuring amount and strength of acids. **-try,** *n.*

---

hat, bah, hāte, hāre, crawl ; pen, ēve, hēre ; it, īce, fīre ; on, bōne, boil, bōre, howl ; foot, fōōd, bōōr, hull, tūbe, pūre.

acidosis (asidō'sis), *n. Med.*, excessively acid condition of blood and tissues.

acidulous, -lent (asid'ūləs, -lənt), *adj.* sharp in taste. **-late,** *v.t.*

acierage(as'iərij), *n.* process of steel-plating. **-rate,** *v.t.* make into steel.

aciform (as'ifawm), *adj.* needle-shaped.

acinaciform (asinas'ifawm), *adj.* having shape of scimitar.

aciniform (asin'ifawm), *adj.* shaped like cluster of grapes ; full of seeds.

acinous, -ose (as'inəs, -ōs), *adj.* containing small seeds or drupes.

acipenser (asipen'sə), *n.* sturgeon. **-id, -ine,** *adj.*

aclastic (aklas'tik), *adj.* non-refractive.

aclinic (aklin'ik), *adj.* app. to line passing through all points where there is no magnetic inclination. **a.line,** magnetic equator.

acne (ak'ni), *n.* irruption of pimples on face, back and chest. **a.rosacea,** *n.* redness and swelling of face, *espec.* nose.

acology (akol'əji), *n.* science of med. remedies ; aceology. **-logic,** *adj.*

acolous (akō'ləs), *adj.* limbless.

acolyte (ak'əlīt), *n. R.C.*, candle-bearer and assistant at Mass.

acomia (akō'miə), *n.* baldness. **-mous,** *adj.*

aconite (ak'ənīt), *n.* the monk's-hood or wolf's-bane plant.

aconitine (akon'itin, -ēn), *n.* poisonous alkaloid obtained from aconite.

acopic (akop'ik), *n. & adj. Med.*, curative of fatigue.

acor (ā'kōr), *n. Med.*, stomach acidity.

acoria (akōr'iə), *n. Med.*, morbid appetite for food.

à corps perdu (ah kōr par'dü), *Fr.*, "with lost body" ; impetuously ; in desperation.

acosmism (akoz'mizm), *n.* doctrine denying existence of universe distinct from God. **-mic,** *adj.* unorganised. **-mist,** *n.*

acotyledon (ākotilē'dn), *n.* plant without differentiated seed lobes. **-ous** (-led'ənəs, -lē'-), *adj.*

acouasm (akōō'azm), *n.* ringing noise in head.

acoumeter (akow'mitə, -kōō'-), *n.* instr. measuring keenness of hearing. **-try,** *n.*

à coup sûr (ah kōō sür'), *Fr.*, "with sure stroke."

acoustic (akōō'stik), *adj.* pert. to the hearing, to sound and its transmission ; worked by sound or echoes. **a. mine,** mine detonated by sound waves from ship's engines. **-ian** (-ish'ən), *n.* expert in acoustics. **-s,** *n.* science of sound laws ; properties of audibility of a building.

acquittance (akwit'əns), *n.* payment of, or release from, debt ; full receipt.

acracy (ak'rəsi), *n.* anarchy.

acratia (akrā'shiə), *n.* impotence.

acrimonious (akrimō'niəs), *adj.* bitter ; caustic ; angry. **-ny** (ak'riməni), *n.*

acritochromacy (akritəkrō'məsi), *n.* colour-blindness.

acroaesthesia (akrōesthē'zhiə), *n. Med.*, increase in sensitiveness ; pain in extremities.

acroamatic (akrōəmat'ik), *adj.* oral ; secret ; abstruse.

acrocephalous, -lic (akrəsef'ələs, -sifal'ik), *adj.* having pointed skull. **-ly,** *n.*

acrogenous (akroj'inəs), *adj. Bot.*, growing at summit.

acrolith (ak'rəlith), *n.* statue with wooden trunk and stone head and extremities.

acrologic (akrəloj'ik), *adj.* pert. to initials. **-gy** (-ol'əji), *n.*

acromegaly (akrəmeg'əli), *n.* gigantism ; enlargement of extremities, head, jaw, etc., due to excess secretion of pituitary gland. **-lic** (-al'ik), *adj.*

acromonogrammatic (akrəmonəgrəmat'ik), *adj.* app. to verse in which each line begins with letter with which preceding line end ed.

acronychal, -ycal, -ichal, -ical (akron'ikəl), *adj. Astron.*, happening at sunset, *espec.* of star whose rising is at sunset. **a.place,** opposition of planet.

acronyx (ak'rəniks), *n.* ingrowing nail.

acropathy (akrop'əthi), *n.* disease of extremities.

acrophobia (akrəfō'biə), *n.* dread of heights.

acropodium (akrəpō'diəm), *n.* pedestal of statue.

acropolis (akrop'əlis), *n.* fortified

elevated part of city, *espec.* of Athens. **-itan** (-pol′itən), *adj.*

acroscopic (akrəskop′ik), *adj. Bot.*, facing, or moving to, apex.

acroteleutic (akrətelū′tik), *n.* end of psalm ; words added to end of psalm ; doxology.

acroteric (akrəter′ik), *adj.* pert. to or affecting the extremities.

acroterion, -ium (akrəter′iən, -iəm), *n. Archit.*, ornament or its pedestal at angle of pediment.

acrotic (akrot′ik), *adj.* pert. to surface. **-ism** (ak′-), *n.* failure of pulse.

A.C.T.H., *abbr.* of adreno-cortico-trophic hormone, a secretion of the pituitary gland which stimulates the adrenal cortex to produce cortisone.

actinism (ak′tinizm), *n.* property of solar radiation of causing chemical change. **-nic** (-tin′ik), *adj.* ; **a.glass,** glass opaque to actinic rays.

actinium (aktin′iəm), *n.* rare radio-active element.

actino-chemistry (aktinə-kem′-istri), *n.* chem. study of actinism.

actinograph (aktin′əgraf), *n.* instr. for calculating time of photog. exposures.

actinoid (ak′tinoid), *adj.* star-shaped ; like rays.

actinology (aktinol′əji), *n.* science of chem. effects of light.

actinometer (aktinom′itə), *n.* instr. measuring heating power of the sun's rays ; *Photog.*, instrument for calculating exposure times. **-try,** *n.*

actinomorphic, -phous (aktinəmaw′-fik, -əs), *adj* having symmetrically radiated shape.

actinomycin (aktinəmī′sin), *n.* antibiotic produced by a soil fungus.

actinomycosis (aktinəmīkō′sis), *n.* parasitic disease in men and cattle resulting in inflammation of jaw ; "lumpy jaw."

actinophone (aktin′əfōn), *n.* instr. in which sound is produced by actinic rays. **-nic** (-fon′ik), *adj.*

actinotherapy (aktinəther′əpi), *n.* use of ultra-violet and other actinic rays in med. treatment.

actuary (ak′tūəri), *n.* expert on insurance statistics and tables of expectation of life. **-rial** (-ār′iəl), *adj.*

actum ut supra (act′əm ut sōōp′rə), *Lat.*, "done as above" (*abbr.* a.u.s.).

aculeate (akū′liət), *adj. Bot.*, bearing many sharp points ; *Zoo.*, having sting ; incisive.

aculeiform (akū′liifawm), *adj.* thorn-shaped.

acumen (ak′ūmen, -ū′mən), *n.* quickness to perceive ; shrewdness.

acuminate (akū′minət), *adj.* pointed ; tapering ; (-āt), *v.t.* sharpen ; *v.i.* end in point.

acuminulate (akūmin′ūlət), *adj.* very sharply pointed ; ending in minute point.

acupressure (ak′ūpreshə), *n.* pressing needle across blood vessel to stop haemorrhage.

acupuncture (ak′ūpungktūr), *n.* inserting a needle into flesh, etc., as med. remedy.

acutorsion (akū′ūtawshn), *n.* twisting artery with needle to stop bleeding.

acyanopsia (āsiənop′siə), *n.* colour blindness towards blue.

acyesis (āsie′sis), *n.* sterility of female. **-etic** (-et′ik), *adj.*

acyrology (asirol′əji), *n.* incorrect diction. **-gical,** *adj.*

adactylous (adak′tiləs), *adj.* lacking fingers, toes or claws. **-lia** (ādak-til′iə, ad-), **-lism,** ″.

adamant (ad′əmənt), *n.* exceptionally hard substance ; *adj.* impenetrable ; immovable. **-tine** (-an′tīn, -tin), *adj.*

adaxial (adaks′iəl), *adj.* on, beside, or turned towards, axis.

ad captandum (vulgus) (ad kaptan′-dəm, vul′gəs), *Lat.*, "to capture" the affection or suit the taste (of the crowd).

addendum (adend′əm), *n.* (*pl.* **-da**) something added ; appendix.

addio (ahdē′ō), *It.*, adieu.

additament (adit′əmənt), *n.* thing added. **-ary** (-men′təri), *adj.*

addititious (aditish′əs), *adj.* pert. to, or resulting from, addition ; *Astron.*, app. to force increasing gravitation between planet and satellite.

additive (ad′itiv), *adj.* pert. to addition ; *Gram.*, signifying addition of similar elements or of new thought ; *Phil.*, marked by addition and not union ; *n.* something added.

---

adduce (adūs′), *v.t.* bring forward as evidence. **-nt,** *adj.* drawing towards.

adeciduate (adēsid′ū āt), *adj.* evergreen.

adelphogamy (adəlfog′əmi), *n.* form of marriage in which brothers have common wife or wives.

ademonist (adē′mənist), *n.* person denying existence of demons or the Devil.

ademption (ademp′shn), *n. Law,* revoking by testator, donor, etc., of legacy, donation, etc., by previously paying sum or parting with object bequeathed.

adenia (adē′niə), *n. Med.,* enlargement of glands.

adeniform (aden′ifawm, ad′ən-), *adj.* gland-shaped.

adenitis (adinī′tis), *n.* inflammation of glands.

adenoid (ad′inoid), *adj.* pert. to or like gland. **-s,** *n.pl.* enlargement of lymphatic tissues at back of throat.

adenology (adinol′əji), *n.* study of glands. **-gical,** *adj.*

adenoma (adinō′mə), *n.* tumour of gland or like a gland. **-tous,** *adj.*

adenopathy (adinop′əthi), *n.* glandular disease.

adenose (ad′inōs), *adj.* gland-like; having many glands.

adenotomy (adinot′əmi), *n.* incision into or removal of gland.

adephagous (adef′əgəs), *adj. Med.,* having morbid appetite for food.

adespoton (ades′pətən), *n.* anonymous saying, poem, etc.

ad eundem (gradum) (ad ēun′dəm, grā′dəm), *Lat.,* (admitted) "to same (rank)," *espec.* to same degree at different university.

à deux (ah dö′), *Fr.,* "for two"; *Mus.,* for two hands.

adevism (ad′ivizm), *n.* denial of legendary gods.

ad finem (ad fin′em), *Lat.,* "to the end" *(abbr.* **ad fin.).**

ad hanc vocem (ad hank vok′em), *Lat.,* "to this word" *(abbr.* **a.h.v.)**

adhibit (adhib′it), *v.t.* grant admittance to; apply; attach. **-tion,** *n.*

ad hoc (ad hok), *Lat.,* "to this"; for the present purpose alone; not provable by reference to other phenomena.

ad hominem (ad hom′inem), *Lat.,*

"to the man"; appealing to prejudice or passions; illogical.

ad hunc locum (ad hunk lok′əm), *Lat., Law,* "at this place"; on this passage *(abbr.* **ad loc.**; **a.h.l.**).

adiabatic (ādiəbat′ik, ad-), *adj.* without losing or gaining heat. **a.gradient,** rate of change in temperature of rising or falling air.

adiabolist (ādiab′əlist), *n.* person denying existence of the Devil.

adiactinic (adiaktin′ik), *adj.* not transmitting actinic rays.

adiaphoresis (ādiafərē′sis), *n.* absence or lack of perspiration. **-etic** (-et′ik), *n.* & *adj.* (drug) preventing perspiration.

adiaphoron (adiaf′əron), *n. (pl.* **-ra**), matter of indifference; *Theol.,* religious observance left to conscience; amoral matter. **-rism,** *n.* belief in doctrine of adiaphora. **-rist,** *n.* **-ristic,** *adj.* app. to certain controversies on religious observances. **-rous,** *adj.* neutral; indifferent.

adiapneustia (adiapnū′stiə), *n.* defective perspiration.

adiathermic (adiathō′mik), *adj.* impervious to heat. **-mancy,** *n.*

ad infinitum (ad infinī′təm), *Lat.,* "to infinity"; for ever; without limit *(abbr.* **ad inf.**).

ad interim (ad in′tərim), *Lat.,* "at interval"; meanwhile; for the present *(abbr.* **ad int.**).

adios (adiōs′; Sp., ahdhiōs′), *Sp.,* adieu.

adipescent (adipes′ənt), *adj.* becoming fatty.

adipic (adip′ik), *adj. Chem.,* pert. to fatty or greasy substance.

adipocere (ad′ipəsēr), *n.* fatty substance occurring in dead bodies in moist places. **-rous** (-pos′ərəs), *adj.*

adipose (ad′ipōz, -ōs), *adj.* fat. **a.tissue,** connective fat-storing tissue. **-sis** (-ō′sis), *n.* fatness; fatty degeneration. **-sity** (-os′iti), *n.*

adipsy, -sia (ad′ipsi, -ip′siə), *n.* lack of thirst. **-sic,** *adj.* **-sous,** *adj.* quenching thirst.

adit (ad′it), *n.* entrance, *espec.* horizontal passage into mine.

adjutator (aj′ōōtātə), *n.* helper.

adjutor (ajōō′tə), *n.* helper. **-ious,** **-y** (aj′ōōtəri), *adj.*

adjuvant (aj′oovənt), *adj.* helping; *Med.,* remedial; *n.* such drug.

ad libitum (ad lib'itəm), *Lat.*, "at one's pleasure"; as much or long as desired; *Mus.*, according to desire of performer (*abbr.* ad lib.).

ad-lib, *v.i.* & *t.* speak impromptu, *espec.* (of actors) jokes, words, etc., not written or rehearsed, or to replace forgotten lines; *adj.* said on the spur of the moment; *n.* an ad-lib statement.

ad locum (ad lok'əm), *Lat.*, "at the place" (*abbr.* ad loc.).

admaxillary (admaks'iləri), *adj.* near or connected with jaw.

admeasurement (admezh'əmənt), *n.* act or result of measuring; apportionment; dimensions.

admensuration (admensūr ā'shn), *n.* admeasurement.

adminicle (admin'ikl), *n.* aid; support; corroboration; *Numismatics*, ornament round figure on coin. **-cular** (-ik'ūlə), *adj.* **-culate** (-ik'ūlāt), *v.t.* corroborate. **-culation**, *n.*

adnascent (adnas'ənt), *adj.* growing on something else. **-nce**, *n.*

adnate (ad'nāt), *adj.* closely attached; related; grown together congenitally. **-tion**, *n.*

ad nauseam (ad naw'siam), *Lat.*, "to nausea"; until disgust is felt.

adnominal (adnom'inəl), *adj.* pert. to adnoun.

adnomination (adnominā'shn), *n.* punning.

adnoun (ad'nown), *n.* adjective, *espec.* used as noun.

adobe (adō'bi), *n.* unburnt sundried brick; dwelling of a.; clay used for a.; *adj.* built of a.

Adonic (adon'ik), *adj.* pertaining to Adonis; app. to metrical foot comprising a dactyl followed by a spondee or trochee.

adonise (ad'əniz), *v.i.* & *t.* ornament; adorn oneself.

adoptionism (adop'shənizm), *n.* doctrine that Christ was Son of God by adoption and not birth. **-ist**, *n.* & *adj.* **-tian**, *adj.*

adoral (adōr'əl), *adj.* near to mouth.

adosculation (adoskūlā'shn), *n.* sexual impregnation by contact only; wind-pollination.

adoxography (adoksog'rəfi), *n. Lit.*, fine writing on trivial or base subject.

adoxy (ad'oksi), *n.* belief neither orthodox nor heterodox.

adrectal (adrek'təl), *adj.* close to rectum.

ad rem (ad rem'), *Lat.*, "to the thing"; to the purpose; pertinent.

adrenal (adrē'nəl), *adj.* close to kidney; suprarenal, *espec.* app. to ductless glands above kidneys. **-in(e)**, *n.* hormone of a. gland; preparation from such secretion or synthetic drug used as haemostatic and heart stimulant.

adrenin(e) (adren'in, -ēn), *n.* hormone of adrenal glands.

adscititious (adsitish'əs), *adj.* supplementary; auxiliary.

adsorb (adzawb'), *v.t.* attract and hold to surface (minute particles of mixture or molecules of gas or liquid). **-ate**, *n.* substance or molecules adsorbed. **-ent**, *n.* & *adj.* (substance) adsorbing. **-rption**, *n.*

adsum (ad'səm), *Lat.*, "I am present."

adulation (adūlā'shn), *n.* excessive flattery; abject worship. **-tory**, *adj.*

adumbrate (ad'umbrāt), *v.t.* shadow forth; outline; sketch out. **-ant**, **-tive**, *adj.* **-tion**, *n.*

aduncate, **-cous** (adung'kāt, -kəs), *adj.* hook-shaped; crooked; *v.i.* curve inward. **-city** (-un'siti), *n.* inward curvature.

ad unguem (ad ung'gwem), *Lat.*, "to the finger nail"; to a nicety; with great exactitude; to minute detail.

ad usum (ad ūs'əm), *Lat.*, "to usage"; according to custom (*abbr.* ad us.).

ad valorem (ad vəlōr'em), *adj.* in proportion to value, *espec.* of import duties of a percentage of the value of the imports (*abbr.* ad val.).

advehent (ad'viənt), *adj.* afferent.

advenient (advē'niənt), *adj.* due to outside causes. **-nce**, *n.*

adventitious (adventish'əs), *adj.* added from without; not essential; accidental; casual; *Med.*, acquired; *Bot.*, adventive.

adventive (adven'tiv), *n.* & *adj Bot.*, (plant) not completely naturalised or growing out of natural habitat.

ad verbum (ad vɜ'bəm), *Lat.*, "to the word"; word for word.

adversaria (advəsār'iə), *n.pl.* collection of notes and comments; commonplace book.

adversative (advə'sətiv), *n.* & *adj.* *Gram.*, (word or clause) expressing opposition or antithesis.

ad vitam aut culpam (ad vī'tam ˌwt kul'pam), *Lat.*, "to life or misdeed"; so long as good behaviour lasts.

advowee (advow'ē), *n.* eccl. patron; holder of advowson.

advowson (advow'zn), *n.* right to present to church living.

~dynamic (ādīnam'ik), *adj.* lacking strength; causing weakness. **-mia** (-nā'miə), **-my** (-dī'nəmi), *n.*

~dytum (ad'itəm), *n.* inner sanctuary of temple; secret room.

~dz(e) (adz), *n.* axe with rounded blade set at right angles to handle; *v.t.* cut with a.

aedile (ē'dīl), *n.* head of anct. Rom. office of works. **-lity** (-il'iti), *n.* a.'s office.

aedoeology (ēdiol'əji), *n.* study of generative organs.

aegagrus (ēgag'rəs), *n.* mountain goat of Asia Minor; paseng.

aeger (ē'jə), *Lat. adj.* "sick"; *n.* student's certificate of illness.

aegilops (ē'jilops), *n.* stye in inner corner of eye.

aegis (ē'jis), *n.* protection; shield, *espec.* of classical gods.

aegrotat (ē'grōtat), *Lat.*, "he is ill"; *n.* certificate of student's illness for absence from university lectures or examination. a.degree, degree given to student absent from examination by reason of illness.

aeneous (ā ē'nēəs), *adj.* like brass.

Aeolian (ē ō'liən), *adj.* pertaining to Aeolis or Aeolus, god of the winds; carried or caused by wind. A.harp, mus. instr. played by the winds.

aeolipyle, **-pile** (ēol'ipīl), *n.* first steam engine, with globe made to revolve by steam jets, described in 1st cent. A.D.; kind of blowpipe.

aeolistic (ē ōlis'tik), *adj.* long-winded.

aeolotropic (ē ōlətrop'ik), *adj.* having different physical properties in different positions or directions. **-py** (-ot'rəpi), *n.*

aepyornis (ēpiaw'nis), *n.* large fossil bird of Madagascar.

aere perennius (ēr'i pərən'iəs), *Lat.*, "more lasting than brass."

aerobe (ār'ōb, ā ēr'-), *n.* (*pl.* **-bia**) organism growing only in presence of oxygen. **-bic,** *adj.* **-biosis,** *n.* such growth or existence.

aerodonetics (āˌrədonet'iks, ā ēr'-), *n.* science of gliding.

aerodromics (āˌrədrom'iks, ā ēr'-), *n.* science of mechanical flight.

aerodynamics (āˌrədīnam'iks, ā ēr'-), *n.* science of forces acting on bodies in motion in air.

aerodyne (ār'ədīn, ā ēr'-), *n.* heavier-than-air aircraft kept up by its movement through air.

aerogenic (āˌrəjen'ik, ā ēr'-), *adj.* derived from air; gas-forming. **-nesis,** *n.*

aerolite, **-lith** (ār'əlīt, ā ēr'- ; -lith), *n.* meteorite.

aerology (ārol'əji, ā ēr'-), *n.* study of physical properties of atmosphere, *espec.* meteorological.

aeromancy (ār'əmansi, ā ēr'-), *n.* divination by the air; weather forecasting. **-ntic,** *adj.*

aeromechanics (ārəmikan'iks, ā ēr'-), *n.* science of mechanical properties of gases.

aerometer (ārom'itə, ā ēr'-), *n.* instr. measuring weight or density of gases. **-try,** *n.* such measurement; pneumatics.

aerophilately (ārəfilat'ili, ā ēr'-), *n.* collecting of air-mail stamps and covers.

aerophore (ār'əfor, ā ēr'-), *n.* apparatus for inflating lungs, *espec.* of still-born child.

aerophyte (ār'əfīt, ā ēr'-), *n.* plant obtaining all nourishment from the air; epiphyte.

aeropleustic (ārəplōō'stik, ā ēr'-), *adj.* pert. to aerial navigation.

aeroscope (ār'əskōp, ā ēr'-), *n.* instr. measuring purity of air. **-py** (-os'kəpi), *n.* observation of varying air conditions.

aerose (ēr'ōs, erōs'), *adj.* brassy.

aerosol (ār'əsol, ā ēr'-) *n.* mist-like suspension of minute particles in air or gas.

aerostat (ār'əstat, ā ēr'-), *n.* lighter-than-air craft; balloonist. **-ic,** *adj.* **-ics,** *n.* science of gases in equilibrium; aerial navigation. **-ion,** *n.* act of navigating a.

aerotherapeutics (ārətherəpū'tiks, ā ēr'-), *n.* med. treatment by modifying atmospheric pressure.

aerugo (erōō'gō), *n.* rust, *espec.* of copper and brass; verdigris. **-ginous** (-jinəs), *adj.*

---

aesculaceous (ēskūlā'shəs), *adj.* pert. to or like horse-chestnut ; belonging to the horse-chestnut family of plants.

Aesculapian (ēskūlā'piən), *adj.* pert. to Aesculapius, the god of medicine ; medical. **A. snake,** non-venomous Eur. snake, once sacred to Aesculapius.

Aesopian, -pic (ēsō'piən, -op'ik), *adj.* pert. to or in the style of Aesop or his fables.

aesthesia (ēsthē'zhiə), *n.* sensibility.

aesthesis (ēsthē'sis), *n.* sense perception.

aesthesiogenic (ēsthēziəjen'ik), *adj.* causing sensation.

aesthesiometer (ēsthēziom'itə), *n.* instr. measuring acuteness of sense perception. **-try,** *n.*

aesthete (ēs'thēt), *n.* lover of beauty, *espec.* to an exaggerated degree.

aesthetic (ēsthet'ik), *adj.* pert. to beauty or appreciation of beauty, or to pure sensation ; *n.* science of sense cognition. **-ism** (-isizm), *n. Phil.,* doctrine that principle of beauty is alone fundamental. **-s,** *n.* department of phil. dealing with beauty.

aestival (ē'stivəl, es'-), *adj.* of summer. **-vation,** *n. Zoo.,* sleepiness in animals during summer ; *Bot.,* arrangement of organs in flower bud.

aetat (ē'tat), *Lat., abbr.* of **aetatis,** *abbr.* of **anno aetatis suae,** "in the year of his age" ; aged (*abbr.* **aet.**).

aether, *see* ether.

aetiology, et- (ētiol'əji), *n.* science of causes of natural phenomena. **-gical,** *adj.*

aevia (ē'viə), *Mus., abbr.* of alleluia.

afebrile (āfē'bril), *adj.* free from fever.

afferent (af'ərənt), *adj.* carrying towards, *espec.* of nerves carrying impulses to centres.

affiche (afēsh'), Fr. *n.* poster ; placard. **-ché** (-ā), *adj.* advertised ; posted up.

affidavit (afidā'vit), *n.* written statement made on oath.

affiliate (afil'iāt), *v.t.* attach to ; adopt into ; unite ; fix paternity of or on. **-tion,** *n.* ; **a.order,** order by court fixing paternity of illegitimate child and requiring maintenance from man affiliated.

affinal (afī'nəl), *adj.* related by marriage ; having same source.

affinity (afin'iti), *n.* close relationship ; attraction ; resemblance ; *Law,* relationship by marriage ; *Chem.,* force causing elements to combine.

affirmation (afəmā'shn), *n. Law,* solemn declaration by person who refuses to take the oath for reasons of conscience. **-mant,** *n.* person making a.

afflatus (aflā'təs), *n.* divine breath ; inspiration. **-tion,** *n.* act of breathing upon ; inspiration.

affluent (af'looənt), *adj.* wealthy ; *n.* tributary to a river. **-nce,** *n.* wealth.

afflux (af'luks), *n.* flowing towards or together.

affranchise (afran'chīz), *v.t.* liberate.

affreux (afrə'), Fr. *adj.* frightful.

affricate (afrik'āt), *v.t.* rub ; grate on ; (af'-), *n. Phon.,* sound, as *th* or *j,* comprising a stop developing into a fricative. **-tion,** *n.*

affusion (afū'zhn), *n.* pouring liquid on, *espec.* in baptismal ceremony or as med. treatment.

aficionado (ahfēthiənah'dhō), Sp. *n.* keen follower of sport; "fan."

à fond (ah fawn'), Fr., "to the bottom" ; thoroughly.

a fortiori (ā fawshiōr'ī), *Lat.,* "by the stronger"; with better reason ; all the more.

Afrikaans (afrikahns'), *n.* S. African Dutch language.

Afrikander (afrikan'də), *n.* white native of S. Africa, *espec.* Dutch. **A.Bond,** Dutch political organization (1881-1911) of S. Africa.

afterbirth (ahf'təbəth), *n.* membrane covering foetus, expelled after birth.

afterdamp (ahf'tədamp), *n.* gas (mixture of carbon dioxide and nitrogen) remaining after explosion of fire-damp in mine ; choke-damp.

aftermath (ahf'təmath, -mahth), *n.* events (*espec.* unpleasant) following ; second crop of hay.

aga, agha (ā'gə, ah'-), Turk. *n.* high officer in Mohammedan community.

agalactia (agəlak'shiə), *n. Med.,* absence or lack of milk secretion. **-tic, -tous,** *adj.*

agami (ag'əmi), *n.* crane-like bird of S. America ; trumpeter.

agamic (agam'ik), adj. non-sexual.

agamogenesis (agəməjen'isis), n. non-sexual reproduction. -netic (-jinet'ik), adj.

agamous (ag'əməs), adj. lacking sexual organs; agamic; cryptogamous.

agamy (ag'əmi), n. lack of marriage or sexual reproduction.

agape (ag'əpi), n. "love-feast," an early Christian ceremony commemorating the Last Supper. Agapemone (agəpem'ənē), n. "abode of love"; former religious communal settlement, based on free love.

agar-agar (ā'gah-ā'gah), n. nutritive jelly obtained from sea-weeds; "Bengal isinglass"; sea-weed yielding a.

agaric (ag'ərik, -ar'ik), n. species of mushroom-like fungus. -iform (-is'ifawm), adj. mushroom-shaped.

agathism (ag'əthizm), n. doctrine that ultimate end of all things is good, though means may be evil.

agave (əgā'vi), n. sev. tropical Amer. fibre-yielding plants; Amer. aloe.

agenda (ajen'də), n.pl. (sing. -dum; pl. takes sing. verb) list of subjects to be dealt with at meeting.

agenesis (ājen'isis), n. incomplete development of body or part of body; agennesis. -sic (-es'ik), adj.

agennesis (ajənē'sis), n. sterility in the male. -netic (-et'ik), adj.

agent provocateur (ahzhahń' provokatār'), Fr., spy employed to provoke suspected persons to break the law so that they may be arrested.

ageotropic (ajiətrop'ik), adj. Bot., turning away from the earth; apogeotropic. -ism (-ot'rəpizm), n.

ageustia, -sia (agū'stiə, -siə), n. absence of sense of taste. -sic, -tic, adj.

aggeration (ajərā'shn), n. heaping up; mound raised by prehistoric man. -rose, adj. in heaps; having many heaps.

agglomerate (aglom'ərāt), v.i. & t. collect, espec. into a mass; adj. so collected; clustered; n. Geol., rock comprised of angular volcanic fragments. -ant, n. causing to a. -tion, n.

agglutinate (aglōo'tināt), v.i. & t. join firmly; thicken; make like glue; coagulate; Philol., make compound words by additions. -nin, n. substance in blood causing coagulation. -nogen, n. substance causing production of agglutinin. -tive, adj. app. to agglutinated words or languages containing many such words. -tion, n.

agio (ā'jiō, aj'-), n. charge made when cash is given for paper currency, or one currency is exchanged for another. -tage, n. such exchange; speculation; brokerage.

aglet, aig- (ag'lit, ā'-), n. metal tag on lace or as adornment; Bot., catkin.

aglossal, -ate (aglos'əl, -ət), adj., lacking tongue. -sia, n.

aglutition (aglōotish'n), n. state of being unable to swallow.

agmatology (agmətol'əji), n. Med., study and treatment of fractures.

agminate (ag'minət), adj. grouped.

agnail (ag'nāl), n. "hangnail"; sore at the nail; whitlow.

agnate (ag'nāt), adj. having same male forefather; allied; Law, related on father's side; n. such relative.

agnathous (ag'nəthəs), adj. lacking jaws. -thia (-ā'thiə), n.

agnation (agnā'shn), n. kinship.

agnomen (agnō'men), n. additional name. -mination (-nom-), n. surname; punning; alliteration.

agnostic (agnos'tik), n. one who denies that there can be any knowledge of God or of supernatural things; adj. pert. to a.; non-dogmatic. -ism (-sizm), n.

agnosy (ag'nəsi), n. ignorance.

agometer (agom'itə), n. instr. measuring elec. resistance.

agomphious (agom'fiəs), adj. toothless. -phiasis (-fī'əsis), -phosis, n. looseness of teeth.

agonic (agon'ik), adj. app. to line drawn through all places where there is no magnetic declination.

agonism (ag'ənizm), n. competition (espec. athletic) for prize; great effort. -ist, n. -istic, adj. athletic; strained for effect.

agoraphobia (agərəfō'biə), n. morbid fear of open spaces.

agouti (agōo'ti), n. guinea-pig-like S. Amer. rodent; adj. having the brownish, grizzled colour of the a.

agraffe (agraf'), *n.* hook, *espec.* on piano-string to prevent rattle.

agraphia (agraf'iə), *n.* inability to write due to form of aphasia.

agrarian (agrār'iən), *adj.* pert. to agric. and the land ; *n.* believer in a policy of equal distribution of land. -**ism**, *n.* such policy.

agrestic, -tial (agres'tik, -tiəl), *adj.* of the countryside ; rustic. -**tian**, *n.* such person.

agricolist (agrik'əlist), *n.* farmer. -**lous**, *adj.* agricultural.

agriology (agriol'əji), *n.* study of savage customs. -**gist**, *n.*

agrobiology (agrəbiol'əji), *n.* biology of crop-plants in relation to soil control.

agrology (agrol'əji), *n.* scientific study of soils. -**gic(al)**, *adj.*

agronomy (agron'əmi), *n.* scientific management of land, *espec.* of raising of crops. -**mic** (-om'ik), *adj.*

agrostology (agrostol'əji), *n. Bot.*, study of grasses. -**gic(al)**, *adj.* -**tography**, *n.* description of grasses.

agrypnia (agrip'niə), *n.* sleeplessness. -**notic** (-not'ik), *n.* & *adj.* (stimulant) causing wakefulness.

aguardiente (ahgwahdien'tā), *n.* strong Sp. brandy distilled from potatoes, etc.

agynary, -rious (aj'inəri, -nār'iəs), *adj. Bot.*, lacking female organs.

aheliotropic (əheliətrop'ik), *adj.* tending to turn away from light; apheliotropic. -**pism** (-ot'rə-pizm), *n.*

ahypnia (ahip'niə) *n.* insomnia.

A.I., *abbr.* of artificial insemination (*see* insemination) ; **A.I.D.**, artificial insemination from known donor.

aide-memoire (ād-məmwahr'), Fr. *n.* "reminder"; memorandum ; diplomatic note clearly stating a government's view, policy, etc., on a particular matter.

aiger (ē'gə), *n.* tidal wave in river ; bore.

aigrette (ā'gret), *n.* spray of feathers; any object in that shape ; egret.

aiguille (ā'gwil), *n.* sharp point ; peak.

ailantus, -thus (āilan'təs, -thəs), *n.* Oriental tree, "tree of heaven," yielding food for silkworms. -**tery**, *n.* a. grove. -**tic, -thine, -tine**, *adj.*

aileron (ā'lərən), *n.* movable surface of aeroplane, *espec.* of wing, moved in steering.

aîné (ā'nā), Fr. *adj.* (*fem.* -**ée**) elder ; senior.

ait (āt), *n.* small island in river or lake ; eyot.

akinesia (akinē'zhiə), *n.* paralysis of motor nerves. -**sic**, *adj.*

à la (ah lah), *Fr.*, "in the manner as" ; *sl. abbr.* of à la mode.

ala (al'ə, ā'-), *n.* (*pl.* -**ae**) wing-shaped projection.

alabamine (aləbam'ēn), *n.* rare halogen-like element, No. 85, also called as*t*atine.

alabaster (al'əbahstə, -ast-), *n.* formerly carbonate of lime from which vases and boxes were made ; box made of such substance ; *mod.*, kind of gypsum ; *adj.* of a. ; very smooth and white. -**trine**, *adj.*

à la belle étoile (ah lah bel ātwahl'), *Fr.*, "under the beautiful star"; in the open air at night.

à la carte (ah lah kaht'), *Fr.*, chosen from the menu.

alalia (alā'liə), *n.* loss of speech.

à la mode (ah lah mod'), *Fr.*, "in fashion"; chic.

à la mort (ah lah mōr'), *Fr.*, "to the death"; mortally.

alar(y) (ā'lə, -əri), *adj.* like or pert. to a wing or shoulder.

alastrim (alas'trim), *n.* disease like, or mild form of, smallpox.

alate (al'āt), *adj.* winged.

alation (alā'shn), *n.* state of having wings ; disposition of wings in insect.

alaudine (alaw'din, -īn), *adj.* belonging to bird family which includes the skylark ; like or pert. to skylark.

alb (alb), *n.* long white priestly garment.

albacore, -ic- (al'bəkōr, -ik-), *n.* sev. tunny-like marine fishes ; tunny ; species of mackerel.

albedo (albē'dō), *n.* degree of whiteness ; *Photog.*, reflecting power of a surface ; *Astron.*, ratio of solar light reflected from a body to total amount it receives. -**graph**, *n. instr.* measuring a.

albescent (albes'ənt), *adj.* becoming white ; whitish.

albicant (al'bikənt), *adj.* growing white. -**cation**, *n.*

albificative (al'bifikātiv), *adj.* able

---

hat, bah, hāte, hāre, crawl ; pen, ēve, hēre ; it, īce, fīre ; on, bōne, boil, bōre, howl ; foot, fōod, bōor, hull, tūbe, pūre.

to whiten. -tion, *n.* act of whitening.

albiflorous (albiflōr'əs), *adj.* having white flowers.

albino (albē'nō), *n.* person or animal with white skin and hair and pinkish eyes ; plant deficient in pigment. -nal, -nic (-bin'ik), -tic (-not'ik), *adj.* -nism (al'-), *n.*

alborado (albōrah'dhō), Sp. *n.* morning song.

albuginea (albūjin'iə), *n.* white of eye ; white fibrous tissue. -neous, *adj.* like white of eye or egg. -nitis, *n.* inflammation of a.

albugo (albū'gō), *n. Med.*, white spot on cornea of eye ; leucoma ; *Bot.*, white rust.

albumen (al'būmən), *n.* white of egg ; substance surrounding embryo in seed.

albumin (al'būmin), *n.* protein forming chief constituent of animal and plant tissues.

albuminate (albū'mināt), *n.* kind of protein resulting from action of acid or alkali on albumins ; compound of albumin with other substance.

albuminoid (albū'minoid), *adj.* like albumen ; *n.* protein ; sev. substances like protein. -nous, *adj.* pert. to albumen or albumin.

albuminuria (albūminūr'iə), *n.* presence of albumin in urine.

alburnum (albʉ'nəm), *n.* sap-wood.

alcahest (al'kəhest), *n.* universal solvent sought by alchemists.

Alcaic (alkā'ik), *adj.* written in metre used by Alcaeus. A.ode, ode of four strophes, of four lines each, with four accents in each line. -s, *n.pl.* verses in that metre.

alcaid(e) (alkād'), *n.* governor of Sp., Moorish, etc., prison or fort.

alcalde (alkal'di), *n.* Sp. sheriff, mayor, etc.

alcazar (alkəzah', -kaz'ə, -kah'thar), Sp. *n.* palace ; castle ; citadel, *espec.* that of Toledo.

alcovinometer (alkəvinom'itə), *n.* instr. measuring alcoholic strength of wine. -try, *n.*

alcyon, *see* halcyon.

Aldine (awl'din), *adj.* printed by Aldus Manutius or his son or grandson at Venice in 15th and 16th centuries.

aleatory (ā'liətəri), *adj.* dependent on chance ; pert. to gambling or luck.

ale-conner (āl'konə), *n.* official supervising sale, measure and quality of ale.

alectryomachy (alektriom'əki), *n.* cock-fighting.

alegar (al'igə, ā'li-), *n.* sour ale ; vinegar made from ale.

alembic (alem'bik), *n.* anct. distilling apparatus ; purifying or transforming apparatus or act. -ate, *v.t.* distil.

alethiology (alēthiol'əji), *n.* study of nature of truth.

aleurometer (alūrom'itə), *n.* instr. measuring gluten content of flour. -try, *n.*

aleurone (alūr'ōn), *n.* protein granules in plant seeds ; external protein layer of cereal seeds.

alevin (al'əvin), *n.* young fish, *espec.* salmon just hatched.

alexandrine (aliksan'drīn), *n.* type of verse having six iambics ; kind of mosaic invented by Alexander Severus, emperor of Rome ; *adj.* pert. to a., or to Alexander the Great, or popes named Alexander.

alexia (aleks'iə), *n.* inability to read due to aphasia.

alexin (aleks'in), *n.* bacteriolytic substance. -ic, *adj.*

alexipharmic (aleksifah'mik), *n.* & *adj.* (antidote) against poisoning.

alexipyretic (aleksipīret'ik), *n.* & *adj.* (drug) curative of fever.

alexiteric (aleksiter'ik), *n.* & *adj.* preventive of contagion ; antidote against poison.

alfalfa (alfal'fə), *n.* clover-like forage crop ; lucerne.

alfresco (alfres'ko), *adj. & adv.* in open air.

alga (al'gə), *n.* (*pl.* -ae) seaweed ; *pl.* division of cryptogamic plants.

algaroba, -rroba (algərō'bə), *n.* locust-tree ; carob ; mesquite. -bin, *n.* dyestuff obtained from carob.

algazel (algəzel'), *n.* horned antelope of Nigeria.

algedonic (aljidon'ik), *adj.* pert. to pain, *espec.* in association with pleasure. -s, *n.* science of pleasure and pain.

algefacient (aljifā'shənt), *adj.* cooling.

algesia (aljē'zhiə), *n.* sensitiveness to pain. -etic (-et'ik), *adj.* causing pain. -sic, *adj.* -sis (-sis), *n.* pain sensation.

algid (al'jid), *adj.* chilly, *espec.* during fever. -ity, *n.*

algific (aljif'ik), *adj.* making cold.

alginuresis (aljinūr ē'sis), *n. Med.*, painful urination.

algivorous (aljiv'ərəs), *adj.* feeding on algae.

algogenic (algəjen'ik), *adj.* producing pain.

algolagny, -nia (algəlag'ni, -ə), *n.* taking pleasure in inflicting or enduring pain. -nic, *adj.* -nist, *n.*

algology (algol'əji), *n.* study of algae.

algometer (algom'itə), *n.* instr. measuring sensitivity to pain. -try, *n.*

algophilia (algəfil'iə), *n.* algolagny. -list (-of'ilist), *n.*

algophobia (algəfō'biə), *n.* morbid dread of pain.

algor (al'gaw), *n.* coldness ; shivering fit in fever.

algorism (al'gərizm), *n.* art of calculating, *espec.* in Arabic numeration ; arithmetic.

algous (al'gəs), *adj.* pert. to algae.

Alhambra (alham'brə), *n.* building in Moorish style, *espec.* palace at Granada. -resque, *adj.* in style of the A.

alias (ā'liəs), *adj.* otherwise called ; *n.* assumed name ; *adv.* at other times.

alibi (al'ibī), *n.* plea that, at the time when act was committed, one was elsewhere than at the place where act was committed ; proof of such a plea.

alible (al'ibl), *adj.* nourishing. -bility, *n.*

alienism (ā'liənism), *n.* study of mental disease. -ist, *n.* expert in a.

aliferous (alif'ərəs), *adj.* having wings.

aliform (al'ifawm), *adj.* like a wing.

aligerous (alij'ərəs), *adj.* winged.

aliment (al'imənt),*n.* food ; nourishment. -al (-men'tal), *adj.* affording food. -ary, *adj.* pert. to food ; nourishing ; a.canal, digestive tract from mouth to anus. -ation, *n.* act of feeding or being fed. -ative, *adj.* nourishing. -ive, *adj.*

alimentotherapy (alimentəther'əpi), *n. Med.*, treatment by dieting.

alimony (al'iməni), *n.* allowance paid by a spouse for other's support pending, during or after separation or divorce.

aliped (al'iped), *adj.* having winged feet ; *n.* such animal.

aliphatic (alifat'ik), *adj.* pert. to fat ; *Chem.*, app. to group of organic compounds, including the fats, having open-chain structure.

aliquant (al'ikwənt), *n.* & *adj.* (number) not dividing exactly into another number ; not aliquot.

aliquot (al'ikwot), *n.* & *adj.* (number) contained an exact number of times in another number ; equal share ; *v.i.* & *t.* divide into equal parts.

aliter (al'itə), Lat. *adv.* "otherwise" ; *Law*, requiring a different rule.

alizarin (aliz'ərin), *n.* red dye formerly obtained from madder root.

alk (alk), *n.* resin obtained from turpentine tree.

alkahest, *see* **alcahest.**

alkalescent (alkəles'ənt), *adj.* somewhat alkaline. -ncy, *n.*

alkali (al'kəlī), *n. Chem.*, substance having property of neutralising acids.

alkalify (al'kəlifī, -kal'ifī), *v.t.* change into alkali.

alkalimeter (alkəlim'itə), *n.* instr. measuring strength or amount of alkali in mixture. -try, *n.*

alkaline (al'kəlin), *adj.* pert. to, like or consisting of alkali. -nity (-in'iti), *n.*

alkalise (al'kəlīz), *v.t.* make alkaline.

alkaloid (al'kəloid), *n.* nitrogenous basic compound of vegetable origin. -al, *adj.* -ometry, *n.* measurement of alkaloids ; administration and dosage of alkaloids.

alkalosis (alkəlō'sis), *n.* abnormally high alkalinity of blood and tissues.

alkanet (al'kənet), *n.* dyer's bugloss ; red dye obtained from that plant.

allamotti (aləmot'i), *n.* stormy petrel (also called **allamonti** and **allamoth**).

allantiasis (aləntī'əsis), *n.* sausage poisoning.

allantois (alan'tōis), *n.* sac-like foetal membrane developing into umbilical cord and forming part of placenta. -toic (-tō'ik), -toid, *adj.* pert. to a. ; sausage-shaped.

allative (al'ətiv), *n.* & *adj. Gram.*, (case) expressing motion towards.

---

allegory (al'igəri), *n.* story or other representation in which the subject is expressed metaphorically or personified; parable. -rical (-or'ikl), *adj.* -rise, *v.t.* -rism, *n.* interpreting Scripture as allegory. -rist, *n.*

allelomorph (alē'ləmawf, -lel'-), *n. Biol.*, one of a pair of alternative contrasting inheritable characteristics; gene carrying that characteristic. -ic, *adj.* -ism, *n.*

allergy (al'əji), *n. Med.*, abnormal sensitivity towards a substance or germ, due to prior inoculation with that substance or germ; anaphylaxis. -gen, *n.* substance causing a. -gic (-ō'jik), *adj.*

alliaceous (aliā'shəs), *adj.* having smell or taste of garlic; belonging to the onion family of plants.

allicient (alish'ənt), *n.* & *adj.* (thing) attracting. -ncy, *n.*

alligation (aligā'shn), *n.* act or state of attaching or being attached; *Arith.*, arch. method of solving "mixture" problems; "rule of mixtures."

allision (alizh'n), *n.* intentional collision, *espec.* of ships.

alliteration (alitərā'shn), *n.* lit. device wherein several or all words in phrase or sentence begin with same sound. -rate, *v.i.* & *t.* -tive, *adj.*

allocatur (alokā'tə), *n. Law*, (certificate of) allowance of costs.

allochromatic (aləkrəmat'ik), *adj.* pert. to change of colour; variable in colour.

allochroous (alok'rōəs), *adj.* changing in colour.

allochthonous (alok'thənəs), *adj.* not autochthonous; formed elsewhere.

allocution (aləkū'shn), *n.* formal speech; action of speaking; *R.C.,* formal papal address to College of Cardinals. -te, *v.i.* make such speech. -tive (-ok'ūtiv), *adj.* hortative.

allodium (alō'diəm), *n.* property under absolute control; freehold; *Amer.*, estates in fee simple. -dial, *adj.*

allo-erotism (al'ō-er-'ətizm), *n. Psych.*, love of other person or object; opp. of auto-erotism.

allogamy (alog'əmi), *n.* cross-fertilisation. -mous, *adj.*

allogeneous (aləjēn'iəs), *adj.* different in kind. -neity (-jinē'iti), *n.*

allograph (al'əgraf), *n.* writing, *espec.* signature, for another; opp. of autograph.

allolalia (aləlā'liə), *n.* form of aphasia in which words are spoken at random. -ic (-al'ik), *adj.*

allomerism (alom'ərizm), *n. Chem.,* variation in constitution without variation in form. -rous, *adj.*

allonge (əlonj'), *n. Comm.,* slip of paper attached to bill of exchange for additional endorsements.

allonym (al'ənim), *n.* other person's name assumed by writer; work published under an a. -ous (-on'iməs), *adj.*

allopathy (alop'əthi), *n. Med.,* treatment of disease by remedies producing symptoms different from those of disease treated; opp. of homoeopathy; *erron.,* orthodox medical treatment. -thic (-ath'ik), *adj.* -thist, *n.*

allosematic (aləsimat'ik), *adj.* having imitative protective coloration.

allotheism (al'əthēizm), *n.* worship of strange gods.

allotropy (alot'rəpi), *n.* existence of an element in more than one form. -pe, *n.* form taken by allotropic element. -pic(al) (-op'ik, -l), *adj.*

alluvion (alōō'viən), *n.* impact of water on shore; flood; alluvium.

alluvium (alōō'viəm), *n. (pl.* -iums, -ia) matter deposited by river or flood. -vial, *adj.*

almacentor, *see* almucantar.

almagest (al'məjest), *n.* comprehensive treatise or textbook, *espec.* on astronomy, gen. the treatise of Ptolemy.

alma mater (al'mə mā'tə), *Lat.,* "fostering mother"; one's school or university.

almandine (al'məndin, -in), *n.* kind of violet-coloured garnet.

alme, -meh, -mai (al'mā), *n.* Egyptian dancing girl.

almira (almir'ə), Anglo-Ind. *n.* furniture for storing, *e.g.* cupboard or chest.

almonds (ah'məndz), *n.pl. Med.,* the tonsils.

almoner (ah'mənə, al'mənə), *n.* official who distributes alms; hospital official who interviews prospective patients, etc. -nry, *n.* place for alms distribution; a.'s office.

almucantar (almūkan'tə), *n.* *Astron.*, circle of celestial sphere parallel with horizon ; parallel of altitude ; telescope that, in rotating, sweeps out curves of this kind.

alnico (al'nikō), *n.* permanent magnet alloy of aluminium, nickel and cobalt, with some iron and sometimes copper.

aloe (al'ō), *n.* bitter fruit of sev. plants used in preparation of purgative. **-s,** *n.* such purgative. **-tic** (-ōet'ik), *adj.* pert. to a.

alogia (alō'jiə), *n.* speech defect due to mental deficiency.

alogism (al'əjizm), *n.* illogical statement.

alopecia (aləpē'siə, -shə), *n.* baldness. **a.areata,** loss of hair in small patches.

alopecoid (aləpē'koid, -op'ikoid), *adj.* fox-like.

alpenglow (alp'ənglō), *n.* reddish light at sunset or sunrise on mountain-tops, *espec.* occurring before appearance or after disappearance of sun.

alpestrine (alpes'trin), *adj.* pert. to alpine zone.

alpha (al'fə), *n.* first letter (A, α) of Gr. alphabet. **a. and omega,** first and last ; entirely ; quintessence. **a. particle,** positively charged particle, the nucleus of a helium atom. **a. ray,** a ray or beam of a. particles.

alphenic (alfen'ik), *n.* *Med.,* sugarcandy.

alsike (al'sik), *n.* pink-flowered clover, grown as forage.

alsinaceous (alsinā'shəs), *adj.* like or pert. to chickweed ; belonging to chickweed family of plants.

alt (alt), *n.* & *adj.* *Mus.,* (note) in first octave above the treble stave.

altarage (awl'tərij), *n.* offerings at altar ; payment for masses for dead ; certain payments to priest.

altazimuth (altaz'iməth), *n.* instr. measuring altitude and azimuth of heavenly bodies.

alterative (awl'tərətiv), *adj.* causing change ; *Med.,* changing gradually to healthy state ; *n.* drug or other treatment changing nutritional processes.

alter ego (al'tə ē'gō, eg'ō), *Lat.,* "other self" ; close friend ; confidant.

alterity (alter'iti, awl-), *n.* state of being different.

alternator (awl'tənātə), *n.* machine generating alternating electric current.

althea (althē'ə), *n.* rose of Sharon.

althing (awl'thing), *n.* parl. of Iceland.

altiloquence (altil'əkwəns), *n.* pompous, high-sounding speech.

altimeter (altim'itə), *n.* instr. for taking or showing altitude.

altisonant (altis'ənənt), *adj.* high-sounding.

altissimo (altis'imō), *n.* & *adj.* *Mus.,* (note) in the second octave above the treble stave.

altivolant (altiv'ələnt), *adj.* flying high.

alto-relievo (al'tō-rilē'vō), *n.* carving in high relief, *i.e.* in which the figures, etc., project more than half their proportions from the background.

altruism (al'trōoism), *n.* principle of regard for others ; self-sacrifice. **-ist,** *n.* **-istic,** *adj.*

alum (al'əm), *n.* sulphate of aluminium used in dyeing, as an astringent, etc.

alumina (alōōm'inə), *n.* oxide of aluminium.

aluminium (alūmin'iəm), *n.* light, malleable white metal, resistant to organic salts, obtained by heating a. oxide. **-nic,** *adj.*

aluminosis (alūminō'sis), *n.* lung disease due to inhaling aluminium dust.

aluminous (alōō'minəs), *adj.* pert. to alumina.

aluminum (alū'minəm), Amer. *n.* aluminium.

alumnus (alum'nəs), *n.* (*pl.* -ni ; *fem.* -na, *pl.* -ae) member of university or college.

alveary (al'viəri), *n.* beehive ; outer canal of ear.

alveola (alvē'ələ), *n.* (*pl.* -ae) *Bot.,* small cavity, *espec.* in surface of an organ.

alveolar (alvē'ələ, al'-), *adj.* pert. to alveolus ; bearing alveolae ; *Phon.,* pronounced with tongue and alveolus ; *n.* sound so pronounced ; *pl.* the a. arch. **a. arch,** tooth-bearing part of upper jaw.

alveolate (alvē'əlāt, al'-), *adj.* having many deep cavities ; like a honey-comb.

alveolus (alvē'ələs), *n.(pl.* -li) *Anat.*, small cavity ; tooth socket ; air-cell, etc. ; *Phon.*, upper front tooth ridge.

alviducous (alvidū'kəs) *adj.* purgative.

alvine (al'vīn, -vin), *adj.* pert. to belly or intestines.

amadavat (amədəvat'), *n.* Ind. song-bird ; strawberry finch.

amadelphous (amədel'fəs), *adj.* gregarious.

amadou (am'ədōō), *n.* form of tinder prepared from fungi; "German tinder" ; punk.

amah (ah'mah), Anglo-Ind. *n.* wet-nurse.

amaldar, *see* **amildar.**

amandine (aman'din, am'-), *n.* albumin in sweet almonds ; cold cream composed of that substance.

amanous (am'ənəs), *adj.* lacking hands.

amanuensis (amanūen'sis), *n.* (*pl.* -ses) employee who writes from dictation ; secretary.

amaranth (am'əranth), *n.* myth. plant that never fades ; love-lies-bleeding ; purple colour. **-ine,** *adj.* unfading ; eternal ; purple.

amarthritis (amahthrī'tis), *n.* arthritis of sev. joints.

amasthenic (aməsthen'ik), *adj.* bringing light rays into one focus.

amatol (am'ətol), *n.* explosive composed of T.N.T. and ammonium nitrate.

amaurosis (amŏr ō'sis), *n.* loss of sight without noticeable change in eye, due to failure of optic nerve ; gutta serena. **-otic** (-ot'ik), *adj.*

ambage (am'bij), *n.* circuitous path or approach ; circumlocution. **-gious** (-bā'jəs), **-gitory** (-baj'itəri), *adj.*

ambary (ambah'ri), *n.* fibre-yielding plant of E. Indies.

ambergris (am'bəgrēs), *n.* substance obtained from intestines of sperm-whale, found in the sea and used in perfumes.

ambidexter, -trous (ambideks'tə, -rəs), *adj.* able to use both hands with equal facility ; *n.* such person. **-erity** (-er'iti), *n.*

ambient (am'biənt), *adj.* surrounding ; *n.* such thing, *espec.* atmosphere.

ambiguous (ambig'ūəs), *adj.* of uncertain meaning. **-uity** (-ū'iti), *n.*

ambilaevous (ambilē'vəs), *adj.* ambi-sinister.

ambilateral (ambilat'ərəl), *adj.* of both sides.

ambisinister, -trous (ambisin'istə, -rəs), *adj.* left-handed in both hands ; awkward.

ambivalence (ambiv'ələns), *n.* simultaneous attraction and repulsion. **-nt,** *adj.* feeling a.

amblosis (amblō'sis), *n.* abortion. **-otic** (-lot'ik), *adj.* causing a.

amblyopia (ambliō'piə), *n.* partial loss of sight not due to disease of eye ; early stage of amaurosis.

ambosexous (ambōseks'əs), *adj.* hermaphrodite.

ambrosia (ambrō'ziə), *n.* *Myth.*, food of the gods ; any very pleasant food. **-l,** *adj.*

ambry (am'bri), *n.* niche ; cupboard, *espec.* containing sacred vessels in chancel.

ambsace (ām'zās), *n.* double ace ; lowest score ; bad luck.

ambulant (am'būlənt), *adj.* walking, continuing active. **-ation,** *n.*

ambulatory (am'būlətri), *n.* enclosed space, *espec.* in monastery, for walking ; *adj.* pert. to walking.

ameba, *see* **amoeba.**

âme damnée (ahm dan'ā), *Fr.*, "lost soul" ; dupe ; tool ; devoted follower.

amelification (amelifikā'shn), *n.* formation of tooth-enamel.

ameloblast (amel'əblast), *n.* enamel-producing cell of tooth.

amende (amahnd'), *Fr.* *n.* fine ; reparation. **a.honorable** (onōrah'-bl), public apology ; full reparation for dishonour.

amenia (amē'niə), *n.* amenorrhoea.

amenity (əmē'niti), *n.* attractiveness ; pleasantness ; *pl.* pleasant conditions or surroundings.

amenorrhoea (amenərē'ə), *n.* abnormal absence or arrest of menstruation.

a mensa et thoro (ā men'sə et thor'ō), *Lat.*, "from table and bed" ; app. to judicial separation of husband and wife.

ament(um) (ament', -əm), *n.* catkin. **-taceous,** *adj.* like or composed of catkins. **-tal,** *adj.* pert to catkins. **-tiferous,** *adj.* bearing catkins. **-tiform,** *adj.* catkin-shaped.

amerce (amœs'), *v.t.* punish, *espec.* by fine. **-ciable,** *adj.* **-ment,** *n.*

ə=*er* in *father* ; ē=*er* in *pert* ; th=*th* in *thin* ; dh=*th* in *then* ; zh=*s* in *pleasure* ; k=*ch* in *loch* ; ǹ=Fr. nasal *n* ; ū=Fr. *u.*

americium (amərish'iəm), *n.* artificial element (No. 95), made by bombarding uranium or plutonium with helium ions.

amesace, *see* ambsace.

ametropia (amitrō'piə), *n.* abnormality in optical refraction. **-pic** (-op'ik), *adj.*

amiantus, -thus (amian'təs, -thəs), *n.* asbestos with silky fibres. **-thine,** *adj.*

amice (am'īs), *n.* R.C., white linen square covering shoulders of celebrant priest; garment or badge of a religious order.

amicicide (amī'sisīd), *n.* murder or murderer of a friend.

amicron (amī'kron, -mik'-), *n.* smallest microscopically detectable particle.

amicus curiae (amī'kəs kūr'ī'ē), *Lat.,* "friend of the court"; person invited or allowed to assist court on points of law.

amigo (ahmē'gō), Sp. *n.* (*pl.* **-gos** ; *fem.* **-ga**) friend.

amildar (am'əldah), Anglo-Ind. *n.* native revenue collector or factor.

amine (am'ēn), *n.* compound derived from ammonia.

amino-acid (amē'nō-as'id, am'inō-), *n.* one of many acids forming the principal ingredients of protein.

amitosis (amitō'sis), *n.* direct cell division. **-totic** (-ot'ik), *adj.*

ammeter (am'ētə), *n.* instr. measuring amperage of elec. current.

ammonite (am'onīt), *n.* fossil cephalopod with whorled shell. **-tiferous,** *adj.* containing ammonites.

ammophilous (amof'iləs), *adj.* sand-loving.

ammotherapy (aməther'əpi), *n.* med. treatment by sand baths.

amnesia (amnē'zhiə), *n.* loss of memory. **-emonic** (-imon'ik), **-etic** (-et'ik), *adj.*

amnesty (am'nisti), *n.* general pardon.

amnion (am'niən), *n.* innermost membrane enclosing foetus. **-iota** (-ō'tə), *n.pl.* vertebrates having a. **-iotic** (-ot'ik), *adj.*

amoeba (amē'bə), *n.* (*pl.* **-ae, -as**) unicellular animal, composed of microscopic mass of naked protoplasm; lowest form of animal life.

amoebaean (amēbē'ən), *adj.* app. to verse in which two persons speak alternately.

amoeban (amē'bən), *adj.* pert. to amoeba. **-bic, -biform, -boid,** *adj.* **-bicide,** *n.* substance killing amoebas.

amoret (am'əret), *n.* female lover; love-making; love-poem, etc.

amorphous (amaw'fəs), *adj.* without shape; irregularly shaped; *Chem.,* lacking crystalline structure; *Biol.,* lacking differentiation in structure; *Geol.,* not divided into strata. **-phism,** *n.*

amortise (amaw'tīz), *v.t.* nullify debt, *gen.* by forming a sinking fund; alienate lands in mortmain. **-ment,** *n.* *Archit.,* topmost member of a building; slanting top of buttress, etc. **-sation,** *n.*

amour (amoor'), Fr. *n.* love-affair. **-ette,** *n.* petty amour.

amour-propre (amoor-prop'r), Fr. *n.* self-love; self-respect.

ampelideous (ampilid'iəs), *adj.* of or like the vine.

ampelopsis (ampilop'sis), *n.* Virginia creeper.

ampelotherapy (ampəlather'əpi), *n.* *Med.,* grape cure.

ampere, -ère (am'pār, ahñ'-), *n.* unit of intensity of elec. current (current produced by one volt acting through resistance of one ohm) (*abbr.* amp.). **a.hour,** unit of quantity of elec. current (quantity flowing in one hour at one amp.).

ampersand (am'pəsand), *n.* sign (&) for *and.*

amphibian (amfib'iən), *n.* & *adj.* (animal) able to live both on land and in water; (vehicle) able to alight on or take off from, or to travel on, both land and water.

amphibious (amfib'iəs), *adj.* amphibian. **-iety** (-ī'iti), *n.*

amphibole (am'fibōl), *n.* rock-forming silicate similar to asbestos and hornblende.

amphibolic (amfibol'ik), *adj.* able to turn backwards or forwards, *espec.* of joints and limbs; ambiguous; like amphibole.

amphibolite (amfib'əlīt), *n.* rock composed of amphibole; hornblende.

amphibology (amfibol'əji), *n.* ambiguous speech; equivocation; quibble.

amphiboly (amfib'əli), *n.* amphibology. **-lous,** *adj.*

amphibrach (am'fibrak), *n.* metrical

foot of one short, one long and one short syllable.

amphichroic (amfikrō'ik), *adj.* producing two colours. **-chrome,** *n.* such a plant. **-chromatic,** *adj.* **-chromy,** *n.*

amphicoelous (amfisē'ləs), *adj. Zoo.,* having both surfaces concave.

amphictyonic (amfiktion'ik), *adj.* app. to anct. Gr. council of state-deputies. **-ny** (-ik'tiəni), *n.* league of adjacent states.

amphicyrtic (amfisə'tik), *adj.* with both sides convex.

amphigean (amfijē'ən), *adj.* occurring in both hemispheres ; *Bot.,* with flowers arising from root-stock.

amphigony (amfig'əni), *n.* sexual reproduction. **-nic** (-on'ik), **-nous,** *adj.*

amphilogism (amfil'əjizm), *n.* amphibology.

amphimacer (amfim'əsə), *n.* metrical foot comprising one long, one short and one long syllable.

amphimixis (amfimiks'is), *n.* interbreeding ; joining of germ plasm of two individuals in sexual reproduction.

amphiont (am'fiont), *n.* zygote.

amphipodous (amfip'ədəs), *adj. Zoo.,* having both walking and swimming feet.

amphiprostyle (amfip'rəstīl, -prō'-), *n. & adj.* (building) with columns at each end but not at sides.

amphirhinal (amfirī'nəl), *adj.* with two nostrils.

amphisbaena (amphisbē'nə), *n.* myth. double-headed serpent ; kind of worm-like lizard.

amphiscian (amfish'ən), *n. & adj.* (inhabitant) of torrid zone.

amphivorous (amfiv'ərəs), *adj.* both carnivorous and herbivorous.

amphora (am'fərə), *n.* (*pl.* **-ae, -as**) vase with two handles, of Gr. or Rom. origin ; standard liquid measure of nine galls. (Gr.) and six galls. (Rom.). **-ral, -rous,** *adj.* **-ric** (-or'ik), *adj.* app. to sound made by blowing into an a., or sound resembling that.

amphoteric (amfətər'ik), *adj.* of both kinds ; *Chem.,* reacting as either alkali or acid.

amplectant (amplek'tənt), *adj. Bot.,* clasping tightly.

ampliative (am'pliətiv), *adj.* supplementary. **-tion,** *n.* enlargement.

amplitude (am'plitūd), *n.* spaciousness ; plenty ; breadth ; amount of displacement of vibrating body or oscillating current ; *Astrol.,* angular distance between heavenly body at rising or setting and east or west point of horizon ; *Astron.,* arc of horizon between foot of vertical circle through heavenly body and east or west point. **a. modulation,** radio transmission by varying the amplitude (height or depth) of carrier wave (*abbr.* **A.M.**),

ampulla (ampul'ə), *n.* anct. Rom. flask with two handles and globular body, *espec.* such flask used at coronation of Eng. monarchs to contain holy oil. **-aceous, -ar,** *adj.* ampulla-shaped.

amyctic (amik'tik), *n. Med.,* irritating.

amyelotrophy (amīilot'rəfi), *n.* atrophy of spinal cord.

amygdala (amig'dələ), *n.* any almond-shaped formation in body, *e.g.* tonsil. **-laceous, -late,** *adj.*

amygdalin (amig'dəlin), *n.* glucoside in bitter almonds and kernels of certain fruits. **-e,** *adj.* pert. to almonds. **-loid,** *adj.* almond-shaped ; pert. to tonsils ; *n.* basaltic rock with almond-shaped cavities.

amylaceous (amilā'shəs), *adj.* starchy.

amyloid (am'iloid), *n.* food containing starch ; *adj.* starchy ; app. to disease in which lardaceous substance arises from degenerated cells.

amylolysis (amilol'isis), *n.* conversion of starch into soluble products in digestive process. **-ytic** (-it'ik), *adj.*

amylopsin (amilop'sin), *n.* digestive ferment in pancreatic juice.

amylose (am'ilōs), *n.* starch-forming substance.

amyotrophy (amiot'rəfi), *n.* atrophy of muscle.

amyous (am'iəs), *adj.* lacking muscle.

ana (a'nə, ah'nə), *n.* collection of sayings by, or stories and facts about, a person (often a suffix, *e.g.* Dickensiana).

anabaptist (anəbap'tist), *n.* believer in adult baptism. **-ism,** *n.* such belief ; re-baptism.

ə=*er* in *father* ; ē=*er* in *pert* ; th=*th* in *thin* ; dh=*th* in *then* ; zh=*s* in *pleasure* ; k=*ch* in *loch* ; ṅ=Fr. nasal *n* ; ü=Fr. *u.*

anabas (an'əbas), *n.* Ind. climbing fish.

anabasis (anab'əsis), *n.* (*pl.* -ses) upward journey; military advance, *espec.* of Persians and Greeks under Cyrus (401 B.C.); work by Xenophon describing the march of the 10,000 Greek mercenaries; *Med.*, first phase of disease; increase of fever. -atic (-at'ik), *adj.* increasing; ascending; *Meteor.*, moving upwards.

anabiosis (anəbī ō'sis), *n.* return to life after seeming death. -otic (-ot'ik), *n.* & *adj.* tonic.

anabolism (anab'əlizm), *n.* constructive chem. processes in living creatures. -ic (-bol'ik), *adj.* -ise, *v.i.*

anacamptic (anəkamp'tik), *adj.* reflecting or reflected. -s, *n.* study of reflection of sound and light waves. -tometer (-om'itə), *n. Med.,* instr. measuring strength of reflex actions.

anacardic (anəkah'dik), *adj.* pert. to cashew nut.

anacatharsis (anəkathah'sis), *n.* vomiting; expectoration. -rtic, *n.* & *adj.* (drug) causing a.

anachorism (anak'ərizm), *n.* thing foreign or not suited to a country; thing impossible or absurd geographically.

anachronism (anak'rənism), *n.* error in chronology, *espec.* of dating event before its correct date; thing impossible or absurd by reason of such error. -istic, -nic (-on'ik), -nous, *adj.*

anaclasis (anak'ləsis), *n. Med.,* forced bending of limb. -astic (-as'tik), *adj.* elastic; pert. to refraction. -astics, *n.* study of refraction.

anaclitic (anəklit'ik), *adj.* dependent; marked by dependence on other faculty, phenomenon, etc.

anacoluthon (anəkəlōō'thən), *n. Gram.,* lack of sequence; passing to a new subject, or sentence-construction, without completing first one. -thia, *n.* such practice. -thic, *adj.*

anaconda (anəkon'də), *n.* python of S. Amer. and Ceylon; any boa-like snake.

Anacreontic (anakrion'tik), *adj.* pert. to Anacreon, Gr. poet; *n.* bacchanalian poem. -s, *n.pl.* verses in the style of Anacreon.

anacrusis (anəkrōō'sis), *n.* unaccented syllable(s) at beginning of verse-line, or such notes at beginning of piece of music. -ustic (-us'tik), *adj.*

anacusia, -sis (anəkū'zhiə, -sis), *n.* complete deafness. -sic (-sik), *adj.*

anadem (an'ədəm), *n.* band; wreath; fillet.

anadenia (anədē'niə), *n.* deficiency in gland activity; lack of glands.

anadiplosis (anədiplō'sis), *n.* rhet. device of repetition of last word of one clause at beginning of next.

anadipsia (anədip'siə), *n. Med.,* abnormal thirst. -sic, *adj.*

anadromous (anad'rəməs), *adj.* ascending, *espec.* of fish that ascend rivers to spawn.

anaematosis (anēmətō'sis), *n.* pernicious anaemia.

anaemia (ənē'miə), *n.* lack of blood. **pernicious** *or* **primary a.,** disease resulting in rapid destruction of red corpuscles. -ic, *adj.*

anaemotrophy (animot'rəfi), *n.* insufficient nourishment of blood.

anaeretic, -er- (aniret'ik), *adj.* destructive.

anaerobe (an'ār ōb, -ār'-, -ā'er-), *n.* organism able to live without, or unable to live in presence of, oxygen. -bic, *adj.* -biosis, *n.* such existence. -biotic, *adj.*

anaerophyte (anār'əfit, -ā er'-), *n. Bot.,* anaerobic plant.

anaesthesia, -sis (anesthē'zhiə, -sis), *n.* loss of feeling; unconsciousness; act of causing such state for med. purposes. -iant, *n.* anaesthetic. -iology, *n.* study of a.

anaesthetic (anesthet'ik), *n.* & *adj.* (drug) causing anaesthesia. -tise (-ēs'thitīz), *v.t.* administer a. to. -tist, *n.* person administering a.

anagalactic (anəgəlak'tik), *adj. Astron.,* beyond our galaxy; not galactic.

anagenesis (anəjen'isis), *n.* tissue regeneration.

anaglyph (an'əglif), *n.* ornament in bas relief; stereoscopic pictures in complementary colours viewed through glasses, etc., of same colours, one to each eye. -y (-ag'lifi), *n.* art of carving a.

anaglypta (anəglip'tə), *n.* moulded decoration of walls and ceilings. -tics, *n.* art of carving in bas relief.

anagnorisis (anagnōr'isis), *n.* denouement in play, arising from recognition.

anagoge, -gy (anəgō'ji), *n.* spiritual exaltation ; *Med.*, rejection upwards of blood, etc. **-gic(al)** (-oj'ik, -l), *adj.* mystical. **-gics,** *n.* mystical interpretation of Bible.

anagraph (an'əgraf), *n.* catalogue. **-y** (-ag'rəfi), *n.* making of a.

anakinetic (anəkinet'ik), *adj.* restorative of energy.

anal (ā'nəl), *adj.* pert. to or near the anus.

analects (an'əlekts), *n. pl.* collection of writings ; literary gleanings. **-tic,** *adj.*

analeptic (anəlep'tik), *n. & adj. Med.,* restorative.

analgesia, -sis (analjē'ziə, -sis), *n.* absence of pain ; art of banishing pain. **-sic** (-ē'sik, -es'ik), *n. & adj.* **-sist,** *n.* anaesthetist.

analgetic (analjet'ik), *n. & adj.* (drug) arresting pain.

analgia (anal'jiə), *n.* analgesia. **-ic,** *adj.* **-ise,** *v.t.*

anallagmatic (anəlagmat'ik), *adj. Math.,* unchanged in shape by inversion.

analogy (anal'əji), *n.* close similarity ; a similar case used in reasoning. **-gical,** *adj.* **-gise,** *v.t. & t.* **-gism,** *n.* reasoning by quoting a. **-gous** (-gəs), *adj.* similar in some respect ; corresponding in function. **-gue** (an'əlog), *n.* analogous thing ; word in other language with same use or meaning.

anamnesis (anamnē'sis), *n.* act of reminiscence, *espec.* of history of med. case. **-nestic** (-nes'tik), *adj.* mnemonic.

anamorphic (anəmaw'fik), *adj.* changing into a more complex form. **-phism,** *n.* such geol. change.

anamorphosis (anəmawfō'sis), *n.* distorted image only recognisable if viewed through appropriate device ; method of making such images ; *Biol.,* evolution by slow changes ; *Bot.,* abnormal change of shape. **-oscope,** *n.* device for viewing a.

ananas (anah'nas, -nā'-), *n.* pineapple.

anandrious (anan'driəs), *adj.* impotent.

anandrous (anan'drəs), *adj. Bot.,* without stamens.

ananym (an'ənim), *n.* name written backwards as pseudonym.

anapaest, -pest (an'əpēst), *n.* metrical foot of two short syllables followed by one long syllable. **-ic,** *adj.*

anapeiratic (anəpīrat'ik), *adj. Med.,* caused by long or excessive use, *espec.* of paralysis.

anaphia (anā'fiə), *n.* loss of sense of touch.

anaphora (anaf'ərə), *n.* rhet. device of repeating word or phrase at beginning of successive clauses ; *Astron.,* oblique ascension. **-ric** (-or'ik), *adj. Gram.,* referring to word occurring earlier.

anaphrodisia (anafrədiz'iə), *n.* absence of sexual desire. **-c,** *n. & adj.* (drug) reducing sexual desire.

anaphroditic (anafrədit'ik), *adj.* asexually produced. **-tous** (-dī'təs) *adj.* pert. to anaphrodisia.

anaphylaxis(anəfilaks'is),*n.* allergy; extreme sensitivity caused by previous inoculation. **-actic,** *adj.* **-actogen,** *n.* substance causing a.

anaplasty (an'əplasti), *n.* plastic surgery. **-tic,** *adj.*

anapnoea, -nea (anapnē'ə), *n.* recovery of breathing.

anapnograph (anap'nəgraf), *n.*instr. measuring breathing movements.

anapnoic (anapnō'ik), *adj.* pert. to or restoring breathing.

anaptotic (anaptot'ik),*adj. Philol.,* with weakened or no case inflections.

anarthrous (anah'thrəs), *adj. Zoo.,* non-jointed ; *Gram.,* without the article (of Gr. nouns).

anasarcous (anəsah'kəs), *adj.* dropsical.

anaseismic (anəsīz'mik, -sis'-), *adj.* pert. to earthquake with vertical movement.

anastalsis (anəstal'sis), *n.* reversed peristalsis ; styptic action. **-ltic,** *adj.* styptic.

anastasis (anas'təsis), *n.* convalescence.

anastigmat (anas'tigmat), *n.* an anastigmatic lens. **-ic,** *adj.* not astigmatic ; corrective of astigmatism.

anastomosis (anastəmō'sis), *n.* (*pl.* **-ses**) intercommunication between branches of blood-vessels, nerves, etc., or of rivers ; formation of network. **-motic** (-mot'ik), *adj.*

ə=*er* in *father* ; ə̄=*er* in *pert*; th=*th* in *thin* ; dh=*th* in *then* ; zh=s in *pleasure* ; k=*ch* in *loch* ; .ṅ=Fr. nasal *n* ; ü=Fr. *u.*

anastrophe (anas'trəfi), *n.* rhet. device of reversing natural order of words ; inversion.

anathema (anath'imə), *n.* (*pl.* -s) curse, gen. by eccl. authorities ; act of cursing; thing cursed ; object of hatred ; (*pl.* -ata) consecrated thing; offering to deity. -tic (-at'ik), *adj.* -tise, *v.t.* -tism, *n.*

anatocism (anat'əsizm), *n.* compound interest; taking such interest.

anatomy (anat'əmi), *n.* study of structure of body ; art of dissecting ; structure ; analysis ; skeleton ; very thin person. -mical (-om'ikl), *adj.* -mise, *v.t.* dissect ; analyse. -mist, *n.*

anatopism (anat'əpizm), *n.* incongruous placing.

anatreptic (anətrep'tik), *adj.* defeating ; overturning.

anatripsis (anətrip'sis), *n.* friction as med. treatment. -psology, *n.* use of a. -ptic, *adj.*

anaudia (anaw'diə), *n.* loss of voice.

anbury, am- (an'bəri, am'-), *n.* soft tumour of horses ; "finger and toe" disease of turnips ; "clubroot."

anchorite, -ret (ang'kərīt, -it), *n.* (*fem.* -ress, -ritess, **ancress**) hermit, ascetic. -tic(al) (-it'ik, -l), *adj.* -tism, *n.*

anchovy (anchō'vi), *n.* small Mediterranean fish of herring family ; paste, etc., made from a. **a.pear**, mango-like West Ind. fruit and tree.

anchusa (angkū'sə), *n.* alkanet.

ancien régime (ahn'siaṅ rā'zhēm), *Fr.*, political and social state before the Fr. revolution ; former (gen. evil) times.

anchylosis (ankilō'sis), *n.* union of bones or hard parts ; stiffness so caused. -ose, *v.t.* grow together (of bones).

ancillary (ansil'ari), *adj.* subordinate ; auxiliary.

ancipital, -tous (ansip'itəl, -əs), *adj.* having two faces or edges ; double-headed ; twofold.

ancistroid (ansis'troid), *adj.* having shape of hook.

anconeal (angkō'niəl), *adj.* pert. to the elbow. -nitis (-ənī'tis), *n.* inflammation of elbow. -noid (ang'kənoid), *adj.* like an elbow.

ancoral (ang'kərəl), *adj.* like an anchor; hooked.

ancress, *see* **anchorite**.

ancylostomiasis, *see* **ankylostomiasis**.

andiron (an'dīrn), *n.* support for logs, fire-irons, or spit ; fire-dog.

andranatomy (andrənat'əmi), *n.* human anatomy.

androcentric (andrəsen'trik), *adj.* with the male element dominating.

androcephalous (andrəsef'ələs), *adj.* with human head.

androcracy (androk'rəsi), *n.* domination of society by men. -atic (-at'ik), *adj.*

androgen (an'drəjen), *n.* substance producing masculine characteristics ; male sex hormone. -ic (-jen'ik), *adj.* -ous (-oj'inəs), *adj. Bot.*, producing males.

androgynal, -nous (androj'inəl, -nəs), *adj.* hermaphrodite. -ne (an'drəjīn, -in), *n.* hermaphrodite ; effeminate man ; masculine woman. -neity (-nē'iti), -nism, -ny, *n.*

android (and'roid), *n.* machine in form of human being ; robot ; *adj.* man-like. -al, *adj.*

androkinin (androk'inin), *n.* male sex hormone.

androlepsy, -sia (an'drəlepsi, -lep'siə), *n.* seizure of foreign subjects to enforce claim for justice or other right against their nation.

andromania (andrəmā'niə), *n.* excessive sexual desire in female.

andromorphous (andrəmaw'fəs), *adj.* having man's shape or appearance.

androphagous (androf'əgəs), *adj.* cannibal.

androphobia (andrəfō'biə), *n.* dread or hatred of men.

androphonomania (andrəfōnəmā'-niə), *n.* homicidal mania.

androphorous (androf'ərəs), *adj. Zoo.*, having male organs.

androsphinx (an'drəsfingks), *n.* figure with man's head and lion's body.

anele (anēl'), *v.t.* anoint ; administer extreme unction to.

anelectric (anilek'trik), *n. & adj.* (body) not electrified by friction or parting rapidly with its electricity.

anemia, *see* **anaemia**.

anemochord (anem'əkawd), *n.* kind of pianoforte having strings vibrated by air currents.

---

hat, bah, hāte, hāre, crawl ; pen, ēve, hēre ; it, īce, fīre ; on, bōne, boil, bōre, howl ; foot, fŏŏd, bŏŏr, hull, tūbe, pūre.

anemograph (anem'əgraf), *n*. instr. recording strength or speed of wind. -gram, *n*. record made by an a.

anemometer (animom'itə), *n*. instr. measuring strength and speed of wind. -trograph (aneməmet'-rəgraf), *n*. instr. recording strength, speed and direction of wind. -try, *n*.

anemopathy (animop'əthi), *n*. med. treatment by inhalation.

anemophilous (animof'iləs), *adj*. *Bot*., pollinated by wind. -le (-nem'əfil, -fil), *n*. such plant. -ly, *n*. such pollination.

anemoscope (anem'əskōp), *n*. instr. indicating direction of wind.

anencephaly, -lia (anensef'əli, -sifā'liə), *n*. state of lacking a brain. -lic (-sifal'ik), -lous (-sef'ələs), *adj*.

anenterous (anen'tərəs), *adj*. lacking intestine or stomach.

anepia (anē'piə), *n*. loss or absence of power of speech.

anergy, -gia (an'əji, -ō'jiə), *n*. absence of energy; loss of immunity.

aneroid (an'əroid), *adj*. not using liquid. a.barometer, instr. measuring atmospheric pressure by recording the movements of the surface of an air-tight box. -ograph, *n*. recording a barometer.

anesis (an'isis), *n*. *Med*., abatement of symptoms; *Mus*., tuning to lower pitch.

aneuria (anūr'iə), *n*. lack of nervous energy. -ic, *adj*.

aneurin (an'ūrin), *n*. vitamin B₁.

aneurism, -ysm (an'ūrizm), *n*. swelling of artery. -al, -atic, *adj*.

anfractuose, -uous (anfrak'tū ōs, -ūəs), *adj*. wavy; snake-like; *Bot*., spiral-shaped. -osity (-os'iti), *n*.

angary (ang'gəri), *n*. right of belligerent to take or destroy property of neutral.

angelica (anjel'ikə), *n*. aromatic plant yielding oil used in med. and cookery; sugared stalks of a.; green liqueur flavoured with a. oil.

angelolater (ānjəlol'ətə), *n*. worshipper of angels. -try, *n*. such worship.

angelus (an'jiləs), *n*. prayer(s) said at early morning, noon and sunset. a.bell, bell calling to prayer at such times.

angiitis (anjiī'tis), *n*. *Med*., inflammation of vessel.

angina (anjī'nə), *n*. quinsy; any inflammation of throat or trachea. a.pectoris, spasm of the chest resulting from disease of heart or arteries. -niform (-jin'ifawm), *adj*. resembling a. pectoris. -noid, -nose, -nous (an'jin-), *adj*.

angioid (an'jioid), *adj*. like blood or lymph vessel.

angiology (anjiol'əji), *n*. study of blood and lymphatic system.

angioma (anjiō'mə), *n*. tumour due to dilated blood vessels. -tosis, *n*. state of having many a. -tous, *adj*.

angiospasm (an'jiəspazm), *n*. sudden contraction of blood vessels. -astic, *adj*.; *n*. substance causing a.

angiosperm (an'jiəspōm), *n*. flowering plant with seeds in closed seed-vessel; *pl*. natural division containing plants of such kind, the highest forms of plant life. -al, -atous, -ic, -ous, *adj*.

angiotomy (anjiot'əmi), *n*. dissection of or incision into blood vessel.

Anglice (ang'glisi), *adv*. in English.

angola (anggō'lə), *n*. and *adj*. angora.

angora (anggōr'ə), *n*. long-haired goat of Asia Minor; material made from a. hair; *adj*. long-haired (of cat, rabbit, etc.).

angostura, -gus- (anggəstūr'ə), *n*. Brazilian tree and its bark; tonic fluid extracted from the bark.

angstrom (ang'strom), *n*. *Phys*., unit of length of light waves, one hundred-millionth of a centimetre.

anguiform (ang'gwifawm), *adj*. having shape of snake.

anguilliform (anggwil'ifawm), *adj*. having shape of eel. -loid, *adj*. like an eel.

anguine, -eal, -eous (ang'gwin; anggwin'iəl, -iəs), *adj*. pert. to or like a snake.

angulometer (anggūlom'itə), *n*. instr. measuring external angles.

anguria (anggūr'iə), *n*. gourd; watermelon.

anhaematosis, -hem- (anhēmətō'-sis), *n*. incomplete or incorrect blood formation.

anhedonia (anhidō'niə), *n*. inability to be happy.

anhelation (anhilā'shn), *n*. shortness of breath. -lous (-hē'ləs), *adj*. panting.

anhidrosis (anhidrō'sis), *n.* lack or absence of perspiration. **-otic** (-ot'ik), *n.* & *adj.* (drug) checking perspiration.

aniconic (anīkon'ik), *adj.* without idols. **-nism** (-ī'kənizm), *n.* worship of object symbolising but not representing god; iconoclasm.

anicular (anik'ūlə), *adj.* like an old woman.

anidian (anid'iən), *adj.* shapeless.

anil (an'il), *n.* W. Ind. plant yielding indigo; indigo.

anile (an'īl, ā'-), *adj.* like a very old woman; imbecile.

anilic (anil'ik), *adj.* pert. to anil.

aniline (an'ilīn, -lin, -lēn), *n.* substance obtained from indigo, nitro-benzene, etc., used in manuf. of dyes; *adj.* app. to dye prepared with a. **-nism** (-linizm), *n.* disease due to inhaling fumes in aniline manuf.

anility (anil'iti), *n.* state of being anile.

animadvert (animadvöt'), *v.i.* take notice; comment; criticise; reprove. **-rsion,** *n.*

animalcule (animal'kūl), *n.* (*pl.* **-s,** **-lae**) microscopic animal, or, *erron.,* plant. **-lar, -line, -lous,** *adj.*

animastic (animas'tik), *adj.* spiritual; animate; *n.* psychology.

animatism (an'imətizm), *n.* belief that inanimate objects, etc., have personality and will, but not soul.

animative (an'imətiv, -māt-), *adj.* giving life; animistic.

animism (an'imizm), *n.* belief in the possession of a soul by inanimate objects; belief in existence of soul separate from matter; spiritualism. **-ist,** *n.* **-istic,** *adj.*

animus (an'iməs), *n.* strong hostility; *Law,* intention.

anion (anī'ən, an'i-), *n.* negatively charged ion. **-ic** (-on'ik), *adj.*

anise (an'is), *n.* Egyptian plant yielding aniseed. **-sate,** *v.t.* flavour with aniseed.

aniseed (an'isēd), *n.* dried fruit of anise; cordial made from it; *adj.* containing a. **-sic** (-is'ik, -ī'sik), *adj.* pert. to anise.

anisometropia (anīsəmetrō'piə), *n.* condition of eyes having unequal refractive power. **-pe,** *n.* person suffering from a. **-pic** (-op'ik), *adj.*

anisosthenic (anīsosthen'ik), *adj.* of unequal strength.

anker (ang'kə), *n.* liquid measure, *espec.* Dutch, of 8½ imperial gallons; cask holding that amount.

ankus (ang'kəs), Ind. *n.* elephant goad with hook and spike.

ankylosis, *see* **anchylosis.**

ankylostoma (angkilost'əmə), *n.* lockjaw.

ankylostomiasis (angkilostəmī'əsis), *n.* infestation with threadworms.

ankyroid (angkīr'oid), *adj.* having shape of hook.

anlace (an'lās), *n.* short doubleedged sword or long dagger.

anna (an'ə), Ind. *n.* coin valued at sixteenth part of rupee; onesixteenth.

annates (an'āts, -its), *n.pl.* first fruits; *Eccl.,* a year's income of benefice.

annatto (anat'ō), *n.* reddish dye used for colouring foodstuffs; tropical Amer. tree from seeds of which it is obtained.

anneal (anēl'), *v.t.* strengthen; temper, *espec.* by subjecting to great heat and slow cooling.

annectant (anek'tənt), *adj.* connecting; *Biol.,* linking, *espec.* of species.

annelid (an'ilid), *n.* worm composed of annular segments. **-an** (-el'idən), **-ian** (-lid'iən), **-ous** (-el'idəs), *adj.* **-lism,** *n. Zoo.,* annular structure. **-loid,** *adj.* like an annelid.

annihilate (anī'ilāt), *v.t.* totally destroy; reduce to nothing. **-tion,** **-tor,** *n.* **-tive, -tory,** *adj.*

annodated (an'ədātid), *adj.* S-shaped.

anno hebraico (an'ō hebrā'ikō), *Lat.,* "in the Hebrew year" (*abbr.* A.H.).

anno hegirae (an'ō hej'irē), *Lat.,* "in the year of the hegira"; Mohammedan date (*abbr.* A.H.).

annomination (anominā'shn), *n.* play on words; pun; alliteration.

anno mundi (an'ō mun'di), *Lat.,* "in the year of the world"; dating from creation, fixed by Archbp. Ussher at 4004 B.C. (*abbr.* A.M.).

anno orbis conditi (an'ō aw'bis con'diti), *Lat.,* "in the year of the creation" (*abbr.* a.o.c.).

annos vixit (an'ōs viks'it), *Lat.,* "lived (so many) years"; was aged (*abbr.* a.v.).

annotine (an'ōtīn, -in), *n.* one-year-old, *espec.* bird after first moult.

anno urbis conditae (an'ō ə'bis kon'dītē), *Lat.*, "in the year of the foundation of the city (Rome)," dated at 753 B.C. (*abbr.* A.U.C.) *See* ab urbe condita.

annuent (an'ūənt), *adj.* nodding, *espec.* of muscles that nod the head.

annuity (anū'iti), *n.* yearly income, *espec.* for life. **-tant,** *n.* person receiving annuity.

annul (anul'), *v.t.* cancel ; invalidate ; destroy. **-ment,** *n.*

annular (an'ūlə), *adj.* pert. to, forming or having shape of a ring. **a. eclipse,** eclipse of sun in which a ring of its surface surrounds the moon. **-late,** *adj.* marked with rings ; having rings of colour ; annular. **-lation,** *n.* **-y,** *n.* ring-finger.

annulet (an'ūlit), *n.* small ring ; *Archit.,* fillet or ring round column, *espec.* on Doric capital.

annulism (an'ūlizm), *n.* ringed structure.

annulose (an'ūlōs), *adj.* ringed ; composed of rings.

annulus (an'ūləs), *Lat. n.* anything having shape of ring.

annunciate (anun'shiāt, -siāt), *v.t.* announce ; proclaim. **-tion,** *n.* announcement of the Incarnation to Mary, mother of Jesus ; feast celebrated on Lady-day (March 25) ; **a.lily,** madonna lily ; **a.style,** old style of dating years as beginning on March 25. **-tive, -tory,** *adj.*

annus mirabilis (an'əs mirah'bilis), *Lat.,* "wonderful year," *espec.* (in England) 1666.

anoa (anō'ə), *n.* wild ox of Celebes.

anocathartic (anəkathah'tik), *n.* & *adj.* (drug) causing vomiting or expectoration.

anode (an'ōd), *n.* *Elec.,* positive terminal ; electrode by which current enters, or to which electrons flow. **a.battery,** battery supplying current between a. and cathode of thermionic valve. **-dal, -dic** (-od'ik), *adj.* **-dise** (an'ədīz), *v.t.* coat with protective film electrolytically.

anodont (an'ədont), *n.* hingeless and toothless bivalve ; freshwater mussel.

anodontia (anədon'shiə), *n.* absence of teeth.

anodyne (an'ədīn), *n.* & *adj.* (drug) reducing pain. **-nia** (-din'iə, -dī'-), *n.* absence of pain. **-nic** (-in'ik), **-nous** (-od'inəs), *adj.*

anoesia (anō ē'zhiə), *n.* imbecility.

anoesis (anō ē'sis), *n.* *Psych.,* mere reception of impressions without intellectual effort.

anoestrum (anē'strəm), *n.* period between "heats" in animals. **-rous,** *adj.*

anoetic (anōet'ik), *adj.* pert. to anoesis.

anogenic (anəjen'ik), *adj.* *Geol.,* formed from below ; plutonic.

anolis, **-li** (anō'lis, -li),*n.* chameleon-like W. Ind. and Amer. lizard.

anolyte (an'əlīt), *n.* *Elec.,* portion of electrolyte about anode.

anomalism (anom'əlizm), *n.* state or instance of being anomalous.

anomalistic (anoməlis'tik), *adj.* *Astron.,* pert. to anomaly. **a. month,** interval between two perigees of moon. **a.year,** interval between two perihelion passages of Earth.

anomalous (anom'ələs), *adj.* self-contradictory ; abnormal ; out of harmony ; irregular. **-ly,** *n.* ; *Astron.* : true a., angle subtended at centre of sun by planet and the perihelion it has passed ; **mean a.,** angle between perihelion and position that planet would occupy if it revolved in circular orbit with uniform velocity.

anomy (an'əmi), *n.* lack of law and order ; act contrary to natural law ; miracle.

anon (ənon'), *adv.* presently ; as soon as possible ; at a later date ; *n.* & *a'lj. abbr.* of anonym(ous).

anonym (an'onim), *n.* anonymous person ; pseudonym. **-ity** (-im'iti), *n.* act or state of concealing name ; unknown authorship. **-ous** (-on'-iməs), *adj.* of unknown name or origin ; unnamed.

anoopsia (anōopsiə), *n.* upward squint.

anopheles (anof'ilēz), *n.* kind of mosquito. **-line,** *adj.*

anopia (anō'piə), *n.*defective vision ; lack or deficiency of eyes.

anopisthographic (anəpisthəgraf'ik), *adj.* bearing writing, etc., on one side only.

anopsia (anop'siə), *n.* blindness ; anoopsia.

anorchous (anaw'kəs), *adj.* lacking testicles. **-chism**, *n.* **-chus**, *n.* such person.

anorexy, -xia (an'əreksi, -reks'iə), *n.* lack of appetite. **-ectic, -ectous**, *adj.*

anorthography (anawthog'rəfi), *n.* inability to write correctly due to imperfect muscular co-ordination. **-phic**, *adj.* contrary to rules of orthography.

anosmia (anos'miə), *n.* loss of sense of smell. **-matic, -mic**, *adj.*

anosphresia (anosfrē'zhiə), *n.* loss of sense of smell.

anotia (anō'shə), *n.* absence of ears. **-tus**, *n.* person lacking ears.

anourous, *see* **anurous**.

anoxaemia (anoksē'miə), *n.* condition resulting from insufficient aeration of blood; mountain sickness. **-ic**, *adj.*

anoxia (anoks'iə), *n.* deficiency of oxygen; condition due to this, *espec.* in flying at great heights. **-xic**, *adj.*

anoxybiosis (anoksībī'ō'sis), *n.* anaerobiosis. **-otic** (-ot'ik), *adj.*

ansate (an'sāt), *adj.* having a handle. **-tion**, *n.* handlemaking.

anserine, -rous (an'sərīn, -in ; -rəs), *adj.* like or pert. to a goose; foolish.

antacid (antas'id), *n.* & *adj.* curative of acidity, *espec.* intestinal.

antalgic (antal'jik), *n.* & *adj.* (drug) alleviating pain.

antalkali (antal'kəlī), *n.* substance neutralising alkali. **-ne**, *adj.*

antanaclasis (antənak'ləsis), *n.* repetition of word from earlier phrase, *espec.* of same word with different meaning.

ant-apex (ant'āpeks), *n.* *Astron.*, point 180° from that towards which sun is moving.

antapology (antəpol'əji), *n.* reply to apology.

antarthritic (antahthrit'ik), *n.* & *adj.* (drug) used against gout.

antecedaneous (antisidā'niəs), *adj.* before in time.

antecedent (antisē'dnt), *adj.* before in time ; prior ; *Mus.*, event happening prior to ; *Gram.*, subject of fugue stated in first part ; *Gram.*, previous word, *espec.* one to which pronoun, etc., refers ; *pl.* personal history ; ancestry. **-ence**, *n.*

antedate (antidāt', an'-), *v.t.* date, or assign a date to, a document,

etc., earlier than its correct date ; precede in point of time ; anticipate.

antediluvian, -ial (antidīloo'viən, -iəl), *adj.* pert. to period before the flood ; old-fashioned ; out-of-date.

antelocation (antilōkā'shn), *n.* *Med.*, forward displacement of an organ.

antelucan (antilōo'kən), *adj.* before dawn.

antelude (an'tilōod, -lūd), *n.* prelude ; "curtain-raiser."

antemetic (antimet'ik), *n.* & *adj.* preventive of vomiting.

ante mortem (an'ti maw'tem), *Lat.*, "before death."

antemundane (antimun'dān), *adj.* before the Creation ; before one's birth.

antenatal (antinā'tl), *adj.* before birth.

antenna (anten'ə), *n.* *Zoo.* (*pl.* **-ae**), sensitive outgrowth on head of insect, crustacean, etc. ; *Rad.* (*pl.* **-as**), aerial. **-l, -ry**, *adj.* **-niferous, -te**, *adj.* bearing a. **-niform**, *adj.* a.-shaped. **-nule**, *n.* small a.

antenuptial (antinup'shəl), *adj.* before marriage.

antepaschal (antipas'kəl), *adj.* before Easter or the Passover.

antepast (an'tipast), *n.* foretaste.

antependium (antipen'diəm), *n.* altar frontal ; similar cloth on pulpit or lectern.

antepenult (antipinult', -pē'-), *n.* antepenultimate syllable or word. **-imate**, *adj.* last but two.

antephialtic (antifial'tik), *n.* & *adj.* preventive of nightmare.

anteprandial (antiprand'iəl), *adj.* before dinner.

anterior (antēr'iə), *adj.* before in time ; in front. **-ity** (-or'iti), *n.*

antetype (an'titīp), *n.* prototype.

antevenient (antivē'niənt), *adj.* preceding.

antevocalic (antivəkal'ik), *n.* immediately preceding a vowel.

anthelion (anthē'liən, ant-hē'-), *n.* (*pl.* **-ia**) kind of solar halo opposite sun ; antisun.

anthelmintic (anthelmin'tik), *n.* & *adj.* (remedy) used against intestinal worms.

anthemion (anthē'miən), *n.* (*pl.* **-ia**) flat cluster of leaves or flowers as ornament in art ; *Archit.*, honeysuckle ornament.

anthemis (an'thimis), *n.* tonic obtained from camomile flowers.

anther (an'thə), *n. Bot.*, male, pollen-bearing organ of flower. **-al,** *adj.* **-idium** (*pl.* **-ia**), *n.* male organ in cryptogams. **-iferous,** *adj.* bearing a. **-oid,** *adj.* like an a. **-ozoid,** *n.* male sexual element in lower plants; spermatozoid.

anthesis (anthē'sis), *n.* full bloom.

anthoid (an'thoid), *adj.* flower-like.

anthology (anthol'əgi), *n.* collection of literary pieces. **The A.,** collection of some 4,500 poems of anct. Greece. **-gical,** *adj.* **-gise,** *v.t.* **-gist,** *n.*

anthomania (anthəmā'nia), *n.* great love of flowers.

anthophilous, **-lian** (anthof'iləs, -fil'iən), *adj.* flower-loving; feeding on flowers.

anthophorous (anthof'ərəs), *adj. Bot.,* flower-bearing.

anthorism (an'thərizm), *n.* counter-definition.

anthotaxy (an'thətaksi), *n. Bot.,* disposition of flowers in cluster.

anthozoan (anthəzō'ən), *n.* sea-anemone; coral polyp; any creature of the natural class Anthozoa. **-zoic,** *adj.* **-zooid,** *n.* coral polyp. **-zoon,** *n.*

anthracaemia (anthrəsē'miə), *n.* anthrax.

anthracolithic (anthrəkəlith'ik), *adj.* containing anthracite or graphite.

anthracometer (anthrəkom'itə), *n.* instr. measuring amount of carbon dioxide in mixture. **-try,** *n.*

anthracosis (anthrəko'sis), *n.* presence of coal dust in lungs; miner's phthisis.

anthracothere (an'thrəkəthēr), *n.* fossil pachyderm.

anthracotic (anthrəkot'ik), *adj.* pert. to anthracosis.

anthrax (an'thraks), *n.* boil; severe infectious disease of cattle and sheep, communicable to human beings.

anthropic(al) (anthrop'ik, -l), *adj.* pert. to Man.

anthropocentric (anthrəpəsen'trik), *adj.* regarding Man as centre of universe. **-ism,** *n.*

anthropogenesis (anthrəpəjen'isis), *n.* study of human generation or evolution. **-etic** (-jinet'ik), *adj.* **-ny** (-oj'ini), *n.* study of Man's origin.

anthropogeography (anthrəpəjiog'-rəfi), *n.* study of geographical distribution of Man.

anthropoglot(an'thrəpəglot,-thrō'-), *n.* animal with human-like tongue; parrot.

anthropoid (an'thrəpoid), *adj.* resembling man; *n.* such ape. **-al,** *adj.*

anthropolatry (anthrəpol'ətri), *n.* worship of a human being; conception of God in human shape.

anthropolith, -ite (an'thrəpəlith, -īt; -thrō'-), *n.* petrified human remains.

anthropology (anthrəpol'əji), *n.* science of natural history of Man. **-gical,** *adj.* **-gist,** *n.*

anthropometry (anthrəpom'itri), *n.* measurement of parts and functions of human body.

anthropomorphism (anthrəpəmaw'-fism), *n.* representation of a god in human form; ascribing human characteristics to non-human things. **-phic,** *adj.* **-phise,** *v.t.* **-phist, -phite,** *n.* **-phosis,** *n.* transformation into human shape. **-phous,** *adj.* resembling Man.

anthroponomy, -mics (anthrəpon'-əmi, -nom'iks), *n.* study of human conduct.

anthropopathy (anthrəpop'əthi), *n.* ascribing human feelings to a god or inanimate object. **-thic** (-path'-ik), *adj.* **-thite,** *n.*

anthropophagi (anthrəpof'əjī), *n.pl.* (*sing.* **-gus**) cannibals. **-gic, -gous** (-gəs), *adj.* **-gism, -gy,** *n.* **-gist, -gite,** *n.*

anthropophuism (anthrəpof'ūizm), *n.* ascribing human nature to God. **-istic,** *adj.* **-physite,** *n.*

anthropopithecus (anthrəpəpith'-ikəs), *n.* conjectural animal forming "missing link" between Man and apes.

anthropopsychism (anthrəpəsī'-kizm), *n.* ascribing human-like soul to nature.

anthroposociology (anthrəpəsōsiol'-əji), *n.* study of effect of environment on race, and vice versa.

anthroposophy (anthrəpos'əfi), *n.* knowledge of human nature; human wisdom; form of mysticism akin to theosophy. **-ist,** *n.*

anthropotheism (anthrəpəthē'izm), *n.* belief that gods have human nature or are only deified men.

anthropotomy (anthrəpot'əmi), *n.* human anatomy. -mical (-om'ikl), *adj.* -mist, *n.*

anthropozoic (anthrəpəzō'ik), *adj. Geol.*, characterised by human existence, *espec.* the Quaternary period.

anthus (an'thəs), *n.* meadow pipit, titlark.

antiaditis (antiādī'tis), *n.* tonsilitis.

antibacchius (antibak'iəs), *n.* metrical foot of two long and one short syllables. -chic, *adj.*

antibasilican (antibəsil'ikən), *adj.* opposed to principle of monarchy.

antibiosis (antibī ō'sis), *n.* association between organisms causing injury to one of them. -ont (-bī'ont), *n.* organism living in a. -otic (-ot'ik), *n.* & *adj.* (substance) active against disease bacteria, obtained from a living organism such as a mould (fungus) or bacterium.

antiblastic (antiblas'tik), *adj.* opposing growth, *espec.* of harmful substances; giving natural immunity.

antibody (an'tibodi), *n.* substance in blood that neutralises specific harmful substances.

antibrachial (antibrā'kiəl), *adj.* pert. to forearm.

antibromic (antibrō'mik), *n.* & *adj.* (substance) destroying offensive odours.

anticachectic (antikakek'tik), *n.* & *adj.* (drug) used against cachexy.

antichresis (antikrē'sis), *n.* (*pl.* -es) possession and enjoyment of mortgaged property by mortgagee in lieu of interest payments.

anticausotic (antikawsot'ik), *n.* & *adj.* (drug) used against high fever.

antichthones (antik'thənēz), *n. pl.* inhabitants of antipodes.

anticlastic (antiklas'tik),*adj.* having transverse and opposite curvatures of surface.

anticlimax (antiklī'maks), *n.* weak ending; sudden descent to the ridiculous; bathos.

anticline (an'tiklīn), *n. Geol.*, upward fold. -nal, *adj.* -norium, *n.* arch-shaped group of a. and synclines.

anticous (antī'kəs), *adj.* turning away from axis.

anticonvellent (anticonvel'ənt), *n.* & *adj.* (drug) used against convulsions.

anticryptic (antikrip'tik), *adj. Zoo.*, having protective resemblance to environment.

anticyclone (antisī'klōn), *n.* area of high atmospheric pressure, from which winds flow outwards in a clockwise direction in N. hemisphere.

antidactyl (antidak'til), *n.* anapaest.

antidetonant (antidet'ənənt), *n.* anti-knock element in motor spirit.

anti-ethnic (antieth'nik), *adj.* against Gentiles.

antifebrile (antifē'brīl), *n.* & *adj.* preventive or curative of fever.

antigalactic (antigəlak'tik), *n.* & *adj.* preventive of milk-secretion.

antigen (an'tijen), *n.* substance causing production of antibody.

antihydropic (antihīdrop'ik), *n.* & *adj.* (drug) used against dropsy.

anti-icteric (anti-ikter'ik), *n.* & *adj.* (drug) used against jaundice.

anti-knock (antinok'), *n.* & *adj.* (substance) preventing detonation of fuel in internal combustion engine.

antilapsarian (antilapsār'iən), *n.* & *adj.* (person) denying doctrine of the fall of Man.

antilegomena (antiligō'minə), *n.pl.* N.T. books not in early Christian canon.

antilibration (antilībrā'shn), *n.* counterpoising.

antilogarithm (antilog'əridhm), *n.* number of which logarithm is a power of 10 or other base (*abbr.* antilog.).

antilogism (antil'əjizm), *n. Log.*, statement containing three propositions two of which contradict the third.

antilogous (antil'əgəs), *adj.* self-contradictory; inconsistent. -gy (-ji), *n.*

antilyssic (antilis'ik), *n.* & *adj.* (drug) used against hydrophobia.

antimetabole (antimetab'əli), *n.* repetition of words or ideas in different order.

antimetathesis (antimetath'isis), *n.* repetition of parts of antithesis in reverse order. -thetic (-thet'ik), *adj.*

antimnemonic (antinimon'ik), *n.* & *adj.* (thing) injuring the memory.

antimony (an'timəni), *n.* a brittle, crystalline, whitish mineral; metal obtained from a. and used in alloys. -nic (-mon'ik), -nious (-mō'niəs), adj. -niferous, adj. yielding a.

antineuritic (antinūrit'ik), n. & adj. preventive of neuritis, espec. app. to vitamin B or food containing it.

antinomy (antin'əmi), n. legal contradiction; contradiction between logical conclusions. -me (an'tinōm), n. contradictory law or conclusion. -mic (-nom'ik), adj. -mist, n. person opposed to law.

antiodontalgic (antiōdontal'jik), n. & adj. (drug) used against toothache.

anti-orgastic (antiawgas'tik), n. & adj. sedative.

antipaedobaptist (antipēdəbap'tist), n. & adj. (person) denying validity of infant baptism.

antiparallelogram (antiparəlel'əgram), n. quadrilateral with two sides parallel and two not parallel.

Antipasch(a) (an'tipask, -ə), n. Low Sunday; first Sunday after Easter.

antipastic (antipas'tik), adj. pert. to or like dishes, aperitifs, etc., served before main courses of dinner. -to, It. n. appetiser; hors d'oeuvres.

antipathy (antip'əthi), n. dislike. -thetic (-thet'ik), -thic (-path'ik), adj.

antiperistasis (antiperis'təsis), n. opposition; resistance; denying an inference while admitting the fact on which it is based. -tatic (-at'ik), adj.

antipharmic (antifah'mik), adj. alexipharmic.

antiphlogistic (antifləjist'ik), n. & adj. (drug) used against inflammation; opposed to phlogiston theory. -tian, n. such person.

antipodagric (antipədag'rik), adj. used against gout. -ron, n. such remedy.

antipodes (antip'ədēz), n.pl. region on other side of globe; exact opposite. -dal, -dic (-od'ik), adj. diametrically opposite. -ean, adj.

antipruritic (antiprūrit'ik), n. & adj. (drug) alleviating itching.

antipsoric (antipsor'ik), n. & adj. (drug) used against the itch.

antipudic (antipū'dik), adj. covering private parts of body.

antipyic (antipī'ik), n. & adj. (treatment) preventive of suppuration.

antipyretic (antipīret'ik), n. & adj. (drug) preventing or reducing fever; febrifuge. -pyrin, n. one drug of this kind. -resis (-rē'sis), n. treatment of fever with such drugs.

antipyrotic (antipīrot'ik), n. & adj. (treatment) used against burns.

antirachitic (antirakit'ik), adj. preventive of rickets, espec. app. to vitamin D or food containing it.

antiscians (antish'ənz), n.pl. persons living on opposite sides of equator but in same longitude.

antiscolic (antiskol'ik), adj. anthelmintic.

antiscorbutic (antiskawbū'tik), n. & adj. preventive of scurvy, espec. app. to vitamin C or food containing it.

antisemite (antisē'mīt), n. opponent of Jews. -tic (-imit'ik), adj. -tism (-em'itizm), n.

antisideric (antisīder'ik), n. & adj. (substance) counteracting effect of iron.

antispast (an'tispast), n. metrical foot comprising an iambus followed by a trochee.

antistrophe (antis'trəfē), n. stanza answering strophe in Gr. chorus, recited during movement from left to right; repetition of words in reverse order; turning opponent's argument against him. -phic (-of'ik), adj.

antistrumatic (antistrōomat'ik), n. remedy for scrofula. -mous, adj.

antithalian (antithəlī'ən, -ā'liən), adj. disapproving of festivity and laughter.

antithesis (antith'isis), n. (pl. -ses) opposite; contrast; Lit., device of parallel but contrasted phrases or sentences. -thetical, adj.

antithrombin (antithrom'bin), n. substance in blood preventing coagulation of blood.

antitoxic (antitoks'ik), adj. neutralising poison. -in, n. antibody, espec. obtained from infected animal.

anti-trade (an'titrād), n. westerly wind prevailing beyond 40° N. and S.; westerly wind of upper air above trade winds.

antitropic (antitrop'ik), adj. Zoo., symmetrically reversed, as right and left hands. -pe (an'titrōp), *n.* such appendage. -py (-it'rəpi), *n.* state of being antitropic.

antitype (an'titīp), *n.* object or person prefigured by the type or symbol. -pic(al) (-ip'ik, -l), *adj.*

antitypy (antit'ipi), *n.* resistance to penetration.

antivenene, -nin (antiven'ēn, -in), *n.* serum used against snake-bite.

antizymic (antizim'ik), *n. & adj.* preventive of fermentation. -motic (-ot'ik), *n.*

antoecial (antē'shəl), *adj.* app. to places in opposite hemispheres but in same lat. and long. -ians, *n.pl.* persons living in such places.

antonomasia (antənəmā'zhiə), *n.* lit. device of using descriptive epithet or phrase instead of person's name ; using proper name as epithet.

antonym (an'tənim), *n.* word of opposite meaning. -mous (-on'-iməs), *adj.* -my, *n.*

antral (an'tral), *adj.* pert. to antrum.

antrorse (an'traws), *adj.* turning upward and forward.

antrum (an'trəm), *n.* (*pl.* -ra) sinus ; cavity, *espec.* leading into nose.

antrycide (an'trisīd), *n.* chem. insecticide *espec.* used against tsetse fly.

anuresis (anūr ē'sis), *n.* absence or deficiency of urine. -etic (-et'ik), *adj.*

anurous (anūr'əs), *adj.* lacking a tail, *espec.* app. to frog.

anury, -ria (an'ūri, -ūr'iə), *n.* anuresis.

anus (ā'nəs), *n.* opening at posterior end of alimentary canal.

anutraminosa (anūtrəminō'sə), *n.* vitamin deficiency.

aorist (ā'ərist, ār'-), *n. & adj.* Gram., (tense) signifying happening in unrestricted or unspecified past. -ic, *adj.* indefinite ; pert. to a.

aorta (āaw'tə), *n.* main artery from left ventricle of heart. -l, -tic, *adj.*

aosmic (āoz'mik, -os'-), *adj.* free from odour.

à outrance (ah ōōtrahṅs'), *Fr.*, "to the utmost" ; to the death.

apaesthesia (apesthē'zhiə), *n.* loss of feeling in limb. -thetic (-et'ik), *adj.* -thetise (-ēs'thitīz), *v.t.* cause a. in.

apagoge (apəgō'ji), *n.* Math., argument by reductio ad absurdum. -gic(al) (-oj'ik, -l), *adj.*

apanage, app- (ap'ənij), *n.* perquisite ; right, *espec.* of high office ; provision made for younger offspring.

apandry (apan'dri), *n.* male impotence.

apartheid (apahrt'hīd), S. African *n.* policy of segregating racial groups, *espec.* in S. Africa.

aparthrosis (apahthrō'sis), *n.* diarthrosis.

apatetic (apətet'ik), *adj. Zoo.,* having protective imitative coloration or shape.

apathy (ap'əthi), *n.* indifference ; insensibility ; intellectual dullness. -thetic (-et'ik), *adj.* -thic, *adj.* without sensation.

apellous (apel'əs), *adj. Med.,* skinless ; circumcised.

apepsy, -sia (apep'si, -ə), *n.* indigestion. -ptic, *adj.*

aperient (aper'iənt), *n. & adj.* laxative (medicine).

aperitif (aper'itēf), *n.* appetiser, gen. alcoholic. -tive, *n. & adj.* aperient.

aphaeresis (afer'isis), *n.* cutting off beginning of word. -retic (-iret'ik), *adj.*

aphagia (afā'jiə), *n.* inability to swallow.

aphasia (afā'zhiə), *n.* loss of powers of speech and of memory of words, due to injury to speech area of brain. -c, *n.* person so afflicted.

aphelion (afē'liən), *n.* (*pl.* -lia) point in orbit most distant from sun. -ian, *adj.*

apheliotropic (afēliətrop'ik), *adj.* aheliotropic. -pism (-ot'rəpizm), *n.*

aphemia (afē'miə), *n.* loss of power of articulate speech ; motor aphasia.

aphesis (af'isis), *n.* loss of unaccented vowel at beginning of word. -etic (-et'ik), *adj.* -sism, *n.* word so shortened.

aphid, *see* aphis.

aphis (af'is, ā'-), *n.* (*pl.* -ides, af'idēz), plant-louse ; insect family including greenfly, etc. -idian (-id'iən), *n. & adj.* -idivorous (-iv'ərəs), *adj.* feeding on a.

aphlogistic (afləjis'tik), *adj.* flameless.

aphnology (afnol'əji), *n.* science of wealth.

aphonia (afō'niə), n. loss of voice. -ic (-on'ik), adj. -nous (af'ənəs), adj. voiceless.

aphoria (afor'iə), n. Med., sterility.

aphorism (af'ərism), n. brief wise saying ; maxim ; definition. -istic, adj.

aphotic (afō'tik), adj. without light. -ism, n. -totropic, adj. turning away from light.

aphrasia (afra'zhiə), n. inability to speak, or to make intelligible phrases.

aphrodisiac (afrədiz'iak), n. & adj. (drug) inducing sexual desire. -ian, adj. pert. to love or Venus.

Aphrodite (afrədī'ti), n. Venus, goddess of love ; sea-mouse ; meerschaum-like white mineral. -tous, adj. pert. to sexual desire.

aphtha (af'thə), n. (pl. -ae) disease called "thrush," characterised by white spots in mouth. -thic, adj.

aphthong (af'thong), n. letter in word not sounded (as b in doubt).

aphthous (af'thəs), adj. pert. to aphtha ; a.fever, foot-and-mouth disease.

aphylly (afil'i), n. absence of leaves. -lous, adj.

apiaceous (apiā'shəs), adj. parsley-like ; belonging to plant family including carrot, parsley, etc.

apian (ā'piən), adj. pert. to bees.

apiary (ā'piəri), n. place where bees are kept ; collection of beehives. -rian (-ār'iən), adj. pert. to bee-keeping. -rist, n. bee-keeper.

apical (ā'pikl, ap'ikl), adj. at·the summit. -cad (ap'-), adv. towards the summit.

Apician (apish'n), adj. pert. to or like Apicius, a famous epicure ; gluttonous ; luxurious.

apicilar, -llary (apis'ilə, -il'əri), adj. Bot., at the apex.

apiculture (ā'pikultūr), n. bee-keeping.

apinoid (ap'inoid), adj. Med., clean.

apiology (āpiol'əji), n. study of bees.

apivorous (āpiv'ərəs), adj. eating bees.

aplanat (ap'lənat), n. aplanatic lens. -ic, adj. lacking spherical aberration. -ism (-an'ətizm), n.

aplasia (aplā'zhiə), n. Med., incomplete development -stic, adj.

aplotomy (aplot'əmi), n. simple surgical cut.

apnoea (apnē'ə), n. cessation of breathing. -l, -oeic, adj.

apneumatic (apnūmat'ik), adj. without air ; pert. to exclusion of air.

apocalypse (apok'əlips), n. revelation, gen. of St. John the Divine. -lyptic(al), adj. pert. to a. ; mysterious ; a.number, the number 666, mentioned in the Revelation.

apocatastisis (apəkatas'tisis), n. restoration ; Med., relapse ; subsidence ; Astron., reversion to same position ; Theol., conversion of whole world to Christianity

apocentre (ap'əsentə), n. point in orbit opposite centre of attraction. -ric, adj. different from archetype. -ricity, n.

apochromat (ap'əkrəmat), n. apochromatic lens. -ic, adj. lacking both spherical and chromatic aberration.

apocope (apok'əpi), n. cutting off end of word. -pate (-āt), v.t. ; (-pət), adj.

apocrisiary (apəkriz'iəri), n. papal secretary or nuncio.

apocrustic (apəkrus'tik), n. & adj. astringent (medicine).

apochrypha (apok'rifə), n.pl. books of unknown authorship ; uncanonical books, espec., those of Septuagint and Vulgate. -l, adj. of doubtful origin.

apodal (ap'ədəl), adj. lacking feet. -dan, n. -dia (-ō'diə), n. congenital footlessness.

apodeictic, -dic- (apədīk'tik, -dik'-), adj. evident ; demonstrable ; incontrovertible ; n. study of knowledge and its basis.

apodosis (apod'əsis), n. (pl. -ses) main clause in conditional sentence ; last clause in a sentence.

apodous (ap'ədəs), adj. apodal.

apogaeic, -aic (apəjē'ik, -gā'ik), adj. pert. to apogee.

apogamy (apog'əmi), n. Biol., interbreeding in a separated group which has no characteristic differentiating it from parents ; Bot., non-sexual reproduction.

apogee (ap'ojē), n. point in orbit, espec. moon's, most distant from earth ; zenith ; climax. -geal -gean, adj.

apogeny (apoj'ini), n. Bot., sterility. -nous, adj.

apogeotropic (apəjēətrop'ik), adj. ageotropic. -pism (-ot'rəpizm), n.

apograph (ap'əgraf), *n.* copy; facsimile. -al (-og'rəfəl), *adj.*

apolaustic (apəlaw'stik), *adj.* caring only for pleasure.

apolegamic (apəligam'ik),*adj. Biol.,* pert. to selection, *espec.* sexual.

apologal (ap'əlogəl), *adj.* pert. to apologue.

apologetics (apoləjet'iks), *n.pl.* defence and proof, gen. of Christianity; whole body of such writings. -gist, *n.* author of such writings.

apologue (ap'olog), *n.* parable.

apomecometer (apəmikom'itə), *n.* instr. measuring height and distance.

apomixis (apəmiks'is), *n.* non-sexual reproduction.

aponia (apon'iə), *n.* painlessness. -ic, *adj.*

apopemptic (apəpemp'tik), *n.* & *adj.* valedictory (address).

apophasis (apof'əsis), *n.* rhet. device of emphasising, by pretending to ignore or deny, a fact.

apophlegmatic (apəflegmat'ik), *n.* & *adj.* (drug) causing discharge of mucus.

apophony, -nia (apof'əni, -ō'niə), *n.* ablaut.

apophthegm (ap'əthem, -ofthem), *n.* brief wise saying. -atic (-egmat'ik), *adj.*

apophysis (apof'isis), *n.* offshoot; projecting part, *espec.* of bone. -seal, -sial (-iz'iəl), *adj.* -sitis, *n.* inflammation of a.

apoplexy (ap'əpleksi), *n.* stroke or seizure due to thrombosis or rupture of brain artery. -ectic, *adj.* pert. to, like or symptomatic of apoplexy.

aporia (apōr'iə), *n.* (*pl.* -ae) rhet. device of pretending not to know what to do or say.

aposematic (apəsimat'ik), *adj. Zoo.,* giving warning, app. to coloration, odour, etc., of animals.

aposia (apō'siə), *n. Med.,* lack of thirst.

aposiopesis (apəsīəpē'sis), *n.* oratorical device of suddenly stopping in a speech. -pestic (-es'tik), -petic (-et'ik), *adj.*

apositia (apəzish'iə), *n.* distaste for food. -tic (-sit'ik), *adj.* causing apositia.

apostasy (əpos'təsi), *n.* desertion from religion or other similar

body. -tate. *n.* & *adj.* (person) practising a -atise, *v.i.*

aposteme, -ume (ap'əstēm, -ūm), *n.* abscess. -mate (-os'timāt), *v.i.* & *t.* form an a. -mation, *n.* -matous (-em'ətəs), *adj.*

a posteriori (ā posteriōr'ī), *adj.* derived from experience; empirical; from effect to cause.

apostil(le) (apos'til), *n.* comment; note in margin.

apostolic (apəstol'ik), *adj.* pert. to apostle. a.fathers, immediate disciples of the apostles, *espec.* those leaving writings; the writings of the a. fathers. a. succession, unbroken derivation of episcopal power from the apostles.

apostrophe (apos'trəfi), *n.* sign (') that a letter has been omitted, or of possessive case; *Lit.,* exclamatory or rhetorical address to absent person, abstract quality, etc. -phal, -phic (-of'ik), *adj.* -phise, *v.t.* address in exclamatory or rhetorical fashion; use an apostrophe; omit letter from word.

apotelesm (apot'əlezm), *n.* casting of horoscope. -atic, *adj.*

apothegm, *see* apophthegm.

apotheosis (apothiō'sis), *n.* (*pl.* -ses) deification; ascent to glory; personification of ideal. -e, *v.t.*

apothesis (apoth'isis), *n. Med.,* setting of broken limb; *Archit.,* side-room or cupboard.

apotropaic (apətrəpā'ik), *adj.* averting or combating evil. -aion, *n.* such amulet or offering. -aism, *n.* such magical practice.

apotypic (apətip'ik), *adj.* differing from type.

appanage, *see* apanage.

apparitor (apar'itə), *n.* herald; harbinger; one who appears before court; officer executing order of eccl. court.

appellate (apel'ət), *adj.* app. to person, court, etc., having power to reverse decision of inferior.

appellation (apəlā'shn), *n.* name; rank. -tive (-el'ativ), *n.* & *adj. Gram.,* common (noun).

appendalgia (apendal'jiə), *n.* pain about the vermiform appendix.

appendant (apend'ənt), *n.* & *adj.* (thing) adjunct; attached to; hanging from or to; belonging as of right.

appendectomy (apendek'təmi), *n.* removal of vermiform appendix.

appendix (apen'diks), *n.* (*pl.* -ices) addition, gen. to book; vermiform organ in intestines. -icitis, *n.* inflammation of the a. -icial, -icular, -iculate, *adj.* -icle, *n.* small appendage.

apperception (apəsep'shn), *n.* perception of inner meaning, and of relation of new facts to facts already known; mental assimilation; state of being conscious of perceiving. -ceptive, *adj.* -cipient, *n.*

appersonation (apəsənā'shn), *n.* delusion of insane person that he is another, gen. famous, person.

appetence, -cy (ap'itəns, -i), *n.* strong desire; craving; powerful instinct. -ent, *adj.*

appetible (ap'itəbl), *adj.* desirable. -tition, *n.* yearning.

applanate (ap'lənət), *adj.* flattened. -tion, *n.*

appliqué (ap'likā), *n.* & *adj.* (ornament) let into or laid on; *v.t.* to attach or inlay such ornament.

appoggiatura (apojətūr'ə), *n. Mus.*, short note placed before a longer one. short a., acciaccatura.

apport (apawt'), *n.* tangible object caused to appear by spiritualist medium; production of such object.

apposite (ap'əzit), *adj.* appropriate. -tion, *n.* juxtaposition; *Gram.*, putting two nouns or phrases together as attributive or adjunct terms; relationship of such nouns or phrases. -tive (-oz'itiv), *adj.*

apprehend (aprihend'), *v.t.* arrest; become aware of; understand; anticipate with fear. -nsion, *n.* -nsive, *adj.*

apprise (apprīz'), *v.t.* inform.

apprize (apriz'), *v.t.* appraise, value.

approbate (ap'rəbāt), *v.t.* approve; permit; commend. -tion, *n.* -tory, -tive (ap'-), *adj.*

appropinquation (apropingkwā'-shn), *n.* act of approaching.

appropriate (aprō'priət), *adj.* apt; suitable; (-āt), *v.t.* take exclusively; assign to special use; steal. -tion, *n.*; A. Act, *Parl.*, act of assigning to govt. depts. money voted in Supply. -tive, *adj.* -tor, *n.*

approver (aprōō'və), *n.* person turning King's (Queen's) evidence.

approximate (aproks'imət, -mit), *adj.* very close to; almost exact; (-māt), *v.i.* & *t.* be or make a.; approach. -tion, *n.* -tive, *adj.*

appui (apwē'), *n.* & *v.t.* support, *espec.* in mil. use. point of a., fixed object in line with which troops form up.

appulse (apuls'), *n.* act of striking against; *Astron.*, close approach of two celestial objects.

appurtenance (apɜ'tinəns), *n.* belonging; appendage; subsidiary right; *pl.* apparatus; paraphernalia. -ant, *adj.* belonging to by right; accessory.

a priori (ā pri ōr'ī), *adj.* not derived from experience; deductive; lacking proof; from cause to effect. -ist, *n.* person using such arguments. -ity (-or'iti), *n.*

apropos (aprəpō'), *adj.* & *adv.* apt; to the point; opportunely. a.of, with reference to.

apse (aps), *n.* rounded extension at end of building, *espec.* at east end of church; *Astron.*, apsis. a.line, line joining apsides.

apselophesia, -sis (apseləfē'zhiə, -sis), *n.* loss or deficiency of sense of touch.

apsidal (ap'sidl), *adj.* having shape of apse; pert. to apsides.

apsis (ap'sis), *n.* (*pl.* -ides) *Astron.*, point at which heavenly body is most or least distant from centre of attraction. higher a., most distant point. lower a., least distant point.

apsychia (apsik'iə, -ī'kiə), *n.* unconsciousness. -ical (ap'-), *adj.* not needing conscious thought.

apteral (ap'tərəl), *adj.* having columns at front or back only; apterous. -ran, *n.* wingless arthropod. -roid, *adj.* with only rudimentary wings. -rous, *adj.* lacking wings.

apteryx (ap'tɜriks), *n.* tailless, flightless bird of N.Z.; kiwi. -ygial (-ij'iəl), *adj.* wingless; finless.

aptote (ap'tōt), *n.* indeclinable noun. -tic (-ot'ik), *adj.* uninflected.

aptyalism, -lia (aptī'əlizm, -ā'liə), *n.* lack or absence of saliva.

apyretic (āpīret'ik, ap-), *adj.* without fever. -exy, -exia, *n.* absence or abatement of fever.

apyrous (apīr'əs), *adj.* non-inflammable.

aqua-fortis (ak'wə-faw'tis), *Lat.*, "strong water"; nitric acid, *espec.* weak nitric acid used by etchers; etching done with a. -t, *n.* etcher using a.

aquapuncture (ak'wəpungktūr), *n. Med.*, injection of water under skin.

aqua pura (ak'wə pūr'ə), *Lat.*, "pure water," *espec.* distilled.

aqua regia (ak'wə rē'jiə), *Lat.*, "royal water"; mixture of hydrochloric and nitric acids, used by alchemists to dissolve gold.

aquarelle (akwərel'), *n.* painting in water-colour, *espec.* transparent; painting in which water-colours are applied through stencils. -list, *n.* artist painting a.

aquatic (akwat'ik, -wot'-), *n. & adj.* (plant) living in or by water; *n.pl.* water sports.

aquatint (ak'wətint), *n.* kind of engraving with aqua fortis having effect of water-colour drawing.

aqua vitae (ak'wə vī'tē), *Lat.*, "water of life"; strong spirits.

aqueduct (ak'widukt), *n.* channel carrying water, *espec.* in shape of bridge.

aqueous (ā'kwiəs, ak'-), *adj.* pert. to water; *Geol.*, deposited in or by water.

aquiferous (akwif'ərəs), *adj.* carrying, yielding or containing water.

aquiform (ak'wifawm), *adj.* watery; liquid.

aquiline (ak'wilīn), *adj.* eagle-like; like beak of eagle.

Aquilo (ak'wilō), *Lat.*, north or north-east wind.

arabesque (arəbesk'), *n. & adj.* (decoration) having intertwined scrollwork patterns, *espec.* of leaves, flowers, etc.

arable (ar'əbl), *n. & adj.* (land) used or suitable for ploughing.

arachnid (arak'nid), *n.* creature of the natural class Arachnida, including spiders, mites, etc.; *adj.* of or resembling a spider. -ism, *n.* condition arising from bite of poisonous spider.

arachnoid (arak'noid), *adj.* like a spider; like a spider's web. a.membrane, thin middle membrane enveloping brain.

arachnology (araknol'əji), *n.* study of arachnids.

arachnophagous (araknof'əgəs), *adj.* eating spiders.

araeometer, are- (ariom'itə), *n.* hydrometer. -try, *n.*

araneidan (arənē'idən), *n.* spider; *adj.* pert. to spiders. -eiform, *adj.* shaped like a spider. -eology (-ăniol'əji), *n.* study of spiders.

araneous (arā'niəs), *adj.* like a spider's web; transparent; delicate.

araphorostic, -phostic (arəfəros'tik, -fos'-), *adj.* seamless.

araroba (arərō'bə), *n.* tree of Brazil with striped timber; zebra-wood.

aration (arā'shn), *n.* ploughing.

araucaria (arawkār'iə), *n.* monkey-puzzle tree; genus of conifers including it.

arbalest (ahr'bəlest), *n.* cross-bow with mechanism for drawing string; cross-staff. -er, *n.* soldier using a.

arbiter (ah'bitə), *n.* (*fem.* -tress) judge, *espec.* one chosen by disputing parties. a.elegantiae, *Lat.*, "judge of taste," *espec.* G. Petronius, supervisor of Nero's entertainments. a.morum, *Lat.*, "judge of conduct."

arbitrage (ah'bitrahzh, -rij), *n. Comm.*, simultaneously buying stock, etc., in cheaper market and selling in dearer: *v.i.* practise a. -ger, -geur, *n.* person engaged in a.

arbitrament (ahbit'rəmənt), *n.* judicial decision; power to make decision.

arbitrary (ah'bitrəri), *adj.* discretionary; capricious; tyrannical.

arbitrate (ah'bitrāt), *v.i. & t.* judge; settle quarrel. -tion, *n.*; a. of exchange, *Comm.*, arbitrage of currency; remittance of money to one country through another where exchange rate is more favourable. -tor, *n.*

arbitrium liberum (ahbit'riəm lib'-ərəm), *Lat.*, "free will."

arblast (ah'blahst), *n.* arbalest.

arboraceous (ahbərā'shəs), *adj.* pert. to or like a tree.

arboreal (ahbor'iəl), *adj.* pert. to trees, or living in trees.

arboreous (ahbor'iəs), *adj.* having many trees.

arborescent (ahbəres'ənt), *adj.* branched; having shape or growth like a tree. -nce, *n.*

arboretum (ahbərē'təm), *n.* (*pl.* -ta) botanical garden devoted to trees.

arborical (ahbor'ikl), *adj.* pert. to trees.

arboricole (ahbor'ikōl), *adj.* living in trees. -**line** (-ik'əlīn), -**lous** (-ik'ələs), *adj.* growing on trees.

arboriculture (ah'bərikultūr), *n.* tree-cultivation. -**ral**, *adj.* -**rist**, *n.*

arboriform (ah'bərifawm, -bor'-), *adj.* shaped like a tree.

arborise (ah'bərīz), *v.i.* & *t.* take on or give tree-like shape.

arborous (ah'bərəs), *adj.* pert. to trees; composed of trees. -**roid**, *adj.* like a tree; branched.

arbor vitae (ah'bə vītē), *n.* a coniferous evergreen shrub.

arbuscle, -**cula** (ah'busl, -bus'kūlə), *n.* dwarf tree; shrub-like tree. -**cular**, *adj.*

arbuscule (ahbus'kūl), *n.* tuft.

arbustum (ahbus'təm), *n.* (*pl.* -**ta**) copse; orchard.

arbutus (ahbū'təs, ah'-), *n.* strawberry tree.

arcana (ahkā'nə), *n.pl.* (*sing.* -**num**) mysteries; secrets; *sing.* universal remedy; elixir of life. -**ne** (-kān'), *adj.* secret.

arcate (ah'kāt), *adj.* shaped like a bow. -**ture**, *n.* small or blind arcade.

arc-boutant (ark-bōotahń') Fr. *n.* (*pl.* **arcs-boutants**) flying buttress.

archaean (ahkē'ən), *adj.* prehistoric; of extreme age; *Geol.*, app. to all pre-Cambrian rocks.

archaeolatry (ahkiol'ətri), *n.* worship of archaic customs, expressions, etc.

archaeolithic (ahkialith'ik), *adj.* pert. to earliest stone age.

archaeology (ahkiol'əji), *n.* study of remains of past human life. -**gical**, *adj.* -**gist**, *n.*

archaeopteryx (ahkiop'təriks), *n.* fossil bird with reptilian characteristics.

archaeornis (ahkiaw'nis), *n.* fossil, beakless, reptile-like bird.

archaeozoic (ahkiəzō'ik), *adj.* living in the earliest geological era.

archaic (ahkā'ik), *adj.* ancient; primitive; out of date. -**ism**, *n.* such thing, *espec.* word or phrase; use of such thing. -**istic**, *adj.*

archebiosis (ahkibiō'sis), *n.* abiogenesis.

archecentric (ahkisen'trik), *adj.* pert. to archetype.

archelogy (ahkel'əji), *n.* study of first principles.

archetype (ahk'itīp), *n.* original pattern. -**pal**, *adj.*

arch-flamen (ahch-flā'men), *n.* high priest; archbishop.

archididascalian (ahkididaskā'liən), *adj.* pert. to headmaster of school.

archil (ah'kil, -chil), *n.* dye obtained from certain lichens; lichens yielding a.

archimage, -**gus** (ah'kimāj, -mā'gəs), *n.* (*pl.* -**gi**) head magician; chief Parsee priest.

archimandrite (ahkiman'drīt), *n.* superior of large monastery of Gr. Church; abbot.

Archimedian (ahkimē'diən), *adj.* pert. to or inverted by Archimedes. **A.drill**, drill in which a nut is slid up and down a coarse spiral thread. **A.screw**, apparatus for raising water, consisting of a cylinder enclosing a screw.

archipelago (ahkipel'əgō), *n.* (*pl.* -**es**, -**s**) group or string of islands; sea containing many islands. -**gian** (-ā'jiən), -**gic** (-aj'ik), *adj.*

architectonic (ahkitekton'ik), *adj.* pert. to architecture, or to the systematisation of knowledge; resembling architecture; structural; showing constructive ability. -**s**, *n.* science of architecture; constructive skill.

architis (ahkī'tis), *n.* inflammation of rectum.

architrave (ah'kitrāv), *n.* beam resting directly on columns; epistyle; moulding at head and sides of window or doorway.

archives (ah'kīvz), *n.pl.* public records; place where such are kept. -**vist** (-ivist), *n.* keeper of archives.

archivolt (ah'kivolt), *n.* curved moulding on face of arch.

archizoic (ahkizō'ik), *adj.* pert. to earliest living things.

archology (ahkol'əji), *n.* theory of origins; science of government.

archon (ah'kən), *n.* chief magistrate of anct. Athens. -**tic**, *adj.*

arciform (ah'sifawm), *adj.* shaped like an arch.

arctation (ahktā'shn), *n. Med.*, constriction, *espec.* of anus, causing constipation.

arctogaeal, -**geal**, -**gaean**, -**gean** (ahktəjē'əl, -ən), *adj.* pert. to the region including Europe, Africa, Asia and N. America.

ə=*er* in *father*; ō=*er* in *pert*; th=*th* in *thin*; dh=*th* in *then*; zh=*s* in *pleasure*; k=*ch* in *loch*; ń=Fr. nasal *n*; ü=Fr. *u*.

arctoid (ahk'toid), *adj*. like a bear.

arcuate, -al (ah'kū̆ at, -ūəl), *adj*. bow-shaped. -tion, *n*.

arcus senilis (ah'kəs sinī'lis), *Lat*., "senile ring"; whitish ring round iris in eyes of old people.

areca (ar'ikə, -rē'-), *n*. sev. palm trees, *espec*. the betel. a.nut, betel-nut.

arefaction (arifak'shn), *n*. act of drying; state of being dry. -fy, *v.t*.

arenaceous (arinā'shəs), *adj*. like or consisting of sand; growing in sand.

arenation (arinā'shn), *n*. use of sand as med. remedy.

areng (areng'), *n*. E. Ind. sago-producing palm.

arenicolous (arinik'ələs), *adj*. living in sand.

arenilitic (arenilit'ik), *adj*. pert. to sandstone.

arenoid (ar'inoid), *adj*. like sand.

arenose, -ous (ar'inōs, -əs), *adj*. sandy; containing much sand.

areography (ārīog'rəfi), *n*. description of surface of planet Mars.

areola (arē'ələ), *n*. (*pl*. -ae) circular coloured border, *espec*. round pupil of eye, pustule or nipple; small circumscribed space; interstice. -r, -te, *adj*. -tion, *n*.

areology (ārīol'əji), *n*. study of planet Mars.

areometer, *see* araeometer.

Areopagus (ariop'əgəs), *n*. in anct. Athens the highest legal tribunal; hill where this court sat; any important tribunal. -gite (-jīt), *n*. member of such court. -gitic (-jit'ik), *adj*.

aretaics (arita'iks), *n*. science of virtue.

arête (arāt'), Fr. *n*. sharp ridge of mountain.

Aretinian (aritin'iən), *adj*. of Guido Aretinus (d'Arezzo). A.syllables, names given by him to six tones (*ut, re, mi, fa, sol, la*) of hexachord.

argal (ah'gal), *adv*. therefore (corruption of *ergo*); *n*. argol.

argala (ah'gələ), *n*. adjutant-bird; marabou.

argali (ah'gəli), *n*. Asiatic wild mountain sheep.

argand- (ah'gand-), *adj*. app. to lamps, burners, etc., having tubular wick or flame.

argeelah (ahgē'lah), *n*. argala.

argent (ah'jənt), *n*. & *adj*. silver; silver-like. -al, -ate, -eous, -ic, -ous, *adj*. -ation, *n*. silver coating. -iferous, *adj*. yielding silver. -ine, *n*. silvery metal. -ometer, *n*. instr. measuring strength of silver solutions. -ry *n*. silver plate.

argil (ah'jil), *n*. clay, *espec*. used in pottery. -laceous, -llous, *adj*. containing clay; clay-like. -lliferous, *adj*. yielding or containing clay. -lloid, *adj*. like clay.

argol, -al (ah'gəl), *n*. crust formed on long-kept wine.

argon (ah'gon), *n*. inert gas contained in very small quantity in atmosphere, used to fill electric light bulbs.

argonaut (ah'gənawt), *n*. companion of Jason in the Argo; any heroic sailor; paper nautilus.

argosy (ah'gəsi), *n*. large merchant ship; merchant fleet.

argot (ah'gō), Fr. *n*. slang or jargon, *espec*. of criminals, tramps, etc. -ic (-ot'ik), *adj*.

arguria, -yria (ahjur'iə, -ir'-), *n*. silver-poisoning.

Argus (ah'gəs), *n*. monster with a hundred eyes; careful watcher; Asiatic pheasant. A.-eyed, ever-watchful.

argute (ah'gūt), *adj*. quick; sharp; shrill; astute; subtle.

argyrocephalous (ahjirəsef'ələs), *adj*. with silvery or shining head.

aria (ah'riə, ar'-), *n*. melody, *espec*. solo for voice in opera or oratorio.

arietinous (ariet'inəs), *adj*. having shape of ram's head.

arietta (ahriet'ə, ar-), *n*. short aria.

ariose (ar'iōs), *adj*. characterised by or like melody.

arioso (ariō'sō), *n*. *Mus*., song-like instrumental piece; solo pert. to both aria and recitative; *adj*. melodious.

arista (aris'tə), *n*. (*pl*. -ae) awn. -te, *adj*.

aristarchy (ar'istahki), *n*. government by best men.

aristology (aristol'əji), *n*. art or science of dining. -gical, *adj*. -gist, *n*.

aristulate (aris'tūlət), *adj*. having short arista.

arithmogram (arith'məgram), *n*. number composed of numerical values assigned to letters in a word. -graph, *n*. calculating machine.

-graphy (-og'rəfi), *n.* representing a number with letters having numerical values. **-mania**, *n.* obsession with numbers, *espec.* compulsion to count things. **-meter**, *n.* multiplying machine.

armadillo (ahmədil'ō), *n.* burrowing animal of S. and Cent. Amer. with bony armour, and able to roll into a ball for protection ; *adj.* app. to other creatures with such ability.

Armageddon (ahməged'n), *n.* tremendous conflict ; war that will precede the end of the world.

armature (ah'mətūr), *n.* armament ; *Bot.,* defensive outgrowth ; *Elec.,* piece of iron placed on poles of permanent magnet ; piece of iron whose movement, due to magnetic attraction, actuates apparatus or machinery ; rotating part of dynamo or elec. motor ; stationary part of revolving field alternator.

armiferous (ahmif'ərəs), *adj.* carrying weapons or arms.

armiger (ah'mijə), *n.* (*pl.* **-ri**, **-mij'-əri**) armour-bearer ; knight's squire ; person bearing heraldic arms. **-al**, **-ous** (-mij'ərəl, -əs), *adj.*

armillary (ah'miləri, -mil'-), *adj.* like, pert. to or composed of rings. **a.sphere**, celestial globe composed only of rings marking equator, tropics, etc. **-ate**, *adj. Bot.,* ringed.

armipotent (ahmip'ətənt), *adj.* having strong armament. **-nce**, *n.*

armisonant, **-nous** (ahmis'ənənt, -nəs), *adj.* resounding with the clash of arms.

armoire (ahmwahr'), Fr. *n.* cupboard ; wardrobe.

armorial (ahmor'iəl), *adj.* pert. to or bearing heraldic arms. **a. bearings**, coat-of-arms.

armory (ah'məri), *n.* heraldry. **-rist**, *n.* expert in heraldry.

arnatto, **-otto**, *see* annatto.

arnee, **-ni**, **-na** (ah'nē, -nə), *n.* Ind. wild buffalo.

arnica (ah'nikə), *n.* genus of plants including the mountain tobacco ; tincture obtained from mountain tobacco used for bruises, etc.

arpeggio (ahpej'ō), *n. Mus.*, number of notes sounded in rapid succession ; playing in such fashion. **-iando**, *adj.* in such manner. **-iation**, *n.*

arquebus(e), **har-** (ah'kwibəs,hah'-),

n. anct. hand gun supported on tripod. **-ier** (-bū'ziə), *n.* soldier armed with a.

arrack (ar'ak, ərak'), *n.* strong liquor of the East, manuf. from coco-palm, rice, sugar-cane, etc.

arraign (ərān'), *v.t.* call to account ; bring before judicial court. **-ment**, *n.* indictment.

arrant (ar'ənt), *adj.* unmitigated ; infamous.

arras (ar'əs), *n.* tapestry, *espec.* covering wall. **-ene**, *n.* embroidery material of silk and wool.

arrect (arekt'), *adj.* raised up ; attentive.

arrêt (arā'), Fr. *n.* judgment ; decree ; arrest.

arrha (ar'ə), *n.* (*pl.* **-ae**) pledge ; earnest money. **-l**, *adj.*

arrhizal (arī'zəl), *adj.* rootless.

arrière-ban (ar'iār-bahn'), Fr. *n.* summoning by king of his feudatories and their vassals to military service ; vassals so called ; the nobility.

arrière-pensée (ar'iār-pahn'sā), Fr. *n.* hidden meaning ; ulterior motive ; mental reservation.

arris (ar'is), *n.* sharp edge formed by two angled surfaces, *espec.* edge of fluting on column. **a.fillet**, wedge raising slates round chimney or skylight. **a.rail**, rail of triangular section. **-wise**, *adj.* edgewise.

arriviste (arēvēst'), Fr. *n.* pushful, ambitious person.

arrogate (ar'ogāt), *v.t.* take or claim beyond one's rights. **-tion**, *n.*

arrondissement (arawñdēs'mahñ), Fr. *n.* largest subdivision of a Fr. department.

arrosive (arō'siv), *adj.* gnawing. **-sion**, *n.*

arroyo (aroi'ō), Sp. *n.* small stream ; dry stream bed ; gulley.

arsinotherium (ahsinəther'iəm), *n.* rhinoceros-like fossil mammal.

arsis (ah'sis), *n.* (*pl.* **-ses**) *orig.,* unstressed part of metrical foot ; *mod.,* accented syllable ; *Mus.,* unaccented part of bar.

artefact, *see* artifact.

arterial (ahtēr'iəl), *adj.* like an artery ; main (of roads). **-ise**, *v.t.* transform into arterial blood ; give arteries to.

artery (ah'təri), *n.* vessel conveying blood from the heart ; main channel. **-riography,** *n.* description of arterial system. **-riology,** *n.* study of or treatise on arteries. **"-rio-sclerosis,** *n.* hardening of artery walls. **-riotomy,** *n.* dissection of arteries : opening an artery.

artesian (ahtē′ziən), *adj.* app. to wells bored perpendicularly through imporous to porous strata ; *Amer.,* app. to any deep well.

arthritis (ahthrī′tis), *n.* inflammation of joint. **-rectomy,** *n.* excision of joint. **-rography,** *n.* description of joints. **-rology,** *n.* study of joints ; deaf and dumb language. **-tic** (-it′ik), *adj.*

arthropod (ah′thrəpod), *n.* & *adj.* (creature) of natural division Arthropoda, having jointed legs. **-al, -an, -ous** (-op′əd-), *adj.*

arthrosis (ahthrō′sis), *n.* joint or articulation connecting two bones. **-sia** (-zhia), *n.* arthritis.

articular (ahtik′ūlə), *adj.* pert. to joints.

articulate (ahtik′ūlət), *adj.* spoken clearly ; having power of speech, *espec.* fluent and expressive ; divided into syllables ; segmented ; jointed ; (-āt), *v.t.* & *i.* speak clearly ; connect or be connected by or at joints. **-tion,** *n.* clear speech ; jointing. **-tive, -tory,** *adj.* **-tor,** *n.*

artifact (ah′tifakt), *n.* object of human manufacture ; condition caused by human interference. **-itious,** *adj.*

artifice (ah′tifis), *n.* ingenuity ; skill ; trickery. **-r** (-if′isə), *n.* craftsman ; mechanic in army.

artisan (ahtizan′), *n.* workman ; journeyman ; mechanic.

arum (ār′əm), *n.* large-spathed plant, called "cuckoo-pint" or "lords and ladies." **a.**lily, calla lily.

arundinaceous (arundinā′shəs), *adj.* like or pert. to a reed. **-iferous,** *adj.* bearing reeds. **-neous** (-in′iəs), *adj.* reedy.

aruspex, *see* **haruspex.**

arvicoline (ahvik′əlin, -in), *adj.* living in the fields or countryside. **-culture,** *n.* cultivation of fields.

Aryan (ār′iən), *n.* & *adj.* *Philol.,* Indo-European, Indo-Germanic or Indo-Iranian (language) ; prehistoric Cent. Asiatic person or tribe speaking that language ;

erron. applied to "Nordic" race, *espec.* non-Jewish. **-ism,** *n.* belief in the existence of A. race ; belief that A. race and its descendants were or are superior to non-A. peoples.

as (as), *n.* (*pl.* **asses**) copper coin of anct. Rome ; weight of 12 oz. ; measure equivalent to one foot or one acre.

asafoetida (asəfē′tidə), *n.* gum with garlic-like smell obtained from roots of certain E. Ind. plants.

asbestos (azbes′təs), *n.* uninflammable material manuf. from fibrous amphibole. **-tic, -tine,** *adj.* **-toid, -tous,** *adj.* **-tinise,** *v.t.* make uninflammable.

ascarid (as′kərid), *n.* (*pl.* **-es,** -ar′idēz) roundworm. **-riasis** (-ī′əsis), *n.* disease caused by infestation with a. **-ricide** (-ar′isid), *n.* substance destroying ascarides.

ascendant, -ent (asend′ənt), *adj.* rising into power ; powerful ; *Astron.,* moving towards zenith ; *Astrol.,* immediately above eastern horizon ; *n.* powerful or preeminent position ; *Astrol.,* degree of zodiac above eastern horizon at birth of child ; horoscope. **House of the a.,** from 5° of zodiac to 25° below a. ; **Lord of the a.,** planet in house of the a.

ascetic (aset′ik), *n.* & *adj.* (person) practising severe abstinence ; austere. **-ism** (-sizm), *n.*

ascian (ash′iən), *n.* inhabitant of torrid zone.

ascidian (asid′iən), *n.* sea-squirt. **-ioid,** *adj.* like an a.

ascites (asī′tēz), *n.* abdominal dropsy.

asclepiad (asklē′piad), *n.* metrical verse invented by Asclepiades, comprising a spondee, two or three choriambi and an iambus. **-ean, -ic,** *adj.*

Asdic (az′dik), *n.* apparatus for locating submarines by measuring direction and time-lag of echoes of sound waves reflected by their hulls.

aseismic (asīz′mik, -sīs′-), *adj.* free from earthquakes. **-ity,** *n.* **-matic,** *adj.* reducing or withstanding effect of earthquakes.

asepsis (asep′sis), *n.* absence of poisonous matter and organisms ; method of causing such condition

---

hat, bah, hāte, hāre, crawl ; pen, ēve, hēre ; it, īce, fīre ; on, bōne, boil, bōre, howl ; foot, fōōd, bōōr, hull, tūbe, pūre.

in surgery ; sterilising. -ptic, adj. ; n. substance causing or in state of a. -pticise, -ptify, v.t.

asexual (asek'shooəl, ā-), adj. non-sexual ; sexless. -ity, n.

ashlar (ash'lə), n. squared building stone ; stonework composed of a. ; thin, dressed stone for facing rough wall. -ing, n. partition in attic to cut off angle made by rafters and floor.

asinine (as'inīn), adj. pert. to the ass ; stupid ; fatuous. -ninity (-nin'iti), n.

asitia (asish'iə), n. distaste for food.

askari (as'kəri), n. native E. African soldier in army of European state.

asomatous (asō'mətəs), adj. incorporeal ; lacking body. -tophyte, n. Bot., plant in which body and reproductive cells are undifferentiated.

asonia (asō'niə), n. inability to hear sounds of certain pitches.

asparaginous (aspəraj'inəs), adj. pert. to, like or eaten like asparagus.

asperate (as'pərət), adj. rather rough ; (-āt), v.t. make rough. -tion, n.

asperge (aspōj'), v.t. sprinkle. -s (-jēz), n. R.C., ceremony of sprinkling holy water.

aspergil, -ill(um) (as'pəjil, -il'əm), n. R.C., brush-like implement used to sprinkle holy water. -liform, adj. shaped like an a. ; brush-shaped.

aspergillus (aspəjil'əs), n. minute fungus forming mould. -losis, n. animal disease caused by a.

asperity (asper'iti), n. roughness, espec. of behaviour.

aspermatism (aspə'mətizm), n. failure of male generative powers. -tic (-mat'ik), adj.

asperse (aspəs'), v.t. slander ; calumniate. -sion, n. ; R.C., act of springling holy water. -sive, -sory, adj.

aspersorium (aspəsōr'iəm). n. R.C., vessel holding holy water ; aspergil.

asperulous (asper'ūləs), adj. Bot., rather rough.

asphalt (as'falt, -fawlt ; pop., ash'felt), n. black bituminous substance found natural in pitch lakes, and manuf. from tar, etc. ; substance composed of a. with gravel, sand, etc., used for paving, watercourses, etc. ; adj. made of or covered with a. ; v.t. cover or impregnate with a. -ic, adj.

aspheterism (asfet'ərizm), n. communism.

asphodel (as'fədel), n. kind of liliaceous plant ; daffodil ; Lit., flower of the Elysian fields. bog a., Brit. grass-like moorland plant.

asphyxia, -xy (as fiks'iə, -si), n. suffocation. -al, adj. -ant, n. & adj. (substance) causing a. -ate, v.i. & t. -ator, n. substance causing a. ; apparatus for testing drains by filling with. smoke ; fire extinguisher using carbonic acid gas. -yctic, -yctous, adj.

aspidate (as'pidāt), adj. shield-shaped.

aspirate (as'pirət), n. sound (h) made by breathing out ; consonant combined with h sound ; adj. so pronounced ; (-āt), v.t. pronounce with initial h sound ; move or draw by suction. -tor, n. any suction machine, espec. for withdrawing gas, or for separating corn from chaff ; Med., instr. for withdrawing fluids by suction from body.

aspirin (as'pirin), n. drug (acetyl-salicylic acid) removing pain and fever.

asportation (aspawtā'shn), n. removal, espec. crime of removing property.

assapan(ick) (asəpan', -ik), n. flying squirrel of N. Amer.

assart (asaht'), v.t. Law, make arable by clearing trees, etc. ; n. land so treated ; action of assarting. -ment, n.

assary (as'əri), n. small copper coin of anct. Rome ; as.

assecuration (asekūr ā'shn), n. marine insurance. -tor, n.

assentaneous (asəntā'niəs), adj. acquiescent.

assentation (asəntā'shn), n. ready, insincere assent. -ious, adj. willing to assent. -tor, n. flatterer ; one assenting insincerely or conniving. -tory (-sen'tətəri), adj.

assentor (asen'tə), n. Law, voter (not proposer or seconder) endorsing nomination of candidate for election.

asseverate (asev'ərāt), *v.t.* affirm; declare. **-tion, -tor,** *n.* **-tive, -tory,** *adj.*

assibilate (asib'ilāt), *v.t.* pronounce with sibilant sound or hiss. **-tion,** *n.*

assiduity (asidū'iti), *n.* unremitting care; unflagging or obsequious attention. **-uous** (-id'ūəs), *adj.*

assiento (asien'tō), Sp. *n.* contract; treaty, *espec.* with Spain for supplying slaves to Sp. Amer. **-tist,** *n.* party to a contract; member of company supplying slaves under an assiento.

assign (asīn'), *v.t.* allot; appoint; select; attribute; transfer legally; *n.* assignee.

assignat (as'ignat, asēnyah'), Fr. *n.* promissory note secured on state lands, issued during Fr. revolution.

assignation (asignā'shn), *n.* appointment to meet; rendezvous; *Law,* formal transference; nomination of assignee; interest transferred; paper money.

assignee (asīnē'), *n.* agent; representative; person to whom something is assigned.

assignment (asīn'mənt), *n.* deed of transfer; act of assigning; commission, *espec.* of a journalist.

assignor, -er (asīnōr', -ī'nə), *n.* person assigning.

assimilate (asim'ilāt), *v.i.* & *t.* make or become similar; compare; incorporate; digest; absorb; be incorporated, digested, or absorbed. **-tion, -tor,** *n.* **-tive, -tory,** *adj.*

assize (asīz'), *n.* legislative assembly; decree, gen. one fixing weights, measures and prices, *espec.* of bread and ale; trial; *Scot.,* trial by jury; jury. **-r,** *n.* person fixing weights and measures; *Scot.,* juror. **-s,** *n.pl.* court of sessions held periodically in all counties; court-room for such courts.

assoil(zie) (asoil', -yi), *v.t.* pardon; absolve; acquit; release. **-ment,** *n.*

assonance (as'ənəns), *n.* similarity between sounds; kind of rhyme in which only vowels are identical. **-ant,** *adj.* **-ate,** *v.i.*

assuage (aswāj'), *v.t.* soothe; mitigate; appease. **-asive,** *adj.* **-ment,** *n.*

assuetude (as'witūd), *n. Med.,* habituation to harmful influences.

assumpsit (asum'sit), *n. Law,* contract (not under seal) founded on a consideration; suit for breach of such contract.

assumption (asum'shn, -sump'-), *n.* act of assuming or putting on; pride; supposition; *R.C.,* ascent of Virgin Mary into heaven, and feast (Aug. 15) of that event; *Law,* assumpsit. **-tious,** *adj.* assuming. **-tive,** *adj.* assumed; arrogant.

assurgent (asə'jənt), *adj.* ascending; *Bot.,* upward curving. **-ncy,** *n.*

astasia (astā'zhiə), *n.* inability, due to imperfect muscular co-ordination, to keep erect.

astatic (astat'ik), *adj.* unstable; in neutral equilibrium; *Elec.,* not tending to assume a definite position. **a.couple,** pair of magnetised needles of opposite charges. **a. system,** elec. system in which components' polarities cancel out. **-s,** *n.* study of equilibrium of body under known forces. **-tise,** *t.t.* make a.

astatine (as'tətēn), *see* **alabamine.**

asteism (as'tiizm), *n.* polite irony.

asterial (astēr'iəl), *adj.* starlike; *n.* a fossil starfish.

asteriated (astēr'iātid), *adj.* having star-like rays.

asterism (as'tərizm), *n.* constellation of stars; group of asterisks; appearance of star-like reflection by certain crystals. **-al,** *adj.*

asteroid (as'təroid), *n.* small planet revolving between Jupiter and Mars; planetoid; any star-like body; *adj.* star-shaped; pert. to or like a starfish. **-al,** *adj.*

asthenia (asthē'niə, -thinī'ə; as'thini), *n.* debility. **-ic** (-then'ik), *adj.* weak; weakening. **-nology,** *n.* study of diseases due to a.

asthenopia (asthinō'piə), *n.* optical weakness, *espec.* muscular. **-ic** (-op'ik), *adj.*

astigmatism (astig'mətizm), *n.* defect in curvature of lens or of cornea of eye, causing unequal focusing. **-mometer,** *n.* instr. measuring amount of a. **-tic** (-mat'ik), *adj.*

astomatous, -mous (astom'ətəs, as'təməs), *adj.* lacking mouth or skin pores. **-mia** (-ō′miə), *n.* absence of mouth.

astraean (astrē′ən), *adj.* astral; *n.* star coral.

astragal (as′trəgəl), *n.* ankle-bone; rounded beading or moulding on column; *pl.*, dice. **-ar** (-ag′ələ), *adj.* **-omancy** (-ag′ələmansi), *n.* divination by ankle-bones or dice. **-us** (-ag′ələs), *n. Med.*, aukle-bone.

astral (as′trəl), *adj.* pert. to or like stars; heavenly; spiritual; of a non-tangible substance of which a. body is composed. **a.body,** semi-spiritual body believed by theosophists to accompany physical body in life and survive it at death; soul. **a.lamp,** shadowless lamp resembling an argand-lamp.

astraphobia, -pophobia (astrəfō′biə, -pəfō′biə), *n.* morbid fear of thunder and lightning.

astrict (astrikt′) *v.t.* astringe. **-ion,** *n.* **-ive,** *adj.*

astringe (astrinj′), *v.t.* bind; brace; restrict; constipate.

astringent (astrin′jənt), *adj.* causing to contract: binding; styptic; tonic; constipating; *n.* such medicine or lotion. **-ncy,** *n.*

astrognosy (astrog′nəsi), *n.* knowledge of fixed stars.

astrogony (astrog′əni), *n.* theory of the origin of the stars.

astrograph (as′trəgraf), *n.* photographic telescope. **-y** (-og′rəfi), *n.* mapping or describing the stars.

astroid (as′troid), *adj.* star-shaped.

astrolabe (as′trəlāb), *n.* anct. astron. instr. for taking altitudes. **-bical** (-lab′ikəl), *adj.*

astrolatry (astrol′ətri), *n.* worship of stars.

astrolithology (astrəlithol′əji), *n.* study of meteorites.

astrologaster (astrol′əgastə), *n.* fraudulent astrologer.

astrology (astrol′əji), *n.* study of supposed influence of stars on human life; *arch.*, astronomy. **-ger,** *n.* one who tells fortunes from the stars. **-gical,** *adj.*

astro-meteorology (as′trō-mētiərol′-əji), *n.* study of supposed effect of heavenly bodies on weather.

astrometer (astrom′itə), *n.* instr. measuring relative brightness of stars. **-try,** *n.* measurement of heavenly bodies.

astrophil (as′trəfil), *n.* person fond of learning about stars.

astrophotometer (astrəfətom′itə), *n.* instr. measuring light of stars.

astrophysics (astrəfiz′iks), *n.* study of composition of heavenly bodies. **-cal,** *adj.*

astucious (astū′shəs), *adj.* astute. **-city,** *n.*

astylar (astī′lə), *adj. Archit.,* lacking columns.

asymptote (as′imtōt), *n.* line approaching a curve but meeting it only at infinity. **-tic** (-ot′ik), *adj.*

asynchronous (asing′krənəs), *adj.* not occurring at same time. **a.machine,** elec. generator which can run at a speed not an exact multiple of the frequency of the circuit. **-nism,** *n.*

asyndeton (asin′diton), *n.* rhet. device of omitting conjunctions. **-tic** (-det′ik), *adj.*

asynergy, -gia (asin′əji, -ō′jiə), *n. Med.,* lack of co-ordination, *espec.* of muscles.

asyngamy (asing′gəmi), *n. Bot.,* failure to effect cross-fertilisation due to asynchronous development of flowers. **-mic** (-am′ik), *adj.*

asyntactic (asintak′tik), *adj.* breaking rules of syntax or grammar.

asystole (asis′təli), *n.* cessation of contraction of heart. **-lic** (-ol′ik), *adj.* **-lism,** *n.*

atabal, att- (at′əbal), *n.* Moorish drum.

atactic (atak′tik), *adj.* asyntactic; irregular; pert. to ataxy. **-tiform,** *adj.* resembling ataxy.

ataghan (at′əgan), *n.* yataghan.

ataraxy, -xia (at′əraksi, -aks′iə), *n.* indifference; stoicism; imperturbability.

atavism (at′əvizm), *n.* reversion to remote ancestral type; "throwback"; recurrence of hereditary feature after an interval of a generation or more. **-ic** (-av′ik), *adj.* pert. to remote ancestor. **-st,** *n.* person or thing marked by a. **-stic,** *adj.*

atavus (at′əvəs), Lat.*n.* "ancestor," *espec.* grandfather; *Biol.,* remote ancestor whose characteristics recur in atavism.

ataxaphasia (ataksəfə′zhiə), *n.* inability, due to imperfect muscular co-ordination, to speak sentences.

ataxy, -xia (ataks'i, -ə), *n.* irregularity; *Med.*, inability to co-ordinate muscles or other parts; condition arising therefrom. **locomotor a.**, a. as it affects walking muscles. **-xic,** *adj.*

atebrin (at'ibrin), *n.* anti-malarial drug also called mepacrine.

ateknia (atek'niə), *n.* childlessness.

atelectasis (atilek'təsis), *n.* incomplete dilatation or collapse of lungs.

atelier (atel'iā, atlyā'), Fr. *n.* studio; workshop.

ateliosis (ateliō'sis), *n.* imperfect development; dwarfism.

athanasia, -sy (athənā'zhiə, -than'əsi), *n.* immortality.

Athanasian (athənā'shn), *adj.* pert. to Athanasius, 4th cent. archbp. of Alexandria; *n.* follower of Athanasius. **A. Creed,** long creed in Anglican service, beginning *Quicunque vult.* **-ism,** *n.*

atheling (ath'əling), *n.* Anglo-Saxon noble; prince, *espec.* heir apparent.

athenaeum (athənē'əm), *n.* club having learned members; library.

athermanous (athə'mənəs), *adj.* impervious to radiant heat. **-nacy,** *n.*

athermic (athə'mik), *adj.* without heat. **-mous,** *adj.* athermanous.

atheroma (athərō'mə), *n.* (*pl.* -ata) soft, curdy tumour; fatty degeneration of inner lining of arteries. **-sia, -tosis,** *n.* **-tous,** *adj.*

athetise (ath'itīz), *v.t.* condemn as spurious. **-tesis,** *n.*

athetosis (athitō'sis), *n.* nervous twitching of fingers and toes. **-sic, -toid,** *adj.*

athrepsia (athrep'siə), *n.* complete debility in children. **-ptic,** *adj.*

athymy, -mia (ath'imi; -im'iə, -ī'miə), *n.* melancholy.

athyria (athīr'iə), *n.* absence of thyroid gland; lack of thyroid secretion. **-reosis,** *n.* condition due to a.

atlantes (atlan'tēz), *n.pl.* male figures used as columns.

atmiatry (atmī'ətri), *n.* med. treatment by inhalation, etc., of vapours.

atmocausis (atməkaw'sis), *n.* med. treatment by application of steam. **-autery,** *n.* apparatus used in a.

atmogenic (atməjen'ik), *adj.* Geol., of atmospheric origin.

atmograph (at'məgraf), *n.* instr. recording movements of respiration; recording atmometer.

atmology (atmol'əji), *n.* study of laws of watery vapour. **-gic(al),** *adj.* **-gist,** *n.*

atmolysis (atmol'isis), *n.* method of separating gases of different densities. **-yse** (at'məliz), *v.t.*

atmometer (atmom'itə), *n.* instr. measuring rate of evaporation into atmosphere. **-tric** (-et'rik), *adj.* **-try,** *n.*

atmospherics (atməsfer'iks), *n.pl.* interference in reception of radio signals due to electrical disturbances in the atmosphere.

atocia (atō'shiə), *n.* female sterility.

atokous (at'əkəs), *adj.* lacking offspring.

atoll (at'ol, -ol'), *n.* island formed of a coral reef surrounding a lagoon.

atom (at'm), *n.* ultimate unit of matter; smallest particle of element, constituent of molecule; any very small thing or quantity.

atomechanics (atəmikan'iks), *n.* study of motions of atoms.

atomic (atom'ik), *adj.* of atoms. **a.bomb,** bomb of which the immense destructive power is due to sudden release of energy by nuclear fission of uranium, plutonium, etc., atoms. **a.number,** number representing the magnitude of the positive charge on the nucleus of an atom of an element, *i.e.* the number of protons in the nucleus, or the number of electrons in the atom; numerically equal to the number denoting the position of an element in the periodic table. **a.pile,** apparatus in which the energy of nuclear fission is controlled and released gradually; nuclear reactor. **a. weight,** weight of an atom of an element on a scale on which the weight of an oxygen atom is 16. **-ity** (atəmis'iti), *n.* number of atoms in molecule of an element.

atomism (at'əmizm), *n.* theory of atoms. **-ise,** *v.t.* reduce to atoms; study in greatest detail. **-iser,** *n.* pump-like instr. producing fine spray. **-ist,** *n.* **-istic,** *adj.*

atomy (at'əmi), *n.* very small creature; very thin or contemptible person; skeleton.

---

atonal (atō'nəl), *adj. Mus.*, composed in accordance with theory of atonality. **-ity,** *n. Mus.*, theory in which the scale consists of twelve semitones of equal value.

atonic (aton'ik), *n. & adj.* unaccented or voiceless (sound) ; surd ; *Med.*, lacking tone or energy. **-ity,** **-nia** (-ō'niə), **-ny** (at'əni), *n.*

atopic (atop'ik), *adj. Med.*, displaced ; allergic. **-py** (at'əpi), *n.* allergy.

atrabilious (atrəbil'iəs), *adj.* very melancholic ; hypochondriac. **-larian,** *n.* such person ; person suffering from biliousness. **-larious,** *adj.* **-liar(y),** *adj.* ; **a.capsules,** suprarenal glands.

atrament (at'rəmənt), *n.* blacking ; ink. **-al,** **-ary,** **-ous,** *adj.*

atraumatic (atrawmat'ik, ā-), *adj.* designed to avoid injury.

atrepsy (at'rəpsi), *n.* athrepsia. **-ptic** (-ep'tik), *adj.*

atresia (atrē'zhiə), *n.* lack or closing of a passage of the body. **-etic** (-et'ik), **-sic,** *adj.*

atrial (ā'triəl), *adj.* pert. to atrium.

atrichia (atrik'iə), *n.* baldness.

atrium (ā'triəm),*n.* main courtyardlike room of Rom. house ; cavity of heart or ear.

atrophy (at'rəfi), *n.* wasting or paralysis due to lack of nutrition or exercise ; *Biol.*, loss of organ due to disuse ; *v.i. & t.* suffer or cause a. **-phic** (-of'ik), **-phous,** *adj.*

atropine (at'rəpēn, -in), *n.* poisonous alkaloid obtained from deadly nightshade roots and leaves. **-pism,** *n.* condition due to abuse of a.

atrous (ā'trəs), *adj.* jet black.

attaché (atash'ā), *Fr. n.* person attached to embassy.

attachment (atach'mənt), *n. Law,* taking of person or property by order of court. **a. of debts,** receipt by creditor of moneys owed to debtor.

attainder (atān'də), *n.* loss of civil rights, formerly result of outlawry or death sentence. **bill of a.,** act of Parl. pronouncing such sentence.

attaint (atānt'), *v.t.* pass sentence of attainder on ; sully ; attach disgrace to ; infect ; *adj.* convicted ; attainted ; *n.* dishonour ; misfortune. **-ure,** *n.*

attar (at'ah), *n.* oil distilled from rose petals ; any perfume derived from flowers.

attemper (atem'pə), *v.t.* alter quality by addition or mixture ; moderate ; adapt. **-ament,** *n.* **-ate,** *v.t.* moderate temperature. **-ator,** *n.* apparatus for moderating temperature.

attenuate (aten'ū āt), *v.t.* make thin; dilute ; weaken ; (-ət), *adj.* thin ; tapering ; rarified. **-tion,** *n.* **-tor,** *n.* resistance diminishing amplitude of oscillations in elec. circuit. **-uant,** *adj.* diluting ; *n.* drug diluting the blood.

attestation (atestā'shn), *n.* witnessing ; giving evidence ; declaration on oath. **a.clause,** declaration by witnesses to document that the signatures were witnessed by them. **-ant,** *n. & adj.*

Attic (at'ik), *n. & adj.* (dialect) of Athens or Attica ; classic. **A.salt,** typically Athenian wit. **A.order,** *Archit.*, column with square plinth. **-ism** (-sizm), *n.* refined language ; polished phrase.

attingent (atin'jənt), *adj.* touching.

attollent (atol'ənt), *adj.* raising up, *espec.* of muscles.

attorney (atə'ni), *n.* accredited agent in law or finance ; solicitor ; *Amer.*, counsel or solicitor. **power of a.,** authorization to act as agent. **by a.,** by proxy. **A.General,** chief law officer of Crown. **-ship,** *n.*

attornment (atən'mənt), *n.* assignment ; acknowledgment by tenant of landlord's rights.

attrahent (at'rəhənt), *adj.* attracting ; drawing towards or forward ; *n.* such thing or muscle ; *Med.*, irritant increasing action in part to which it is applied.

attrition (atrish'n), *n.* wearing away ; rubbing or scraping ; *R.C.*, incomplete repentance. **war of a.,** campaign of wearing down enemy's morale and resistance. **-tive** (-ī'tiv), *adj.* causing a. **-tus** (-ī'təs), *n.* pulverised matter.

aubade (ōbahd'), *Fr. n.* mus. piece performed at or describing dawn.

aubergine (ōbārzhēn'), *Fr. n.* fruit of egg plant.

au courant (ō kōōrahn'), *Fr.*, "in the current" ; up-to-date, *espec.* in information.

---

auctorial (awktōr'iəl), *adj.* pert. to an author.

aucupate (aw'kūpāt), *v.i.* & *t.* hunt birds; pursue vigilantly.

audile (aw'dīl), *n.* person whose mental processes are stimulated more strongly by hearing than by other senses; *adj.* pert. to such persons; auditory.

audio-frequency (aw'diō-frē'kwənsi), *n.* frequency between 15 and 20,000 cycles per sec., *i.e.* the frequency of normally audible sound waves.

audiometer (awdiom'itə), *n.* instr. testing sensitivity of hearing and audibility of sounds. **-tric** (-et'rik), *adj.* **-try,** *n.*

audiphone (aw'difōn), *n.* instr. for the deaf placed against the teeth.

audit (aw'dit), *n.* examination, *espec.* of business accounts; report on such examination; *v.t.* make such examination. **a.ale,** special strong ale used at certain Oxford colleges on audit day. **-or,** *n.* person who audits; listener. **-orial,** *adj.*

auditory (aw'ditəri), *adj.* pert. to hearing; *n.* audience; auditorium.

au fait (ō fā'), *Fr.,* "to the fact"; having complete and up-to-date knowledge; conversant.

au fond (ō fawn'), *Fr.,* "at bottom"; fundamentally.

Augean (awjē'ən), *adj.* pert. to Augeas, King of Elis, in Gr. myth., whose stables were not cleaned for thirty years; filthy.

au grand sérieux (ō grahn sāriə'), *Fr.,* "with great seriousness"; quite seriously.

augur (aw'gə), *n.* prophet; soothsayer; omen; *v.i.* & *t.* predict; portend. **-al** (-ūrəl), *adj.* **-y** (-ūri), *n.* art of prophecy or divination; omen.

august (awgust'), *adj.* majestic; venerable; awe-inspiring.

Augustan (awgus'tən), *adj.* pert. to Augustus Caesar and his age, *espec.* literature of his reign; of any classical or golden age of literature; *n.* writer in such age.

auk (awk), *n.* short-winged seabird, *espec.* the extinct great and the little a. **-let,** *n.* small auk.

au lait (ō lā'), *Fr.,* "with milk."

aularian (awlār'iən), *adj.* pert. to hall; *n.* member of a hall at Oxford or Cambridge.

aulete (aw'lēt), *n.* flautist. **-tic** (-et'ik), *adj.*

aulic (aw'lik), *adj.* courtly; ceremonious. **a.council,** body established c. 1500 to assist in govt. of Holy Roman Empire. **-ism** (-sizm), *n.* courtly refinement.

aumbry, aumry (awm'bri, -ri), *n.* ambry.

aumildar, *see* **amildar.**

au naturel (ō natūrel'), *Fr.,* "in natural" (style); simply; without additions, *espec.* of cooking; nude.

aura (ōr'ə), *n.* emanation; atmosphere surrounding a thing or person; personality; light breeze; *Elec.,* air current due to electrical discharge from sharp point; *Med.,* sensation warning of onset of epileptic fit, hysteria, etc.

aural (ōr'əl), *adj.* pert. to ear or hearing.

aurantiaceous (ōrantiā'shəs), *adj.* like or pert. to orange or plant group containing it.

aurate (ōr'āt), *adj.* having ears or ear-like appendages; gilded.

aurea mediocritas (ōr'iə mēdiok'-ritas), *Lat.,* "the golden mean."

aureate, -eous (ōr'iət, -iəs), *adj.* golden-coloured; ornate. **-tion,** *n.*

aureity (ōr ē'iti), *n.* properties of gold.

aureola (ōr ē'ələ), *n.* heavenly crown; aureole.

aureole (ōr'iōl), *n.* halo; bright circle of light; aureola; *Astron.,* solar corona. **-line,** *adj.* gold-coloured.

aureomycin (ōriōmī'sin), *n.* antibiotic produced by a soil fungus.

aureus (ōr ē'əs), *n.* (*pl.* -ei) gold coin of anct. Greece and Rome, at first valued at about £1.

auric (ōr'ik), *adj.* pert. to, like or composed of gold; aural; pert. to aura.

auricle (ōr'ikl), *n.* external ear; ear-shaped appendage; upper cavity of heart.

auricomous (ōrik'əməs), *adj.* having golden hair; making hair golden.

auricular (ōrik'ūlə), *adj.* pert. to hearing, or to the ear; spoken secretly. **a.finger,** the little finger.

---

hat, bah, hāte, hāre, crawl; pen, ēve, hēre; it, īce, fīre; on, bōne, boil, bōre, howl; foot, fōōd, bōōr, hull, tūbe, pūre.

auriculate (ōrik´ūlāt), *adj.* having ears or ear-shaped outgrowths; lobed; ear-like.

aurific (ōrif´ik), *adj.* producing gold. **-ation**, *n.* working with gold.

auriferous (ōrif´ərəs), *adj.* containing gold.

auriform (ōr´ifawm), *adj.* ear-shaped.

aurify (ōr´ifi), *v.t.* change into gold.

auriga (ōr i´gə), *n.* charioteer. **-l**, *adj.* **-tion** (-igā´shn), *n.* art of driving a chariot.

auriphrygia (ōrifrij´iə), *n.* gold embroidery. **-te,** *adj.*

auriscope (ōr´iskōp), *n.* instr. for examining ear. **-scopy** (-is´kəpi), *n.*

aurist (ōr´ist), *n.* specialist on the ear and its diseases.

aurochs (ōr´oks), *n.* extinct wild ox; *erron.,* European bison.

aurora (ōr ōr´ə), *n.* dawn; reddish glow in sky before sunrise. **a.borealis,** luminosity in sky in Arctic region due to atmospheric electricity; northern lights. **a. australis,** same phenomenon in Antarctic region; southern lights. **-l, -rean,** *adj.*

aurous (ōr´əs), *adj.* pert. to, containing or made of gold.

aurulent (ōr´oolənt), *adj.* gold-coloured.

auscultate (aws´kultāt), *v.i.* & *t. Med.,* listen to sounds in human body; examine in this manner. **-tion**, *n.* **-tive,** *adj.* **-tor,** *n.* person practising auscultation; stethoscope. **-tory,** *adj.*

auslaut (ows´lowt), *n.* final sound of syllable or word.

auspice (aws´pis, os´pis), *n.* omen, *espec.* of good fortune; *pl.,* patronage; protection. **-cate** (-kāt), *v.i.* & *t.* predict; give good start to. **-cious** (-pish´əs), *adj.* promising well; favourable; important.

Auster (aws´tə), *Lat.,* south wind; southern latitudes.

austere (awstēr´, ostēr´), *adj.* strict in moral outlook; extremely simple; without ornamentation; severe; sharp. **-ity** (-er´iti), *n.*

austral (aws´trəl, os´trəl), *adj.* of the south; moist and warm.

autacoid (aw´təkoid), *n.* hormone. **-al,** *adj.*

autarch (aw´tahk), *n.* despot. **-y,** *n.*

autarky (aw´tahki), *n.* national economic self-sufficiency.

autism (aw´tizm), *n.* constant day-dreaming. **-s´**, *n.* **-stic,** *adj.*

autobahn (aw´.əbahn; Ger., ow´-), Ger. *n.* "motor-way"; trunk road for fast traffic.

autocephalous (awtəsef´ələs), *adj. Eccl.,* self-governing. **-lia** (-ā´liə), **-lity** (-al´iti), **-ly,** *n.*

autochthon (awtok´thən), *n.* native; aboriginal species. **-al, -ous,** *adj.* **-y,** *n.*

autocrat (aw´təkrat), *n.* sole ruler; despot. **-ic,** *adj.* **-racy** (-ok´rəsi), *n.* **-rix,** *n.* empress of Russia.

auto-da-fé (awtōdahfā´), Sp. *n.* (*pl.* **autos-** . . . .) "act of faith"; promulgation and execution of sentence of Inquisition.

autodidact (aw´tədīdakt, -dīd-), *n.* self-taught person. **-ic,** *adj.*

autodynamic (awtədīnam´ik), *adj.* acting under its own power.

auto-erotism (aw´tō-er´ətizm), *n. Psych.,* sexual self-love.

autogamy (awtog´əmi), *n.* self-fertilisation. **-mic** (-gam´ik) **-mous,** *adj.*

autogenesis (awtəjen´isis), *n.* spontaneous generation. **-neal** (-jē´niəl), **-netic** (-jinet´ik), **-nous** (-oj´inəs), *adj.*

autogeny (awtoj´ini), *n.* self-generation.

autognosis (awtognō´sis), *n.* self-knowledge. **-ostic** (-os´tik), *adj.*

autointoxication (awtōintoksikā´-shn), *n.* absorption of poisons produced in body.

autokinesis (awtəkīnē´sis, -kin-), *n.* voluntary or automatic movement. **-etic** (-et´ik), *adj.*

autolatry (awtol´ətri), *n.* self-worship.

automation (awtəmā´shn), *n.* control of machines by other machines, electronic devices, etc., instead of by human beings.

automaton (awtom´ətən), *n.* (*pl.* **-ta**) automatic mechanism, *espec.* one effecting complex actions; robot; person who acts like a machine. **-tism,** *n.* machine-like action or routine; involuntary action; belief that actions are not controlled by conscious mind. **-tous,** *adj.*

autometry (awtom´itri), *n.* measurement or judgment of self. **-tric** (-et´rik), *adj.*

automorphic (awtəmaw´fik), *adj.* formed after its or one's own pattern. **-phism,** *n.*

automotive (awtəmō′tiv), *adj.* self-propelling.

autonomy (awton′əmi), *n.* power or right to govern oneself or itself; free-will. **-mic** (-om′ik), *adj.* spontaneous; involuntary. **-mous,** *adj.* self-governing.

autonym (aw′tənim), *n.* writer's own name; work published under own name.

autopathy (awtop′əthi), *n.* undiagnosible disease; introspection. **-thic** (-ath′ik), *adj.* resulting from diseased part itself.

autophagy, -gia (awtof′əji, -ā′jiə), *n.* sustaining life by living on the body's tissues. **-gi** (jī), *n.pl.* creatures able to feed themselves immediately after birth or hatching. **-gous** (-gəs), *adj.*

autophobia (awtəfō′biə), *n.* fear of solitude.

autophony (awtof′əni), *n.* apparent distortion of one's own voice due to infection or stoppage of ears; sound of auscultator's voice as reverberating in patient's chest.

autophyte (aw′təfīt), *n.* plant able to organise its foodstuffs; non-saprophytic plant. **-ytic**(-it′ik), *adj.*

autoplasty (aw′təplasti), *n.* grafting tissue from patient's own body. **-tic,** *adj.*; *Biol.,* pert. to self-adaptation to environment.

autopsy (aw′topsi, -op′si), *n.* personal examination, *espec.* post-mortem. **-ptic,** *adj.* derived from personal observation. **-sic,** *adj.*

autoschediasm (awtəshē′diazm), *n.* improvisation. **-ase,** *v.i.* **-stic,** *adj.*

autoskeleton (aw′təskelitən), *n.* internal skeleton.

autosome (aw′təsōm), *n.* non-sexual chromosome.

autosoteric (awtəsəter′ik), *adj.* obtaining salvation through oneself. **-ism** (-ot′ərizm), *n.*

autostrada (aw′təstrahdə), It. *n.* "motor-way"; autobahn.

autotelic (awtətel′ik), *adj.* having itself as its only purpose.

autothaumaturgist (awtəthaw′mətējist), *n.* person pretending to be mysterious or notable.

autotheism (awtəthē′ism), *n.* belief in self-subsistence of God the Son; deification of oneself.

autotherapy (awtəther′əpi), *n. Med.,* treatment of patient by himself or by application of his secretions.

autotrophic (awtətrof′ik), *adj. Bot.,* nourishing itself; autophytic.

autotropic (awtətrop′ik), *adj. Bot.,* tending to grow in straight line. **-pism** (-ot′rəpizm), *n.*

autotype (aw′tətīp), *n.* facsimile; true copy. **-py,** *n.* process of producing such copies.

autrefois acquit (ōtrəfwah ak′ē), *Fr.,* "formerly acquitted"; *Law,* plea that defendant has already been acquitted on the charge. **a.convict,** plea that he has already been convicted on the charge.

autres temps, autres moeurs (ō′trə tahn, ō′trə mərs), *Fr.,* "other times, other customs."

auxanometer (awksənom′itə), *n.* instr. measuring rate of growth of plants.

auxesis (awksē′sis), *n.* hyperbole. **-etic** (-et′ik), *adj.*

auxin (awks′in), *n.* chem. substance increasing growth of plants; plant hormone.

auxograph (awks′əgraf), *n.* instr. recording variations in volume.

auxology (awksol′əji), *n.* science of growth.

auxotonic (awksəton′ik) *adj.* according or due to growth.

ava (ah′və), *n.* strong liquor of Sandwich Is.; plant from which it is obtained.

aval (ā′vəl), *adj.* pert. to grandparent(s).

avatar (av′ətah), *n.* incarnation of deity, *espec.* Hindu; manifestation; deification.

ave (ah′vā, ā′vi), *Lat.,* "hail!" **a.atque vale,** hail and farewell. **A.Maria,** *n.* prayer to the Virgin Mary.

avellaneous (avələ′niəs), *adj.* hazel.

avenaceous (avinā′shəs), *adj.* pert. to or like oats. **-niform** (-en′-ifawm), *adj.* like oats in shape.

avenous (avē′nəs), *adj.* lacking veins.

aventurine (aven′tūr in, -in), *n.* glass containing golden or green flecks; quartz containing mica-flakes.

average (av′ərij), *n. Comm.,* loss to owners due to damage to ship or cargo at sea; assessing of incidence of such loss in proportion among interested parties. **particular a.,** incidence of such loss, due to unavoidable accident, upon

---

hat, bah, hāte, hāre, crawl; pen, ēve, hēre; it, īce, līre; on, bōne, boil, bōre, howl; foot, fōōd, bōōr, hull, tūbe, pūre.

particular goods or interests. **general a.,** incidence of such loss, due to intentional damage to ship and cargo done to safeguard ship at sea, upon ship and cargo generally. **a.adjuster,** professional assessor of marine insurance claims who apportions them among owners, underwriters, etc.

averaging (av'ərijing), *n. Comm.,* operation of increasing transactions on Stock Exchange when market goes against the operator to maintain price at level desired.

Avernal (avē'nəl), *adj.* pert. to Avernus, an Italian lake, or the infernal regions.

averruncate (avərung'kāt), *v.t.* avert. **-tion,** *n.* **-tor,** *n.* pruning tool for trees.

avian (ā'viən), *adj.* pert. to birds.

avicide (av'isīd), *n.* killing of birds.

avicula (avik'ūlə), *n.* kind of pearloyster.

avicular (avik'ūlə), *adj.* pert. to birds.

aviculture (ā'vikultūr), *n.* rearing of birds.

avifauna (āvifaw'nə), *n.* birdlife of a region.

avigation (avigā'shn), *n.* aerial navigation. **-te,** *v.i.* **-tor,** *n.*

avine (ā'vīn, -in), *adj.* pert. to birds.

avion (aviawn'), Fr. *n.* "aeroplane." **par a.,** *Fr.,* "by aeroplane"; stamp placed on correspondence sent by air.

avital, -tic (av'itəl, -ī'təl ; -it'ik), *adj.* ancestral.

avitaminosis (avitəminō'sis), *n.* condition due to vitamin-deficiency. **-otic** (-ot'ik), *adj.*

avocado (avəkah'dō), *n.* pearshaped W. Ind. fruit; alligator pear.

avocation (avəkā'shn), *n.* calling away; diversion; hobby; vocation. **-tive** (-ok'ətiv), *adj.* **-tory** (-ok'ətri), *adj.* recalling.

avocet, -set (av'əset), *n.* long-legged wading bird with upturned beak.

avolitional (avəlish'ənəl), *adj.* involuntary.

avulsion (avul'shn), *n.* act of pulling away; portion torn off. **-ive,** *adj.*

avuncular (avung'kūlə), *adj.* of or like an uncle.

awn (awn), *n.* "beard" of grass, barley, etc.; spiky outgrowth; *v.t.* strip of awns.

axifugal (aksif'ūgəl), *adj.* centrifugal.

axil (aks'il), *n.* upper angle between leaf and stem, or branch and trunk.

axilla (aksil'ə), *n.* (*pl.* -ae) armpit; shoulder; axil. **-nt,** *adj.* forming or growing in an axil. **-ry,** *adj.* of arm-pit; of or growing in an axil.

axiniform (aksin'ifawm), *adj.* having shape of axe-head.

axiology (aksiol'əji), *n.* study of ultimate values. **-gical,** *adj.* **-gist,** *n.*

axiom (aks'iəm), *n.* necessary and accepted truth; basic and universal principle. **-atic,** *adj.*

axion (aks'iən, -ī'ən), *n.* brain and spinal cord.

axolotl (aks'əlotl), *n.* larval salamander of Mexico and W. America.

axonometry (aksənom'itri), *n.* measurement of or by axes. **-tric** (-et'rik), *adj.*

axophyte (aks'əfīt), *n.* stem-bearing plant.

axunge (aks'unj), *n.* medicinal lard or grease.

ayah (ī'ə, ā'ə), *n.* native Ind. nurse or servant.

aye-aye (ī'ī), *n.* species of lemur of Madagascar.

azan (azahn'), *n.* Moham. call to prayer.

azimuth (az'iməth), *n.* angular distance, measured along horizon, of object from north or south points; angle between meridian and the great circle which passes through both zenith and heavenly body. **a.compass,** magnetic compass having sights for taking the a. **a.circle,** quadrant of great circle through zenith and nadir. **motion in a.,** motion of an astron. instr. about a vertical axis. **-al,** *adj.*

azofication (āzəfikā'shn), *n.* nitrogenisation of soil by bacteria. **-fier,** *n.* bacterium causing a. **-fy,** *v.t.* cause a.

azoic (azō'ik), *adj.* lacking life, *espec.* of geol. period.

azoology (azōol'əji), *n.* study of inanimate nature.

azote (az'ōt), *n.* nitrogen. **-taemia,** *n.* excess of nitrogen in blood. **-tic** (-ot'ik), **-tous** (-ō'təs), *adj.* **-tise,** *v.t.* combine with nitrogen. **-tism,** *n.* **-torrhoea,** *n.* excess of nitrogen in bodily discharges. **-turia,** *n.* excess of nitrogen in urine.

azulejo (athoolā'ho), Sp. *n.* brightly coloured tile of Near East, Spain and Holland.

azygous (azī'gəs), *adj.* unpaired; odd.

azym(e) (az'īm, -im), *n.* unleavened bread ; Passover cake ; *pl.* feast of such bread. **-mite,** *n.* believer in use of unleavened bread at Holy Communion. **-mous,** *adj.* unleavened.

B

Baal (bā'əl), *n.* (*pl.* **-im**) local god of anct. Semitic tribes ; idol. **-ath,** *n.* such goddess. **-ism,** *n.* idolatry.

babiroussa, -russa, -rusa (babiroo'sə), *n.* tusked wild hog of E. India ; horned-hog.

babu, -boo (bah'boo), Anglo-Ind. *n.* title of Hindu gentleman ; Mr. ; English-speaking Hindu, *espec.* used contemptuously. **b.-English,** incorrect English written by b.

babuina (babū ē'nə), *n.* female baboon.

babul (bab'ool), *n.* gum-arabic tree of E. Ind. and Arabia.

baccaceous (bakā'shəs), *adj.* like a berry ; bearing berries.

baccalaureate (bakəlor'iət), *n.* degree of Bachelor. **-rean,** *adj.* pert. to a Bachelor.

baccate (bak'āt), *adj.* pulpy ; like a berry ; bearing berries.

bacchanal (bak'ənəl), *adj.* pert. to Bacchus, god of wine, and rites in his worship ; *n.* drunkard ; reveller ; votary of Bacchus. **-ia** (-ā'liə), *n.pl.* festival of Bacchus ; drunken behaviour. **-ian,** *adj.* **-ianism,** *n.* habitual drunken behaviour.

bacchant (bak'ənt), *n.* (*pl.* **-es**) priest or votary of Bacchus. **-e** (-an'ti), *n.* such priestess or female votary. **-ic,** *adj.*

bacchic (bak'ik), *adj.* pert. to Bacchus and bacchanalia ; drunken ; jovial ; *n.* drinking song.

bacchius (bəkī'əs), *n.* (*pl.* **-ii**) metrical foot of one long followed by two short syllables.

bacciferous (baksif'ərəs), *adj.* bearing berries. **-iform,** *adj.* berry-shaped. **-ivorous,** *adj.* feeding on berries.

bacillus (bəsil'əs), *n.* (*pl.* **-li**) rod-shaped bacterium, *espec.* causing disease. **-laemia,** *n.* presence of b. in blood. **-lary,** *adj.* rod-shaped ; caused by b. **-licide,** *n.* substance

killing b. **-liform,** *adj.* rod-shaped. **-ligenic,** *adj.* caused by b. **-losis,** *n.* infection with b. **-luria,** *n.* presence of b. in urine.

backwardation (bakwədā'shn), *n.* *Comm.,* postponement by seller of delivery of stock ; premium paid to buyer for such postponement.

Baconian (bākō'niən), *adj.* pert. to Francis Bacon (1561–1626), his inductive system of philosophy, etc. ; *n.* & *adj.* (person) believing that Bacon was author of the plays attributed to Shakespeare. **-ism,** *n.* Bacon's inductive system.

bacteria (baktēr'iə), *n.pl.* (sing. **-ium**) universally present microscopic unicellular organisms. **-ial, -ian, -ious,** *adj.*

bacteriaemia (baktēriē'miə), *n.* presence of bacteria in blood.

bactericide (baktēr'isīd), *n.* substance destroying bacteria. **-dal,** *adj.*

bacterin (bak'tərin), *n.* bacterial extract or vaccine.

bacteriogenic, -nous (baktēriəjen'ik, -oj'inəs), *adj.* caused by bacteria.

bacteriology (baktēriol'əji), *n.* study of bacteria.

bacteriolysin (baktēriəli'sin), *n.* antibody causing destruction of bacteria. **-sis** (-ol'isis), *n.* decomposition caused by bacteria ; destruction of bacteria. **-ytic** (-it'ik), *adj.*

bacteriophage (baktēr'iəfāj), *n.* destroyer of bacteria in intestines. **-gic, -gous** (-of'əgəs), *adj.* **-gy** (-of'əji), *n.*

bacterioscopy (baktērios'kəpi), *n.* examination of bacteria with microscope. **-pic** (-op'ik), *adj.* **-pist,** *n.*

bacteriosis (baktēriō'sis), *n.* bacterial plant disease.

bacteriostasis (baktēriəstā'sis), *n.* prevention of growth of bacteria. **-atic** (-at'ik), *adj.*

bacteriotherapy (baktēriəther'əpi), *n.* med. treatment with bacteria. **-peutic,** *adj.*

bacteriotoxin (baktēriətoks'in), *n.* poison destroying or preventing growth of bacteria; poison produced by bacteria.

bacteriotropic (baktēriətrop'ik), *adj.* affecting bacteria.

bacteritic (baktērit'ik), *adj.* caused or marked by bacteria. **-roid,** *adj.* like bacteria.

baculus (bak'ūləs), *n.* stick; rod; symbol of power. **-liferous,** *adj.* bearing canes, reeds, etc. **-liform,** *adj.* rod-shaped. **-line,** *adj.* pert. to rod or punishment therewith.

badigeon (bədij'ən), *n.* mixture of plaster and ground stone, or glue and sawdust, for repairing masonry and woodwork respec.; *v.t.* repair with b.

badinage (bad'inahzh), Fr. *n.* banter.

baffy (baf'i), *n.* wooden deep-faced golf club used to give loft to ball.

bagasse (bəgas'), *n.* dry residue, *espec.* of sugar cane and beet after extraction of juice, and plants after removal of fibre.

baggala (bag'ələ), *n.* Arabian two-masted vessel; dhow.

bagnio (ban'yō), It. *n.* bath house; prison; brothel.

baguette (baget'), *n.* small astragal moulding; narrow rectangular cut gem; *adj.* cut into such shape.

bahadur (bəhah'door), *n.* Ind. title of respect; *sl.,* self-important official.

bailee (bālē'), *n.* person receiving goods in trust.

bailey (bā'li), *n.* outer wall of castle; space between outer and inner walls.

bailie (bā'li), *n.* Scot. civic officer, equiv. of alderman. **-iary, -iery,** *n.* jurisdiction of b.

bailiff (bā'lif), *n.* sheriff's officer; agent or steward of estate. **-ry,** *n.* office of b. **bum-b.,** *n. sl.* sheriff's officer.

bailiwick (bā'liwik), *n.* jurisdiction of sheriff or bailie.

bailment (bāl'mənt), *n.* delivery of goods in trust. **-lor,** *n.* person delivering such goods.

bain-marie (ban-marē'), *n.* (*pl.* **bains-....**) vessel holding hot water in which other vessels are placed; double boiler.

bakal (bəkawl'), *n.* Oriental shop-keeper.

bakelite (bā'kəlit), *n.* solid thermo-setting plastic of universal use made from phenols and formaldehyde. **-lise,** *v.t.* make into b. **-iser,** *n.*

baksheesh, -shish (bak'shēsh), Pers. *n.* tip; alms.

balachong, -chan (bal'əchong, -an), Indo-Chin. *n.* fishy condiment used with rice.

balaghat (baləgaht'), Anglo-Ind. *n.* high tableland.

balalaika (baləli'kə), *n.* triangular guitar-like mus. instr. of Russia.

balandra (bələn'drə), *n.* single-masted Sp. cargo ship.

balaneutics (balənū'tiks), *n.* balneology.

balaniferous (balənif'ərəs), *adj.* bearing acorns.

balanism (bal'ənizm), *n.* use of suppositories or pessaries.

balanoid (bal'ənoid), *adj.* acorn-shaped; pert. to acorn barnacles; *n.* acorn barnacle.

balata (bal'ətə), *n.* elastic gum obtained from milk-tree of Brazil.

balatron (bal'ətron), *n.* clown. **-ic,** *adj.*

balaustine (bəlaw'stin), *n.* pomegranate tree.

balbuties (balbū'shiēz), *n. Med.,* stammering.

baldachin(o), -kin, -quin (bal'dəkin, -kē'nō), *n.* silk and gold fabric; fabric canopy over throne, altar, etc.; stone canopy over altar.

bald-faced (bawld'-fāst), *adj.* with white face or facial mark.

baldric(k) (bawl'drik), *n.* shoulder belt for sword, etc. **b.-wise,** *adj.* worn like a b., *i.e.,* over one shoulder and under opposite arm.

baleen (balēn'), *n.* whalebone.

balefire (bāl'fīr), *n.* bonfire; beacon; funeral pyre.

baline (bəlēn'), *n.* coarse wool or cotton stuff; sacking.

balistarius (balistār'iəs), *n.* (*pl.* **-ii**) crossbow-man.

balistraria, ball- (balistrār'iə), *n.* cross-shaped opening in fortress wall for discharge of arrows.

balize (balēz'), *n.* pole bearing beacon, etc., on sea-shore.

ballade (balahd'), *n.* poem of one or more sets of three-, seven- or eight-lined stanzas, with envoi of four or five lines. **b.royal,** stanzas of seven or eight decasyllabic lines ; rime royal.

ballerina (balərē′nə), *n.* female ballet dancer.

balletomane (bal′etəmān), *n.* person fanatically devoted to ballet. **-nia,** *n.*

ballista (balis′tə), *n.* (*pl.* **-ae**) anct. mil. catapult for throwing rocks, fire, etc. **-tic,** *adj.* pert. to projectiles. **-tician,** *n.* student of ballistics. **-tics,** *n.* science of projectiles.

ballistite (bal′istīt), *n.* kind of smokeless explosive power.

ballon d'essai (balawn′ desā′), *Fr.* "trial balloon" ; tentative experiment made to discover what the fate of an action would be.

ballonet(te) (bal′ənet), *n.* interior, variable-volume gasbag of airship or balloon.

ballottement (bəlot′mahn, -mənt), *n.* diagnosis of pregnancy by sharp pressure, causing movement of foetus. **renal b.,** diagnosis of floating kidney by same means.

balmoral (balmor′əl), *n.* name of Scot. cap, boot and petticoat.

balneal (bal′niəl), *adj.* pert. to bathing. **-ary,** *n.* bathing-place ; medicinal spring.

balneation (balniā′shn), *n.* bathing. **-tory** (bal′niətri), *adj.*

balneography (balniog′rəfi), *n.* treatise on baths. **-pher,** *n.* author of b.

balneology (balniol′əji), *n.* science of med. application of baths. **-gical,** *adj.* **-gist,** *n.*

balneotherapy (balniəther′əpi), *n.* treatment by natural waters. **-peutic,** *adj.* **-peutics,** *n.*

baluchitherium, -there (bəloochi-thēr′iəm, -ēr′), *n.* (*pl.* **-ia**) gigantic rhinoceros-like fossil mammal of Cent. Asia.

bambino (bambē′nō), It. *n.* baby, *espec.* figure of infant Christ.

banal (bā′nəl), *adj.* trivial ; trite. **-ity** (bənal′iti), *n.*

banausic (banaw′sik), *adj.* pert. to or characteristic of a workshop.

bancus superior (bang′kəs sooper′-iaw), *Lat.,* "upper bench" ; *Law,* King's (Queen's) Bench (*abbr.* **banc. sup.**).

bandana, -nna (bandan′ə), *n.* coloured spotted handkerchief.

banderilla (bandərēl′ya), Sp. *n.* dart stuck into bull at bull-fight.

-lero (-ār′ō), *n.* bull-fighter wielding b.

banderol(e), -drol (band′ərol, -drol), *n.* small streamer, flag or banner.

bandicoot (ban′dikoot), *n.* large Ind. rat ; small, kangaroo-like Austral. animal.

bandobast (ban′dəbast), Anglo-Ind. *n.* practical, detailed organisation ; settlement.

bandog (ban′dog), *n.* fierce dog on chain ; mastiff.

bandolier, -leer (bandəlēr′), *n.* shoulder belt carrying cartridges. **-lero,** *n.* bandit.

bandoline (ban′dəlin, -ēn), *n.* gummy, scented hair-fixative.

bandonion (bandō′niən), *n.* large concertina.

bandore (ban′dor, -dōr′), *n.* anct. lute-like mus. instr. **-durria,** *n.* Sp. instr. of same type.

bandy (ban′di), *n.* any Ind. horse-drawn conveyance ; form of hockey.

banghy, -gy (bang′gi), *n.* Ind. porter's shoulder yoke. **b.post,** parcel post.

banian, see **banyan.**

banket (bang′kit), *n.* gold-bearing conglomerate rock of S. Africa.

bank-rate (bangk′rāt), *n.* discount rate as fixed by central or State bank.

bankshall (bangks′hawl), Anglo-Ind. *n.* warehouse ; port official's office.

banneret (ban′ərit), *n.* knight, *espec.* knighted for valour in battle ; such order of knighthood.

bannock (ban′ək), *n.* flat, round, unleavened Scot. loaf. **mashlum b.,** b. made of mixed meal.

banquette (bahnket′, bang-), *n.* firing-step in trench ; narrow seat ; raised sidewalk.

banshee (ban′shē), *n.* female spirit, *espec.* of Ireland, whose wailing foretells death.

banstickle (ban′stikl), *n.* three-spined stickleback.

bant (bant), *v.i. sl.* diet for slimness.

banteng (ban′teng), *n.* wild ox of Malaya.

bantling (bant′ling), *n.* brat ; illegitimate child.

banxring (bangks′ring), *n.* squirrel-like E. Ind. mammal.

banyan, -ian (ban′yan), *n.* native Ind. trader, *espec.* attached to

European firm; Hindu trading caste who eat no meat; Ind. flannel coat; sacred Ind. tree, with aerial roots; covering a vast area. **b.days,** days when ship's crew received no meat; any period of poor feeding.

banzai (banzī'), *Jap.*, hurrah! long live (the Emperor)!

baobab (bā'əbab), *n.* huge W. Afric., Ind. and Austral. tree, yielding rope fibre and edible fruit; monkey-bread tree.

baptistery, -try (bap'tistri), *n.* part of church where baptism is performed, formerly a separate building.

baragnosis (baragnō'sis), *n.* loss of ability to perceive weight.

barathea (barəthē'ə), *n.* worsted fabric with twill hopsack weave; silk or silk-and-worsted fabric with lightly ribbed or pebbled weave.

barbastelle (bahbəstel'), *n.* long-eared species of bat.

barbate (bah'bāt), *adj.* bearded; tufted; barbed; having awns.

barbecue (bah'bikū), *n.* frame on which meat is cooked or dried; animal roast whole; outdoor oven or other cooking apparatus; *Amer.*, large open-air party at which cooking is done out of doors, *espec.* of animal roast whole; *v.t.* roast whole; cook, dry or cure on a b.

barbel (bah'bəl), *n.* fleshy appendage on head of certain fishes; carp-like fish having a b. **-llate,** *adj.* bristly.

barbet (bah'bit), *n.* brightly plumaged toucan-like tropical bird of Old World; kind of long-haired poodle.

barbette (bahbet'), *n.* gun platform behind parapet; armoured protection of gun platform on ship.

barbican (bah'bikən), *n.* tower on or beyond outer wall of city or castle.

barbicel (bah'bisel), *n.* small outgrowth on barbule.

barbigerous (bahbij'ərəs), *adj.* having beard.

barbital (bah'bitəl), *n.* barbitone. **-ism,** *n.* condition due to abuse of b.

barbiton (bah'biton), *n.* (*pl.* **-ta**) anct. Gr. lyre-like mus. instr.

barbitone (bah'bitōn), *n.* a sleep-inducing drug; veronal.

barbiturate (bahbit'ūr āt), *n.* powerful sleep-inducing drug. **-ric** (-ūr'ik), *adj.* denoting acid, also called malonyl urea, from which b. is derived.

barbotine (bah'bətin), *n.* kaolin paste used to ornament pottery.

barbule (bah'būl), *n.* hooked outgrowth on barb of feather. **-late,** *adj.* barbellate.

barcarole, -lle (bahkərōl'), *n.* gondolier's song.

bardolatry (bahdol'ətri), *n.* excessive worship of Shakespeare and his works. **-ter,** *n.* such worshipper.

barège, -ège (barāzh), *n.* light fabric of silk, or cotton, and worsted; mineral water from Barèges, in the Pyrenees.

barge-board (bahj'bawd), *n.* board over gable, covering ends of rafters.

bargoose (bah'gōōs), *n.* sheldrake.

baric (bar'ik), *adj.* pert. to weight; barometric; pert. to barium.

barium (bār'iəm), *n.* white metallic element. **b.meal,** drink containing a compound of barium which is opaque to X-rays, taken before or during X-ray examination of digestive tract.

barker (bah'kə), *Amer. n.* person shouting wares, etc.; tout; *sl.*, pistol.

barley-break (bah'li-brāk), *n.* Old Eng. catching game.

barleycorn (bah'likawn), *n.* grain of barley; third part of inch. **John B.,** personification of barley and of spirituous liquor.

barm (bahm), *n.* yeast; froth on surface of fermenting liquor.

Barmecide (bah'misīd), *adj.* illusory; *n.* one who gives such presents. **B.feast,** mock banquet of empty dishes, or any similar illusion. **-dal,** *adj.*

barnacle (bah'nəkl), *n.* limpet-like marine crustacean; pincers holding horse's nose while it is shod; *pl., sl.,* spectacles. **b.goose,** large black-and-white Arctic wild goose.

barodynamic (barədinam'ik), *adj.* pert. to the phys. behaviour of dams, bridges, and other very heavy constructions. **-s,** *n.* study of this.

barognosis (barognō'sis), *n.* ability to perceive weight.

barogram (bar'əgram), *n.* recording made by barograph.

barograph (bar'əgraf), *n.* instr. continuously recording atmospheric pressure.

barology (barol'əji), *n.* science of weight and gravitation.

barometer (bərom'itə), *n.* instr. registering atmospheric pressure, *espec.* for weather forecasting. **-tric(al)** (-et'rik, -l), *adj.* pert. to atmospheric pressure or barometer. **-trograph** (barəmet'rəgraf), *n.* barograph. **-try,** *n.*

baron and feme (bar'ən ənd fēm), *Fr., Law,* husband and wife. ·

baroque (bərok', -ōk'), *n.* grotesque ; extravagant ; *n.* contorted style of archit. of late Renaissance (17th–18th cent.); similar irregular style of mus. composition.

baroscope (bar'əskōp), *n.* weatherglass. **-pic(al)** (-op'ik, -l), *adj.*

barothermograph (barəthē'məgraf), ·*n.* instr. recording simultaneously pressure and temperature, *espec.* atmospheric.

barothermohygrograph (barəthēmə-hī'grəgraf), *n.* instr. recording simultaneously atmospheric pressure, temperature and humidity.

barouche (bərōōsh'), *n.* four-wheeled four-seater carriage with folding hood and separate driver's seat. **-t** (-ooshā'), **-tte** (-ooshet'), *n.* light b.

baroxyton (baroks'iton), *n. Mus.,* large bass brass wind instr.

barque, -rk (bahk), *n.* three-masted vessel with square-rigged mizzen mast ; any small ship.

barquentine, -ken-, -kan- (bah'kəntēn), *n.* three-masted vessel with square-rigged foremast and fore-and-aft rigged main and mizzen masts.

barracoon (barəkōōn'), *n.* enclosure in which slaves or convicts were confined.

barracoota, -couta, -cuda (barəkōō'tə, -də), *n.* pike-like tropical sea fish.

barrage (bar'ahzh), *n.* dam ; barrier of heavy gunfire aimed at and along a line ; **box b.,** standing b. on three sides of an area ; **creeping b.,** barrage in which range is gradually extended ; **standing b.,** such fire with fixed range. **balloon b.,** number of captive balloons flown close together, their cables intended to deter low-flying aircraft. **b. balloon,** one such balloon.

barratry (bar'ətri), *n.* unlawful action by captain or seamen injuring owner or freighter of ship ; inciting to litigation or riot ; simony. **-tor,** *n.* person habitually entering into quarrels and lawsuits. **-tous, -trous,** *adj.* quarrelsome ; guilty of b.

barrette (baret'), *n.* hair-clip.

barrico (bərē'kō), *n.* keg.

bar sinister (bah sin'istə), *n.* mark of bastardy.

bartizan (bah'tizən, -zan'), *n.* small overhanging turret.

barton (bah'tən), *n.* farmyard ; manor farm ; fowl-yard.

barycentre (bar'isentə), *n.* centre of gravity. **-tric,** *adj.*

baryecoia (bariikoi'ə), *n. Med.,* hardness of hearing.

baryphony, -nia (barif'oni, -ō'niə), *n.* difficulty of speech. **-nic** (-on'ik), *adj.*

barysphere (bar'isfēr), *n.* area of earth underlying lithosphere.

barythymia (barithim'iə), *n.* nervous depression.

basalt (bas'awlt, bās'-), *n.* greenish-black igneous rock, often forming columns. **-ic, -ine,** *adj.* **-iform, -oid,** *adj.* like b. ; column-like.

bas bleu (bah blē'), *Fr.,* "blue stocking."

bascule (bas'kūl), *n.* balanced lever. **b.-bridge,** drawbridge raised by falling counterpoises, as Tower Bridge, London.

base (bās), *n. Chem.,* compound combining with acid to form salt.

bashaw (bashaw'), *n.* pasha.

bashi-bazouk (bashibazōōk'), *n.* Turkish mercenary soldier.

basial (bā'ziəl), *adj.* pert. to kissing. **-ate,** *v.t.* kiss. **-ation,** *n.*

basic (bā'sik), *adj. Chem.,* app. to salt with base atomically greater than acid ; having alkaline reaction. **-sicity,** *n.* power of acid to combine with bases.

basifugal (bāsif'ūgəl), *adj. Bot.,* growing away from base, or at apex only.

basil (baz'il), *n.* aromatic herb of mint family.

basilic (bəsil'ik), *adj.* royal ; *n.* basilica.

basilica (bəsil'ikə), *n.* rectangular building with colonnades along its length, dividing it into nave and aisles ; early Christian church ;

R.C., church having certain liturgical privileges. **-n**, *adj.*

basilicon (bəsil'ikən), *n.* kind of ointment.

basilisk (baz'ilisk, bas'-), *n.* mythical fire-breathing reptile or one whose stare turned persons to stone; cockatrice; tree-lizard of Cent. Amer.; *anct.* brass cannon. **-scan, -scine** (-*is* īn. -i..), *adj.*

basipetal (bāsip'itəl), *adj. Bot.*, growing from top to base.

basket-fish (bah'skit-fish), *n.* kind of starfish; sea-spider.

bas-relief (basrilēf', bah-), *n.* carving in low relief, *i.e.*, in which figures stand out less than half their proportion from background.

basset (bas'it), *n.* short-legged hound used in badger- and hare-hunting; gambling c rd game like faro; *Geol.*, edge of outcrop. **b.-horn**, tenor clarinet.

bassinet(te) (bas'inet), *n.* hooded cradle or perambulator of wicker.

basso-rilievo (bas'ō-rilia'vō), It. *n.* bas-relief.

basta (bas'tah), It. *excl.* enough!

bastard (bas'təd, bah'stəd), *n.* illegitimate child; spurious object; *adj.* counterfeit; hybrid. **-ise**, *v.t.* declare illegitimate. **-y**, *n.* illegitimacy.

bastille, -ile (bastēl'), *n.* prison or fortress, *espec.* that of Paris (destroyed by revolutionaries, July 14, 1789).

bastinado (bastinā'dō), *n.* (*pl.* **-oes**) beating on soles of feet; *v.t.* administer such punishment.

bastion (bas'tiən), *n.* earthwork projecting outwards from fortification.

batata (batā'tə, -ah'tə), *n.* sweet potato.

bateau (batō'), Fr. *n.* (*pl.* **-eaux,** -ōz') Canadian flat-bottomed river boat. **b. bridge**, pontoon bridge.

bathetic (bathet'ik), *adj.* pert. to or like bathos.

bathic (bath'ik), *adj.* pert. to depths, *espec.* of sea.

bathmism (bath'mizm), *n.* energy or force of growth. **-ic**, *adj.*

batholith, -ite (bath'əlith, -īt), *n. Geol.*, mass of intruded igneous rock below surface and of great depth.

bathometer (bathom'itə), *n.* bathymeter.

bathos (bath'os, bā'-), *n.* anti-climax with humorous effect; spurious pathos; triteness.

bathyal (bath'iəl), *adj.* pert. to zone of sea from 600 feet to abyssal zone.

bathybic (bathib'ik), *adj.* pert. to or dwelling in deepest zone of sea.

bathycolpian, -pic (bathikol'piən, -pik), *adj.* having deep bosom.

bathylimnetic (bathilimnet'ik), *adj.* living at bottom of lake or marsh.

bathymeter (bathim'itə), *n.* instr. for deep-sea sounding. **-tric** (-et'rik), *adj.* pert. to vertical distribution of organisms in sea. **-try**, *n.* process of measuring depths of sea.

bathyorographical (bathiōrəgraf'-ikl), *adj.* pert. to or showing depths below and heights above sea level.

bathypelagic (bathipəlaj'ik), *adj.* living in deep sea.

bathyseizm (bath'isīzm), *n.* earthquake taking place at great depth.

bathysmal (bathiz'məl), *adj.* pert. to deepest part or bottom of sea.

bathysophical (bathisof'ikl), *adj.* pert. to knowledge of deep-sea life and conditions.

bathysphere (bath'isfēr), *n.* kind of diving bell for descending to great depths in sea.

batiste (batēst'), *n.* fine linen; cambric; fine cotton or wool fabric, *espec.* as treated for use as antiseptic dressing.

batophobia (batəfō'biə), *n.* fear of heights, or of being close to high buildings.

batrachian (batrā'kiən), *adj.* pert. to frogs or toads; *n.* a frog or toad. **-choid**, *adj.* like a frog or toad. **-chophagous**, *adj.* eating frogs or toads. **-chophobia**, *n.* fear of frogs or toads.

batta (bat'ə), Anglo-Ind. *n.* addition to pay, *espec.* soldier's; agio, *espec.* on out-of-date coins.

battels (bat'əls), *n.pl.* accounts of Oxford college, *espec.* for provisions.

batter (bat'ə), *v.i. Archit.*, recede as it rises (of a wall); *n.* such inclination. **b.rule**, plumb-line of such walls, falling within base.

battology (batol'əji), *n.* an unnecessary repetition. **-gical**, *adj.* **-gise**, *v.i.* **-gist**, *n.*

battue (batoo', -tū'), *n.* driving of game towards guns; shooting-party of that kind; massacre of helpless persons.

batture (batŭr'), *n.* raised bed of sea or river.

baudekyn (baw'dikin), *n.* baldachin.

bauxite (bōz'īt, bawks'-, bowks'-), *n.* earthy mineral compound yielding aluminium.

bavardage (bavahdazh'), Fr. *n.* idle chatter.

bavian (bā'viən), *n.* poetaster; baboon.

bawd (bawd), *n.* procuress. **-ry,** *n.* obscene talk. **-y,** *adj.* obscene.

baya (bəyah'), *n.* Ind. weaver-bird.

bayadere (bahyədēr'), *n.* Hindu dancing girl; *adj.* app. to brightly coloured striped fabrics.

bayberry (bā'beri), *n.* fruit of bay-tree; *Amer.*, fruit of wax-myrtle; species of W. Ind. pimento, yielding bay oil or rum.

bayete (bahyā'tə), *Zulu,* salutation to king; hail!

bayou (bī'ōō), *Amer. n.* marshy branch of river, lake or bay; slow-flowing stream.

baysalt (bā'sawlt), *n.* salt obtained from sea-water.

bazigar (bahzigah'), *n.* nomadic Ind. gypsy.

bazooka (bəzōō'kə), *n.* anti-tank rocket projector.

B.C.G., *abbr.* of bacillus Calmette-Guérin, injected to give protection against tuberculosis.

bdellium (del'iəm), *n.* myrrh-like gum-resin; Ind. and African tree yielding it.

bdelloid (del'oid), *adj.* pert. to leech; leech-like in appearance; *n.* leech. **-ometer,** *n.* cupping-glass for surg. bleeding. **-otomy,** *n.* surg. application of leeches.

beadhouse, bede- (bēd'hows), *n.* almshouse housing beadsmen.

beadle (bē'dl), *n.* officer of parish, church, court, etc., for keeping order; mace-bearer. **-dom,** *n.* petty officialdom.

bead-roll (bēd'rōl), *n. R.C.,* list of persons to be prayed for; any list or catalogue; rosary.

beadsman, bede- (bēdz'mən), *n.* monk; pensioner or almshouse inmate who prays for benefactor.

beagle (bē'gl), *n.* small hound used in hare-hunting; *pl.* pack of harriers. **-ling,** *n.* hunting on foot with b.

beakiron (bē'kiən), *n.* bickern.

beambird (bēm'bəd), *n.* spotted flycatcher; garden warbler.

bean-tree (bēn'trē), *n.* Austral. chestnut tree; carob tree.

bear (bār), *n. Comm.,* speculator on Stock Exchange who desires a fall in price; *v.t.* cause fall in price of.

bearing-rein (bār'ing-rān), *n.* rein that compels horse to arch its neck.

beastlings (bēst'lingz), *n.pl.* beestings.

beata (biā'tə), *n. (pl.* -tae), *R.C.,* female beatified person.

beatify (biat'ifī), *v.t.* make blessed or happy; *R.C.,* confer title of "blessed," preliminary to canonisation. **-fic** (-if'ik), *adj.* saintly. **-fication,** *n.*

beatitude (biat'itūd), *n.* blessedness; bliss; *pl.* blessings in Matt. v.

beatus (biā'təs), *n. (pl.* -ti) *R.C.,* male beatified person.

beau (bō), *n. (pl.* -x, bōz) lover; dandy. **b.geste,** magnanimous action; polite gesture. **b.ideal,** one's highest conception of excellence or virtue. **b.monde,** fashionable society.

beaux-arts (bōzahr'), Fr. *n.pl.* "fine arts."

bebeerine (biber'in, -ēn), *n.* bibirine.

béchamel (bāshəmel'), *n.* white sauce thickened with cream.

bêche-de-mer (bāsh-də-mār'), *n.* species of holothurian used for food in China; sea-cucumber; sea-slug; trepang.

bechic (bek'ik, bē'-), *adj.* curative of cough.

becket (bek'it), *n.* hook-like device of rope, wood or metal to secure ship's ropes, etc.

bedeguar, -gar (bed'igah), *n.* mossy rose-gall; dog rose.

bedel(l) (bē'dl), *n.* beadle at universities.

bee-bread (bē'-bred), *n.* mixture of honey and pollen stored by bees for food.

beele (bēl), *n.* miner's pick with two sharp ends. **-man,** *n.* worker using a b.

beestings (bēs'tingz), *n.pl.* first milk of cow after birth of calf.

beeswing (bēz'wing), *n.* thin crust on old port; any old wine.

beg (beg), *n. (fem.* -ani, bā'gəni) Turk. and Ind. title of honour.

begohm (beg'ōm), *n.* one thousand million ohms.

beguine (begēn'), *n.* member of religious order of lay sisters, *espec.* of Belgium ; rumba-like dance of Fr. W. Indies. **-nage,** *n.* convent of b.

begum (bē'gəm), *n.* Moham. woman of high rank.

behaviourism (bihā'vyərizm), *n.* psych. theory that all mental processes result from external stimuli and association of ideas. **-rist,** *adj.* ; *n.* believer in such theory.

behemoth (bē'imoth, -hē'-), *n.* gigantic animal, mentioned in Job xl ; hippopotamus.

bejan (bē'jən), *n.* freshman at Scot. university.

belay (bilā'), *v.i.* secure rope by coiling it round a projection. **-ing pin,** short wooden post to which ropes are secured.

belcher (bel'chə), *n.* coloured, spotted neckerchief.

belemnite (bel'əmnīt), *n.* bullet-shaped molluscan fossil. **-tic** (-it'ik), *adj.*

belemnoid (bel'əmnoid), *adj.* dart-shaped.

bel esprit (bel esprē'), Fr. *n.* (*pl.* **beaux esprits,** bōz-) genius ; witty person ; wit.

bel-étage (belātahzh'), Fr. *n.* main storey of building.

belladonna (belədon'ə), *n.* deadly nightshade ; narcotic drug obtained from that plant. **b.lily,** bulbous plant of S. Africa with lily-shaped flowers. **b.ointment, plaster,** etc., pain-relieving medicaments containing the drug b.

belle (bel), *n.* beautiful woman ; noted beauty. **b.amie,** mistress.

belleric (bəler'ik), *n.* kind of myrobalan.

belles-lettres (bel-let'r), *n.* writings of solely literary or aesthetic value, *espec.* essays, etc. **-trist,** *n.* writer or student of b. **-tristic,** *adj.*

bellicism (bel'isizm), *n.* war-mindedness.

bellicose (bel'ikōs), *adj.* desirous of fighting ; war-like. **-sity** (-os'iti), *n.*

belliferous (bəlif'ərəs), *adj.* bringing war.

belligerent (bəlij'ərənt), *adj.* making war ; *n.* person or nation engaged in warfare. **-nce,** **-ncy,** *n.*

belling (bel'ing), *n.* deer's cry at mating time.

bellipotent (belip'ətənt), *adj.* powerful in war.

bellonion (bəlō'nion), *n.* mechanical mus. instr. consisting of drums and trumpets.

bellote, ball- (bəlōt'), *n.* holm-oak acorn.

bell-wether (bel'wedhə), *n.* sheep with bell attached to the neck leading the flock.

beloid (bē'loid), *adj.* arrow-shaped.

belonoid (bel'ənoid), *adj.* needle-shaped.

beltein, **-tane** (bel'tān), *n.* anct. Celtic May-day festival.

beluga (bilōō'gə), *n.* white sturgeon ; kind of dolphin, also called white whale.

belvedere (bel'vidēr), *n.* turret, or open shelter on roof, giving fine view ; summer-house.

bencher (ben'chə), *n.* senior member of an Inn of Court.

bench-mark (bench'-mahk), *n.* surveyor's mark at known position, from which measurements are calculated ; datum level.

bend sinister (bend sin'istə), *n.* diagonal line on coat of arms indicating bastardy.

Benedicite (benidī'siti), *n.* canticle beginning "O all ye works of the Lord," sung when Te Deum is omitted.

benedick (ben'idik), *n.* newly married husband, *espec.* one formerly a confirmed bachelor.

benediction (benidik'shn), *n.* blessing ; act of blessing ; *R.C.*, rite of blessing the people with the monstrance. **-al,** **-ary,** *n.* collection of b. **-tive,** **-tory,** *adj.*

Benedictus (benedik'təs), *n.* canticle beginning "Blessed be the Lord God of Israel" ; *R.C.*, canticle beginning "Benedictus qui venit in nomine Domini."

benefic (benef'ik), *adj.* favourable, *espec.* astrol.

benefice (ben'ifis), *n.* church living ; *v.t.* endow with a b. **-d,** *adj.,* holding a b.

beneficial (benifish'l), *adj.* advantageous ; bringing good. **b. interest,** right to enjoy property, though it be legally invested in another. **-ary,** *n.* person receiving benefits ; legatee under will ;

ə=*er* in *father* ; ē̄=*er* in *pert* ; th=*th* in *thin* ; dh=*th* in *then* ; zh=*s* in *pleasure* ; k=*ch* in *loch* ; ñ=Fr. nasal *n* ; ü=Fr. *u.*

holder of benefice; *adj.* holding by feudal tenure.

beneficiate (benifish'iāt), *v.t.* prepare for smelting. -tion, *n.*

beneplacito (beniplas'itō), *Lat.* "during pleasure."

benet (ben'it), *n.* R.C.; exorcist.

benevolence (binev'ələnts), *n.* charitableness; former loan demanded by certain Eng. kings. -nt, *adj.*

Bengali, -lee (bengaw'li), *adj.* pert. to Bengal, *espec.* native language.

bengaline (beng'gəlēn, -lēn'), *n.* silk, silk-and-wool or silk-and-cotton transversely corded fabric.

Bengal light (ben'gawl līt), *n.* signal firework, with brilliant blue light.

benign (binīn'), *adj.* kin ly; favourable; wholesome; *Med.*, mild; not malignant. -ant (-ig'nənt), *adj.* -ance (-ig'nəns), -ity (-ig'niti), *n.*

benison (ben'izn, -sn), *n.* blessing.

benjamin (ben'jəmin), *n.* gum benz.in and ree yielding it; man's tight coat.

Benthamism (ben'thəmizm), *n.* utilitarian doctrine of Jeremy Bentham (1748-1832) that the greatest happiness of the greatest number is most desirable. -mite, *n.* adherent of B.

benthos (ben'thos), *n.* sea-bottom's flora and fauna. -thic, -thoic (-thō'ik), -thonic, *adj.*

ben trovato (ben trəvah'tō), *It.*, "well invented"; *adj.* well expressed; *n.* such speech or thought.

benzedrine (ben'zidrin, -zē'-), *n.* vasoconstrictor drug, also called amphetamine, which relieves hay fever, catarrh, etc., and, taken internally, increases physical and mental activity.

benzene (benzēn', ben'-), *n.* hydrocarbon (phenylhydride) distilled from coal-tar.

benzine (ben'zin, -zēn'), *n.* petrollike distillate of petroleum, used as solvent; coal-tar oil containing benzene.

benzoin (ben'zoin, -zōin, -zō'in), *n.* balsamic resin used in perfumery, etc., and in med. as compound tincture called friar's balsam; bitter-almond-oil camphor, found in gum benzoin. -ic (-o'ik), *adj.*

benzol(e) (ben'zol, -zōl), *n.* benzene; coal-tar oil containing benzene. -late, -lise, *v.t.* mix or treat with b.

benzoline (ben'zəlin, -ēn), *n.* benzine; petrol; impure benzene.

berberia (bəbēr'iə), *n.* beri-beri.

berberine (bə'bərēn, -in), *n.* tonic alkaloid obtained from barberry and other plants.

berceuse (bārsəs'), Fr. *n.* cradlesong; lullaby.

bere (bēr), *n.* four-rowed barley.

beretta, *see* biretta.

bergamask (bə'gəmahsk), *n.* kind of country dance.

bergamot (bə'gəmot), *n.* kind of pear; essence obtained from rind of kind of pear-shaped orange; fruit and tree yielding such essence; snuff scented with such essence.

bergère (bārzhār'), Fr. *n.* "shepherdess"; kind of 18th-century chair and sofa. -tte (-zhəret'), *n.* kind of country song or dance.

beriberi (ber'iber'i), *n.* Eastern disease, similar to peripheral neuritis, due to deficiency of vitamin B_1.

berlin (bəlin'), *n.* four-wheeled twoseater roofed carriage, with seat or platform behind. **B.spirit,** coarse spirit distilled from potatoes, beetroot, etc. **B.wool,** fine, dyed wool for tapestry, etc. -e, *n.* kind of motor car body with glass partition between driver's and passengers' seats.

berm (bəm), *n.* narrow ledge; *Amer.,* canal bank opposite towing path.

bernicle (bən'ikl), *n.* barnaclegoose.

bersaglieri (bārsahlyār'i), *n.pl.* (*sing.* -re) It. sharpshooter corps.

berserk (bə'sək, bəsək'), *adj.* frenzied; wild, *espec.* of fighting. -er, *n.* person fighting thus, *espec.* Norse warrior; *adj.* berserk.

bestial (bes'tiəl), *adj.* animal-like; base. -ise, *v.t.* -ity (-al'iti), *n.* *Law,* sexual intercourse with animal.

bestiarian (bestiār'iən), *n.* animal-lover, *espec.* opposed to vivisection. -ism, *n.*

bestiary (bes'tiəri), *n.* medieval book, *espec.* illustrated, on beasts.

beta (bē'ta), *n.* second letter of Gr. alphabet (B, β). **b.particle,** negatively-charged particle; electron. **b.ray,** a beam or stream of b. particles. -tron, *n.* apparatus in which electrons are accelerated electromagnetically to very high energies to form a beam of beta rays for bombarding atomic nuclei and generating high-voltage X-rays.

betel (bē'tl), *n.* Asiatic palm, yielding nut which is wrapped in leaf of same tree and chewed; areca.

bête noire (bāt nwahr'), *Fr.*, "black beast"; pet abomination; bugbear.

bethel (beth'əl), *n.* sacred place; nonco formist chapel.

bêtise (bātēz'), *Fr. n.* foolishness; foolish or stupid act.

béton (bet'ən, bātawñ'), *n.* concrete made by mixing gravel with cement and sand.

bettong (betong'), *n.* kind of Austral. kangaroo-rat.

betulin(ol) (bet'ūlin, -ol, -ōl), *n.* resinous extract of birch bark; birch camphor.

bey (bā), Turk. *n.* governor; title of honour. -**lic**, -**lik**, *n.* area of bey's jurisdiction.

bezel (bez'əl), *n.* sloping edge of cutting tool; edge and facet of cut gem; flanged groove holding watch- or clock-glass; *v.t.* grind to edge; bevel.

bezoar (bizō'ə), *n.* stone-like mass found in stomach of ruminants. **b.antelope, goat,** etc., animals in which b. are found. **b.stone,** such mass used in East as antidote to poison. -**dic** (-ah'dik), *adj.*

bhandar (bahn'dah), Hindu *n.* store; library. -**i,** *n.* store-keeper; treasurer.

bhang (bang), Ind. *n.* dried leaves and twigs of Ind. hemp, chewed, smoked and made into infusion or sweetmeat; hashish.

bheesty, -tie (bē'sti), Anglo-Ind. *n.* servant who draws and carries water.

bhungi(ni) (bung'gi, -ni), *n.* Hindu street-sweeper.

bialate (bīal'āt), *adj.* with two wings.

biarchy (bī'ahki), *n.* rule by two persons.

bibacious (bibā'shəs), *adj.* fond of drinking. -**city,** *n.*

bibcock (bib'kok), *n.* tap, with nozzle bent downwards.

bibelot (bib'lō), *n.* small object of art; trinket; curio.

bibi (bē'bē), Hind. *n.* lady; Mrs.

bibirine (bibēr'in, -ēn), *n.* quinine-like extract of bark of S. Amer. greenheart tree.

bibitory (bib'itəri), *adj.* pert. to drinking.

biblioclasm (bib'liəklazm), *n.* destruction of books; destructive criticism of Bible. -**st,** *n.* person so destroying or criticising.

bibliogenesis (bibliəjen'isis), *n.* production of books.

bibliognost (bib'liognost), *n.* person having deep knowledge of books. -**ic,** *adj.*

bibliogony (bibliog'əni), *n.* bibliogenesis.

bibliography (bibliog'rəfi), *n.* list of books on one subject or by one author; scientific study of books and writings; historical work on books. -**pher,** *n.* compiler of such work. -**phical,** *adj.*

biblioklept (bib'liəklept), *n.* book-thief. -**omania,** *n.* kleptomania towards books.

bibliolater (bibliol'ətə), *n.* worshipper of books, or of letter of Bible. -**trous,** *adj.* -**try,** *n.* such worship.

bibliology (bibliol'əji), *n.* book-lore; Biblical literature. -**gical,** *adj.* -**gist,** *n.*

bibliomancy (bib'liəmansi), *n.* divination by reference taken at random in book, *espec.* in the Bible.

bibliomania (bibliəmā'niə), *n.* strong desire for collecting books. -**iac,** -**ne,** *n.* person with such desire.

bibliopegy (bibliop'iji), *n.* art of book-binding. -**gic** (-ej'ik, -ē'jik), *adj.* -**gist,** *n.* book-binder.

bibliophagy (bibliof'əji), *n.* devouring of books. -**gic** (-aj'ik), *adj.* -**gist,** *n.* person devouring books.

bibliophile (bib'liəfil, -il), *n.* lover of books. -**lism,** -**ly** (-of'ilizm, -li), *n.* love of books. -**lic** (-il'ik), -**listic,** *adj.* -**list,** *n.*

bibliophobia (bibliəfōbiə), *n.* hatred of books. -**be,** *n.* person hating books.

bibliopoesy (bibliəpō'isi), *n.* making of books.

bibliopole (bib'liəpōl), *n.* bookseller, *espec.* of rare books. -**ery** (-ōl'ri), -**lism,** -**ly** (-op'əlizm, -li), *n.* selling of books. -**lar** (-ō'lə), -**lic** (-ol'ik), *adj.* -**list** (-op'əlist), *n.* -**listic,** *adj.*

bibliosoph (bib'liəsof), *n.* bibliognost.

bibliotaph (bib′liətaf), *n.* person keeping his books secret or locked up. **-ic**, *adj.*

bibliothec(a) (bib′liəthek, -ək′ə), *n.* library. **-al** (-ek′l), *adj.* **-cary** (-oth′əkəri), *n.* librarian. **-thetic**, *adj.* pert. to arrangement of books.

biblus, **-los** (bib′ləs); *n.* papyrus.

bibulous (bib′ūləs), *adj.* fond of drink; drunken; sponge-like. **-osity**, *n.*

bicameral (bīkam′ərəl), *adj.* having two Chambers or Houses. **-ism**, *n.* **-rist**, *n.* person advocating such legislative system.

bicapitate (bīkap′itāt), *adj.* two-headed.

bicarbonate (bīkah′bənət), *n.* acid carbonate, *espec.* of soda, which is used as antacid.

bice (bīs), *n.* green or blue pigment.

bicentenary (bīsentē′nəri, -sen′tin-), *n.* two hundredth anniversary; *adj.* pert. to two centuries. **-nnial** (-en′iəl), *adj.* occurring every two hundred years; lasting two hundred years.

bicephalous (bīsef′ələs, -sifal′ik), *adj.* having two heads.

bichord (bī′kawd), *adj. Mus.*, having two strings, *espec.* two strings for each note.

bicipital (bīsip′itəl), *adj.* pert. to biceps; bifurcating. **-tous**, *adj.* having two heads or extremities.

bickern (bik′ən), *n.* anvil pointed at both ends.

bicollateral (bīkəlat′ərəl), *adj.* having two sides the same. **-ity**, *n.*

biconic (bīkon′ik), *adj.* having shape of two cones with bases together.

biconjugate (bīkon′jūgāt), *adj. Bot.*, having a pair each member of which is divided into a pair.

bicorn (bī′kawn), *adj.* having two horns or points. **-nate**, **-nous**, *adj.*

bicrural (bīkrūr′əl), *adj.* two-legged.

biddery, **bidree** (bid′ri), *n.* alloy of several metals on which gold and silver are inlaid.

bident (bī′dent), *n.* two-pronged instr.; sheep aged two years. **-al**, **-ate**, *adj.* having two prongs or teeth. **-iculate**, *adj.* having two small teeth.

biduous (bid′ūəs), *adj.* lasting two days.

bien aimé (bianāmā′), Fr. *n.* (*fem.* **-mée**) "well beloved" (person).

bien aise (bianāz′), Fr. *n.* "well being"; comfort.

bien-être (bianā′tr), Fr. *n.* "well being."

biennial (bīen′iəl), *adj.* lasting two years; occurring every two years; *n.* plant living for two years and flowering in the second. **-ium**, *n.* (*pl.* **-ia**) two years.

bienséance (biansāahns′), Fr. *n.* proper, correct or fitting thing; *pl.* the proprieties.

bifacial (bīfā′shl), *adj.* having distinct upper and lower surfaces; having both sides the same; having two faces.

bifarious (bīfār′iəs), *adj.* in two rows; twofold; pointing in two directions.

bifer (bī′fə), *n.* plant flowering or fruiting twice a year. **-ous**, *adj.*

bifid(ate) (bī′fid, -āt), *adj.* divided into two portions; forked. **-dity**, *n.*

bifilar (bīfī′lə), *adj.* having two threads, *espec.* of measuring instr.

bifocal (bīfo′kl), *adj.* with two foci, *espec.* app. to spectacle lens of which upper part is used for viewing distant and lower part for near objects; *n.* such lens.

bifurcate (bī′fəkāt), *v.i.* & *t.* split into two branches or forks; *adj.* (-fək′ət) so divided. **-tion**, *n.* one of the forks.

bigeminate (bījem′ināt), *adj.* biconjugate. **-nal**, *adj.* arranged in pairs.

bigener (bī′jinə), *n.* hybrid arising from two genera. **-ic** (-er′ik), **-rous** (-jen′ərəs), *adj.* pert. to two genera.

bigential (bījen′shəl), *adj.* with two races.

bigg (big), Scot. *n.* four-rowed barley.

bigot (big′ət), *n.* person with fixed and intolerant belief. **-ed**, *adj.* **-ry**, *n.* such belief.

bigrid (bī′grid), *adj.* app. to thermionic valve having two grids and combining functions of two valves.

bijou (bē′zhōō), *n.* (*pl.* **-x**, -ōōz) jewel; piece of jewellery; *adj.* small and well-formed. **-terie** (-ōō′tri), *n.* jewellery.

bijugate, **-gous** (bī′jəgāt, -gəs), *adj.* having two overlapping heads, said of coin struck to two persons; *Bot.*, with two pairs of leaflets.

---

hat, bah, hāte, hāre, crawl; pen, ēve, hēre; it, īce, fīre; on, bōne, boil, bōre, howl; foot, fōōd, bōōr, hull, tūbe, pūre.

bikh (bik), Hind. *n.* aconitine.

bilabiate (bīlā'biət), *adj.* having two lips. **-ial**, *adj.*; *Phon.*, formed with both lips ; *n.* such consonant.

bilateral (bilat'ərəl), *adj.* having or pert. to two sides ; of two parties or States. **-ism, -ity,** *n.* b. symmetry.

bilberry (bil'bəri), *n.* moorland plant with edible blue berries ; blaeberry ; whortleberry.

bilbo (bil'bō), *n.* sword.

bilboes (bil'bōz), *n.pl.* fetters, *espec.* long iron bar with sliding shackles used to imprison persons on ship.

bildar (bildah'), Anglo-Ind. *n.* navvy ; camp servant.

bile (bīl), *n.* bitter digestive fluid emanating from liver ; melancholy ; anger. **b.stone,** gall-stone.

bilge (bilj), *n.* lowermost part of interior of ship ; widest part of barrel ; *v.i.* & *t.* leak in that part ; make hole in bilge. **b.water,** foul water in ship's bilge.

bilharziasis (bilhahzī'əsis), *n.* tropical disease due to certain parasitic worms or blood flukes.

biliary (bil'iəri), *adj.* pert. to bile. **-lic,** *adj.* **-lification,** *n.* formation of b.

bilinear (bilin'iə), *adj.* having, pert. to or between two lines.

bilingual (biling'gwəl), *adj.* speaking, in or pert. to two languages. **-uist,** *n.* person speaking two languages.

biliteral (bilit'ərəl), *adj.* consisting of or using two letters ; *n.* such linguistic root.

bill (bil) : **b.-broker,** dealer in b. of exchange. **b. of adventure,** declaration that merchandise shipped is not property of shipowner, whose liability is limited to safe delivery. **b. of costs,** solicitor's account of charges. **b. of exchange,** negotiable order to pay cash on or before certain date. **b. of health,** statement of health, *espec.* as to infectious diseases, of persons aboard ship. **b. of indictment,** statement of accusation in criminal court. **b. of lading,** acknowledgment by ship's master that goods have been received on board, and promise of safe delivery. **b. of sale,** document transferring title to goods, *espec.* as security for loan. **b. of sight,** outline description of

goods being imported. **b. of sufferance,** permission to load or unload at certain ports without payment of duty. **true b.,** statement by grand jury that there was a prima facie case against accused.

billabong (bil'əbong), Austral. *n.* river creek ; backwater ; watercourse.

billet-doux (bilidoo'; Fr., bēyādoo'), Fr. (*pl.* billets-....), "loveletter."

billion (bil'yən), *n.* a million millions ; *Amer.* & *Fr.*, a thousand millions.

billon (bil'ən), *n.* alloy of precious with larger quantity of base metal.

bilocation (bilōkā'shn), *n.* existence, or power to exist, in two places simultaneously.

biloquist (bil'əkwist), *n.* person with power of speaking in two distinct voices.

biltong (bil'tong), S. African *n.* strips of dried meat.

bimanous, -nal (bim'ənəs ; bim'ənəl, bimā'nəl), *adj.* having two hands ; pert. to human species. **-nual** (biman'ūəl), *adj.* requiring or using two hands.

bimarine (bīmərēn'), *adj.* situated between seas.

bimaxillary (bīmaks'iləri), *adj.* pert. to both jaws.

bimensal (bīmen'səl), *adj.* occurring every two months.

bimestrial (bīmes'triəl), *adj.* occurring every two months ; lasting two months.

bimetallism (bīmet'əlizm), *n.* currency system in which both gold and silver are standard money. **-ic** (-al'ik), *adj.* **-ist,** *n.* advocate of b. **-istic,** *adj.*

bimillenary (bīmil'inəri), *n.* space of two thousand years. **-nium** (-en'iəm), *n.* (*pl.* -ia) two thousand years.

binal (bī'nəl), *adj.* double ; twin.

binary (bī'nəri), *adj.* double ; dual. **b.converter,** machine converting alternating into direct current. **b.fission,** division of cell into two equal parts. **b.measure,** *Mus.*, common time. **b.star,** two stars revolving round a common centre. **b.theory,** chem. theory defining every acid as a hydrogen compound with radicle, and every salt as hydrogen compound with hydrogen replaced by a metal.

ə=*er* in *father* ; ē=*er* in *pert* ; th=*th* in *thin* ; dh=*th* in *then* ; zh=*s* in *pleasure* ; k=*ch* in *loch* ; n=Fr. nasal *n* ; ü=Fr. *u.*

binate (bī'nāt), *adj.* double ; in couples. **-tion,** *n.* celebration by a priest of Mass twice on same day.

binaural (binŏr'əl), *adj.* pert. to or for use with two ears.

bine (bīn), *n.* flexible shoot of climbing plant, *espec.* hop.

binghi (bing'gi), Austral. *n. sl.* aborigine.

binnacle (bin'əkl), *n.* fixed case or stand for ship's compass. **b.list,** list of sick men on man-of-war.

binocle (bin'əkl), *n.* binocular instr.

binocular (binok'ūlə, bī-), *adj.* pert. to or for two eyes. **-ate,** *adj.* having two eyes. **-ity,** *n.* **-s,** *n. pl.* field glasses.

binomial (bīnō'miəl), *adj.* having two names, *espec.* of scientific nomenclature giving two names, genus and species, to each species ; *Math.,* composed of two algebraic terms joined by $+$ or $-$. **b.theorem,** formula for fin ing any power of a b. expression. **-ism,** *n.* use of b. nomenclature.

binominal (bīnom'inəl), *adj.* having two names ; binomial, *espec.* of scientific nomenclature. **-nous,** *adj.* having two interchangeable names.

binotic (bīnō'tik, -ot'ik), *adj.* binaural.

binotonous (bīnot'ənəs), *adj.* consisting of two notes.

binturong (bin'tūrong), *n.* Asiatic civet with prehensile tail.

biobibliography (bīəbibliog'rəfi), *n.* bibliography with biographical notes.

biocentric (bīəsen'trik), *adj.* having life as its centre or main principle.

biochem'stry (bīəkem'istri), *n.* chemistry of living organisms.

biocoenosis, -cen- (bīəsēnō'sis), *n.* (*pl.* **-ses**) association of living creatures in a certain area. **-otic** (-ot'ik), *adj.*

biodynamics (bīədīnam'iks), *n.* study of activities of living organisms. **-cal,** *adj.*

bio-electric (bī ōilek'trik), *adj.* pert. to plant or animal electricity.

biogen(e) (bī'əjen, -ēn), *n.* ultimate component part of protoplasm.

biogenesis (bīəjen'isis), *n.* theory that life derives only from living matter. **-etic** (-jinet'ik), *adj.* ; **b.law,** recapitulation theory. **-t,** *n.* adherent of b.

biogenous (bīoj'inəs), *adj.* produced from living organism ; giving life.

biogeny (bīoj'ini), *n.* history of evolution of living organisms ; bicgenesis.

biogeography (bīəjiog'rəfi), *n.* study of geographical distribution of plants and animals. **-phic(al),** *adj.*

biognosy, -os's (bīog'nəsi, -nō'sis), *n.* sciences of life collectively.

biograph (bī'əgraf), *n.* early form of cinematograph.

biokinetics (bīəkinet'iks), *n.* study of changes during development of organism.

biolinguistics (bīəlinggwis'tiks), *n.* study of relations between physiology and speech.

biolith, -lite (bī'əlith, -līt), *n.* rock formed by living organisms.

biology (bīol'əji), *n.* science of life of plants and animals. **-gical,** *adj.* **-gism,** *n.* biological theory ; use of biological terms. **-gist,** *n.*

bioluminescence (bīəlōōmines'əns), *n.* production of light by living creatures.

biolysis (bīol'isis), *n.* destruction of life or organic substance. **-ytic** (-it'ik), *adj.*

biomagneti m (bīəmag'nitizm), *n.* animal magnetism. **-tic,** *adj.*

biomathematics (bīəmathimat'iks), *n.* math. principles used in biology.

biometrics, -try (bīəmet'riks, -om'-itri), *n.* calculation f length of human life ; statistical biology. **-tric,** *adj.* **-trician,** *n.* student of b.

bion(t) (bī'on, -t), *n.* physiologically independent living organism.

bionergy (bion'əji), *n.* vital force.

bionomics (bīənom'iks), *n.* study of relations of living organisms to environment ; ecology. **-ic,** *adj.* **-ist,** *n.* student of b.

bionomy (bīon'əmi), *n.* bionomics; physiolcgy.

biophagous (bīof'əgəs). *adj.* feeding on living orgai isms. **-gy** (-ji), *n.*

biophor(e) (bī'əfŏr), *n.* biogen.

biophysics (bīəfiz'iks), *n.* physics of living organisms.

biophyte (bī'əfīt), *n.* plant consuming living organi ms.

bioplasm (bī'əplazm), *n.* living protoplasm. **-ic,** *adj.* **-plast,** *n.* minute portion of bioplasm.

biopsy (bī'opsi), *n.* med. examination of living tissue taken from body.

biorgan (bī'awgən), *n.* physiological organ.

bios (bī'os), *n.* organic life ; constituent of yeast, causing its growth.

bioscope (bī'əskōp), *n.* form of cinematograph. -py (-os'kəpi), *n.* med. examination of body for presence of life.

biosis (bīō'sis), *n.* life, as distinguishing living organisms.

biosphere (bī'əsfēr), *n.* region of earth, air and water occupied by living organisms.

biostatics (bīəstat'iks), *n.* study of physiological relations between structure and function.

biostatistics (bīəstətis'tiks), *n.* vital statistics.

biostratigraphy (bīəstrətig'rəfi), *n.* determination of age, etc., of sedimentary strata from fossils which they contain.

biota (bīō'tə), *n.* flora and fauna of a region.

biotaxy (bī'ətaksi), *n.* biological classification.

biotic (bīot'ik), *adj.* vital ; pert. to life. -ism (-sizm), *n.* phil. theory that ultimate reality is Life. -s, *n.* study of activities of living organisms.

biotin (bī'ətin), *n.* growth-promoting vitamin of the vitamin B complex, found in liver and yeast.

biotomy (bīot'əmi), *n.* vivisection.

biotope (bī'ətōp), *n.* area having uniform conditions and supporting a particular, uniform association of animal life.

biparous (bip'ərəs), *adj.* bringing forth two offspring at a birth.

bipartile (bīpah'tīl), *adj.* divisible into two parts. -ient, *adj.* so dividing.

bipartite (bīpah'tīt), *adj.* having two parts ; between two parties. -tion, *n.*

biped (bī'ped), *n. & adj.* (creature) having two feet. -al, *adj.* -ality, *n.*

bipennate (bīpen'āt), *adj.* having two wings.

bipod (bī'pod), *n.* support or stand with two legs.

bipolar (bīpō'lə), *adj.* having or pert. to two poles ; occurring in both polar regions ; equidistant north and south of equator. -ity, *n.*

biquadratic (bīkwodrat'ik), *adj.* Math., of the fourth power ; *n.*

number's fourth power ; equation involving fourth power of unknown quantity.

biramose, -mous (bīrā'mōs, -məs), *adj.* divided into two branches.

bireme (bī'rēm), *n. & adj.* (galley) having two banks of oars.

biretta (biret'ə), *n. R.C.,* cleric's square cap.

bis (bis), *adv.* twice ; in two places ; *Mus.,* direction to repeat ; Fr. *excl.* (bēs), encore ! ; *n.* duplicate.

bise (bēz), *n.* cold, dry north wind of Switzerland, Italy and S. France.

biserial (bīsēr'iəl), *adj.* in two rows.

bisexual (bīseks'ūal), *adj.* of two sexes ; hermaphrodite. -ism, -ity, *n.*

bish (bish), *n.* bikh.

bismarine (bismərēn'), *adj.* bimarine.

bismillah (bismil'ə), Arab. *excl.* in the name of Allah !

bismuth (biz'məth), *n.* hard, brittle, reddish-white metallic element, used in alloys and, as carbonate, for dyspepsia, etc. b.meal, dose of bismuth salts, which are opaque to X-rays, taken to show abnormality in alimentary canal in X-ray photograph. -ic (-ū'thik, -uth'ik), *adj.*

bisonant (bisō'nənt, bī'-), *adj.* having two sounds.

bisontine (bī'səntīn, -in), *adj.* pert. to bison.

bisque (bisk), *n.* point allowed to tennis player ; stroke(s) allowed to golfer ; extra turn allowed to croquet player ; kind of rich thick soup ; pottery fired but not glazed. b.oven, oven for firing pottery.

bissext (bis'ekst), *n.* intercalary day. -ile, *adj.* containing the b. ; intercalary ; *n.* leap-year.

bistort (bis'tawt), *n.* a plant with twisted astringent root ; snakeweed.

bistoury (bis'toori), *n.* small, narrow surgical knife. -rnage, *n.* a method of castration.

bistre (bis'tə), *n.* brown pigment derived from wood soot.

bisulcate (bīsul'kət), *adj.* with two grooves ; cloven.

bisyllabic (bīsilab'ik), *adj.* consisting of two syllables. -ble (-il'əbl), *n.* such word, prefix, etc.

bitheism (bīthē'izm), *n.* belief in two gods.

bitonality (bītōnal'iti), *n. Mus.*, use of two keys simultaneously.

bittern (bit'ən), *n.* heron-like wading birds with booming call.

bitts (bits), *n.pl.* pairs of posts on deck of ship for fastening ropes.

bitumen (bit'ūmən), *n.* mineral pitch ; *sev.* partly oxygenated hydrocarbons ; asphalt ; pigment obtained from asphalt. **-minate, -minise** (-ū'mināt, -īz), *v.t.* cement with or convert into b. **-minoid,** *adj.* like b. **-minous,** *adj.* like or containing b.

biune (bī'ūn, -ū'niəl), *adj.* combining two in one. **-nity,** *n.*

bivalent (biv'ələnt), *adj. Chem.,* with valency of two ; *n. Biol.,* double chromosome. **-ncy,** *n.*

biventral (bīven'trəl), *adj.* with two bellies.

biverbal (bīvē'bəl), *adj.* relating to two words ; punning.

bivious (biv'iəs), *adj.* offering two paths or directions.

bivocal (bīvō'kl), *n.* diphthong. **-ise,** *v.t.* place between two vowels.

bivouac (biv'ŏŏak), *n.* temporary camp without tents ; *v.i.* (**-acked, -acking,** etc.) pitch such camp.

bizarre (bizah'), *adj.* fantastic ; outlandish ; incongruous. **-rie,** *n.*

black (blak), **-ball,** *v.t.* vote against, *espec.* by placing a black ball in ballot box ; reject for membership ; exile. **-cock,** *n.* male of black grouse. **-fellow,** *n.* Austral. aborigine. **-leg,** *n.* person who works when his fellows are on strike ; swindler. **-list,** *n.* list of persons under suspicion or with bad credit, etc. ; *v.t.* place on such a list. **-strap,** Amer. *n.* mixture of rum and molasses ; cheap wine. **-water,** *n.* infectious tropical fever. **b.belt,** southern (negro) states of U.S.A. **b.draught,** strong purge. **b.jack,** leather wine container ; *Amer.,* small oak ; life preserver (weapon). **b.letter,** Old English or Gothic type. **b.pudding,** kind of sausage containing blood. **B.Rod,** chief officer of House of Commons.

blain (blān), *n.* sore ; blister.

blandiloquence (blandil'əkwəns), *n.* complimentary language or speech.

blank verse (blank vēs), *n.* rhymeless decasyllabic iambic line.

blasé (blah'zā), Fr. *adj.* bored ; sophisticated ; having exhausted all pleasures.

blastogenesis (blastəjen'isis), *n.* reproduction by budding ; theory of inheritance of characters through germ-plasm. **-etic** (-jinet'ik), **-nic,** *adj.* pert. to germ cells.

blattnerphone (blat'nəfōn), *n.* system, invented by Ludwig Blattner (*d.* 1935), of recording sound on a steel tape electro-magnetically, and of reproducing sound by same process.

blauwbok (blow'bok), S. African *n.* extinct antelope with bluish coat.

blazon (blā'zon), *n.* coat of arms ; banner, etc., bearing heraldic device ; *v.t.* delineate or describe such object ; adorn ; announce loudly. **-ment,** *n.* **-ry,** *n.* art of delineating such objects ; colourful display.

bleak (blēk), *n.* small fresh-water fish having very silvery scales.

bleeder (blē'də), *n.* person suffering from haemophilia.

blende (blend), *n.* zinc sulphide ; name of sev. lustrous metallic sulphides.

blendling (blend'ling), *n.* hybrid. **-dure,** *n.* mixture.

blennoid (blen'oid), *adj.* like mucus. **-ogenic, -ogenous,** *adj.* generating mucus. **-orrhoea,** *n.* mucus discharge.

blenny (blen'i), *n.* long, slender, spiny-rayed marine fish.

blepharal (blef'ərəl), *adj.* pert. to eyelids. **-rism, -rospasm,** *n.* muscular spasm of eyelid. **-ritis,** *n.* inflammation of eyelids.

blesbok (bles'bok), *n.* species of S. African antelope with white facial spot.

bletonism (blet'ənizm), *n.* faculty of water divining.

blewit (blōō'it), *n.* kind of edible toadstool.

blip (blip), *n.* spot of light on radar screen.

blissom (blis'əm), *adj.* with strong sexual desires ; in rut.

Blitzkrieg (blits'krēg), Ger. *n.* "lightning war" ; sudden devastating all-out attack ; *abbr.* **blitz,** *n.* heavy air-raid, *espec.* series of Ger. raids on London in 1940-41 ; an all-out attack or campaign ; *v.t.* to launch or maintain a b. on ; to bomb from the air.

blockhouse (blok'hows), *n.* small fortified building.

block-system (blok'sistəm), *n.* method of railway signalling by which one section of line never carries more than one train.

bloom (bloom), *n.* *Metall.*, bar of puddled iron. **-ary, -ery,** *n.* place where such bars are manufactured; forge into which iron passes after first melting.

blucher (bloo'chə, -kə), *n.* leather half-boot.

blue (bloo) : **-book,** *n.* Parl. publication, bound in blue covers ; *Amer.,* book giving particulars of government servants or prominent persons ; *adj.* app. to dull, dry literary style. **-nose,** *n.* native of Nova Scotia. **-stocking,** *n.* learned, studious woman, *espec.* with literary pretensions. **b.disease,** cyanosis. **b.laws,** strict Puritanical laws of certain U.S. states ; any such laws. **b.peter,** ship's blue flag with white square in centre flown as signal for sailing, etc. **b.pill,** strong purgative containing mercury. **b.ribbon,** highest honour or prize in competition ; chief competition of its kind ; badge formerly worn by members of teetotal organisation.

blunge (blunj), *v.i.* mix clay and water for pottery ; blend. **-r,** *n.* apparatus for such mixing.

blurb (blɜb), *n.* *sl.* publisher's laudatory advertisement or description of book ; any advance notice or advertisement.

boa (bō'ə), *n.* large non-venomous snake killing by constriction ; long woman's scarf, *espec.* of feathers. **b.constrictor,** Brazilian python.

Boanerges (bōanə'jēz), *n.* "sons of thunder" ; fiery orator with loud voice.

bobbery (bob'əri), Anglo-Ind. *n.* disturbance ; uproar.

bobbinet, bobbin-net (bob'inet), *n.* cotton net imitating lace.

bobolink (bob'əlingk), *n.* N. Amer. songbird, also called reed-bird, rice-bunting, and skunk-bird.

bob-sleigh (bob'-slā), *n.* long sports sleigh carrying sev.. persons ; *Amer.,* sleigh consisting of two short ones joined together ; one of the two sleighs so joined.

bobstay (bob'stā), *n.* rope attached to and steadying bowsprit.

bocking (bok'ing), *n.* coarse baize ; smoked herring.

bodega (bodē'gə ; Sp., bodhā'gah), Sp. *n.* wine-shop.

Boetian (biō'shən), *adj.* stupid ; dull ; of Boeotia, part of anct. Greece noted for its people's stupidity. **-tarch,** *n.* magistrate of anct. Boeotia.

bogey (bō'gi), *n.* in golf, number of strokes in which a good player should play hole or course.

bohea (bōhē'), *n.* cheapest black tea.

Bohemian (bəhē'miən), *n.* & *adj.* (person) of unconventional, carefree habits, *espec.* artistic or literary ; app. to quarter in which artists or writers live. **-ism,** *n.*

bolar (bō'lə), *adj.* pert. to clay.

bolas (bō'las), Sp. *n.* pair of balls joined by cord, thrown so as to wind round the object of attack.

bolection, **bi-** (bələk'shən, bī-), *n.* projecting part of moulding round panel.

bolero (bolā'ō), *n.* lively Sp. dance ; waist-length jacket.

bolide (bō'lid, -id), *n.* large meteor ; "fire-ball."

bollard (bol'əd), *n.* post to which mooring rope is secured.

bolling (bol'ing), *n.* pollarded tree.

bolometer (bələm'itə), *n.* instr. measuring small amounts of radiant heat electrically. **-ograph** (bō'ləgraf), *n.* photograph made with a b. **-tric** (-et'rik), *adj.*

bolt, *see* **boult.**

bolthead (bolt'hed), *n.* long, straight-necked glass vessel for distilling ; matrass.

bolus (bō'las), *n.* large pill ; any round mass. **b.alba,** china clay.

boma (bō'mə), *n.* large non-venomous snake of W. Africa ; Brazilian boa ; circular fenced-in enclosure in Africa.

bombardon (bombah'dən), *n.* deep. bass double-reeded wind instr.

bombasine, -zine (bombəzēn'), *n.* twilled, black, worsted, worsted-with-silk or worsted-with-cotton dress material. **-zet(te),** *n.* thin smooth-surfaced worsted fabric.

Bombay duck (bombā duk'), *n.* preserved flesh of a pike-like marine fish of East.

bombé (bawn'bā), Fr. *adj.* bulging

or curved outward, *espec.* such furniture, embroidery, etc.

bombic (bom'bik), *adj.* pert. to silkworm.

bombilate, -nate (bom'bilāt, -nāt), *v.i.* buzz ; boom. **-tion,** *n.*

bombous (bom'bəs), *adj.* rounded ; convex.

bombycine (bom'bisin), *adj.* bombic.

bona fide (bō'nə fidi), *Lat.*, "with good faith" : genuine ; in good faith. **-s** (-dēz), *n.pl.* credentials ; honesty ; sincerity.

bonamano (bōnəmah'nō), It. *n.* tip ; pourboire.

bonanza (bənan'zə), Sp. *n.* rich vein or mine ; *Amer.*, something from which much wealth is easily obtained.

bonasus, -ssus (bənā'səs, -as'əs), *n.* aurochs.

bonbonnière (bawṅbon'iār), Fr. *n.* dainty sweetmeat box.

bonce (bons), *n.* large playing marble ; kind of marbles game.

bond (bond), *n.* in masonry, method of placing bricks or stones. **English b.,** laying of bricks in alternate courses of headers and stretchers. **Flemish b.,** methods in which each course comprises alternate headers and stretchers. **-stone,** *n.* stone extending whole depth of wall.

bonded (bon'did), *adj. Comm.,* app. to warehouse, vaults, etc., where dutiable goods are stored, the goods being not chargeable with duty until removed ; app. to such goods.

bongar (bong'gah), *n.* kind of poisonous Ind. snake ; krait.

bongo (bong'gō), *n.* striped antelope of W. and E. Africa.

bonhomie (bonomē'), Fr. *n.* friendliness ; urbane manner.

Boniface (bon'ifās), *n.* inn-keeper.

bonification (bonifikā'shn), *n.* betterment ; payment of bonus. **-form,** *adj.* like or seeming good. **-fy,** *v.t.* improve ; make good.

boning (bō'ning), *n.* judging level by looking along a line of poles. **-rod,** *n.* pole used in boning.

bonito (bənē'tō), *n.* striped tunny ; sev. fishes of mackerel family.

bon mot (bawṅ mō'), *Fr.* (*pl.* **bons mots**), "good word" ; epigram ; witty remark.

bonne (bon), Fr. *n.* female servant.

bonne bouche (bon boosh'), *Fr.* (*pl.* **bonnes bouches**), "good mouth" ; titbit.

bonnet rouge (bon'ā roozh). *Fr.,* "red cap," worn by French revolutionaries ; a revolutionary, or revolutionary movement.

bontebok (bon'tibok), *n.* reddish, white-faced antelope of S. Africa.

bon ton (bawṅ tawṅ'), *Fr.,* "good tone" ; high society ; good breeding.

bon vivant, viveur (bawṅ vēvahṅ', vēvör') *Fr.* (*pl.* **bons vivants,** **viveurs** ; *fem.* **bonne vivante,** -ahṅt'), "good living or liver" ; lover of good food and drink ; gourmet.

bonze (bonz), *n.* Buddhist priest. **-ry,** *n.* Buddhist monastery.

boom (boom), *n.* long spar extending foot of sail. **b.-sail, b.-sheet,** etc., sail, sheet, etc., attached to boom.

boomer (boo'mə), Austral. *n.* male of largest kangaroo species.

boomslang (boom'slang), S. African *n.* (*pl.* -e) large poisonous snake of S. Africa.

boongary (boong'gəri), Austral. *n.* small tree kangaroo.

bora (bor'ə), It. *n.* cold north wind of N. Adriatic.

boracic (bərəs'ik), *adj.* pert. to or derived from borax. **b.acid,** former name for boric acid. **-acous** (bor'əkəs), *adj.*

borage (bur'ij), *n.* rough-stemmed, blue-flowered salad herb.

borasco, -ca, -sque (bərah'skō, -kah, -ask'), *n.* Mediterranean squall.

borax (bor'aks), *n.* a natural salt, also made from soda, used as flux and antiseptic.

bordel (baw'dəl), *n.* brothel.

bordereau (bor'dərō), Fr. *n.* (*pl.* **-x**) invoice ; detailed bill ; memorandum.

bore (bor), *n.* wall of water advancing up narrow estuary at certain tides.

boreal (bor'iəl), *adj.* pert. to Boreas, the north wind ; cold ; of the north. **-ad, -an,** *adj.*

borecole (baw'kōl), *n.* kale.

boron (bor'on), *n.* non-metallic, non-fusible element, found in borax, etc. **-ic,** *adj.* **-ric,** *adj.* pert. to or containing boron ; **b.acid,** such acid, formerly called boracic acid, used as preservative and antiseptic. -rise, v.t. preserve with boric acid.

borough-English (bur'ə-ing'glish), n. custom whereby landed property is inherited by youngest son.

borracha (bərah'shə), Port. n. crude rubber ; rubber tree.

bort (bawt), n. ground diamond fragments, used in polishing, etc. -y, adj.

bortsch, -rsch (bawch, bawsh), Russ. n. mixed soup coloured red with beetroot.

borzoi (baw'zoi), n. Russ. wolf-hound.

bosch (bosh), S. African n. wood ; bush. b.-bok, bush-buck ; kind. of antelope. b.-man, Bushman. b.-vark, kind of wild pig. b.-veldt, bush country.

boskage, -cage (bos'kij), n. thicket of trees or shrubs.

bosket, -quet (bos'kit), n. thicket.

bosky (bos'ki), adj. having trees or shrubs ; sl. tipsy.

bosselated (bos'ilātid), adj. covered with or formed into knobs.

bot(t) (bot), n. parasitical maggot of bot-fly ; pl. disease of horses caused by b.

botargo (bətah'gō), n. relish made from tunny's or mullet's roe.

bo-tree (bō'-trē), n. sacred tree of Ceylon, kind of banyan, yielding caoutchouc ; peepul tree.

botryoid(al) (bot'rioid, -əl), adj. having shape of cluster of grapes. -ose, adj. with flowers in clusters that develop upwards from base.

bottine (botēn'), n. small boot ; surgical boot for correcting def rmity.

bottomry (bot'əmri), n. raising load on ship as security.

botulism (bot'ūlizm), n. sausage-poisoning ; poisoning by any infected preserved meat. -liform, adj. sausage-shaped. -linic, adj.

bouchée (bōō'shā), Fr. n. small patty ; adj. Mus., muted or stopped.

boucherise (bōō'shəriz), v.t. preserve by impregnating with copper sulphate.

bougie (bōōzhē'), Fr. n. wax candle ; flexible med. instr. for insertion into body passages ; suppository.

bouillabaisse (bōōlyabās' ; Fr., bōōyabās'), Fr. n. fish and vegetable stew.

bouilli (bōō'yē). Fr. n. stewed meat.

bouillon (bōō'yawn), Fr. n. clear soup ; broth ; stew.

boule (bōōl), n. roulette-like game.

boule (bōō'lē), n. advisory council or senate of anct. Greece. -uterion, n. (pl. -ia) assembly-place.

boulevard (bōō'livahd ; Fr., bōōl'-vahr), Fr. n. wide avenue, espec. near park or river ; fashionable promenade. -ier, n. man-about-town.

boulimia (bōōlim'iə), n. bulimy.

boult, bolt (bōlt), v.t. sift. -el, n. sifting cloth. -er, n. one who sifts ; sieve ; fishing line with many hooks.

bouquetin (bōōktan'), Fr. n. ibex of the Alps.

bourasque (bōōrask'), n. borasco.

bourdon (bōōr'dən), n. Mus., bass drone, as of bagpipe.

bourgeois (bōōr'zhwah), Fr. n. & adj. (person) of middle class ; n. (bəjois'), size of type : 9 point. petit b., (person) of lower middle class. -ie (-zē'), n. the middle classes.

bourrée (bōōr'ā), Fr. n. quick dance of S. France and Spain.

bourse (bōōrs), n. foreign money-market.

boutonnière (bōōton'iār), Fr. n. small bunch of flowers for button-hole.

bouts-rimés (bōō-rē'mā), Fr. n.pl. "rhymed endings" ; composition of verses to given rhymes ; verses so composed.

bovine (bō'vīn), adj. pert. to cattle ; apathetic ; stupid. -vicide, n. killer of cattle ; butcher. -viform, adj. having shape of cattle. -void, adj. like cattle.

bow-chaser (bow'-chāsə), n. ship's gun for firing ahead.

bowdlerise (bowd'ləriz), v.t. expurgate, espec. too strictly. -isation, -ism, n.

bower-bird (bow'ə-bād), n. Austral. bird which builds and decorates bower-like runs.

bow-head (bō'-hed), n. Greenland whale.

bowline (bō'lin, -in), n. rope steadying upright edge of sail ; knot securing b. to sail. b.bridle, rope securing b. to sail.

bowsprit (bō'sprit), n. spar extending at bows of ship.

ə=er in father ; ē=er in pert; th=th in thin ; dh=th in then ; zh=s in pleasure ; k=ch in loch ; n=Fr. nasal n ; ü=Fr. u.

bowyer (bō'yə), *n.* maker of bows (the weapons).

box-wallah (boks'-wolə), Anglo-Ind. *n.* itinerant pedlar.

boyar (boyah'), *n.* anct. Russ. rank next below prince; Russ. landowner.

boyau (bwoi'ō), Fr. *n.* (*pl.* -x) winding trench; zigzag.

bracciale (braksiā'li), *n.* wall socket or bracket.

brach (brach, brak), *n.* female hunting hound.

brachial (brā'kiəl, brak'-), *adj.* pert. to arm; arm-shaped. **-ate,** *v.i.* swing by arms from place to place; *adj.* having arms. **-ation,** *n.* **-iferous,** *adj.* having arms or branches. **-iotomy,** *n.* amputation of arm.

brachistocephalic, -lous (brakistəsifal'ik, -sef'ələs), *adj.* having skull of which breadth is 85 per cent or more of length.

brachycatalectic (brakikatəlek'tik), *adj.* with two syllables lacking from end; *n.* such verse line.

brachycephalic, -lous (brakisifal'ik, -sef'ələs), *adj.* short-headed; having skull of which maximum breadth is 80 per cent or more of maximum length. **-lism,** *n.*

brachycerous (brakis'ərəs), *adj.* having shorn horns or antennae.

brachydactylous, -lic (brakidak'-tiləs, -til'ik), *adj.* having short digits. **-lism, -ly,** *n.*

brachygraphy (brakig'rəfi), *n.* shorthand. **-pher,** *n.* stenographer. **-phic(al),** *adj.*

brachylogy (brakil'əji), *n.* condensed expression; laconic speech.

brachymetropy, -pia (brakimet'rəpi, -ō'piə), *n.* shortsightedness. **-pic** (-op'ik), *adj.*

brachypodous (brakip'ədəs), *adj.* having short legs or stalk.

brachypterous (brakip'tərəs), *adj.* having short wings.

brachyure (brak'iūr), *n.* short-tailed animal, bird, etc. **-ran,** *n.* a crab.

bract (brakt), *n.* leaf from axil of which flower is produced. **-eal,** *adj.* bract-like. **-eate,** *adj.* bearing bracts. **-eiform,** *adj.* bract-shaped. **-eole,** *n.* small bract; bract at base of flower. **-eolate,** *adj.* having bracteoles. **-eose,** *adj.* having many bracts.

braggadocio (bragədō'shō), *n.* boasting; braggart. **-ian,** *n.* & *adj.*

brahman, *see* **brahmin.** **-y,** *see* **brahminee.**

brahmin (brah'min), *n.* male member of priestly caste of Hindus; learned person; pedant. **b.ox,** humped ox sacred to Hindus. **-ee,** *n.* female member of such caste. **-ism,** *n.*

brahminee (brah'minē), *adj.* belonging to Hindu priestly caste. **b.bull,** brahmin ox. **b.duck,** ruddy sheldrake. **b.kite,** sacred Ind. bird of prey.

Braidism (brā'dizm), *n.* hypnotism.

brail (brāl), *v.t.* truss sail; haul up. **-s,** *n.pl.* cords on edge of sail for trussing.

branchial, -iac (brang'kiəl, -iak), *adj.* pert. to gills. **-iate, -iferous,** *adj.* having gills. **-icolous,** *adj.* living in gills. **-iform,** *adj.* gill-shaped.

branchiopod (brang'kiəpod), *n.* kind of crustacean with gills on feet. **-an, -ous** (-op'ədən, -əs), *adj.*

brandling (brand'ling), *n.* striped earthworm used by anglers.

brandy-pawnee (bran'di-paw'nē), Anglo-Ind. *n.* brandy and water.

brank(s) (brangk, -s), *n.* kind of bridle fixed to head of nagging woman as punishment; scold's bridle; *Scot.,* mumps.

brant (brant), *n.* brent.

brash (brash), *n.* slight sickness; broken pieces of rock or ice; collection of fragments; *adj.* brittle; lifeless; rash. **water-b.,** pyrosis.

brassage (brah'sij), *n.* charge for minting coin, difference between value of metal, with cost of minting, and face value.

brassard (bras'ahd), *n.* armlet; arm-badge.

brassie (brah'si), *n.* wooden golf-club with brass sole.

brassy (brah'si), *n.* bib.

brattice (brat'is), *n.* partition, *espec.* in mine gallery to regulate ventilation or support sides or roof; *v.t.* erect b. **b.cloth,** canvas sheet for regulating ventilation in mine.

bravado (brəvahd'ō), *n.* ostentatious show of boldness; braggart.

bravura (brəvoōr'ə), *n. Mus.,* exceptional skill; boldness; brilliance; passage needing this.

---

hat, bah, hāte, hāre, crawl; pen, ēve, here; it, īce, fīre; on, bōne, boil, bōre, howl; foot, fōōd, bōōr, hull, tūbe, pūre.

braxy (braks'i), *n.* apoplectic disease of sheep ; meat of sheep dead from disease, *espec.* from b. ; *adj.* sick with or dead from this disease.

braze (brāz), *v.t.* solder with zinc and brass alloy ; cover with brass ; *n.* joint so soldered.

breastsummer, *see* bressummer.

breccia (brech'iə), *n. Geol.*, aggregate of angular rock fragments. **-l**, *adj.* **-tion**, *n.* making into b.

brehon (brē'hon, bre'-), *n.* judge of anct. Ireland. **b.law**, anct. Irish legal code.

bressummer (bres'əmə), *n.* beam or girder over opening and supporting a wall.

brettice (bret'is), *n.* brattice.

breve (brēv), *n.* papal letter ; brief ; mark (⌣) indicating a short vowel ; *Mus.*, note equiv. of two semibreves.

brevet (brev'it), *n.* commission giving army officer honorary higher rank. **-cy**, *n.* such rank.

breveté (brevtā'), Fr. *adj.* patented.

breviary (brē'viəri, brev'-), *n.* short prayer-book of R.C. Church.

breviate (brē'viət), *n.* summary ; precis.

brevicaudate (brevikaw'dət), *adj.* having short tail.

brevier (brivēr'), *n.* size of type : 8-point.

brevifoliate (brevifō'liət), *adj.* having short leaves. **-ilingual**, *adj.* having short tongue. **-iloquence**, *n.* laconic manner of speech. **-iped**, *adj.* having short legs. **-ipennate**, *adj.* having short wings.

brewster (broo'stə), *n.* brewer. **B.Sessions**, court hearing applications for liquor trade licences.

Briarean (brī ar'iən), *adj.* pert. to Briareus, monster in Gr. legend with hundred hands ; having many hands.

bric-à-brac (brik'-ə-brak), *n.* odds and ends of furniture, antiquities, china, art, etc.

bricole (brik'əl, -ōl'), *n.* indirect stroke, *espec.* in tennis, in which ball is hit against wall or rebounds from it ; and billiards, in which ball hits cushion between the two contacts of a cannon.

bridewell (brīd'wəl), *n.* prison ; house of correction.

brig (brig), *n.* two-masted, square-rigged ship.

brigantine (brig'əntēn), *n.* two-masted ship, square-rigged on foremast only.

brilliant (bril'yənt), *n.* smallest size of type : 3½-point.

brinjal, -aul (brin'jawl), Anglo-Ind. *n.* fruit of egg-plant.

brinjarry (brinjah'ri), Anglo-Ind. *n.* itinerant seller of grain and salt.

brioche (brēosh'), Fr. *n.* rich, unsweetened, bread-like roll.

briqué (brē'kā), Fr. *n.* negro half-caste with red hair.

brisling (bris'ling), *n.* small, sardine-like fish.

Bristol-fashion (bris'təl-fash'ən), *adj.* in good order.

britannia metal (britan'yə met'l), *n.* cheap white alloy of copper, zinc, antimony and bismuth, with lead.

British-warm (brit'ish-wawm), *n.* army officer's overcoat.

britzka (brit'skə), *n.* single-seated, four-wheeled, hooded Polish carriage.

Brobdingnagian (brobdingnag'iən, -ā'jiən), *adj.* pert. to Brobdingnag, a country of giants in Swift's *Gulliver's Travels* ; gigantic ; *n.* giant.

brocard (brok'əd ; Fr., brō'kahr), *n.* axiom ; maxim ; caustic remark.

brocatel(lo) (brokətel', -ō), *n.* kind of variegated marble ; thick figured silk used in upholstery.

broch (brok), *n.* ancient N. Scot. stone tower.

broché (brō'shā), Fr. *adj.* with raised pattern.

brochure (broshūr'), *n.* booklet ; pamphlet.

brock (brok), *n.* badger. **-et**, *n.* stag in its second year ; Brazilian pronged deer. **-faced**, *adj.* having white mark on face.

broderie (brō'drē), Fr. *n.* embroidery-like pattern. **b.anglaise** (ahn'glāz), mixture of solid and open-work embroidery.

brogan (brō'gən), *n.* coarse, strong shoe ; brogue.

brokerage (brō'kərij), *n. Comm.,* commission taken by agent, *espec.* on sale or purchase of shares, etc.

bromate (brō'māt), *n.* salt of bromic acid.

bromatology (bromətol'əji), *n.* treatise on or study of food.

---

bromic (bro'mik), *adj.* containing bromine. **b.silver**, bromyrite.

bromide (bro'nĭd), *n.* compound of bromine ; silver b., used in photography ; sedative drug composed of bromine and potassium hydrate; person using this drug ; trite statement ; meaningless adjective ; dull, tedious person. **-dic** (-id'ik), *adj.*

bromidrosis (brōmidrō'sis), *n.* strongly smelling perspiration.

bromine (bro'min), *n.* non-metallic chlorine-like element found in sea-water and mineral springs. **-mise**, *v.t.* compound with b.; prepare photographic plate with bromide. **-mism**, *n.* condition due to excessive use of bromide. **-nated**, *adj.* compounded with b.

bromyrite (bro'mirĭt), *n.* natural bromide of silver ; bromic silver.

bronchi (brong'ki), *n.pl.* (*sing.* **-chus**) divisions of windpipe, one leading to each lung. **-al**, *adj.* **-ectasis**, *n.* dilatation of b. **-tis** (-i'tis), *n.* inflammation of b. **-tic** (-it'ik), *adj.*

bronchocele (brong'kəsēl), *n.* goitre.

bronchopulmonary (brongkəpul'mənəri), *adj.* pert. to bronchial tubes and lungs.

bronchos (brong'kəs), *n.* temporary loss of voice.

bronchotomy (brongkot'əmi), *n.* incision into larynx or trachea.

brontephobia, -toph- (brontifō'biə, -təf-), *n.* dread of thunder and lightning.

brontide (bron'tĭd), *n.* sound like distant thunder, due to seismic causes.

brontograph (bron'təgraf), *n.* instr. recording discharges of atmospheric electricity. **-gram**, *n.* record made by b.

brontology (brontol'əji), *n.* study of thunder. **-ometer**, *n.* brontograph.

brontosaurus (brontəsor'əs), *n.* gigantic fossil dinosaur.

brose (brōz), Scot. *n.* kind of porridge ; broth. **Athole-b.**, mixture of whisky and honey.

brothel (broth'l), *n.* house inhabited by prostitutes.

brouette (brooet'), Fr. *n.* small two-wheeled carriage ; kind of four-seater motor car.

brougham (broo'əm, brō'-, broom), *n.* small one-horse four-wheeled

closed carriage with unroofed driver's seat ; kind of limousine-like motor car body with driver's seat uncovered.

Brownian (brow'niən), *adj.* app. to movement, discovered by Robert Brown (1773–1858), of minute particles suspended in fluid, due to collisions between them and molecules of fluid.

Brownist (brow'nist), *n.* follower of Robert Browne (d. 1663), founder of Congregationalism ; *adj.* pert. to his principles ; congregationalist ; Brunonian. **-ism**, *n.*

brucin(e), -na (broo'sin, -ēn- -inə), *n.* strychnine-like poison derived from nux vomica plant.

bruit (broot), *n.* sounds in chest symptomatic of disease ; rumour ; *v.t.* report ; spread abroad.

Brum (brum), *abbr.* of Brummagem.

brumal (broo'məl), *adj.* pert. to brume or winter.

brumby, -bie, -bee (brum'bi), Austral. *n.* wild horse.

brume (broom), *n.* mist or fog. **-mous**, *adj.*

Brummagem (brum'əjəm), *n. sl.* Birmingham ; *adj.* tawdry ; counterfeit.

brunneous (brun'iəs), *adj.* dark brown.

Brunonian (broonō'niən), *adj.* app. to theory that disease arises solely from action of external stimuli on body, held by John Brown (1735–1788) ; *n.* Brownist. **-nism**, *n.*

brusque (brusk), *adj.* blunt in speech or conduct. **-rie**, *n.*

brutum fulmen (broo'təm fool'men), *Lat.*, "unfeeling thunder" ; empty threat.

bryology (brīol'əji), *n.* study of mosses and liverworts ; plant life of such kind of a region. **-gical**, *adj.* **-gist**, *n.* **-ophyte**, *n.* moss or liverwort.

Brythonic (brīthon'ik, brith-), *adj.* Welsh ; of anct. Cambria or Cornwall ; of the language group including Breton, Cornish and Welsh.

bubal(is) (bū'bəl, -bā'lis), *n.* kind of African antelope. **-line**, *adj.*

bubo (bū'bō), *n.* (*pl.* -oes) swelling with inflammation of lymphatic gland, *espec.* of groin. **-nalgia**, *n.* pain in groin. **-nic** (-on'ik), *adj.*

buccal (buk'l), *adj.* pert. to mouth or cheek.

buccan (buk'ən, -kan'), *n.* framework over which meat is roasted or dried ; *v.t.* dry meat on a b.

buccate (buk'ət), *adj.* with protruding cheeks.

buccinal (buk'sinəl), *adj.* having shape or sound of trumpet. **-ator,** *n.* muscle forming cheek-wall. **-atory,** *adj.*

buccula (buk'ūlə), *n.* (*pl.* **-ae**) double chin.

bucentaur (būsen'taw), *n.* mythical creature, half-man, half-ox ; Venetian doge's state barge.

Buchmanism (buk'mənizm), *n.* religious principles and methods enunciated by F. N. D. Buchman (*b.* 1878), founder of the "group movement," including open confession and testimony. **-nite,** *n.* adherent of B.

bucket-shop (buk'it-shop), *n.* office of outside broker who is not a member of the Stock Exchange.

bucolic (būkol'ik), *adj.* rustic ; pert. to shepherds ; *n.pl.* pastoral poems. **-liast** (-ō'liast), *n.* writer of bucolics.

buddle (bud'l), *n.* sloping trough, etc., for washing crushed ore ; *v.t.* wash on a b.

budgerow (buj'ərō), Anglo-Ind. *n.* heavy flat-bottomed Ganges barge.

budzat, -art (bud'zaht), Anglo-Ind. *n.* ne'er-do-well.

bufonite (bū'fənit), *n.* toadstone.

buhl (bool), Ger. *n.* inlaying of gold, brass, tortoiseshell, mother of pearl, etc., on furniture ; piece of furniture so inlaid.

buhrstone (bə'stōn), *n.* burr-stone.

bulbil (bul'bil), *n.* small bulb ; large, fleshy, axillary bud from which plant may be grown.

bulbul (bool'bool), Pers. *n.* songthrush of Orient ; nightingale.

bulger (bul'jə), *n.* wooden golf-club with convex face.

bulimy, -mia (bū'limi, -im'iə), *n.* insatiable hunger. **-mic** (-im'ik), *adj.* voracious. **-mious** (-im'iəs), *adj.* suffering from b.

bulkhead (bulk'hed), *n.* vertical partition in ship between cabins or watertight compartments. **collision b.,** foremost b.

bull (bool), *n.* Comm. Speculator in shares who desires a rise in price.

bullace (bool'is), *n.* small wild plum fruit and tree.

bullary (bool'əri), *n.* collection of papal bulls.

bullate (bool'ət), *adj.* puckered ; with blistered appearance. **-tion,** *n.*

bullhead (bool'hed), *n.* sev. small, large-headed spinous marine fishes, *espec.* the miller's thumb.

bulliform (bool'ifawm), *adj.* bullate.

bullion (bool'yən), *n.* gold or silver in the mass, *espec.* uncoined. **-ist,** *n.* upholder of metallic currency.

bullroarer (bool'rōrə), *n.* wooden instr. making a roaring sound, used by Austral. and other aborigines, gen. to cause rain ; whizzing-stick ; lightning-stick.

bum-bailiff, *see* bailiff.

bumboat (bum'bōt), *n.* small harbour boat carrying provisions, etc., to ship.

bumicky (bum'iki), *n.* cement mixed with stone fragments for repairing masonry.

bummalo (bum'əlō), *n.* small S. Asiatic fish ; Bombay duck.

bund (bund), Anglo-Ind. *n.* quay ; esplanade ; embankment. **-er,** *n.* quay ; harbour ; port.

bundobust, *see* bandobast.

bunt (bunt), *n.* kind of fungus attacking wheat ; middle of sail or fish-net when slack. **b.-line,** furling rope.

buonamano, *see* bonamano.

buphthalmia (bufthal'miə), *n.* enlargement of eye. **-ic,** *adj.*

buran (boorahn'), *n.* sudden violent storm of Cent. Asia.

burbot (bə'bət), *n.* long, slender, freshwater fish of cod family ; eel-pout.

bureaucracy (būrō'krəsi, -rok'-), *n.* government by permanent officials ; officialdom. **-crat** (būr'əkrat), *n.* **-cratic** (-at'ik), *adj.* **-cratise,** *v.t.* **-cratism, -cratist,** *n.*

burette (būret'), *n.* graduated glass measuring tube ; Eccl., sacramental cruet.

burgee (bəjē'), *n.* small triangular pennant of yacht, etc.

burgensic (bəjen'sik), *adj.* pert. to citizen or freeman of borough.

burgeon (bə'jən), *n.* & *v.i.* bud ; sprout.

burgrave (bö'grāv), *n.* former Ger. commander of a town or castle; title of honour equiv. of count. **-viate,** *n.* jurisdiction of b.

burin (būr'in), *n.* engraver's tool; graver. **-ist,** *n.* engraver.

burlap (bö'lap), *n.* kind of sacking canvas; coarse, vari-coloured curtain fabric.

burletta (bŏlet'ə), It. *n.* light comic opera.

burnettise (bö'nitīz), *v.t.* saturate with zinc chloride solution to prevent decay. **-sing,** *n.* such process, invented by Sir W. Burnett.

burnous (bö'nōōs), *n.* Moorish hooded cloak.

burra (bur'ah), Hind. *adj.* great, used as title of respect. **b.sahih,** important official; manager, chief.

burro (boor'ō), Sp.-Amer. *n.* donkey.

burrow-duck (bur'ō-duk), *n.* sheldrake.

burrstone (bö'stōn), *n.* flinty rock used for millstones; millstone made of b.

bursal (bö'səl), *adj.* pert. to synovial sac; pert. to state's revenue.

bursar (bö'sə), *n.* college or school treasurer; holder of bursary. **-ial** (-ār'iol), *adj.* **-y,** *n.* office of bursar; scholarship at school or university.

burse (bös), *n.* purse; bourse; bursary; *R.C.,* purse-like container of Communion cloth. **-sicle,** *n. Bot.,* purse-shaped pod. **-siculate,** *adj.* having shape of small purse. **-siform,** *adj.* purse-shaped.

bursitis (bösi'tis), *n.* inflammation of synovial sac.

burucha (booruch'ə), *n.* borracha.

'bus-bar (bus'-bah), *n. Elec.,* main conductor on switch board.

bush (boosh): **-buck,** *n.* small African spiral-horned antelope. **-man,** *n.* S. African aborigine. **-master,** *n.* large S. Amer. poisonous snake. **b.cat,** serval. **b.lawyer,** N.Z. bramble.

bushido (bōō'shēdō), Jap. *n.* code of honour of Jap. military class; chivalry.

buskin (bus'kin), *n.* high boot; thick-soled boot (also called cothurnus) worn by actors in anct. Gr. tragedy; classic tragedy.

bustard (bus'təd), *n.* large cranelike bird of Europe; *Amer. & Can.,* the Canada goose. **great b.,** largest European land bird.

but-and-ben (but'-n-ben), Scot. *n.* two-roomed dwelling.

butte (but), Amer. *n.* steep, isolated hill.

butyric (būtir'ik), *adj.* pert. to butter. **-raceous, -rous,** *adj.* like, producing or containing butter. **-rometer,** *n.* instr. measuring fat content of milk.

buzzard (buz'əd), *n.* kind of falcon; *Amer.,* kind of vulture.

bwana (bwah'nah), Swahili *n.* master.

by-blow (bī'blō), *n.* side blow; illegitimate child.

byssus (bis'əs), *n.* filamentous tuft ("beard") by which molluscs attach themselves; fine flax and fabric woven from it. **-saceous,** *adj.* consisting of fine threads; like a b. **-sal,** *adj.* **-siferous,** *adj.* having a b.; tufted. **-sine,** *adj.* silky; the fabric b. **-sogenous,** *adj.* producing a b. **-soid,** *adj.* like a b.; fibrous; cottony.

bywoner (bī'vōnə), S. African *n.* sub-tenant of farm; agricultural labourer.

C

caaing whale (kah'ing wāl), *n.* kind of dolphin, also called blackfish or pilot-whale.

cabal (kəbal'), *n.* political coterie or intrigue; *v.i.* form a cabal.

cabala, cabb- (kab'ələ -bah'-), *n.* occult knowledge; mystery; mystical interpretation of Scriptures. **-lic** (-al'ik), *adj.* **-lism, -list,** *n.* **-listic,** *adj.* mysterious.

caballero (kabalyār'ō), Sp. *n.* knight; gentleman.

caballine (kab'əlīn, -in), *adj.* equine.

cabobs (kabobz'), *n.pl.* roast meat, *espec.* small pieces cooked on skewers.

cabochon (kab'ōshawn), Fr. *n.* convex-cut, polished stone. **en c.,** cut in that manner.

caboose (kəboos'), *n.* ship's galley; *Amer.*, guard's or engineer's van on goods train.

cabriole (kab'riōl), *n.* outward curving leg, with ornamental foot, of Queen Anne furniture.

cabriolet (kabriōlā'), *n.* one-horse, two wheeled, single- or two-seater carriage; motor car body with folding hood and fixed sides.

cacaesthesia (kakesthē'zhiə), *n.* morbid sensation.

ca' canny (kah kan'i, kaw), *v.i.* move cautiously; *n.* extreme caution: limitation of output by workmen; *adj.* cautious; mean.

cacao (kakā'ō), *n.* cocoa tree and seed.

cachaemia (kəkē'miə), *n.* poisoned condition of blood. -mic, *adj.*

cachalot (kash'əlot, -lō), *n.* sperm whale.

cache (kash), *n.* secret hiding-place.

cachectic (kəkek'tik), *adj.* pert. to cachexy.

cachet (kash'ā), Fr. *n.* distinctive mark or quality; seal.

cachexy, -xia (kəkeks'i, -ə), *n.* generally unhealthy physical or mental state. -xic, *adj.*

cachinnate (kak'ināt), *v.i.* laugh harshly and loudly. -tion, -tor, *n.* -tory (-in'ətəri), *adj.*

cachucha (kəchoō'chə), *n.* quick Sp. dance, with castanet accompaniment.

cacidrosis (kakidrō'sis), *n.* malodorous perspiration.

cacique, caz- (kəsēk'), *n.* S. Amer., Mex., and W. Ind. native chieftain.

cacodemon, -dae- (kakədē'mən), *n.* evil spirit. -ia (-dimō'niə), -omania (-mɔnəmā'niə), *n.* insanity in which patient believes himself to be possessed by evil spirit. -iac (-dimō'niak), *adj.*

cacodoxy (kak'ədoksi), *n.* heterodoxy.

cacoepy (kak'ōipi, -ō'ipi), *n.* incorrect pronunciation. -pist, *n.* -pistic, *adj.*

cacoethes (kakō ē'thēz), *n.* strong desire; bad habit. -thic (-eth'ik), *adj.*

cacogastric (kakəgas'trik), *adj.* dyspeptic.

cacogenics (kakəjen'iks), *n.* study or process of racial deterioration. -nic, *adj.*

cacography (kakog'rəfi), *n.* incorrect spelling or writing. -pher, *n.* bad speller. -phic(al), *adj.*

cacology (kakol'əji), *n.* incorrect diction.

caconym (kak'ənim), *n.* bad or wrongly derived name. -ic, *adj.*

cacophony (kakof'əni), *n.* unpleasant, discordant noise. -nic (-on'ik), -nous, *adj.* -nist, *n.* composer of such music.

cacuminal (kakū'minəl), *adj.* pert. to point, top or crown. -ate, *v.t.* sharpen. -ation, *n.* -nous, *adj.* pointed.

cadastre (kədas'tə), *n.* register of lands, their values and owners. -tral, *adj.* -tration, *n.* making a c.

cadaver (kad'əvə, -av'ə, -ā'və), *n.* corpse. -ic (-av'ərik), *adj.* pert. to corpses. -ous (-av'ərəs), *adj.* deathly pale; gaunt.

cadence (kā'dəns), *n.* rhythmical fall or modulation; *Mus.,* close of phrase, *espec.* final chords. -ntial (-en'shəl), *adj.*

cadenza (kəden'zə), *n. Mus.* virtuoso passage immediately preceding close of work or section.

cadi (kah'di), *n.* inferior Moham. judge.

cadre (kah'dr), Fr.*n.* permanent regimental unit capable of expansion.

caducary (kədū'kəri), *adj. Law,* passing by forfeiture, lapse, etc.

caduceus (kadū'siəs), *n. (pl. -ei)* winged wand entwined with snakes, borne by Mercury; herald's wand of office. -ean, *adj.*

caduciary (kədū'siəri), *n.* caducary property.

caducous (kədū'kəs), *adj.* of short duration; *Bot.,* dying when function is completed; deciduous. -city (-siti), *n.*

caecum (sē'kəm), *n. (pl. -ca)* blind outgrowth at junction of large and small intestines, terminating in vermiform appendix. -cal, *adj.* -ciform (sēs'ifawm), *adj.* shaped like a c. -city, *n.* blindness.

caenogenesis (sēnəjen'isis), *n.* development in individual of processes not common to its species. -etic (-jinet'ik), *adj.*

Caesarean, -ian (sēzār'iən), *adj.* pert. to Julius Caesar (102–44 B.C.) or other emperor. **C.** cut, operation *or* section, liberation of infant in childbirth by cutting abdomen and womb.

ə=*er* in *father*; ē=*er* in *pert*; th=*th* in *thin*; dh=*th* in *then*; zh=*s* in *pleasure*; k=*ch* in *loch*; ñ=Fr. nasal *n*; ü=Fr. *u*.

caesaropapacy (sēzərəpā'pəsi), *n.* secular possession of highest eccl. power.

Caesarotomy (sēzərot'əmi), *n.* the Caesarean cut.

caesious (sē'ziəs), *adj.* pale blue-green.

caespitose (ses'pitōs), *adj.* cespitous.

caesura (sizūr'ə), *n.* natural pause in verse-line. **masculine c.**, c. following stressed syllable of foot. **feminine c.**, c. occurring in un-stressed part of line. **-l,** *adj.*

caffeine (kaf'iin, -ēn), *n.* tonic alkaloid occurring in tea, coffee, etc. **-nism,** *n:* condition due to excessive drinking of coffee.

caftan (kaf'tən), *n.* long and wide-sleeved, girdled gown of Asia Minor and Levant.

caiman, cay- (kā'man), *n.* Cent. and S. Amer. alligator.

cainozoic (kīnəzō'ik), *n.* & *adj. Geol.*, tertiary.

caique (kīē'k), *n.* long, narrow, oared Turkish boat.

cairngorm (kārn'gawm), *n.* yellowish-brown variety of quartz, *espec.* found in Scot. Cairngorm mt.

caisson (kā'son), *n.* underwater water-tight chamber for bridge-building, etc.; hydraulic lift for raising ship; *Mil.*, ammunition wagon. **c.disease**, condition, marked by pain, paralysis or death, due to over-rapid lowering of air pressure after working in compressed air; "the bends."

calabash (kal'əbash), *n.* gourd.

calamary (kal'əməri), *n.* squid.

calamus (kal'əməs), *n.* feather quill; reed used as pen; Malacca and rattan cane palm.

calash (kəlash'), *n.* kind of four-seater carriage with hood; *Can.*, two-wheeled single-seater driving carriage.

calathiform (kal'əthifawm, kəlath'-), *adj.* cup-shaped.

calcaneus (kalkā'niəs), *n.* heel bone. **-eal, -ean,** *adj.*

calcareous (kalkār'iəs), *adj.* pert. to limestone; consisting of carbonate of lime.

calcariferous (kalkərif'ərəs), *adj.* spurred. **-form** (-ar'ifawm), **-rine,** *adj.* spur-shaped.

calceiform (kal'siifawm, -sē'-), *adj.* slipper-shaped.

calcicole (kal'sikōl), *n.* plant thriving on limy soil.

calcicosis (kalsikō'sis), *n.* lung disease due to inhaling limestone dust.

calciferous (kalsif'ərəs), *adj.* yielding lime or calcite. **-fic,** *adj.*

calciform (kal'sifawm), *adj.* pebble-shaped.

calcifuge (kal'sifūj), *n.* plant thriving on soil not rich in lime.

calcify (kal'sifī), *v.i.* & *t.* convert or be converted into lime.

calcimine (kal'simīn, -in), *n.* & *v.t.* whitewash.

calcine (kal'sin), *v.i.* & *t.* convert or be converted into powder or lime by burning; roast. **-nation,** *n.* **-natory,** *adj.*; *n.* vessel for calcination.

calcite (kal'sīt), *n.* calcium carbonate; limestone; Iceland spar.

calcium (kal'siəm), *n.* soft white metal occurring in limestone, gypsum, etc.

calcivorous (kalsiv'ərəs), *adj.* app. to plants thriving on limestone.

calcography (kalkog'rəfi), *n.* chalk-or pastel-drawing. **-pher,** *n.* pastel artist. **-phic(al),** *adj.*

calculus (kal'kūləs), *n.* (*pl.* **-li**) *Med.*, stone-like concretion; *Math.*, method of calculation. **-lary, -lous,** *adj.* **-liform,** *adj.* pebble-shaped.

calèche (kəlesh'), Fr. *n.* calash.

calefacient (kalifā'shənt), *adj.* heating. **-action,** *n.* **-active,** *adj.* **-actory,** *adj.*; *n.* warm room or vessel.

calelectricity (kalilektris'iti), *n.* electricity caused by changes in temperature. **-ric(al),** *adj.*

calendal (kalen'dəl), *adj.* pert. to calends.

calender (kal'ində), *n.* & *v.t.* mangle or press, *espec.* to produce glazed surface.

calends (kal'endz), *n.pl.* first day of month in anct. Roman calendar. at Greek **c.**, never.

calenture (kal'əntūr), *n.* sunstroke, or other fever or delirium due to heat. **-ral,** *adj.* **-rist,** *n.*

calescent (kəles'ənt), *adj.* becoming warm. **-nce,** *n.*

calibre (kal'ibə), *n.* diameter, *espec.* of gun bore; capacity; quality. **-brate,** *v.t.* determine or correct graduations of measuring instr. **-bration,** *n.* act of calibrating; graduations on measuring instr.

---

calicular, -ate (kəlik'ūlə, -ət), adj. cup-like.

caliduct (kal'idukt), n. conduit for hot fluid.

caligo (kəli'gō), n. dim-sightedness. -ginous (-ij'inəs), adj. dim; obscure.

caliology (kaliol'əji), n. study of birds' nests. -gical, adj. -gist, n.

calipash (kal'ipash), n. turtle's carapace, or flesh next to it.

caliph (kā'lif), n. ruler of Islam. -ate, n. office and succession of c.

calix (kā'liks), n. (pl. -ices) cup; chalice.

calligraphy, cali- (kalig'rəfi), n. handwriting; penmanship. -pher, -phist, n. -phic(al), adj.

callipers, cali- (kal'ipəz), n.pl. instr. with two curved legs for measuring diameter, thickness, etc.

callipygian, -gous (kalipij'iən, -i'gəs), n. having well-shaped buttocks.

callisection (kalisek'shən), n. vivisection of anaesthetised animals.

callisteia (kalistī'ə), Gr. n.pl. beauty prizes.

callisthenics, cali- (kalisthen'iks), n. strengthening and beautifying exercises.

calodemon, -dae- (kalədē'mən), n. good spirit.

calomel (kal'əməl), n. strong purgative, compound of mercury, acting on liver.

caloric (kal'ərik), n. heat. -rie, n. unit of heat: amount of heat needed to raise 1 gramme of water through 1° C.; great c., 1,000 calories. -rifacient, -rific, adj. producing heat. -rifics, n. study of heat. -rify (-or'ifi), v.t. heat. -rigenic, adj. generating heat. -rimeter, n. apparatus measuring quantities of heat; vessel of copper, etc., used in this.

calotte (kəlot'), n. skull cap, espec. of R.C. clergy. -otin (-otañ'), n. wearer of c.; R.C. adherent.

calumet (kal'ūmit), n. Amer. Ind. tobacco pipe of peace.

calumniate (kəlum'niāt), v.t. slander. -ious, -tory, adj. -ny (kal'əmni), -tion, -tor, n.

calvarial (kalvār'iəl), adj. pert. to crown of head.

calvities (kalvish'iēz), n. baldness. -vous, adj.

calx (kalks), n. (pl. -lces) heel; lime; oxide.

calypso (kəlip'sō), n. W. Ind. song of marked, uneven rhythm, improvised on some topical subject.

calyx (kā'liks), n. (pl. -lices) outer whorl of gen. green floral leaves (sepals) in flower. -ycate, adj. having c. -yciform (-is'ifawm), adj. calyx-shaped. -ycine (-isin), adj. pert. to c.; like a cup. -ycoid (-ikoid), adj. calyx-like.

camaraderie (kamərah'dərē), Fr. n. comradeship; good fellowship.

camarilla (caməril'ə -rēl'ya), n. political secret society, espec. of king's favourites.

cambial (kam'biəl), adj. pert. to cambium. -iform, adj. like cambium in nature or function. -iogenetic, adj. producing cambium.

cambism (kam'bizm), n. theory of comm. exchange. -ist, n. person dealing in bills of exchange. -istry, n. study of international exchange.

cambium (kam'biəm), n. soft enveloping tissue of trees from which new tissues are formed.

camelopard (kamel'əpahd), n. giraffe.

cameralism (kam'ərəlizm), n. economic theory in which public revenue is sole measure of national prosperity. -ist, n. adherent of c. -istic, adj. pert. to public revenue. -istics, n. study of national finance.

camera lucida (kam'ərə lōō'sidə), n. instr. containing prism by which image of object is projected on to flat surface, where it may be traced.

camera obscura (kam'ərə obskūr'ə), n. box or chamber with lens throwing on to screen image of object outside.

camerate(d) (kam'ərāt, -id), adj. divided into chambers. -tion, n. division into chambers; vaulting.

cameriere (kaməryār'ā), It. n. (pl. -ri: fem. -ra, pl. -re) valet; waiter.

camerlingo, -engo (kaməling'gō, -eng'-), n. papal treasurer.

camion (kam'iən; Fr., kam'yawñ), n. flat, low, four-wheeled truck or dray.

camisade, -do (kam'isād, -ō), n. attack by night.

camlet (kam'lit), n. fine dress

fabric of silk and camel-hair, or wool and goat's hair. -een, -ine, *n*. imitation c. of hair and worsted.

camomile, cham- (kam'əmīl), *n*. common daisy-like plant, yielding drug of wide use. c.tea, infusion of c. flowers.

camorra (kəmor'ə), *n*. secret terrorist organisation, *espec*. of 19th cent. Italy. -rism, -rist, *n*.

campanile (kampənē'lē) *n*. isolated bell-tower. -liform (-il'-), -niform (-an'ifawm), *adj*. bell-shaped.

campanology (kampənol'əji), *n*. study and knowledge of bells ; bell-making ; bell-ringing. -gical, *adj*. -gist, *n*. -nist, *n*. expert on bells.

campanulate, -lar, -lous (kampan'ūlət, -lə, -ləs), *adj*. bell-shaped.

campestral, -rial (kampes'trəl, -riəl), *adj*. pert. to or thriving on level ground.

campus (kam'pəs), Amer. *n*. grounds of school or college.

canaille (kanī'), Fr. *n*. the mob ; rabble.

canard (kanahd'), *n*. baseless rumour ; hoax.

canasta (kənas'tə), *n*. elaborate form of rummy (card-game) with partners.

canaster (kənas'tə), *n*. coarse tobacco.

cancellate(d) (kan'silāt, -id), *adj*. marked with network of lines. -lous, *adj*. with sponge-like structure.

cancriform (kang'krifawm), *adj*. crab-shaped ; *Med*., cancer-like. -ivorous, *adj*. feeding on crabs. -izans, *adj*. moving crab-wise or backwards ; *Mus*., having theme repeated backwards. -roid, *adj*. crab-like ; cancer-like.

candent (kan'dənt), *adj*. white-hot.

candescent (kandes'ənt), *n*. glowing. -nce, *n*.

canephorus (kanē'fərəs), *n*. (*pl*. -ri) sculpture of a young man or woman carrying a basket on head.

canescent (kanes'ənt), *adj*. becoming white ; hoary. -nce, *n*.

cang(ue) (kang), *n*. wooden yoke, inscribed with list of his offences, hung round criminal's neck in China.

canicular (kənik'ūlə), *adj*. pert. to dog star or dog days.

canine (kā'nīn, kan'-), *adj*. pert. to

dog ; *n*. pointed tooth next to incisors. -iniform (-in'ifawm), *adj*. like a canine tooth. -inity, *n*.

canities (kənish'iēz), *n*. whiteness of hair.

cannabis (can'əbis), *n*. sev. plants of E., including C. sativa, the Indian hemp-plant, yielding hemp, hashish, marijuana and bhang. -bic, *adj*. hempen. -bism, *n*. addiction to or poisoning by hashish or bhang.

cannel (kan'əl), *n*. kind of fine, brightly burning coal.

cannellate(d) (kan'ilāt, -id), *adj*. fluted. -elure, *n*. groove, *espec*. in cartridge.

cannular, -ate (kan'ūlə, -ət), *adj*. hollow ; tubular.

canon (kan'ən), *n*. law ; code, *espec*. eccl. ; criterion ; authentic or accepted books *espec*. of Bible ; list ; *Mus*., part-song in which opening passage is strictly repeated. -ical (kənon'ikl), *adj*. according to eccl. law ; authentic ; legal. -icals, *n.pl*. clergyman's costume or robes. -ics, *n*. study of canon of Bible.

canonise (kan'ənīz), *v.t*. make a saint. -sation, *n*.

canonist (kan'ənist), *n*. expert on canon law ; strict adherent of rules.

canopus (kanō'pəs), *n*. (*pl*. -pi) anct. Egyptian vase for holding viscera of dead. -pic, *adj*.

canorous (kənōr'əs), *adj*. sweet-sounding.

cantaloup(e) (kan'təloop), *n*. kind of small melon.

cantative (kan'tətiv), *adj*. pert. to or for singing. -tory, *adj*. pert. to singer or singing.

cantatrice (kahntətrēs'), Fr. *n*. female singer.

canthal (kan'thal), *adj*. pert. to canthus.

cantharides (kanthar'idēz), *n.pl*. med. preparation of dried Spanish flies. -dal, *adj*. -date, *v.t*. treat with c. -dean, -dian, *adj*. made of or like c. -dism, *n*. condition due to excessive use of c.

canthus (kan'thəs), *n*. angle between eyelids at corner of eye.

canticle (kan'tikl), *n*. short psalm ; holy song.

cantilever (kan'tilēvə), *n*. projecting bracket. c.bridge, bridge composed of two or more c., not supporting each other, as Forth Bridge.

cantle (kan'tl), *n.* slice; hinder saddle-bow.

cantonment (kanton'mənt, -tōōn'-, kan'-), *n.* troops' camp or barracks; small military town.

cantor (kan'tōr), *n.* singer; choir-leader; precentor. **-al, -ial,** *adj.* pert. to the north, or precentor's, side of choir.

canzone (kantsō'nā), *n.* song; lyric; song-like instr. piece. **-t** (-ənet'), *n.* short song or melody.

caoutchouc (kow'chook), *n.* rubber, *espec.* pure. **-in(e)** (-sin), *n.* rubber oil.

capacitance (kəpas'itəns), *n.* Elec., ratio of the charge on a conductor to the potential it acquires; ratio of the charge on a condenser's positive plate to the potential difference between its positive and negative plates. **-tor,** *n.* elec. condenser.

cap-à-pie (kap'-ə-pē), *adj.* from head to foot.

caparison (kəpar'izn), *n.* armour; harness; trappings; *v.t.* place such coverings upon.

capeador (kapāadhawr'), Sp. *n.* bullfighter carrying red cloak.

capercailzie, -llie, -lye (kapəkāl'yi), *n.* largest grouse bird.

capias (kap'ias), *n.* writ of arrestment.

capillary (kəpil'əri), *adj.* pert. to or like a hair; *n.* minute hair-like blood-vessel. **-aceous, -lose** (kap'-), *adj.* hairy; bristly. **-liform,** *adj.* hair-like. **-rimeter,** *n.* instr. measuring liquid by action of capillarity. **-rity** (-ar'iti), *n.* movement of liquid up or down when in contact with solid, due to surface tension.

capistrate (kəpis'trət), *adj.* hooded.

capitate (kap'itāt), *adj.* head-like. **-tim,** *adv.* per head. **-tion,** *n.* counting or levying by the head, *i.e.* per person; poll tax. **-tive,** *adj.* per person.

capitular(y) (kəpit'ūlə, -ri), *adj.* pert. to cathedral chapter; *n.* statute or member of such chapter.

capitulate (kəpit'ūlāt), *v.i.* surrender on terms. **-tion,** *n.* surrender; terms of surrender or agreement;

summary; *pl.* agreements between other powers and government of Turkish empire and countries formerly belonging thereto, securing to foreign nationals certain legal privileges. **-tory,** *adj.*

capon (kā'pən), *n.* castrated cock, *espec.* fattened for table. **-ise,** *v.t.* castrate.

caporal (kapəral'), *n.* coarse tobacco.

capote (kəpōt'), *n.* lady's long hooded cloak.

capreolate (kap'riəlāt, -rē'-), *adj.* having tendrils.

capric (kap'rik), *adj.* pert. to goat. **-rid,** *n.* goat.

caprificate (kap'rifikāt, -if'-), *v.t.* improve (cultivated figs) by artificial pollination from wild figs. **-fig,** *n.* wild fig. **-tion,** *n.*

caprifoliaceous (kaprifōliā'shəs), *adj.* pert. to or like honeysuckle; belonging to honeysuckle family of plants.

caprine (kap'rīn), *adj.* pert. to or like goat. **-nic** (-in'ik), *adj.*

capriole (kap'riōl), *n.* leap and kick by trained horse.

capripede (kap'ripēd), *n.* satyr.

capsicum (kap'sikəm), *n.* sev. pepper-yielding plants; chili.

capsule (kap'sūl), *n.* sac-like membrane; box-like vessel; small round container; hollow gelatine ball, etc., containing medicine, for swallowing. **-lar,** *adj.* **-liferous, -ligerous, -logenous,** *adj.* producing c.

captation (kaptā'shn), *n.* attempt to obtain applause or recognition.

captious (kap'shəs), *adj.* fault-finding.

capybara (kapibah'rə), *n.* the largest rodent, a guinea-pig-like, webbed-footed mammal of S. America.

carabiniere (karəbinyār'ā), It. *n.* (*pl.* **-ri**) policeman; soldier armed with carbine.

caracal (kar'əkal), *n.* lynx of Africa and Asia.

caracole (kar'əkōl), *n.* half turn by trained horse; caper; *v.i.* make such turn.

carapace (kar'əpās), *n.* exo-skeleton; protective shell of tortoise, etc. **-cic,** *adj.*

caravanserai, -sary (karəvan'sərī), *n.* Eastern inn, *espec.* for accommodation of caravans.

---

e=*er* in *father*; ə̄=*er* in *pert*; th=*th* in *thin*; dh=*th* in *then*; zh=*s* in *pleasure*; k=*ch* in *loch*; ṅ=Fr. nasal *n*; ü=Fr. *u.*

caravel, carv- (kar'əvel, kah'v-), n. small three- or four-masted ship of 15th and 16th cent.; Turkish battleship.

carbacidometer (kahbəsidom'itə), n. instr. measuring quantity of carbon dioxide in air.

carbasus (kah'bəsəs), n. lint; gauze.

carbohydrate (kahbəhi'drāt), n. Chem., compound of carbon, hydrogen and oxygen, essential to life, including starch, sugar, cellulose, etc.

carbon (kah'bən), n. element occurring in coal, asphalt, etc., and as diamond and graphite, and manuf. as lamp-black, charcoal, etc. c.dioxide, gas breathed out by humans and absorbed by plants; carbonic acid gas. c.monoxide, poisonous, colourless, odourless gas produced by incomplete combustion of carbon fuels. -aceous, adj.

carbonari (kahbənah'ri), n.pl. (sing. -ro) members of secret 19th-cent. It. republican association. -sm, -st. n.

carbonic (kahbon'ik), adj. pert. to carbon. -iferous, adj. containing coal. -ise, v.i. & t. convert into carbon; char.

carborundum (kahbərun'dəm), n. polishing substance compounded of silicon and carbon.

carboy (kar'boi), n. large wicker-covered bottle.

carbuncle (kah'bungkl), n. large boil; garnet cut en cabochon. -cular (-ung'kūlə), adj.

carburet (kahbūret'), v.t. combine or charge with carbon. -ration, n. charging air with enough fuel vapour to render mixture explosive. -tter, -ttor, n. device for mixing fuel with air in internal combustion engine.

carcajou (kah'kəzhōō), n. wolverine; cougar; N. Amer. badger

carcanet (kah'kənet), n. jewelled necklace or collar.

carcinology (kahsinol'əji), n. study of crustaceans. -omorphic, adj. like a crab or crustacean. -ophagous, adj. feeding on crabs.

carcoon (kahkōōn'), Anglo-Ind. n. clerk.

cardamon, -om (kah'dəmən, -əm), n. seeds and fruit of an E. Ind. plant, used in med. as stimulant, etc.

cardiac (kah'diak), adj. pert. to heart; n. stimulant for heart or stomach. -ialgia, n. heartburn. -iant, n. heart stimulant.

cardinal (kah'dinəl), n. & adj. (app. to) simple numbers, 1, 2, 3, etc.; app. to N., S., E., and W. points of compass.

cardiology (kah:diol'əji), n. study of heart and its diseases. -iograph, n. instr. recording heart's movements. -iography, n. description of heart. -ioid, adj. heart-shaped. -iometry, n. measurement of heart. -iopathy, n. heart disease. -iotomy, n. incision into heart or upper end of stomach. -itis, n. inflammation of cardiac tissue.

cardophagus (kahdof'əgəs), n. (pl. -gi) eater of thistles; donkey.

careen (kərēn'), v.i. & t. heel over; turn on side for repairs.

carême (karem'), Fr. n. Lent.

caret (kar'et), n. mark (ʌ) indicating omission.

caribou (kar'ibōō), n. N. Amer. and Greenland reindeer.

caricology (karikol'əji), n. study of sedges. -cography, n. description of sedges.

caricous (kar'ikəs), adj. fig-like.

caries (kā̆r'iēz), n. decay of bone or tooth.

carillon (kar'ēyawn, kar'ilən), Fr. n. peal of bells. -eur (-nər'), -ist, n. player on c.

carinate (kar'ināt), adj. like or having a keel. -nal, -niform (-in'ifawm), adj. keel-shaped. -tion, n.

cariole, carr- (kar'iōl), n. light one-horse carriage or cart; Can., kind of sleigh.

carious (kā̆r'iəs), adj. pert. to caries; decayed.

caritative (kar'itətiv), adj. charitable.

carmagnole (kahrmanyōl'), Fr. n. wide-lapelled, buttoned jacket of Piedmont; costume of Jacobin French revolutionaries, including the c., red cap and tricolour sash: a Fr. revolutionary song.

carminative (kah'minətiv), n. & adj. (medicine) expelling wind.

carnal (kah'nəl), adj. pert. to flesh; worldly; sensual; sexual. -ism, -ity, n.

carnelian (kahne'liən), n. hard, red variety of chalcedony.

carneous (kah'niəs) adj. like or of

flesh; flesh-coloured. -nic, *adj.* carnal. -niferous, *adj.* bearing flesh. -nifex, *n.* executioner. -nification, *n.* conversion into flesh. -nificial, *adj.* pert. to executioner or butcher. -niform, *adj.* flesh-like. -nify, *v.t.* convert into or like flesh. -nivore, *n.* fl sh-eating animal or plant. -nivorous, *adj.* flesh-eating. -nose, *adj.* fleshy.

carob (kar'əb), *n.* Mediterranean plant yielding bean used in cattle food; "locust"; algarroba.

carom (kar'əm), Amer. *n.* cannon (in billiards); *v.i.* cannon; rebound.

carotene (kar'ətēn), *n.* yellowish-red hydrocarbon giving colour to carrots, butter, etc., and converted into vitamin A in the body.

carotid (kərot'id), *n. & adj.* (artery) conducting blood to head. -tic, *adj.* comatose.

carpal (kah'pəl), *adj.* pert. to carpus.

carpe diem (kah'pi dī'em), *Lat.,* "enjoy the day"; seize opportunity; "make hay while sun shines."

carpel (kah'pəl), *n. Bot.,* pistil; organ forming part of pistil. -llary, *adj.* -llate, *adj.* having c. -pid(ium), *n.* small c.

carpitis (kahpī'tis), *n.* arthritis of carpus.

carpogenous (kahpoj'inəs), *adj.* fruit-producing. -olith, -olite, *n.* fossil fruit or seed. -ology, *n.* study of fruit structure. -ophagous, *adj.* feeding on fruit.

carpus (kah'pəs), *n. (pl.* -pi) wrist; small bones of wrist.

carrack (kar'ək), *n.* galleon.

carrageen (kar'əgēn), *n.* kind of dark red branched sea-weed; Irish moss.

carronade (karənād'), *n.* kind of short, light ship's gun.

carron oil (kar'ən oil), *n.* lotion, composed of limewater and linseed oil, formerly used for burns.

carte blanche (kahrt blahnsh'), *Fr.,* "white card"; permission to act freely. c. de visite (də vēzēt'), small size (about 3½ in. by 2½ in.) of photograph. c. du pays (-dü pā'ē), map; lay of land.

cartel (kahtel'), *n.* association of industrialists or political parties; agreement, *espec.* between nations

at war; duel challenge. -ise, *v.t.* -ist, *n.*

cartilage (kah'tilij), *n.* gristle. -ginoid (-aj'inoid), *adj.* like c. -ginous (-aj'inəs), *adj.* pert. to or composed of c.

cartography (kahtog'rəfi), *n.* drawing of maps. -pher, *n.* map-drawer. -phic, *adj.*

cartomancy (kah'təmansi), *n.* divination or fortune-telling by playing-cards.

carton pierre (kahr'tawn piar'), *Fr.,* kind of papier-mâché imitative of stone or bronze.

cartouch(e) (kahtōōsh'), *n.* scroll- or shield-shaped or oval ornamentation; oval figure containing anct. Egyptian king's name and titles; cartridge-case.

caruncle (kar'ungkl), *n.* fleshy outgrowth, -cular, -culous (-ung'kūlə, -s), *adj.* -culate, *adj.* having c.

caryatid (kariat'id), *n.* sculptured female figure acting as pillar. -al, -tic, *adj.*

casaque (kazak'), *Fr. n.* cassock; blouse.

casein (kā'sēin), *n.* essential albumin of milk. acid c., curd. -eate, *v.t.* become cheese-like. -eation, *n.* - efy, *v.i. & t.* become or make cheese-like. -ic, *adj.* like cheese.

casemate (kās'māt), *n.* bomb-proof room in fortification.

caseous (kā'siəs), *adj.* like cheese.

casern(e) (kəzēn'), *n.* garrison's barracks.

cashew (kash'ōō), *n.* tropical Amer. tree yielding valuable gum, bark and nut; acajou.

cassation (kasā'shn), *n.* annulment. court of c., highest Fr. court of appeal.

cassava (kasah'və), *n.* tropical plant with roots yielding starch used in tapioca making; manioc.

cassideous (kasid'iəs), *adj.* helmet-shaped.

cassidony(kas'idəni), *n.* Fr. lavender.

cassiterite (kəsit'ərit), *n.* native dioxide of tin, the chief ore of tin.

cassowary (kas'əweri), *n.* emu-like bird of Australasia. c.tree, casuarina.

castanean, -ian (kastā'niən), *adj.* pert. to chestnut. -eous, *adj.* chestnut-coloured.

castellan (kas'tələn), *n.* castle governor. -y, *n.* jurisdiction of c.

castellar (kastel'ə), *adj.* pert. to or like a castle.

castellate(d) (kas'təlāt, -id), *adj.* battlemened; turreted; castle-like in appearance. -**tion,** *n.*

castigate (kas'tigāt), *v.t.* punish, *espec.* by beating. -**tion, -tor,** *n.* **-tive, -tory,** *adj.*

castor (kah'stə), *n.* substance derived from beaver and used in perfumery; hat, *espec.* of beaver fur. -**y,** *n.* brown colour obtained from c.

castral (kas'trəl), *adj.* pert. to camp.

castrametation (kastrəmetā'shn), *n.* camping; laying out camp.

castrate (kastrāt'), *v.t.* remove testicles or glands; render sexually impotent. **-tion,** *n.* **-to** (-ah'tō), It. *n.* (*pl.* **-ti**) treble or alto male singer whose voice was prevented from breaking by castration.

castrensian (kastren'siən), *adj.* castral.

casuarina (kasūərē'nə,, *n.* Austral. oak; beefwood.

casuist (kazh'ūist), *n.* sophist; resolver of questions of conscience. **-ry,** *n.* study of rules of right and wrong; application of such rules to particular cases; false reasoning, *espec.* on moral matters.

casus belli (kā'səs bel'ī), *Lat.,* "case of war"; justification for declaring war.

catabaptist (katəbap'tist), *n.* opponent of infant baptism.

catabasis (katab'əsis), *n.* (*pl.* **-ses**) decline of disease. **-atic** (-at'ik), *adj.*

catabolism (katab'əlizm), *n.* destructive chem. processes in living creatures. **-lic** (-bol'ik), *adj.* **-lise,** *v.t.*

catachresis (katəkrē'sis), *n.* use of wrong words. **-estic** (-es'tik), *adj.*

catachthonian, -nic (katakthō'niən, -on'ik), *adj.* subterranean.

cataclasm (kat'əklazm), *n.* breaking down. **-ic,** *adj.* **-stic,** *adj.*; *Geol.,* pert. to granulation of rocks.

cataclysm (kat'əklizm), *n.* catastrophe; upheaval. **-al, -ic,** *adj.*

catacoustic (katəkoō'stik), *adj.* pert. to echoes. **-s,** *n.* study of echoes.

catadioptric (katədīop'trik), *adj.* pert. or due to both reflection and refraction of light. **-s,** *n.* study of such phenomena.

catadromous (kətad'rəməs), *adj.*

migrating from fresh to salt water to spawn.

catafalque (kat'əfalk, -fawlk), *n.* fixed bier for lying-in-state.

catakinetic (katəkinet'ik), *adj.* destructive of energy.

catalactic (katəlak'tik), *adj.* pert. to exchange. **-s,** *n.* study of comm. exchange.

catalectic (katəlek'tik), *adj.* lacking a syllable at end.

catalepsy (kat'əlepsi), *n.* rigid or trance-like fit. **-ptic** (-ep'tik), *adj.* **-ptiform,** *adj.* like c.

catalexis (katəleks'is), *n.* state of being catalectic.

catalpa (katal'pə), *n.* ornamental Amer. and Asiatic tree; Indian bean.

catalysis (kətal'isis), *n.* alteration in speed of chem. reaction due to introduction of a substance which remains unchanged. **-yse** (kat'əlīz), *v.t.* **-yst, -yte** (kat'əlist, -īt), *n.* such introduced substance. **-ytic** (-it'ik), *adj.*; *n.* catalyst; alterative.

catamaran (katəmaran'), *n.* raft-like boat; log-raft; boat with twin hulls; virago.

catamenia (katəmē'niə), *n. Med.,* menstruation. **-l,** *adj.*

catamount(ain) (kat'əmownt, -in), *n.* wild cat.

catapasm (kat'əpazm), *n. Med.,* remedial powder.

cataphoresis (katəfərē'sis), *n.* movement, due to application of electricity, of particles through fluid; injection of drugs electrically. **-etic** (-et'ik), *adj.*

cataplasm (kat'əplazm), *n.* poultice.

cataplexy (kat'əpleksi), *n.* catalepsy-like trance or fit due to shock; motionlessness in animals feigning death.

catastaltic (katəstal'tik), *n.* & *adj.* (drug) exercising restraint; astringent.

catastasis (kətas'təsis), *n.* (*pl.* **-ses**) climax or culmination of drama.

catastrophe (katəs'trəfi), *n.* serious calamity; disaster; *Lit.,* denouement or unravelling of drama after climax. **-phic** (-of'ik), *adj.* **-phism,** *n. Geol.,* theory that sudden isolated upheavals were responsible for geological changes. **-phist,** *n.* believer in such theory.

catchment (kach'mənt), *n.* thing catching or being caught; reservoir. **c.basin,** area draining into reservoir, etc. ; river basin.

catchpole, -poll (kach'pōl), *n.* bumbailiff.

catechesis (katikē'sis), *n.* (*pl.* **-ses**) catechism ; such writings or speeches. **-etic(al)** (-et'ik, -l), *adj.*

catechism (kat'ikizm), *n.* oral questioning ; cross-examination ; teaching by question and answer. **-ise,** *v.t.* **-ist,** *n.* teacher by c. ; native Christian teacher.

catechu (kat'ichoo), *n.* astringent substance extracted from fruit, wood or leaves of sev. tropical plants including acacias and areca palm.

catechumen (katikū'mən), *n.* person receiving instruction, *espec.* in religion. **-ate, -ism,** *n.* status of a c. **-ical** (-en'ikl), *adj.*

category (kat'igəri), *n.* class ; order. **-rical** (-or'ikəl), *adj.* explicit ; in detail ; absolute ; **c.imperative,** phil. principle of Kant—an action willed to be good in itself, and not only good as a means to an end. **-rise,** *v.t.* classify.

catena (katē'nə), *n.* chain ; series. **-noid** (kat'inoid), **-nular, -nulate** (-en'ūlə, -ət), *adj.* chain-like. **-rian** (-ār'iən), *adj.* pert. to chain or catenary. **-ry,** *adj.* chain-like ; *n.* curve assumed by chain suspended between two points. **-te** (kat'ināt), *v.t.* join together like a chain ; *adj.* chain-like. **-tion,** *n.*

catharsis (kathah'sis), *n.* (*pl.* **-ses**) purging ; *Lit.,* purging of emotions by tragedy. **-rtic,** *n.* & *adj.* pur-. gative.

cathedra (kathē'drə), *n.* throne ; bishop's or professor's chair. **ex c.,** *Lat.,* "from the chair" ; authoritative. **-tic** (-at'ik), *adj.*

catheter (kath'itə), *n. Med.,* tube introduced into bladder through urethra. **-ise,** *v.t.*

cathode (kath'ōd), *n.* negative terminal ; electrode by which current leaves. **c.particle,** electron. **c.ray,** stream of electrons from cathode to anode in discharge tube ; **c.r.tube,** vacuum tube in television receiver on fluorescent end of which (the screen) picture is created by c. rays. **-dic** (-od'ik), *adj.* **-dograph,** *n.* X-ray photograph.

catholicon (kathol'ikən), *n.* panacea.

catholyte (kath'əlīt), *n.* portion of electrolyte about cathode.

cation (kat'īən), *n.* positively charged ion moving towards cathode in electrolysis.

catogenic (katəjen'ik), *adj. Geol.,* formed from above ; sedimentary.

catoptric (katop'trik), *adj.* pert. to reflection of light. **-romancy,** *n.* divination by gazing into mirror or crystal. **-s,** *n.* study of reflection.

caucus (kaw'kəs), *n.* small powerful committee, *espec.* in political party ; meeting of such com-. mittee.

caudal (kaw'dəl), *adj.* pert. to tail. **-ad,** *adv.* towards tail. **-ate,** *adj.* tailed. **-diform,** *adj.* tail-like.

caul (kawl), *n.* membrane sometimes covering head of new-born infant, and regarded as lucky.

cauline (kaw'līn), *adj. Bot.,* growing on stem. **-iform,** *adj.* like a stem. **-igenous,** *adj.* borne on stem. **-lescent,** *adj.* with aerial stem. **-lome,** *n.* stem structure of plant. **-lotaxy,** *n.* disposition of branches on stem.

cause célèbre (kōz sāleb'r), *Fr.* (*pl.* **causes célèbres**) "famous lawsuit," *espec.* one creating much public stir.

causerie (kō'zərē), *Fr. n.* "chat" ; writing in conversational tone.

caustic (kaw'stik), *adj.* burning ; corroding ; biting ; sarcastic ; *n.* burning substance. **-ity** (-is'iti), *n.*

cautery (kaw'təri), *n.* med. instr. used for searing wounds, etc. ; use of such instr. **-rant,** *adj.* ; **-rise,** *v.t.*

cavatina (kavətē'nə), *n.* simple song or melody.

cave (kā'vi), *Lat.,* "beware" ; look out ! **c.canem,** "beware of the dog." **keeping c.,** acting as look-out.

caveat (kā'viat), *n.* injunction to stop proceedings ; warning. **c. emptor,** *Lat.,* "let the purchaser beware."

cavernicolous (kavənik'ələs), *adj.* living in caves. **-nulous** (-ə'nūləs), *adj.* full of small cavities.

caviar(e) (kav'iah), *n.* pickled sturgeon's roe ; any rare, delicate or generally unappreciated thing.

cavicorn (kav'ikawn), *adj.* with hollow horns.

cavil (kav'il), v.i. find fault; n. querulous objection.

cavo-relievo (kā'vō-rilē'vō), n. sculpture in which highest part is level with surface of stone; hollow relief.

cavy (kā'vi), n. sev. small rodents; guinea-pig.

cavman, see caiman.

cecidiology (sisidiol'əji), n. study of insect galls. **-gist,** n. **-logenous,** adj. causing galls.

cecil (ses'il), n. forcemeat ball.

cedilla (sidil'ə), n. comma-like mark (ç) indicating that c is pronounced sibilant.

cedrate (sē'drāt), n. citron.

celation (silā'shn), n. concealment. **-ti e** (scl'ətiv), adj.

celibate (sel'ibət), n. & adj. unmarried (person). **-acy,** n. unmarried state. **-tarian, -tist,** n. & adj. (person) advocating celibacy. **-tic** (-at'ik), adj. **-tory,** n. celibate.

celidography (selidog'rəfi), n. description of sun's or planet's surface markings. **-pher,** n.

cellulose (sel'ūlōs), n. starch-like carbohydrate largely forming cell walls of plants, wood, paper, etc. **-sic,** adj. **-sity,** n.

celt (selt), n. prehistoric edged stone, bronze or iron implement. **-iform,** adj. celt-shaped.

cembalo (sem'bəlō), n. dulcimer; harpsichord; any mus. instr. with hammers to strike strings. **-list,** n. player on a c.

cenacle (sen'əkl), n. dining-room.

cenobite (sen'əbīt), n. member of religious community; monk. **-by,** n. convent or monastery. **-ian** (-ō'biən), **-tical** (-it'ikl), adj. **-tism,** n. cenobitical state or practice.

censer (sen'sə), n. receptacle for incense.

cental (sen'təl), n. measure of weight equiv. of 100 lb.

centaur (sen'tör), n. myth. creature, half-man, half-horse; expert horseman. **-ial, -ian, -ic,** adj.

centenary (sentē'nəri, sen'tinəri), adj. pert. to or lasting 100 years; n. one hundredth anniversary. **-nnial** (-en'iəl), adj. pert. to or lasting 100 years. **-rian** (-inār'iən), n. person aged 100 years or more.

centesimal (sentes'iməl), adj. counting or counted by hundredths. **-mate,** v.t. punish by punishing

(espec. executing) every hundredth man. **-mation,** n.

centimetric (sentimet'rik), adj. less than 1 metre in length (of very short radio and radar waves).

cento (sen'tō), n. anthology of short quotations; any patchwork-like composition. **-nical** (-on'ikl), adj. **-nism,** n. composition of a c.

centrifugal (sentrif'ūgəl), adj. tending to move away from centre. **-ge** (sen'trifūj), n. machine for separating substances of different densities by centrifugal force; v.t. separate by this means. **-ipetal** (-ip'itəl), adj. tending to move towards centre.

centrobaric (sentrəbar'ik), adj. pert. to centre of gravity.

centuple (sen'tūpəl), adj. hundredfold; v.t. increase a hundredfold. **centuriate** (sentūr'iət), adj. divided into hundreds. **-tion,** n.

centurion (sentūr'iən), n. anct. Roman captain of an army company.

cepaceous (sipā'shəs), adj. like an onion.

cephalic (sifal'ik), adj. pert. to head. **c.index,** 100 times maximum breadth of skull divided by maximum length. **-lad** (sef'-), adv. towards head. **-late** (sef'-), adj. having a head. **-ligation,** n. situation of leading organs or functions in head. **-logram** (sef'-), n. outline of head.

cephalopod (sef'ələpod), n. & adj. (mollusc, as octopus, squid, etc.) with arm-like tentacles attached to head.

cephalothorax (sefələthör'aks), n. body, or head with thorax, of spiders, crustaceans, etc. **-acic** (-as'ik), adj.

cephalous (sef'ələs), adj. cephalate.

ceraceous (sirā'shəs), adj. like wax. **-ral** (sēr'əl), adj. pert. to wax or cere.

ceramic (siram'ik), adj. pert. to pottery; n. a pottery article. **-ist** (ser'-), n. maker of or expert on pottery. **-mography,** n. historical or descriptive work on pottery. **-s,** n. art of making pottery.

cerate (sēr'āt), n. med. unguent composed of wax, lard, etc.; adj. having a cere. **-d,** adj. covered with wax.

ceratoid (ser'ətoid), *adj.* horny; like or shaped like horn.

ceraunograph (seraw'nəgraf), *n.* instr. recording thunder and lightning. **-ophore**, *n.* instr. recording thunder by sound.

Cerberic, -rean (sā'bərik, -ēr'iən), *adj.* pert. to Cerberus, three-headed dog in classical myth. that guarded Hades' gates; vigilant; dragon-like.

cercal (sə'kl), *adj.* caudal.

cere (sēr), *n.* wax; wax-like protuberance at base of upper part of bird's bill.

cerebellum (seribel'əm), *n.* part of brain projecting at back; "little brain." **-lar**, *adj.*

cerebrum (ser'ibrəm), *n.* brain, *espec.* fore part. **-ral**, *adj.* **-rate, v.i.** think deeply; reason. **-ration**, *n.* **-ro-spinal**, *adj.* pert. to brain and spinal cord.

cerements (sēr'mənts), *n.pl.* grave-clothes.

ceriferous (serif'ərəs), *adj.* yielding wax.

cernuous (sə'nūəs), *adj.* drooping; hanging.

cerography (sirog'rəfi), *n.* writing on wax; painting with wax colours; encaustic painting. **-oplastics**, *n.* wax modelling.

cerous (sēr'əs), *adj.* pert. to or like a cere.

certes (sətz, -tēz), *adv.* certainly.

certiorari (səshior ar'ī), *n.* writ for transference of hearing to superior court, or calling for production before superior court of records of a lower court.

cerulean (seroo'liən), *adj.* sky-blue; dark blue. **-eous**, *adj.* sky-blue. **-escent**, *adj.* bluish.

cerumen (sərŏo'mən), *n.* wax of ear. **-miniferous**, *adj.* yielding c. **-minous**, *adj.* pert. to c.

ceruse (ser'ōos, -ōōs'), *n.* white lead.

cervical (kə'vikl, sə'-; səvī'kl), *adj.* pert. to the neck.

cervine (sə'vīn), *adj.* pert. to or like deer. **-icorn**, *adj.* bearing, or branched like antlers.

cervisial (səvis'iəl), *adj.* pert. to beer.

cervix (sə'viks), *n.* (*pl.* **-ices**) neck; narrow mouth.

cesious (sē'ziəs), *adj.* blue-grey.

cespitous (ses'pitəs), *adj.* like turf; tufted. **-titious**, *adj.* composed of turf.

cetacean (sitā'shn), *n.* & *adj.* (mammal) of the natural order that includes whales, dolphins and porpoises. **-ceous**, *adj.* like or pert. to a whale. **-tic** (sē'tik), *adj.* pert. to whales. **-ticide**, *n.* person killing whales. **-tology**, *n.* study of whales.

cetane (sē'tān), *n.* an oil found in petroleum. **c.number**, number representing ignition value of diesel oil, being the percentage of cetane in a mixture used for testing by comparison.

chaconne (shakon'), *n.* quiet old Sp. dance.

chaetiferous (kētif'ərəs), *adj.* bearing bristles. **-igerous, -topherous**, *adj.*

chagrin (shag'rin, shəgrēn'), *n.* disappointment annoyance; vexation; *v.t.* (shəgrēn'), disappoint deeply; annoy.

chaise (shāz), Fr. *n.* light, two-wheeled carriage, *espec.* with suspended body. **c.longue** (-lawng'), long chair with footrest; couch.

chalastic (kəlas'tik), *n.* & *adj.* laxative.

chalcedony (kalsed'əni, kal'sid-), *n.* blue or grey variety of quartz. **-nic** (-on'ik), **-nous** (-ed'ənəs), *adj.*

chalcography (kalkog'rəfi), *n.* engraving on brass or copper. **-olithic**, *adj.* pert. to copper or bronze age. **-otript**, *n.* person who takes rubbings of ornamental brasses.

chalicosis (kalikō'sis), *n.* stone-cutters' lung disease, due to inhaling stone dust.

chalone (kal'ōn), *n.* glandular secretion curbing activity. **-nic** (-on'ik), *adj.* pert. to c.; restraining.

chalybeate (kəlib'iət), *adj.* containing salts of iron; *n.* such water, medicine, etc.

chamecephalic, -lous (kamisifal'ik, -sef'ələs), *adj.* having a flattened skull. **-lus**, *n.* (*pl.* **-li**) such person. **-ly**, *n.* such condition.

chamfer (cham'fə), *n.* groove; bevel; *v.t.* cut c. in, cut off angles of, round off. **-ed**, *adj.*

chamma (cham'ah), *n.* cloak-like Abyssinian garment.

champaign (cham'pān), *n.* plain; any level expanse; *adj.* pert. to such country.

ə=*er* in *father*; ə̄=*er* in *pert*; th=*th* in *thin*; dh=*th* in *then*; zh=*s* in *pleasure*; k=*ch* in *loch*; n̄=Fr. nasal *n*; ü=Fr. *u.*

champerty (cham'pəti), *n. Law.*, crime of aiding another's lawsuit in order to share in gains therefrom. **-tous,** *adj.*

champignon (champin'yən ; Fr. shahṅpēn'yawṅ), *n.* mushroom.

champlevé (shamp'ləvā ; Fr. shahṅ'ləvā), *n. & adj.* (enamel) bearing indentations filled with colour.

chancre (shang'kə), *n.* syphilitic ulcer. **-riform,** *adj.* like a c. **-roid,** *n.* local sore resembling a c. **-rous,** *adj.* like or having c.

chandoo (chandōō'), Ind. & Chin. *n.* prepared opium.

chantage (chahn'tij), *n.* blackmail.

chanter (chahn'tə), *n.* pipe of bagpipe on which the air is played.

chantry (chahn'tri), *n.* chapel, priest or endowment for singing masses.

chaparajos, -rej- (chaparah'hōs, -rā'-), Sp.-Mex. *n.pl.,* cowboys' leather leg-coverings ; "chaps."

chapatty (chəpat'i), *n.* chupatti.

chapelle ardente (shapel' ahr-dahṅt'), *Fr.,* "burning chapel" ; framework bearing burning candles over coffin or at catafalque.

chapbook (chap'book), *n.* small popular book, formerly of songs, etc., sold by pedlars. **-man,** *n.* pedlar.

chargé d'affaires (shah'zhā dafār'), *n. (pl.* chargés .....) ambassador at minor court; assistant or deputy to ambassador.

charism (kar'izm), *n.* divinely bestowed attribute or power. **-atic,** *adj.*

charivari (shahrivah'ri), *n.* medley, *espec.* of noises ; mock musical performance with whistles, utensils, etc.

charlatan (shah'lətən), *n.* impostor ; quack. **-ic** (-an'ik), *adj.* **-ism, -ry,** *n.*

charnel-house (chah'nəl-hows), *n.* place where dead bodies or bones are deposited.

charpoy (chah'poi), Anglo-Ind. *n.* light bedstead.

charqui (chah'ki); *n.* dried strips of meat ; jerked beef. **-qued,** *adj.* cut into strips and dried.

chasmogamy (kazmog'əmi), *n.* opening of flower for fertilisation. **-mic** (-am'ik), **-mous,** *adj.*

chasmophilous (kazmof'iləs), *adj.*

fond of crannies and crevices. **-phyte,** *n.* such plant.

chasuble (chaz'ūbl), *n.* outermost eccl. vestment without sleeves.

chatelaine (shat'əlān), *n.* woman owner, occupier or caretaker of castle ; ring attached to belt for carrying keys, etc.

chatoyant (shətoi'ənt), *adj.* with lustre that seems different colours in different lights ; *n.* stone which shines with a wavy band of light ; cat's-eye.

chatta (chat'ə), Anglo-Ind. *n.* umbrella.

chatty (chat'i), Anglo-Ind. *n.* waterpot.

chaus (kā'əs), *n.* wild cat, *espec.* of Ind. and Africa.

chaussure (shōsūr'), Fr. *n.* foot covering.

chauvinism (shō'vinizm), *n.* aggressive patriotism ; jingo. **-ist,** *n.* **-istic,** *adj.*

chebec(k) (shəbek'), *n.* xebec.

chee-chee (chē'chē), Anglo-Ind. *n.* Eurasian half-caste ; kind of Eng. spoken by c.

chef-d'oeuvre (shā-də'vr), Fr. *n. (pl.* chefs .....) masterpiece. **c. de cabinet** (shef də kab'enā), private secretary. **c. de train** (shef də traṅ), railway guard.

cheiropody, -ology, etc., *see* **chiropody, -ology,** etc.

cheliferous (kēlif'ərəs), *adj.* claw- or pincer-bearing. **-form,** *adj.* claw- or pincer-shaped.

chelonian (kilō'niən), *n. & adj.* (pert. to) tortoise or turtle. **-nid,** *n.* sea turtle.

chemin-de-fer (shəmaṅ' də fār'), Fr. *n.* "road of iron" ; railway ; a kind of baccarat.

chemokinesis (keməkinē'sis), *n.* increase in activity caused chemically. **-olysis,** *n.* decomposition chemically caused. **-otaxis,** *n.* movement of organism towards or away from chemical substance. **-otherapy,** *n.* med. treatment by chemicals attacking disease-producing organism. **-otropism,** *n.* growth towards or away from chemical substance.

chemurgy (kem'əji), *n.* industrial organic chemistry.

chéri (shār ē'), Fr. *n. & adj. (fem.* -ie) beloved.

chersonese (kə'sənēz), *n.* peninsula.

chert (chĕrt), *n.* flint-like concretions in limestone.

chervil (chĕr'vil), *n.* a salad herb with curled léaves.

cheval-de-frise (shəval' də frēz'), *n.* (*pl.* chevaux- .....) spiked bar on wall or window-sill. c. de bataille (-də batī'), war-horse; hobby-horse. c.glass, full-length mirror in frame.

chevalier (shevalēr'), *n.* knight; cavalier; gallant.

chevaline (shev'əlin), *adj.* equine; *n.* horse flesh.

chevelure (shevlūr'), Fr. *n.* head of hair.

cheveril, -el (chev'əril, -əl), *n.* & *adj.* (made of) kind of kid leather.

chevet (shəvā'), Fr. *n.* east end of church; end of chancel.

cheville (shəvēl'; Fr., -vē'), *n.* unnecessary word, *espec.* used to extend verse line.

chevon (shev'ən), *n.* goat's flesh.

chevrette (shevret'), *n.* kind of thin kid leather.

chevron (shev'rən), *n.* V-shaped or Λ-shaped bar or stripe.

chevrotain (shev'rətān), *n.* small deer-like mammal of E. Ind. and Africa ; mouse-deer.

chez (shā), Fr. *prep.* at the house or home of.

chiaroscuro (kīərəskūr'ō, -ōor'ō), *n.* use of light and shade in art; use of similar contrast in writing, etc. -rist, *n.* artist skilled in c.

chiasmus (kīaz'məs), *n.* (*pl.* -mi) inversion of order of corresponding elements of two antitheses so that they fall into correspondence as

a b b a . -stic, *adj.*

chibouk, -que (chibōōk'), *n.* long Turk. smoking pipe.

chicane (shikān'), *n.* & *v.i.* & *t.* cheat ; trick ; (use) subterfuge. -ry, *n.*

chicle (chik'l; Sp., chē'klā), *n.* rubber-like gum, main ingredient of chewing gum, obtained from Cent. Amer. sapodilla tree. -ro (-ār'ō), Sp.-Amer. *n.* gatherer of c.

chico (chē'kō), Sp. *n.* "little one"; my friend.

chicory (chik'əri), *n.* a wild endive; succory ; its powdered root added to coffee.

chiffonier (shifənēr'), *n.* sideboard ; chest of drawers.

chignon (shinon'; shēnyon'; Fr., shēn'yawṅ), *n.* knot or "bun" of hair ; pad over which hair is arranged.

chigoe (chig'ō), *n.* W. Ind. and S. Amer. flea ; chigger ; jigger.

chihuahua (chēwah'wah), *n.* very small Mex. dog. c.pine, Mex. timber tree.

chikara (chikah'rə), *n.* Ind. gazelle or kind of antelope.

chiliad (kil'iad), *n.* one thousand (years). -al, -ic, *adj.* -iagon, *n.* thousand-sided figure. -iasm, *n.* belief in second incarnation of Christ as king of world ; millenarianism. -iast, *n.* adherent of such belief. -iastic, *adj.* -iomb, *n.* sacrifice of one thousand animals.

chillum (chil'əm), Anglo-Ind. *n.* hookah ; bowl of hookah ; tobacco-smoking. -chee, *n.* brass wash basin.

chimera, -aera (kīmēr'ə, kim-), *n.* imaginary monster ; bogy ; impossible idea. -rical (-er'ikl), *adj.* imaginary ; fanciful ; fantastic.

chinch (chinch), *n.* bed-bug.

chinchilla (chinchil'ə), *n.* small, squirrel-like S. Amer. rodent ; its soft fur ; *adj.* app. to soft-furred grey varieties of rabbit, cat, etc.

chine (chīn), *n.* backbone ; cut of meat adjoining backbone ; saddle ; ridge ; small ravine ; *v.t.* cut into pieces.

chinoiserie (shēnwaz'rē), Fr. *n.* example of Chinese manners, art, etc.

chinook (chinōok'), *n.* warm dry wind blowing down E. side of Rocky Mts.

chionablepsia (kīənəblep'siə), *n.* snow blindness.

chipmunk (chip'mungk), *n.* N. Amer. ground or striped squirrel.

chiragra (kīrag'rə), *n.* gout of the fingers.

chiral (kīr'əl), *adj.* pert. to hand ; turning to either left or right. -ity (-al'iti), *n.* -rapsia, *n.* massage.

chiropody (kīrop'ədi), *n.* care of feet (*orig.*, of feet and hands). -dous, *adj.* with prehensile feet. -ocosmetics, *n.* beautifying the hands. -ognomy, -omancy, *n.* palmistry. -ograph, *n.* written bond or indenture. -ography, *n.* handwriting. -ology, *n.* study of hand. -onomy, *n.* art of gesture with hands. -opractic, -opraxis, n. manipulation of joints, espec. of spine, as med. remedy. -othesia, n. laying on of hands in eccl. ceremony. -otomy, n. election by show of hands ; Eccl., use of hand in blessing, etc.

chirurgeon (kīr ə'jən), n. arch., surgeon. -ery, n. surgery. -gic, adj.

chitin (kī'tin), n. horny substance forming outer surface of most insects, crustaceans, etc. -oid, adj. like c. -ous, adj.

chives (chīvz), n.pl. onion-like plant used in salad and for flavouring.

chlamys (klam'is, klā'-), n. horseman's loose cloak of anct. Greece. -ydate, adj. having a mantle. -ydeous, adj. Bot., pert. to floral envelope.

chloraemia, -anaemia (klōrē'miə, -anē'-), n. chlorosis.

chloral (klōr'əl), n. oily liquid obtained from chlorine and alcohol ; (properly c. hydrate) sleeping draught obtained from chloral. -ism, n. condition due to abuse of c. -ride, n. compound of chlorine. -rinate, n. treat with chlorine to bleach or sterilise. -rine, n. poisonous green gaseous element, used as bleach, disinfectant, etc.

chlorochrous (klōr'əkrəs), adj. greenish.

chloromycetin (klōrəmī'sitin), n. antibiotic produced by a soil fungus. -ramphenicol, n. synthetic form of c.

chlorophyll (klōr'əfil), n. green colouring matter of plants. -aceous, -ose, adj. -iferous, -igerous, adj. containing c. -igenous, adj. producing c. -oid, adj. like c. -plast(id), n. portion of protoplasm containing c., active in photosynthesis.

chlorosis (klōr ō'sis), n. anaemia in young women ; green sickness ; similar condition of plants, due to lack of light. -otic (-ot'ik), adj. lacking chlorophyll.

choanoid (kō'ənoid), adj. funnel-shaped.

chokedamp (chōk'damp), n. asphyxiating gas, mainly carbon dioxide, of mines.

chokidar, -kidar (chōk'dah, -idah), Anglo-Ind. n. watchman.

chokra (chō'krah), Anglo-Ind. n. office boy.

cholecyst (kol'isist), n. gall bladder. -ic, adj. -itis, n. inflammation of gall bladder.

cholelithiasis (kolilithī'əsis), n. production of gall-stones.

choler (kol'ə), n. anger ; bile. -ric (-er'ik), adj. pert. to choler ; easily angered.

cholera (kol'ərə), n. severe disease or temporary affection of stomach and intestines. Asiatic c., such acute epidemic fatal disease, due to bacteria. European c., or c. morbus, acute biliousness, due to heat and injudicious diet. -ic (-a'ik), adj. -riform, -roid, adj. like c. -rigenous, adj. causing c.

cholesterin(e), -rol (kəles'tərin, -rol), n. fatty alcohol occurring in bile and nervous tissue, and forming gall-stones.

choliamb (kō'liam), n. iambic trimeter having trochee or spondee in third foot. -ic (-bik), adj.

cholic (kol'ik), adj. pert. to bile.

choller (chol'ə), n. double chin.

chololith (kol'əlith), n. gall-stone. -ic, adj.

chômage (shō'mahzh), Fr. n. work stoppage ; slump ; unemployment.

chondral (kon'ərəl), adj. cartilaginous. -ric, adj. -rification, n. conversion into cartilage. -rogenesis, n. production of cartilage. -roid, adj. like cartilage. -rosis, n. formation of cartilage. -rostean, -rosteous, adj. with cartilaginous skeleton.

chorale (korahl'), n. hymn tune.

chorditis (kawdī'tis), n. inflammation of vocal chords.

chorea (korē'ə), n. nervous disease marked by involuntary twitchings. c.minor, St. Vitus's dance. -eic, -l, -tic, adj. -eiform, -eoid, adj. like c.

choree, -eus (kor'ē, -ē'əs), n. trochee.

choreography (koriog'rəfi), n. arrangement of dances for stage ; representation of dance movements by a kind of notation. -pher, n. dance arranger. -phic, adj.

choreutic (kor oo'tik), adj. like or pert. to chorus.

chorial (kor'ial), adj. pert. to chorion.

choriamb (kor'iam), n. metrical foot comprising a trochee and an iambus. -ic, adj.

hat, bah, hāte, hāre, crawl ; pen, ēve, hēre ; it, īce, fīre ; on bōne, boil, bōre, howl ; foot, fōod, bōor, hull, tūbe, pūre.

choric (kor'ik), adj. pert. to chorus in anct. Gr. tragedy.

chorion (kōr'iən), n. membrane enclosing amnion. -ic, adj.

choripetalous (kōripet'ələs), adj. with petals separated. -isepalous, adj. with sepals separated.

chorograph (kōr'əgraf), n. instr. finding position of a place from angles enclosed by lines between it and three other known places.

chorography (kōrog'rəfi), n. geographical description of a region. -rology, n. study of geographical distribution. -rometry, n. surveying of land.

chose jugée (shōz zhü'zhā), Fr., "judged thing"; settled matter, on which further argument is useless. c. in action, Law, thing, such as mortgage, debt, etc., in respect of which there is a right of legal action. c. in possession, thing, as goods and chattels, in ownership.

chota hazri (chō'tə haz'ri), Anglo-Ind. n. light breakfast.

choultry (chōol'tri), Anglo-Ind. n. caravanserai; colonnade.

chowder (chow'də), Amer. n. mixed meat, fish, vegetable and clam stew.

chowry (chow'ri), Anglo-Ind. n. whisk or fan for removing flies.

chrematistic (krēmətis'tik), adj. pert. to gaining of money. -s, n. study of money.

chrestomathy (krestom'əthi), n. collection of short written passages, espec. in foreign language; phrasebook. -thic (-ath'ik), adj. pert. to useful knowledge.

chrism (krizm), n. holy oil. -al, adj. -ation, n. application of c. -atory, n. vessel holding c.; adj. pert. to chrismation.

chromaesthesia (krōmesthē'zhiə), n. mental association of colours with tastes, sights, sounds, figures, etc.

chromascope (krō'məskōp), n. instr. showing colour's effects.

chromatic (krəmat'ik), adj. pert. to colour; Mus., using tones outside the key in which it is written, espec. the half-tones; n. an accidental. -ity (-is'iti), n. degree or state of having colour. -s, n. study of colour.

chromatin (krō'mətin), n. protoplasmic substance in cell nucleus, forming chromosomes and carrying hereditary characters.

chromatism (krō'mətizm), n. occurrence of abnormal coloration.

chromatography (krōmətog'rəfi), n. treatise on colours. -ology, n. study of colours.

chromatopathy (krōmətop'əthi), n. disease causing abnormal coloration of skin.

chromatoptometer (krōmətoptom'itə), n. instr. measuring eye's sensitiveness to colour. -try, n.

chromatosis (krōmətō'sis), n. chromatism of skin.

chromogen (krō'məjen), n. substance developing into colouring matter of plants. -ic, adj. producing colour.

chromolithograph (krōməlith'əgraf), n. coloured lithograph. -y, n.

chromophilous, -lic (krōmof'iləs, -əfil'ik), adj. Chem., readily staining. -phobe, adj. staining only slightly.

chromophotography (krōməfətog'rəfi), n. colour photography.

chromosome (krō'məsōm), n. coloured particle of chromatin, gen. of definite number and shape for a species, occurring in cell nucleus.

chromosphere (krō'məsfēr), n. layer of glowing gas surrounding sun or a star.

chromotypography (krōmətīpog'rəfi), n. printing in colours. -oxylography, n. printing in colours from wooden blocks.

chronogram (kron'əgram), n. phrase or sentence certain letters of which form a date, gen. in Roman figures. -mmatic, adj. -mmatist, n. composer of c.

chronograph (kron'əgraf), n. stopwatch. -y, n. recording of intervals of time.

chronology (krənol'əji), n. science of dates; arrangement in order of time of occurrence. -gical, adj.

chronometer (krənom'itə), n. timepiece, espec. of exceptional accuracy. -tric (-et'rik), adj. -try, n. measuring of time and divisions of time.

chronopher (kron'əfə), n. elec. contact maker for transmitting time signals.

chronophotography (kronəfətog'rəfi), n. taking of a set of photographs of a moving object at regular intervals.

chronoscope (kron'əskōp), *n.* instr. measuring very small intervals of time ; chronometer in which figures are seen through apertures in dial. **-py** (-os'kəpi), *n.*

chronostichon (krənos'tikon), *n.* chronogrammatic line of verse.

chronothermometer (kronəthəmom'itə), *n.* chronometer whose rate is altered by temperature changes.

chronotropic (kronətrop'ik), *adj.* affecting rate of pulse. **-pism** (-ot'rəpizm), *n.*

chrysalis (kris'əlis), *n.* (*pl.* **-ses**) motionless stage of insect's life, in which it has a hard covering ; pupa. **-lid**, *adj.* **-loid**, *adj.* like a c.

chrysanthous (krisan'thəs), *adj.* yellow-flowered.

chryselephantine (kriselifan'tīn, -in), *adj.* made of or ornamented with ivory and gold.

chrysoaristocracy (krisōaristok'rəsi), *n.* plutocracy.

chrysocarpous (krisəkah'pəs), *n.* having yellow fruit.

chrysochlorous (krisəklor'əs), *adj.* greenish-gold in colour.

chrysochrous (kris'əkrəs), *adj.* golden yellow.

chrysocracy (krisok'rəsi), *n.* plutocracy.

chrysography (krisog'rəfi), *n.* writing in letters of gold. **-pher**, *n.*

chrysolite (kris'əlīt), *n.* olive-green or yellow crystal used as gem ; olivine.

chrysology (krisol'əji), *n.* economic study of precious metals and their value.

chrysophilist, -lite (krisof'ilist, -līt), *n.* lover of gold.

chrysopoetics (krisəpōet'iks), *n.* manufacture of, or transmutation into, gold.

chrysoprase (kris'əprāz), *n.* green variety of chalcedony used as gem.

chrystocrene (kris'təkrēn), *n. Geol.,* rock formation resembling glacier.

chtonian (thō'niən), *adj.* pert. to Gr. gods of underworld.

chucker, *see* **chukker.**

chuddar (chud'ə), Anglo-Ind. *n.* large head-shawl.

chukker (chuk'ə), *n.* one of the periods into which game of polo is divided.

chupatty (chōōpah'ti), Anglo-Ind. *n.* unleavened cake or pancake.

chuprassi (chōōprah'si), Anglo-Ind. *n.* attendant ; government official's servant.

churrus (chur'əs), Ind. *n.* hemp resin ; leather bag for drawing water from well.

chyle (kīl), *n.* milky fat-containing fluid secreted into blood by lactic vessels in small intestine. **-laceous,** *adj.* **-lific,** *adj.* producing c. **-liform,** *adj.* like c. **-locauly,** *n. Bot.,* possession of fleshy stems. **-lophylly,** *n.* possession of fleshy leaves. **-lopoiesis,** *n.* production of c. **-lous,** *adj.* consisting of c.

chyme (kīm), *n.* semi-liquid partly digested food leaving stomach. **-miferous,** *adj.* containing c. **-mification,** *n.* conversion of food into c. **-mous,** *adj.*

chypre (shēpr), *n.* mixture of resins, etc., used in perfumery.

cibation (sība'shn), *n.* feeding. **-arian,** *adj.* pert. to mouth. **-arious,** *adj.* pert. to food.

cibophobia (sībəfō'biə), *n.* dislike for food.

cicada (sika'də), *n.* locust ; harvest-fly.

cicatrice, -rix (sik'ətris, -iks), *n.* scar. **-cial,** *adj.* **-cle,** *n.* small scar. **-cose,** *adj.* scarred. **-rise,** *v.i.* & *t.* heal ; grow over.

cicerone (sisərō'ni ; *It.* chicherō'nā), *It. n.* (*pl.* **-ni**) guide. **-nage,** *n.*

ciconine, -nian (sik'ənīn, -in ; -ō'niən), *adj.* like or pert. to a stork.

ci-devant (sē-dəvahń'), Fr. *adj.* former ; ex-.

cilia (sil'iə), *n.pl.* (*sing.* **-ium**) eyelashes ; hair-like outgrowths of microscopic organisms or cells, acting as organs of propulsion. **-ry,** *adj.* ; c.**muscle,** muscle compressing or extending lens of eye in accommodation. **-te,** *adj.* having fine hairs.

cilice (sil'is), *n.* hair-cloth.

cillosis (silō'sis), *n.* muscular spasm of upper eyelid.

cimex (sī'meks), *n.* (*pl.* **-ices**) bedbug. **-micide,** *n.* substance destroying bed-bugs.

Cimmerian (simēr'ian), *adj.* pert. to Cimmeria, in Gr. legend a kingdom of gloom and mist ; dark ; gloomy.

cinchona (sinkō'nə), *n.* S. Amer.

hat, bah, hāte, hāre, crawl ; pen, ēve, hēre ; it, īce, fīre ; on, bōne, boil, bōre, howl ; foot, fōōd, bōōr, hull, tūbe, pūre.

tree with bark yielding quinine; Peruvian bark. **-nic** (-on'ik), *adj.* **-nine** (sin'kanēn), *n.* quinine-like alkaloid extracted from c. bark. **-nism,** *n.* condition due to over-use of quinine and other extracts of c. bark.

cincture (singk'tūr), *n.* girdle.

cinemograph (sinē'magraf), *n.* instr. recording speed, *espec.* of wind.

cinenchymatous (sinengkim'ətəs), *adj.* laticiferous.

cinerary (sin'ərəri), *adj.* pert. to ashes, *espec.* of cremated body. **-rium** (-ār'iəm), *n.* place where ashes of cremated bodies are deposited.

cinerial (sinēr'iəl), *adj.* pert. to, like or coloured like ashes. **-reous, -ritious,** *adj.* like ashes.

cingulate (sing'gūlət), *adj.* having girdle. **-ar,** *adj.* ring-shaped.

cinnabar (sin'əbah), *n.* natural sulphide of mercury, the chief source of mercury. **-ic, -ine,** *adj.*

cinquecento (chingkwichen'tō), It. *adj.* sixteenth-century; *n.* work or style of art produced then. **-tism,** *n.* **-tist,** *n.* It. artist of 16th cent.; student of It. art of that period.

cinquefoil (singk'foil), *n.* sev. plants having leaves divided into five lobes; archit. decoration resembling such leaf.

cipolin (sip'əlin), *n.* green-streaked white marble.

cippus (sip'əs), *n.* (*pl.* **-pi**) small column marking burial-place or landmark.

circa (sū'kə), Lat. *prep.* "about" (*abbr.* c.).

Circean (sūsē'ən), *adj.* pert. to Circe, an enchantress in anct. Gr. myth; bewitching; causing degradation.

circinate (sū'sinət), *adj.* ring-shaped; rolled into a close spiral.

circumambient (sōkəmam'biənt), *adj.* surrounding on all sides. **-ncy,** *n.*

circumambulate (sōkəmam'būlāt), *v.t.* walk round. **-tion, -tor,** *n.*

circumaviate (sōkəmā'viāt), *v.t.* fly round. **-tion, -tor,** *n.*

circumcise (sū'kəmsīz), *v.t.* remove foreskin of; purify. **-sion,** *n.*

circumcrescent (sōkəmkres'ənt), *adj.* growing over or round. **-nce,** *n.*

circumdiction (sōkəmdik'shən), *n.* circumlocution.

circumferentor (sēkəmfəren'tə), *n.* surveyor's angle-measuring compass instr.

circumflex (sū'kəmfleks), *n.* & *adj.* (app. to) accent (^) indicating length of vowel; curved; arched. **-ion,** *n.*

circumfluent (sōkəmfloo'ənt), *adj.* flowing round. **-nce** (-um'-flooəns), *n.*

circumforaneous (sōkəmfərā'niəs), *adj.* wandering, *espec.* from street to street; vagrant.

circumfulgent (sōkəmful'jənt), *adj.* shining about or round.

circumfuse (sōkəmfūz'), *v.t.* surround with liquid; pour round. **-sion,** *n.*

circuminsular (sōkəmin'sūlə), *adj.* surrounding an island.

circumjacent (sōkəmjā'sənt), *adj.* surrounding. **-nce, -ncy,** *n.*

circumlittoral (sōkəmlit'ərəl), *adj.* next to shore.

circumlocution (sōkəmləkū'shn), *n.* roundabout phrase or talk. **-tory** (-lok'ūtəri), *adj.*

circummigrate (sōkəmmīgrāt'), *v.i.* wander from place to place. **-tion,** *n.*

circumnavigate (sōkəmnav'igāt), *v.t.* sail round. **-tion, -tor,** *n.* **-tory,** *adj.*

circumoesophagal (sōkəmēsof'əgəl), *adj.* about or along the gullet.

circumpolar (sōkəmpō'lə), *adj.* about or at N. or S. Pole.

circumscribe (sū'kəmskrīb), *v.t.* enclose; limit. **-ription,** *n.* **-riptive,** *adj.*

circumsolar (sōkəmsō'lə), *adj.* revolving round sun.

circumspect (sū'kəmspekt), *adj.* cautious. **-ion,** *n.* **-ive,** *adj.*

circumstantial (sōkəmstan'shəl), *adj.* detailed; inessential; pert. to circumstances. **c. evidence,** evidence of circumstances that make it extremely probable that event has occurred. **-iate,** *v.t.* prove or support with details. **-ity,** *n.* **-s,** *n.pl.* incidentals; details.

circumvallation (sōkəmvalā'shn), *n.* surrounding trench or rampart.

circumvent (sōkəmvent'), *v.t.* outwit; prevent by strategy. **-ion,** *n.*

circumviate (səkum'viāt), *v.t.* travel round.

circumvolant (səkum'vələnt), *adj.* flying round.

circumvolute (səkum'vəlōōt), v.t. twist; wind round. -tion, n. revolution; fold; circumlocution. -tory (sōkəmvol'ūtəri), adj.

circumvolve (sēkəmvolv'), v.i. & t. revolve (round). -lution (-vəlū'-shn), n.

cirrate (sir'āt), adj. having tendrils.

cirrhosis (sirō'sis), n. Med., hardened or fibrous condition, espec. of liver. -otic (-ot'ik), adj.

cirriped (sir'iped), n. parasitic marine crustacean, as barnacle. -ropodous, adj.

cirrus (sir'əs), n. (pl. -ri) tendril; high, fine, thin cloud. -ro-cumulus, n. small cumulus clouds at great height; mackerel sky. -rose, adj. cirrate. -ro-stratus, n. layer of stratus cloud at great height. -ro-velum, n. sheet of cirrus cloud covering sky.

cisalpine (sisal'pīn), adj. on this side of the Alps, espec. on the southern or Roman side. -andine, adj. on this side of the Andes. -atlantic, adj. on this side of the Atlantic Ocean. -elysian, adj. on this side of Elysium or heaven. -gangetic, adj. on this (west) side of Ganges. -marine, adj. on this side of the sea. -montane, adj. on this side of mountains; desiring limitation of papal power. -oceanic, adj. on this side of ocean. -pontine, adj. on this side of bridges, i.e. on north side of Thames. -rhenane, adj. on this side of the Rhine.

cistus (sis'təs), n. rock rose.

citation (sītā'shn), n. summons; quotation; enumeration. -tory (sī'-), adj.

cithara (sith'ərə), n. anct. lyre-like stringed mus. instr. -rist, n. player on c.

either(n)(sidh'ə,-n), n. lute; cithera; zither, etc. -rcedic, adj.

citreous (sit'riəs), adj. lemon-coloured. -ric, adj. pert. to or derived from lemons and other acid fruit. -rine, adj. lemon-coloured. -ron, n. large lemon-like fruit. -rous, -rus, adj. pert. to or like citron.

civet (siv'it), n. musk-like substance, used as perfume, obtained from c. cat. c.cat, banded and spotted cat-like animal of Africa.

civic (siv'ik), adj. pert. to city or citizenship. -s, n. principles of good citizenship. -vism, n. citizenship.

cladoptosis (kladoptō'sis), n. annual shedding of twigs. -dose, adj. branched.

clairaudient (klāraw'diənt), adj. able to hear sounds not actually present, as spirit communications, etc. -nce, n.

clair de lune (klār' də lūn), Fr., "moonlight"; greenish-blue colour.

clairsentient (klārsen'shənt), adj. able to perceive sensations not actually present. -nce, n.

clairvoyant (klārvoi'ənt), n. & adj. (person) able to see objects not actually present; having "second sight." -nce, n.

clamant (klā'mənt), n. loud; insistent. -atory, -morous (klam'-), adj. loud.

clancular (klang'kūlə), adj. clandestine.

clandestine (klandes'tin), adj. secret; illicit.

claque (klak), n. group of paid applauders. -ur (-kə'), n. member of c.

clashee (klash'i), Anglo-Ind. n. Ind. sailor or erector of tents.

clastic (klas'tik), adj. detachable into component parts; Geol., composed of fragments.

clathrate (klath'rāt), adj. lattice-like. -roid, adj. -rose, adj. marked with lattice-like lines or grooves.

claudent (klaw'dənt), adj. shutting.

claudicate (klaw'dikāt), v.i. limp. -ant, adj. -tion, n.

claustral (klaw'strəl), adj. cloistral. -ation, n. confinement, espec. in convent.

claustrophobia (klawstrəfō'biə), n. dread of enclosed spaces.

clavate (klav'āt), adj. club-shaped. -tion, n.

clavecin (klav'isin), n. harpsichord; carillon keyboard.

clavelise (klav'ilīz), v.t. inoculate with sheep pox. -sation, n.

claviature (klav'iətūr), n. keyboard; fingering system.

clavicembalo (klavichem'bəlō), n. (pl. -li) harpsichord.

clavichord (klav'ikawd), n. piano-forte-like mus. instr., preceding pianoforte, with horizontal strings.

clavicle (klav'ikl), n. collar-bone. -cotomy, n. incision through c

-cular (-ik'ūlə); adj. -culate, adj. having c.

clavicytherium (klavisithēr'iəm), n. harpsichord-like mus. instr.

clavier (klav'iə), n. claviature ; any stringed mus. instr. with keyboard.

claviger (klav'ijə), n. club-bearer ; key-keeper or caretaker. -ous, adj.

clavis (klav'is), n. (pl. -ves) key ; glossary.

clavus (klā'vəs), n. (pl. -vi) purple stripe worn on toga by persons of high rank in anct. Rome ; corn (on foot).

claymore (klā'mōr), Scot. n. large double-edged sword ; erron. broadsword with basket hilt.

clearance (klēr'əns), n. Comm., official statement that dues have been paid, and permit to sail or move goods. c. inwards, c. to vessel in port having discharged cargo. c. outwards, c. to vessel about to sail.

clearcole (klēr'kōl), n. mixture of size and whiting.

cledonism (klē'dənizm), n. using circumlocution to avoid speaking words deemed unlucky.

cleek (klēk), n. golf-club with iron head.

cleg (kleg), n. gadfly ; horse-fly.

cleistogamy (klīstog'əmi), n. Bot., self-fertilization without opening of flower. -genous (-oj'inəs), adj. having such flowers. -mous, adj.

clem (klem), dial. v.i. & t. starve. -mmed, adj. famished.

clemency (klem'ənsi), n. mercy ; mildness. -nt, adj.

clepsydra (klep'sidrə), n. water-clock.

clerestory (klēr'stori), n. windowed part of nave wall rising above aisle roof.

clerihew (kler'ihū), n. short nonsensical or satirical poem, gen. of four lines of varying length, and espec. biographical, invented by E. Clerihew Bentley.

cleromancy (klēr'əmansi), n. divination by casting lots. -onomy, n. inheritance.

clevis (klev'is), n. any securing device, U-shaped and with a pin between the extremities.

clew (kloo), n. corner of sail to which ropes are attached ; v.t. haul on c. when changing sail.

cliché (klē'shā), n. trite or hackneyed phrase ; stereotype plate.

climacteric (klīmak'tərik), adj. critical ; forming a turning-point or crisis ; n. turning-point, espec. in life of individual, gen. reckoned at 21, 35, 49, 63 and 81 years of age ; "change of life," menopause. grand c., 63rd or 81st year of life. -al, adj.

climatotherapy (klīmətəther'əpi), n. treatment of disease by living in particular climate. -peutic, adj.

clinamen (klīnā'mən), n. (pl. -mina) bias.

clinical (klin'ikl), adj. pert. to sickbed.

clinocephalic, -lous (klīnəsifal'ik, -sef'ələs), adj. having a saddle-shaped skull. -lus, n. (pl. -li) such person. -ly, n.

clinology (klīnol'əji), n. study of organism's retrograde development after passing maturity. -gic, adj.

clinometer (klīnom'itə), n. instr. measuring angle of slope. -tric (-et'rik), adj. -try, n.

clinquant (kling'kənt), adj. glittering ; showy ; n. tinsel ; meretricious work of art.

clipper (klip'ə), n. fast sailing ship with large sails.

clithridiate (klithrid'iat), adj. keyhole-shaped.

clitoris (klī'təris), n. small erectile, penis-like organ of female, near mouth of vagina. -ritis, n. inflammation of c.

cloaca (klō ā'kə), n. (pl. -ae) sewer ; watercloset ; Zoo., passage or chamber receiving all bodily excretions in birds, reptiles, etc. -l, adj.

cloisonné (klwahzon'ā), n. & adj. (app. to) enamel with colour applied in spaces partitioned off by wires.

cloister (kloi'stə), n. roofed, colonnaded walk with one side open, of monastery, cathedral, etc.; monastery or convent ; v.t. shut up, as in a convent. -tral, adj.

clonic (klon'ik), adj. irregularly spasmodic. -ity (-is'iti), n.

closure (klō'zhūr), n. Parl., motion that "the question be now put" which, if carried, ends debate on subject.

clou (kloo), Fr. n. "nail" ; cynosure.

clough (kluf), n. gully.

clumber (klum′bə), n. short-legged heavy kind of spaniel.

clupeoid (kloo′pioid), n. & adj. (fish) like a herring.

clypeate (klip′iət), adj. shaped like a buckler. -peiform, adj.

clysis (klī′sis), n. Med., washing-out of body cavity.

clysmian (kliz′miən), adj. pert. or due to flood. -mic, adj. cleansing.

clyster (klis′tə), n. Med., rectal liquid injection for relieving constipation or introducing nourishment ; v.t. give c. to.

cnemis (nē′mis), n. shin bone. -mial, adj.

coaction (kōak′shən), n. compulsion. -tive, adj.

coadjument (kōaj′ūmənt), n.mutual aid.

coadjutor (kōaj′ūtə), n. (fem. -trix) helper ; abettor. -tant, adj.

coadjuvant (kōaj′ūvənt), adj. co-operating. -ncy, n.

coadunate (kōad′ūnāt), v.t. combine into one ; (-nət), adj. united. -tion, n. -tive, adj.

coagment (kōagment′), v.t. cement together.

coagulate (kōag′ūlāt), v.i. & t. solidify ; clot. -ant, -lin, n. substance causing coagulation. -lum, n. clot. -tion, n. -tive, adj. causing c.

coalesce (kōəles′), v.i. grow together; combine into one. -nce, n. -nt, adj.

coapt(ate) (kōapt′, -āt), v.t. join or fit together. -ation, n.

coarctate (kōahk′tāt), adj. closely pressed together. -tion, n. constriction.

coati (kōah′ti), n. raccoon-like animal of S. and Cent. Amer.

coaxial (kōaks′iəl), adj. having a common axis. c.cable, cable in which central conductor is surrounded by tubular conductor, the insulation between them being mostly air.

coble (kob′l), n. flat, single-masted N. Sea fishing boat.

cocciferous (koksif′ərəs), adj. bearing berries.

coccus (kok′əs), n. (pl. cocci, kok′si) spherical bacterium.

coccyx (kok′siks), n. bone at base of spinal column. -ygeal (-ij′iəl), adj. pert. to or near c.

cochineal (kochin′ēəl), n. scarlet dye obtained from dried insects.

cochlea (kok′liə), n. (pl. -ae) spirally coiled part of ear. -r, adj. pert. to c. ; spirally shaped. -re (-ār′i), n. Med., spoonful. -riform (-ar′ifawm), adj. spoon-shaped. -te, adj. like a screw or snail's shell.

cockatrice (kok′ətrīs), n. basilisk.

cocket (kok′it), n. official seal ; shipper's clearance ; customs duty.

cocotte (kokot′), Fr. n. flirt ; prostitute ; kind of casserole.

coctile (kok′til, -il), adj. baked.

codex (kō′deks), n. (pl. -dices) collection of anct. MSS., espec. Biblical.

codicil (kod′isil, kō′-), n. clause added to and altering will ; any additional clause or provision. -llary, adj.

codon (kō′don), n. small bell; trumpet mouth.

coefficient (kōifish′ənt), n. contributive force or person ; Math., quantitative expression or number.

coelacanth (sē′ləkanth), n. large, spiny, bony-plated fish—probable link between fishes and amphibious reptiles—believed to have become extinct 60 million years ago, of which live specimens were caught in 1952.

coelanaglyphic (sēlanəglif′ik), adj. pert. to cavo-relievo.

coeliac (sē′liak), adj. pert. to coelom.

coelialgia (sēlial′jiə), n. pain in belly.

coelom (sē′ləm), n. body cavity. -ate (-ō′māt), adj. having a c. -ic, adj.

coemption (kōemp′shən), n. gaining monopoly in a commodity by buying all available supplies ; "cornering." -tor, n. person practising c.

coenaculous (sēnak′ūləs) adj. fond of eating. espec. suppers.

coenaesthesis (sēnesthē′sis), n. Psych., sensation as a whole.

coenotrope (sē′nətrōp), n. Psych., conduct characteristic of a group.

coerce (kō ōs′), v.t. force ; constrain. -cion, n. -cive, adj.

coessential (kōisen′shəl), adj. formed from same substance.

coetaneous (kōitā′niəs), adj. contemporary.

coeval (kō ē′vəl), n. & adj. (person or thing) of same age ; of same length of time.

cogent (kō'jənt), *adj.* compelling; forceful; convincing. **-ncy,** *n.*

cogitate (koj'itāt), *v.i.* & *t.* think deeply; consider seriously. **-table,** *adj.* conceivable. **-tabund,** *adj.* deep in thought. **-tion,** *n.* **-tive,** *adj.* contemplative; having power of thought.

cognate (kog'nāt), *adj.* having same ancestry; closely related; *n.* word of same origin; *Law,* relation on mother's side. **-tion,** *n.* such relationship.

cognisance (kon'izəns, kog'-), *n.* extent of knowledge; notice, *espec.* judicial; awareness; distinctive badge. **-nt,** *adj.* taking notice; having knowledge. **-se,** *v.t.* perceive; take notice of.

cognition (kognish'ən), *n.* mental act of perceiving; knowledge. **-al,** *adj.* **-tive,** *adj.* able to perceive or know.

cognomen (kognō'men), *n.* family name; nickname. **-minal** (-nom'-inəl), *adj.*; *n.* namesake. **-minate,** *v.t.*

cognoscente (kōnyōshen'tā), It. *n.* (*pl.* -ti) connoisseur.

cognovit (kognō'vit), *n. Law,* admission by defendant of justice of plaintiff's case.

cohabit (kōhab'it), *v.i.* live together, *espec.* as man and wife. **-ant,** *n.* person cohabiting. **-ation,** *n.*

cohere (kōhēr'), *v.i.* adhere together; be united or consistent. **-nce,** *n.* **-nt,** *adj.* sensible; intelligible. **-r,** *n. Rad.,* early form of detector, based on an imperfect contact.

cohesion (kōhē'zhən), *n.* force uniting parts; interdependence. **-ive** (-siv), *adj.*

cohibit (kōhib'it), *v.t.* restrain. **-tion,** *n.* **-tive,** *adj.*

cohort (kō'hawt), *n.* company of soldiers, numbering from 300 to 600 in anct. Roman army.

coif (koif, kwof), *n.* close-fitting cap or hood, *espec.* of women; skull cap; any headdress.

coiffeur (kwafə̄'), *n.* (*fem.* -euse, -ə̄z') hair-dresser. **-fure,** *n.* hair-dressing; a manner of dressing the hair.

coign (koin), *n.* corner; angle; viewpoint.

coinstantaneous (kōinstəntā'niəs), *adj.* occurring at same instant. **-eity** (-stantənē'iti), *n.*

coir (koir, kwahr), *n.* fibre obtained from coconut husk.

coition (kōish'n), **-tus** (kōish'n, kō'itəs), *n.* sexual intercourse.

col (kol), *n.* pass between mountain peaks.

colation (kəlā'shn), *n.* filtering.

colchicum (kol'kikəm, -chik-), *n.* meadow saffron; autumn crocus. **-cine** (-sēn), *n.* extract of c. used as specific against gout.

coleopterous (koliop'tərəs), *adj.* pert. to beetles and weevils; having hard anterior wings. **-ran,** *n.* such insect. **-roid,** *adj.* beetle-like. **-rology,** *n.* study of c. insects.

coleslaw (kōl'slaw) *n.* chopped cabbage salad.

colibri (kol'ibrē), Sp. *n.* humming-bird.

colic (kol'ik), *n.* spasmic pain in intestines; *adj.* pert. to colon.

coliform (kol'ifawm, kō'-), *adj.* like a sieve.

colitis (kəlī'tis), *n.* inflammation of colon.

collate (kolāt'), *v.t.* compare closely; classify.

collateral (kəlat'ərəl), *adj.* derived from same main stock but subsidiary; secondary; *n.* such relative or happening. **c.security,** *Comm.,* additional security against loan.

collation (kəlā'shn), *n.* act of collating; bestowal of benefice; contribution; light meal, *espec.* cold. **-tive** (kol'ətiv), *adj.* having power to bestow benefice. **-tor,** *n.*

collectivism (kəlek'tivizm), *n.* theory of communal control of means of production; evolutionary socialism. **-st,** *n.* & *adj.*

collegium (kəlē'jiəm), *n.* managing board or committee.

colletic (kəlet'ik), *n.* & *adj.* adhesive (substance).

colliform (kol'ifawm), *adj.* neck-like.

colligate (kol'igāt), *v.t.* bind together; collate facts for deduction of principle therefrom. **-tion,** *n.*

collimate (kol'imāt), *v.t.* make parallel; adjust into line; adjust line of sight. **-tion,** *n.* **-tor,** *n.* device in optical instr. for adjusting line of sight or producing parallel rays.

collinear (kəlin'iə), *adj.* lying along same line. **-eate,** *v.t.* aim at; place in line with. **-eation,** *n.*

collingual (kəling'gwəl), *adj.* of same language.

collocal (kəlō'kəl), *adj.* in same place.

collocate (kol'əkāt), *v.t.* arrange; place side by side. -tion, *n.* -tive, *adj.*

collocution (koləkū'shn), *n.* conversation. -tor, *n.* speaker in c.

colloid (kol'oid), *n.* & *adj.* jelly-like (substance). -al, *adj.*

colloquy (kol'əkwi), *n.* conversation; dialogue. -quial (kəlō'kwiəl), *adj.* pert. to ordinary speech. -quialism, *n.* non-literary word or phrase; slang; use of such words or phrases. -quise, *v.i.* converse; use colloquialisms.

collusion (kəlōō'zhn), *n.* secret fraudulent agreement. -ive, *adj.*

collutory (kol'ūtəri), *n.* mouthwash.

colluvies (kəlū'viēz), *n.* collection of filth. -ial, *adj.*; *Geol.*, pert. to rocks formed of many kinds of fragments.

collyrium (kəlir'iəm), *n.* (*pl.* -ia) eye wash or ointment; suppository.

colocynth (kol'əsinth), *n.* kind of cucumber forming ingredient of purgative; "bitter apple."

colon (kō'lən), *n.* part of large intestine from caecum to rectum; punctuation mark (:). -ic (-on'ik), *adj.*

colophon (kol'əfən), *n.* device, *espec.* printer's or publisher's emblem, on book; statement at end of book of printer's name and other particulars of publication.

colophony (kəlof'əni), *n.* rosin.

coloratura (kolərətūr'ə; It., kōlōrahtōōr'ə), *n.* & *adj.* highly ornamented, virtuoso (mus. passage); singer, *espec.* soprano, of such music.

colossus (kəlos'əs), *n.* (*pl.* -si) gigantic statue or person. -sal, *adj.*

colostomy (kəlos'təmi), *n.* permanent opening made into colon.

colostrum (kolos'trəm), *n.* mother's first milk. -ral, -ric, -rous, *adj.*

colotomy (kəlot'əmi), *n.* surgical incision into colon.

colporteur (kolpawtə'), *n.* itinerant seller or giver of books, *espec.* religious literature. -tage, *n.*

colubrine (kol'ūbrīn, -in), *adj.* snake-like; cunning. -riform, -roid, *adj.* snake-shaped.

colugo (kəlōō'gō), *n.* flying lemur.

columbaceous (koləmbā'shəs), pert. to pigeons. -barium, *n.* collection of pigeon-holes; cinerarium. -bine, *adj.* like a dove. -boid (-um'boid), *adj.* like a pigeon.

columnist (kol'əmnist, -əmist), *n.* writer of newspaper column.

colure (kol'ūr), *n.* celestial circle intersecting other at poles. **equinoctial c.**, such circle passing through equinoctial points. **solstitial c.**, such circle at right angles to equinoctial c.

colytic (kəlit'ik), *adj.* restraining; antiseptic.

coma (kō'mə), *n.* stupor.

comate (kō'māt), *adj.* hairy.

comatose (kō'matōs), *adj.* pert. to, in or tending to coma.

comburent (kəmbūr'ənt), *adj.* burning; *n.* substance aiding combustion. -rivorous, *adj.* consuming by burning.

comephorous (kəmef'ərəs), *adj.* bearing hair.

comestibles (kəmes'tiblz), *n.pl.* victuals.

comiferous (kəmif'ərəs), *adj.* tufted.

comity (kom'iti), *n.* civility; friendliness.

commatic (kəmat'ik), *adj.* divided into short stanzas or lines; pert. to comma. -tism, *n.*

comme il faut (kom ēl fō'), *Fr.*, "as is necessary"; as it should be; according to good manners; immaculate.

commensal (kəmen'səl), *adj.* living and feeding together; *n.* such organism; symbiont. -ism, -ity, *n.*

commensurable (kəmen'sūrəbl), *adj.* measurable by same standard; proportionate. -ate, *adj.* proportionate; *v.t.* make proportionate. -ation, *n.*

commère (kom'ār), Fr. *n.* gossiping woman; female compère. -rage, *n.* gossip.

commination (kominā'shn), *n.* denunciation; cursing; threatening. -tive (kom'-), -tory (-min'ətəri), *adj.*

comminute (kom'inūt), *v.t.* pulverise. -tion, *n.*

commis (kom'ē), Fr. *n.* agent; deputy; assistant, *espec.* apprentice waiter.

commiserate (kəmiz'ərāt), *v.t.* express sympathy with or pity for. -tion, *n.* -tive, *adj.*

commissar (kom'isah), *n.* former title of a chief of a Russ. government department. **-ial** (-ār'iəl), *adj.* **-iat** (-ār'iət), *n.* army department of food and stores; supply. **-y,** *n.* commissariat chief; deputy; appointee.

commissure (kom'ishoor), *n.* seam; joint; cleft. **-ral,** *adj.*

commodious (kəmō'diəs), *adj.* spacious; convenient.

commodore (kom'ədōr), *n.* commander of squadron; senior captain in shipping line.

commonalty (kom'ənəlti), *n.* common people.

commorant (kom'ərənt), *n.* & *adj.* (person) residing or dwelling. **-ncy,** *n.*

commonition (komənish'n), *n.* warning.

commorient (kəmōr'iənt), *adj.* dying together; *n.* such person.

communiqué (kəmū'nikā), *n.* written communication; dispatch, *espec.* official.

commutation (komūtā'shn), *n.* act of commuting; *Amer.,* issuing of season ticket. **c.ticket,** season ticket.

commutator (kom'ūtātə), *n. Elec.,* device transforming alternating current produced by dynamo into direct current, *espec.* segmented drum bearing brushes which collect the current.

commute (kəmūt'), *v.t.* exchange *espec.* for something less, or many small amounts for one large amount; substitute a lighter penalty for. **-r,** *Amer. n.* season ticket holder.

comose (kō'mōs), *adj.* with tuft of hair. **-moid,** *adj.* like a tuft of hair. **-mous,** *adj.* hairy.

compaternity (kompətə'niti), *n.* relationship in spirit between godparents, and between them and actual parents.

compatible (kəmpat'ibl), *adj.* in agreement, accordance or proportion. **-bility,** *n.*

compatriot (kompat'riət, -pāt'-), *n.* fellow-countryman.

compeer (kom'pēr), *n.* equal; peer.

compellation (kompəlā'shn), *n.* calling upon by name; manner in which person is addressed. **-tive** -(-el'ətiv), *adj.* ; *n.* name by which person is addressed.

compendium (kəmpen'diəm), *n.* (*pl.* **-ia**) summary; epitome. **-ious,** *adj.* containing much in small space.

complaisant (kom'plizənt, -ant'; kəmplā'zənt), *adj.* obliging; desirous of pleasing. **-nce,** *n.*

complanate (kom'plənət), *adj.* level. **-tion,** *n.* act of levelling.

complement (kom'plimənt), *n.* full number or amount; addition that makes up full number; one of two equal things that complete each other; *Gram.,* addition to complete a predicate; *v.t.* complete. **-al, -ary,** *adj.*

completory (kəmplē'təri), *n.* compline.

complin(e) (kom'plin), *n. R.C.,* last service or prayer of day.

complot (kom'plot), *n.* plot; conspiracy; *v.i.* & *t.* plot; conspire.

composite (kom'pəzit), *n.* & *adj.* (thing) composed of a number of parts; compound. **-tive** (-poz'-itiv), *adj.* synthetic.

compos mentis (kom'pəs men'tis), *Lat.,* sane. **non c. m.,** insane; not responsible for actions.

compossible (kəmpos'ibl), *adj.* able to coexist or coincide with other thing.

compost (kom'post, -ōst), *n.* fertilising mixture; *v.t.* give c. to; mix to form a c.

compotation (kompətā'shn), *n.* drinking-party. **-tor,** *n.* **-tory,** *adj.*

compôte (kom'pōt), *n.* mixed fruit with syrup; mixed savoury dish. **-tier** (kawṅpō'tiā), *Fr. n.* dish for c.

comprador(e) (kom'prədōr), *n.* Ind. native major-domo; Chinese native agent or manager.

comprecation (komprikā'shn), *n.* prayer meeting.

compte rendu (cawṅt rahṅ'dü), *Fr.,* "account rendered"; report.

compunction (kəmpungk'shn), *n.* remorse; regret. **-tious,** *adj.*

compurgation (kompəgā'shn), *n.* vindication. **-tory,** *adj.*

con amore (kon amōr'i), *It.,* "with love"; with enthusiasm.

conarium (kənār'iəm), *n.* pineal gland. **-ial,** *adj.*

conation (kənā'shn), *n.* mental striving. **-tive** (kon'ətiv), *adj.* ; *Gram.,* expressing endeavour.

concamerated (konkam'ərātid), *adj.* divided into chambers. **-tion,** *n.* vaulting; vaulted roof.

concatenate (konkat'ināt), *v.t.* link together; form into series; *adj.* linked together. **-tion**, *n.* chain; sequence; series.

concave (kong'kāv), *adj.* curving inwards; hollow. **-vity** (-av'iti), *n.*

concavo-convex (kongkā'vō-kon'-veks), *adj.* with one side concave and other convex. **-concave**, *adj.* concave on both sides.

concentric (konsen'trik), *adj.* having a common centre. **-ity** (-is'iti), *n.*

concept (kon'sept), *n. Psych.*, idea, *espec.* one comprehending all its associations; mental image. **-ual**, *adj.* **-ualism**, *n.* phil. theory that universal truths exist as mental concepts.

concertante (konchātahn'tā), *adj. Mus.*, exhibiting or needing great skill and brilliancy; virtuoso; *n.* concerto for more than one soloist.

concerto (konchār'tō), *n.* mus. composition for soloist and orchestra. **c.grosso**, c. for more than one soloist.

conch (kongk, konch), *n. (pl. -s, -es)* spiral shell. **-ate**, **-ic**, *adj.* having a c. **-iferous**, *adj.* bearing a c. **-iform**, *adj.* shell-shaped. **-itic**, *adj.* containing shells. **-itis**, *n.* inflammation of external ear. **-oid**, *adj.* shell-like; *n.* simple curve. **-ology**, *n.* study of shells.

conchyliated (kongkil'iātid), *adj.* obtained from molluscs. **-liferous**, *adj.* bearing a shell.

concierge (kawn'siārzh), Fr. *n.* doorkeeper; caretaker.

conciliabule (konsil'iabūl), *n.* secret meeting of plotters.

conciliar (konsil'ia), *adj.* pert. to council.

concinnate (konsin'āt), *adj.* harmonious; fit; elegant. **-nity**, *n.*

concision (konsizh'n), *n.* division; schism.

conclamation (konkləmā'shn), *n.* shouting together. **-mant** (-klā'mənt), *adj.*

conclave (kong'klāv), *n.* meeting, *espec.* secret or solemn; R.C., meeting of cardinals for election of pope; rooms in which such meeting is held.

concolorate (konkul'ərāt), *adj.* having same colour on both sides.

concomitant (konkom'itant), *n. & adj.* accompanying (thing or circumstance). **-nce**, *n.*; R.C.,

existence of both body and blood of Christ in one element of Eucharist. **-ncy**, *n.*

concordance (kankaw'dəns), *n.* index of words, *espec.* of Bible.

concordat (konkaw'dat), *n.* amicable agreement; treaty.

concordia discors (konkaw'dia dis'-kaws), *Lat.*, "discordant concord"; armed truce.

concours d'élégance (kawn'kōōr dā'lāgahns), *Fr.*, "meeting of elegance"; competition or rally with prizes for neatness, beauty, etc., *espec.* of motor cars.

concresce (kankres'), *v.i.* grow together; coalesce. **-nce**, *n.* **-rement** (kon'-), *n.* concretion.

concrete (konkrēt'), *v.i.* solidify; coalesce. **-tion**, *n.* mass formed by coalescence; stone-like formation in bodily organ. **-tionary**, **-tive**, *adj.*

concubine (kong'kūbin), *n.* woman living with man without marriage; mistress. **-nage** (-kū'binij), *n.* **nal**, **-nary**, *adj.*

concubitant (kankū'bitənt), *adj.* marriageable. **-ncy**, *n.* **-tous**, *adj.* **-tus**, *n.* coition.

concupiscent (kankū'pisənt), *adj.* having strong sexual desires. **-nce**, *n.* lust.

condign (kəndīn'), *adj.* deserved; adequate; appropriate.

condominium (kondəmin'iəm), *n.* joint rule by two states or persons. **-nate** (-dom'ināt), *adj.*

condottiere (kondotiār'ā), It. *n.* **(pl. -ri)** mercenary soldier; captain of mercenary band.

conductitious (konduktish'əs), *adj.* hired; for hire.

conduit (kun'dit, kon'-, -dwit), *n.* channel for liquid, *espec.* water supply; channel or tube for elec. wire.

condyle (kon'dīl), *n.* knuckle-like prominence at end of bone. **-lar** (-ilə), *adj.* **-loid**, *adj.* near or shaped like c.

confelicity (konfilis'iti), *n.* pleasure in others' happiness.

conferva (konfʉ'və), *n.* greenish algae on surface of stagnant water. **-l**, **-void**, **-vous**, *adj.*

confidant (konfidant'), *n. (fem. -te)* confidential friend.

configuration (kənfigūrā'shn), *n.* general outline or appearance. **-al**, **-rate**, **-tive**, *adj.*

confiteor (kənfit'iōr), *Lat.*, "I confess"; prayer confessing sins.

confluent (kon'flooənt), *adj.* flowing together; combining; *n.* such stream. **-nce, -ux,** *n.*

confrère (kon'frār; Fr. kawṅ'frār), *n.* colleague; associate; fellow.

confute (kənfūt'), *v.t.* prove to be wrong; overcome in argument. **-tation** (kon-), *n.*

congé (kawṅ'zhā), Fr. *n.* leave, *espec.* to go; dismissal; bow. **c. d'élire** (-dā́lēr'), permission to elect.

congee (kon'jē), *n.* congé; Anglo-Ind., conjee.

congelation (konjilā'shn), *n.* act or state of freezing solid.

congener (kon'jinə), *n.* person or thing of same kind. **-acy** (-jen'-ərəsi), *n.* **-ic** (-er'ik), **-ous** (-jen'-ərəs), *adj.*

congenetic (konjinet'ik), *adj.* having common origin.

congenital (kənjen'itəl), *adj.* existing at or dating from birth.

congeries (kənjer'iēz), *n.* conglomeration; heap or mess.

conglobate (kənglō'bāt), *adj.* ball-shaped; *v.i. & t.* form or be formed into a ball-shaped mass. **-tion,** *n.*

conglobulate (kənglob'ūlāt), *v.t.* form into a ball. **-tion,** *n.*

conglomerate (kənglom'ərāt), *n. Geol.,* rock formed of rounded fragments; anything composed of particles from diverse sources; *v.t.* form into mass or ball; (-ət), *adj.* formed into a mass; concentrated. **-tion,** *n.*

conglutinate (konglōō'tināt), *v.t.* join together; glue; (-ət), *adj.* stuck together. **-ant,** *n. & adj.* glueing or healing (substance). **-tion,** *n.* **-tive,** *adj.*

congou (kong'gōō), *n.* kind of black China tea.

congruent, -uous (kong'grooənt, -əs), *adj.* in agreement or correspondence; *Geom.,* exactly coincident. **-nce, -uity** (-ōō'iti), *n.*

conic (kon'ik), *adj.* pert. to cone. **c.section,** *Math.,* curve formed by intersection of plane and right circular cone. **-s,** *n.* study of c. sections.

conicopoly (konikop'əli), Anglo-Ind. *n.* S.E. Ind. native clerk.

conifer (kō'nifə), *n.* cone-bearing

tree. **-fication,** *n.* making or becoming cone-shaped, tapering or pyramidal. **-form,** *adj.* cone-shaped. **-ous** (-if'ərəs), *adj.*

conjee (kon'jē), Anglo-Ind. *n.* liquid of boiled rice. **c.house,** mil. prison or guard-room.

conjugal (kon'joogəl), *adj.* pert. to marriage. **-gacy,** *n.* **-gate,** *v.i. & t.* conjoin; *Gram.,* name inflections of verb; *adj. Bot.,* paired. **-gation,** *n. Biol.,* union of cells in reproduction; *Gram.,* group of verbs with same inflections. **-gative,** *adj.*

conjunction (kənjungk'shn), *n.* joining together; coincidence; *Gram.,* word used to connect words, phrases or sentences; *Astron.,* position of heavenly body when its longitude is same as another's. **-al, -tive,** *adj.*

conjunctiva (konjungktī'və), *n.* membrane lining eyelid and joining it with eyeball. **-l,** *adj.* **-vitis,** *n.* inflammation of c.

connate (kon'āt), *adj.* congenital; joined together from birth. **-tal,** *adj.* **-tion,** *n.* **-tural,** *adj.* congenital; having same nature.

connive (kənīv'), *v.i.* permit tacitly; wink (at). **-vance,** *n.*

connote (kənōt'), *v.t.* imply; suggest. **-tation,** *n.* **-tative,** *adj.*

connubial (kənū'biəl), *adj.* pert. to marriage. **-ity,** *n.*

connumerate (kənū'mərāt), *v.t.* count together. **-tion,** *n.*

conoid (kon'oid), *n. & adj.* somewhat conical (object). **-al,** *adj.*

conquistador (konkwis'tədōr), *n.* conqueror, *espec.* Sp. conqueror of Cent. and S. Amer.

consanguinity (konsanggwin'iti), *n.* blood-relationship. **-neal, -neous,** *adj.*

consecution (konsikū'shn), *n.* logical advance in argument; sequence. **-tive** (-ek'ūtiv), *adj.* following in uninterrupted or logical order.

consenescence (konsines'əns), *n.* growing old together.

consensus (kənsen'səs), *n.* harmony; agreement; unanimity; general trend. **-sion,** *n.* unanimity. **-sual,** *adj.* based on agreement only.

consentaneous (konsentā'niəs), *adj.* agreeing; unanimous; suitable. **-eity** (-ənē'iti), *n.*

consentient (kənsen'shənt), *adj.* agreeing; unanimous. **-nce,** *n.*

conservatoire, -tory, -torium (konsō'vətwah, -ō'vətəri, -tōr'iəm), n. school of music and elocution.

consignificant (konsignif'ikənt), adj. synonymous; meaningless unless used with another word. -cation, n. meaning in context. -ly, v.t.

consilient (konsil'iənt), adj. agreeing in inferences drawn from different premises. -nce, n.

consistory (kənsis'təri), n. council chamber; papal senate; eccl. court; adj. pert. to a c. -rial (-ōr'iəl), adj.

consociate (konsō'shiāt), v.i. & t. associate; ally; unite; adj. associated; n. associate. -tion, n. -tive, adj.

Consols (kon'solz), n.pl. abbr. of consolidated annuities; Brit. funded government securities.

consonance (kon'sənəns), n. agreement; harmony. -ant, -nous, adj. -ate, v.t. sound in harmony.

consortium (konsaw'shiəm), n. (pl. -tia) partnership; association; cartel.

conspecies (konspē'shēz), n. species belonging to same genus; variety. -cific (-spisif'ik), adj. belonging to same species.

conspectus (kənspek'təs), n. general view or outline; summary.

conspue (konspū'), v.t. spurn; despise.

constate (kənstāt'), v.t. establish upon positive evidence. -tion, n. -tory, adj.

constringe (kənstrinj'), v.t. cause to contract; constrict. -nt, adj. -ncy, n.

construe (kənstrōō), v.t. translate; interpret; analyse grammatically in order to explain meaning.

consubstantial (konsəbstan'shəl), adj. having or formed from same substance. -iation, n. presence of Christ's body in Holy Communion bread and wine. -ity, n. -tive, adj.

consuetude (kon'switūd), n. established custom. -dinal, adj. -dinary, adj.; n. book of customs and laws of an association, espec. of monastic life.

consummate (kənsum'ət), adj. perfect; entirely complete; (kon'səmāt), v.i. & t. complete; fulfil; be or reach culmination. -tion, -tor, n. -tive, -tory, adj.

contabescent (kontəbes'ənt), adj. wasting away. -nce, n.

contadino (kontadē'nō), It. n. (pl. -ni; fem. -na, pl. -ne) peasant.

contagion (kəntā'jən), n. transmission of disease by contact; disease so transmitted; diseasetransmitting agent; polluting influence. -gious, adj.

contango (kontang'gō), n. Comm. charge paid by purchaser for postponing payment from one settling day to next; v.i. permit such postponement. c.day, the day, second before settling day, on which such arrangements are made.

conte (kawnt), Fr. n. short story. c. pieux (-pēō'), moral story. -ur (-ər'), writer of c.

contect (kəntekt'), v.t. cover. -ion, n.

contemn (kəntem'), v.t. treat with contempt; scorn. -er, -or (-em'ə, -em'nə), n.

contemporaneous (kəntemporā'niəs), adj. existing at same time. -neity (-ənē'iti), n. -rary (-em'pərəri), adj. of same or present time; n. such person; living person; newspaper, etc., published at present day. -rise, v.t. cause to occur at same time.

contention (kənten'shn), n. quarrel; strife; opinion, belief. -tious, adj. quarrelsome; controversial.

conterminous (kontō'minəs), adj. having common boundary, extent or termination. -nant, adj. ending together. -nate, adj.

context (kon'tekst), n. words or passages immediately preceding and following a word or passage. -ual, adj.

contiguous (kəntig'ūəs), adj. adjacent; touching. -uity, n.

continence (kon'tinəns), n. selfrestraint, espec. sexual. -nt, adj.

contingent (kəntin'jənt), adj. possible; able to take place; accidental; conditional; n. full number of draft of troops. c. liability, Comm., one that may have to be assumed in certain circumstances. -ncy, n. possibility; event that may take place; close relationship.

continuum (kəntin'ūəm), n. (pl. -nua) something that is entirely continuous and homogeneous, and can be described only by reference to other things; something containing one common recognisable factor in a multitude of parts or variations. **space-time c.**, area of four dimensions (three of space, and one of time) in which everything may be determined.

contorniate (kəntaw'niət), *adj.* with groove round edge; *n.* such medallion.

contour (kon'tōōr), *n.* outline; line passing through all places of same altitude. **c.map**, map bearing such lines.

contraband (kon'trəband), *n. & adj.* smuggled (goods); goods which it is forbidden to carry or import. **s. of war**, goods supplied to a belligerent and seizable by another. **absolute c.**, goods of a kind intended for war use only, *e.g.* armaments. **conditional c.**, goods which only become c. of war if specifically intended for war use, *e.g.* food, etc. **-age**, **-ism**, *n.* **-ist**, *n.*

contrabass (kon'trəbās), *n. & adj.* (voice or instr.) one octave lower than bass; double-bass.

contra bonos mores (kon'trə bon'ōs mōr'ēz), *Lat.*, "against good morals"; harmful to public morality.

contraceptive (kontrəsep'tiv), *n. & adj.* preventive of conception. **-tion**, *n.* birth control by use of c.

contractile (kəntrak'tīl), *adj.* able or causing to grow smaller. **-lity** (-il'iti), *n.*

contradistinguish (kontrədisting'-gwish), *v.t.* differentiate by reference to opposites. **-nct**, *adj.* so differentiated. **-nction**, *n.*

contrahent (kon'trəhənt), *n. & adj.* (party) entering into contract.

contra mundum (kon'trə mu'ı'dəm), *Lat.*, "against the world"; in defiance of all accepted belief.

contra pacem (kon'trə pā'sem), *Lat.*, "against the peace."

contrapuntal (kontrəpun'təl), *adj.* pert. to counterpoint. **-tist**, *n.* expert in counterpoint.

contravene (kontrəvēn'), *v.t.* infringe; oppose. **-ntion** (-ven'shn), *n.*

contretemps (kawn'trətahn), Fr. *n.* unlooked-for mishap; awkward situation.

controvert (kon'trəvət'), *v.t.* dispute; doubt. **-rsial**, *adj.* about which

there is dispute. **-rsialist**, *n.* disputer. **-rsy** (kon'-), *n.* dispute.

contubernal (kəntū'bənəl), *n. & adj.* cohabiting (person).

contumacious (kontūmā'shəs), *adj.* obstinate; rebellious. **-cy** (kon'-), *n.* **-ity** (-as'iti), *n.* such act.

contumely (kon'tūmili), *n.* insult; contempt. **-lious**, (-ē'liəs), *adj.*

contuse (kəntūz'), *v.t.* bruise. **-sion**, *n.* **-sive**, *adj.*

conurbation (konəbā'shn), *n.* city surrounded by large number of urban districts.

convection (kənvek'shn), *n.* conveying; movement of particles of fluid due to alterations in density, *espec.* caused by heat. **-tive**, *adj.*

convenances (kawn'vənahns), Fr. *n.pl.* the proprieties; conventions.

conventicle (kənven'tikl), *n.* chapel; meeting-house; nonconformist assembly. **-cular** (-ik'ūlə), *adj.*

conventual (kənven'tūəl), *adj.* pert. to convent; *n.* inmate of convent.

conversant (kon'vəsənt), *adj.* closely acquainted; having deep knowledge. **-nce**, *n.*

conversazione (konvəsatsiō'nā), *n.* (*pl.* -ni) social gathering.

converse (kon'vəs), *n. & adj.* opposite.

convex (kon'veks), *adj.* curving outwards. **-ity**, *n.*

convexo-concave (kənveks'ō-kong'-kāv), *adj.* convex on one side and concave on other. **-convex**, *adj.* convex on both sides.

conveyance (kənvā'əns), *n.* Law, act or document by which title to property is transferred. **-cing**, *n.* **-r**, *n.* lawyer dealing in such business.

convivial (kənviv'iəl), *adj.* pert. to banquet; festive; jolly. **-ity**, *n.* **-ve** (kon'vīv), *n.* fellow-guest at banquet.

convocation (konvəkā'shn), *n.* act of calling together, or assembly of persons; eccl. conference; assembly of graduates of university. **-al**, *adj.*

convolute (kon'vəlōōt), *adj.* spiral; *v.i. & t.* twist; contort. **-tion**, *n.* spiral shape; one coil of spiral.

cony, **-ney** (kō'ni), *n.* rabbit.

co-opt (kō-opt'), *v.t.* make fellow-member. **-ation**, **-ative**, *adj.*

copaiba (kəpī'bə), *n.* kind of oily resin. **-bic**, **-aivic**, *adj.*

ə=*er* in *father*; ɜ=*er* in *pert*; th=*th* in *thin*; dh=*th* in *then*; zh=*s* in *pleasure*; k=*ch* in *lock*; n̈=Fr. nasal *n*; ü=Fr. *u*.

copal (kō'pəl), *n.* kind of resin used in varnishes, etc.

coparcener (kōpah'sinə), *n.* joint heir. **-nary**, *n.* & *adj.*

Copernican (kəpā'nikən), *adj.* pert. to Copernicus, and his theory of the solar system that earth rotates on own axis and revolves round sun.

cophosis (kəfō'sis), *n.* deafness.

copperas (kop'ərəs), *n.* sulphate of iron; green vitriol.

copra (kop'ra), *n.* dried kernels of coconuts yielding coconut oil.

copraemia (koprē'miə), *n.* poisoning resulting from chronic constipation.

coprolalia (koprəlā'liə), use of obscene language. **-c**, *n.* person practising c.

coprolite (kop'rəlīt), *n.* fossilised faeces, *espec.* of fish. **-lith**, *n.* hard mass of faecal matter. **-tic** (-it'ik), *adj.*

coprology (koprol'əji), *n.* study of filth or faeces, or of obscene literature.

coprophagy (koprof'əji), *n.* feeding on dung. **-gan** (-gən), *n.* dung beetle. **-gous** (-gəs), *adj.*

coprophilia (koprəfil'iə), *n.* love of obscenity. **-lous** (-of'iləs), *adj.* living in or feeding on dung.

coprostasis (kopros'təsis), *n.* constipation.

coprozoic (koprəzō'ik), *adj.* living in dung.

Copt (kopt), *n.* Egyptian Christian. **-ic**, *adj.*; *n.* language derived from anct. Egyptian.

copula (kop'ūlə), *n.* link; verb, *espec.* part of *to be*, linking subject and predicate. **-r**, *adj.*

copulate (kop'ūlāt), *v.i.* unite in sexual intercourse. **-tion**, *n.* **-tive**, *adj.*; *Gram.*, app. to conjunctions which join like terms, implying addition and co-ordination. **-tory**, *adj.*

copyhold (kop'ihōld), *n.* tenure of manor land at will of lord of manor; land so held. **-er**, *n.* holder of such land.

coquillage (kōkēyahzh'), Fr. *n.* shell-like decoration.

coquito (kəkē'tō), *n.* Chilean palm yielding sap, seeds and fibre.

coracle (kor'əkl), *n.* light round wicker boat covered with skin.

coram populo (kor'am pop'ūlō),

Lat., "in the presence of the public"; for appearance's sake. **c.judice**, before a judge. **c.paribus**, before one's equals or peers.

corbel (kaw'bl), *n.* supporting projection from wall.

corbiculate (kawbik'ūlət), *adj.* like a small basket; pert. to bee's pollen-holding organ.

cordate (kaw'dāt), *adj.* heart-shaped. **-diform**, *adj.*

Cordelier (kawdəlēr'; Fr., kordel'-yā), *n.* Franciscan monk; member of Fr. revolutionary club.

cordillera (kor ilyar'ə), *n.* main mountain range or system of a continent. **-n**, *adj.*

cordite (kaw'dīt), *n.* smokeless explosive powder compounded of guncotton, nitro-glycerine and vaseline.

cordon bleu (kor'dawn blə'), *Fr.* "blue ribbon."

cordovan (kaw'dəvən), *n.* Cordova leather, orig. of goatskin, later of pig and horse skin.

cordwainer (kawd'wānə), *n.* shoemaker.

coriaceous (koriā'shəs), *adj.* like or consisting of leather.

coriander (korian'də), *n.* plant yielding seeds used in med. and in pickles.

corinne (kərin'), *n.* gazelle.

corkage (kaw'kij), *n.* charge made by hotel keeper for serving bottle of wine, or for consumption in his hotel of bottle purchased elsewhere.

corm (kawm), *n.* swollen bulblike subterranean part of stem, bearing buds. **-el**, *n.* small c. **-oid**, *adj.* like c. **-ophyte**, *n.* plant with stem and root. **-ous**, *adj.* producing c.

cornea (kaw'niə), *n.* transparent horny substance protecting eyeball. **-eous**, *adj.* horny. **-l**, *adj.*

cornelian (kawniē'liən), *n.* carnelian.

cornemuse (kawn'mūz), *n.* anct. bagpipe-like instr.

corniculate (kawnik'ūlət), *adj.* having horns or horn-like outgrowths.

cornific (kawnif'ik), *adj.* producing horn or horns. **-ation**, *n.* **-form**, *adj.* horn-shaped. **-nigerous**, *adj.* bearing horns.

cornucopia (kawnūkō'piə), *n.* (*pl.* **-ae**, **-s**) horn, or source, of plenty; horn-shaped container.

cornute (kaw'nūt), *v.t.* cuckold;

adj. with horn-like outgrowths. -d, adj. horned; horn-shaped.

corolla (kərol'ə), n. the petals of a flower collectively. -ceous, adj.

corollary (kərol'əri), n. fact or proposition that follows naturally from one already proved: result. -rial (-ār'iəl), adj.

corollate (kor'əlāt), adj. having a corolla. -liferous, adj. -liform, -line, adj. shaped like a corolla.

corona (kərō'nə), n. (pl. -ae) coloured ring, due to diffraction, seen round sun or moon; luminous envelope surrounding sun; Phon., tip of tongue.

coronal (kor'ənəl), adj. pert. to corona or crown of head; n. coronet; fillet.

coronach (kor'ənak), Scot. n. dirge.

coronary (kor'ənəri), adj. crown-shaped. c.artery, artery supplying heart tissues with blood. c. thrombosis, formation of clot in c.artery.

coronoid (kor'ənoid), adj. beak-shaped.

corozo (kərō'zō), n. sev. tropical New World palms, espec. ivory palm.

corporal (kaw'pərəl), adj. pert. to body. -ity, n. state of having a body. -ate, adj.

corporeal (kawpōr'iəl), adj. physical; pert. to or having a body; tangible. -ity, -reity, n.

corporify (kawpor'ifi), v.t. embody; solidify. -fication, adj.

corposant (kaw'pəzənt), n. flame-like elec. discharge from ship's masts, steeples, etc., in thundery weather; St. Elmo's fire.

corpus (kaw'pəs), n. (pl. -pora) body, espec. of written works on a certain subject. c.delicti (-dēlik'-tī), basic fact necessary to prove crime to have been committed; erron., body of murdered person. c.vile (-vī'li), worthless thing.

corpuscle (kaw'pusl), n. particle; minute portion or body. -cular (-us'kūlə), adj. -culated, adj. having c. -culous, adj. containing c.

corral (kəral', -ahl'), n. enclosure for horses, cattle, etc.; v.t. drive into a c.

corregidor (kərej'idor), n. Sp. magistrate.

correlate (kor'ilāt), v.i. & t. have or demonstrate close relationship; bring into relation or accord; n. one of two things or propositions that necessitates or implies the other. -tion, n. -tive (-el'ətiv), n. & adj.

correption (kərep'shn), n. shortening in pronunciation.

corrie (kor'i), n. round hollow in hillside.

corrigendum (korijen'dəm), n. (pl. -da) thing to be corrected; erratum.

corrigible (kor'ijibl), adj. capable of correction.

corrivate (kor'ivāt), v.t. make to flow together. -tion, n.

corrobboree, -obo-, -ri (kərob'ərē), n. Austral. aborigines' festivity and dance; any noisy gathering; uproar.

corroborant (kərob'ərənt), n. & adj. Med., tonic.

corroborate (kərob'ərāt), v.t. confirm. -tion, n. -tive, adj.; n. corroborant. -tory, adj.

corsage (kaw'sahzh), n. part of dress over bust; bouquet worn on dress.

corsetier (kōrs'tyā), Fr. n. (fem. -ière, -yār) corset-maker.

cortège (kawtāzh'), n. procession, espec. funeral.

Cortes (kaw'tez), n. Sp. Parliament.

cortex (kaw'teks), n. outer part, rind; grey matter of the brain. -ticate, -ticose, -ticous, adj. having c. or bark. -ticiferous (-tisif'ərəs), adj. forming c. or bark. -ticiform, adj. like bark.

cortinate (kaw'tināt), adj. cobweb-like. -narious, adj.

cortisone (kaw'tizōn), n. hormone, essential to life, secreted by cortex of adrenal glands; synthetic equivalent of this obtained from ox-bile or sisal.

corundum (kərun'dəm), n. exceptionally hard mineral, crystallised alumina, used, when transparent, as gem.

coruscate (kor'əskāt), v.i. sparkle; flash. -ant (-us'kənt), adj. -tion, n.

corvée (kōr'vā), n. exaction of unpaid labour.

corvette (kawvet'), n. flush-decked warship, next below frigate in size; small, fast, submarine-chasing warship.

corvine (kaw'vīn), adj. pert. to or like a crow. -viform, c.-void, adj.

corybant (kor'ibant), n. priest, votary or attendant of Cybele, sanct. goddess of nature. -ic, adj. pert. to wild and noisy rites performed by c.; n. wild, frenzied dance.

corymb (kor'im), n. flat-topped raceme-like inflorescence. -iate, -iform, -ose, -ous, adj. -iferous adj. bearing c.

coryphaeus (korife'əs), n. (pl. -aei) chorus-leader; spokesman. -phée (-fā'), n. leading woman dancer in ballet.

coryza (kərī'zə), n. cold in head.

cosaque (cosahk'), Fr. n. cracker.

cosher, see kosher.

cosmesis (kozmē'sis), n. preservation of bodily beauty, espec. of face. -etic (-et'ik), n. & adj. -etician, n. maker of cosmetics: beauty practitioner. -etology, n. manuf., sale, etc., of cosmetics.

cosmic (koz'mik), adj. pert. to cosmos. c. rays, elec. charged particles of high energy—protons, electrons, mesons, etc.—falling on Earth from outer space.

cosmocracy (kozmok'rəsi), n. government of whole world. -crat, n. ruler over world. -cratic, adj.

cosmogenesis (kozməjen'isis), n. theory of origin of universe. -gony (-mog'əni), n.

cosmopolitan (kozməpol'itən), adj. of all races and regions of world; able to mingle with all races, creeds and classes; n. such person. -ism, n. -te (-op'əlit), n. cosmopolitan person. -tic, adj. -tics, n. world politics. -tism, n.

cosmorama (kozmərah'mə), n. series of views of different parts of world. -mic (-am'ik), adj.

cosmos (koz'mos), n. universe; system of universe; order. -mosophy, n. theory of cosmos. -mosphere, n. material universe. -motellurian, adj. pert. to both heaven and earth. -motheism, n. attribution of divinity to the cosmos; identifying God with world.

cossid (kos'id), Anglo-Ind. n. mounted courier.

costal (kos'təl), adj. pert. to ribs. -ard, n. ribbed variety of apple. -ate, adj. having ribs; ridged. -gia (-al'jiə), n. pain in ribs. -tectomy, n. removal of rib. -tellate, adj. finely ribbed.

costive (kos'tiv), adj. constipated.

coteau (kō'tō), n. (pl. -x) divide between valleys; valley-side.

coterie (kō'təri), n. exclusive set of persons; clique.

coterminous, see conterminous.

cothurnus (kəthə'nəs), n. (pl. -ni) buskin. -nal, -nian, adj. pert. to c. or tragedy. -nate, adj. wearing c.

cotillion, -lon (kətil'yən), n. quadrille-like dance.

cotitular (kōtit'ūlə), n. one of patron saints of a church dedicated to more than one.

cotyledon (kotilē'dən), n. first, embryonic seed leaf of plant. -al, -ary, -ous (-ed'ənəs), adj. -loid, adj cup-shaped.

couchant (kōō'shahń, kow'chənt), adj. lying, espec. with head raised.

cougar (kōō'gah), n. large, brown Amer. wild cat; puma.

coulée, -lee (kōō'lā, -lē), n. steep dry gully; Geol., flow of lava.

coulisse (kōōlēs'), Fr. n. groove, espec. in timber for thing to slide in; back-stage place; lobby.

couloir (kōōl'wahr), Fr. n. deep cleft in mountain; corridor.

coulomb (kōōlom'), n. quantitative unit of elec.: the amount of elec. charge conveyed by current of one amp. in one second. -meter, n. instr. measuring c.

counter-irritant (kown'tə-ir'itənt), n. application or action irritating body surface to relieve internal congestion.

counterpoint (kown'təpoint), n. Mus., melody added to or woven in with another; combining of melodies; mus. composition in which melodies are combined.

counterpoise (kown'təpoiz), n. equal and opposite weight or force; v.t. counterbalance.

counterpole (kown'təpōl), n. exact opposite.

coup (kōō), Fr. n. "stroke"; successful action; stroke of business. c. de grâce (-də grahs'), finishing blow; fatal blow. c. de main (-dəmań), sudden violent onslaught. c.d'essai (-desā'), experiment. c.d'état (-dātah'), sudden action whereby government is changed; short revolution, espec. bloodless. c.d'oeil (-dö'ē), swift survey or glance; what is thus seen. c. de soleil (-də solā'ē), sunstroke. **c. de théâtre** (-də tāah'tr), sudden dramatic or sensational action.

coupé (kōō'pā), *n.* small closed four-wheeled carriage with outside driver's seat; two-door saloon motor car body; moving rapier, in fencing, to other side of opponent's rapier.

courtesan, -zan (kawtizan'), *n.* high-class prostitute.

couscous (koos'koos), *n.* African gruel-like dish.

couturier (kōōtŪr'iā), Fr. *n.* (*fem.* -ière, -iā̄r) dressmaker.

couveuse (kōōvēz'), Fr. *n.* incubator for human infants.

couvre-feu (kōō'vrə-fə̄), Fr. *n.* curfew; scuttle-shaped device for covering fire at curfew.

coverture (kuv'ətŪr), *n. Law,* status of married woman.

covin(e) (kuv'in), *n.* collusion; fraud. **-nous,** *adj.*

cowle (kowl), Anglo-Ind. *n.* written promise or agreement.

cowrie, -ry (kow'ri), *n.* small sea shell used as money in E. Ind. **c.bird,** Ind. weaver bird.

coxalgy, -gia (koks'alji, -al'jiə), *n.* pain in hip. **-gic,** *adj.* **-xitis,** *n.* inflammation of hip joint.

coyote (kī'ōt,-ō'ti), *n.* small N. Amer. wolf; prairie wolf.

coypu (koi'pōō), *n.* S. Amer. webbed-footed rodent, and its fur; nutria.

cozen (kuz'ən), *v.i.* & *t.* cheat. **-age,** *n.*

crachoir (krash'wahr), Fr. *n.* spittoon.

crambo (kram'bō), *n.* game in which a rhyme has to be found to a given word. **dumb c.,** form of c. in which rhyming words are acted in dumb show.

crampon (kram'pon), *n.* boot-spike for climbing ice; spiked grip for carrying blocks of stone, ice, etc.; *Bot.,* aerial root.

cranium (krā'niəm), *n.* skull, *espec.* part enclosing brain. **-ial,** *adj.* **-iate,** *adj.* having a skull. **-iology,** *n.* study of c. **-iometry,** *n.* measurement of c.

crannog (kran'og), *n.* prehistoric Scot. and Ir. lake-dwelling.

cranny (kran'i), Anglo-Ind. *n.* English-writing Bengali clerk; half-caste E. Indian.

crapulent, -lous (krap'Ūlənt, -ləs), *adj.* sick through eating or drinking to excess. **-nce,** *n.*

crasis (krā'sis), *n.* constitution; blending; diphthongisation of two vowels.

crassamentum (krasəmen'təm), *n.* clot of blood.

crassilingual (krasiling'gwəl), *adj.* with thick tongue.

crassitude (kras'itŪd), *n.* coarseness; grossness.

cratometer (krətom'itə), *n.* instr. measuring power of magnification. **-try,** *n.*

creancer (krē'ənsə), *n.* guardian; mentor.

creatic (kriat'ik), *adj.* pert. to flesh or meat. **-tophagous,** *adj.* flesh-eating.

crèche (krāsh), *n.* public nursery.

credence (krē'dəns), *n.* belief; *Eccl.,* small table or sideboard for sacred vessels.

credentials (kriden'shəls), *n.pl.* documents proving identity or honesty; letters of recommendation.

crédit foncier (krā'dē fawn'syā), Fr., "landed credit"; loan on mortgage, repaid in annual instalments. **c.mobilier** (-mōbēl'yā), loan on personal property; banking company for such and other loans.

credo (krē'dō), *n.* creed; belief.

cremnophobia (kremnəfō'biə), *n.* dread of precipices.

crenate (kren'āt), *adj.* scalloped. **-tion. -ture,** *n.*

crenellated (kren'əlātid), *adj.* having battlements. **-tion,** *n.*

crenitic (krinit'ik), *adj.* pert. to mineral springs. **-notherapy,** *n.* med. treatment by mineral springs.

crenulate (kren'Ūlət), *adj.* minutely crenate. **-tion,** *n.*

creole (krē'ōl), *n.* person born in tropical region of European descent, *espec.* descendant of early Fr. or Sp. settlers; half-breed; W. Ind. language or native.

creophagous (krēof'əgəs), *adj.* carnivorous. **-agia** (-ā'jiə), **-gism** (-jizm), **-gy** (-ji), *n.* eating of flesh. **-gist,** *n.*

crepitate (krep'itāt), *v.i.* crackle. **-tant,** *adj.* **-tion, -tus,** *n.*

crepuscular (kripus'kūlə), *adj.* pert. to twilight; appearing or active

at twilight. **-cle, -cule,** *n.* twilight.
-line, *adj.*

crescograph (kres'kəgraf), *n.* instr.
recording plant growth.

cresset (kres'it), *n.* hanging light-
giving brazier.

cretaceous (kritā'shəs), *adj.* pert. to
or like chalk.

cretic (krē'tik) *n.* amphimacer.

cretify (kret'ifi), *v.t.* change into
chalk or lime. **-faction, -fication,** *n.*

cretin (kret'in), *n.* mentally and
physically deficient person, gen.
a large-headed dwarf, whose condition is due to deficient thyroid
secretion. **-ic, -ous,** *adj.* **-ism,** *n.*

Cretism (krē'tizm), *n.* conduct like
that of people of Crete; lying.

crevasse (krivas'), *n.* deep chasm
in glacier.

crewel (kroo'əl), *n.* thin embroidery
worsted. **c.-work,** *n.*

cribriform (krib'rifawm), *adj.* like
a sieve. **-ral, -rose,** *adj.* **-ration,** *n.*
sifting.

cri de coeur (krē də kər'), *Fr.,* "cry
of heart"; deeply-felt, passionate
request or complaint.

crime passionel (krēm pasyŏnel'),
Fr., "crime of passion," *i.e.* due
to love or jealousy.

crimp (krimp), *n.* person luring or
"shanghai-ing" sailors aboard
vessel; *v.t.* so to obtain sailors for
ship. **-age,** *n.* rate paid to c.

crinal (krī'nəl), *adj.* hairy. **-natory,
-nite, -nitory,** *adj.*

crinoid (krī'noid, krin-), *adj.* like a
lily in shape.

crinose (krī'nōs), *adj.* hairy. **-sity,** *n.*

criophore (krī'əfor), *n.* sculptured
figure of man carrying ram.
-osphinx, *n.* sphinx with ram's
head.

crispate (kris'pāt), *adj.* curled;
crisped. **-tion, -ture,** *n.* curling;
shudder.

cristate (kris'tāt), *adj.* bearing
crest. **-tiform,** *adj.* crest-shaped.

criterion (kritēr'iən), *n.* (*pl.* **-ia**)
principle of criticism; standard
with which facts and ideas are
compared.

criticaster (krit'ikastə), *n.* inferior
critic.

critique (kritēk'), *n.* written criticism; review.

croceous (krō'shəs), *adj.* saffron
yellow in colour.

Croesus (krē'səs), *n.* name of

exceedingly rich king of Lydia in
6th cent. **B.C.**; any very rich
person.

Cro-Magnon (krō-man'yawn), *adj.*
app. to a European Stone Age race.

cromlech (krom'lek), *n.* prehistoric
monument, comprising a flat stone
resting horizontally on two vertical stones or circle of stones.

crore (kror), Anglo-Ind. *n.* ten
million, *espec.* of rupees, *i.e.*
100 lacs.

crosier, -oz- (krō'zhiə), *n.* shep-
herd's-crook-like staff borne by
abbot or bishop.

cross-staff (kros'-stahf), *n.* anct.
nautical instr. for taking altitudes.

crotaline (krot'əlin, -īn; krō-), *adj.*
pert. to rattle-snake. **-lic, -liform**
(-al'-), **-loid,** *adj.* like a rattlesnake.

croton (krō'tən), *n.* E. Ind. tree
with seeds yielding an oil used as
purge, etc.

crounotherapy (krōōnəther'əpi), *n.*
med. treatment by mineral waters.

croupier (krōō'piə; *Fr.,* krōōp'yā),
n. collector of stakes at gaming
table.

cruciate (krōō'shiət), *adj.* cross-
shaped or Y-shaped; marked
with cross; *v.t.* mark with cross.
-tion, *n.* torture; cruciate state.

crucible (krōō'sibl), *n.* vessel for
fusing metals; melting-pot; *v.t.*
melt in a c.

crucifer (krōō'sifə), *n.* person bearing cross; cruciferous plant. **-ous**
(-if'ərəs), *adj. Bot.,* app. to mustard
family of plants (brassicas), in
flowers of which four equal-sized
petals are arranged in form of
cross.

cruciform (krōō'sifawm), *adj.* cross-
shaped.

cruentation (krōōentā'shn), *n.* ooz-
ing of blood, *espec.* from dead
body.

cruorin (krōō or'in), *n.* haemoglobin.

crural (krōōr'əl), *adj.* pert. to leg,
espec. thigh.

cruse (krōōz), *n.* small earthenware
pot.

crustacean (krustā'shn), *n.* animal
with hard shell. **-ceology,** *n.* study
of c. **-ceous,** *adj.* having a shell;
like a crust or a crab.

crymodinia (krīmədin'iə), *n.* rheumatism due to cold. **-otherapy,** *n.*
use of cold as med. treatment.

---

cryogen (krī'əjen), *n*. freezing mixture or agent. **-y** (-oj'əni), *n*. refrigeration.

cryolite (krī'əlīt), *n*. aluminium-yielding mineral of Greenland.

cryometer (krīom'itə), *n*. instr. measuring very low temperatures.

cryophorus (krīof'ərəs), *n*. instr. demonstrating freezing of water by its evaporation. **-ric** (-or'ik), *adj*.

cryoscopy (krīos'kəpi), *n*. determination of freezing points. **-pe** (-ōp), *n*. instr. used in c. **-pic** (-op'ik), *adj*.

cryptaesthesia (kriptesthē'zhiə), *n*. clairvoyance. **-etic** (-et'ik), *adj*.

cryptarch (krip'tahk), *n*. secret ruler. **-y**, *n*.

cryptic (krip'tik), *adj*. mysterious; secret; concealing.

crypto- (krip'tō-), *prefix* hidden, secret; *sl. n*. a crypto-Communist, secret member of Communist party or sympathiser with Communism.

cryptodynamic (kriptədīnam'ik), *adj*. having hidden power.

cryptogam (krip'təgam), *n*. non-flowering or non-seeding plant. **-ian, -ic, -ous** (-og'əməs), *adj*.

cryptogenic (kriptəjen'ik), *adj*. of unknown origin. **-netic** (-jinet'ik), *adj*.

cryptogram (krip'təgram), *n*. writing in code. **-grapher**, *n*. writer of or expert on c. **-graphic, -mmatic, -mmic**, *adj*. **-graphy**, *n*.

cryptology (kriptol'əji), *n*. secret language.

cryptonym (krip'tənim), *n*. secret name. **-ous** (-on'iməs), *adj*.

cryptophyte (krip'təfīt), *n*. cryptogam.

cryptorhetic (kriptərē'tik), *adj*. endocrine. **-esis**, *n*.

cryptous (krip'təs), *adj*. cryptic; like a crypt.

cryptozoic (kriptəzō'ik), *adj*. living hidden, or in darkness.

crystallomancy (kris'tələmansi), *n*. telling fortunes by crystal-gazing.

crystic (kris'tik), *adj*. *Geol*. pert. to ice.

crystograph (kris'təgraf), *n*. painting or writing on glass.

ctenoid (tē'noid, ten'-), *adj*. with comb-like edge. **-niform**, *adj*. comb-like.

ctetology (tētol'əji), *n*. biol. study of acquired characteristics.

cubeb (kū'beb), *n*. dried fruit of a pepper plant, used for catarrh.

cubism (kū'bizm), *n*. geometrical style of painting expressing abstract form. **-ist**, *n*.

cubit (kū'Lit), *n*. measure of length (length of forearm), equiv. of 18 in. **-al**, *adj*. pert. to elbow or forearm.

cuckold (kuk'old), *n*. husband who is ignorant of wife's adultery; *v.t*. make a c. of. **-ry**, *n*.

cuculine (kū'kūlin, -īn), *adj*. pert. to or like a cuckoo. **-iform**, *adj*. like a cuckoo.

cucullate (kū'kəlāt, -kul'ət), *adj*. hooded; hood-shaped. **-liform**, *adj*. hood-shaped.

cuculoid (kū'kūloid), *adj*. like a cuckoo.

cucumiform (kūkū'mifawm), *n*. cucumber-shaped.

cucurbit (kūkə'bit), *n*. gourd-like chem. vessel, main part of still or alembic. **-ine**, *adj*. like gourd seed in shape.

cudbear (kud'bār), *n*. kind of archil.

cui bono? (kū'i bō'nō), *Lat*. "to whose good?"; "to whose profit?"; to what purpose?

cuirass (kwiras'), *n*. armour for breast and back. **-ier** (kūrasēr'), *n*. horse-soldier wearing c.

cuisine (kwēzēn'), Fr. *n*. "kitchen"; cooking; feeding arrangements. **-nary**, *adj*. **-nier** (-nyā), *n*. (*fem*. **-nière, -nyar**) cook.

cul-de-sac (kool-də-sak', kul-; Fr., kü-də-sak'), *n*. (*pl.* .....sacs; Fr., culs.....) blind alley.

culiciform (kūlis'ifawm), *adj*. like a mosquito. **-fuge**, *n*. substance killing mosquitoes.

culinary (kū'linəri), *adj*. pert. to cooking.

cullion (kul'yən), *n*. rascal; orchid root; man orchid.

culm (kulm), *n*. grass stem. **-inal**, *adj*.

culminate (kul'mināt), *v.i*. reach peak or climax; *Astron*., reach meridian; be directly overhead. **-ant**, *adj*. **-tion**, *n*.

culpable (kul'pəbl), *adj*. at fault; criminal. **-bility**, *n*.

culverin (kul'vərin), *n*. kind of anct. small cannon.

culvert (kul'vət), *n*. drain; conduit.

culvertage (kul'vətij), *n*. villeinage.

culvertail (kul'vətāl), *n*. dovetail.

ə=*er* in *father*; ō=*er* in *pert*; th=*th* in *thin*; dh=*th* in *then*; zh=*s* in *pleasure*; k=*ch* in *loch*; ṅ=Fr. nasal *n*; ü=Fr. *u*.

cumbly (kum'bli), Anglo-Ind. *n.* harsh woollen cloth ; blanket.

cum grano salis (kum grā'nō sā'lis), *Lat.*, "with a grain of salt" ; with caution or incredulity.

cummerbund (kum'əbund), *n.* wide sash round waist.

cumshaw (kum'shaw), Chin. *n.* tip ; gratuity.

cumulative (kū'mūlətiv), *adj.* increasing ; growing by successive additions ; gathering strength as it grows ; expressing addition.

cumulus (kū'mūləs), *n.* (*pl.* -li) rounded, flat-based mass of cloud at middle altitude. **-lo-cirrus**, *n.* small c. cloud at great height. **-lo-cirro-stratus**, *n.* thunder cloud. **-lo-stratus**, *n.* c. cloud with stratuslike base.

cumulose (kū'mūlōs), *adj.* containing small heaps. **-lous**, *adj.* pert. to or like cumulus.

cunabular (kūnab'ūlə), *adj.* pert. to cradle or original dwelling ; pert. to incunabula.

cunctation (kungktā'shn), *n.* delay. **-tor**, *n.* procrastinator.

cuneiform (kūnē'ifawm), *adj.* wedge-shaped ; app. to such anct. alphabet and inscriptions. **-eal**, **-eate** (kū'-), *adj.* wedge-shaped.

cunicular (kūnik'ūlə), *adj.* pert. to underground passages or burrows ; burrow-dwelling.

cupel (kū'pəl, -pel'), *n.* small dish, *espec.* of bone ash, or furnace hearth for cupellation. **-lation**, *n.* refining or separating precious metals.

cupidity (kūpid'iti), *n.* avarice.

cupola (kū'pələ), *n.* dome, *espec.* small.

cupping (kup'ing), *n. Med.*, drawing blood by causing partial vacuum over surface of skin. **c.glass**, glass used in c.

cupreous (kū'priəs), *adj.* pert. to or like copper.

cupressineous (kūpresin'iəs), *adj.* pert. to or like the cypress.

cupric (kū'prik), *adj.* app. to compounds of bivalent copper. **-ro-nickel**, *n.* alloy of copper and nickel used for making "silver" and "nickel" coins. **-rous**, *adj.* app. to compounds of univalent copper.

cupulate (kū'pūlāt), *adj.* cup-shaped ; having a cup-shaped appendage. **-liform**, *adj.* cup-shaped.

curacao (kūr'əsō), *n.* Dutch liqueur made from orange peel.

curare (kūrah'ri), *n.* vegetable extract used as arrow poison by S. Amer. Ind.

curassow (kūr'əsō), *n.* turkey-like bird of S. and Cent. America.

curculionid (kəkūlion'id), *n.* snout beetle ; weevil.

curé (kūr'ā), Fr. *n.* parish priest; vicar.

curette (kūret'), *n.* surg. instr. for scraping sides of body cavity ; *v.t.* use a c. **-tage**, *n.* use of a c.

curialism (kūr'iəlizm), *n.* ultramontanism.

curiescopy (kūries'kəpi), *n.* radioscopy with radioactive substance. **-etherapy**, *n.* med. treatment by radium.

curiology (kūriol'əji), *n.* picture-writing. **-gic(al)**, *adj.* **-gics** (-oj'iks), *n.*

curium (kūr'iəm), *n.* one of the transuranic elements.

curratow (kūr'rətō), *n.* fibre from wild pineapple of Brazil.

curricle (kur'ikl), *n.* light two-horse two-wheeled carriage. **-cular** (-ik'ūlə), *adj.* pert. to carriages and driving ; pert. to curriculum.

currier (kur'iə), *n.* leather-dresser.

currycomb (kur'ikōm), *n.* metal comb for grooming horse.

cursive (kə'siv), *adj.* running, flowing ; *n.* script with rounded letters joined together.

cursorial (kəsōr'iəl), *adj.* used for walking or running **-rious**, *adj.*

cursory (kə'səri), *adj.* quick ; superficial.

curtal (kə'tl), *adj.* short ; curtailed ; *n.* person wearing short garment ; animal with docked tail.

curtate (kə'tāt), *adj.* shortened ; short. **c.distance**, *Astron.*, distance of heavenly body from sun or earth in ecliptic plane. **-tion**, *n.* difference between c. distance and true distance.

curtilage (kə'tilij), *n.* courtyard ; land attached to house.

curucucu (kōōr ōōkōō'kōō), *n.* bushmaster.

curule (kūr'ōōl), *adj.* app. to curved-legged chair occupied by high officials of anct. Rome. **c.leg**, outward curving furniture leg.

curvet (kō'vit), *n.* & *v.i.* leap; bound; leap of trained horse with forelegs first raised, immediately followed by raising of hind legs.

curvilinear (kōvilin'iə), *adj.* pert. to or within curved lines.

curvulate (kə'vūlāt), *adj.* slightly curved.

cushat (kush'ət, koosh'-), *n.* wood-pigeon or ring-dove.

cush-cush (koosh'-koosh), *n.* kind of yam.

cusp (kusp), *n.* prominence; crown of tooth; sharp point. **-al**, *adj.* **-ate**, *adj.* having cusps. **-id**, *n.* canine tooth. **-idal**, *adj.* **-idate**, *adj.* coming to a point.

cuspidor (kus'pidor), Amer. *n.* spittoon.

custodian (kustō'diən), *n.* keeper; warden. **-ial**, *adj.* **-iam**, *n.* grant of crown lands.

custos morum (kus'tos mōr'əm), *Lat.*, "keeper of morals"; censor. **c.rotulorum**, keeper of the rolls. **c.sigilli**, keeper of great seal.

cutaneous (kūtā'niəs), *adj.* pert. to the skin, *espec.* its surface.

cutcha, *see* **kutcha**.

cutchery, **-rry** (kuch'əri, -er'i), Anglo-Ind. *n.* office; court-house.

cuticle (kū'tikl), *n.* epidermis; hardened epidermis round nail. **-cular** (-ik'ūlə), *adj.* **-culate**, *adj.* having c. **-tification**, *n.* formation of c. **-tigeral**, *adj.* skin-bearing.

cutis anserina (kū'tis ansərī'nə), *Lat.*, "goose-flesh."

cuvée (kü'vā), Fr. *n.* vintage.

cyaneous (siā'niəs), *adj.* sky-blue.

cyanometer (siənom'itə), *n.* instr. measuring blueness. **-tric** (-et'rik), *adj.* **-try**, *n.*

cyanopathy (siənop'əthi), *n.* cyanosis. **-thic** (-ath'ik), *adj.*

cyanosis (siənō'sis), *n.* heart condition or disease causing blueness of surface of body; blue disease. **-otic** (-ot'ik), *adj.*

cyanotype (siən'ətip), *n.* blue-print.

cyathiform (siath'ifawm, si'əth-), *adj.* cup-shaped.

cybernetics (sībənet'iks), *n.* comparative study of control and communication in living organisms and machines.

cyclarthrosis (siklanthrō'sis), *n.* (*pl.* **-ses**) pivot joint. **-odial**, *adj.*

cyclitis (sikli'tis), *n.* inflammation of ciliary muscle.

cyclometer (siklom'itə), *n.* instr. measuring arcs of circles or revolutions of bicycle wheel.

cyclone (si'klōn), *n.* any storm in which wind is rotary; *Meteor.*, area of low pressure into which winds flow in anti-clockwise direction in N. hemisphere; hurricane; typhoon; *erron.* tornado. **-nic** (-on'ik), *adj.* **-nology**, *n.* study of c. **-noscope**, *n.* instr. determining c.'s centre.

Cyclopean (siklō'piən, -əpē'ən), *adj.* pert. to the Cyclopes, a myth. race of one-eyed giants; gigantic; having one median eye.

cyclophoria (sikləfor'iə, sik-), *n.* squint due to weakness of an eye muscle.

cycloplegia (sikləplē'jiə, sik-), *n.* paralysis of ciliary muscle. **-gic** (-ē'jik, -ej'ik), *adj.*

cyclorama (siklərah'mə), *n.* circular panorama surrounding spectator; curved backcloth of stage used to indicate vast spaces. **-mic** (-am'ik), *adj.*

cyclostyle (sik'ləstil), *n.* apparatus for printing copies from a handwritten stencil.

cyclothymia (sikləthi'miə, sik-), *n.* mental condition of alternating moods of extreme gaiety and depression. **-me**, *n.* person having such moods. **-imic** (-im'ik), *adj.*

cyclotomy (siklot'əmi, sik-), *n.* incision into ciliary muscle. **-me** (sik'lətōm, sik'-), *n.* instr. used in c. **-mic** (-om'ik), *adj.*

cyclotron (sik'lətron), *n.* apparatus in which ions are accelerated to high energies for bombarding atomic nuclei in nuclear fission processes.

cyesis (si ē'sis), *n.* pregnancy. **-siology**, *n.* med. study of c.

cygnet (sig'nit), *n.* young swan. **-neous**, *adj.* swan-like.

cyllosis (silō'sis), *n.* (*pl.* **-ses**) congenital deformity, *espec.* clubfoot.

cymaphen (si'məfen), *n.* telephone receiver.

cymbiform (sim'bifawm), *adj.* boat-shaped. **-bate**, *adj.* **-bocephalic**, **-lous**, *adj.* having head with forehead receding and back projecting.

cyme (sim), *n.* inflorescence in which axes end in single flower only, *e.g.* phlox. **-miferous**, *adj.* producing c.

cymograph (sī'məgraf), *n.* instr. for tracing outlines of projections, profiles, etc.

cymoid (sī'moid), *adj.* like a cyme.

cymometer (sīnom'itə), *n.* instr. measuring frequency of electric waves. **-oscope**, *n.* instr. detecting elec. waves.

cymose (sī'mōs), *adj.* cymoid. **-mous**, *adj.*

Cymric (kim'rik), *adj.* Welsh. **-ru**, *n.* Wales.

cymule (sī'mūl), *n.* small cyme.

cynanche (sinang'ki), *n.* any inflammatory disease of throat, etc.

cynanthropy (sinan'thrəpi), *n.* form of insanity in which patient imagines himself to be a dog.

cynarctomachy (sinahktom'əki), *n.* bear-baiting with dogs.

cynegetics (sinijet'iks), *n.* hunting.

cyniatrics (siniat'riks), *n.* study of canine diseases.

cynocephalous, -lic (sinəsef'ələs, -sifal'ik ; si-,, *adj.* having dog-like head or face. **-lus**, *n.* flying lemur ; myth. ape with dog's head.

cynoid (sī'noid, sin'-), *adj.* dog-like. **-nopodous**, *adj.* having dog-like claws. **-norrhodon**, *n.* dog-rose.

cynosure (sin'əshoor, sī'- ; -zhoor), *n.* guiding star ; object of common interest. **-ral**, *adj.*

cyphonism (sī'fənizm), *n.* pillorying as punishment.

cyprian (sip'riən), *adj.* lecherous ; *n.* prostitute.

cyprine (sip'rīn, -in), *adj.* pert. to the cypress.

cyprinoid (sip'rinoid, -ī'noid), *adj.* pert. to or like a carp.

cypseline (sip'silīn, in), *adj* pert. to or like a swift. **-loi**, *adj.*

cyst (sist), *n.* sac-like outgrowth containing fluid or semi-fluid matter ; capsule ; vesicle. **-al, -ic**, *adj.* **-itis**, *n.* inflammation of bladder. **-oid**, *adj.* like a bladder. **-olith**, *n.* stone in the bladder. **-ology**, *n.* study of c. **-oscope**, *n.* instr. for examining bladder. **-ose, -ous**, *adj.*

Cytherean (sidhərē'ən), *adj.* pert. to Venus ; *n.* votary of Venus.

cytitis (siti'tis), *n.* inflammation of skin.

cytoblast (sī'təblast), *n. Biol.,* cell nucleus. **-oderm**, *n.* cell wall. **-ogamy**, *n.* cell conjugation. **-ogenous**, *adj.* cell-producing. **-oid**, *adj.* cell-like. **-ology**, *n.* study of cells. **-olysis**, *n.* dissolution of cells. **-ophagy**, *n.* phagocytosis. **-oplasm**, *n.* substance of cell excluding nucleus. **-osome**, *n.* body of cell excluding nucleus.

czardas (shah'dash), *n.* a Hungarian dance that increases in speed.

czigany (chēgah'ni), Hung. *n.* gypsy.

D

dabchick (dab'chik), *n.* little grebe.

da capo (dah kah'pō), *It.,* "from the beginning" ; *Mus.,* instruction to repeat from start (*abbr.* D.C.)

dacoit (dəkoit'), *n.* brigand of India and Burma. **-age, -y**, *n.* robbery by d. or by a gang.

dacryops (dak'riops), *n.* wateriness of eye.

dactyl (dak'til), *n.* metrical foot comprising one long followed by two short syllables ; *Zoo.,* digit. **-ate**, *adj.* like a finger. **-ic**, *adj.* ; *n.* verse of dactyls.

dactylioglyph (daktil'iəglif), *n.* engraver of gems, *espec.* for rings. **-ic**, *adj.* **-liography**, *n.* study of gem engraving. **-liology**, *n.* study of finger-rings.

dactylitis (daktilī'tis), *n.* inflammation of fingers and toes.

dactylogram (daktil'əgram), *n.* finger-print. **-graphy**, *n.* study of finger-prints.

dactyloid (dak'tiloid), *adj.* like a finger.

dactylology (daktilol'əji), *n.* sign language ; deaf and dumb language.

dactylomegaly (daktiləmeg'əli), *n.* abnormal largeness of fingers and toes.

dactylonomy (daktilon'əmi), *n.* counting on the fingers.

dactyloscopy (daktilos'kəpi), *n.* comparison of finger-prints for identification.

daedal (dē'dəl), *adj.* complicated ; showing or needing skill ; artistic ; variegated. **-ian** (-ā'liən), *-ic* (-al'ik), *adj.* pert. to Daedalus, in Gr. myth., designer of the labyrinth of Crete and inventor of flying wings ; skilful ; ingenious ; labyrinthine. -ist, n. aviator.

daemon (dē'mən), n. inward spirit ; personality ; genius. -ic (-on'ik), adj.

dagoba, -aba (dagō'bə, -ā'bə ; dah'gəbə), n. shrine holding Buddhist relics.

daguerreotype (dəger'ətĭp), n. early 19th-cent. kind of photograph invented by L. J. M. Daguerre.

dahabeeyah, -beah (dahhabē'yah), n. sailing house-boat of Nile.

Dail Eireann (doil ār'in ; Ir., dhawl yār'ən), Ir., lower house of Irish parliament.

daimon (dī'mən), n. daemon.

dairi (dīr'ē), Jap. n. mikado and his court.

dak, see dawk.

dalmatic (dalmat'ik), n. kind of outer eccl. vestment ; similar vestment worn by king at coronation.

dalton (dawl'tən), n. unit of mass, equiv. of one-sixteenth of mass of oxygen atom.

daman (dam'an), n. small herbivorous animal of Palestine, called cony in O.T.

damascene, -skeen (daməsēn', -skēn'), v.t. ornament (metal) with wavy patterns ; adj. pert. to such art or to damask. d.blade, sword made in Damascus or ornamented with damascening.

damassé (dam'əsā), Fr. n. & adj. (fabric) with damask-like weave. -sin, n. damask with patterns in gold or silver.

damier (dam'yā), Fr. n. large-squared pattern.

damine (dā'mĭn, -in), adj. like a f. llow deer or its antlers.

dammer (dam'ah), n. kauri gum ; sev. other resins from Austral. and E. Ind. trees.

damnosa hereditas (damnō'sə hered'itas), Lat., "burdensome inheritance."

damnum fatale (dam'nəm fətā'li), Lat., Law, loss resulting from act of God.

dapicho, -co (dap'ichō, -kō), n. kind of S. Amer. rubber.

dapifer (dap'ifə), n. bearer of meat to table ; steward.

dargah, see durgah.

darnel (dah'nəl), n. tall, awned grass, a weed of corn-fields.

dartre (dah'tə), n. any eczema-like skin disease. -rous, adj.

darwan (dəwahn'), Anglo-Ind. n. doorkeeper.

dashpot (dash'pot), n. shock-resisting device, using air or liquid.

dastur, see dustoor.

dasypoedes (dasipē'dēz), n.pl. birds having downy young. -dal, -dic, adj. -phyllous, adj. with thick or downy leaves.

dasyure (das'iūr), n. small, marten-like Austral. marsupial.

dation (dā'shn), n. act of giving ; conferment.

dative (dā'tiv), adj. Gram., signifying indirect object or giving to ; Law, capable of being given ; dismissible ; n. such gram. case. -val (-ī'vəl), adj.

dato, -tto (dah'tō), n. Malay tribal chieftain.

datum (dā'təm), n. (pl. -ta) known or accepted fact used as basis for argument, etc. ; point, line, position, etc., in relation to which others are fixed, espec. low-water level.

datura (datūr'ə), n. narcotic, poisonous weed of nightshade family, of India and other countries ; jimson weed. -rism, n. d. poisoning.

dauphin (daw'fin ; Fr., dō'faṅ), n. French king's eldest son. -e (-ēn), -ess, n. d.'s wife.

davenport (dav'ənpawt), n. small writing table ; Amer., sort of settee, espec. convertible into bed.

davit (dav'it), n. ship's small crane, espec. for lowering boats.

dawk (dawk), Anglo-Ind. n. relay system for post or transport ; post. d.boat, mail boat. d.bungalow, rest-house for travellers.

D.D.T., abbr. of dichlor-diphenil-trichlorethane, a powerful insecticide.

de aequitate (dē ekwitā'ti), Lat., "by equity" ; by justice if not by right.

dealate (dē ā'lāt), v.t. rob or divest of wings. -tion, n.

dealbation (dēalbā'shn), n. whitening.

deambulatory (dēam'būlətəri), n. ambulatory ; adj. wandering.

deassimilation (dēəsimilā'shn), n. catabolism.

débâcle (dābah'kl), Fr. n. complete

rout or failure; stampede; ice-break; flood.

debarrass (dibar'əs), *v.t.* disembarrass.

debauch (dibawch'), *v.t.* seduce; *n.* orgy. **-ed** (-osht'), *adj.* dissolute. **-ee**, *n.* libertine. **-ery**, *n.* sensual indulgence; drunkenness. **-ment**, *n.* act of debauching.

debellate (dibel'āt), *v.t.* conquer. **-tion**, **-tor**, *n.*

debenture (diben'tūr), *n.* official certificate of right to receive payment; bond; any company security other than shares. d.stock, class of shares, holders of which are guaranteed repayment but cannot demand it until default or winding up of company.

debility (dibil'iti), *n.* weakness. **-tant**, *n.* (substance) reducing energy or excitement. **-tate**, *v.t.* weaken. **-tation**, *n.* **-tative**, *adj.*

debonair(e), **-nnaire** (debənār'), *adj.* urbane; genial; jaunty.

debouch (dibōōsh'), *v.i.* issue into open place; *n.* outlet. **-ment**, *n.* act of debouching; river mouth.

debris, **dé-** (deb'rē), *n.* broken or burnt remains; fragments; rubbish.

début (dābü'), Fr. *n.* first appearance; entrance into society. **-ant** (-tahn), *n.* (*fem.* **-ante**, -tahnt'), person making debut.

decachord (dek'əkawd), *n.* & *adj.* (mus. instr.) having ten strings.

decad (dek'əd), *n.* group of ten. **-al**, *adj.* **-e** (dikād', dek'əd), *n.* period of ten years.

decadent (dek'ədənt), *adj.* deteriorating; declining in strength or virtue; *n.* such person, *espec.* late 19th-cent. Fr. writer of morbid sensuous style. **-nce**, *n.*

decadescent (dekədes'ənt), *adj.* tending to become decadent.

decadic (dikad'ik), *adj.* pert. to decimal system.

decagon (dek'əgən), *n.* 10-sided plane figure. **-al** (dikag'ənəl), *adj.*

decahedron (dekəhē'drən), *n.* 10-sided solid figure. **-ral**, *adj.*

decalescence (dekəles'əns), *n.* sudden increase at certain temperature in amount of heat absorbed by heating bodies.

decalogue (dek'əlog), *n.* Ten Commandments.

decalvant (dikal'vənt), *adj.* depilatory.

decameral (dikam'ərəl), *adj.* divided into ten. **-rous**, *adj. Bot.*, having parts in tens.

decameter (dikam'itə), *n.* verse line of ten feet.

decanal (dikā'nəl), *adj.* pert. to deacon; on the dean's (*i.e.* south) side of choir. **-nate** (dek'ənāt), *n.* deanery.

decapod (dek'əpod), *n.* ten-legged crustacean, including shrimps, lobsters, etc. **-al**, **-an**, **-ous** (-ap'-), *adj.*

decarch (dek'ahk), *n.* member of decarchy; commander over ten. **-y**, *n.* rule by or ruling body of ten persons.

decarnate (dikah'nət) *adj.* divested of bodily form.

decastich (dek'əstik), *n.* ten-line poem.

decasyllable (dek'əsiləbl), *n.* verse line or word of ten syllables. **-bic** (-ab'ik), *adj.*

decathlon (dikath'lən), *n.* athletic contest of ten running, jumping and field events.

decatise (dek'ətiz), *v.t.* cause to uncurl by steaming or damping.

decemvir (disem'və), *n.* member of decemvirate. **-al**, *adj.* **-ate**, *n.* ruling body of ten persons.

decennial (disen'iəl), *adj.* occurring every ten years; consisting of ten years. **-nary**, *adj.* decennial; *n.* decennium. **-nium**, *n.* (*pl.* **-ia**) period of ten years.

decibel (des'ibel), *n.* unit of intensity of sound.

deciduous (disid'ūəs), *adj.* falling off at certain season, *espec.* at end of growing period; shedding leaves in autumn.

decillion (disil'yən), *n.* a million nonillions (10^{60}); *Amer.* & *Fr.*, a thousand nonillions (10^{33}).

decimate (des'imāt), *v.t.* kill large number of; kill one-tenth of; punish by punishing or executing every tenth man chosen by lot. **-tion**, *n.*

decimestrial (desimes'triəl), *adj.* consisting of or lasting ten months.

decimosexto (desiməseks'tō), *see* sextodecimo.

déclassé (dāklas'ā), Fr. *adj.* (*fem.* **-ée**) fallen or degraded from social class.

declension (diklen'shn), *n.* decline; *Gram.*, group of nouns with same

---

hat, bah, hāte, hāre, crawl; pen, ēve, hēre; it, īce, fīre; on, bone, boil, bōre, howl; foot, fōōd, bōōr, hull, tūbe, pūre.

inflection ; naming the inflections of nouns. -al, *adj.*

declination (deklinā´shn), *n.* bending ; turning aside ; angle between magnetic needle and geographical meridian ; *Astron.*, angular distance from equator. -**te** (dek´-), *adj.* bent to one side.

declivity (dikliv´iti), *n.* downward slope. -**tous**, -**vate** (dek´), -**vous** (-ī´vəs), *adj.*

decoct (dikokt´), *v.t.* boil ; infuse ; extract essence by boiling ; reduce. -**tion**, *n.* -**tive**, *adj.*

decollate (dikol´āt), *v.t.* behead. -**tion**, *n.*

décolleté (dākol´tā), Fr. *adj.* (*fem.* -**ée**) low-necked. -**tage**, *n.* such dress ; edge of low-cut neck.

décor (dā´kor), *n.* decoration, etc., of theatre stage ; design of scenery and dresses.

decorticate (dēkaw´tikāt), *v.t.* divest of bark, peel, husk, skin, etc. ; flay ; (-ət), *adj.* lacking such outer layer. -**tion**, -**tor**, *n.*

decorum (dikōr´əm), *n.* suitability ; seemliness ; good behaviour ; etiquette. -**rous** (dek´ərəs, -ōr´əs), *adj.*

decrement (dek´rimənt), *n.* decrease ; waste.

decrepit (dikrep´it), *adj.* infirm ; worn-out.

decrepitate (dikrep´itāt), *v.t.* make to crackle by roasting. -**tion**, *n.*

decrepitude (dikrep´itūd), *n.* state of being decrepit.

decrescent (dikres´ənt), *adj.* decreasing gradually. -**nce**, *n.*

decretal (dikrē´təl), *n.* decree, *espec.* papal ; *adj.* pert. to decree. -**ist**, *n.* student of d. -**tive**, -**tory**, *adj.* pert. to or like a decree.

decrudescence (dēkrōōdes´əns), *n.* diminution in disease.

decubitus (dikū´bitəs), *n.* act or attitude of lying down. -**tal**, *adj.* pert. to or resulting from d.

decuman (dek´ūmən), *adj.* every tenth.

decumbence, -**cy** (dikum´bəns, -i), *n.* decubitus. -**biture**, *n.* confinement to bed. -**nt**, *adj.*

decuple (dek´ūpl), *adj.* tenfold ; arranged in tens ; *n.* such amount ; *v.i.* & *t.* multiply by ten.

decurrent (dikur´ənt), *adj.* running downward ; elapsing. -**nce**, *n.*

decursive (dikə´siv), *adj.* decurrent.

decurtate (dikə´tāt), *adj.* shortened ; *v.t.* curtail. -**tion**, *n.*

decurve (dikəv´), *v.i.* & *t.* curve downward. -**vation**, *n.*

decussate (dikus´ət), *adj.* X-shaped ; *v.i.* & *t.* cross in X-shape. -**tion**, *n.*

dedition (dedish´n), *n.* surrender.

deemster (dēm´stə), *n.* Manx judge. -**ship**, *n.*

de-esis (di-ē´sis), *n.* rhet. invocation.

de facto (dē fak´tō), *Lat.,* "in fact" ; actual ; done or existing, whether rightfully or not.

defalcate (dē´falkāt, -fal´- ; -fawl-), *v.i.* embezzle. -**tion**, *n.* embezzlement ; amount embezzled.

defamation (defəmā´shn), *n.* injury to character ; calumny. -**tory** (-am´ətri), *adj.*

defeasance (difē´zəns), *n.* *Law,* nullification ; condition on performing which provision is nullified. -**d**, -**sible**, *adj.* able to be annulled ; having such condition.

defecate (def´ikāt), *v.i.* & *t.* refine ; remove impurities from ; excrete ; *adj.* purified. -**ant**, *n.* purifying agent. -**tion**, -**tor**, *n.*

defenestration (difenistrā´shn), *n.* throwing of a person or thing out of window.

deferrise (dēfer´īz), *v.t.* remove iron from. -**sation**, *n.*

defervesce (dēfəves´), *v.i.* become cool ; lose interest. -**nce**, *n.* -**nt**, *adj.* pert. to or causing cooling ; *n.* such drug.

de fide (dē fī´di), *Lat.,* "of the faith" ; *R.C.,* accepted and taught by church as revelation.

deflagrate (def´ləgrāt, dē´-), *v.i.* & *t.* burn up suddenly. -**tion**, -**tor**, *n.*

deflation (diflā´shn), *n.* *Econ.,* restriction or reduction of purchasing power and means of exchange, causing rise in value of money and fall in prices. -**ary**, *adj.* -**ist**, *n.* advocate of d.

deflocculate (diflok´ūlāt), *v.t.* break into small pieces ; disentangle. -**lant**, -**lent**, *adj.*

deflorate (diflor´āt), *v.t.* deflower. -**tion**, *n.*

deflower (diflow´ə), *v.t.* ravish ; rupture hymen, *espec.* as primitive ceremony ; strip of flowers.

defluent (def´looənt), *adj.* flowing down. -**uvium**, *n.* falling of hair. -**uxion**, *n.* discharge of mucus from nose.

---

defoliate (difō'liāt), *v.i.* & *t.* lose, or strip of, leaves ; *adj.* stripped of leaves. -tion, -tor, *n.*

dégagé (dāgah'zhā), Fr. *adj.* (*fem.* -ée) "disengaged" ; at ease.; unworried.

degauss (dēgows'), *v.t.* de-magnetise by surrounding with elec. charged wire or coil, *espec.* ships to prevent their detonating magnetic mines.

deglutinate (diglōō'tināt), *v.t.* un-stick ; remove glue or gluten from. -tion, *n.*

deglutition (dēglōōtish'n), *n.* act or power of swallowing. -tious, *adj.* -tive, -tory, *adj.* aiding d.

de gratia (dē grā'shiə), *Lat.*, "by favour."

dehaematise (dihē'mətiz), *v.t.* re-move blood from. -hepatise, *v.t.* remove liver from.

dehiscent (dihis'ənt), *adj.* gaping ; discharging contents (*e.g.* seeds) by bursting open. -nce, *n.*

dehydrate (dēhī'drāt), *v.i.* & *t.* remove or lose water from ; desic-cate ; remove or lose hydrogen and oxygen in amounts to form water. -tion, -tor, *n.*

deicide (dē'isīd), *n.* killer or des-troyer, or killing or destruction, of a god, *espec.* of Christ.

deictic, dic- (dīk'tik), *adj.* directly proving or demonstrating.

Dei gratia (dē'ī grā'shiə), *Lat.*, "by the grace of God" (*abbr.* D.G.).

Dei judicium (dē'ī jōōdish'iəm), *Lat.*, "judgment of God" ; trial by ordeal.

deiparous (dēip'ərəs), *adj.* giving birth to a god or Christ.

deipnosophist (dīpnos'əfist), *n.* per-son expert in art of table talk. -ic, *adj.* -ism, *n.*

deipotent (.ēip'ətənt), *adj.* with god-like power.

deism (dē'izm), *n.* belief in God's existence but not in revealed religion. -ist, *n.* -istic, *adj.*

dejecta (dijek'tə), *n.pl. Med.*, excre-ments. -tory, *n.* & *adj.* purgative. -ture, *n.* excrement.

déjeuner (dā'zhənā), Fr. *n.* lun-cheon ; breakfast. petit d., break-fast.

de jure (dē jōōr'i), *Lat.*, "by right" ; rightful.

dekarch, see **decarch**.

delactation (lēlaktā'shn), *n.* wean-ing ; cessation of milk flow.

delation (dilā'shn), *n.* laying infor-mation against a person. -tor, *n.* informer. -torian, *adj.*

delectus (dilek'təs), *n.* chresto-mathy.

delendum (dilen'dəm), *n.* (*pl.* -da) thing to be deleted.

deleterious (delitēr'iəs), *adj.* harm-ful.

delicatessen (delikətes'n), *n.pl.* cooked, tinned or bottled foods ; shop selling such food.

deligation (dēligā'shn), *n.* bandag-ing.

delignate (dilig'nāt), *v.t.* remove wood or woody matter from.

delimit (dēlim'it), *v.t.* fix boundaries of. -ation, *n.*

delinquent (diling'kwənt), *n.* & *adj.* (person) falling off from standard of duty or morals. -ncy, *n.*

deliquesce (dēlikwes'), *v.i.* melt away. -nce, *n.* -nt, *adj.*

delirium (dilēr'iəm, -ir'-), *n.* disor-dered state of mind, due to fever, etc. ; wild excitement. d.tremens, extreme d. due to alcoholism, marked by violent tremors and hallucinations. -iant, -ifacient, *n.* & *adj.* (substance) causing d. -ious, *adj.* -ration (delirā'shn), *n.* mental aberration ; delirium.

delitescent (delites'ənt), *adj.* latent. -nce, -ncy, *n.*

deloul (delōōl'), *n.* quick-moving riding camel of Arabia.

Delphian, -ic (del'fiən, -fik), *adj.* pert. to oracle of Delphi ; am-biguous ; having several uses.

delta (del'tə), *n.* fourth letter of Gr. alphabet (Δ δ) ; Δ-shaped area of alluvium at river-mouth. -ic (-ā'ik), -tic, *adj.* -tification, -tion, *n.* formation of deltas. -toid, *adj.* Δ-shaped ; *n.* such shoulder muscle.

demagogue (dem'əgog), *n.* orator addressing himself to, or using arguments such as to stir, the masses. -gic (-gik, -jik), *adj.* -gism (-gizm), -gy (-gi, -ji), *n.*

demarcate (dēmah'kāt, dē'-), *v.t.* delimit. -tion, *n.*

démarche (dā'mahrsh), Fr. *n.* de-cisive step or action, *espec.* diplo-matic, and initiating new policy.

demegoric (dēmigor'ik), *adj.* pert. to demagogic speech.

démenti (dāmah'tē), Fr. *n.* official denial.

dementia (dimen'shiə), *n.* insanity; any abnormal mental state. **d.praecox** (-prē'koks), form of insanity with complete loss of interest in life and of emotions.

demephitise (dēmef'itīz), *v.t.* purify (air). **-sation,** *n.*

demersal (dimā'səl), *adj.* sinking to bottom. **-sion,** *n.*

demesne (dimēn'), *n.* estate; territory; unrestricted possession of land. **-nial,** *adj.*

demijohn (dem'ijon), *n.* large bottle with wicker case.

demi-monde (dem'i-mond), *n.* class of women of doubtful reputation. **-dain,** *adj.* **-daine,** *n.* woman of that class.

demi-rep (dem'i-rep), *n.* demimondaine.

demisang(ue) (dem'isang), *n.* halfbreed; first cross.

demise (dimīz'), *n.* death; act of conveying estate; *v.t.* convey estate, *espec.* by will.

demiurge (dem'iəj), *n.* inferior god who created world; creative power or spirit. **-geous, -gic,** *adj.*

demogenic (dēməjen'ik), *adj.* app. to societies based on citizenship rather than kinship.

demography (dimog'rəfi), *n.* study of population statistics. **-pher, -phist,** *n.* **-phic(al),** *adj.*

demology (dimol'əji), *n.* study of human activities. **-gical,** *adj.*

demonetise (dēmun'itīz), *v.t.* divest (coin, etc.) of its value or withdraw from circulation; abandon (gold, etc.) as currency. **-sation,** *n.*

demonifuge (dimon'ifūj), *n.* charm against evil spirits.

demonolatry (dēmənol'ətri), *n.* worship of demons, and good and evil spirits. **-ater,** *n.* demon-worshipper. **-logy,** *n.* study of demons.

demophil(e) (dem'əfil, -īl), *n.* friend of people; person fond of crowds or the masses. **-phobe,** *n.* person disliking the masses or crowds.

Demos (dē'mos), *n.* personification of democracy or the masses.

demotic (dimot'ik), *adj.* pert. to common people; app. to simplified style of Egyptian writing. **-s,** *n.* sociology.

demulcent (dimul'sənt), *n. & adj.* soothing (substance), **-lsify,** *v.t.* extract from an emulsion. **-lsion,** *n.* soothing.

demurrage (dimur'ij), *n.* delay by freighter of a vessel's loading, departure, etc.; payment for such delay. **-rer,** *n. Law,* objection to pleading.

denarius (dinār'iəs), *n. (pl.* **-rii)** anct. Roman coin of silver or, later, copper; penny (*abbr.* d.).

denary (den'əri, dē'-), *adj.* of ten; tenfold; decimal; *n.* ten; group of ten; one tenth.

dendrachate (den'drəkāt), *n.* moss agate.

dendral (den'drəl), *adj.* living in trees; arboreal. **-riform,** *adj.* treelike; branched.

dendrite (den'drīt), *n.* tree-shaped mark made by another mineral in stone or crystal; nerve-cell outgrowth conducting impulse inwards. **-tic** (-it'ik), *adj.* like a d.; tree-like. **-tiform,** *adj.* branched.

dendrograph (den'drəgraf), *n.* instr. recording growth of tree's girth. **-y,** *n.* such recording; treatise on trees.

dendroid (den'droid), *adj.* treeshaped.

dendrology (dendrol'əji), *n.* study of or treatise on trees. **-gic(al), -gous, -gist,** *n.*

dendrometer (dendrom'itə), *n.* instr. measuring tree's height and girth.

dendron (den'dron), *n.* dendrite (of nerve-cell).

dendrophilous (dendrof'iləs), *adj.* fond of or inhabiting trees.

denehole (dēn'hōl), *n.* shaft, with chambers at base, sunk in chalk regions, of anct. origin.

dengue (deng'gā), *n.* kind of fever of hot regions; break-bone fever.

denigrate (den'igrāt), *v.t.* blacken; slander. **-tion, -tor,** *n.*

denizen (den'izən), *n.* inhabitant; naturalised person or thing; *v.t.* naturalise; people; colonise. **-ation, -zation,** *n.*

de nouveau (də nōō'vō), *Fr.,* "again"; afresh.

de novo (dē nō'vō), *Lat.,* "from the beginning"; afresh.

dentagra (dentag'rə), *n.* toothache; dentist's forceps.

dentate (den'tāt), *adj.* with toothed edge, or tooth-like prominences. **-telated,** *adj.* with small notches. **-ticulate,** *adj.* with small tooth-like prominences.

dentigerous (dentij'ərəs), *adj.* bearing teeth.

dentilingual (dentiling'gwəl), *n.* & *adj.* (sound) pronounced (as *th*) with tongue against teeth. -loquy (-il'əkwɪ), *n.* speaking with teeth clenched.

dentinasal (dentinā'zəl), *n.* & *adj.* (sound) pronounced (as *n*) with nasal passage open and tongue against upper teeth or teeth-ridge.

dentine (den'tēn, -in), *n.* bone-like substance forming tooth; dental ivory.

dentiphone (den'tifōn), *n.* audiphone.

dentition (dentish'n), *n.* teeth development; characteristic arrangement or nature of animal's teeth.

denumeration (dinūmərā'shn), *n. Math.*, determination of number of things able to fulfil certain conditions. -tive, *adj.*

deobstruent (dēob'strooənt), *n.* & *adj.* (medicine) removing obstacles; purgative.

deodar (dē'ədah), *n.* Ind. cedar.

deontology (dēontol'əji), *n.* science of moral duty. -gical, *adj.* -gist, *n.*

deoppilate (dēop'ilāt), *v.i.* & *t.* remove obstructions (from). -ant, *n.* & *adj.* -tion, *n.* -tive, *adj.*

deordination (dēawdinā'shn), *n.* disorder; abnormality.

deorsum (dēaw'səm), Lat. *adv.* downward. -version, *n.* turning downward.

depascent (dipas'ənt), *adj.* eating.

Deo volente (dē'ō vəlen'ti), Lat., "God being willing" (*abbr.* D.V.).

dépaysé (dāpā'ēzā), Fr. *adj.* (*fem.* -ée) "away from natural country or environment"; lost; out of one's element.

depilation (depilā'shn), *n.* removal of hair. -lous (dep'-), *adj.* bald. -tory (-pil'ətəri), *adj.* used to remove hair; *n.* such substance.

deploy (diploi'), *v.i.* & *t.* spread out into one line. -ment, *n.*

deponent (dipō'nənt), *n.* person giving evidence or making affidavit; *adj. Gram.*, app. to verbs with active meaning and passive form.

deposition (dēpəzish'n), *n. Law,* sworn testimony.

depotentiate (dēpəten'shiāt), *v.t.* divest of power; weaken. -tion, *n.*

de profundis (dē prəfun'dis), Lat., "from the depths"; *adj.* expressing deep misery; *n.* 130th Psalm.

depurate (dep'ūrāt), *v.t.* purify. -ant, *n.* & *adj.* -tion, *n.* -tive, *n.* & *adj.*

deracinate (diras'ināt), *v.t.* uproot. -tion, *n.*

de règle (də rā'gl), Fr. "by rule"; according to custom or propriety.

dereliction (derilik'shn), *n.* failure to perform duty.

deric (der'ik), *adj.* pert. to skin.

de rigueur (də rēgēr'), Fr., according to or demanded by etiquette; comme il faut.

derma, -mis (dɜ'mə, -is), *n.* layer of skin, containing nerves and blood vessels, beneath epidermis. -mad, *adv.* towards skin. -mal, -matic, -matine, *adj.* pert. to skin.

dermatitis (dɜmətī'tis), *n.* inflammation of skin or derma.

dermatoglyphics (dɜmətəglif'iks), *n.* study of fingerprints and other skin patterns. -graph, *n.* fingerprint or other impression of skin markings. -graphy, *n.* description of skin.

dermatoid (dɜ'mətoid), *adj.* skin-like.

dermatology (dɜmətol'əji), *n.* study of skin and skin diseases. -gical, *adj.* -gist, *n.*

dermatome (dɜ'mətōm), *n.* instr. for cutting skin. -mic (-om'ik), *adj.*

dermatomycosis (dɜmətəmikō'sis), *n.* skin disease due to vegetable parasite.

dermatopathy, -thia (dɜmətop'əthi, -əpath'iə), *n.* skin disease. -thic, *adj.*

dermatophyte (dɜ'mətəfīt), *n.* disease-causing fungus parasite of skin. -tic (-it'ik), *adj.* -tosis, *n.*

dermatoplasty (dɜ'mətəplasti), *n.* plastic surgery of skin.

dermatosis (dɜmətō'sis), *n.* skin disease.

dermographia, -ism (dɜməgraf'iə, -og'rəfizm), *n.* condition in which slight pressure, as of writing, on skin causes red mark. -phic, *adj.*

dermoid (dɜ'moid), *adj.* skin-like.

dermutation (dɜmūtā'shn), *n.* alteration of dermal tissue. -tive, *adj.*

dernier cri (dārn'yā krē'), Fr., "last cry"; latest fashion; newest discovery.

derogate (der'əgāt), *v.i.* & *t.* reduce value (of) ; detract. **-tion**, *n.* **-tory** (-rog'ətəri), *adj.* disparaging.

derrick (der'ik), *n.* simple deck crane, gen. of pulley attached to spar ; tower-like erection over oil well.

derringer (der'injə), *n.* short, wide-barrelled pistol.

desacralise (dēsā'krəliz), *v.i.* & *t.* divest of supernatural qualities ; remove tabu. **-sation**, *n.*

descant (des'kant), *n. Mus.*, melody ; part-song ; treble ; counterpoint ; simple counterpoint sung by trebles ; *v.i.* comment ; discourse.

deshabillé (dāzabē'ya), Fr. *adj.* partly clad ; *n.* such state.

desiccate (des'ikāt), *v.t.* dry up ; preserve by drying. **-ant**, *n.* & *adj.* **tion**, **-tor**, *n.* **-tive**, **-tory**, *adj.*

desiderate (disid'ərāt), *v.t.* desire strongly ; regard as lacking. **-tion**, *n.* **-tive**, *adj.* **-tum**, Lat. *n.* (*pl.* **-ta**) desired thing ; condition ; thing regarded as lacking.

desiderium (desidēr'iəm), Lat. *n.* yearning.

desinent(ial) (des'inənt, -en'shəl), *adj.* terminal. **-nce**, *n.* ending.

desipient (disip'iənt), *adj.* foolish. **-nce**, *n.*

desition (disish'n), *n.* ending ; cessation. **-sistive**, *adj.* final.

desman (des'mən), *n.* aquatic mole-like animal of Russia and Pyrenees ; its fur.

desmid (des'mid), *n.* species of algae. **-ian**, *n.* **-iology**, *n.* study of d.

desmology (desmol'əji), *n.* study of ligaments or bandaging. **-motomy**, *n.* cutting or anatomy of ligaments.

despumate (dispū'māt, des'-), *v.i.* & *t.* remove scum ; throw off like or in scum ; foam. **-tion**, *n.*

desquamate (des'kwəmāt), *v.i.* & *t.* peel off, or cause to peel off, in scales. **-tion**, **-tory**, *n.* **-tive**, *adj.*

desucration (dēsūkrā'shn), *n.* removal of sugar.

desuetude (dē'switūd), *n.* disuse ; obsolescence.

desultory (des'əltri), *adj.* aimless ; lacking method or application ; digressive.

détente (dā'tahṅt), Fr. *n.* relaxation ; ease of strained political relations.

detergent (ditə'jənt), *n.* & *adj.*

cleansing (substance), *espec.* powdered soap substitute. **-nce**, **-ney** *n.* power to cleanse.

determinism (ditə'minizm), *n.* phil. theory that acts of will arise from deciding causes ; fatalism ; theory that present conditions are so by necessity.

detersion (ditə'shn), *n.* act of cleansing. **-sive**, *n.* & *adj.* detergent.

detinue (det'inū), *n. Law*, illegal detention of another's personal property ; writ for recovering such detained property.

detoxicate (dētoks'ikāt), *v.t.* remove poison or its effects from. **-ant**, *n.* & *adj.* **-tion**, **-tor**, *n.*

detritus (ditrī'təs), *n.* debris ; fragments worn away, *espec.* of rock. **-tal**, *adj.* **-ted**, *adj.* worn thin. **-tion** (-ish'n), *n.*

de trop (di trō'), *Fr.*, "too much" ; unwanted ; in the way.

detrude (ditrōōd'), *v.t.* push down or out.

detruncate (ditrung'kāt), *v.t.* cut short ; lop. **-tion**, *n.*

detrusion (ditrōō'zhn), *n.* act of detruding. **-usive**, *adj.*

deus ex machina (dē'əs eks mā'-kinə), *Lat.*, "a god from a machine" ; interference by divine power to set right a situation ; any artificial method of solving difficulty.

deuterium (dūtēr'iəm), *n.* heavy hydrogen, the oxide of which is heavy water used to slow down neutrons emitted in nuclear fission.

deuterogamy (dūtarog'əmi), *n.* remarriage after spouse's death. **-mist**, *n.*

deuteropathy (dūtərop'əthi), *n.* secondary illness. **-thic** (-ath'ik), *adj.*

deutoplasm (dū'təplazm), *n.* yolk of egg. **-ic**, *adj.*

devaluate (dēval'ū āt), *v.t.* reduce value of, *espec.* of currency in terms of other currencies. **-tion**, *n.*

devise (divīz'), *v.t. Law*, bequeath (real estate) by will. **-see**, *n.* person to whom property is bequeathed. **-sor**, *n.* person bequeathing property.

devoir (dəv'wahr), Fr. *n.* duty ; best of which one is capable ; *pl.* respects ; attentions ; courtesy.

dewan, di- (diwahn'), Anglo-Ind. *n.* native prime minister or minister of finance ; native business manager or major-domo. **-ee, -i,** *n.* d.'s office.

dewlap (dū'lap), *n.* loose skin hanging at throat.

dexter (deks'tə), *adj.* on right-hand side ; presaging good ; honest ; *Her.*, on right-hand side of wearer of shield. **-ity** (-er'iti), *n.* adroitness ; deftness. **-ous,** *adj.* adroit ; deft.

dextral (deks'trəl), *adj.* on right-hand side. **-ity,** *n.* use of right limb, eye, etc., more than left. **-ly,** *adv.* towards right-hand side.

dextrin (deks'trin), *n.* gummy carbohydrate, manuf. from, and resulting from digestion of, starch ; starch gum. **-ate,** *v.t.* make into or mix with d. **-ous,** *adj.*

dextrocular (dekstrok'ūlə), *adj.* using right eye more than left. **-ity** (-ar'iti), *. n.* **-oduction,** *n.* moving eyes to right.

dextrogyratory (dekstrəjīr'ətəri), *adj.* turning to the right. **-tion,** *n.*

dextrorotatory (dekstrərō'tətəri), *adj.* turning to the right, *espec.* turning plane of polarised light to right.

dextrorse (deks'traws), *adj.* spirally turning to the right. **-sal,** *adj.*

dextrose (deks'trōs), *n.* glucose ; grape sugar.

dextrosinistral (dekstrəsin'istrəl), *adj.* extending to right and left ; app. to left-handed person using right hand for writing.

dextrous (deks'trəs), *adj.* dexterous.

dextroversion (dekstrəvō'shn), *n.* turn to the right.

dhai (dah'ē), Hind. *n.* wet-nurse ; midwife.

dhal (dahl), Anglo-Ind. *n.* porridge of pulse.

dhanuk (dah'nook), Hind. *n.* member of low Ind. caste.

dhobi, -by, -bey, -bie, -bee (dō'bi), Anglo-Ind. *n.* washer-woman.

dhole (dōl), *n.* Ind. wild hog.

dhoti, -ooti, -ty, -tie, -tee (dō'ti, dōō'-), Anglo-Ind. *n.* Hindu loin-cloth.

dhow (dow), *n.* Arab sailing ship with lateen sails.

dhurra, see **durra.**

diabetes (dīabē'tēz), *n.* disease due to lack of insulin. **d.mellitus** *or* **sugar d.,** form of d. in which urine contains sugar. **-tic** (-et'ik), *adj.* ;

n. sufferer from d. **-togenic,** *adj.* causing d. **-togenous,** *adj.* caused by d.

diablerie (diah'blərē), Fr. *n.* "devilry" ; sorcery ; black magic ; mischievous act.

diabolism (dīab'əlizm), *n.* devil worship ; black magic ; devilish behaviour. **-larch,** *n.* king of the devils. **-lepsy,** *n.* devil-possession. **-lic(al)** (-bol'ik, -l), *adj.* pert. to devils. **-list,** *n.* student or teacher of d. **-lology,** *n.* study of or belief in devils ; doctrine about devils.

diabrosis (dīəbrō'sis), *n.* perforation, *espec.* by ulcer. **-otic** (-ot'ik), *n.* & *adj.* corrosive (thing).

diachoretic (dīəkəret'ik), *adj.* aperient.

diachronic (dīəkron'ik), *adj.* pert. to time since world's creation.

diachylon (dīak'ilən), *n.* kind of sticking plaster.

diaclasis (dīəklā'sis), *n.* fracture ; refraction. **-astic,** *adj.*

diaconal (dīak'ənəl), *adj.* pert. to deacon. **-ate,** *n.* deacon's jurisdiction or office, the order of deacons.

diacope (dīak'əpi), *n.* deep incision.

diacrisis (dīəkrī'sis), *n. Med.,* change in secretion during illness ; discharge aiding diagnosis. **-ritic** (-it'ik), *adj.* distinctive ; aiding diagnosis ; *n.* such symptom.

diacritical (dīəkrit'ikəl), *adj.* distinctive ; app. to mark distinguishing sound of letter.

diactinal (dīak'tinəl), *adj.* two-rayed ; with both ends pointed.

diactinic (dīaktin'ik), *adj.* able to transmit actinic rays. **-nism,** *n.*

diadem (dī'ədem), *n.* crown ; fillet.

diadermic (dīədə'mik), *adj.* pert. to penetration through skin.

diaeresis, dier- (dīer'isis, -ēr'-), *n.* (*pl.* **-ses)** mark (¨) placed over vowel to indicate change in pronunciation or that it is pronounced separately (*e.g.* co̎pt) ; such separate pronunciation of vowels. **-etic** (-et'ik), *adj.* pert. to d. ; dividing ; caustic.

diaglyph (dī'əglif), *n.* intaglio. **-ic, -yptic,** *adj.*

diagnose (dī'əgnōz), *v.t.* determine disease from study of symptoms ; arrive at any such conclusion. **-sis** (-ō'sis), *n.* (*pl.* **-ses)** act or result of diagnosing. **-stic** (-os'tik), *adj.*

pert. to or aiding diagnosis ; *n.* symptom ; distinctive mark. -stician, *n.* expert at diagnosis.

diagraphics (dīagraf'iks), *n.* art of drawing diagrams.

dialectic(s) (dīəlek'tik, -s), *n.* art of logical and analytical argument. -cal, *adj.* pert. to or given to d. ; logical. -cian (-ish'ən), *n.* person skilled in d.

diallelus (dīəlē'ləs), *n.* (*pl.* -li) arguing in a circle.

dialysis (dīal'isis), *n.* (*pl.* -ses) separation ; decomposition. -yse, *v.t.* -ytic (-it'ik), *adj.*

diamb (dī'am), *n.* verse foot of two iambi.

diamesogamous (dīəmisog'əməs), *n. Bot.*, not self-pollinated.

diamond (dī'əmənd), -*n.* size of type : 4 or 4½ point.

diandrous (dīan'drəs), *adj. Bot.*, having two stamens.

dianoetic (dīənōet'ik), *adj.* pert. to reasoning.

diapason (dīəpā'zn), *n.* loud, harmonious burst of music ; entire gamut or compass ; organ-stop sounding the octaves of the note played.

diaper (dī'əpə), *n.* linen with regular repetitive pattern ; such pattern ; napkin, sanitary towel ; *v.t.* ornament with d. patterns.

diaphanous (dīaf'ənəs), *adj.* transparent ; filmy. -neity, *n.* -nometer, *n.* instr. measuring transparency of air, etc. -noscopy, *n.* illumination from within of body cavities for med. examination.

diaphoretic (dīafəret'ik), *n.* & *adj.* (drug) causing perspiration. -esis (-ē'sis), *n.* perspiration.

diaphragm (dī'əfram), *n.* vibrating disk in telephone, radio, etc., instr.; muscular partition between abdomen and chest ; any thin partition or dividing membrane. -atic (-agmat'ik), *adj.*

diapnoic (diapnō'ik), *n.* & *adj.* mild(ly) diaphoretic.

diapyesis (dīəpī ē'-is), *n.* discharge of pus. -etic (-et'ik), *n.* & *adj.*

diarchy (dī'ahki), *n.* government by two rulers. -chial, -chic, *adj.*

diarthrosis (dīahthrō'sis), *n.* joint permitting free movement.

diastase (dī'ə-tās), *n.* digestive ferment converting starch into sugar. -tatic, *adj.*

diastole (dīas'təli), *n.* heart dilatation, alternating with systole. -lic (-ol'ik), *adj.*

diastomatic (dīəstomat'ik), *adj.* through pores.

diastrophe (dīas'trəfi), *n. Geol.*, deformation, upheaval, etc., of earth's crust. -phic (-of'ik), *adj.* -phism, *n.* such geol. process ; result of d. ; any such process of upheaval or drastic change.

diasyrm (dī'əsəm), *n.* rhet. device of damning by faint praise.

diathermic (dīəthə'mik), *adj.* transmitting heat rays. -macy, -mancy, -maneity, *n.* -manous, -mous, *adj.* -mometer, *n.* instr. measuring diathermacy. -motherapy, *n.* med. treatment by diathermy. -my, *n.* heating, by elec. means, of subcutaneous tissues ; elec. current used in diathermy.

diathesis (dīath'isis), *n.* (*pl.* -ses) congenital susceptibility or aptitude ; predisposing factor. -etic (-et'ik), *adj.*

diatom (dī'ətom), *n.* species of algae. -aceous, *adj.* containing many d.

diatomic (dīətom'ik), *adj.* comprising two atoms ; bivalent. -ity (-is'iti), *n.*

diatonic (dīəton'ik), *adj. Mus.*, containing no accidentals ; denoting the standard 8-tone scale.

diatribe (dī'ətrīb), *n.* violent speech or writing ; denunciation.

dicaeology (dīsiol'əji), *n.* rhet. device of defending oneself by pleading justification.

dicephalous (dīsef'ələs), *adj.* two-headed. -lism, *n.* -lus, *n.* (*pl.* -li) such monster.

dicerous (dis'ərəs), *adj.* having two antennae or horns.

dichogamy (dīkog'əmi), *n.* coming to maturity at different times of male and female elements of plant or animal, to avoid self-fertilisation. -mic (-am'ik), -mous, *adj.*

dichord (dī'kawd), *n.* two-stringed mus. instr.

dichotomy (dīkot'əmi), *n.* division into two. -mal, -mic (-om'ik), -mous, *adj.* -ise, *v.t.* divide into two or more parts ; analyse.

dichromatic (dīkrəmat'ik), *adj.* of or in two colours ; partially colour-blind. -tism (-krō'-), *n.* substance's property of presenting different colours at different thicknesses.

dicotyledon (dīkotilē'dən), *n.* plant having two cotyledons. **-ary, -ous** (-lē'-, -led'-), *adj.*

dicoumarin (dīkōō'mərin), *n.* chem. compound which prevents or delays clotting of blood.

dicrotic (dīkrot'ik), *adj.* pert. to second pulse dilatation. **-tism** (dī'krətizm, dik'-), *n.*

dictum (dik'təm), *n.* (*pl.* **-ta**) axiom; saying; apophthegm.

didactic (dīdak'tik), *adj.* intended or intending to teach; moral. **-ism** (-sizm), *n.* **-s,** *n.* art of teaching.

didascalic, -lar (didaskal'ik, -as'-kələ; dī'-), *adj.* didactic; pert. to teaching.

didelphian (dīdel'fiən), *n.* & *adj.* marsupial. **-phic, -phous,** *adj.*

didymous, -mate (did'iməs, -mət), *adj.* growing in pairs.

diectasis (dīek'təsis), *n.* lengthening verse line by introducing extra syllable.

dielectric (dīilek'trik), *n.* & *adj.* *Elec.*, non-conducting (substance). **-al,** *adj.*

dies faustus (dī'ēz faw'stəs), *Lat.,* "auspicious or favourable day." **d.infaustus,** unlucky day.

dies irae (dī'ēz īr'ē), *Lat.,* "day of wrath"; day of judgment; Lat. hymn or that subject.

dies non (juridicus) (dī'ēz non joorid'ikəs), *Lat.* (*pl.* .....juridici, -sī), "not lawful day"; day on which no law-court business takes place.

dietary (dī'itəri), *adj.* pert. to diet; *n.* diet chart; food allowance. **-tetic,** *adj.* dietary. **-tetics,** *n.* science of diet. **-tician, tist, -titian,** *n.* expert on dietetics. **-totherapy,** *n.* med. dietary prescription.

differentia (difərən'shiə), *n.* (*pl.* **-ae**) distinguishing mark.

differential (difərən'shəl), *adj.* pert. to or denoting difference; distinguishing; *n.* distinguishing mark; difference; any mechanical device allowing for or using differences in size, speed, etc., of component parts.

diffident (dif'idənt), *adj.* shy; modest. **-nce,** *n.*

diffinity (difin'iti), *n.* absence of affinity.

diffluent (dif'looənt), *adj.* flowing away or melting with ease. **-nce,** *n.*

diffract (difrakt'), *v.t.* break up into portions. **-ion,** *n.* breaking up of light into coloured bands when it passes through narrow opening or by edge of solid body, etc.; **d.grating,** fine grating causing diffraction of light.

diffrangible (difran'jibl), *adj.* able to be diffracted.

diffugient (difū'jiənt), *adj.* dispersing.

digamma (dī'gamə), *n.* early Gr. letter (F). **-mic,** *adj.*

digamy (dig'əmi), *n.* deuterogamy. **-mist,** *n.* **-mous,** *adj.*

digastric (dīgas'trik), *adj.* biventral.

digenesis (dijen'isis), *n.* successive sexual and non-sexual reproduction. **-etic** (-et'ik), *adj.*

digeny (dij'ini), *n.* sexual reproduction. **-nous,** *adj.*

dight (dīt), *adj.* clad; *v.t.* clothe.

digit (dij'it), *n.* figure from 0 to 9; unit; finger or toe. **-al,** *adj.*

digitalis (dijitā'lis), *n.* heart stimulant obtained from foxglove leaves. **-m,** *n.* condition due to over-use of d.

digitate (dij'itāt), *adj.* having or resembling fingers. **-tion,** *n.*

digitigrade (dij'itigrād), *adj.* walking on toes only; *n.* such animal.

digitise (dij'itīz), *v.t.* finger; point at.

digladiation (dīgladiā'shn), *n.* fight; dispute.

diglot(tic) (dī'glot, -ot'ik), *adj.* bilingual **-ttist,** *n.* such person.

digoneutic (dīgənū'tik), *adj.* double-brooded.

digonous (dig'ənəs), *adj.* with two angles.

digraph (dī'graf), *n.* two letters with one sound only (*e.g.* ph). **-ic,** *adj.*

dilatory (dil'ətəri), *adj.* procrastinating; slow.

dilettante (dilitan'ti), *n.* (*pl.* **-ti**) amateur of fine arts; superficial lover or practiser of art. **-tism,** *n.*

dilogy (dil'əji), *n.* intentional ambiguity; emphatic repetition of word, etc.

diluent (dil'ūənt), *n.* & *adj.* diluting (agent).

diluvial (dīlōō'viəl, dil-), *adj.* pert. to or caused by the Flood or any inundation. -vianism, n. belief that certain geol. facts are explainable by the Deluge.

dime (dīm), Amer. n. coin worth tenth part of dollar; ten-cent piece.

dimeter (dim'itə), n. verse line of two feet. -tric (dīmet'rik), adj.

dimidiate (dimid'iāt, dī-), v.t. halve. -tion, n.

diminutive (dimin'ūtiv), n. & adj. (word or form of word) signifying smallness; very small (person or thing).

dimissory (dim'isəri; dīmis'-), adj. giving permission to go; dismissing.

dimorphism (dīmaw'fizm), n. occurrence of noticeable differences between two creatures of same species; dual personality. -phic, -phous, adj.

dingo (ding'gō), n. (pl. -es) Austral. wild dog.

dinic(al) (din'ik, -l), adj. pert. to vertigo.

dinosaur (dī'nəsōr), n. huge fossil reptile. -ian, adj. -othere, n. extinct elephant-like mammal.

dioecious (diē'shəs), adj. having male and female organs in separate individuals. -cism, n.

dioestrum (diē'strəm, -es'-), n. period between "heats." -rous, adj.

dionym (dī'ənim), n. name containing two terms. -al (-on'iməl), adj. binomial.

Dionysiac (dīənis'iak), adj. pert. to Dionysus, anct. Gr. god of wine, and his wild rites; ba chanalian.

dioptometer (dīoptom'itə), n. instr. measuring refractive power of eye.

dioptre, -ter (dīop'tə), n. unit of power of lens, the reciprocal of the focal length in metres. -ric (-op'trik), adj. pert. to refraction of light; transparent. -roscopy, n. measurement of refractive power of eye. -s, n. study of refraction of light.

diorama (dīərah'mə), n. lighted painting(s) and figures so disposed and viewed as to appear real scenes. -mic (-am'ik), adj.

diorthosis (dīawthō'sis), n. correction; straightening, espec. of deformed limbs. -otic (-ot'ik), adj.

diotic (dīot'ik, -ō'tik), adj. affecting both ears.

diphyletic (difilet'ik), adj. descended from two genealogical lines.

diphyodont (dif'iədont), adj. having two successive sets of teeth.

diplegia (dīplē'jia), n. paralysis of corresponding parts on both sides of body.

diplocephalus (dipləsef'ələs), n. double-headed monster. -lous, adj. -ly, n.

diplograph (dip'ləgraf), n. instr. for writing two lines or two types of writing at once. -y, n.

diploid (dip'loid), adj. double, espec. having double normal chromosome number. -y, n. such state.

diplopia (diplō'piə), n. double vision. -pic (-op'ik), adj.

diplopod (dip'ləpod), n. millipede. -ic, adj.

dipnoous (dip'nōəs), adj. having both lungs and gills. -noan, n. such fish; lungfish.

dipody (dip'ədi), n. verse measure of two feet; -dimeter.

dipsetic (dipset'ik), n. & adj. (thing) causing thirst.

dipsomania (dipsəmā'niə), n. uncontrollable desire for drink, espec. alcohol. -c, n. sufferer from d. -cal (-mənī'əkəl), adj.

dipsosis (dipsō'sis), n. great thirst due to disease.

dipterous (dip'tərəs), adj. having two wings. -ral, adj.; Archit. having double colonnade. -ran, n. such fly. -rology, n. study of two-winged insects.

diptote (dip'tōt), n. Gram., noun with two cases only.

diptych (dip'tik), n. paintings on a pair of hinged tablets used as altar-piece; list of persons commemorated in church service written on a pair of hinged tablets.

directoire (dērektwahr'), adj. signifying style of low-necked, high-waisted dress, and curving Oriental furniture, of the Directory period (1795–99) of France.

dirigent (dir'ijənt), adj. guiding.

dirigible (dir'ijibl), adj. capable of being steered; n. such balloon. rigid d., airship.

diriment (dir'imənt), n. Law, nullification.

disagio (disā'jiō, -aj'-), n. charge made for exchanging depreciated or foreign money.

discalced (diskalst'), adj. bare-foot.

-ceate, n. & adj. bare-foot (friar or nun).

discarnate (diskah'nət), adj. having no body; (-āt), v.t. deprive of bodily existence. -tion, n.

discept (disept'), v.i. discuss; dispute. -ation, -ator, n.

discerp (disōp'), v.t. tear off, or to pieces. -ible, -tible, adj. -tion, n.

discigerous (diskij'ərəs), adj. bearing a disc.

discinct (disingkt'), adj. partly or loosely clad; having belt removed.

discission (disizh'n, -sh'n), n. incision; open cut.

discobolus, -los (diskob'ələs), n. discus-thrower; famous anct. statue of discus-thrower.

discrete (diskrēt', dis'-), adj. separate; composed of separable parts; v.t. separate.

disculpate (diskul'pāt), v.t. exculpate. -tion, n. -tory, adj.

disembogue (disimbōg'), v.i. & t. debouch; discharge into sea, etc.; eject.

diseuse (dēzōz'), Fr. n. (masc. -seur, -zŏr') reciter.

disgeneric (disjiner'ik), adj. of different kind or genus.

dishabille, de- (disabēl', des-), n. déshabillé; negligée.

disjecta membra (disjek'tə mem'brə), Lat., "scattered fragments"; scattered or disjointed quotations.

disjection (disjek'shn), n. dispersion; scattering.

disjunction (disjungk'shn), n. act of separating; state of being separated. -tive, adj. expressing or requiring alternation, separation or contrast; n. Gram., such conjunction.

disomus (disō'məs), n. (pl. -mi) monster with two bodies. -matous (-som'ətəs, -sō'-), adj. having two bodies.

disparate (dis'pərət), adj. fundamentally different; unequal. -rity (-ar'iti), n.

dispendious (dispen'diəs), adj. extravagant; costly.

dispermous (dispō'məs), adj. having two seeds. -my, n. union of two sperm cells and one ovum.

disseminate (disem'ināt), v.t. spread; scatter; broadcast; diffuse. -tion, n. -tive, adj.

dissepiment (disep'imənt), n. partition, espec. of tissue. -al, adj.

dissident (dis'idənt), adj. disagreeing; different; n. such person. -nce, n.

dissilient (disil'iənt), adj. bursting open or apart.

dissimulate (disim'ūlāt), v.i. & t. feign; pretend. -tion, n. -tive, adj.

dissociate (disō'shiāt), v.t. separate into constituent parts; split up. -tion, n. Chem., separation of a compound into components; Psych., splitting of personality.

dissonant (dis'ənənt), adj. discordant; harsh. -nce, n.

dissyllable (dis'siləbl), n. word or verse foot of two syllables. -bic (-ab'ik), adj.

distaff (dis'tahf), n. staff to which flax, etc., is attached in hand-spinning; woman's work. d.side, female side.

distal (dis'təl), adj. away from point of attachment or axis.

distich (dis'tik), n. verse couplet. -ous, adj. arranged in two rows.

distrain (distrān'), v.i. seize goods in default of payment. -t, n.

distrait (dēs'trā), Fr. adj. inattentive; abstracted.

distributary (distrib'ūtəri), n. river branch flowing away from main stream.

dit (dē), Fr. adj. "said"; commonly known as; reputed to be.

dithecal (dithē'kl), adj. having two cells. -cous, adj.

ditheism (dī'thēizm), n. belief in two equal gods, espec. one good and one evil. -ist, n. -istic(al), adj.

dithyramb (dith'iram), n. Dionysiac song; ecstatic poem or harangue. -ic, adj. wild and impassioned.

ditokous (dit'əkəs), adj. producing two offspring at a birth, or offspring of two kinds.

ditrichotomous (dītrikot'əməs), adj. divided into two or three parts.

dittograph (dit'əgraf), n. letter of word repeated unintentionally in writing or copying. -ology, n. two different interpretations of same text.

diuretic (dī ūret'ik), n. & adj. (drug) increasing urination. -esis, n. copious urination.

diurnal (dī ō'nəl), adj. daily; of a day or daylight; lasting one day; Bot., app. to flowers opening by day only. -nation, n. sleeping or torpidity during daylight.

---

diuturnal (dī ūtē'nəl), adj. lasting long time. -nity, n.

divagate (dī'vəgāt), v.i. wander; digress. -tion, n.

divaricate (dīvar'ikāt), v.i. bifurcate; adj. wide-spreading. -tion, n. bifurcation; straddling; disagreement; ambiguity.

diverticulum (dīvətik'ūləm), n. blind passage or branch; caecum. -lar, adj. -late, adj. having a d.

divertissement (dēvār'tēsmahṅ), Fr. n. amusing diversion; light entertainment, play, music, etc.

divot (div'ət), n. turf; small piece of turf torn up by golfing stroke.

divulse (divuls'), v.t. rend apart. -sion, n. -sive, adj.

dixi (diks'ī), Lat., "I have spoken"; let that suffice or settle the matter. -t, "he has spoken"; person's statement, espec. without corroboration.

docent (dō'sənt), adj. teaching; didactic.

docimasy (dō'siməsi), n. experimental testing or inquiry. -mology, n. treatise on d. -stic (-as'tik), adj.

doctrinaire (doktrinār'), adj. dogmatic; disregarding practical facts or difficulties in one's devotion to a theory or doctrine; n. such person. -rism, n.

doctrinarian (doktrinār'iən), n. & adj. doctrinaire. -ism, n. -ry (dok'-), adj. doctrinaire; having abstract beliefs.

dodecafid (dōdek'əfid), adj. divided into 12 parts.

dodecagon (dōdek'əgən), n. 12-sided plane figure. -al (-ag'ənəl), adj.

dodecahedron (dōdikəhē'drən), n. 12-sided solid figure. -ral, -ric, adj.

dodecarch (dō'dikahk), n. member of dodecarchy. -y, n. government by 12 persons.

dodecasyllable (dōdikəsil'əbl), n. word or verse line of twelve syllables. -bic (-ab'ik), adj.

doge (dōj), n. former leading magistrate of Venice or Genoa. -garessa (-g-), n. d.'s wife. -gate (-gāt, n. d.'s office.

dogma (dog'mə), n. fundamental doctrine or belief. -tic (-at'ik), adj. pert. to d.; asserting positively; based on assumption. -tise, v.i. make dogmatic statements. -tism, -tist, n.

dokhma (dok'mə), Pers. n. stone wall on which Parsee dead are exposed; "tower of silence."

dolabrate, -riform (dələ'brāt, dol'-əbrāt; -ab'rifawm), adj. shaped like axe-head.

dolce far niente (dol'chā fahr nien'tā), It., "sweet to do nothing"; pleasant idling.

doldrums (dol'drəmz), n.pl. area of calm and light winds about equator; mood of depression or boredom.

dolent (dō'lənt), adj. mournful.

dolichocephalic, -lous (dolikəsifal'ik, -sef'ələs), adj. long-headed; having skull of which maximum breadth is less than 80 per cent of maximum length. -lus, n. (pl. -li) such person. -ly, n. -oblong, n. such blond "Nordic" person.

dolichocercic (dolikəsē'sik), adj. having long forearms.

dolichocnemic (dolikoknē'mik), adj. having long legs.

dolichofacial (dolikəfā'shəl), adj. having long face.

dolichopodous (dolikop'ədəs), adj. having long feet.

dolichoprosopic (dolikəprəsop'ik, -sō'pik), adj. having very long and narrow face.

dolioform (dō'liəfawm), adj. shaped like a barrel.

dolman (dol'mən), n. long Turkish outer robe; short hussar's jacket worn over shoulder. d.sleeve, large-armholed sleeve.

dolmen (dol'men), n. cromlech. -ic, adj.

dolomite (dol'əmīt), n. magnesian limestone containing white marble. -tic (-it'ik), adj.

dolorific (dolərif'ik), adj. causing sorrow or pain.

dolose, -lous (dō'lōs, -ləs), adj. Law, of evil intent.

dolus malus (dō'ləs mā'ləs), Lat., "bad deceit"; fraud; evil intent. d.bonus, "good or permissible deceit."

dominical (dəmin'ikl), adj. pert. to Christ or Sunday. d.letter, letter denoting Sunday and used in calculating Easter date.

dominie (dom'ini), Scot. n. school master; Amer. (dō'-) parson.

donga (dong'gə), S. African n. gully.

donjon (don'jon), n. castle keep.

dooly, -lie (dōō'li), Anglo-Ind. n. kind of rough litter.

---

dop (dop), S. African *n.* kind of coarse brandy ; cup for holding diamond during cutting.

Doric (dor'ik), *adj.* pert. to Dorian race of anct. Greece ; rustic ; broad in speech ; *n.* such dialect, *espec.* N. Eng. or Scot. **-rism,** *n.* Doric idiom or custom.

dormer (daw'mə), *n.* window projecting vertically from roof with gable-like covering.

dormition (dawmish'n), *n.* act of falling asleep ; death. **-tive** (daw'-), *n.* & *adj.* soporific.

dormy, -mie (daw'mi), *adj.* winning in golf by as many holes as remain to play.

dorsal (daw'səl), *adj.* pert. to, on or at the back ; *n.* hanging behind throne, etc., or against wall. **-sad,** *adv.* towards the back.

dorsiventral (dawsiven'trəl), *adj.* having differentiated front and back, or upper and lower, surfaces. **-ity,** *n.*

doryphorus, -ros (dərif'ərəs), *n.* sculptured figure of spear-bearer.

dos-à-dos (dōz-ah-dō'), Fr. *adj.* back to back ; *n.* such seat, etc.

dosimetry (dōsim'itri), *n.* measurement of doses ; med. system in which very few drugs in strictly regulated doses are prescribed.

dot (dōt, dot), Fr. *n.* dowry. **-al,** *adj.* **-ation.** *n.* endowment.

dotterel, -trel (dot'rəl), *n.* sev. kinds of plover, including ringed plover.

douane (dooahn'), Fr. *n.* customs house. **-nier** (-ahn'yā), *n.* customs official.

double entendre (dōō'bl ahñtahñ'dr), *Fr.,* word or phrase having double meaning ; using such words.

doublette (dōōblet'), Fr. *n.* artist's copy of own work.

douceur (dōōsēr'), Fr. *n.* "sweetness, sweetener" ; bribe ; gratuity ; gentleness of manner.

doulocracy, du- (dōōlok'rəsi, dū-), *n.* government by slaves.

do ut des (dō ut dēz), *Lat.,* "I give that you may give" ; reciprocal agreement or concession.

dowager (dow'əjə), *n.* woman with title, etc., deriving from deceased husband.

dowel (dow'əl), *n.* connecting pin, gen. of wood.

doxastic (doksas'tik), *adj.* pert. to opinion.

doxography (doksog'rəfi), *n.* anct. Gr. collection of philosophical extracts. **-pher,** *n.* **-phical,** *adj.*

doxology (doksol'əji), *n.* short hymn giving praise to God, *espec.* stanza beginning "Praise God, from whom all blessings flow." **-gical,** *adj.* **-gise,** *v.i.* & *t.* give praise to God.

doyen (doi'ən; dwah'yən), *n.* (*fem.* **-nne**) senior member.

drachma (drak'mə), *n.* (*pl.* **-ae**) anct. Gr. coin and weight ; mod. Gr. coin.

Draconian, -nic (drəkō'niən, -on'ik), *adj.* pert. to Draco, Athenian lawgiver (7th cent. B.C.) and his severe and cruel laws ; harsh, oppressive.

draconic (drəkon'ik), *adj.* like or pert. to a dragon.

draconites, -ntites (drakəni'tēz), -ti'tēz), *n.* serpent-stone, a jewel supposed to be found in dragon's head.

dracontian, -tine (drəkon'shiən ; -tin, -tīn), *adj.* draconic.

dragoman (drag'əman), *n.* guide and interpreter. **-ate,** *n.* d.'s office. **-ic,** *adj.*

dragonnade (dragənād'), *n.* cruel persecution ; violent invasion or punitive expedition.

dramamine (dram'əmēn), *n.* chem. drug used against sea-sickness.

dramatis personae (dram'ətis pəsō'ı.ē), *Lat.,* "characters of the drama."

dramaturgy (dram'ətəji), *n.* composition and production of dramas. **-gic,** *adj.* **-ge, -gist,** *n.*

dree (drē), Scot. *v.i.* & *t.* endure. d. one's weird, endure one's fate ; "grin and bear it."

drepaniform (drep'ənifawm), *adj.* like a sickle in shape. **-noid,** *adj.* like a sickle.

dripstone (drip'stōn), *n.* stalactite or stalagmite ; *Archit.,* stone projection for throwing off rain water.

droit (drwah), Fr. *n.* "right" ; law ; justice. **d.administratif,** law stating right of government agents to be liable to administrative tribunals only. **d. au travail,** right to work. **d. du seigneur,** feudal lord's right to enjoy female vassal on her wedding night. **-ural**

(droi'tūral), adj. pert. to right to property.

dromic(al) (drom'ik, -l), adj. pert. to foot-race course; with long, narrow plan.

dromometer (drəmom'itə), n. any speed-measuring instr.

droshki (drosh'ki), n. light one-horse four-wheeler Russ. carriage, espec. one in which passengers ride astride a saddle-like seat.

drosometer (drəsom'itə), n. instr. measuring amount of dew. -ograph (dros'-), n. such recording instr.

drosophila (drəsof'ilə), n. the fruit-fly, used in genetic experiments because of its quick breeding.

drumlin (drum'lin), n. long glacially-formed hill. -loid, adj. like a d.

drupe (drōōp), n. Bot., single-seeded stoned fruit with fleshy or dry covering, as cherry or almond. -let, -ole, n. small d. -paceous, adj. pert. to, like, or bearing d. -piferous, adj. bearing d.

dryad (drī'ad), n. wood nymph. -ic, adj.

dry-bob (drī'bob), n. Etonian who plays cricket or football.

drysalter (drī'sawltə), n. dealer in dried goods, foods, chemicals, etc. -y, n.

dualism (dū'əlizm), n. Phil., theory that ultimate reality comprises two elements, e.g. mind and matter; Theol., belief in two equal and opposite principles, as good and evil, or in dual constitution of man, as composed of spirit and matter. -istic, adj.

duarchy, see diarchy.

dubash (doobahsh'), Anglo-Ind. n. native guide or guard.

dubiety (dūbī'iti), n. doubt; doubtful matter. -ious, adj. doubtful; suspicious; questionable. -iosity, n. -itation, n. doubting; hesitation. -itative, adj. signifying doubt.

ducat (duk'ət), n. former gold and silver coin of sev. countries.

Duce (dōō'chā), It. n. chief; leader.

ductile (duk'tīl), adj. easily hammered or drawn out into long thin strip; easily led. -lity (-il'iti), n.

ductless (dukt'lis), adj. Med., endocrine.

dudheen (dooden'), Ir. n. clay pipe.

duenna (dūen'ə), n. chaperone; governess.

duffel (duf'l), n. coarse heavy-nap woollen cloth.

dug (dug), n. udder; teat; breast.

dugong (dōō'gong), n. small seal-like aquatic mammal.

duiker (dī'kə), S. African n. cormorant. -bok, n. small African antelope.

dulce domum (dul'si dō'məm), Lat., "sweet home."

dulcify (dul'sifī), v.t. sweeten; mollify. -fication, n. -igenic, adj. yielding sweetness.

dulosis (dūlō'sis), n. enslavement, espec. of certain ant species. -otic (-ot'ik), adj.

dulse (duls), n. kind of red Scot. and Ir. seaweed used as food.

duma (dōō'mə), n. parliament of Czarist Russia.

dumdum (dum'dum), adj. app. to bullet with soft nose, expanding on contact, first made at Dumdum, India.

dumose, -mous (dū'mōs, -məs), adj. bushy. -osity, n.

dunga, don- (doong'gə, dong'-), n. Ind. dug-out boat with sail.

dunlin (dun'lin), n. species of sand-piper.

dunnage (dun'ij), n. packing material for protecting cargo.

duodecillion (dūədisil'yən), n. a million undecillions (10^{72}); Amer. & Fr., a thousand undecillions (10^{40}).

duodecimal (dūədes'iməl), adj. pert. to twelve or twelfths; in groups of twelve. d. system, arithmetical system similar to decimal but based on scale of twelve and twelfths. -mo, n. size of books, about 5¼ in. by 8¼ in. (abbr. 12mo.).

duodenum (dūədē'nəm), n. part of small intestine leading from stomach. -nal, adj. -nitis, n. inflammation of d.

duomachy (dūom'əki), n. fight between two persons.

Duralumin (dūral'ūmin), n. a very strong aluminium alloy.

dura mater (dūr'ə mā'tə), n. outer membrane enclosing brain.

duramen (dūrā'mən), n. heartwood of tree.

duress (dūres'), n. imprisonment; restraint; compulsion by threats.

durgah (dŏ'gah), Hind. *n.* Moham. saint's shrine or tomb.

durian, -ion (dŏŏr'iən), *n.* E. Ind. fruit with prickly rind and pleasant edible pulp.

durity (dūr'iti), *n.* hardness. **-rometer,** *n.* instr. measuring hardness.

durra (dur'ə), *n.* Ind. millet.

durwaun (dəwawn'), *n.* darwan.

dustoor(y) (dustŏŏr', -i), Anglo-Ind. *n.* custom ; usual fee.

dustuk, -uck (dus'tuk), Anglo-Ind. *n.* passport.

duumvir (dūum'və), *n.* (*pl.* **-i, duoviri**) member of duumvirate. **-al,** *adj.* **-ate,** *n.* governing body of two men.

dwale (dwāl), *n.* deadly nightshade.

dyad (dī'ad), *n.* set of two ; bivalent atom, etc. ; *adj.* consisting of two ; bivalent. **-ic,** *adj.*

dyarchy (dī'ahki), *n.* dual form of government. **-ic(al),** *adj.*

dygogram (di'gəgram), *n.* graph showing amount, at all positions, of deflection of compass due to iron of ship.

dynameter (dīnam'itə), *n.* instr. measuring telescope's magnifying power.

dynamic (dīnam'ik), *adj.* pert. to or marked by power, energy, movement or change. **-mism,** *n.* energy; drive ; phil. theory of forces as constituting universe. **-mist,** *n.* expert on dynamics or believer in dynamism. **-s,** *n.* study of motion and of forces causing or changing motion.

dynamogenesis (dīnəməjen'isis), *n.* production of power. **-nic, -nous** (-oj'inəs), *adj.*

dynamometer (dīnəmom'itə), *n.* instr. measuring power.

dynamomorphic (dīnəməmaw'fik), *adj.* pert. to changes due to physical forces.

dyne (dīn), *n.* unit of force : force causing mass of one gramme to undergo acceleration per second of one centimetre per second.

dyotheism (dī'əthēizm), *n.* ditheism.

dysaesthesia (disesthē'zhiə), *n.* loss of sense of touch. **-etic** (-et'ik), *adj.*

dysarthrosis (disahthrō'sis), *n.* diseased or abnormal condition of joint.

dyschroa, -oia (dis'krŏə, -roi'ə), *n.* skin discoloration.

dyschromatoptic (diskrōmətop'tik), *adj.* colour-blind. **-psia,** *n.*

dyschronous (dis'krənəs), *adj.* not synchronous.

dyscrasia (diskrā'zhiə), *n. Med.,* constitutional weakness. **-atic, -ic, -l,** *adj.*

dysentery (dis'əntri), *n.* severe bowel disease due to microbes. **-ric** (-er'ik), *adj.*

dysergia (disō'jiə), *n.* deficient muscular co-ordination.

dysgenesis (disjen'isis), *n.* sterility, *espec.* among hybrids. **-ic,** *adj.* **-nic,** *adj.* damaging to hereditary qualities ; causing racial degeneration. **-nics,** *n.* study of such retrograde evolution.

dysidrosis (disidrō'sis), *n.* excessive perspiration ; skin disease attacking soles and palms.

dyskinesia (diskinē'zhiə), *n.* loss of power of voluntary movement. **-etic** (-et'ik), *adj.*

dyslogia (dislō'jiə), *n.* inability to express ideas in speech due to mental deficiency.

dyslogy (dis'ləji), *n.* unfavourable speech ; censure. **-gistic,** *adj.*

dysmenorrhea (dismenərē'ə), *n.* painful menstruation. **-l,** *adj.*

dyspepsia (dispep'siə), *n.* severe indigestion, *espec.* chronic. **-ptic,** *adj.* ; *n.* person suffering from d.

dysphagic (disfaj'ik), *adj.* having difficulty in swallowing. **-gia** (-ā'jiə), *n.*

dysphasia (disfā'zhiə), *n.* impairment of understanding of words, due to brain disease or injury. **-sic,** *adj.*

dysphonia (disfō'niə), *n.* inability to pronounce sounds, due to physical abnormality or disease. **-nic** (-on'ik), *adj.*

dysphoria (disfor'iə), *n.* generalised feeling of being ill or depressed. **-ric** (-or'ik), *adj.*

dysphrasia (disfrā'zhiə), *n.* impairment of speech due to mental deficiency.

dyspnoea (dispnē'ə), *n.* difficult breathing. **-l, -oeic, -oic,** *adj.*

dyssynergia (disinə'jiə, -in'-əji), *n.* dysergia.

dystocia (distō'shiə), *n.* difficult childbirth. **-l,** *adj.*

dystrophy (dis'trəfi, -ō'fiə), *n.* malnutrition. muscular d., faulty nutrition of muscles, leading to paralysis. **-phic** (-of'ik), *adj.*

E

eagre, -ger (ē'gə, ā'-), n. aiger.

easement (ēz'mənt), n. Law, right over another's land.

eau-de-nil (ō-də-nēl'), Fr., "water of Nile" ; a light shade of green.

eau-de-vie (ō-də-vē'), Fr. n. brandy.

eau forte (ō fôrt'), Fr. n. aqua fortis ; etching.

eau sucrée (ō sü'krā), Fr., "sweetened water."

ebeneous (ibē'niəs), adj. pert. to or like ebony.

ebrious, -ose (ē'briəs, -ōs), adj. given to excessive drinking. -osity, n.

ebullient (ibul'iənt), adj. boiling ; effervescent ; exhilarated. -lio-scope, n. instr. for determining boiling point. -lition, -nce, -ncy, n. -litive, adj.

eburnean, -eous (ibə'niən, -əs), adj. like, pert. to or made of ivory. -nated, adj. like ivory. -nation, n. disease in which cartilage or bone becomes like ivory.

ecbatic (ekbat'ik), adj. Gram., signifying result without intention.

ecbolic (ekbol'ik), n. & adj. (drug) helping childbirth or causing abortion.

ecce homo (ek'i hō'mō), Lat., "behold the man !"

ecchymosis (ekimō'sis), n. discoloured spot due to effusion of blood into tissue. -mose, v.t. cause e.

ecclesiarch (iklē'ziahk), n. church ruler. -y, n. government by clerics.

ecclesiastry (iklē'ziəstri), n. church affairs.

ecclesiolatry (iklēziol'ətri), n. worship of or undue devotion to church. -ter, n. such worshipper.

ecclesiology (iklēziol'əji), n. study of eccl. art, decoration, etc. -gical, adj. -gist, n.

eccoprotic (ekəprot'ik), n. & adj. purgative. -ophoric, adj. like a purgative in action.

eccrinology (ekrinol'əji), n. study of excretion and secretion. -ritic, n. & adj. purgative.

ecdemic (ekdem'ik), adj. of foreign origin ; not endemic.

ecdysis (ek'disis), n. moulting of outer skin, etc.

échelon (āsh'lən ; Fr., āsh'lawn), Fr. n. step-like arrangement of troops with divisions parallel but diagonally slightly to rear ; a section of a mil. command or other organisation.

echidna (ikid'nə), n. spined, burrowing, egg-laying, ant-eating mammal of Australasia ; porcupine anteater.

echinal, -noid (ek'inəl, -oid), adj. pert. to or like a sea urchin. -nate(d), adj. prickly. -nid(an), n. sea urchin.

echinoderm (ikī'nədōm, ek'in-) n. spiny-skinned marine animal, as sea urchin, starfish, etc. -nology, n. study of e.

echinulate (ikin'ūlāt, -kī-), adj. having small spines. -liform, adj. like small spines.

echinus (ikī'nəs), n. (pl. -ni) hedgehog ; sea urchin ; Archit., egg-and-dart ornament.

echolalia (ekəlā'liə), n. habitual repetition, like an echo, of others' remarks. -ic (-al'ik), adj. -opraxia, n. habitual repetition of others' actions.

éclaircissement (āklār'sēsmahṅ), Fr. n. full explanation ; enlightenment.

éclat (āklah'), n. brilliancy ; brilliant achievement ; acclaimed success ; exposure, espec. scandalous.

eclectic (iklek'tik), adj. selecting, espec. the best from a number of sources ; comprising selected pieces. -ism (-sizm), n. compounding body of phil. or relig. doctrine from selected beliefs of other systems.

eclipsis (iklip'sis), n. omission of sounds or words in speech ; ellipsis.

ecliptic (iklip'tik), n. Astron. celestial great circle along which sun apparently travels. -al, adj.

eclogue (ek'log), n. pastoral poem.

ecology (ikol'əji), n. biol. study of inter-relationships between living organisms and their environment. -gic(al), adj. -gist, n.

ecophobia (ekəfō'biə, ē-), n. dislike of home.

écru (ek'rōō ; Fr., ākrü'), adj. of a natural, unbleached shade.

ectasis (ek'təsis), n. dilatation. -atic (-at'ik), adj.

ecthlipsis (ekthlip'sis), n. (pl. -ses) omission of sounds in pronouncing a word.

ecthyma (ekthī'mə), n. skin eruption bearing sev. pustules.

ectobatic (ektəbat'ik), adj. efferent.

ectocranial (ektəkrā'niəl), adj. pert. to exterior of skull.

ectoderm (ek'tədɜm), n. outermost membrane and tissue. -al, -ic, adj. -osis, n. disease of the e.

ectogenesis (ektəjen'isis), n. development outside body. -nic, -nous (-oj'inəs), adj.

ectoparasite (ek'təparəsīt), n. parasite on surface of animals. -phyte, n. such plant parasite.

ectopia (ektō'piə), n. Med., displacement of organs, etc. -ic (-op'ik), adj.

ectoplasm (ek'təplazm), n. protoplasmic emanation from spiritualist medium; Biol., outer layer of protoplasm. -ic, adj. -sy (-plasi), n. formation of such emanation.

ectorhinal (ektərī'nəl), adj. pert. to exterior of nose.

ectozoon (ektəzō'on), n. (pl. -zoa) external parasite. -oan, -oic, adj.

ectype (ek'tīp), n. copy; noneternal being or idea. -pography, n. etching in relief.

ecumenical (ēkūmen'ikl, ek-), adj. world-wide; pert. to whole church. -city, n.

edacious (idā'shəs), adj. pert. to eating; gluttonous. -city (-as'iti), n.

edaphic (idaf'ik), adj. pert. to or conditioned by soil; indigenous. -phology, n. study of soils. -phon (ed'-) n. living organisms in soil.

edelweiss (ā'dlvīs), n. small Alpine flower of Switzerland and N.Z.

edema, see oedema.

edeology, see oedeeology.

edulcorate (idul'kərāt), v.t. sweeten; purify, espec. of acids; (-ət), adj. sweetened. -tion, -tor, n. -tive, adj.

effendi (efen'di), n. Turk. title of respect; sir.

efferent (ef'ərənt), adj. carrying away; conveying outwards; n. such nerve, blood-vessel, etc.

effete (efēt'), adj. degenerated; sterile; worn-out.

effloresce (eflōres'), v.i. flower; burgeon; Chem., become powder when exposed to air; develop a powdery crust. -nce, n. -nt, adj.

effluent (ef'looənt), adj. flowing out or away; n. such stream, drain, sewage, etc. -nce, -ux, -uxion, n.

effodient (efō'diənt), adj. burrowing.

effulgent (iful'jənt), adj. radiant; bright. -nce, n.

egalitarian (igalitār'iən), n. & adj. (adherent) of theory of political or social equality. -ism, n.

egest (ijest'), v.t. excrete. -a, n.pl. excrements. -ion, n. -ive, adj.

ego (eg'ō, ē'-), n. I; self; personality. -centric, adj. selfish; seeing only one's own or Man's or individual's viewpoint. -ism, n. selfishness; conceit; egocentric phil. or psych. theory. -ist, n. -istic, adj. -mania, n. excessive egoism. -tism, n. continuous speaking of oneself; self-praise; conceit. -tist, n. -tistic, adj.

egregious (igrē'jəs), adj. outstanding; infamous.

egret (ē'grit, eg'-), n. white heron.

eidetic (idet'ik), adj. vivid; n. person having very vivid mental pictures.

eidolon (idō'lən), n. phantom. -lic (-ol'ik), adj. -lism, n. belief in ghosts. -lology, n. study of mental imagery.

eikonology (īkənol'əji), n. metaphor.

eirenic, ir- (īren'ik, -rē'-), adj. promoting peace. -ism (-sizm), n. such state of mind. -on, n. such act. -s, n. theology aiming at relig. unity.

eisegesis (īsijē'sis), n. incorrect explanation of text, espec. of Bible, by distorting the meaning to fit preconceived ideas. -etical (-et'ikl), adj.

eisteddfod (estedh'vəd), n. (pl. -au, -vod'ī) assembly of Welsh bards, with singing, verse-making, etc.; competitions. -ic, adj. -ism, n.

eiusdem generis, ejus- (ēus'dəm jen'əris, -jus'-), Lat., "of the same kind."

ejecta(menta) (ijek'tə, -men'tə), n.pl. ejected material, espec. from volcano.

ek dum (ek dum), Anglo-Ind. adv. immediately.

élan (ālahń'), Fr. n. eagerness; brilliancy of style; vivacity.

e.vital (-vētal'), creative or "life" force.

elaterid (ilat'ərid), *n.* click beetle.

elaterium (elatēr'iəm), *n.* aperient extracted from a species of cucumber.

elateroid (ilat'əroid), *adj.* pert. to or like elaterid.

elatrometer (elətrom'itə), *n.* instr. measuring pressure of gas.

elchi, -chee (el'chi), Turk. *n.* ambassador.

eldritch (el'drich), *adj.* weird; horrifying.

elecampane (elikampān'), *n.* large yellow-flowered plant, with root from which sweetmeat is made.

electrepeter (ilektrep'itə), *n.* elec. device changing current's direction.

electrode (ilek'trōd), *n.* elec. terminal; either pole of electrolytic cell.

electrodynamics (ilektrədīnam'iks), *n.* study of elec. currents.

electro-encephalograph (ilek'trō-ensef'ələgraf), *n.* apparatus which detects and records elec. activity of the brain (*abbr.* E.E.G.). **-gram,** *n.* such record. **-ic,** *adj.* **-y,** *n.*

electrolier (ilektrəlēr'), *n.* chandelier for elec. lamps.

electrolysis (ilektrol'isis), *n.* decomposition of substance by elec. current. **-yse,** *v.t.* **-yte,** *n.* substance, *espec.* dissolved in liquid, which is separated by current in e. **-ytic** (-it'ik), *adj.*

electromerism (ilektrom'ərizm), *n.* ionisation of gases.

electrometer (ilektrom'itə), *n.* instr. measuring differences of elec. potential. **-tric** (-et'rik), *adj.* **-try,** *n.*

electromotive (ilektrəmō'tiv), *adj.* pert. to elec. motion; causing elec. current. **e.force,** amount of elec. energy; voltage; potential (*abbr.* **e.m.f.**).

electron (ilek'tron), *n.* negatively charged constituent part of atom. **e.microscope,** microscope producing magnified images of things too small to be seen with the most powerful optical microscope, by means of a beam of electrons focused by a magnetic field. **-ic,** *adj.* pert. to electrons; worked by beams of electrons. **-ics,** *n.* study and application of the effects of beams of electrons.

electronegative (ilektrəneg'ətiv), *adj.* negatively charged; passing to anode in electrolysis; acid; *n.* such substance.

electropathy (ilektrop'əthi), *n.* med. treatment by electricity.

electrophoresis (ilektrəfərē'sis), *n.* cataphoresis. **-etic** (-et'ik), *adj.*

electrophorus (ilektrof'ərəs), *n.* (*pl.* **-ri**) instr. consisting of ebonite disc, electrified by friction, and metal plate in which positive elec. is induced from the disc. **-ric** (-for'ik), *adj.*

electropositive (ilektrəpoz'itiv), *adj.* positively charged; passing to cathode in electrolysis; basic; *n.* such substance.

electroscope (ilek'trəskōp), *n.* instr. determining elec. charge and nature of it, *espec.* by diverging gold-leaf strips, etc.

electrostatics (ilektrəstat'iks), *n.* study of stationary (*i.e.* not current) electricity.

electrotherapy, -peutics (ilektrə-ther'əpi, -pū'tiks), *n.* use of electricity in med. treatment.

electrotype (ilek'trətīp), *n.* plate for printing consisting of soft mould covered with metal electrolytically; *v.i.* & *t.* make e. (of). **-py,** *n.*

electuary (ilek'tūəri), *n.* med. remedy in syrup.

eleemosynary (eliēmoz'inəri, eli-mos'-), *adj.* pert. to or like alms; giving, or given as, alms; dependent on alms.

elegiac (eliji'ak), *n.* Pros., verseline of five dactyls with marked caesura; *adj.* pert. to or written in such verse line. **e.couplet,** dactylic hexameter followed by dactylic pentameter. **-s,** *n.* verses written in e. metre or e. couplets.

elench (ilengk'), *n.* fallacious argument, *espec.* seeming true. **-ctic,** *adj.* refuting. **-us,** *n.* syllogistic refutation.

elephantiasis (elifantī'əsis), *n.* disease causing skin, *espec.* of legs, to become hard and thick, and limbs to swell. **-tiac,** *n.* & *adj.* (person) suffering from e. **-tous,** *adj.*

Eleusinian (elūsin'iən), *adj.* pert. to Eleusis, in anct. Greece, and its religious mysteries of initiation.

eleutheromania (elūthərəmā'niə), *n.*

strong desire for freedom. -c, *n.* & *adj.*

elide (ilīd'), *v.t.* suppress or omit in pronunciation. -ision, *n.*

élite (ālēt'), Fr. *n.* chosen few; superior body or class of persons.

elixir (iliks'ə), *n.* highly purified spirit; substance thought to confer immortality or cure all diseases, or transmute into gold.

ellipsis (ilip'sis), *n.* intentional omission of grammatically necessary words. -ptic(al), *adj.*

éloge (ālozh'), Fr. *n.* eulogy; laudatory funeral oration.

elogy, -gium (el'əji, -ō'jiəm), *n.* éloge; laudatory obituary notice.

elute (ilūt'), *v.t.* wash out; purify or separate by washing. -tion, -tor, *n.* -triate, *v.t.* purifying by washing and straining. -triation, -triator, *n.* -uate (cl'-), *n.* material obtained by elution.

eluvium (ilū'viəm), *n.* detritus from weathering of rock. -ial, *adj.*

elver (el'və), *n.* young eel.

elydoric (elidor'ik), *adj.* with both oil and water colours.

Elysian (iliz'iən), *adj.* pert. to Elysium, the heaven of Gr. myth.; ideally happy.

elytron, -rum (el'itrən, -rəm), *n.* (*pl.* -ra) insect's hardened forewing, forming case for hind wing. -ral, *adj.* -riferous, -rigerous, *adj.* bearing e. -riform, *adj.* like e.

em (em), *n.* printer's unit of measurement: width of pica M (one-sixth of inch).

emarcid (imah'sid), *adj.* wilted.

emasculate (imas'kūlāt), *v.t.* weaken; deprive of vigour; render sterile, *espec.* by castration; (-ət), *adj.* effeminate. -tion, *n.* -tive, -tory, *adj.*

embarras de richesses (ahñbarah' də rēshes'), Fr., "embarrassment of riches"; embarrassing surplus. **e. de choix** (-də shwah), multitude difficult to choose from.

emblements (em'blimənts), *n.pl.* Law, growing crops.

emblic (em'blik), *n.* kind of myrobalan.

embolism (em'bəlizm), *n.* Med., obstruction of vessel by clot, etc.; insertion of intercalary day(s), month, etc. -ic, -lic, *adj* -lectomy, *n.* removal of embolus. -liform, *adj.* like a clot. -lus, *n.* (*pl.* -li)

obstructive clot, foreign body, etc.; wedge.

embonpoint (ahñbawñpwañ'), Fr. *n.* corpulence.

embouchement (ahñbōōsh'mahñ), Fr. *n.* opening of passage. -chure (-shūr'), *n.* river mouth; mouthpiece; placing of lips, etc., about mouthpiece of mus. instr.

embryo (em'briō), *n.* partly developed offspring before birth or hatching (in humans, from conception to third month); plant before germination of seed; any partly developed thing. -ctony (-ok'təni), *n.* killing of e. -geny (-oj'əni), *n.* growth of e. -id (-oid), *adj.* like an e. -logy (-ol'əji), *n.* study of e. -nated (-ənātid), *adj.* containing an e. -nic (-on'ik), *adj.* -niform (-on'ifawm), *adj.* shaped like e. -ny (-ī'əni), *n.* production of e. -tomy (-ot'əmi), *n.* mutilation of e. to facilitate birth. -yectomy, *n.* removal of e.

emeer, -mir (emēr'), *n.* Arab ruler or general; descendant of Mohammed. -ate, *n.* jurisdiction of e.

emeritus (imer'itəs), *adj.* retired, but retaining honorary office; *n.* (*pl.* -ti) such professor, etc.

emesis (em'isis), *n.* vomiting. -etic (imet'ik), *n.* & *adj.* (substance) causing vomiting. -etology, *n.* study of emetics and their action.

emiction (imik'shn), *n.* urination, urine. -tory, *n.* & *adj.* (drug) promoting urination.

émigré (ā'mēgrā), Fr. *n.* (*fem.* -ée) person forced to flee, *espec.* from revolution.

emmenagogue (əmen'əgog, -mē'-), *n.* drug aiding menstruation. -gic (-oj'ik), *adj.* -niopathy, *n.* menstruation disorder. -nology (emənol'-), *n.* study of menstruation.

emmetropia (emitrō'piə), *n.* perfect refraction of eye. -pic (-op'ik), *adj.*

emollient (imol'iənt), *n.* & *adj.* softening or soothing (substance). -lescence, *n.*

emolument (imol'ūmənt), *n.* salary; profit.

empaestic, -pai- (empē'stik, -pes'-, -pā'-), *adj.* embossed.

empasm (empaz'm), *n.* scented powder concealing odour of perspiration.

empathy (em'pəthi), *n.* deep sympathetic understanding, *espec.* of non-human beings. **-thic** (-ath'ik), *adj.* **-thise**, *v.i.* & *t.*

emphractic (emfrak'tik), *n.* & *adj.* (substance) closing skin pores. **-raxia, -raxis**, *n.* obstruction, *espec.* of pores.

emphysema (emfise'mə), *n. Med.,* swollen state of tissue due to air or gas. **-tous** (-sem'ətəs, -sē'-), *adj.* so swollen ; bloated ; bladder-like.

emphyteusis (emfitū'sis), *n.* contract granting possession of land for long period on certain conditions. **-eutic,** *adj.*

empiric(al) (empir'ik, -l), *adj.* relying on or derived from experiment or experience only ; ignoring theory or science ; *n.* such thinker or scientist ; quack. **-cism, -cist,** *n.*

emporeutic, -etic (empərōō'tik, -et'ik), *adj.* pert. to trade ; *n.* merchandise.

empressé (ahṅpres'ā), Fr. *adj.* (*fem.* **-ée**) in haste ; eager. **-ment** (-pres'mahṅ), *n.* show of affection.

emption (emp'shn), *n.* buying.

emptysis (emp'tisis), *n.* spitting of blood.

empyaema (empiē'mə), *n.* (*pl.* **-ta**) collection of pus in body cavity, *espec.* in pleural cavity. **-mic,** *adj.*

empyesis (empiē'sis), *n.* eruption of pus-containing pimples.

empyrean (empīr'ē'ən), *n.* & *adj.* (pert. to) the sky ; heaven. **-eal** (-īr'iəl), *adj.*

emulgent (imul'jənt), *adj.* draining ; purifying ; pert. to kidneys ; *n.* drug stimulating bile.

emulsion (imul'shn), *n.* milky fluid ; suspension of oil or resin in watery liquid or vice versa ; any dispersion of one liquid in another ; coating, containing suspended silver salt, of photog. films and plates. **-sify,** *v.t.* convert into e. **-sive,** *adj.*

emunctory (imungk'təri), *n.* & *adj.* excretory (organ).

enallage (enal'əji), *n. Gram.,* exchange of part of speech, gender, tense, etc., for another.

enanthesis (enanthē'sis), *n.* eruption on skin due to internal disease.

enantiopathy (enantiop'əthi), *n.* med. treatment by inducing effect opposite to those of disease being treated. **-thic** (-ath'ik), *adj.*

enantiosis (enantiō'sis), *n.* rhet. device of ironically stating the opposite of what is meant.

enarthrosis (enahthrō'sis), *n.* ball-and-socket joint.

enate (ē'nāt), *adj.* growing out ; *n.* relation on mother's side. **-tic** (inat'ik), *adj.* related on mother's side ; having same mother. **-tion,** *n.* outgrowth ; enatic relationship.

encaenia (ensē'niə), *n.* festival commemorating dedication or foundation.

encaustic (ęnkaw'stik), *adj.* burnt in ; *n.* painting with wax colours fixed by heat.

enceinte (ahṅsaṅt'), Fr. *adj.* pregnant ; *n.* fortification enclosing fortress or town ; cathedral close.

encephalitis (ensefəli'tis), *n.* inflammation of brain. **e. lethargica,** sleeping sickness.

encephalon (ensef'əlon), *n.* (*pl.* **-la**) the brain. **-lograph,** *n.* X-ray photograph of brain. **-loid,** *adj.* brain-like. **-loma,** *n.* brain tumour.

enchiridion (enkīrid'iən), *n.* handbook.

enchorial, -ric (enkōr'iəl, -or'ik), *adj.* native ; domestic.

enchylema (enkilē'mə), *n.* fluid part of protoplasm. **-tous,** *adj.*

en clair (aṅ klār'), *Fr.,* "in clear" ; not in code.

enclave (en'klāv ; Fr., ahṅklav'), *n.* part of a foreign country enclosed in native territory ; (-klāv'), *v.t.* surround land thus. **-ment,** *n.*

enclitic (enklit'ik), *adj.* dependent, *espec.* of word or particle attached to preceding word in pronunciation ; *n.* such word or particle. **-lisis** (eng'klisis), *n.* pronunciation of e. word.

encomic (enkō'mik, -om'-), *adj.* app. to closely curled woolly hair.

encomium (enkō'miəm), *n.* (*pl.* **-ia**) eulogy. **-miast,** *n.* composer of e. **-miastic,** *adj.*

encyclical (ensīk'likl), *n.* & *adj.* (publication) for wide distribution, *espec.* Pope's letter to bishops.

endarchy (en'dahki), *n.* centralised government.

endeictic (endīk'tik), *adj.* demonstrating.

endemic (endem'ik), *adj.* native ; indigenous ; generally present in a particular place or class ; *n.* such

---

disease. -miology (-dēmiol'əji), n. study of e. diseases. -mism (en'dimizm), n.

endive (en'div), n. kind of chicory with curled leaves. French e., e. with blanched leaves for salad.

endocardium (endəkah'diəm), n. membrane lining heart cavities. -disc, -dial, adj. -ditis, n. inflammation of e.

endocrine (en'dəkrin), adj. secreting direct into the blood-stream ; n. such gland. -nic (-in'ik), -nous (-ok'rinəs), adj. -nology, n. study of e. glands and hormones. -nopathy, n. disease due to abnormal hormone secretion. -notherapy, n. med. treatment with hormones.

endogamy (endog'əmi), n. marriage to person of same tribe only. -mic (-gam'ik), -mous, adj.

endogeny (endoj'ini), n. growth from within. -nesis (-jen'isis), n. endogamy. -netic (-jinet'ik), adj. not elastic. -nic (-jen'ik), adj. pert. to geol. processes occurring within earth. -nous, adj.

endoparasite (en'dəparəsit), n. internal parasite. -tic, adj.

endophagy (endof'əji), n. cannibalism among members of same tribe ; erosion of internal tissue.

endophyte (en'dəfit), n. endoparasitic plant. -phytic (-it'ik), adj. -phytous (-of'itəs), adj. living in plants.

endoplasm (en'dəplazm), n. inner layer of protoplasm. -ic, adj. -st, n. cell nucleus.

endoscope (en'dəskōp), n. instr. for med. examination of interior of organ. -pic (-op'ik), adj. -py (-os'kəpi), n. such examination.

endoskeleton (en'dəskelitən), n. internal skeleton. -tal, adj.

endosperm (en'dəspêm), n. albumen in plant seed. -ic, adj.

endothermy (en'dəthêmi), n. surgical introduction of elec. needle or knife into tissues to produce heat. -mic, -mous, adj.

endysis (en'disis), n. development of new hair, feathers, skin, etc.

enema (en'imə), n. (pl. -ta) injection of liquid into rectum.

energumen (enəgū'men), n. person possessed by evil spirit ; fanatic.

enervate (en'əvāt), v.t. weaken. -tion, -tor, n. -tive (-ō'vətiv, en'-), adj.

enfant terrible (ahn'fahn terā'bl), Fr., "terrible child" ; child causing embarrassment by its questions, remarks, etc. ; any such rash person.

enfilade (enfilād'), n. arrangement in parallel rows or avenues ; arrangement of troops, etc., so that raking fire can be directed along length of objective ; v.t. fire upon in such manner.

English (ing'glish), n. size of type : 14-point.

engram (en'gram), n. lasting effect on memory or protoplasm. -mmatic, -mmic, adj. -raphia, -raphy, n. production of e.

enjambement (enjam'mənt ; Fr., ahnjahnb'mahn), n. running-over of sense or sentence from one verse line to next.

ennead (en'iad), n. set of nine. -ic, adj.

ennea-eteric (en'iə-iter'ik), adj. happening every ninth year.

enneagon (en'iəgən), n. nine-sided plane figure. -al (-ag'ənəl), adj.

enneahedron (eniəhē'drən), n. nine-sided solid figure. -ral, adj.

enneatic (eniat'ik), adj. happening once in every set of nine ; every ninth.

ennomic (enom'ik), adj. lawful.

ennui (on'wē), n. boredom. -uyant (-ahn), adj. boring. -uyé, n. & adj. (fem. -uyée) bored (person).

en pantoufles (ahn pahntōō'fl), Fr., "in slippers" ; at ease ; informal(ly).

enphytotic (enfitot'ik), n. & adj. endemic (disease) of plants.

en plein air (ahn plan ār'), Fr., "in open air." e. ρ. jour (-zhōōr'), "in open daylight" ; openly.

en rapport (ahn rapōr'), Fr., "in close relationship" ; in sympathy ; working together harmoniously.

en règle (ahn reg'l), Fr., "in rule" ; in due order.

ensate, -siform (en'sāt, -sifawm), adj. sword-shaped.

ensilage (en'silij), n. storing in silo ; crops so stored. -late, -le, v.t. store in silo. -lation, n.

entablature (entab'lətūr), n. Archit., wall resting on capitals of columns, comprising architrave, frieze and cornice.

entail (ental), v.t. Law, settle on a person and his descendants or certain of them; *n.* estate so settled; line of descendants to whom estate is limited.

entelechy (entel'iki), *n. Phil.*, perfect realisation of end or cause.

enteric (enter'ik), *n.* pert. to intestines; *n.* typhoid fever. **-ritis**, *n.* inflammation of intestines. **-rocly-sis** (-ok'lisis), *n.* injection of liquid into intestines. **-rography**, *n.* description of intestines. **-roid**, *adj.* shaped like intestine. **-rop-tosis**, *n.* dropping and protrusion of intestines.

enthelmintha, **-thes** (enthelmin'thə, -ēz), *n.pl.* intestinal worms. **-thic**, *adj.*

entify (en'tifi), *v.t.* make or regard as separate substance or entity. **-fical**, *adj.* **-fication**, *n.*

entitative (en'titətiv), *adj.* regarded as entity alone, apart from attendant circumstances.

ento-ectad (en'tō-ek'tad), *adv.* outwards from within.

entomic(al) (entom'ik, -l), *adj.* pert. to insects.

entomology (entəmol'əji), *n.* study of insects. **-gical**, *adj.* **-gist**, *n.*

entomophagous (entəmof'əgəs), *adj.* feeding on insects. **-philous**, *adj.* pollinated by insects.

entophyte (en'təfīt), *n.* parasitic plant living within another plant or animal. **-tal**, **-tic** (-it'ik), **-tous** (-of'itəs), *adj.*

entotic (entō'tik, -ot'-), *adj.* pert. to interior of ear. **-optic**, *adj.* pert. to interior of eyeball.

en tous cas (ahṅ too' kah), *Fr.*, "in any circumstances"; bag for general use; all-weather, *espec.* tennis court.

entozoon (entəzō'ən), *n.* (*pl.* **-zoa**) internal parasite. **-zoal**, *adj.* **-zoan**, *n. & adj.* **-zoology**, *n.* study of e.

entre-chat (ahṅ'trəshah), *Fr. n.* dancer's leap in which legs are quickly crossed or heels tapped.

entrée (on'trā; *Fr.*, ahṅ'trā), *n.* permission or right to enter; meat dish served before roast.

entre nous (ahṅ'tr noo), *Fr.*, "between ourselves."

entrepot (ahṅ'trəpō), *Fr. n.* warehouse; importing for re-export.

entrepreneur (ahṅtrəprənēr'), *Fr. n.* (*fem.* **-euse**, **-ōz**) employer; owner of business.

entresol (ahṅ'trəsol), *Fr. n.* mezzanine floor.

entropy (en'trəpi), *n.* amount of unavailable energy in a thermodynamic system; static condition.

enuresis (enūr ē'sis), *n.* inability to control urination; urine discharged involuntarily.

enzootic (enzōōt'ik), *n. & adj.* (disease) attacking animals.

enzyme (en'zīm), *n.* ferment, *espec.* digestive. **-matic**, **-mic**, *adj.*

eoan (iō'ən), *adj.* of dawn or east.

eolation (ēəlā'shn), *n.* geol. action of wind.

eolithic (ēəlith'ik), *adj.* pert. to earliest Stone Age.

eonism (ē'ənizm), *n.* adoption of opposite sex's manners, clothes and mentality.

eozoic (ēəzō'ik), *adj.* containing earliest evidence of animal life.

epact (ē'pakt, ep'-), *n.* difference, represented by a number, between solar and lunar year, or calendar and lunar month; age of moon at start of calendar year. **-al**, *adj.* intercalary.

epagoge (epəgō'ji), *n.* inductive reasoning. **-gic** (-oj'ik), *adj.*

epanadiplosis (epənədiplō'sis), *n.* repetition at end of sentence of word used at beginning.

epanalepsis (epənəlep'sis), *n.* repetition. **-ptic**, *adj.*

epanodos (epan'ədos), *n.* return to theme from digression.

epanorthosis (epənawthō'sis), *n.* emphatic repetition.

epedaphic (epidaf'ik), *adj.* pert. or due to atmospheric conditions.

epeirogeny (epīroj'ini), *n.* geol. formation of continents, oceans, etc. **-nic** (-jen'ik), *adj.*

epenthesis (epen'thisis), *n.* (*pl.* **-ses**) introduction of sound into word; removal of vowel into preceding syllable. **-e**, *v.t.* **-etic** (-et'ik), *adj.*

epergne (ā'pən; *Fr.*, āpārn'), *n.* central ornament on table.

ephectic (efek'tik), *adj.* habitually suspending judgment.

ephelis (efe'lis), *n.* (*pl.* **-lides**, -el'idēz) freckle.

ephemeron (ifem'ərən), *n.* (*pl.* **-ra**) thing, *espec.* insect, living for a day only. **-ral**, **-rous**, *adj.* short-lived. **-rid**, *n.* (*pl.* **-rides**, -er'idēz) may-fly; short-lived publication;

almanac showing daily positions of heavenly bodies.

ephidrosis (efidrō'sis), *n.* copious perspiration.

ephod (ef'od), *n.* garment of Jewish priest.

ephor (ef'or), *n.* magistrate of Sparta; supervisor of public works in mod. Greece. -al, -ic (-or'ik), *adj.* -ate, *n.* office of e.; whole body of e.

epibole (ipib'oli), *n.* rhet. device of beginning sev. clauses with same or similar word.

epicedium (episē'diəm), *n.* (*pl.* -ia) elegy; dirge. -dial, *adj.*

epicene (ep'isēn), *adj.* adapted for use by or common to both sexes; sexless; effeminate; *Gram.,* with one form signifying both male and female; *n.* an e. person.

epichorial (epikōr'iəl), *adj.* belonging to a rural area. -ric (-or'ik), -ristic. *adj.*

epichristian (epikris'tyən), *adj.* pert. to the period immediately after Christ.

epicolic (epikol'ik), *adj.* app. to lower abdomen lying over the colon.

epicrisis (epik'risis), *n.* (*pl.* -ses) critical appreciation of literature; (-krī'-), *Med.,* secondary crisis in disease.

epicure (ep'ikūr), *n.* person taking care over the niceties of food and drink. -an (-ē'ən), *adj.* luxurious; sensual; *n.* such person; follower of phil. of Epicurus, who taught that ultimate moral good is happiness.

epicycle (ep'isīkl), *n.* circle whose centre is on circumference of a greater circle. -lic, *adj.*

epideictic(al) (epidīk'tik, -l), *adj.* displaying.

epidermis (epidē'mis), *n.* outermost layer of skin; *Bot.,* plant's derma. -ma, *n.* outgrowth on e. -mal, -matic, -mic, -mous, *adj.* -moid, *adj.* like e.

epidiascope (epidī'əskōp), *n.* magic lantern for use with opaque as well as translucent objects.

epigamic (epigam'ik), *adj.* attracting opposite sex at breeding time.

epigastrium (epigas'triəm), *n.* part of abdomen lying over the stomach. -rial, -ric, *adj.*

epigeal, -ean (epijē'əl, -n), *adj.* living near the ground.

epigenesis (epijen'isis), *n.* biol. theory of the fresh creation of the embryo. -etic (-et'ik), *adj.* -nist (ipij'inist), -t, *n.*

epigeous (epijē'əs), *adj.* growing on or above ground.

epiglottis (epiglot'is), *n.* throat cartilage protecting the windpipe in swallowing. -tal, -tic, *adj.*

epigonous, -nic (epig'ənəs, -on'ik), *adj.* belonging to later generation or school of thought.

epigraph (ep'igraf), *n.* inscription; quotation at beginning of work or chapter. -y (-ig'rəfi), *n.* study of anct. inscriptions.

epilate (ep'ilāt), *v.t.* remove (hair). -tion, *n.*

epimorphic (epimaw'fik), *adj.* passing several stages of growth in same form.

epimyth (ep'imith), *n.* moral of story.

epinician (epinish'ən), *adj.* in celebration of victory.

epipastic (epipas'tik), *n.* med. dusting powder.

epiphany (ipif'əni), *n.* manifestation, *espec.* of Christ to the wise men; feast celebrating the E. of Christ on Jan. 6.

epiphenomenon (epifinom'inən), *n.* secondary phenomenon associated with and apparently due to another. -nal, *adj.*

epiphora (ipif'ərə), *n.* watering of eyes.

epiphysis (ipif'isis), *n.* (*pl.* -ses) separately ossified portion of bone, joining to main portion later. e.cerebri, pineal body. -sary, -seal (-iz'iəl), *adj.*

epiphyte (ep'ifīt), *n.* non-parasitic plant growing on another. -tal, -tic (-it'ik), -tous, *adj.* -totic, *n.* & *adj.* (disease) common among plants.

epiplexis (epipleks'is), *n.* reproof. -ectic, *adj.*

epiploce (ipip'ləsi), *n.* rhet. climax.

epipolism (ipip'əlizm), *n.* fluorescence. -lic (-ol'ik), *adj.* -lise, *v.t.*

epipterous (epip'tərəs), *adj.* having wings or wing-like projections at apex.

episcopal (ipis'kəpəl), *adj.* pert. to or ruled by bishops. -ian (-ā'liən), *adj.* pert. to episcopal church or government; *n.* member of such church. -pacy, *n.* rule by bishops;

the body of bishops collectively. -pate, *n.* office, see or whole body of bishops. -picide, *n.* murder of bishops. -polatry, *n.* worship of bishops.

epispastic (epispas'tik), *n. & adj.* (substance) causing blister as med. remedy.

epistasis (ipis'təsis), *n.* act of suppressing secretion. -atic (-at'ik), *adj.* suppressing, *espec.* the effect of another factor.

epistaxis (epistaks'is), *n.* nose-bleeding.

epistemology (ipistemol'əji), *n.* branch of phil. dealing with the study of knowledge. -gical, *adj.* -gist, *n.* -mic (-ē'mik, -em'ik), -monic, *adj.* pert. to knowledge; intellectual.

epistolary (ipis'tələri), *adj.* pert. to letters. -lography, *n.* art of letter-writing. -rian (-ār'iən), *n. & adj.* (person) fond of letter-writing.

epistrophe (ipis'trəfi), *n.* repetition of same phrase at end of successive sentences. -al (-ō'fiəl), -phic (-of'ik), *adj.*

epitasis (ipit'əsis), *n.* part. of drama in which action is developed; crisis of disease.

epithalamium, -ion (epithəlā'miəm, -iən), *n. (pl.* -ia) wedding song or poem. -mial, -mic (-am'ik), *adj.* -miast, *n.* composer of e. -my (-al'əmi), *n.* epithalamium.

epithelium (epithē'liəm), *n. (pl.* -ia) cellular membrane covering surface or lining cavity or passage. -ial, *adj.* -ioid, *adj.* like e.

epithesis (ipith'isis), *n.* addition of sound to end of word; straightening of crooked limbs.

epitimesis (epitimē'sis), *n.* adverse criticism; reproof.

epitome (ipit'əmi), *n.* summary; collection of all characteristics, facts, etc., into small space; embodiment, essence. -mic(al) (-om'ik, -l), *adj.* -mise, *v.t.* summarise; represent all essentials of; embody.

epitonic (epiton'ik), *adj.* subjected to too great strain.

epitrope (ipit'rəpi), *n.* ironical giving of permission.

epityphlitis (epitifli'tis), *n.* appendicitis. -ion, *n.* vermiform appendix.

epizeuxis (epizūks'is), *n.* repetition for emphasis.

epizoon (epizō'on), *n. (pl.* -zoa) external parasite. -zoan, *n. & adj.* -zoic, *adj.*

epizootic (epizōot'ik), *n. & adj.* (disease) epidemic among animals.

e pluribus unum (ē ploor'ibəs ū'nəm), *Lat.*, "one out of many"; unity from combination of many parts.

eponym (ep'ənim), *n.* person or his name from which name of race, family, etc., is derived; person whose name is used metaphorically to signify a quality or thing associated with him. -ic, -ous (-on'iməs), *adj.* -y (-on'imi), *n.*

epopee (ep'əpē), *n.* epic poem or poetry. -ean, *adj.* -poest, *n.* writer of epics.

epopt (ep'opt), *n. (pl.* -ae) person initiated into mysteries. -ic, *adj.*

epos (ep'os), *n.* epic poem or poetry; collection of lays dealing with same theme.

epulary (ep'ūləri), *adj.* pert. to banquet. -ation, *n.*

epulosis (epūlō'sis), *n.* formation of scar. -otic(al) (-ot'ik, -l), *n. & adj.* (substance) aiding e.

equine (ē'kwīn), *adj.* pert. to or like a horse. -nate (ek'wināt), *v.t.* inoculate with horse pox.

equinox (ē'kwinoks), *n.* date on which sun crosses equator. autumnal e., such date in autumn (about Sept. 23). vernal e., such date in spring (about March 21). -octial, *adj.* pert. to e., or to place or time having day and night of equal length; equatorial; e.line, celestial equator.

equiparent (ikwip'ərənt), *adj.* having same mutual relationship. -ate, *v.t.* level; equalise.

equipluve (ē'kwiploov), *n.* line on map drawn through all places having same proportion of rainfall in same space of time.

equipoise (ē'kwipoiz), *n.* state of equilibrium; counterpoise; *v.t.* counterpoise.

equipollent (ēkwipol'ənt), *adj.* having equal force or power; having same meaning though differently expressed. -nce, -ncy, *n.*

equisetum (ekwisē'təm), *n. (pl.* -ta) horsetail (plant).

ə=*er* in *father*; ə̄=*er* in *pert*; th=*th* in *thin*; dh=*th* in *then*; zh=*s* in *pleasure*; k=*ch* in *loch*; ñ=Fr. nasal *n*; ü=Fr. *u*.

equitation (ekwitā'shn), *n.* horse-riding. **-tive** (ek'-), *adj.*

equivocal (ikwiv'əkl), *adj.* intentionally ambiguous ; dubious. **-cate**, *v.i.* quibble. **-cation**, **-cator**, *n.* **-ity**, **-oke**, **-oque** (ē'kwivōk), *n.* pun ; ambiguous remark.

equivorous (ikwiv'ərəs), *adj.* eating horse-flesh.

Erastian (iras'tiən), *adj.* pert. to Erastus (1524-83), Swiss theologian, and his doctrine of state government of eccl. matters ; *n.* adherent of that doctrine.

Erebian (erē'biən), *adj.* pert. to Erebos, in Gr. myth. a place of darkness leading to Hades ; pitch dark.

eremic (irē'mik), *adj.* pert. to sandy desert.

eremite (er'imīt), *n.* hermit. **-tage**, *n.* **-tic(al)** (-mit'ik, -l), *adj.*

eremology (erimol'əji), *n.* study of deserts. **-mophyte** (er'-), *n.* plant living in desert.

erethism er'ithizm), *n.* abnormal excitability. **-ic**, **-thistic**, **-thitic**, *adj.*

erg (ēg), *n.* unit of energy : the work done when point of application of force of one dyne moves one centimetre. **-al**, *n.* potential energy. **-asia**, *n.* fondness for work. **-atocracy**, *n.* government by workers.

ergo (ə'gō), Lat. *adv.* "therefore."

ergograph (ə'gəgraf), *n.* instr. measuring muscular work. **-ology**, *n.* study of work's effect on mind and body. **-ophile**, *n.* lover of work. **-ophobia**, *n.* hatred of work.

ergosterol (əgos'tərol, -ōl), *n.* chemical substance in the body developing into vitamin D on exposure to sunlight.

ergot (ə'gət), *n.* fungus disease of cereals, *espec.* rye ; dried fungus causing e., containing drug which contracts blood-vessels, nerves and uterus. **-ic** (-ot'ik), *adj.* **-ise**, *v.t.* **-ism**, *n.* disease due to consuming ergotised grain, etc.

ergusia (əgū'siə, -ziə), *n.* vitamin A.

ericaceous (erikā'shəs), *adj.* pert. to or like heath plant ; belonging to the heath family of plants. **-cetal** (-sē'təl), *adj.* composed of heath plants. **-ceticolous**, *adj.* living on heaths. **-cineous**, *adj.* ericaceous. **-coid** (-koid), *adj.* like a heath plant. **-cophyte** (-ī'kəfīt), *n.* plant growing on heaths.

erinaceous (erinā'shəs), *adj.* like or pert. to a hedgehog.

eriophyllous (ēriəfil'əs), *adj.* with woolly leaves.

eristic (eris'tik), *adj.* pert. to dispute or argument.

erne (ən), *n.* golden or sea eagle.

erode (erōd'), *v.t.* cat or wear away.

erogenesis (erəjen'isis), *n.* production of sexual desire. **-neity** (-jinē'iti), *n.* **-netic** (-jinet'ik), **-nic**, **-nous** (-oj'inəs), *adj.*

erosion (irō'zhn), *n.* act of eroding. **-sive**, *adj.*

erotesis (erətē'sis), *n.* rhet. questioning. **-etic** (-et'ik), *adj.*

erotic (erot'ik), *adj.* pert. to or expressing sexual love ; *n.* such poem, person, etc. **-ism** (-sizm), *n.* **-tism**, *n.* sexual desire. **-tomania** *n.* excessive erotism. **-topathy**, *n.* abnormal erotism.

errant (er'ənt), *adj.* wandering, *espec.* seeking adventure ; mistaking. **-ry**, *n.*

erratum (erā'təm, -rah'-), *n.* (*pl.* **-ta**) mistake, *espec.* printer's or writer's.

errhine (er'īn, -in), *n.* & *adj.* (substance) causing sneezing.

ersatz (ərzahts'), Ger. *n.* & *adj.* substitute.

erubescent (eroobes'ənt), *adj.* becoming red. **-nce**, *n.*

eruca (iroo'kə), *n.* (*pl.* **-ae**) caterpillar. **-ciform** (-sifawm), *adj.* caterpillar-like. **-civorous** (-siv'-ərəs), *adj.* feeding on caterpillars.

eructation (ēruktā'shn), *n.* belching ; belch. **-tive**, *adj.*

erudite (er'oodīt), *adj.* learned. **-tion**, *n.*

erumpent (irum'pənt), *adj.* bursting forth.

erysipelas (erisip'iləs), *n.* disease marked by fever and inflammation of skin, *espec.* of face ; St. Anthony's fire. **-latoid**, **-latous** (-el'ətoid, -əs), *adj.* like e. **-loid**, *n.* non-febrile disease resembling e.

erythema (erithē'mə), *n.* inflammatory redness of skin. **-mic**, **-matous** (-em'ətəs), **-matic** (-mat'-ik), *adj.*

erythraean, **-ean** (erithrē'ən), *adj.* red. **-aemia**, *n.* excessive production of red blood corpuscles. **-rism**, **-rochroism**, *n.* excessive redness of hair, etc. **-rocyte**, *n.*

---

hat, bah, hāte, hāre, crawl ; pen, ēve, hēre ; it, īce, fīre ; on, bōne, boil, būre, howl ; foot, food, boor, hull, tūbe, pūre.

red blood corpuscle. **-rodermia,** *n.* reddening of skin. **-roid,** *adj.* reddish. **-rophobia,** *n.* fear of red light, or of blushing. **-ropia, -ropsia,** *n.* seeing all objects red.

escalade (eskəlad'), *n.* act of scaling wall or crossing moat with ladder.

escalier (eskal'yā), Fr. *n.* staircase. **e.dérobé** (-dārō'bä), secret or back stairs.

escarp (iskahp'), *n.* scarp. **-ment,** *n.* cliff ; cliff-like drop in ground round castle, etc.

eschar (es'kə, -kah), *n.* scab. **-otic,** *n. & adj.* caustic (substance).

eschatology (eskatol'əji), *n.* relig. doctrine concerning final events, as death, resurrection, life hereafter, etc. **-gical,** *adj.* **-gist,** *n.*

escheat (eschēt'), *n.* reversion of land to feudal lord, crown or state, due to failure of heirs ; *v.i. & t.* to revert or cause to revert. **-age,** *n.* right to receive by e.

escritoire (eskritwahr'), *n.* writing-table. **-torial,** *adj.*

esculent (es'kūlənt), *n. & adj.* edible (thing).

escutcheon (iskuch'n), *n.* shield, etc., bearing coat of arms.

esker, -kar (es'kə), *n. Geol.*, ridge of sandy soil sub-glacially deposited.

esodic (isod'ik), *adj.* afferent.

esophagus, *see* oesophagus.

esoteric (esətər'ik), *adj.* capable of being understood only by initiated; abstruse ; confidential. **-ism** (-sizm), **-rism** (-ot'ərizm), *n.*

esotropia (esətrō'pia), *n.* convergent squint. **-pe,** *n.* person having e. **-pic** (-op'ik), *adj.*

E.S P., *abbr.* of extrasensory perception.

espalier (ispal'iə), *n.* lattice, *espec.* for trained fruit tree ; such tree.

esparto (espah'tō), *n.* grass of Spain and N. Africa, used in manuf. of paper, cordage, cloth, etc.

espièglerie (espiāg'lərē), Fr. *n.* mischievousness ; mischievous trick.

esprit (esprē'), Fr. *n.* wit ; vivacity ; quick intelligence. **e. de corps** (-də kōr') loyalty to organisation, corps or fellow-members ; team spirit. **e.fort** (-fōr'), relig. free-thinker.

essorant (es'ərənt), *adj.* soaring.

estaminet (estam'ēnā), Fr. *n.* small café.

estancia (estahn'siah), Sp.-Amer. *n.* ranch. **-ciero** (-siar'ō), *n.* owner of e.

ester (es'tə), *n. Chem.,* salt-like compound formed by replacing acid hydrogen of acid with hydrocarbon radical. **-ify,** *v.t.* convert into e.

esthetic, *see* aesthetic.

estop (istop'), *v.t. Law,* preclude. **-ppage, -ppel,** *n.* prevention of person alleging a fact by his former allegation of the contrary.

estrade (estrahd'), Fr. *n.* dais.

estreat (istrēt'), *v.t. Law,* extract from court's records in order to prosecute ; *n.* copy or extract of record, *espec.* of fines, etc.

esurient (isūr'iant), *adj.* hungry ; starving ; greedy ; *n.* such person. **-nce, -ncy,** *n.*

et alibi (et al'ibī), *Lat.,* "and elsewhere" (*abbr.* et al.). **e.alii** (*fem.* aliae) (et al'iī, -iē), "and others" (*abbr.* et al.).

etesian (itē'zhən), *adj.* occurring annually or periodically, *espec.* such Mediterranean north wind in summer.

ether (ē'thə), *n.* the sky ; space ; *Chem.,* distillation product of alcohol used as solvent, anaesthetic, etc. ; *Phys.,* medium supposed to fill space and transmit light, radio, etc., waves. **-eal** (-ēr'iol), *adj.* pert. to ether ; unearthly ; delicate. **-ic** (-er'ik), *adj.* **-ify,** *v.t.* convert into e. **-ise,** *v.t.* administer e. as anaesthetic to.

ethics (eth'iks), *n.* study of morals and moral principles. **-cal,** *adj.* **-cist** (-sist), *n.*

ethmoid (eth'moid), *adj.* pert. to bones forming nasal cavity and division between nostrils ; of the nasal area ; *n.* such bone. **-al,** *adj.*

ethnology (ethnol'əji), *n.* study of human races. **-gical,** *adj.* **-gist,** *n.* **-nic,** *adj.* pert. to race ; pagan. **-nocracy,** *n.* government by a particular race. **-nodicy,** *n.* comparative study of primitive laws. **-nogeny,** *n.* origin of races. **-nogeography,** *n.* study of geographical distribution of races. **-nography,** *n.* study of racial relations, distribution and origin ; description of human races. **-nomaniac,** *n.* fanatical nationalist.

ə=*er* in *father* ; ō=*er* in *pert*; th=*th* in *thin* ; dh=*th* in *then* ; zh=*s* in *pleasure* ; k=*ch* in *loch* ; ñ=Fr. nasal *n* ; ü=Fr. *u*.

ethology (ithol'əji), *n.* study of manners and customs ; study of character. **-ography**, *n.* description of manners and customs. **-onomics**, *n.* study of economic and ethical principles of citizenship.

ethos (ē'thos), *n.* inherent spirit ; character ; ethical element in literature.

ethyl (eth'il), *n.* a univalent hydrocarbon radical ; a lead-containing compound added to motor spirit to reduce "knocking."

etiolate (ē'tiəlāt), *v.t.* make pale or sickly, *espec.* by depriving of light. **-tion**, *n.*

etiology, *see* **aetiology.**

etui (etwē'), *n.* needle-case ; small case for toilet articles, etc.

etwee, *see* **etui.**

etymology (etimol'əji), *n.* derivation, origin or history of a word ; study of words, their meanings and origins. **-gical**, *adj.* **-gise**, *v.t.* **-gist**, *n.* **-mon**, *n.* word from which another is derived.

eucaine (ūkān'), *n.* synthetic alkaloid used as local anaesthetic.

euchology (ūkol'əji), *n.* prayer-book. **-gical**, *adj.*

eucrasy, -sia (ū'krəsi, -krā'zhiə), *n.* state of general good health.

eudemon, -dae- (ūdē'mən), *n.* good spirit. **-ic** (-dimon'ik), *adj.* causing happiness ; pert. to eudemonism. **-ics**, *n.* conduct based on eudemonism ; study of happiness. **-ism**, *n.* phil. theory that happiness is ultimate moral good and criterion.

eudiaphoresis (ūdiəfərē'sis), *n.* normal perspiration.

eudiometer (ūdiom'itə), *n.* instr. measuring and analysing gases and purity of air. **-tric(al)** (-et'rik, -l), *adj.* **-try**, *n.*

eudipleural (ūdiplōor'əl), *n.* bilaterally symmetrical.

eugenesis (ūjen'isis), *n.* fertility between hybrids. **-esic, -etic** (-jines'ik, -et'-), *adj.*

eugenic (ūjen'ik), *adj.* pert. to improvement of hereditary characteristics ; pert. to production of healthy offspring. **-nist** (ū'jinist), *n.* **-s**, *n.* study of influences promoting, and means to, such improvement and production.

euhemerism (ūhē'mərizm, -hem'-), *n.* belief that myth, gods were deified early heroes. **-ist**, *n.* **-istic**, *adj.*

eulogy (ū'ləji), *n.* laudatory speech or writing ; high praise. **-gious** (-ō'jiəs), *adj.* **-gise**, *v.t.* praise highly. **-gism, -gist**, *n.* **-gistic**, *adj.*

eumenorrhea (ūmenərē'ə), *n.* normal menstruation.

eumerism (ū'mərizm), *n.* collection of similar parts. **-istic**, *adj.*

eumoirous (ūmoir'əs), *adj.* happy because innocent and good. **-riety** (-rī'iti), *n.*

eunomy (ū'nəmi), *n.* state of orderliness and good rule.

eunuch (ū'nək), *n.* castrated man having charge of harem ; majordomo. **-al**, *adj.* **-oid**, *adj.* like an e. ; sexless.

euonymous (ūon'iməs), *adj.* appropriately named. **-my**, *n.*

eupathy (ū'pəthi), *n.* state of contentment and moderation.

eupatrid (ūpat'rid, ū'pə-), *n.* aristocrat, *espec.* of anct. Greece.

eupeptic (ūpep'tik), *adj.* having good digestion. **-psia**, *n.*

euphemism (ū'fimizm), *n.* mild or pleasant-sounding word or phrase, *espec.* substituted for harsher or vulgar one ; such substitution. **-ise**, *v.i.* & *t.* **-ist**, *n.* **-istic**, *adj.*

euphony (ū'fəni), *n.* pleasantness or harmony of sound, *espec.* of words. **-nic** (-on'ik), **-nious** (-ō'niəs), *adj.* **-nise**, *v.t.* **-nism**, *n.* **-nym**, *n.* euphonious synonym.

euphoric (ūfor'ik), *n.* having feeling of fitness and contentment. **-ria** (-ōr'iə), **-ry** (ū'fəri), *n.*

euphrasy (ū'frəsi), *n.* eyebright plant.

euphuism (ū'fūizm), *n.* affected style of writing full of high-flown language and far-fetched metaphors, *espec.* in imitation of Lyly's *Euphues* (1579-80). **-ist**, *n.* writer of such style. **-istic**, *adj.*

eupnoea (ūpnē'ə), *n.* normal breathing.

eupraxia (ūpraks'iə), *n.* correct or normal action. **-actic**, *adj.*

eupsychics (ūsī'kiks), *n.* good education, *espec.* for improvement of human species.

Eurasian (ūrā'shn), *n. & adj.* (person) of mixed European and Asiatic parentage ; common to both Europe and Asia ; signifying Europe and Asia regarded as a whole.

eureka (ūr ē'kə), *Gr.*, "I have found it!"

euripus (ūr ī'pəs), *n.* (*pl.* -**pi**) narrow channel with swift currents.

eurygnathic, -**thous** (ūrignath'ik, -ig'nəthəs), *adj.* with a wide jaw. -**thism**, *n.*

eurythmic, -**rhy**- (ūridh'mik), *adj.* well-proportioned; harmonious. -**al**, *adj.* -**my**, *n.* -**s**, *n.* art of graceful and harmonious movement, *espec.* such free dancing, expressive of musical accompaniment.

eustatic (ūstat'ik), *adj.* unchanged in altitude by geol. action.

eutaxy (ū'taksi), *n.* orderly management. -**xic**, *adj.*

eutechnics (ūtek'niks), *n.* improvement of man's conditions, *espec.* by using natural forces.

eutectic (ūtek'tik), *n.* & *adj.* (alloy) having lowest possible melting point. -**texia**, *n.* state of having low melting point.

euthanasia (ūthənā'zhiə), *n.* pleasant death; painless putting to death of those incurably diseased.

euthenics (ūthen'iks), *n.* study of improvement of human conditions of life, *espec.* to increase efficiency. -**nist**, *n.*

euthermic (ūthə'mik), *adj.* producing warmth.

euthycomic (ūthikom'ik), *adj.* having straight hair.

eutony (ū'təni), *n.* pleasantness of sound of word.

eutrophy (ū'trəfi), *n.* state of being well nourished. -**phic** (-of'ik), *adj.*; *n.* tonic.

eutropic (ūtrop'ik), *adj.* turning with sun.

evagation (ēvəgā'shn), *n.* wandering; depression; departure from etiquette.

evaginate (ivaj'ināt), *v.i.* & *t.* turn inside out; protrude by so turning; *adj.* evaginated. -**tion**, *n.*

evanesce (evənes'), *v.i.* fade away; vanish. -**nce**, *n.* -**nt**, *adj.*

evangel (ivan'jəl), *n.* Gospel; creed; good news; evangelist. -**ic**(**al**) (-el'ik, -l). *adj.* pert. or according to Gospel; Low Church; *n.* Low Church member. -**ise**, *v.t.* convert to belief in Gospel. -**ism**, *n.* missionary work; adherence to Low Church. -**ist**, *n.* writer or preacher of Gospel; missionary; revivalist.

evection (ivek'shn), *n.* alteration in moon's orbit caused by solar attraction. -**al**, *adj.*

eventration (ēventrā'shn), *n.* protrusion of intestines from abdomen; dropped state of abdomen; evisceration.

everglade (ev'əglād), Amer. *n.* grassy, islanded swamp, *espec.* of Florida.

evert (ivōt'), *v.t.* turn inside out; turn outwards. -**rsion**, *n.*

eviscerate (ivis'ərāt), *v.t.* disembowel; divest of strength and force. -**tion**, *n.*

evulgate (ivul'gāt), *v.t.* make widely known. -**tion**, *n.*

evulsion (ivul'shn), *n.* act of uprooting. -**sive**, *adj.*

exacerbate (eksas'əbāt), *v.t.* aggravate; irritate. -**bescent**, *adj.* -**tion**, *n.*

exallotriote (eksəlō'triōt), *adj.* foreign.

exanthema (eksanthē'mə), *n.* (*pl.* -**ta**) disease marked by eruptions and fever, as measles. -**tic** (-thimat'ik), -**tous** (-them'ətəs), *adj.*

exarch (egz'ahk), *n.* viceroy; travelling bishop of E. Church. -**al**, *adj.* -**ate**, *n.* office or jurisdiction of e.

exarticulate (eksahtik'ūlāt), *v.t.* dislocate; cut off at joint. -**tion**, *n.*

exaugurate (egzaw'gūrāt), *v.t.* remove blessing from; profane. -**tion**, *n.*

excalation (ekskələ'shn), *n.* omission or loss of part or unit from series.

excise (iksīz'), *n.* tax on certain commodities made, sold or consumed within a country; license for carrying on certain activities; revenue from such sources; government department collecting e.; *v.t.* cut out. -**sion** (-izh'n), *n.* act of cutting out.

exclave (eks'klāv), *n.* part of a country surrounded by foreign territory.

excoriate (ekskor'iāt), *v.t.* remove skin from; flay. -**tion**, *n.*

excrement (eks'krimənt), *n.* waste matter discharged from body. -**al**, -**ary**, -**itious**, *adj.*

excrescent (ekskres'ənt), *adj.* growing out from main body; redundant. -**ial**, *adj.* -**nce**, *n.* such thing.

---

excrete (ekskrēt'), *v.t.* discharge from body. **-ta.** *n.pl.* excrements. **-tal,** *adj.* **-tion,** *n.* **-tionary, -tive, -tory,** *adj.*

exculpate (eks'kulpāt), *v.t.* clear of blame. **-tion,** *n.* **-tory,** *adj.*

excursus (ekskə̄'səs), *n.* lengthy discussion, *espec.* appended to book; digression.

exeat (eks'iat), *Lat.,* "let him go out"; permission to be absent or late.

execrate (eks'ikrāt), *v.t.* curse; loathe. **-able,** *adj.* loathsome. **-tion,** *n.* **-tive, -tory,** *adj.*

executant (eksek'ūtənt, egz-), *n.* performer. **-tor,** *n.* (*fem.* **-trix**) person carrying out provisions of will.

exegesis (eksijē'sis), *n.* explanation, *espec.* of Bible. **-ete,** *n.* expert on e. **-etic(al)** (-et'ik, -l), *adj.* **-etics,** *n.* science of Biblical e.

exemplum (egzem'pləm), *n.* (*pl.* **-la**) example; moral anecdote. **exempli gratia** (-pli grā'shiə), *Lat.,* "for sake of example"; for example (*abbr.* e.g.).

exsequatur (eksikwā'tə), *n.* document recognising foreign consular officer, or permitting R.C. bishops to rule their church and publish papal bulls.

exequies (eks'ikwiz), *n.pl.* funeral ceremony. **-ial** (-ē'kwiəl), *adj.*

exercitor (maris) (egzē̄'sitə, mar'is), *n.* person having right to ship's profits. **-rial** (-ōr'iəl), *adj.*

exergue (eksōg', egz-), *n.* space at base of figure on coin containing date. **-gual,** *adj.*

exeunt (eks'iənt), *Lat.,* "they go out." **e.omnes** (-om'nēz) "all go out."

exfoliate (eksfō'liāt), *v.i.* & *t.* flake or peel off; develop or unfold like leaves. **-tion,** *n.* **-tive,** *adj.*

exgorgitation (eksgawjitā'shn), *n.* vomited matter.

ex gratia (eks grā'shiə), *Lat.,* "by favour."

exheredate (eksher'idāt), *v.t.* disinherit. **-tion,** *n.*

exigent (eks'ijənt), *adj.* exacting; essential. **-gible,** *adj.* chargeable. **-nce, -ncy,** *n.* urgent need or requirement; necessary condition.

exiguous (eksig'ūəs, egz-), *adj.* sparse; slender. **-uity,** *n.*

existential (eksisten'shəl), *adj.* pert.

to existence. **-ism,** *n.* phil. theory stressing need for the individual to be intensely aware of his own existence and freedom, and of his own responsibility for the nature of his existence. **-ist,** *n.* & *adj.*

eximious (ekshim'iəs), *adj.* select; excellent.

ex jure (eks jōōr'i), *Lat.,* "by right."

ex libris (eks lib'ris), *Lat.,* "from the books (of)"; inscription on book-plate; a book-plate.

exoculate (eksok'ūlāt), *v.t.* blind. **-tion,** *n.*

exodontia (eksədon'shiə), *n.* teeth extraction. **-tist,** *n.*

exodromy (eksod'rəmi), *n.* stabilising movement of exchange. **-mic** (-om'ik), *adj.*

ex officio (eks əfish'iō), *Lat.,* "from the office"; by virtue of one's office.

exogamy (eksog'əmi), *n.* marriage to person not of same tribe, family, etc., only. **-mic** (-am'ik), **-mous,** *adj.*

exogenous (eksoj'inəs), *adj.* growing or originating from outside, or due to external factors. **-netic** (-net'ik), **-nic** (-jen'ik), *adj.*

exopathic (eksəpath'ik), *adj. Med.,* due to external causes.

exophagy (eksof'əji), *n.* cannibalism outside tribe or family. **-gous** (-gəs), *adj.*

exophthalmic (eksofthal'mik), *adj.* pert. to or marked by protrusion of eyeball. **-mos, -mus,** *n.* such condition.

exorcise (eks'awsīz), *v.t.* expel (evil spirit) by rites or use of holy words. **-ism,** *n.* **-ist,** *n.*; *R.C.,* member of a minor order.

exordium (eksaw'diəm), *n.* (*pl.* **-ia**) opening portion of speech or writing. **-dial,** *adj.*

exoskeleton (eks'əskelitən), *n.* external skeleton, *e.g.* shell.

exoteric (eksəter'ik), *adj.* popular; capable of being understood by uninitiated; *n.* uninitiated person. **-ism** (-sizm), *n.*

exothermic (eksəthə̄'mik), *adj.* marked by production of heat. **-mal, -mous,** *adj.*

exotic (eksot'ik, egz-), *adj.* of foreign origin; *n.* such plant.

exotropia (eksətrō'piə), *n.* outward squint.

ex parte (eks pah'ti), *Lat.*, "from a side"; on or for one side only.

expatiate (ekspā'shiāt), *v.i.* speak or write at length. -tion, *n.* -tory, *adj.*

expatriate (ekspat'riāt, -pā'-), *v.t.* exile; *adj.* exiled; *n.* such person. -tion, *n.*

expergefacient (ekspōjifā'shənt), *adj.* awakening. -faction, *n.*

expiscate (ekspis'kāt), *v.t.* fish or search out. -tion, -tor, *n.* -tory, *adj.*

explement (eks'plimənt), *n.* complement.

expletive (eksplē'tiv), *n.* & *adj.* (word) added to expand or fill up; swear-word. -tory (eks'-), *adj.*

exposé (ekspō'zā), Fr. *n.* exposure; full statement or explanation.

ex post facto (eks pōst fak'tō), *Lat.*, "from that which is done afterwards"; by virtue of a thing done later; retrospective.

exprobate (eks'prəbāt), *v.t.* rebuke; reproach. -tion *n.*

expromissor (eksprəmis'ə), *n.* person relieving another of debt by taking it upon himself. -ssion, *n.*

expropriate (eksprō'priāt), *v.t.* deprive of; transfer ownership of. -tion, -tor, *n.*

expugnable (ekspug'nəbl), *adj.* capable of being captured by storm.

expunge (ekspunj'), *v.t.* blot, cross, rub or wipe out. -nction, *n.*

expurgate (eks'pəgāt), *v.t.* remove objectionable portions from; purify. -tion, -tor, *n.* -torial, -tory, *adj.*

exsanguine (ekssang'gwin), *adj.* lacking blood. -nate, *v.t.* drain blood from. -neous, -nous, -uious, *adj.*

exscind (eksind'), *v.t.* cut out; uproot.

exsiccate (eks'sikāt), *v.t.* desiccate. -tion, -tor, *n.* -tive, *adj.*

exstrophy (eks'strəfi), *n. Med.*, turning organ inside out.

exsuccous (ekssuk'əs), *adj.* lacking sap.

exsufflate (ekssuf'lāt), *v.t.* blow away. -tion, *n.* blowing out; forced breathing.

extant (eks'tənt, ikstant'), *adj.* existing.

extempore (ekstem'pəri), *adj.* composed on spur of moment. -raneous, -rary, *adj.* -rise, *v.i.* & *t.*

extensor (eksten'sə), *n.* muscle extending limb.

extenuate (eksten'ū āt), *v.t.* reduce; weaken; excuse. -tion, -tor, *n.* -tive, -tory, *adj.*

exterritorial (eksteritōr'iəl), *adj.* outside territorial boundaries; beyond territorial jurisdiction. -ise, *v.t.* -ity, *n.* exemption from local laws.

extirpate (eks'təpāt), *v.t.* destroy; banish; uproot. -tion, -tor, *n.* -tive, -tory, *adj.*

extradite (eks'trədīt), *v.t.* surrender (criminal) to foreign authority. -table, *adj.* app. to crime warranting such surrender. -tion, *n.*

extragalactic (ekstrəgəlak'tik), *adj.* beyond or outside our galaxy.

extramundane (ekstrəmun'dān), *adj.* outside the known world or universe.

extramural (ekstrəmūr'əl), *adj.* outside the walls or fortifications; outside, but under the aegis of, a university or other institution.

extrasensory (ekstrəsen'səri). *adj.* beyond the senses. **e. perception,** unexplained phenomena such as clairvoyance, telepathy, etc., which are outside or beyond the scope of the senses.

extraterritorial (ekstrəteritōr'iəl), *adj.* exterritorial. -ity, *n.*

extravasate (ekstrav'əsāt), *v.i.* & *t.* flow or filter out; expel from a vessel, *espec.* blood; pour out; *n.* such fluid. -tion, *n.*

extrinsic (ekstrin'sik), *adj.* external; incidental.

extrorse (eks'traws), *adj.* facing away or out.

extrospection (ekstrəspek'shn), *n.* habitual interest in or examination of matters outside oneself. -tive, *adj.*

extrovert, extra- (eks'trəvət), *n.* person given to extrospection.

exuviae (eksū'viē), *n.pl.* cast-off skin, etc., of animal. -iable, -ial, *adj.* -iate, *v.i.* & *t.* slough; shed.

ex-voto (eks-vō'tō), *n.* & *adj.* votive (offering).

eyas (ī'əs), *n.* unfledged bird, *espec.* falcon.

eyot (āt), *n.* ait.

F

fabaceous (fəbā'shəs), *adj.* like a bean.

Fabian (fā'biən), *adj.* pert. to Q. Fabius Maximus, Roman general, and his cautious tactics and avoidance of open battle.

fabiform (fā'bifawm), *adj.* bean-shaped.

façade (fasahd'), *n.* front of building; outward show or semblance.

facetiae (fasē'shiē), *n.pl.* humorous remarks or writings. **-tiation**, *n.* making such remark, etc. **-tious**, *adj.*

facia (fash'ə, fā'-), *n.* name-plate over shop.

facile princeps (fas'ili prin'seps) *Lat.*, "easily first." **f.** descensus Averno, **-ni**, "the road to evil, or Hell, is easy."

facsimile (faksim'ili), *n.* & *adj.* (pert. to) exact copy; *v.t.* make a f. **-lise**, *v.t.* **-list**, *n.*

factice (fak'tis), *n.* vulcanised oil, used as substitute for rubber.

faction (fak'shn), *n.* dissident or self-seeking group; clique; dissension. **-al**, **-tious**, *adj.*

factitious (faktish'əs), *adj.* artificial; spurious.

factitive (fak'titiv), *adj. Gram.*, signifying making something to be; app. to complementary object of such verb.

factotum (faktō'təm), *n.* servant of all work; general assistant. **Johannes F.**, Jack-of-all-trades.

faculty (fak'oolti), *n.* talent; capability; branch of study and its students in university; governing body of university or college; *Eccl.*, permission to add to or alter fabric of church. **-tative**, *adj.* pert. to f.; granting permission; optional; *Biol.*, able to exist in different forms and conditions.

faeces (fē'sēz), *n.pl.* solid excrement; dregs. **-cal** (fē'kəl), *adj.* **-calith**, *n.* stone-like mass of f. **-caloid**, *adj.* like f.

faex (feks), *n.* dregs. **f.populi**, the rabble.

fagaceous (fəgā'shəs), *adj.* belonging to beech family of trees.

fagottist (fəgot'ist), *n.* bassoon-player.

faience (fahyahns'), *n.* glazed decorative earthenware.

fainéant (fā'nāahn), *n.* & *adj.* idle (person). **-nce**, **-ncy** (fā'niəns, -i), *n.*

fait accompli (fāt akawn'plē), *Fr.*, "accomplished deed"; thing done or completed, about which it is too late to argue.

fakir (fakēr'), *n.* Ind. ascetic or mendicant.

falcate (fal'kāt), *adj.* sickle-shaped.

falchion (fawl'chən, -shən), *n.* broad curved sword.

falciform (fal'sifawm), *adj.* falcate. **-cular**, **-culate**, *adj.*

faldstool (fawld'stool), *n.* prayer desk; bishop's round armless chair.

fallacy (fal'əsi), *n.* false idea or argument; illogical statement; deception. **-cious** (-ā'shəs), *adj.* **-lible**, *adj.* liable to err.

Fallopian (fəlō'piən), *adj.* discovered by Fallopius, 16th-cent. It. physician. **F.tube**, tube conveying egg from ovary to womb.

falsidical (fawlsid'ikl), *adj.* giving false impression. **-sification**, *n.* forgery.

fanfaronade (fanfarənād'), *n.* boasting; bluster; blast on trumpets.

fanion (fan'yən), *n.* small marking flag.

fan-tan (fan'-tan'), *n.* Chin. gambling game in which bets are laid on number of objects (as beans) remaining after a known number has been removed.

fantassin (fan'təsin; Fr., fahn-tasan'), *n.* infantryman.

fantoccini (fantəchē'nē), It. *n.pl.* marionettes.

farad (far'ad), *n.* unit of elec. capacity: capacity of condenser, charged with one coulomb, giving potential difference of one volt. **-ic** (-ad'ik), *adj.* app. to certain inductive elec. phenomena discovered by Faraday. **-ism**, *n.* med. application of induced elec. currents.

farceur (fahrsēr'), Fr. *n.* joker.

farcy (fah'si), *n.* disease affecting lymphatic glands of horses and cattle.

---

hat, bah, hāte, hāre, crawl; pen, ēve, hēre; it, īce, fīre; on, bōne, boil, bōre, howl; foot, fōod, bōor, hull, tūbe, pūre.

farina (farī'nə), *n.* flour or meal of cereals, nuts, etc. **-ceous** (-inā'-shəs), *adj.* like or consisting of flour. **-nose**, *adj.* like or yielding flour ; mealy.

farouche (fahrōōsh'), Fr. *adj.* wild ; gauche ; shy.

farrier (far'iə), *n.* horse-shoeing smith. **-y**, *n.* art or place of shoeing horses.

farrow (far'ō), *v.i.* & *t.* give birth (of pigs) ; *n.* act of giving birth to pigs ; litter.

farthingale (fah'dhinggāl), *n.* skirt or petticoat over hoops.

fasces (fas'ēz), *n.* bundle of rods with an axe carried before anct. Roman magistrates, symbolising authority.

fascia (fash'iə), *n.* (*pl.* **-ae**) band ; fillet ; bandage ; band or layer of connective tissue. **-cicle**, *n.* small bundle ; part of book published separately ; collection of written or printed sheets. **-cine**, *n.* bundle of sticks used in building fortifications. **-cism**, *n.* extreme political nationalism, *espec.* of Italy. **-cist**, *n.* **-te**, *adj.* tied round with a band or fillet. **-tion**, *n.*

fasti (fas'ti), Lat. *n.pl.* record ; register ; calendars of anct. Rome.

fastigate (fas'tigāt), *adj.* pointed. **-giate** (-ij'iət), *adj.* narrowing at apex. **-gium** (-ij'iəm), *n.* (*pl.* **-gia**) roof ; top ; gable.

fastuous (fas'tūəs), *adj.* arrogant ; showy.

fata morgana (fah'tə mawgah'nə), *n.* mirage.

fatidic (fətid'ik), *adj.* pert. to prophecy or fortune-telling. **-al**, *adj.* having fatidic powers.

fauces (faw'sēz), *n.pl.* passage from mouth to pharynx. **-cal** (-kəl), *adj.* ; *n.* glottal stop.

faucet (faw'sit), *n.* water tap.

faucial (faw'siəl), *adj.* pert. to fauces. **-citis**, *n.* inflammation of fauces.

fauna (faw'nə), *n.* (*pl.* **-ae**) animal life of region, period, etc. **-l**, *adj.* **-nist**, *n.* expert on f. **-nology**, *n.* study of geographical distribution of animals.

faute de mieux (fōt də miə̄'), *Fr.*, "for want of better."

fauteuil (fōtə̄'ē), *Fr. n.* "arm-chair" ; professorship ; stall seat in theatre.

faux pas (fō pah'), *Fr.*, "false step" ; social solecism ; embarrassing action.

faveolate (fəvē'əlāt), *adj.* honey-combed. **-viform** (fā'-), *adj.* honeycomb-like.

favonian (fəvō'niən), *adj.* pert. to Favonius, in Rom. myth. the west wind ; gentle ; favourable.

favose (fā'vōs), *adj.* faviform.

favus (fā'vəs), *n.* contagious parasitic skin disease.

fealty (fē'əlti), *n.* loyalty ; duty, *espec.* of vassal to feudal lord.

febricant (feb'rikənt), *adj.* causing fever. **-city**, *n.* feverishness. **-rific**, *adj.* feverish ; febricant.

febrifuge (feb'rifūj, fē'-), *n.* & *adj.* (drug) allaying fever. **-gal** (-if'ūgəl), *adj.*

febrile (fē'brīl), *adj.* characterised by or symptomatic of fever ; feverish. **-lity** (-il'iti), *n.*

fecit (fē'sit), *Lat.*, "made (it)."

feculent (fek'ūlənt), *adj.* containing or covered with filth ; faecal ; turbid. **-nce**, *n.*

fecund (fē'kənd, fek'-), *adj.* fertile. **-ate**, *v.t.* make f. **-ity**, *n.*

federal (fed'ərəl), *adj.* pert. to treaty or agreement ; pert. to states united under central government but retaining certain local powers. **-ise**, *v.t.* **-ism**, **-ist**, *n.* **-rate**, *v.i.* & *t.* & *adj.* **-ration**, *n.*

fedora (fidōr'ə), *Amer. n.* man's soft felt hat with curled brim ; trilby.

fee (fē), *n. Law*, feoff. **f.simple**, feoff heritable without restrictions as to heirs ; unconditional use. **f.tail**, entailed feoff.

feldspar (feld'spah), *n.* sev. minerals forming part of all crystalline rocks and decomposing into clay or china clay.

felicide (fē'lisid), *n.* killing of cat.

felicity (filis'iti), *n.* happiness ; well chosen word or phrase. **-cific** (fēlisif'ik), *adj.* making happy. **-tate**, *v.t.* congratulate ; make happy. **-tation**, *n.* **-tous**, *adj.* well chosen ; apt.

feliform (fē'lifawm), *adj.* cat-like. **-ine**, *adj.*

felinophile (fīlī'nəfil), *n.* lover of cats. **-phobe**, *n.* hater of cats.

fellah (fel'ə), *n.* (*pl.* **-een**) Egyptian peasant.

felloe (fel'ō, -i), *n.* wheel's rim or portion of it.

felo de se (fel'ō di sē'), *n.* (*pl.* **felones.....**) self-murder or self-murderer.

felon (fel'ən), *n.* criminal. **-ious** (-ō'niəs), *adj.* **-y,** *n.* serious crime.

felucca (filuk'ə), *n.* fast three-masted Mediterranean vessel, with lateen sails.

feme (fem), *n. Law,* woman. **f.covert** (-kuv'ət), married woman. **f.sole,** unmarried woman or widow.

femicide (fem'isīd), · *n.* killing or killer of woman.

femme (fam), Fr. *n.* woman. **f.fatale** (-fatahl'), "fatal woman"; woman exercising fatal fascination, or seemingly dogged by fate. **f.savante** (-savahnt'), learned woman ; bluestocking.

femur (fē'mə), *n.* thigh bone ; thigh. **-moral** (fem'-), *adj.*

fenestral (fines'trəl), *adj.* pert. to windows ; *n.* window, *espec.* with paper, etc., instead of glass. **-rate,** *adj.* having many openings or windows. **-ration,** *n.* state of being fenestrate ; disposition of windows.

fennec (fen'ek), *n.* small fox of Africa.

feoff (fef, fēf), *n.* heritable land granted by feudal lord ; lord's right in such land. **-ee,** *n.* person to whom f. is granted. **-or, -er,** *n.* grantor of f. **-ment,** *n.* grant of f.

feracious (firā'shəs), *adj.* fecund. **-city,** *n.*

feral (fēr'əl), *adj.* wild ; untamed ; savage ; funereal. **-rae,** *n.pl.* carnivorous animals ; **f.naturae,** *Lat.,* "of a wild nature."

ferash (firahsh'), Anglo-Ind. *n.* lowly servant.

fer-de-lance (far-də-lahns), Fr. *n.* large poisonous snake of S. & Cent. Amer.

feretory (fer'itəri), *n.* shrine ; chapel for bier ; bier.

feria (fēr'iə), *n.* (*pl.* **-ae**) feast day ; holiday ; *Eccl.,* day neither feast nor fast. **-l,** *adj.* ·

ferine (fēr'īn), *adj.* feral.

feringhee, -ghi (fering'gi), Ind. *n.* European, *espec.* Portuguese born in India.

ferity (fer'iti), *n.* wild state ; barbarism.

ferreous (fer'iəs), *adj.* containing, like or pert. to iron.

ferric, -rous (fer'ik, -əs), *adj.* pert.

to or containing iron. **-riferous,** *adj.* yielding iron. **-romagnetic,** *adj.* highly magnetic.

ferruginous (ferōō'jinəs), *adj.* ferreous ; pert. to or coloured like iron rust. **-nate,** *v.t.* stain with iron compound.

ferule (fer'ōōl), *n.* rod or flat ruler for punishment; school discipline. **-laceous,** *adj.* reed-like.

fervescent (fəves'ənt), *adj.* becoming feverish. **-nce,** *n.*

Fescennine (fes'inīn), *adj.* pert. to poetry and inhabitants of anct. Fescennia, Italy ; indecent ; scurrilous.

fescue (fes'kū), *n.* stick used by teacher as pointer ; sev. tall kinds of grass.

festina lente (festī'nə len'ti), *Lat.,* "make haste slowly."

festination (festinā'shn), *n.* haste ; hurrying walk, symptom of some nervous diseases.

festucine (fes'tūsin), *adj.* straw-coloured.

fête champêtre (fet shahṅpet'r), *Fr.,* "country feast"; outdoor entertainment. **f.galante** (-galahṅt'), elegant festival.

fetial (fē'shəl), *adj.* pert. to declaration of war and peace; heraldic.

fetid (fē'tid), *adj.* stinking.

fetlock (fet'lok), *n.* tuft of hair on horse's leg immediately above hoof ; part of leg bearing it.

fetor (fē'tor), *n.* stench.

fetus, *see* **foetus.**

feudal (fū'dəl), *adj.* pert. to feoff or fee ; pert. to medieval social system of overlords and vassals. **-datory,** *n.* & *adj.* (vassal) subject to feudal lord ; (ruler) subject to overlord. **-ism,** *n.* feudal system. **-ist,** *n.* **-istic,** *adj.*

feu de joie (fə' də zhwah), *Fr.,* "fire of joy" ; firing of guns as symbol of joy ; bonfire.

feuilleton (fə'itawṅ), Fr. *n.* feature and criticism page of newspaper ; instalment of serial story. **-ist,** *n.* writer of matter on f. or of serial story.

fiacre (fiak'r), Fr. *n.* small hackney carriage.

fiat (fī'at), *n.* decree ; command ; decision. **f.lux,** *Lat.,* "let there be light."

fibrin (fī'brin), *n.* fibrous protein in

blood formed in clotting. **-ation,** *n.* condition of having excessive f. in blood. **-ogen,** *n.* substance in blood producing f. **-osis,** *n.* disease marked by fibrination.

fibroma (fībrō'mə), *n.* (*pl.* **-ta**) benign fibrous tumour. **-toid,** *adj.* like f. **-tosis,** *n.* disease marked by f.

fibrosis (fībrō'sis), *n.* condition of excessive fibrous formation in organ. **-otic** (-ot'ik), *adj.* **-sitis,** *n.* inflammatory excess of fibrous tissue growth.

fibula (fib'ūlə), *n.* (*pl.* **-ae**) outer, smaller bone of lower leg. **-r,** *adj.*

fichu (fish'ōō), *n.* light shawl for shoulders.

ficiform (fis'ifawm), *adj.* fig-shaped. **-coid** (fi'koid), *adj.* fig-like.

fictile (fik'tīl), *adj.* pert. to pottery ; moulded ; able to be moulded into shape or new shape. **-lity,** *n.*

fictive (fik'tiv), *adj.* imaginative ; imaginary.

fideism (fī'diizm), *n.* reliance on faith alone.

fidicinal (fidis'inəl), *adj.* pert. to stringed mus. instr.

fiducial (fidū'shəl), *adj.* based on faith ; like a trust. **-ciary,** *n. & adj.* (person) holding in trust ; requiring trust ; based on confidence, *espec.* of public ; **f.issue,** currency issued beyond the amount backed by gold.

fief (fēf), *n.* feoff ; that which one rules.

figuline (fig'ūlin, -īn), *adj.* fictile ; *n.* figurine. **-late,** *adj.* made of clay ; fictile.

figurant (fig'ūrənt ; Fr., fēgūrahn'), *n.* ballet dancer ; minor character in play. **-e** (Fr., -ahnt'), *n.* ballet girl.

figurine (figūr'ēn'), *n.* statuette.

filar (fī'lə), *adj.* pert. to thread ; having threads across eye-piece. **-ial, -ian, -ious** (-ār'-), *adj.* pert. or due to thread-worms. **-iasis** (-ī'əsis), *n.* infestation with thread-worms. **-iform** (-ar'-), *adj.* thread-like.

filature (fil'ətūr), *n.* drawing out or reeling of silk threads ; apparatus of factory for f.

filibeg (fil'ibeg), Scot. *n.* kilt.

filibuster (fil'ibustə), *n.* irregular soldier ; freebooter ; *Amer.,* making of interminable obstructive

speech ; such speech or speaker ; *v.i.* make such speech.

filicide (fil'isīd), *n.* killing or killer of own child.

filiciform (filis'ifawm), *adj.* fern- or frond-shaped. **-coid** (fil'ikoid), *adj.* fern-like.

filiferous (filif'ərəs), *adj.* bearing threads. **-form, -lose,** *adj.* thread-like. **-ligerous,** *adj.* flagellate. **-lipendulous,** *adj.* hanging by a thread.

filoselle (fil'əsel), *n.* floss-like silk.

fils (fēs), Fr. *n.* son.

fimbrial (fim'briəl), *adj.* pert. to or having a fringe. **-riate,** *adj.* fringed ; *v.t.* fringe ; hem. **-riation,** *n.* **-ricate,** *adj.* fringed. **-rillate,** *adj.* having small fringe.

fimetic (fimet'ik), *adj.* pert. to dung. **-micolous,** *adj.* living in dung.

fin de siècle (fan də sēek'l), *Fr.* "end of century," *espec.* of 19th cent. ; decadent.

fingent (fin'jənt), *adj.* moulding.

finial (fin'iəl), *adj.* ornament at apex of gable, etc. ; pinnacle.

firkin (fə'kin), *n.* small cask ; measure of capacity : nine gallons.

firman (fə'mən), *n.* Oriental ruler's edict, authorisation, etc.

fiscal (fis'kəl), *adj.* pert. to public revenue. **-ity,** *n.* avarice.

fission (fish'n), *n. Phys.,* splitting, *espec.* of atomic nuclei, accompanied by release of immense energies. **-able,** *adj.* capable of being split, *espec.* unstable minerals used in atomic f. **-sile,** *adj.* easily split ; capable of atomic fission. **-siparous,** *adj.* reproducing by splitting into parts. **-siped,** *adj.* having cloven foot.

fistula (fis'tūlə), *n.* pipe ; very deep ulcer ; pipe-like passage from ulcer to surface or between hollow organs. **-liform,** *adj.* like a f. or pipe. **-lous, -r,** *adj.*

fitch (fich), *n.* hair of polecat ; brush of such hair. **-ew,** *n.* polecat.

fixation (fiksā'shn), *n. Psych.,* establishment in childhood of mental attitude which persists through life ; *pop.,* obsession, established habit.

flabellate (flabel'ət), *adj.* fan-shaped. **-liform,** *adj.* **-tion,** *n.* use of fan to cool.

flaccid (flak'sid), *adj.* flabby. **-ity,** *n.*

flagellate (flaj'ilāt), *v.t.* whip; flog; *adj.* whip-shaped; having whip-like outgrowths. **-ant, -list,** *n.* & *adj.* (person) whipping himself as relig. practice; lashing. **-lum,** *n.* (*pl.* **-la**) whip-like outgrowth; runner of plant. **-tion, -tor,** *n.* **-tory,** *adj.*

flageolet (flajəlet'), *n.* small flute-like mus. instr.

flagitate (flaj'itāt), *v.t.* demand repeatedly. **-tion,** *n.*

flagitious (flajish'əs), *adj.* heinous; villainous.

flagrante delicto (fləgran'ti dilik'tō), *Lat.*, "the crime being still blazing"; in the act of committing crime.

flak (flak), *n.* (*abbr.* of Ger. *Flieger-Abwehr-Kanone*) anti-aircraft fire or guns.

flamen (flā'men), *n.* pagan priest.

flamenco (flameng'kō), *n.* Sp. gypsy style of singing; mus. composition in that style.

flamineous (flamin'iəs), *adj.* pert. to flamen. **-nical,** *adj.*

flammeous (flam'iəs), *adj.* flame-coloured. **-mulated,** *adj.* ruddy. **-mulation,** *n.* flame-coloured or flame-shaped marking.

flâneur (flahnër'), Fr. *n.* idler; trifler.

flatulent (flat'ūlənt), *adj.* pert. to or causing generation of gas in digestive tract; inflated; pretentious. **-nce, -ncy,** *n.* **-tus** (flā'təs), *n.* gas in intestines or stomach.

flautist (flaw'tist), *n.* flute-player.

flavedo (fləvē'dō), *n.* yellowness, *espec.* of plants. **-escent,** *adj.* turning yellow. **-vic(ant)** (flā'-, flav'-), *adj.* yellow; yellowish. **-vid** (flā'-), *adj.* golden yellow.

flense, -nch (flenz, -nch), *v.t.* cut up or skin.

flews (flooz), *n.pl.* pendulous lips; chops.

flexor (fleks'ə), *n.* muscle bending limb. **-xion, -xure,** *n.* act or state of bending or being bent. **-xuose, -xuous,** *adj.* sinuous; zigzag.

floccose (flok'ōs), *adj.* woolly.

flocculate (flok'ūlāt), *v.i.* & *t.* collect into lumps or tufts; *adj.* having hairy tufts. **-lent,** *adj.* woolly; consisting of soft flakes; tufted. **-lence,** *n.* **-lus,** *n.* (*pl.* **-li**) flake; small tuft. **-tion,** *n.*

flora (flor'ə), *n.* (*pl.* **-ae**) plant life of region, period, etc.

florescence (flores'əns), *n.* state or time of flowering. **-nt,** *adj.*

florikan, -ken, -can, -cen (flor'ikən), *n.* small Ind. bustard.

florilegium (flörilē'jiəm), *n.* (*pl.* **-gia**) collection of flowers; description of flora; anthology.

floruit (flor'ooit), *Lat.*, "he flourished"; period during which person lived (*abbr.* fl.); dates of birth and death, *espec.* in brackets after person's name.

flotsam (flot'səm), *n.* floating wreckage; goods lost through wreck.

flügelhorn (flü'glhawn), *n.* bugle with keys; saxhorn-like mus. instr.

fluminous, -ose (floo'minəs, -ōs), *adj.* pert. to or having many rivers.

fluoresce (floorəs'), *v.i.* exhibit fluorescence. **-nce,** *n.* emission of radiation due to absorption of radiation of different wavelength; light, etc., so emitted. **-nt,** *adj.* **-roscope,** *n.* instr. for observing fluorescence. **-roscopy,** *n.*

fluvial (floo'viəl), *adj.* pert. to rivers. **-viatile,** *adj.* **-viograph,** *n.* instr. recording river's rise and fall. **-viology,** *n.* study of water-courses.

fodient (fō'diənt), *adj.* pert. to digging.

foehn (fən), *n.* dry warm wind blowing down mountain-side.

foetid, *see* **fetid.**

foetus (fē'təs), *n.* unborn offspring in later stage of development (in humans, from third month after conception). **-tal,** *adj.* **-tation,** *n.* pregnancy. **-ticide,** *n.* killing of f. **-tiferous,** *adj.* bearing young. **-tiparous,** *adj.* bearing young not fully developed.

foliaceous (fōliā'shəs), *adj.* pert. to, like or consisting of leaves or laminae.

foliate (fōliət), *adj.* like or having leaves; (-āt), *v.i.* & *t.* divide into laminae; beat into thin plate; cover with thin coating. **-tion,** *n.* formation of leaves; state of being f.; act of foliating; number of leaves of book; leaf-like ornamentation.

foliferous (fōlif'ərəs), *adj.* bearing leaves. **-form,** *adj.* leaf-shaped.

folio (fō'lio), *n.* folded sheet of paper; leaf of book, etc.; largest size of book; *v.t.* number pages of.

foliolate (fō'liəlāt), *adj.* pert. to or having leaflets. **-liferous,** *adj.* bearing leaflets.

follicle (fol'ikl), *n.* small deep cavity or sac. **-cular** (-ik'ūlə), *adj.* **-culate,** *adj.* having or enclosed in f. **-culose, -culous,** *adj.* like f.

fomes (fō'mēz), *n.* (*pl.* **-mites,** **-mitēz**) substance carrying infection.

fons et origo (fonz et orī'gō), *Lat.,* "source and origin."

fontinal (fon'tinəl), *adj.* growing by or in springs.

foramen (fərā'men), *n.* (*pl.* **-mina,** **-am'inə**) small orifice. **-minate** (-am'-), *adj.* having f.; *v.t.* pierce. **-minous,** *adj.* having f.

foraneous (fərā'niəs), *adj.* pert. to forum.

force majeure (fōrs mazhər'), *Fr.,* "greater force"; compelling force; unavoidable circumstances.

forcipate (faw'sipāt), *adj.* like forceps. **-piform,** *adj.* shaped like forceps. **-pulate,** *adj.* like small forceps.

forensic (fəren'sik), *adj.* pert. to law courts, argument or rhetoric.

forficate (faw'fikāt), *adj.* forked. **-ciform** (-is'ifawm), *adj.* scissors-shaped. **-culate,** *adj.* forked. **-tion,** *n.*

form(e) (fawm), *n.* page of printed matter ready for impression.

formalin (faw'məlin), *n.* aqueous solution of formaldehyde, a chem. disinfectant and preservative.

formic (faw'mik), *adj.* pert. to ants. **-arian,** *adj.* pert. to ant-hill. **-ary,** *n.* ant-hill. **-ate,** *v.i.* creep or swarm like ants. **-ation,** *n.* feeling as of ants crawling over skin. **-ative,** *adj.* **-ide** (-ṣṭd), *n.* substance destroying ants. **-ivorous** (-siv'-ərəs), *adj.* feeding on ants.

fornicate (faw'nikāt), *v.i.* commit fornication; *adj.* vaulted; arched. **-tion,** *n.* sexual intercourse by an unmarried person; vaulting; vaulted building. **-tor, -trix,** *n.*

fortuitous (fawtu'itəs), *adj.* by or due to chance. **-tism,** *n.* theory that evolutionary adaptations are due to chance. **-tist,** *n.* **-ty,** *n.* chance occurrence.

forum (fōr'əm, *n.* (*pl.* **-ra**) market

place; general meeting place; place for discussion; law courts.

fossarian (fosar'iən), *n.* gravedigger.

fossick (fos'ik), Austral. *v.i.* & *t.* search for by turning or picking over, *espec.* for gold; rummage. **-er,** *n.*

fossorial (fosōr'iəl), *adj.* for use in digging. **-sor,** *n.* grave-digger.

foumart (foo'maht), *n.* polecat.

foveate (fō'viāt), *adj.* pitted. **-tion,** *n.* **-veolate,** *adj.* bearing small pits.

foyer (fwah'yā), Fr. *n.* vestibule.

franchise (fran'chīz), *n.* vote; right to vote; any similar right or privilege; freedom.

francolin (frang'kolin), *n.* S. Asiatic and African partridge.

franc-tireur (frahn-tēr'ər'), Fr. *n.* (*pl.* **francs-tireurs**) member of irregular infantry corps.

frangible (fran'jibl), *adj.* brittle.

fraternise (frat'ərnīz), *v.i.* be friendly, *espec.* with residents in occupied enemy territory, enemy soldiers, etc. **-sation,** *n.*

fratricide (frat'risīd), *n.* killing or killer of brother or sister. **-dal,** *adj.*

frau (frow), Ger. *n.* (*pl.* **-en**) married woman; Mrs.

fräulein (froi'līn), Ger. *n.* unmarried woman; Miss.

freemartin (frē'mahtin), *n.* sterile female twin calf.

freiherr (frī'hār), Ger. *n.* (*pl.* **-n**) baron.

fremitus (frem'itəs), *n.* vibration.

frenetic (frinet'ik), *n.* & *adj.* frantic (person).

frequency (frē'kwənsi), *n.* number of vibrations or cycles of a wave in a given time, *espec.* number of cycles per second. **f.modulation,** radio transmission by varying f. of carrier wave (*abbr.* **F.M.**).

fresco (fres'kō), *n.* water-colour painting on wet plaster; *v.t.* paint in f. **f.secco,** such painting on dry plaster.

fretum (frē'təm), *n.* (*pl.* **-ta**) strait.

friable (frī'əbl), *adj.* easily crumbled.

fricative (frik'ətiv), *n.* & *adj.* (sound) made by friction of breath forced through narrow passage, as *s, f.*

frigoric (frigor'ik), *adj.* pert. to cold. **-giferous** (-jif'-), **-rific,** *adj.* causing cold. **-golabile,** *adj.* susceptible to cold. **-gotherapy,** *n.* med. treatment with cold.

fringilline (frinjil'in, -in), adj. like a finch; belonging to finch family of birds. -laceous, -liform, -loid, adj. finch-like.

frit (frit), n. prepared material from which glass is made.

fritillary (fritil'əri, frit'-), n. several kinds of spotted butterfly and bulbous plant.

frondesce (frondes'), v.i. open leaves. -diferous, -digerous, adj. bearing leaves or fronds. -diform, adj. frond-shaped. -divorous, adj. feeding on leaves. -dose, adj. having or like leaves. -nce, n. -nt, adj.

frontogenesis (frontəjen'isis), n. meeting of two different air currents causing cloud.

fructify (fruk'tifi), v.i. & t. become or make fruitful. -ferous, adj. bearing fruit. -fication, n. -form, adj. like fruit. -tivorous, adj. feeding on fruit.

frumenty (froo'mənti), n. dish of hulled wheat boiled in milk, with sugar. -taceous, adj. like or made of grain.

frutescent (frootes'ənt), adj. like a shrub. -nce, n. -ticetum, n. botanical garden of shrubs. -ticose, adj. -ticulous, adj. like a small shrub.

fucus (fū'kəs), n. (pl. -ci, -sī) kind of flat seaweed; rockweed. -ciphagous, -civorous, adj. eating seaweeds. -coid, n. & adj. (plant) like seaweed. -cous, adj.

Fuehrer, Führer (fü'rər), Ger. n. leader.

fugacious (fūgā'shəs), adj. elusive; ephemeral; volatile. -city (-as'iti), n.

fugleman (fū'glmən), n. soldier standing in front of others to demonstrate drill, etc.; model.

fugue (fūg), n. strictly contrapuntal and highly developed mus. composition; Med., kind of active delirium.

fulciform (ful'sifawm), adj. like a prop.

fulcrum (ful'krəm), n. (pl. -ra) support; point or support on which lever rests. -ral, adj. -rate, adj. having a f.

fulgent (ful'jənt), adj. radiant. -gid, adj. glittering.

fulgurant (ful'gūrənt), adj. like lightning. -rate, v.i. flash. -rating,

adj. Med., app. to intense sudden pains. -rous, adj. flashing.

fuliginous (fūlij'inəs), adj. like soot. -nosity, n.

fuliguline (fūlig'ulin, -in), adj. pert. to or like a sea duck; belonging to sea duck family of birds.

fulmar (fool'mə), n. gull-like sea bird.

fulminate (ful'mināt), v.i. explode; thunder; denounce in loud or violent manner. -ant, adj. Med., developing suddenly. -neous, -nous, adj. pert. to or like thunder and lightning. -tion, -tor, n. -tory, adj.

fulvous (ful'vəs), adj. tawny. -vescent, adj. somewhat f.

fumarole (fū'mərōl), n. volcano's smoke vent.

fumatory (fū'mətəri), n. place for fumigating. -miduct, n. smoke vent.

funambulist (fūnam'būlist), n. tight-rope walker. -late, v.i. -lation, -lator, -lism, n. -latory, adj.

fundamentalism (fundəmen'təlizm), n. belief in the literal truth of all Biblical statements, miracles, etc. -ist, n.

fundiform (fun'difawm), adj. sling-shaped.

fungible (fun'jibl), n. & adj. (thing) mutually interchangeable.

fungicide (fun'jisid), n. substance killing fungus. -gistatic, n. substance preventing fungus growth.

funicular (fūnik'ulə), adj. pert. to small cord, rope or tension. f.railway, cable mountain railway. -niform, adj. cord- or rope-like. -nipendulous, adj. hanging by a rope.

furcate, -cal (fə'kāt, -kəl), adj. branched. -cellate, adj. slightly branched. -tion, n.

furfur (fə'fə), n. scurf. -aceous, -ous, adj. -ation, n. falling of dandruff.

furibund (fūr'ibund), adj. furious.

furlough (fə'lō), n. leave; holiday.

furmety (fə'miti), n. frumenty.

furore (fūr or'i), n. outburst of enthusiasm.

fürst (fürst), Ger. n. (pl. -en) noble next in rank to duke; prince.

furuncle (tūr'ungkl), n. boil. -cular, -culous, adj. -culoid, adj. like a f. -culosis, n. outbreak of boils.

fuscous (fus'kəs), adj. dark in colour; tawny.

fuselage (fū'zilij, -lahzh), n. body of aeroplane.

fusiform (fū'zifawm), adj. spindle-shaped. -soid, adj.

fusion (fū'zhn), n. combination by melting together; Phys., combination of hydrogen atoms to form helium nuclei. f.bomb, bomb of immense destructive power based on this principle; hydrogen bomb.

fustian (fus'tiən), n. coarse cotton cloth; bombast; adj. made of f.; pompous.

fustic (fus'tik), n. tropical Amer. tree yielding yellow dye.

fustigate (fus'tigāt), v.t. beat with cudgel. -tion, -tor, n. -tory, adj.

G

gabbro (gab'rō), n. granular kind of igneous rock. -ic, -itic, adj.

gabelle (gəbel'), Fr. n. tax on salt.

gabion (gā'biən), n. wicker-work cylinder filled with earth or stones for building fortifications, harbour bars, etc. -ade, n. structure made with g.

gadoid (gad'oid), n. & adj. (fish) of the cod family.

gadroon (gadrōōn'), n. form of fluting; Archit., notched moulding.

gaduin (gad'ūin), n. substance occurring in cod-liver oil.

galactic (gəlak'tik), adj. pert. to a galaxy (astron.). -tagogue, n. & adj. (substance) promoting milk secretion. -toid, adj. milk-like. -tometer, n. instr. measuring density of milk. -tophore, n. milk duct. -tophygous, adj. preventing milk secretion. -topoiesis, -togis, n. milk secretion. -torrhoea, n. excessive milk flow.

galanty (gəlan'ti), n. shadow play.

galaxy (gal'əksi), n. Milky Way; island universe, espec. one to which solar system and all visible stars belong; collection of brilliant persons.

galbanum (gal'bənəm), n. asafoetida-like gum resin.

galeate, -eiform (gā'liāt, -ē'ifawm), adj. helmet-shaped.

galena (gəlē'nə), n. natural lead sulphite, main source of lead. -nic(al) (-en'ik, -l), adj. -noid, adj. like g.

galericulate (gəlerik'ūlət), adj. having hat-like covering.

galilee (gal'ilē), n. church porch, or chapel at entrance.

galingale (gal'ingāl), n. ginger-like plant, or sedge, with aromatic root used in med.

galleass (gal'ias), n. large armed 16-cent. vessel with oars and sails.

galliard (gal'iəd), adj. gay; gallant; n. lively 16-cent. dance.

Gallice (gal'isi), adv. in French (style). -cise, v.t. make French. -cism, n. word or phrase borrowed from French; use of such words and phrases.

gallimaufry (galimaw'fri), n. hash of liver and other organs; hotch-potch.

gallinaceous (galinā'shəs), adj. like pheasants and domestic fowls; belonging to the order of birds including those.

gallinule (gal'inūl), n. moor hen.

Gallionic -nian (galion'ik, -ō'niən), adj. pert. to Gallio (Acts xviii); careless; indifferent.

gallivat (gal'ivat), n. E. Ind. galleass.

Gallomania (galəmā'niə), n. fondness for French life, manners, etc. -c, n. -ophile, n. lover of France. -ophobia, n. hatred of France.

galloway (gal'əwā), n. Scot. breed of small horse and black cattle.

galvanic (galvan'ik), adj. pert. to direct current from elec. battery; giving or receiving shock. -nise, v.t. treat with g. current; stimulate into sudden excitement; coat with zinc. -nism, n. current electricity; study of elec. currents and their effects. -nometer, n. instr. measuring small elec. currents. -noscope, n. instr. indicating presence and direction of small elec. currents.

gambade, -do (gambād', -ā'dō), n. horse's leap; caper. -does, n.pl. gaiters, espec. attached to saddle.

gambier (gam'biə), n. yellow dye and astringent substance obtained from a vine of Malaya.

gambit (gam'bit), n. opening moves, espec. of chess.

gamboge (gambōj', -boozh'), *n.* E. Ind. yellow gum resin; reddish yellow colour. **-gian,** *adj.*

gambrel (gam'brel), *n.* horse's hock; kind of roof with pentagonal gable.

gamelotte (gam'ilot), *n.* fibre for paper, etc., obtained from sedge.

gamete (gam'ēt), *n.* sex cell; the reproductive element. **-tic** (-et'ik), *adj.* **-tocyte,** *n.* cell producing g. **-togenesis,** *n.* production of g. **-tophyll,** *n.* leaf bearing sex organs. **-tophyte,** *n.* plant, or stage in plant growth, bearing sex organs.

gamic (gam'ik), *adj.* sexual; requiring or resulting from mating.

gamin (gam'an), Fr. *n.* street urchin.

gamma (gam'ə), *n.* third letter (Γ, γ) of Gr. alphabet. **g.ray,** kind of radioactive ray resembling X-rays. **-cism,** *n.* stuttering over *g* and *k.* **-dion, -tion,** *n.* cross, as swastika, formed of four capital g.

gammexane (gameks'ān), *n.* insecticide, a form of benzene hexachloride.

gamogenesis (gaməjen'isis), *n.* sexual reproduction. **-etic** (-jinet'ik), *adj.* **-ophagia,** *n.* destruction of gamete by other.

gamut (gam'ət), *n.* whole range of musical notes; whole scale from doh to doh; entire range or compass.

gandoura, -durah (gandoor'ə), *n.* short, loose, sleeveless garment of Levant and Asia Minor.

ganglion (gang'gliən), *n.* (*pl.* -ia) mass of nerve cells; nerve centre; small tumour on wrist or ankle. **-ectomy,** *n.* removal of g. **-itis,** *n.* inflammation of g. **-liac, -lial, -liar,** *adj.* **-liate(d),** *adj.* having g. **-Lform, -lioform, -lioid,** *adj.* like g.

gangrene (gang'grēn), *n.* mortification of part of body; *v.i.* & *t.* suffer or cause g. **gas g.,** marked by impregnation of gas caused by bacillus. **-nous,** *adj.* **-scent,** *adj.* tending to become gangrenous.

gangue (gang), *n.* rock or earth yielding ore.

ganister (gan'istə), *n.* kind of flinty rock used for road faces and lining furnaces.

ganj, *see* **gunge.**

ganja (gan'jə), Anglo-Ind, *n.* intoxicant obtained from Ind. hemp.

ganoid (gan'oid), *adj.* app. to hard, smooth, bright fish-scales; having such scales; *n.* fish with such scales.

ganosis (gənō'sis), *n.* reducing shine of marble, *espec.* on naked parts of statue.

gantry (gan'tri), *n.* frame-like support, *espec.* bridge for travelling crane or bearing railway signals.

garçon (gahr'sawn), Fr. *n.* boy; waiter. **g. d'honneur,** best man (at wedding).

garganey (gah'gəni), *n.* kind of teal.

gargantuan (gahgan'tūən), *adj.* vast.

gargoyle (gah'goil), *n.* grotesquely-carved spout projecting from gutter; excessively ugly face or person.

garnishee (gahnishē'), *v.t.* *Law,* attach property by garnishment; *n.* person receiving garnishment. **-shment,** *n.* legal notice requiring person liable to do so not to pay money, etc., to defendant in debt suit, but retain it on plaintiff's behalf; notice calling third party to appear in suit.

garrotte (gərot'), *v.t.* strangle; execute by strangling: *n.* killing by strangling.

garrulous (gar'ooləs), *adj.* talkative. **-lity,** (-oo'liti), *n.*

gasconade (gaskənād'), *v.i.* & *n.* brag.

gasket (gas'kit), *n.* rope for tying furled sail; packing for pistons, etc.

gasogene, gaz- (gas'əjēn, gaz'-), *n.* apparatus for making aerated waters.

gasoline, -ene (gas'əlēn), Amer. *n.* petrol.

gasteropod (gas'tərəpod), *n.* kind of mollusc, including snail, slug, whelk, etc. **-ous** (-op'ədəs), *adj.*

gastral (gas'trəl), *adj.* pert. to stomach. **-gia** (-al'jiə), *n.* pain in stomach.

gastric (gas'trik), *adj.* pert. to stomach.

gastriloquist (gastril'əkwist) *n.* ventriloquist. **-quial** (-ō'kwiəl), *adj.* **-quism,** *n.*

gastritis (gastrī'tis), *n.* inflammation of stomach.

gastrolater (gastrol'ətə), *n.* glutton. **-trous,** *adj.* **-try,** *n.* gluttony.

gastrology (gastrol'əji), *n.* study of stomach and its diseases, etc. **-ger, -gist,** *n.* **-gical,** *adj.*

gastronomy (gastron'əmi), *n*. science of food and cooking. **-me** (-ōm), **-mer**, **-mist**, *n*. **-mical**, *adj*.

gastropod (gas'trəpod), *n*. gasteropod

gastrosophy (gastros'əfi), *n*. gastronomy. **-ph, -pher,** *n*.

gastrostomy (gastros'təmi), *n*. making permanent incision into stomach.

gata (gah'tə), *n*. kind of shark of tropical Atlantic; nurse shark.

gauche (gōsh), Fr. *adj.* "left-handed"; awkward; tactless. **-rie,** *n*. such act or remark.

gaucho (gow'chō), Sp. *n*. S. Amer. cowboy.

gaudeamus (gawdiā'məs), *Lat.*, "let us rejoice"; students' revelry. **g.igitur** (-ij'itə), "let us then make merry."

Gauleiter (gow'lītə), Ger. *n*. political governor of district or province.

gault (gawlt), *n*. heavy clay.

gauss (gows), *n*. elec. unit of magnetic induction, formerly of magnetic intensity.

gavage (gavahzh'), Fr. *n*. forcible feeding.

gavel (gav'əl), *n*. hammer used by auctioneer or chairman; rent; tribute.

gavelkind (gav'əlkīnd), *n*. anct. form of land tenure, with division of estate equally among heirs; such division of estate.

gavial (gā'viəl), *n*. kind of Ind. alligator.

gavotte (gəvot'), *n*. high-stepping Fr. dance.

gazebo (gəzē'bō), *n*. summerhouse; belvedere.

gazogene, *see* gasogene.

geal (jē'əl), *adj*. pert. to the earth.

gecko (gek'ō), *n*. kind of small harmless lizard of warm regions.

geest (gēst), *n*. old superficial alluvial soil.

gegenschein (gā'gənshīn), *n*. soft light in sky opposite sun; counterglow.

gehenna (gihen'ə), *n*. Hell; place of torture.

Geiger-counter (gī'gə-kown'tə), *n*. instrument detecting presence, and recording intensity, of charged particles, radioactivity, cosmic rays, etc.

geisha (gā'shə), *n*. Jap. dancing or singing girl.

geist (gīst), Ger. *n*. spirit; intellectual capacity or bent.

geitonogamy (gītonog'əmi), *n*. pollination of a flower by another on same plant. **-mous,** *adj*.

gekkonid (gek'ənid), *n*. gecko. **-noid,** *adj*.

gelastic (jilas'tik), *adj*. pert. to laughing.

geld (geld), *v.t.* castrate; deprive of vigour. **-ing,** *n*. gelded animal.

gelid (jel'id), *n*. cold; frozen.

gelignite (jel'ignīt), *n*. form of dynamite.

gelogenic (jeləjen'ik), *adj*. producing laughter.

gemel (jem'əl), *adj*. in pairs; twin.

geminate (jem'ināt), *v.i.* & *t*. double; arrange in pairs; *adj*. so arranged. **-niflorous,** *adj*. having paired flowers. **-niform,** *adj*. double. **-nous,** *adj*.

gemma (jem'ə), *n*. (*pl.* **-ae**) kind of bud from which, when separated from parent, new plant can grow. **-ceous,** *adj*. **-miferous,** *adj*. bearing g. or gems. **-miform,** *adj*. like a g. or bud. **-miparous,** *adj*. producing g. **-te,** *adj*. **-tion,** *n*. reproduction by g. or buds. **-moid,** *adj*. like a g.

gemmology (jemol'əji), *n*. study of gems.

gemmule (jem'ūl), *n*. small gemma. **-lation,** *n*. production of g. **-liferous,** *adj*. bearing g.

genappe (jinap'), *n*. kind of worsted used in fringes, etc.

genarch (jen'ahk), *n*. head of family.

gendarme (zhahñdahrm'), Fr. *n*. policeman trained and armed like soldier. **-rie,** *n*. corps of g.

gene (jēn), *n*. part of chromosome transmitting or determining hereditary characteristics.

genealogy (jēnial'əji), *n*. lineage; family tree; study of these. **-gical,** *adj*. **-gise,** *v.i.* & *t*. **-gist,** *n*.

generic (jiner'ik), *adj*. of, pert. to or characterising a genus, sort, or kind.

genesic (jines'ik), *adj*. pert. to generation or genital organs. **-siology** (-ēsiol'əji), *n*. study of heredity or procreation. **-siurgic** (-ēsiə'jik), *adj*. connected with generation.

genet (jen'it, jinet'), *n*. civet-like animal; its spotted fur.

genethliac(al) (jineth′liak, -lī′əkl), *adj.* pert. to nativity and position of star at birth. **-lialogy,** *n.* casting of nativities. **-lic,** *adj.*

genetic (jinet′ik), *adj.* pert. to origin, reproduction and heredity. **-ism** (-sizm), *n.* theory referring to individual or racial history to explain existing conduct, etc. **-ist,** *n.* believer in geneticism ; expert on genetics. **-s,** *n.* study of heredity.

genetous (jen′itəs), *adj.* congenital.

genetrix (jen′itriks), *n.* (*pl.* **-rices,** -ī′sēz) mother.

geniculate (jenik′ūlāt), *adj.* abruptly bent. **-tion,** *n.*

genital (jen′itəl), *adj.* pert. to generation. **-s,** *n.pl.* external organs of reproduction.

genitive (jen′itiv), *adj.* signifying possession or origin ; *n.* such gram. case. **-val** (-ī′vəl), *adj.*

genocide (jen′əsīd), *n.* extermination of a race of people. **-otype,** *n.* species typifying a genus.

genre (zhahn′r), Fr. *n.* kind ; style ; realistic painting of everyday scenes.

gentilitial (jentilish′əl), *adj.* pert. to nation or family ; of high birth. **-tious,** *adj.*

gentoo (jentoo′), Anglo-Ind. *n.* Hindu.

genuflect (jen′ūflekt), *v.i.* bend the knee in worship. **-exion, -ion,** *n.* **-exuous,** *adj.* geniculate. **-or, -ory,** *adj.*

genus (jen′əs, jē′-), *n.* (*pl.* **-nera**) class ; kind ; *Biol.*, category between family and species. **g. homo,** Man.

geocentric (jēəsen′trik), *adj.* pert. to centre of earth ; having earth as centre. **-ism** (-sizm), *n.* belief that earth is centre of universe.

geochrony (jiok′rəni), *n.* chronology used in geology. **-nic** (-on′ik), *adj.*

geocyclic (jēəsīk′lik), *adj.* pert. to earth's rotation or revolution ; revolving round earth.

geode (jē′ōd), *n.* cavity in stone lined with crystals.

geodesy (jiod′isi), *n.* math. study of the earth, its shape, measurements, etc., and the position and area of points and parts of its surface. **-dete, -sist,** *n.* student of g. **-detic** (-et′ik), **-sic** (-es′ik), *adj.*

making allowance for earth's curvature.

geodynamic (jēədīnam′ik), *adj.* pert. to forces within the earth. **-s,** *n.* study of such forces.

geogenous (jioj′inəs), *adj.* growing on ground.

geognosy (jiog′nəsi), *n.* geol. study of materials forming the earth. **-st,** *n.* student of g. **-stic,** *adj.*

geogony (jiog′əni), *n.* theory or study of formation of the earth. **-nic(al)** (-on′ik, -l), *adj.*

geohydrology (jēəhīdrol′əji), *n.* study of subterranean water.

geoid (jē′oid), *n.* figure of the earth. **-al,** *adj.*

geology (jiol′əji), *n.* hist. study of crust of earth, rocks and strata, and life recorded in them. **-gical,** *adj.* **-gist,** *n.*

geomancy (jē′əmansi), *n.* divination by lines and figures. **-ntic,** *adj.*

geomorphic (jēəmaw′fik), *adj.* pert. to or like the form or figure of the earth. **-phogeny,** *n.* study of earth forms. **-phology,** *n.* study of form, nature and evolution on earth's surface.

geophagous (jiof′əgəs), *adj.* eating earth. **-gia** (-ā′jiə), **-gism** (-jizm), **-gy** (-ji), *n.*

geophilous (jiof′iləs), *adj.* living in or on the ground ; growing under the ground.

geophysics (jēəfiz′iks), *n.* physics as applied to geology. **-cal,** *adj.* **-cist,** (-sist), *n.*

geophyte (jē′əfīt), *n.* plant growing in earth.

geopolar (jēəpō′lə), *adj.* pert. to earth's pole(s).

geopolitics (jēəpol′itiks), *n.* study of relationship between geographical situation and politics of a nation.

geoponic(al) (jēəpon′ik, -l), *adj.* agricultural. **-ics,** *n.* science of agriculture.

georama (jēərah′mə), *n.* map of world on inside of globe, viewed from within.

georgic (jaw′jik), *adj.* pert. to agriculture ; rural ; *n.* such poem.

geoscopy (jios′kəpi), *n.* examination of earth and soil. **-pic** (-op′ik), *adj.*

geoselenic (jēəsilen′ik), *adj.* pert. to earth and moon.

geosphere (jē′əsfēr), *n.* solid part of the earth.

geostrophic (jēəstrof'ik), *adj.* pert. to deflection due to earth's rotation.

geotaxis, -taxy (jēətaks'is, -i), *n. Biol.*, movement directed by gravitation. -tactic, *adj.*

geotechnics (jēətek'niks), *n.* study of increasing the habitability of earth.

geotectonic (jēətekton'ik), *adj.* pert. to earth's structure. -s, *n.* structural geology.

geothermal, -mic (jēəthə̄'məl, -mik), *adj.* pert. to heat of earth's interior. -mometer, *n.* instr. measuring such heat.

geotropism, -py (jēot'rəpizm, -pi), *n. Biol.*, growth or movement directed by gravitation, *espec.* towards the earth. -pic (-op'ik), *adj.*

geratic (jirat'ik, gir-), *adj.* pert. to old age and decadence. -tology, *n.* biol. study of decadence.

gerendum (jiren'dəm), *n.* (*pl.* -da) thing to be done.

gerent (jer'ənt), *n.* manager.

gerfalcon (jə̄'fawlkən), *n.* large Arctic falcon.

geriatrics (jeriat'riks, ger-), *n.* med. study of old age and its diseases.

german (jə̄'mən), *adj.* of same. parents; of one's parent's brother or sister. cousin-g., first cousin.

germane (jəmān'), *adj.* relevant; apt.

germicide (jə̄'misīd), *n.* substance destroying germs. -dal, *adj.* -mifuge, *n. & adj.* (substance) expelling germs.

germinal (jə̄'minəl), *adj.* pert. to germ or germination; pert. to embryo.

gerocomy, -mia (jirok'əmi, gir-; jerəkō'miə, ger-), *n.* med. study of old age. -mical (-om'ikl), *adj.*

geromorphism (jerəmaw'fizm, ger-), *n.* having appearance of age greater than one's real age.

gerontic, -tal (jiron'tik, -əl; gir-), *adj. Biol.*, pert. to old age or decadence. -tism, *n.* -tocracy, *n.* government by old men. -togeous (-təjē'əs), *adj.* pert. to Old World. -tology, *n.* study of characteristics of old age.

gerrymander (geriman'də, jer-), *v.t.* divide into electoral wards, etc., in such a way as to gain political advantage; distort or use facts, etc., to gain advantage.

gerund (jer'ənd, -und), *n.* a kind of verbal noun. -ial, *adj.* -ive, *n.* gerundial adjective, expressing (in Lat.) necessity.

gesso (jes'ō), *n.* prepared gypsum or plaster of Paris used in painting; *v.t.* apply g. to.

Gestalt (gəshtalt'), Ger. *n.* (*pl.* -en) integral pattern or system of psych. events as a functional unit.

Gestapo (gəstah'pō), Ger. *n.* (abbr. of *geheime Staats Polizei*) "secret state police"; Ger. political police noted for methods of extreme cruelty.

gestate (jes'tāt), *v.t.* carry in womb. -tion, *n.* such carrying or period of carrying. -tional, -tive, *adj.* -torial, *adj.* pert. to ceremonial carrying-chair. -tory, *adj.* pert. to gestation; pert. to carrying as exercise.

gestic(al) (jes'tik, -l), *adj.* pert. to motion of body, or gestures.

Gesundheit (gəzoont'hīt), Ger. *n.* "good health."

gharry (gar'i), Anglo-Ind. *n.* light horsed carriage. g.-wallah, g. driver.

ghat (gawt), Anglo-Ind. *n.* mountain pass or range; river steps.

ghazi (gah'zē), *n.* Moham. champion; highest Turk. title of honour.

ghee (gē), Hind. *n.* clarified butter.

ghetto (get'ō), *n.* Jewish quarter.

ghoom (gōōm), Anglo-Ind. *v.i.* hunt game at night.

ghurry (gur'i), Anglo-Ind. *n.* interval of time, *espec.* one hour; clock, *espec.* water clock.

giaour (jowr), Turk. *n.* infidel; Christian.

gibbous (gib'əs), *adj.* convex; hump-backed; app. to moon between half and full. -bosity, *n.* -bus, *n.* hump.

gibus (jī'bəs), *n.* opera hat.

gid (gid), *n.* brain disease of sheep.

gigantism (jigan'tizm), *n.* excessive growth; acromegaly. -ticide, *n.* killing or killer of giant. -tomachy, *n.* battle of giants.

gigolo (jig'əlō), *n.* professional dancing partner or escort; man living on prostitute's earnings.

gigot (jig'ət), *n.* leg of mutton.

Gilbertian (gilbə̄'tiən), *adj.* absurd; topsy-turvy, like situations in Gilbert and Sullivan comic operas.

gillaroo (gilərōō'), *n.* Ir. trout.

gillie, gh- (gil'i), *n.* Scot. attendant on hunter.

gilliver (jil'ivə), *n.* wallflower.

gimbals (jim'bəlz, gim'-), *n.pl.* contrivance of rings allowing supported body (*e.g.* ship's compass) to tip in any direction.

gingival (jinji'vəl, jin'ji-), *adj.* pert. to gums; alveolar. **-gia** (-al'jiə), *n.* pain in gums. **-vitis**, *n.* inflammation of gums.

ginglymus (jing'liməs, ging'-), *n.* hinge joint. **-moid**, *adj.* pert. to or like a g.

ginkgo (gingk'gō, jingk'-), *n.* rare Chin. temple tree; maidenhair tree.

ginseng (jin'seng), *n.* Chin. herb with root used in folk medicine.

girandole (jir'əndōl), *n.* cluster of water-jets or fireworks; fountain with spreading spray; any such radiating ornament.

girasol(e) (jir'əsol, -sōl), *n.* heliotrope; sunflower; fire opal.

gittern (git'ən), *n.* cithern.

glabrous (glā'brəs), *adj.* having smooth surface. **-brate**, *adj.* **-brescent**, *adj.* somewhat g.; tending to be g.

glacial (glā'shiəl), *adj.* pert. to ice, ice-age or glacier; crystallised. **-iated**, *adj.* frozen; covered with glaciers; affected by ice action. **-ier** (glas'iə, glā'sh-), *n.* mass of ice moving down valley or spreading over wide area. **-iology**, *n.* geol. study of ice action and ice age.

glacis (glas'i, glā'sis), *n.* gentle slope, *espec.* sloping bank of fortification.

gladiate (glad'iāt, glā'-), *adj.* swordshaped.

glair (glār), *n.* white of egg; any similar substance; *v.t.* cover with g. **-eous**, *adj.*

glanders (glan'dəz), *n.* bacillary gland disease of horses.

glandiform (glan'difawm), *adj.* acorn-shaped. **-ferous**, *adj.* bearing acorns.

glaucescent (glawses'ənt), *adj.* somewhat glaucous.

glaucoma (glawkō'mə), *n.* hardness of eyeball. **-tous**, *adj.*

glaucous (glaw'kəs), *adj.* greygreen; green-blue; yellow-green.

glebe (glēb), *n.* soil; land attached to benefice. **g.house**, parsonage.

gleet (glēt), *n.* mucous discharge, *espec.* from urethra; *v.i.* emit such discharge.

glenoid (glē'noid), *adj.* shaped like a shallow depression.

glirine (glīr'in), *adj.* rodent-like. **-riform**, *adj.*

glissade (glisād', -ahd'), *n.* slide down slope; sliding step; *v.i.* slide.

globulicide (glob'ūlisīd), *n.* & *adj.* (substance) destroying blood corpuscles. **-dal**, *adj.* **-limeter**, *n.* instr. measuring red corpuscles in blood. **-lin**, *n.* kind of protein in blood.

glochidiate, **-deous** (gləkid'iət, -iəs), *adj.* barbed; bristly.

glockenspiel (glok'ənspēl), *n.* xylophone-like mus. instr., *espec.* with metal bars.

glomerate (glom'ərāt), *adj.* collected compactly together. **-tion**, *n.*

gloss (glos), *n.* *Lit.*, explanatory note; false explanation; *v.i.* & *t.* make or add such notes; explain away or wrongly.

glossal (glos'əl), *adj.* pert. to tongue. **-gia** (-al'jiə), *n.* pain in tongue. **-sectomy**, *n.* removal of tongue. **-sitis**, *n.* inflammation of tongue. **-sographer**, *n.* writer of glosses. **-soid**, *adj.* tongue-like. **-solalia**, **-laly**, *n.* gift of tongues. **-sology**, *n.* terminology; study of language; *med.* study of tongue. **-sopathy**, *n.* disease of tongue. **-sophagine**, *adj.* feeding with tongue. **-soplegia**, *n.* paralysis of tongue.

glottis (klot'is), *n.* chink-like space between the vocal cords. **-tal**, *adj.*; **g.stop**, closure and sudden explosive opening of glottis; sound thus caused (as *t* in Lowland Scot.). **-tic**, **-tidean**, *adj.*

glottology (glotol'əji), *n.* study of language. **-ogonic**, *adj.* pert. to origin of language.

glucose (glōō'kōs), *n.* form of sugar; dextrose; kind of syrup made from this. **-caemia**, *n.* occurrence of g. in blood. **-side**, *n.* substance yielding g. on hydrolysis.

glume (glōōm), *n.* dry bract of grass flower. **-maceous**, **-mose**, *adj.* like or composed of g. **-miferous**, *adj.* bearing g.

---

gluside (glōō'sīd), n. saccharin.

gluteal (glōō'tial), adj. pert. to buttocks.

gluten (glōō'tin), n. sticky protein in flour; adj. containing little starch and much g. -ous, adj. -tinous, adj. like or pert. to glue.

glutition (glootish'n), n. act of swallowing.

glycogen (glī'kəjen), n. form of carbohydrate stored in body, found espec. in liver. -esis, n. formation of sugar from g. -ic, -ous (-oj'inəs), adj.

glycose (glī'kōs), n. glucose. -suria, -curesis, n. excretion of sugar in urine.

glyph (glif), n. groove; anct. wall carving. -ic, adj. pert. to sculpture.

glyptic (glip'tik), adj. pert. to carving, espec. of gems. -s, -tography, n. gem-carving. -tology, n. study of gem engravings.

gnathal, -thic (nā'thəl, nath'-; -thik), adj. pert. to jaw. -thism, n. formation of upper jaw; use of such formation as basis for classification. -thonic, adj. flattering.

gneiss (nīs, gn-), n. granite-like metamorphic rock. -ic, -itic, -ose, adj. -oid, adj. like g.

gnomic (nō'mik), adj. pert. to or like aphorisms; Gram., signifying general truth. -mist, n. writer of g. poetry. -mologic, adj. aphoristic. -mology, n. g. writing; collection of g. writings.

gnomon (nō'mon), n. part of sundial casting shadow.

gnosiology (nōsiol'əji, nōz-), n. epistemology.

gnosis (nō'sis), n. spiritual knowledge or insight. -stic, adj. pert. to knowledge or gnosticism; n. adherent of gnosticism. -sticism, n. relig. belief of those claiming gnosis or that freedom was possible through gnosis alone.

Gobinism (gō'binizm), n. theory of the superiority of Aryan or Teutonic race, enumerated by J. A. de Gobineau.

godet (gō'dā), Fr. n. panel inserted to make skirt flare.

godown (gədown'), Anglo-Ind. n. warehouse.

goffer, gauf-, see gopher.

gombroon (gombrōōn'), n. kind of Pers. pottery.

gomphosis (gomfō's's), n. growth of tooth into bone cavity.

gonalgia (gənal'jiə), n. pain in knee.

gonad (gon'ad, gō'-), n. sexual gland; ovary or testis. -al, -ial, -ic, adj.

goneoclinic (goniəklin'ik), adj. app. to hybrid more like one parent than other.

gonfalon (gon'fələn), n. hanging banner. -ier, n. standard-bearer; medieval It. magistrate.

gonion (gō'niən), n. (pl. -nia) angle, espec. of lower jaw. -iometer, n. instr. measuring angles. -iometry, n. trigonometry.

gonitis (gənītis), n. inflammation of knee.

gonoblast (gon'əblast), n. reproductive cell. -ochorism, n. separation of sex. -ocyte, n. gamete-producing cell.

gonorrhoea (gonərē'ə), n. bacterial disease of sexual and urinary tract; clap. -l, -oeic, adj.

gopher (gō'fə, gof'-), v.t. flute edges of; crimp; Amer. n. rat-like burrowing rodent.

goral (gōr'əl), n. Asiatic goat antelope.

gorgon (gaw'gən), n. extremely ugly or terrifying woman. -ian, adj. -ise, v.t. transfix with stare; petrify.

gorsedd (gōr'sedh), n. assembly for giving prizes, degrees, etc., at close of eisteddfod.

goshawk (gos'hawk), n. large, short-winged hawk.

gouache (gwash), n. painting with pigments mixed with gum.

goulash (gōō'lahsh, -ash), n. ragout of veal, etc., with paprika.

gourami (gōōr'əmi), n. large freshwater Malayan food fish.

gourmand (gōōr'mənd; Fr., gōōr'-mahn), n. & adj. gluttonous (person).

gourmet (gōōr'mā), Fr. n. epicure.

governors (guv'ənəz), n.pl. mechanical device, espec. based on centrifugal action of two balls, for controlling speed, etc.

gracile (gras'īl, -il), adj. slender. -lity, n. -scent, adj. becoming g.

gradatim (grədā'tim), Lat. adv. "step by step."

gradin (grā'din; Fr., grad'añ), n. one of a tier of steps, seats, etc.

gradus (grā'dəs), *n.*, *abbr.* of g. ad Parnassum, dictionary used in composition of Latin verses.

graf (grahf), Ger. *n.* (*pl.* -en) title, equiv. of earl, in Ger. and Sweden.

graffito (grafē'tō), *n.* (*pl.* -ti) anct. wall drawing or writing.

grallatory, **-rial** (gral'ətəri, -ōr'iəl), *adj.* pert. to wading birds.

gramicidin (gramisi'din, -is'-), *n.* antibiotic produced by a soil fungus, active against gram-positive bacteria.

graminaceous (graminā'shəs), *adj.* grass-like ; pert. to grass family of plants. **-neal**, **-neous**, *adj.* **-nivorous**, *adj.* feeding on grass. **-nology**, *n.* study of grasses. **-nous**, *adj.* grassy.

grammalogue (gram'əlog), *n.* word represented by one | shorthand sign ; such sign.

grammatolatry (gramatol'ətri), *n.* worship of words or letters, or the letter. **-tor**, *n.*

gram-positive (gram-poz'itiv), *adj.* denoting a class of bacteria stainable by method invented by H. J. C. Gram, Danish physician. **-negative**, *adj.* denoting class of bacteria not stainable thus.

grampus (gram'pəs), *n.* kind of small whale ; blackfish ; killer whale.

grandiloquent (grandil'əkwənt), *adj.* bombastic ; using high-sounding language. **-nce**, *n.* **-quous**, *adj.*

grandisonant (grandis'ənənt), *adj.* sounding great ; pompous. **-nous**, *adj.*

grangerise (grān'jərīz), *v.t.* illustrate, *espec.* by interleaving, with additional pictures. **-ism**, *n.*

granivorous (grəniv'ərəs), *adj.* feeding on grain or seeds.

graphology (grafol'əji), *n.* study of and reading character from handwriting. **-gic(al)**, *adj.* **-gist**, *n.*

graphometer (grafom'itə), *n.* angle-measuring instrument.

graphospasm (graf'əspazm), *n.* writer's cramp.

grapnel (grap'nəl), *n.* small anchor or hook.

graticulate (gratik'ūlāt), *v.t.* divide (pattern, etc.) into squares for easiness of reproduction. **-tion**, *n.*

gratuitous (gratū'itəs), *adj.* done freely ; needless ; groundless. **-ty**, *n.* gift of money ; tip.

gratulatory (grat'ūlātəri), *adj.* congratulating. **-lant**, *adj.* **-tion**, *n.*

gravamen (grəvā'men), *n.* substance of a grievance or charge.

gravedo (grəve'dō), *n.* cold in the head.

gravid (grav'id), *adj.* pregnant.

gravimetric(al) (gravimet'rik, -l), *adj.* pert. to measurement by weight. **-try** (-im'itri), *n.*

great go (grāt gō), *n.* final examination for B.A. degree at Oxford University.

greave (grēv), *n.* armour covering lower leg. **-s**, *n.pl.* tallow refuse.

gregal (grē'gəl), *adj.* pert. to or like a flock.

gregarious (grigār'jəs), *adj.* living in herds ; tending to flock together ; fond of society. **-rian**, *adj.* pert. to the common herd.

gremial (grē'miəl), *adj.* pert. to bosom or lap ; *n.* bishop's apron.

grenadine (gren'əden, -dēn'), *n.* sweet fruit syrup ; light thin dress fabric.

gressorial. **-ious** (gresōr'iəl, -iəs), *adj.* adapted for walking.

griffe (grif), *n.* person of mixed Amer. Ind. and negro blood. **-fado** (-ah'dō), *n.* child of white and quadroon parents.

grilse (grils), *n.* young salmon.

gringo (gring'gō), Sp. Amer. *n.* foreigner ; American ; Englishman.

grisaille (grēzī'), Fr. *n.* glass painted with grey pigment.

griseous (griz'iəs, gris'-), *adj.* grizzled.

grisette (grēzet'), Fr. *n.* gay young working girl.

griskin (gris'kin), *n.* lean loin of pork.

grivet (griv'it), *n.* black and white Abyssinian monkey.

grobian (grō'biən), *n.* lout. **-ism**, *n.*

grognard (grōn'yahr), Fr. *n.* grouser ; old soldier.

gromatic (grəmat'ik), *adj.* pert. to surveying. **-s**, *n.* surveying, *espec.* of camp.

grosbeak (grōs'bēk), *n.* large-billed finch ; hawfinch.

grossulariaceous (grosūlāriā'shəs), *adj.* pert. to or like a gooseberry ; belonging to gooseberry family of plants. **-rious**, *adj.*

groyne (groin), *n.* wooden breakwater.

gruine (grōō'īn, -in), *adj.* like or pert. to crane (bird).

---

grume (grōōm), *n.* clot; clotted liquid. **-mose**, *adj.* comprising a cluster of granules. **-mous**, *adj.* clotted.

gryllid (gril'id), *n.* cricket (insect); *adj.* pert. to or like cricket; belonging to cricket family of insects.

grysbok (grīs'bok), S. Afr. *n.* small reddish antelope.

guaiacum (gwī'əkəm), *n.* resin of a tropical Amer. tree, used as rheumatic remedy.

guanaco (gwahnah'kō), *n.* S. Amer. llama-like animal.

guano (gwah'nō), *n.* sea-birds' excrement used as fertiliser. **-niferous**, *adj.* yielding g.

guava (gwah'və), *n.* apple-like fruit of sev. tropical Amer. shrubs.

gubernatorial (gūbənətor'iəl), *adj.* pert. to governor or government. **-trix** (-ā'triks), *n.* female governor.

guepard(e) (gep'ahd, -ahd'), *n.* cheetah.

guerdon (gɜ'dən), *n.* & *v.t.* reward.

guillemot (gil'limət), *n.* kind of auk-like seabird.

guilloche (gilosh'), *n.* archit. ornament of intertwined curved lines or bands.

guimbard (gim'bahd), *n.* jew's-harp.

guipure (gipūr'), *n.* kind of large-patterned heavy lace.

gules (gūlz), *n.* & *adj.* Her., red.

gulosity (gūlos'iti), *n.* greediness.

gunge (gunj), Anglo-Ind. *n.* market; granary.

gunocracy (gūnok'rəsi), *n.* gynaecocracy.

gunyah (gun'yah), Austral. *n.* aborigine's hut.

gurgitate (gɜ'jitāt), *v.i.* bubble. **-tion**, *n.* ebullition.

gurgulation (gɜgūlā'shn), *n.* gurgling sound; rumble.

gurry (gur'i), *n.* Ind. fortress.

guru (goor'ōō), *n.* Hindu relig. teacher.

gustation (gustā'shn), *n.* act of tasting; sense of taste. **-tory**, *adj.*

gutta (gut'ə), *n.* (*pl.* **-ae**) drop. **g.-percha**, rubber-like substance. **g.rosacea**, acne rosacea. **g.serena**, amaurosis. **-te**, *adj.* like a drop; having spots like drops. **-tiferous**, *adj.* yielding gum. **-tiform**, *adj.* drop-shaped. **-tim**, Lat. *adv.* "drop by drop." **-tion**, *n.* exudation of drops of moisture.

guttule, **-la** (gut'ūl, -ə), *n.* small drop; spot like small drop. **-lous**, *adj.*

gutturotetany (gutərətet'əni), *n.* throat spasm causing stammer.

gyle (gīl), *n.* a brewing of beer; wort; fermenting vat.

gymnosophist (jimnos'əfist), *n.* anct. Ind. ascetic philosopher; nudist. **-phy**, *n.*

gymnosperm (jim'nəspɜm), *n.* flowering plant with naked seed; *pl.* natural division of plants with such seeds. **-ism**, **-y**, *n.* **-ous**, *adj.*

gynaecic, **-nec-** (jinē'sik, jī-, gī-), *adj.* female.

gynaecide, **-nec-** (jir 'isīd, gī'-), *n.* killing or killer of women. **-dal**, *adj.*

gynaecocentric, **-nec-** (jinikəsentrik, jī- gī-), *adj.* with the female element dominating.

gynaecocracy, **-nec-** (jinikok'rəsi, jī-, gī-), *n.* domination of society by women. **-atic** (-at'ik), *adj.*

gynaecolatry, **-nec-** (jinikol'ətri, jī-, gī-), *n.* worship of women.

gynaecology, **-nec-** (jinikol'əji, jī-, gī-), *n.* study of diseases of women. **-gic(al)**, *adj.* **-gist**, *n.*

gynaecomania, **-nec-** (jinikəmā'niə, jī-, gī-), *n.* sexual craving for women.

gynaecomorphous, **-nec-** (jinikəmaw'fəs, jī-, gī-), *n.* having female form or characteristics.

gynaecopathy, **-nec-** (jinikop'əthi, jī, gī-), *n.* any disease of women. **-thic** (-ath'ik), *adj.*

gynandroid (jinan'droid, gī-), *adj.* hermaphrodite; app. to woman of masculine physique. **-dria**, **-drism** **-dry**, *n.* **-drous**, *adj.*

gynarchy (jin'ahki, jī-, gī'-), *n.* government by women. **-chic**, *adj.*

gyniatrics (jiniat'riks, jī-, gī-), *n.* treatment of women's diseases.

gynics (jin'iks, jī'-, gī'-), *n.* knowledge of women.

gynocracy (jinok'rəsi, jī-, gī-), *n.* gynaecocracy.

gynoecium (jinē'siəm, jī-, gī-), *n.* (*pl.* **-cia**) Bot., pistils collectively.

gypsum (jip'səm,, *n.* form of calcium sulphate used in making plaster of Paris; form of alabaster. **-seous**, **-sous**, *adj.* **-siferous**, *adj.* containing g.

gyrfalcon, *see* gerfalcon.

gyrinid (jirī'nid, jī-, gī-), *n.* whirligig beetle; *adj.* like or pert.

to g.; belonging to the g. family of beetles.

gyrocompass (jīr'əkumpəs, gīr'-), *n.* gyroscope with its axis kept horizontal, pointing always to true north.

gyrograph (jīr'əgraf, gīr'-), *n.* instr. recording wheel's revolutions.

gyropilot (jīr'əpīlət, gīr'-), *n.* automatic aircraft pilot comprising two gyroscopes.

gyroscope (jīr'əskōp, gīr'-), *n.* solid wheel rotating in a ring, with its axis free to turn; such apparatus with its axis fixed and acting as compass, stabiliser, etc. **-pic** (-op'ik), *adj.*

gyrostatics (jīrəstat'iks, gīr-), *n.* study of rotating bodies and their properties.

gyve (jīv), *n.* & *v.t.* fetter.

H

habanera (ahbahnār'ə), *n.* slow Cuban dance.

habeas corpus (hā'biəs kaw'pəs), *Lat.*, "that you may have the body"; writ requiring presence of person before judge, court, etc., *espec.* to investigate legality of his detention in custody.

habitant (hab'itənt; Fr., ab'-ētahn), *n.* French settler, or his descendant, in Canada or Louisiana.

habitat (hab'itat), *n.* natural growing- or dwelling-place.

habitué (həbit'ū ā; Fr., abē'tüā), *n.* frequenter.

hachure (hashūr', hash'-), *n.* line used in shading maps to indicate steepness of slope; *v.t.* shade with h.

hacienda (bahsien'də), Sp. *n.* farm; estate.

hackery (hak'əri), Anglo-Ind. *n.* light bullock- or horse-cart.

hackle (hak'l), *n.* cock's long neck feather; part of angler's fly made from h.

Hades (hā'dēz), *n.* abode of dead, or king of underworld, of Gr. myth; Hell. **-ean**, *adj.*

hadj (haj), Arab. *n.* pilgrimage, *espec.* of Moham. to Mecca. **-i**, *n.* Moham. who has made such pilgrimage.

haecceity (hɒksē'iti), *n.* "thisness"; quality of being here at present.

haemachrome (hē'məkrōm, hem'-), *n.* colouring matter of blood.

haemagogue (hē'məgog, hem'-), *n.* & *adj.* (drug) promoting discharge of blood or menstrual flow. **-gic** (-oj'ik), *adj.*

haemal (hē'məl), *adj.* pert. to blood.

haemarthrosis (hēmahthrō'sis,

hem-), *n.* extravasation of blood into joint.

haematal (hē'mətəl, hem'-), *adj.* haemal.

haematencephalon (hēmətensef'-əlon, hem-), *n.* haemorrhage into brain.

haematherm (hē'məthēm), *n.* warm-blooded animal. **-al, -ous, -mato-thermal**, *adj.*

haematic (himat'ik), *n.* & *adj.* (drug) acting on blood; pert. to, like or coloured like blood.

haematid (hē'mətid, hem'-), *n.* red blood corpuscle.

haematite (hē'mətīt, hem'-), *n.* reddish iron ore. **-tic** (-it'ik), *adj.*

haematobic (hēmətō'bik, hem-), *adj.* parasitic in blood. **-bious**, *adj.* **-bium**, *n.* (*pl.* **-ia**) such organism.

haematocryal (hēmətəkrī'əl, hem-), *adj.* cold-blooded.

haematoid (hē'mətoid, hem'-), *adj.* like blood.

haematonic (hēməton'ik, hem-), *n.* & *adj.* (drug) stimulating formation of blood.

haematorrhoea (hēmətərē'ə, hem-), *n.* discharge of blood.

haematose (hē'mətōs, hem'-), *adj.* full of blood.

haemic (hē'mik, hem'-), *adj.* haemal.

haemocyte (hē'məsīt, hem'-), *n.* blood corpuscle.

haemogastric (hēməgas'trik, hem-), *adj.* marked by gastric haemorrhage.

haemoglobin (hēməglō'bin, *n.* colouring matter of blood's red corpuscles. **-bic, -ous**, *adj.*

haemoid (hē'moid, hem'-), *adj.* haematoid.

haemolysis (hēmol'isis), *n.* destruction of red blood corpuscles. **-lytic** (-lit'ik), *adj.*

---

hat, bah, hāte, hāre, crawl; pen, ēve, hēre; it, īce, fīre; on, bōne, boil, bōre, howl; foot, fōōd, bōōr, hull, tūbe, pūre.

haemophilia (hēməfil'iə, hem-), *n.* condition marked by uncontrollable bleeding from smallest cuts. **-c, -le**, *n.* sufferer from h. **-lic,** *adj.*

haemophthalmia (hēmofthal'miə, hem-), *n.* discharge of blood into eye.

haemoptysis (himop'tisis, hem-), *n.* spitting of blood.

haemorrhage (hem'ərij), *n.* discharge of blood. **-gic,** *adj.* **-rhoids,** *n.pl.* piles.

haemospasia (hēməspā'zhiə, hem-), *n.* drawing of blood to part. **-stic,** *n. & adj.*

haemostasia, -sis (hēməstā'zhiə, hem-; himos'təsis), *n.* stopping of haemorrhage ; blood stagnation. **-stat,** *n.* instr. for h. **-static,** *n. & adj.* (agent) for h. ; styptic.

haemotoxic (hēmətoks'ik, hem-), *adj.* causing blood-poisoning. **-xin,** *n.*

haeremai (hahar'āmah'ē), Maori *excl.* welcome !

hageen (həjēn'), *n.* dromedary.

hagiarchy (hag'iahki, hā'j-), *n.* government by priests. **-giocracy,** *n.* government by holy persons.

hagiographa (hagiog'rəfə, hāj-), *n.pl.* O.T. Hebrew scriptures excluding Law and Prophets. **-pher,** **-phist,** *n.* writer of h. ; writer of saints' lives. **-phic,** *adj.* **-phy,** *n.* hagiology.

hagiolatry (hagiol'ətrı, hāj-), *n.* worship of saints. **-ter,** *n.* such worshippers. **-trous,** *adj.*

hagiology (hagiol'əji, hāj-), *n.* description of holy persons or writings ; study or writing of saints' lives ; list of saints. **-gic(al),** *adj.* **-gist,** *n.*

hagioscope (hag'iəskōp, hā'j-), *n.* opening in transept wall for viewing altar. **-pic** (op'ik), *adj.*

ha-ha (hah'-hah), *n.* sunk fence.

hajib (hah'jib), Arab. *n.* Moham. court chamberlain.

haji, *see* **hadj.**

hakeem (həkēm'), Arab. *n.* Moham. physician.

Hakenkreuz (hah'kənkroits), Ger. *n.* swastika.

hakim (hah'kim), *n.* Moham. judge or ruler ; hakeem.

halation (halā'shn), *n.* spreading of light, seen as bright blur at edges in photographs.

halcyon (hal'siən), *n.* sea bird supposed to calm the waves while nesting on them ; kingfisher,

espec. Austral. ; *adj.* tranquil. **h.days,** calm period of 14 days at winter solstice ; any peaceful period. **-ian** (-ō'niən), **-ic** (-on'ik), *adj.*

halfpace (hahf'pās), *n.* dais ; small landing on staircase.

halibios (halibī'os), *n.* collective life of sea. **-otic** (-ot'ik), *adj.*

halicore (halik'əri), *n.* dugong.

halide (hal'īd, hā-), *n.* compound of halogen with other element or radical.

halieutic(al) (haliū'tik, -l), *adj.* pert. to fishing. **-cs,** *n.* art of fishing.

halitosis (halitō'sis), *n.* foul breath.

halitus (hal'itəs), *n.* breath ; exhalation. **-tuous,** *adj.* **-tuosity,** *n.*

halle (al), Fr. *n.* central market.

hallel (hal'el, həlāl'), Heb. *n.* psalm(s) of praise.

hallux (hal'əks), *n.* (*pl.* **-uces**) big toe ; hind toe of birds. **-ucal,** *adj.*

halobios (haləbī'os), *n.* halibios. **-otic** (-ot'ik), *adj.*

halogen (hal'əjen), *n.* element or radical that unites directly with metal to form a salt, *e.g.* bromine, chlorine, fluorine, iodine. **haloid** (hal'oid), *adj.* like salt ; *n.* halide. **-olimnic,** *adj.* app. to sea creatures adapted to fresh-water life. **-omancy,** *n.* divination by salt. **-ophilous,** *adj.* growing in salt water. **-oxene,** *adj.* not unable to live in salt water.

hamadryad (hamədrī'ad), *n.* wood nymph associated with one particular tree ; king cobra.

hamal (hamahl', -awl'), Turk. *n.* porter ; litter-bearer ; male servant.

hamartiology (həmahtiol'əji), *n.* division of theology dealing with sin. **-gist,** *n.*

hamate (hā'māt), *adj.* hooked ; hook-like. **-miform,** *adj.* hook-shaped. **-mirostrate,** *adj.* with hooked beak.

hammam (hamahm'), Turk. *n.* Turkish bath.

hamster (ham'stə), *n.* rat-like rodent with large cheek pouches.

hamstring (ham'string), *n.* tendon at back of knee or hock ; *v.t.* lame by cutting h. ; render incapable of action.

hamular (ham'ūlə), *adj.* hamate. **-late, -lose, -lous,** *adj.* having small hook.

handsel (han'səl), *n.* gift, *espec.* at New Year ; first money taken at shop ; earnest money ; *v.t.* give h. ; inaugurate with gift, etc. ; attempt for first time. **-ller,** *n.* cheap-jack.

hanif (hanēf'), Arab. *n.* orthodox Moslem. **-ism,** *n.*

hapaxanthous (hapaksan'thəs), *adj.* having one flowering period only.

haplography (haplog'rəfi), *n.* accidental omission of letters, words or lines in copying.

haploid (hap'loid), *adj.* single ; *Biol.,* having the specific chromosome number ; *n.* such cell. **-y,** *n.* state of being h.

haplology, -laly (haplol'əji, -əli), *n.* omission of syllable(s) of word in pronunciation. **-gic,** *adj.*

haplotype (hap'lətīp), *n.* single species contained in a genus.

haptic (hap'tik), *adj.* pert. to sense of touch. **-s,** *n.* psych. study of sensations. **-tometer,** *n.* instr. measuring tactile sensitiveness.

hara-kiri (hah'rə-kir'i), Jap. *n.* suicide by disembowelling.

harengiform (həren'jifawm), *adj.* shaped like a herring.

hariolate (har'iəlāt), *v.i.* prophesy ; tell fortunes. **-tion,** *n.*

harlot (hah'lət), *n.* prostitute. **-ry,** *n.* prostitution ; lewdness ; lewd story.

harmattan (hahmətan'), *n.* dry east wind blowing from Sahara.

harmonic (hahmon'ik), *n.* overtone.

harpagon, -go (hah'pəgon, -gō), *n.* grapnel ; harpoon.

harquebus(e), *see* **arquebus(e).**

hartal (hahtahl'), Hind. *n.* general strike.

hartebeest (hah'tibēst), *n.* large S. African antelope.

hartshorn (hahts'hawn), *n.* plantain ; sal volatile.

haruspex (har'əspeks, -us'-), *n.* (*pl.* **-pices**) soothsayer, *espec.* divining by sacrifice's entrails. **-pical, -picate,** *adj.* **-pication, -picy** (-isi), *n.*

haslet (has'lit), *n.* animal's fry or entrails, *espec.* braised.

haslock (has'lok), *n.* wool on sheep's throat.

hastate (has'tāt), *adj.* spear-shaped ; like blade of halberd.

hatchment (hach'mənt), *n.* diamond-shaped escutcheon bearing deceased person's arms.

hathi (hah'ti), Hind. *n.* elephant.

hauberk (haw'bŏk), *n.* tunic-like coat of mail.

haulm (hawm, hahm), *n.* stalks of potatoes, beans, etc.

Hausfrau (hows'frow), Ger. *n.* housewife.

haustorial (hawstŏr'iəl), *adj.* having a sucking proboscis. **-tellate,** *adj.*

haute école (ōt ākōl'), Fr., "high school" ; mastery of difficult horsemanship.

hauteur (hōtə'), *n.* haughty manner.

haut monde (ō'mawṅd'), Fr., "high world" ; high society. **h.ton** (-tawṅ'), high fashion ; bon ton.

havelock (hav'lok), *n.* cloth hanging from back of soldier's cap as protection against sun.

havildar (hav'ildah), Anglo-Ind. *n.* sepoy sergeant.

haysel (hā'səl), *n.* haymaking season.

header (hed'ə), *n.* brick placed with end towards face of wall.

hebamic (hibam'ik), *adj.* pert. to Socratic method.

hebdomadal (hebdom'ədəl), *adj.* weekly ; consisting of a week. **-dary,** *adj.*

hebephrenia (hēbifrē'niə), *n.* dementia praecox occurring at puberty. **-nic** (-en'ik), *adj.*

hebetate (heb'itāt), *v.i.* & *t.* make or become blunt or dull ; *adj.* dull-witted. **-tion,** *n.* **-tive,** *adj.*

hebetic (hibet'ik), *adj.* pert. to or occurring at puberty.

hebetude (heb'itūd), *n.* stupidity. **-dinous,** *adj.*

hecatomb (hek'ətom), *n.* sacrifice of one hundred animals ; wholesale slaughter.

hecatontarchy (hekəton'tahki), *n.* government by 100 persons.

hectic (hek'tik), *adj.* habitual, *espec.* in wasting diseases ; consumptive ; *pop.,* excited ; feverish ; gay.

hectograph (hek'təgraf), *n.* duplicating machine using gelatine slab ; *v.t.* duplicate with a h. **-ic,** *adj.* **-y,** *n.*

hederaceous (hedərā'shəs), *adj.* pert. to or like ivy. **-rate,** *adj.* crowned with ivy. **-ric** (-er'ik), *adj.* **-riferous,** *adj.* bearing ivy. **-riform,** *adj.* shaped like ivy leaves. **-rigerent,** *adj.* bearing or ornamented with ivy. **-rose,** *adj.* having much ivy.

hat, bah, hāte, hāre, crawl ; pen, ēve, hēre ; it, īce, fīre ; on, bōne, boil, bōre, howl ; foot, fōod, bōor, hull, tūbe, pūre.

hedonic (hidon'ik), adj. pert. to pleasure. **-nism** (hē'dən-), n. phil. doctrine that pleasure is sole moral good; life of pleasure. **-nist**, n. **-nistic**, adj. **-nology**, **-gy**, n. ethical or psych. study of pleasure.

hegemony (hej'imǝni, hijem'-, hē'-), n. leadership; authority. **-nic** (-imon'ik), adj.

hegira, **hej-** (hijīrǝ, hej'-), n. Moham. era, dating from Mohammed's flight from Mecca, A.D. 622; flight.

heifer (hef'ǝ), n. cow that has not calved.

heinous (hē'nǝs), adj. hateful; atrocious; unpardonable.

helcology (helkol'ǝji), n. Med., study of ulcers. **-coid**, adj. ulcerlike. **-cosis**, n. ulceration. **-cotic**, adj.

heliacal (hili'ǝkl), adj. near or pert. to sun.

helical (hel'ikl), adj. spiral; pert. to helix. **-ciform** (-is'ifawm), **-cine** (-sīn), **-coid**, adj. **-cometry**, n. measurement of spirals.

helicopter (hel'ikoptǝ), n. aeroplane with horizontal propellers, able to rise and descend vertically.

heliocentric (hēliǝsen'trik), adj. pert. to centre of sun; having sun as centre. **-ism** (-sizm), **-ity** (-is'iti), n.

heliochrome (hē'liǝkrōm), n. photograph in natural colours. **-mic**, adj. **-moscope**, n. device producing h. **-my**, n. colour photography.

helioelectric (hēliōilek'trik), adj. pert. to electricity radiated from sun.

heliofugal (hēliof'ūgǝl), adj. moving away from sun.

heliograph (hē'liǝgraf), n. mirror apparatus for signalling by flashes of light; v.i. & t. signal with a h. **-gram**, n. message sent by h. **-ic**, adj.

helioid (hē'lioid), adj. like the sun.

heliolater (hēliol'ǝtǝ), n. sun-worshipper. **-trous**, adj. **-try**, n.

heliology (hēliol'ǝji), n. astron. study of sun. **-gist**, n.

heliometer (hēliom'itǝ), n. micrometer measuring short interstellar distances. **-tric** (-et'rik), adj. **-try**, n.

heliophilous (hēliof'ilǝs), adj. attracted by sunlight. **-lia** (-il'iǝ), **-liac**, n.

heliophobia (hēliǝfō'biǝ), n. dread or avoidance of sunlight; excessive sensitiveness to sunlight. **-be**, n. **-bic**, adj.

heliophyte (hē'liǝfīt), n. plant flourishing in sunlight. **-tic** (-it'ik), adj.

helioscope (hē'liǝskōp), n. instr. for observing sun. **-pic** (-op'ik), adj. **-py** (-os'kǝpi), n.

heliosis (hēliō'sis), n. sunburn of plants; sunstroke.

heliotaxis (hēliǝtaks'is), n. movement towards or away from sunlight. **-tactic**, adj.

heliotherapy (hēliǝther'ǝpi), n. med. treatment by sunlight.

heliotropism (hēliot'rǝpism), n. growth or movement directed by sunlight; growth towards the sun. **-pic** (-op'ik), adj.

helium (hē'liǝm), n. non-inflammable, lighter-than-air, inert gas.

helix (hē'liks, hel'-), n. (pl. -ices) any spiral-formed object; rim of outer ear; snail-shell; screwthread.

hellebore (hel'ibōr), n. sev. kinds of plant, espec. the Christmas rose; alkaloid poison extracted from h.'s root.

Hellene (hel'ēn), n. Greek. **-nic** (-en'ik), adj. **-nise**, v.t. make Greek in manner or character. **-nism**, n. Gr. culture, idiom or language. **-nist**, n. expert on Gr. literature.

helminth (hel'minth), n. intestinal worm. **-agogue**, n. anthelmintic. **-iasis**, **-ism**, n. infestation with h. **-ic**, adj. **-oid**, adj. like h. **-ology**, n. study of h. **-ous**, adj. infested with h.

helobious (hilō'biǝs), n. dwelling in marshes. **-odes** (-ō'dēz), n. marsh fever; adj. marshy.

heloma (hilō'mǝ), n. Med., corn. **-osis**, n. state of having corns.

helot (hel'ǝt), n. slave, espec. of Sparta. **-ism**, **-ry**, n. slavery.

helotomy (hilot'ǝmi), n. cutting of corns.

helve (helv), n. handle; hilt.

Helvetian, **-tic** (helvē'shn, -et'ik), n. & adj. Swiss (person).

hematite, **hemorrhage**, etc., see haematite, haemorrhage, etc.

hemeralopia (hemǝrǝlō'piǝ), n. ability to see only in faint or no light; day blindness. **-pe**, n. **-pic** (-op'ik), adj.

hemerology, **-gium** (hemǝrol'ǝji, -ǝlō'jiǝm), n. calendar.

hemialgia (hemial'jiǝ), n. pain in

one half of body or head. **-micrania**, *n*. h. of the head. **-mifacial**, *adj*. pert. to one side of face. **-miplegia**, *n*. paralysis of one half (left or right) of body.

hemiptera (hemip'tərə), *n.pl.* order of insects containing the bugs. **-ral, -roid, -rous**, *adj*. **-ran, -ron**, *n*. bug. **-rology**, *n*. study of h.

hemistich (hem'istik), *n*. half a verse line. **-al**, *adj*.

hemitery, -ria (hem'itəri, -ēr'ia), *n*. congenital malformation. **-ratic**, *adj*.

hendecagon (hendek'əgon), *n*. 11-sided plane figure. **-ahedron**, *n*. 11-sided solid figure. **-asyllable**, *n*. verse line of 11 syllables.

hendiadys (hendī'ədis), *n*. use of two nouns joined by *and* instead of a noun and an adjective.

henism (hen'izm), *n*. phil. belief that existence is of one kind only.

henogeny, -nesis (henoj'ini, -əjen'-isis), *n*. ontogeny.

henotic (henot'ik), *adj*. promoting harmony or peace.

henry (hen'ri), *n*. unit of elec. inductance : inductance of circuit in which one volt is induced by current varying at one ampere per second.

heortology (hēawtol'əji), *n*. study of relig. festivals, year, etc. **-gion** (-ō'jiən), *n*. calendar of feast days.

hepatic (hipat'ik), *adj*. pert. to or like liver ; *n*. liver medicine ; liverwort. **h.gas**, hydrogen sulphide. **-ology**, *n*. bot. study of liverworts. **-titis**, *n*. inflammation of liver. **-toid**, *adj*. like liver.

hephaestic, -tian (hifes'tik, -tiən), *adj*. pert. to Hephaestus, Gr. god of fire and iron-working ; pert. to smiths.

heptachord (hep'təkawd), *n*. seven-tone mus. scale ; interval of a major seventh.

heptad (hep'tad), *n*. group of seven.

heptagon (hep'təgən), *n*. 7-sided plane figure. **-al** (-ag'ənəl), *adj*.

heptahedron (heptəhēdrən), *n*. 7-sided solid figure. **-dral**, *adj*.

heptameride (heptam'ərīd, -id), *n*. writing in seven parts. **-meter**, *n*. verse line of seven feet. **-rous**, *adj*. having seven divisions ; *Bot*., having the parts of flower in sevens. **-tapody**, *n*. heptameter.

heptarch (hep'tahk), *n*. member of

heptarchy. **-al, -ic**, *adj*. **-y**, *n*. government by seven persons ; group of seven allied but independent kingdoms, *espec*. of Anglo-Saxon England.

heptastich (hep'təstik), *n*. poem or stanza of seven lines.

heptasyllable (hep'təsiləbl), *n*. verse line or word of seven syllables. **-bic** (-ab'ik), *adj*.

heptateuch (hep'tətūk), *n*. first seven books of Bible.

hepteris (heptēr'is), *n*. galley with seven banks of oars.

heraclean (hərəklē'ən), *adj*. herculean.

herbarium (hərbār'iəm), *n*. collection of dried plant specimens ; museum or room holding it. **-rial**, *adj*.

herbicide (hə'bisīd), *n*. weed-killer.

herbivorous (həbiv'ərəs), *adj*. feeding on plants. **-re**, *n*. such animal. **-rity**, *n*.

herculean (hēkū'liən, -lē'ən), *adj*. pert. to Hercules and his labours ; of or requiring enormous strength. **-lanean, -lanian**, *adj*.

hereditament (hered'itəmənt, -dit'-), *n*. inheritance ; hereditable property. **-table**, *adj*. capable of being inherited.

heresiarch (hirē'siahk, her'-), *n*. leading heretic. **-siography, -siology**, *n*. study of or treatise on heresies.

heresy (her'isi), *n*. unorthodox relig. belief. **-retic(al)** (her'ətik, -ret'ikl), *n*. & *adj*. **-reticate, -reticise**, *v.t.* denounce as heretic. **-reticide**, *n*. killer or killing of heretic.

heriot (her'iət), *n*. payment to feudal lord on death of tenant.

herisson (her'isən), *n*. pivoted beam with iron spikes, protecting wall, passage, etc. ; soldier's punishment of being made to sit astride a h.

heritor (her'itə), *n*. owner ; inheritor. **-retrix, -ritrix**, *n*. heiress.

hermaphrodite (həmaf'rədīt), *n*. & *adj*. (person, plant, etc.) with characteristics, *espec*. generative organs, of both sexes. **h.brig**, brigantine. **-tic** (-it'ik), *adj*. **-tism**, *n*.

hermeneutic (həminū'tik), *adj*. explaining ; interpreting. **-s**, *n*. definition of laws of interpretation of Scriptures.

hermetic (həmet'ik), *adj.* pert. to magic or alchemy ; air-tight.

hernia (hə̄'niə), *n.* rupture. **-iorrhaphy,** *n.* surg. operation for h. **-te,** *v.i.* protrude as h. **-tion,** *n.*

heroin (her'oin, hiro'-), *n.* preparation of morphia.

herpes (hə̄'pēz), *n.* eczema-like skin inflammation, *espec.* shingles, cold sores, etc. **-etic** (-et'ik), *adj.* **-etiform,** *adj.* like h. ; like a reptile. **-etography,** *n.* study of herpetic disease ; treatise on reptiles. **-etophobia,** *n.* dread of reptiles.

Herrenvolk (her'ənfolk), Ger. *n.* "master race" ; superior nation.

hertzian (hə̄t'siən), *adj.* app. to wireless waves, etc., experimented on by Heinrich Hertz.

herzog (hert'sōg), Ger. *n.* (*pl.* **-e**) duke.

Hesperian (hesper'iən), *adj.* pert. to Hesperia (Italy or Spain) or Hesperus, the evening star ; western.

Hessian (hes'iən), *adj.* pert. to Hesse ; *n.* kind of coarse sacking ; mercenary soldier. **H.boot,** high tasselled boot. **H.fly,** fly with larva harmful to wheat.

hesternal (hestə̄'nəl), *adj.* pert. to yesterday.

hesychastic (hesikas'tik), *adj.* soothing. **-asm,** *n.* omphaloskepsis.

hetaera (hitē̄r'ə, -ī̄r'ə), *n.* (*pl.* **-ae, -ai**) paramour. **-ria,** *n.* (*pl.* **-ae**) society ; club. **-rism,** *n.* concubinage ; primitive communal ownership of women. **-rocracy,** *n.* government by paramours, or by Fellows of college.

heterise (het'ərīz), *v.t.* transform. **-sm,** *n.* variation.

heterochiral (hetərəkī̄r'əl), *adj.* laterally inverted.

heterochromatic (hetərəkrəmat'ik), *adj.* pert. to or having different colours. **-mia, -my,** *n.* state of being h. **-mous,** *adj.* **-rosis,** *n.* abnormal coloration.

heterochthonous (hetərok'thənəs), *adj.* not autochthonous.

heteroclite (het'ərəklīt), *adj.* abnormal ; irregular ; *n.* such word, thing or person.

heterodox (het'ərədoks), *adj.* not orthodox. **-y,** *n.* such belief or behaviour.

heterodyne (het'ərədīn), *n.* *Rad.*, production of "beats" by super-

imposition of oscillations of slightly different frequency upon the waves being received ; use of this "beat" frequency in wireless reception ; interference, *espec.* whistle, due to h. ; *v.i.* produce h. ; cause interference by h.

heteroepy (het'əroipi, -ō'ipi), *n.* pronunciation different from standard. **-pic** (-ep'ik), *adj.*

heteroerotism (hetəroer'ətizm), *n.* sexual love for another person. **-tic** (-ot'ik), *adj.*

heterogeneous (hetərəjē'niəs), *adj.* comprising different parts or qualities ; diverse. **-neity** (-ē'iti), *n.* **-nesis** (-jen'isis), *n.* parthenogenesis ; abiogenesis ; alternation of generations. **-nous** (-oj'inəs), *adj.* originating elsewhere ; of different origin. **-ny** (-oj'ini), *n.* heterogeneous collection.

heterography (hetərog'rəfi), *n.* spelling different from standard, or in which same letter represents different sounds.

heterolateral (hetərəlat'ərəl), *adj.* pert. to opposite sides.

heterologous (hetərol'əgəs), *adj.* differing ; comprising different parts or parts in different proportions. **-gic(al),** *adj.* **-gy,** *n.*

heteromorphic (hetərəmor'fik), *adj.* of abnormal form ; having different forms. **-phism,** *n.* **-phous,** *adj.*

heteronomous (hetəron'əməs), *adj.* not autonomous. **-my,** *n.*

heteronym (het'ərənim), *n.* word having same spelling as, but different sound and meaning from, another ; exactly equivalent word in other language. **-ous** (-on'iməs), *adj.*

heteroousia (hetərō ōō'sia, -ow'-), *n.* difference of substance. **-n,** *adj.* ; *n. Theol.*, adherent of belief that Son is of different substance from Father.

heteropathy (hetərop'əthi), *n.* allopathy ; excessive sensitivity. **-thic** (-ath'ik), *adj.*

heterophemy (het'ərəfēmi, -of'imi), *n.* accidental speaking or writing of words different from those meant. **-mise,** *v.i.* **-mism, -mist,** *n.*

heterophoria (hetərətor'iə), *n.* squint due to weak muscle. **-ric** (-or'ik), *adj.*

heterophyte (het'ərəfīt), *n.* plant dependent on another. **-tic** (-it'ik), *adj.*

heterosexual (hetərəseks'ūəl), *adj.* not homosexual ; sexually normal. **-ity,** *n.*

heterotaxis (hetərətaks'is), *n.* abnormality in arrangement. **-tactic, -tactous, -xic,** *adj.*

heterotelic (hetərətel'ik), *adj.* not autotelic.

heterotrichosis (hetərətrikō'sis), *n.* having variegated coloured hair.

heterotropia (hetərətrō'piə), *n.* squint.

heuristic (hūris'tik), *adj.* revealing ; leading to discovery ; *n.* such argument.

hetman (het'mən), *n.* Cossack or Polish commander or ruler.

hexachord (heks'əkawd), *n.* six-tone mus. scale ; interval of major sixth.

hexad (heks'ad), *n.* group of six. **-ic,** *adj.*

hexaemeron, -hem- (heksəem'əron, -hem'-), *n.* six days of Creation ; treatise on or history of h. **-ric** (-er'ik), *adj.*

hexagon (heks'əgən), *n.* 6-sided plane figure. **-al** (-ag'ənəl), *adj.*

hexagram (heks'əgram), *n.* six-pointed star.

hexahedron (heksəhē'drən), *n.* 6-sided solid figure. **-dral,** *adj.*

hexameron (heksam'əron), *n.* hexaemeron. **-ral, -rous,** *adj.* having six parts ; *Bot.,* having parts of flower in sixes.

hexameter (heksam'itə), *n.* verse-line of six feet. **-tral, -tric** (-et'-), *adj.*

hexarchy (heks'ahki), *n.* group of six allied but independent states.

hexastich (heks'əstik), *n.* poem or stanza of six lines. **-ic,** *adj.* **-ous,** *adj. Bot.,* six-ranked.

hexasyllable (heks'əsiləbl), *n.* verse-line or word of six syllables. **-bic** (-ab'ik), *adj.*

hexateuch (heks'ətūk), *n.* first six books of Bible.

hexeris (heksēr'is), *n.* galley with six banks of oars.

hexicology (heksikol'əji), *n.* ecology.

hiatus (hīā'təs), *n.* gap ; pause, *espec.* between vowels.

hibernacle (hī'bənakl), *n.* winter quarters. **-cular** (-ak'ūlə), *adj.*

hibernal (hībə'nəl), *adj.* pert. to winter. **-ate** (hī'-), *v.i.* pass winter in torpid state or warm climate.

Hibernian (hībə'niən), *n.* & *adj.* Irish (person).

hic jacet (hik jā'sit), *Lat.,* "here lies" ; epitaph. **h.sepultus** (-sipul'təs), "here is buried."

hidalgo (hidal'gō), Sp. *n.* gentleman ; noble of lower rank.

hidrosis (hidrō'sis), *n.* perspiration, *espec.* excessive. **-otic** (-ot'ik), *n.* & *adj.* (drug) causing perspiration.

hiemal (hī'iməl), *adj.* pert. to winter.

hieracosphinx (hīərā'kəsfingks), *n.* sphinx with head of hawk.

hierarch (hī'erahk), *n.* chief priest. **-ic,** *adj.* **-y,** *n.* body of chief priests ; body of persons in authority in ranks from highest to lowest ; such ranking of officials, objects or facts.

hieratic (hīərat'ik), *adj.* priestly, *espec.* applied to anct. Egyptian writing used for religious works.

hierocracy (hīərok'rəsi), *n.* government by clerics. **-cratic** (-at'ik), *adj.*

hierodule (hī'ərədūl), *n.* anct. Gr. temple slave. **-lic,** *adj.*

hieroglyph (hī'ərəglif), *n.* picture of object representing sound or word in anct. Egyptian writing. **-ic,** *n.* & *adj.* **-ics,** *n.* such picture-writing ; illegible handwriting. **-ology,** *n.* study of h. **-y,** *n.* writing with h.

hierogram (hī'ərəgram), *n.* sacred symbol. **-mmat(e),** *n.* writer of sacred annals or hieroglyphics.

hierography (hīərog'rəfi), *n.* writing on relig. subjects. **-rology,** *n.* relig. knowledge or tradition ; hagiology.

hieromachy (hīərom'əki), *n.* quarrel between clerics. **-mancy,** *n.* divination by sacrificed objects.

Hieronymic, -ian (hīərənim'ik, -iən), *n.* pert. to or by St. Jerome (4th-5th cent. A.D.).

hierophant (hī'ərəfant), *n.* priest ; person engaged in or explaining relig. mysteries. **-ic,** *adj.*

hierurgy (hī'ərəji), *n.* relig. worship or work. **-gical,** *adj.*

hinny (hin'i), *n.* hybrid of stallion and she-ass.

hinterland (hin'təland), *n.* inland area behind coast or coastal town.

hippiater (hip'iātə), *n.* horse-doctor. **-tric** (-at'rik), *adj.* **-try** (-atri, -ī'ətri), *n.*

hippocampus (hipəkam'pəs), *n.* (*pl.* -pi) sea-horse. **-pal, -pine,** *adj.*

hippocras (hip'əkras), *n.* medieval spiced wine.

---

hat, bah, hāte, hāre, crawl ; pen, ēve, hēre ; it, īce, fīre ; on, bōne, boil, bōre, howl : foot, fōōd, bōōr, hull, tūbe, pūre.

hippocrepiform (hipəkrep'ifawm), adj. shaped like a horseshoe.

hippogriff, -gryph (hip'əgrif), n. fabulous winged monster with body of horse.

hippoid (hip'oid), adj. pert. to or like a horse.

hippology (hipol'əji), n. study of the horse. **-gical**, adj. **-gist**, n.

hippophagous (hipof'əgəs), adj. eating horse-flesh. **-gi** (-ji), n.pl. eaters of horse-flesh. **-gism, -gy,** n.pl.

hippophile (hip'əfīl, -il), n. lover of horses or horse-riding. **-phobia**, n. dread of horses.

hippotomy (hipot'əmi), n. horse's anatomy. **-mical** (-om'ikl), adj. **-mist**, n.

hircarra(h) (həkah'rə), Pers. n. spy; messenger.

hircine (hə'sīn, -in), adj. pert. to or like goats; indecent. **-nous**, adj. with goat-like odour.

hirrient (hir'iənt), n. & adj. trilled (sound), as r.

hirsute (hə'sūt), adj. hairy. **-ties** (-ū'shiěz), **-tism**, n. undue hairiness.

hirudinean (hirədin'iən), n. & adj. (pert. to) leech. **-ne**, adj. **-noid** (-ōō'dinoid), adj. like a leech.

hirundine (hirun'dīn, -in), adj. pert. to or like a swallow; n. such bird. **-nous**, adj.

Hispanic (hispan'ik), adj. Spanish. **-cism**, n. Sp. idiom. **-nophile**, n. & adj. (person) fond of Spain, Spanish life, etc.

hispid (his'pid), adj. bristly. **-ity**, n. **-ulate, -ulous**, adj. with minute bristles.

histamine (his'təmēn), n. vasoconstrictive substance created in tissue at site of injury, ultimate cause of hay fever, nettlerash, and other allergic disorders. **anti-h.**, adj. denoting drug given to remedy allergy.

histology (histol'əji), n. study of or treatise on organic tissue. **-gical**, adj. **-gist**, n. **-lysis**, n. decay of such tissues. **-tography**, n. description of such tissues.

historiographer (histōriog'rəfə), n. historian, espec. one specially appointed. **-phic(al)**, adj. **-phy**, n. **-riometry**, n. statistical study of history.

histrionic (histrion'ik), adj. pert. to or like stage-acting; theatrical.

-ism (-sizm), n. art of acting. **-nism**, n. theatrical manner. **-s,** n.pl. theatrical presentation, manners or language.

hoatzin, -act- (hōat'sin, -akt'-), n. S. Amer. crested bird; stinkbird.

hobson-jobson (hob'sən-job'sən), n. Anglicised word or language corrupted from Oriental word or words.

hodiernal (hōdiə'nəl), adj. pert. to to-day.

hodometry (hodom'itri), n. measurement of length of ship's voyage. **-trical**, adj.

hogget (hog'it), n. boar in its second year; year-old sheep or colt; fleece of year-old sheep.

hogmanay (hog'mənā), Scot. n. New Year's Eve; gift, espec. cake, made on that day.

hoi polloi (hoi pəloi'), Gr., "the many"; the masses; the mob.

holagogue (hol'əgog), n. drug expelling all morbid humours.

holarctic (holahk'tik, hōl-), n. whole arctic region.

holism (hō'lizm), n. phil. theory that evolutionary factors are entities and not constituents. **-istic**, adj.

holm (hōm), n. river island; river plain.

holobaptist (holəbap'tist, hōl-), n. believer in baptismal immersion.

holocaust (hol'əkawst), n. burnt-offering of whole animal; wholesale destruction or death by fire. **-al, -ic**, adj.

holocrine (hol'əkrīn), n. & adj. solely secretory (gland); (gland) secreting its own cells.

holocryptic (holəkrip'tik), adj. undecipherable.

holograph (hol'əgraf), n. writing wholly in handwriting of its author. **-ic**, adj.

holophote (hol'əfōt), n. apparatus for directing most or all of available light in one direction. **-tal**, adj.

holophrase (hol'əfrāz), n. single word expressing complex idea. **-sis** (-of'rəsis), n. use of h. **-stic**, adj.

holoplexia (holəpleks'ia, hōl-), n. general paralysis.

holosteric (holəster'ik), adj. entirely solid.

holothurian (holəthūr'iən, hōl-), n. sea cucumber.

ə=er in father; ō̄=er in pert; th=th in thin; dh=th in then; zh=s in pleasure; k=ch in loch; ñ=Fr. nasal n; ü=Fr. u.

holotony, -nia (həlot'əni, holə-tō'nิə), *n.* general tetanus. **-nic** (-on'ik), *adj.*

hombre (om'brā), Sp. *n.* fellow; man.

homeostasis, *see* **homoeostasis.**

Homeric (hōmer'ik), *adj.* pert. to Homer, Gr. epic poet; epic; heroic.

homicide (hom'isīd), *n.* killing or killer of human being. **-dal,** *adj.*

homily (hom'ili), *n.* moral discourse; sermon. **-letic(al),** *adj.* **-letics,** *n.* study of sermons; art of preaching. **-liarium, -liary,** *n.* book of sermons. **-list, -lite,** *n.* preacher.

hominal (hom'inəl), *adj.* pert. to Man. **-niform,** *adj.* having human shape. **-nivorous,** *n.* man-eating. **-noid,** *n.* & *adj.* man-like (animal).

homocentric(al) (hōməsen'trik, -l), *adj.* concentric.

homochiral (hōməkīr'əl), *adj.* identical in form.

homochromatic (hōməkrəmat'ik), *adj.* pert. to or having one colour. **-mic, -mous** (-krō'mik, -məs), *adj.* of same colour. **-my,** *n.*

homodyne (hō'mədīn, hom'-), *adj. Rad.,* pert. to detection of wireless wave with wave of exactly same frequency.

homoeochromatic (hōmiəkrəmat'-ik), *adj.* having same or similar colour.

homoeochronous (hōmiok'rənəs), *adj.* developing at same period of offspring's as of parent's life.

homoeogenous (hōmioj'inəs), *adj.* of same or similar kind.

homoeopathy (hōmiop'əthi), *n.* treatment of disease by medicines producing in a healthy body symptoms similar to those of disease treated; treatment by extremely small doses. **-th, -thician, -thist,** *n.* **-thic,** *adj.*

homoeophony (hōmiof'əni), *n.* similarity of sound.

homoeostasis (hōmiəstā'sis), *n.* automatic maintenance by an organism of normal temperature, chemical balance, etc., within itself. **-stat,** *n.* machine capable of same kind of self-regulation.

homoeoteleutic (hōmiətelū'tik), *adj.* having same or similar endings. **-ton,** *n.* use of such words in close proximity.

homoeozoic (hōmiəzō'ik), *adj.* hav-ing same or similar living organisms.

homoerotism (hōmōer'ətizm), *n.* homosexuality.

homogeneous (homəjē'niəs), *adj.* of same kind; comprising similar parts; uniform. **-neity,** *n.* **-nesis** (-jen'isis), *n.* reproduction with successive generations alike. **-nise** (həmoj'inīz), *v.t.* make h., *espec.* of milk, etc.

homogenous (homoj'inəs), *adj.* having structural resemblance due to common ancestor. **-ny,** *n.*

homograph (hom'əgraf, hō'-), *n.* word having same spelling as, but different meaning from, another. **-ic,** *adj.* having different symbol for each sound. **-y,** *n.*

homoiousia (homoiō'siə), *n.* similarity in substance. **-n,** *adj.*; *n. Theol.,* adherent to belief that Son is of essentially similar but not identical substance with Father.

homolateral (hōməlat'ərəl, hom-), *adj.* on the same side.

homologate (həmol'əgāt), *v.i.* & *t.* confirm; approve; agree. **-tion,** *n.*

homologoumena (həmələgoo'minə, -gow'-), *n.pl.* Biblical books included in early Christian canon.

homologous (həmol'əgəs), *adj.* exactly or relatively corresponding in structure. **-gise,** *v.t.* make h. **-gue** (hom'əlog), *n.* such thing. **-gy** (-ji), *n.*

homomerous, -ral (həmom'ərəs, -əl), *adj.* having similar parts.

homomorphic (homəmaw'fik, hōm-), *adj.* similar in form. **-phism, -phy,** *n.* **-phous,** *adj.*

homonym (hom'ənim), *n.* word of same pronunciation as, but different meaning from, another; namesake. **-ic, -ous** (-on'iməs), *adj.* **-y,** *n.*

homoousia (hōmō ōō'siə, -ow'-; hom-), *n.* sameness of substance. **-n,** *adj.*; *n. Theol.,* adherent to belief that Son is of same substance with Father.

homophone (hom'əfōn), *n.* letter having same sound as another; word having same pronunciation as, but different spelling and meaning from, another. **-nic** (-on'ik), **-nous** (-of'ənəs), *adj.* **-ny,** *n.* sameness of sound.

homophylic (hōməfil'ik, hom-), *adj.* of same race. **-ly** (-of'ili), *n.* similarity due to common ancestry.

homo sapiens (hō'mō sā'pienz), *Lat.*, "thinking man"; Man; the human species. **h.vulgaris** (-vulgār'is), the common or average man.

homosexual (homəseks'ūəl, hōm-), *n.* & *adj.* (person) having sexual desire for person of same sex. **-ism, -ity, -ist,** *n.*

homotaxis (hōmətaks'is, hom-), *n.* similarity of arrangement. **-tactic, -xeous, -xial, -xic,** *adj.*

homunculus (həmung'kūləs), *n.* (*pl.* **-li**) little man; dwarf; human embryo. **-cle.** *n.* **-lar,** *adj.*

hong (hong), Chin. *n.* foreign trading establishment in China; warehouse.

honnête homme (onet om'), *Fr.*, "honest man"; respectable middle-class man.

honorarium (onərār'iəm), *n.* (*pl.* **-ia**) fee; gift of money. **-ry,** *adj.* given as an honour; without reward or salary.

hookum (hook'əm), Anglo-Ind. *n.* command; instructions. **jo h.,** "according to your commands."

hoopoe (hoo'pō, -poo), *n.* curved-billed, large-crested bird of Old World.

Hoosier (hoo'zhə), Amer. *n.* & *adj.* (native) of Indiana.

hoplite (hop'līt), *n.* armoured infantryman of anct. Gr. **-lomachy,** *n.* fighting in heavy armour.

horal (hōr'əl), *adj.* pert. to hour(s); hourly. **-rary,** *adj.* marking the hours; hourly; lasting for an hour only.

Horatian (hərā'shiən), *adj.* pert. to Horace, Lat. poet, and his elegant style.

hordeaceous (hawdiā'shəs), *adj.* pert. to or like barley. **-deiform** (-ē'ifawm), *adj.* having shape of barley-grain.

horme (haw'mi), *n.* Psych., vital energy directed to an active purpose. **-mic,** *adj.* **-mist,** *n.* believer in h. as fundamental psych. factor.

hormone (haw'mōn), *n.* secretion of endocrine gland.

hornblende (hawn'blend), *n.* dark-coloured variety of amphibole, containing aluminium and iron.

hornbook (hawn'book), *n.* anct. child's schoolbook comprising al-phabet, digits, etc., on parchment covered with sheet of horn.

horography (hərog'rəfi), *n.* account of the hours; art of constructing timepieces. **-pher,** *n.*

horologe (hor'əlōj), *n.* timepiece. **-ger, -gist** (-ol'-), *n.* watch-maker. **-gic** (-oj'ik), *adj.* **-gy** (-ol'əji), *n.* clock-making; science of measuring time. **-rometry** (-om'itri), *n.* measurement of time.

horoscope (hor'əskōp), *n.* diagram showing position of stars at person's birth, etc.; divination of fortune from such diagram. **-pic(al)** (-op'ik, -l), *adj.* **-pist,** *n.* **-py** (-os'kəpi), *n.*

horrendous (hərən'dəs), *adj.* horrible. **-nt** (hor'ənt), *adj.* bristling. **-rescent,** *adj.* expressing horror.

horripilation (horipilā'shn), *n.* bristling of hair or creeping of flesh, due to cold, fright, etc. **-te,** *v.i.* & *t.* cause or suffer h.

horrisonant (horis'ənənt), *adj.* making horrible sound.

hors de combat (or də kawn'bah), *Fr.*, "out of the fight"; disabled.

hortative (haw'tətiv), *adj.* exhorting; urging. **-tory,** *adj.* marked by exhortation.

hortensial, -sian (hawten'shəl, -ən), *adj.* pert. to, grown in or suited to a garden.

horticulture (haw'tikultūr), *n.* gardening. **-ral,** *adj.* **-rist,** *n.*

hortulan (haw'tūlən), *adj.* pert. to garden.

hortus siccus (haw'təs sik'əs), *Lat.*, "dry garden"; herbarium.

hospice (hos'pis), *n.* travellers' rest-house, *espec.* kept by relig. order.

hospitate (hos'pitāt), *v.i.* & *t.* welcome; be guest. **-tion,** *n.*

hotchpot (hoch'pot), *n.* Law, a returning to a common lot or fund for subsequent equal division, *espec.* of advances received by children of person dying intestate.

hôtel de ville (ōtel' də vēl'), *Fr.*, "town-hall." **h.Dieu** (-dyə'), hospital.

houbara (hoobah'rə), *n.* ruffed bustard.

houri (hoor'i, how'-), *n.* beautiful nymph of Moham. paradise.

housel (how'zəl), *v.t.* administer Holy Communion to.

howadji (howaj'i), Arab. *n.* traveller; merchant; Mr.

ə=er in *father*; ō=er in *pert*; th=th in *thin*; dh=th in *then*; zh=s in *pleasure*; k̯=ch in *loch*; n̄=Fr. nasal n; ü=Fr. u.

howdah (how′dah), *n.* seat on elephant.

hsien sheng (shyen sheng), *Chin.*, "older than I"; Mr.; teacher.

hubris (hū′bris), Gr. *n.* arrogance, insolent conceit. -**tic,** *adj.*

huguenot (hū′gənō), *n.* French Protestant.

humanism (hū′mənizm), *n.* human nature; study of the humanities; Renaissance culture; phil. doctrine concentrating on human ideals and perfectibility. -**ist,** *n.*

humanities (hūman′itiz), *n.pl.* polite learning; classical literature, *espec.* Lat.

humectant (hūmek′tənt), *n.* & *adj.* moistening (substance). -**tation,** *n.*

humerus (hū′mərəs), *n.* bone of upper arm. -**ral,** *adj.* pert. to the shoulder; brachial.

humid (hū′mid), *adj.* moist. -**ity,** *n.*

humour (hū′mə), *n. Med.,* body fluid; skin affection due to blood disorder; *arch.,* one of four body fluids—blood, phlegm, bile and atrabile—believed to determine health and character. -**oral,** *adj.*

humus (hū′məs), *n.* soil containing decayed vegetable matter. -**mous,** *adj.*

hurgila (həgē′lah), Hind. *n.* adjutant bird.

hurley, -**ly** (hə′li), *n.* Ir. game like hockey; stick used in it.

hurling (hə′ling), *n.* hurley.

hustings (hus′tingz), *n.* platform or place for political electioneering speeches; election proceedings.

huzoor (həzoor′), Ind. *n.* master; sir, used as title by servant.

hyaline (hī′əlin, -in), *adj.* glassy; transparent. -**lescent,** *adj.* becoming or somewhat glassy. -**loid,** *adj.* like glass. -**lopterous,** *adj.* with transparent wings.

hybris (hī′bris), *n.* hubris.

hydatid (hī′dətid), *n.* fluid-filled cyst, *espec.* containing tape-worm larva. -**inous,** *adj.* -**tiform,** *adj.* like a hydatid. -**tigenous,** *adj.* producing h.

hydra (hī′drə), *n.* many-headed monster in Gr. myth.; small freshwater polyp. -**roid,** *n.* & *adj.* (like a) polyp.

hydracid (hīdras′id), *n.* oxygen-less acid.

hydraemia (hīdrē′miə), *n.* exces-

sively watery condition of blood. -**ic,** *adj.*

hydragogue (hī′drəgog), *n.* & *adj.* (drug) causing discharge of water.

hydrargiric (hīdrahjir′ik), *adj.* pert. to mercury. -**ria,** -**riasis,** -**rism,** -**rosis,** *n.* mercurial poisoning.

hydrate (hī′drāt), *n. Chem.,* compound formed with water. -**ric,** *adj.* pert. to or containing hydrogen. -**ride,** *n.* compound formed with hydrogen.

hydraulic (hīdraw′lik), *adj.* pert. to moving fluids; pert. to mechanical action of water; conveyed or worked by water. -**s,** *n.* study of fluids in motion.

hydriotaphia (hīdriətaf′iə), *n.* urn burial.

hydro (hī′drō), *n. abbr.* of hydropathic.

hydrocarbon (hī′drəkahbən), *n.* compound of hydrogen and carbon.

hydrocephalus, -**ly** (hīdrəsef′ələs, -li), *n.* water on the brain. -**lic** (-sifal′ik), -**lous,** *adj.* -**loid,** *adj.* like h.

hydroconion (hīdrəkō′niən), *n.* atomiser.

hydrocyanic (hīdrəsian′ik), *adj.* prussic (acid).

hydrodynamics (hīdrədīnam′iks), *n.* mechanical study of fluids, *espec.* their motion and action.

hydroelectric (hīdrōilek′trik), *adj.* pert. to generation of, or generating, electricity by water-power. -**ity,** *n.*

hydrogenic (hīdrəjen′ik), *adj. Geol.,* formed by water. -**geology,** *n.* study of geol. action of water.

hydrognosy (hīdrog′nəsi), *n.* historical description of earth's water surface.

hydrography (hīdrog′rəfi), *n.* description, surveying and mapping of water surface of earth, with its depths, tides, etc. -**pher,** *n.* -**phic,** *adj.*

hydrokinetics (hīdrəkinet′iks), *n.* study of changes of motion of fluids.

hydrology (hīdrol′əji), *n.* study of water of earth's surface, *espec.* subterranean. -**gic(al),** *adj.*

hydrolysis (hīdrol′isis), *n.* (*pl.* -**ses**) chem. decomposition by addition of water. -**ysate,** *n.* product of h. -**yse,** *v.t.* -**yst,** *n.* substance causing h. -**ytic,** *adj.*

hydromechanics (hīdrəmikan'iks), *n.* study of laws of fluids in equilibrium and motion.

hydrometer (hīdrom'itə), *n.* instr. measuring specific gravity and density of liquids. **-tric(al)** (-et'rik, -l), *adj.* **-try,** *n.*

hydropathy (hīdrop'əthi), *n.* med. treatment by baths and mineral waters. **-th, -thist,** *n.* **-thic** (-ath'ik), *adj.* ; *n.* establishment for such treatment ; spa.

hydrophanous (hīdrof'ənəs), *adj.* becoming transparent when immersed in water. **-ne,** *n.* such kind of opal.

hydrophid (hī'drəfid), *n.* sea snake. **-phoid,** *adj.*

hydrophobia (hīdrəfō'biə), *n.* morbid dread of water ; rabies. **-be, -bist,** *n.* **-bic, -bous,** *adj.*

hydrophone (hī'drəfōn), *n.* instr. for detecting sounds through water.

hydrophyte (hī'drəfīt), *n.* plant growing in or by water. **-tic** (-it'ik), *adj.*

hydropic(al) (hīdrop'ik, -l), *adj.* dropsical. **-pigenous,** *adj.* causing dropsy.

hydroplane (hī'drəplān), *n.* fast flat-bottomed motor boat, skimming over water ; seaplane.

hydroponics (hīdrəpon'iks), *n.* cultivation of plants without soil, by supporting them in chem. solution containing all ingredients necessary for growth.

hydropot (hī'drəpot), *n.* water-drinker.

hydrops(y) (hī'drops, -i), *n.* distension of organ by fluid. **-ptic,** *adj.*

hydroscopist (hīdros'kəpist), *n.* water diviner.

hydrosphere (hī'drəsfēr), *n.* earth's envelope of watery vapour, or water surface.

hydrostatics (hīdrəstat'iks), *n.* study of pressure and equilibrium of fluids.

hydrotaxis (hīdrətaks'is), *n.* movement towards or away from water.

hydrotechny (hī'drətekni), *n.* use of water for driving machinery, etc. **-nic(al),** *adj.* **-nologist,** *n.*

hydrotherapeutic (hīdrətherəpū'tik), *adj.* hydropathic. **-s,** *n.* hydropathy.

hydrothermal (hīdrəthē'məl), *adj.* pert. to hot water and its geol. action.

hydrotic (hīdrot'ik), *n. & adj.* (drug) expelling water or phlegm.

hydrotimetry (hīdrətim'itri), *n.* measurement of hardness of water. **-ter,** *n.* instr. used in h. **-tric** (-et'rik), *adj.*

hydrous (hī'drəs), *adj.* containing water.

hydrozoan (hīdrəzō'ən), *n.* polyp. **-oal, -oic,** *adj.*

hyetal (hī'itəl), *adj.* pert. to rain. **-tograph,** *n.* rain gauge ; chart of average rainfall. **-tography,** *n.* study of rainfall distribution. **-tology,** *n.* study of all precipitation. **-tometer,** *n.* rain gauge. **-tometrograph,** *n.* recording hyetometer.

hygiology (hījiol'əji), *n.* hygienic science. **-gist,** *n.*

hygric (hī'grik), *adj.* pert. to moisture.

hygrometer (hīgrom'itə), *n.* instr. measuring humidity of air. **-ograph,** *n.* recording h.

hygrophanous (hīgrof'ənəs), *adj.* seeming transparent when wet, and opaque when dry. **-neity** (-nē'iti), *n.*

hygrophilous (hīgrof'iləs), *adj. Bot.,* living in water or moist places.

hygrophthalmic (hīgrofthal'mik), *adj.* moistening the eye.

hygrophyte (hī'grəfīt), *n.* hygrophilous plant.

hygroscope (hī'grəskōp), *n.* instr. showing variations in humidity. **-pic** (-skop'ik), *adj.* absorbing moisture, *espec.* of dust particles, etc., on which atmospheric moisture condenses to form rain and fog.

hygrostat (hī'grəstat), *n.* apparatus for regulating humidity of air. **-ics,** *n.* study of measurement of humidity.

hygrothermal (hīgrəthē'məl), *adj.* pert. to heat and humidity. **-mograph,** *n.* instr. recording humidity and temperature.

hyle (hī'li), Gr. *n.* matter. **-lic,** *adj.* material. **-lism,** *n.* materialism.

hylomorphism (hīləmaw'fizm), *n.* materialist conception of universe. **-phic(al),** *adj.* **-phist,** *n.* **-phous,** *adj.* having material form.

hylopathism (hīlop'əthizm), *n.* belief in capability of matter to affect spirit. **-ist,** *n.*

hylophagous (hīlof'əgəs), *adj.* eating wood. **-otomous,** *adj.* cutting or boring in wood.

hylotheism (hīləthē'izm), n. identification of God with matter or universe. -ist, n. -istic(al), adj.

hylozoism (hīlozō'izm), n. belief that all matter has life. -ist, n. -istic(al), adj.

hymen (hī'men), n. membrane partly closing vagina; maidenhead. -al, adj.

hymeneal (hīminē'əl), adj. pert. to Hymen, god of marriage; nuptial; n. nuptial song.

hymenopterous (hīminop'tərəs), adj. having four membranous wings. -ra, n.pl. (sing. -ron) order including such insects. -rist, n. student of h. -rology, n. study of h.

hymenotomy (hīminot'əmi), n.cutting of hymen.

hyoid (hī'oid), n. & adj. (pert. to) U-shaped bone at base of tongue.

hyoscine (hī'əsēn), n. sleep-inducing drug obtained from plants of nightshade family. -scyamine (-sī'əmēn), n. similar drug obtained from henbane.

hypaesthesia (hipesthē'zhiə), n. incomplete sensory power.

hypaethral (hipē'thrəl, hī-), adj. roofless.

hyperacusis, -ia (hīpərəkū'sis, -zhiə), n. abnormal keenness of hearing.

hyperaemia (hīpərē'miə), n. excess of blood in a part. -mic, adj.

hyperaesthesia (hīpəresthē'zhiə), n. excessive sensitivity. -etic (-et'ik), adj.

hyperalgesis, -sia (hīpəraljē'sis, -zhiə), n. undue sensitiveness to pain.

hyperaphia (hīpərā'fiə), n. abnormal keenness of touch.

hyperbaton (hīpə'bətən), n. (pl. -ta) inversion of normal word order. -tic (-at'ik), adj.

hyperbola (hīpə'bələ), n. curve formed when cone is cut by plane which makes angle with the base greater than that made by side of cone.

hyperbole (hīpə'bəli), n. extravagant rhet. exaggeration. -lical (-ol'ikl), adj. -lise, v.i. & t. use h. -lism, n.

hyperborean (hīpəbor'iən), n. & adj. (dweller) in extreme north or cold.

hyperbulia (hīpəbū'liə), n. undue eagerness for action; rashness.

hypercatalectic (hīpəkatəlek'tik),

adj. having extra syllable(s) at end of verse line. -lexis, n.

hypercathexis (hīpəkətheks'is), n. desire amounting to mania for an object.

hypercritical (hīpəkrit'ikl), adj. excessively critical; captious. -cise (-sīz), v.i. & t.

hyperdulic (hīpədū'lik), adj. venerating Virgin Mary highest of all human beings. -lia, n.

hypergamy (hīpə'gəmi), n. marriage with person of same or higher caste only.

hypermeter (hīpə'mitə), n. hypercatalectic verse line; person above average height. -tric(al) (-et'rik, -l), adj.

hypermetropia (hīpəmetrō'piə), n. longsightedness. -pic(al) (-op'ik, -l), adj. -py (-met'rəpi), n.

hyperopia (hīpərō'piə), n. hypermetropia. -pe, n. -pic (-op'ik), adj.

hyperosmia (hīpəroz'miə, -os'-), n. abnormal keenness of sense of smell. -mic, adj.

hyperpiesis, -sia (hīpəpiē'sis, -zhiə), n. high blood pressure. -etic (-et'ik), adj.

hyperpnoea (hīpəpnē'ə, -ənē'ə), n. abnormally fast breathing.

hypertension (hīpəten'shn), n. high blood pressure. -sive, adj.

hyperthyroidism (hīpəthīr'oidizm), n.excessive thyroid activity, resulting in exophthalmic goitre.

hypertrichosis (hīpətrikō'sis), n. excessive hairiness.

hypertrophy (hīpə'trəfi), n. excessive growth of a part; v.i. grow to abnormal size. -phic, -phied, adj.

hyphaeresis (hīfēr'isis, -er'-), n. omission of sound, syllable or letter from word.

hyphaema, -mia (hīfē'mə, -miə), n. anaemia; extravasation of blood.

hypnagogic (hipnəgoj'ik), adj. causing sleep; occurring while falling asleep or waking.

hypnaesthesis (hipnesthē'sis), n. impaired sensitivity. -etic (-et'ik), adj.

hypnoetic (hipnōet'ik), adj. pert. to logical but unconscious mental processes.

hypnogenesis (hipnəjen'isis), n. production of hypnosis. -etic (-jinet'ik), adj.

hypnoid (hip'noid), adj. sleep-like.

hypnology (hipnol'əji), n. study of

sleep and hypnosis. **-gic(al)**, *adj.* **-gist**, *n.*

hypnopompic (hipnəpom'pik), *adj.* preventing or dispelling sleep ; occurring while waking.

hypnosis (hipnō'sis), *n.* (*pl.* **-ses**) sleep-like state induced by suggestion. **-otic** (-ot'ik), *adj.* ; *n.* & *adj.* (drug) producing sleep. **-otise** (hip'nətiz), *v.i.* & *t.* **-otism, -otist,** *n.* **-otoid,** *adj.* like h.

hypobole (hipob'əli, hī-), *n.* rhet. device of anticipating objections in order to refute them.

hypobulia (hīpōbū'liə, hip-), *n.* diminution in ability to act or decide. **-lic,** *adj.* lacking willpower.

hypocathexis (hīpōkətheks'is, hip-), *n.* abnormal absence of desire for an object.

hypocaust (hī'pəkawst, hip'-), *n.* anct. air chamber or series of chambers for heating rooms.

hypochondria (hīpōkon'driə, hip-), *n.* morbid nervous depression ; continual and causeless anxiety about one's health, *espec.* concerning imaginary illnesses. **-c,** *adj.* ; *n.* person suffering from h. **-l,** *adj.* **-ry,** *n.*

hypocorisma (hīpəkəriz'mə, hip-), *n.* pet name. **-ristic(al),** *adj.*

hypodermic (hīpədə'mik), *adj.* pert. to or entering tissue beneath skin ; *n.* such injection or syringe. **-mal, -matic, -mous,** *adj.*

hypodynamia (hīpōdīnā'miə, hip-), *n.* diminution in strength. **h.cordis,** h. of the heart.

hypogastric (hīpōgas'trik, hip-), *adj.* pert. to lower middle abdominal region. **-rium,** *n.* that region.

hypogeal (hīpəjē'əl, hip-), *adj.* subterranean. **-gean,** *adj.* growing underground. **-geic,** *adj.* **-geiody** (-ī'ədi), *n.* surveying underground.

hypogene (hī'pəjēn, hip'-), *adj.* *Geol.,* plutonic. **-nic** (-en'ik), *adj.*

hypogeous (hīpəjē'əs, hip-), *adj.* hypogean. **-geum,** *n.* (*pl.* **-gea**) underground part of building.

hypoglottis (hīpōglot'is, hip-), *n.* underpart of tongue. **-glossitis,** *n.* inflammation of h.

hypohaemia (hīpōhē'miə, hip-), *n.* anaemia.

hypometropia (hīpōmetrō'pia, hip-), *n.* shortsightedness.

hyponychial (hīpōnik'iəl, hip-), *adj.* underneath finger- or toe-nail.

hypophonic, -nous (hīpəfon'ik, -of'ənəs ; hip-), *adj. Mus.,* acting as accompaniment.

hypophrenia (hīpōfrē'niə, hip-), *n.* feeble-mindedness. **-nic** (-en'ik), *adj.*

hypophyll (hī'pəfil, hip-), *n.* bract.

hypophysis (hīpof'isis, hip-), *n.* pituitary gland. **-seal, -sial** (-iz'iəl), *adj.* **-sectomy,** *n.* removal of h. **-seoprivic, -seoprivous,** *adj.* due to deficient pituitary secretion.

hypostasis (hīpos'təsis, hip-), *n.* (*pl.* **-ses**) support ; hypostatised substance ; essential substance ; *Med.,* sediment ; hyperaemia of an organ ; *Theol.,* substance of the Trinity ; person of the Trinity ; whole personality of Christ. **-tatic** (-at'ik), *adj.* **-tatise,** *v.t.* regard as separate substance ; assume (hypothetical thing) to be real.

hyposthenia (hīpōsthē'niə, hip-), *n.* debility. **-nic** (-en'ik), *adj.*

hypostrophe (hīpos'trəfi, hip-), *n.* *Med.,* relapse or turning over ; *Rhet.,* return to main theme after digression.

hyposynergia (hīpōsinə'jiə, hip-), *n.* incomplete co-ordination.

hypotenuse (hīpot'ənūs), *n.* side opposite right angle in right-angled triangle.

hypothecate (hīpoth'ikāt, hip-) *v.t.* mortgage ; deposit as security. **-cary,** *adj.* **-tion,** *n.* **-tory,** *adj.*

hypothermal (hīpōthə'məl, hip-), *adj.* tepid ; pert. to lowering of temperature. **-mia, -my,** *n.* abnormally low body temperature. **-mic,** *adj.*

hypothesis (hīpoth'isis), *n.* (*pl.* **-ses**) assumption ; conjecture ; supposition ; theory. **-e,** *v.i.* & *t.* **-etical** (-et'ikl), *adj.*

hypothyroidism (hīpōthīr'oidizm), *n.* deficient thyroid activity, resulting in cretinism.

hypotrichosis (hīpōtrikō'sis, hip-), *n.* lack of hair.

hypotrophy (hīpot'rəfi, hip-), *n.* incomplete growth ; atrophy.

hypotyposis (hīpətīpō'sis, -tip-), *n.* vivid description.

hypsiloid (hip'siloid, -sī'-), *adj.* like Gr. letter upsilon (Υ).

hypsography (hipsog'rəfi), *n.* topographical relief, and its observation ; the representation of this on maps. **-ometry**, *n.* measurement of heights above sea-level. **-ophobia**, *n.* dread of heights.

hyson (hī'sən), *n.* kind of green tea of China.

hyssop (his'əp), *n.* kind of mint, remedy for bruises.

hysteralgia (histəral'jiə), *n.* neuralgia of womb. **-rectomy**, *n.* removal of womb. **-rodynia**, *n.* pain in womb.

hysteresis (histərē'sis), *n.* lag in the effect of a change of force, *espec.* in magnetisation. **-retic** (-ret'ik), *adj.*

hysterogen(ic) (his'tərəjen, -en'ik), *adj.* produced or developed later; causing hysteria.

hysteroid (his'təroid), *adj.* like womb or hysteria.

hysteron proteron (his'təron prō'təron), *n.* inversion of natural order or sense, *espec.* of words; fallacy of proving or explaining a proposition with one presupposing or dependent on it.

hysteropathy (histərop'əthi), *n.* disease of womb. **-rorrhexis**, *n.* rupture of womb. **-rotomy**, *n.* Caesarean cut.

I

iamatology (īamətol'əji), *n.* med. study of remedies.

iamb(us) (ī'amb, īam'bəs), *n.* (*pl.* **-bi**) metrical foot of one short followed by one long syllable. **-bic**, *adj.* pert. to or composed of i.; *n.* line of i. **-bist**, *n.* writer of i.

iatric(al) (īat'rik, -l), *adj.* medical. **-traliptics**, *n.* med. treatment by rubbing with oil. **-trology**, *n.* medical science or treatise. **-trotechnics**, *n.* practical therapeutics.

Iberian (ībēr'iən), *adj.* pert. to Sp.-Port. peninsula; *n.* anct. inhabitant of that region.

ibex (ī'beks), *n.* wild goat, *espec.* with long, backward-curved horns; bouquetin; aegagrus.

ibidem (ibī'dem), *Lat. adv.*, "in the same place" (*abbr.* **ibid.**).

ibis (ī'bis), *n.* large heron-like wading bird, with down-curved bill.

Icarian (īkār'iən), *adj.* pert. to Icarus in Gr. myth., who, in flying too near sun, met his death; flying dangerously high; over-ambitious.

ichabod (ik'əbod), *Heb.*, "the glory has departed."

ichneumon (iknū'mən), *n.* mongoose, *espec.* Egyptian species believed to suck crocodiles' eggs. **i.fly**, fly whose larva parasitises other insect's larva. **-mous**, *adj.* parasitic.

ichnography (iknog'rəfi), *n.* map; ground plan; making of maps and plans. **-phic(al)**, *adj.*

ichnology (iknol'əji), *n.* geol. study of fossil footprints. **-nomancy**, *n.* divination by footprints.

ichor (ī'kōr, -kə), *n.* watery fluid discharged from wound; fluid supposed to fill veins of Gr. and Lat. gods. **-ous**, *adj.* **-rrhoea**, *n.* discharge of pus-like fluid.

ichthus, -ys (ik'thəs, -is), *n.* amulet or talismanic carving in shape of fish. **-thyic**, *adj.* pert. to fishes. **-thyism**, *n.* fish-poisoning. **-thyofauna**, *n.* fish life of region. **-thyoid**, *adj.* fish-like. **-thyology**, *n.* study of fishes. **-thyography**, *n.* treatise on fishes. **-thyolatry**, *n.* worship of fishes. **-thyomorphic**, *adj.* fish-shaped. **-thyophagy**, *n.* eating of fish. **-thyopolist**, *n.* fishmonger. **-thyornis**, *n.* toothed fossil bird of Amer. **-thyosaur(us)**, *n.* large fossil marine reptile. **-thyotoxism**, *n.* fish-poisoning.

icon (ī'kon), *n.* sacred or monumental image, statue, painting, etc. **-ic** (-on'ik), *adj.* **-ism**, *n.* worship of images. **-oclasm**, *n.* image-breaking; attacking of established beliefs. **-oclast**, *n.* person practising iconoclasm. **-ography**, *n.* representation in art or diagrams; description of representational works of art. **-olatry**, *n.* image-worship. **-ology**, *n.* study of i.; symbolism. **-omachy**, *n.* objection to worship of i. **-omatic**, *adj.* pert. to picture-writing in which characters represent names or phonetic values and not objects. **-ometer**, *n.* instr. finding distance or size of object by measuring its image; instr. for finding photog. focus; direct view-finder. **-oplast**, *n.* image-maker. **-oscope**, *n*. part of television camera where light is converted into electric waves.

icosahedron (īkəsəhē'drən), *n*. 20-sided solid figure. **-dral**, *adj*. **-sian**, *adj*. pert. to 20.

icteric (ikter'ik), *adj*. pert. to jaundice; *n*. remedy for jaundice. **-rine**, **-ritious**, **-ritous**, *adj*. yellowish. **-roid**, *adj*. like jaundice; yellow. **-rus**, *n*. jaundice.

ictus (ik'təs), *n*. stress in verse; *Med*., fit; sudden pulsation or stroke. **-tic**, *adj*.

id (id), *n*. *Psych*., instinctive energies and tendencies; subconscious mind.

idée fixe (ēdā' fēks), *Fr*., "fixed idea"; obsession; mus. motif.

idem (ī'dem), *Lat*., "the same" (*abbr*. **id**.).

ideogeny (idioj'ini, īd-), *n*. study of origin of ideas. **-netic** (-əjinet'ik), *adj*. initiating ideas. **-nical**, *adj*. **-nous**, *adj*. of mental origin.

ideogram, **-graph** (ī'diəgram, -af; id'-), *n*. symbol in picture-writing representing idea of thing; any symbol universally recognised. **-graphy**, *n*.

ideology (īdiol'əji, id-), *n*. science of ideas; theory, *espec*. impractical; body of ideas on a subject or of a class, race, political party, etc. **-gical**, *adj*.

ideophone (ī'diəfōn, id'-), *n*. group of sounds conveying an idea; spoken word or phrase. **-nous** (-of'ənəs), *adj*.

ides (īdz), *n.pl*. 13th or 15th day of month in anct. Rom. calendar. **i. of March**, unlucky or fatal day.

id est (id est), *Lat*., "that is" (*abbr*. **i.e.**).

idasm (id'iazm), *n*. idiosyncrasy.

idiochromatic (idiəkrəmat'ik), *adj*. having characteristic coloration.

idiocrasy, **-sis** (idiok'rəsi, -krā'sis), *n*. constitutional peculiarity.

idioelectric(al) (idiōilek'trik, -l), *adj*. able to be electrified by friction.

idiograph (id'iəgraf), *n*. trademark. **-ic(al)**, *adj*.

idiologism (idiol'əjizm), *n*. personal peculiarity of speech.

idiom (id'iəm), *n*. language or dialect peculiar to a people, region, class, etc.; linguistic expression peculiar to itself in form, grammar, etc. **-atic**, *adj*. **-ology**, *n*. study of i.

idiomorphic, **-phous** (idiəmaw'fik, -fəs), *adj*. having its own peculiar or proper form.

idiopathy (idiop'əthi), *n*. peculiar characteristic; disease not caused by another. **-thetic**, **-thic(al)**, *adj*.

idiophonic (idiəfon'ik, id-), *adj*. pert. to ideophone.

idioplasm (id'iəplazm), *n*. part of protoplasm bearing hereditary characteristics; germ plasm. **-atic**, **-ic**, *adj*.

idiospasm (id'iəspazm), *n*. localised cramp. **-astic**, *adj*.

idiosyncrasy (idiəsing'krəsi), *n*. mental or physical peculiarity; eccentricity; special sensitivity to a drug. **-ratic(al)** (-at'ik, -l), *adj*.

idiothermous, **-mic** (idiəthə'məs, -mik), *adj*. warm-blooded. **-my**, *n*.

idioticon (idiot'ikən), *n*. dialect dictionary.

idolothyte (īdol'əthīt), *n*. & *adj*. (sacrifice) offered to idol. **-tic** (-it'ik), *adj*.

idolum (īdō'ləm), *n*. (*pl*. **-la**) phantom; fallacy.

idoneous (īdō'niəs), *adj*. appropriate. **-neity** (īdənē'iti), *n*.

ignavy, **-via** (ig'nəvi, -nā'viə), *n*. laziness.

igneous (ig'niəs), *adj*. pert. to fire; *Geol*., due to action of heat within the earth. **-nescent**, *n*. & *adj*. (substance) throwing off sparks when struck; sparkling; inflamed. **-nicolist**, *n*. fire-worshipper. **-nify**, *v.t*. burn.

ignis fatuus (ig'nis fat'ūəs), *Lat*., "foolish fire"; light produced over marshland; will-o'-the wisp; any misleading idea or thing.

ignivomous (igniv'əməs), *adj*. vomiting fire.

ignominy (ig'nəmini), *n*. dishonour. **-nious**, *adj*.

ignorantism (ig'nərəntizm), *n*. obscurantism.

iguana (igwah'nə), *n*. large lizard, *espec*. of tropical Amer. **-nian**, *adj*. **-nodon**, *n*. kind of dinosaur.

ileum (il'iəm), *n*. last part of small intestine. **-eac**, *adj*. **-eitis**, *n*. inflammation of i. **-eus**, *n*. complete obstruction of intestine.

ilex (ī'leks), *n*. holm-oak; holly genus.

iliac (il'iak, ī'-), *adj*. pert. to the loins. **-us** (-i'əkəs), *n*. flexor muscle of thigh.

ilicic (ilis´ik), *adj.* pert. to holly.

ilium (il´iəm, ī´-), *n.* bone forming part of pelvis ; hip bone.

illation (ilā´shn), *n.* inference ; act of inferring. -tive (il´ətiv, -ā´tiv), *adj.* ; *n.* such word (as *therefore*).

illinition (i.linish´n), *n.* act of rubbing on.

imagism (im´əjizm), *n.* poetical doctrine of the use of precise images but entire freedom of form and subject-matter. -ist, *n.*

imago (imā´gō), *n.* (*pl.* -es, -gines) adult form of insect.

imam, -aum (imahm´), Arab. *n.* priest in charge of Moham. mosque ; title of sev. Moham. rulers or leaders. -ah, *n.* office of i. -ate, *n.* jurisdiction of i. -ic, *adj.*

imbat (im´bat), Turk. *n.* periodical cool wind of Cyprus and Levant.

imbreviate (imbrē´viāt), *v.t.* draw up as a brief ; enroll.

imbricate (im´brikāt), *adj.* overlapping ; *v.i.* & *t.* be or make i. -tion, *n.* intricacy. -tive, *adj.*

imbroglio (imbrō´liō), *n.* confused or embarrassing situation or state.

imbrue (imbrōō´), *v.t.* dye ; soak.

imbue (imbū´), *v.t.* soak ; dye ; impregnate ; permeate.

immanent (im´ənənt), *adj.* indwelling ; inherent ; all-pervading. -nce, *n.*

immeability (imiəbil´iti), *n.* state of being impassable or lacking power to pass.

imminent (im´inənt), *adj.* happening in near future ; threatening. -nce, *n.*

imminution (iminū´shn), *n.* diminution.

immolate (im´əlāt), *v.t.* sacrifice, *espec.* by killing. -tion, -tor, *n.*

immortelle (imawtel´), *n.* everlasting dried flower.

immure (imūr´), *v.t.* imprison ; entomb.

impacable (impā´kəbl), *adj.* not pacifiable.

impaction (impak´shn), *n.* obstruction,. or lodgment of matter, in passage.

impair (im´pār ; Fr., añpār´), *n.* odd number ; (wager on) odd numbers in roulette.

impanation (impanā´shn), *n.* introduction or embodiment of Christ's body in Communion bread. -te (-ā´nāt), *adj.*

imparity (impar´iti), *n.* disparity. -risyllabic, *n.* & *adj.* (word) having different number of syllables in different cases.

impasse (impahs´ ; Fr., añ´pas), *n.* deadlock ; blind alley.

impasto (impas´tō), *n.* application of pigment thickly, in painting ; such pigment.

impavid (impav´id), *adj.* without fear. -ity, *n.*

impeccable (impek´əbl), *adj.* without fault. -cant, *adj.* without sin.

impecunious (impikū´niəs), *adj.* poor. -iosity, *n.*

impedance (impē´dəns), *n. Elec.*, apparent resistance to flow of alternating current.

impedimenta (impedimen´tə), *n.pl.* luggage. -l, -ry, *adj.* hindering.

impennate (impen´āt), *n.* & *adj.* (pert. to) penguin.

imperial (impēr´iəl), *n.* pointed beard

imperscriptible (impəskrip´tibl), *adj.* not recorded.

impest (impest´), *v.t.* infect with plague. -ation, *n.*

impetigo (impiti´gō), *n.* pustulous skin disease. -ginous (-ij´inəs), *adj.*

impetrate (im´pitrāt), *v.t.* ask for ; obtaining by asking. -tion, -tor, *n.* -tive, *adj.*

impetus (im´pitəs), *n.* impulse ; push ; tendency of moving body to continue moving.

impi (im´pi), *n.* Kaffir army or battalion.

impignorate (impig´nərāt), *v.t.* mortgage ; pawn ; (-ət), *adj.* pawned. -tion, *n.*

implement (im´pliment), *v.t.* fulfil ; (-ənt), *n.* tool ; utensil. -al, *adj.* -ation, *n.*

implicit (implis´it), *adj.* implied though not expressed ; without question or doubt.

imponderable (impon´dərəbl), *adj.* incapable of being weighed ; *n.* such thing, *espec.* spiritual value. -rous, *adj.* weightless.

importune (impawtūn´), *v.i.* & *t.* ask persistently ; solicit for homosexual purposes. -nate (-paw´-tūnət), *adj.* -nity, *n.*

impostumate, -thum- (impos´tū-māt), *v.i.* & *t.* form or inflict an abscess. -tion, *n.*

impotent (im´pətənt), *adj.* weak ; powerless ; sexually incapable ; *n.* such man.

imprecate (im'prikāt), *v.i.* & *t.* pray for (evil) ; curse. **-tion**, *n.* **-tory**, *adj.*

impresario (imprizah'riō), *n.* manager of entertainment.

impressionism (impresh'ənizm), *n.* artistic doctrine of expressing without detail the artist's subjective impression of subject. **-ist**, *n.*

imprimatur (imprimā'tə), *n.* licence to print ; approval.

imprimis (imprī'mis), Lat. *adv.*, "in the first place."

improcreant (imprō'kriənt), *adj.* sexually impotent.

impromptu (impromp'tū), *n.* & *adj.* extempore (composition).

impropriate (imprō'priāt), *v.t.* transfer (eccl. revenue) to layman. **-tion**, **-tor**, **-trix**, *n.*

improvise (im'prəvīz), *v.i.* & *t.* invent or compose without forethought ; extemporise. **-sate** (-ov'izāt), *v.i.* & *t.* **-sation**, **-sator**, *n.* **-torial**, **-tory**, *adj.*

impudicity (impūdis'iti), *n.* shamelessness.

imshi (im'shi), Arab. *excl.* go away !

imsonic (imson'ik), *adj.* onomatopoeic.

inamorato (inamərah'tō), It. *n.* (*fem.* **-ta**) lover ; beloved person.

inanition (inanish'n), *n.* emptiness ; starvation ; exhaustion.

in articulo mortis (in ahtik'ūlō maw'tis), *Lat.*, "at the point of death."

incalescent (inkəles'ənt), *adj.* becoming warm or warmer. **-nce**, **-ncy**, *n.*

in camera (in kam'ərə), *Lat.*, "in private chamber" ; in secret ; in private.

incandesce (inkandes'), *v.i.* & *t.* become white, glow, or make to glow, with heat. **-nt**, *adj.*

incanous (inkā'nəs), *adj.* covered with soft white hairs.

incarcerate (inkah'sərāt), *v.t.* imprison. **-tion**, **-tor**, *n.*

incardinate (inkah'dināt), *v.t.* make cardinal ; receive (priest) from another diocese.

incarnadine (inkah'nədīn, -in), *adj.* crimson : flesh-coloured ; *v.t.* dye crimson.

incest (in'sest), *n.* sexual intercourse between close relatives. **-uous**, *adj.*

inchoate (in'kō āt), *v.t.* begin ; inaugurate ; initiate ; (-ət) *adj.*

just begun ; imperfect. **-oacy**, *n.* **-tion**, *n.* beginning. **-tive**, *adj.* signifying commencement.

incipit (insip'it), *Lat.*, "here begins."

incisor (insī'zə), *n.* cutting tooth at front of mouth. **-ial**, **-y**, *adj.*

inclination (inklinā'shn), *n.* *Mag.*, angle between horizon and magnetic needle moving vertically ; magnetic dip.

incognito (inkog'nitō), *adj.* & *adv.* (*fem.* **-ta**) with identity concealed ; under assumed name ; *n.* such person (*abbr.* incog.).

incrassate (inkras'āt), *v.t.* thicken ; *adj.* thickened. **-tion**, *n.* **-tive**, *adj.*

increment (in'krimənt), *n.* increase ; profit. **-al**, *adj.*

incretion (inkrē'shn), *n.* internal secretion ; hormone. **-ary**, **-tory**, *adj.*

incroyable (ankrwahyahb'l), Fr. *n.* fop.

incubus (in'kūbəs, ing'-), *Lat.* *n.* (*pl.* **-bi**) "nightmare" ; burden ; oppression ; *Med.*, nightmare.

inculpate (in'kulpāt), *v.t.* blame ; involve in blame. **-tion**, *n.* **-tive**, **-tory**, *adj.*

incumbent (inkum'bənt), *adj.* lying ; resting upon as a duty ; *n.* holder of benifice ; vicar. **-ncy**, *n.*

incunabula (inkūnab'ūlə), *n.pl.* (*sing.* **-lum**) early printed books, *espec.* printed before A.D. 1500 ; any early or beginning period. **-list**, *n.* student of i. **-r**, *adj.*

incuse (inkūz'), *n.* & *adj.* (impression, *espec.* on coin) stamped in.

indaba (indah'bə), Zulu *n.* palaver ; conference.

indagate (in'dəgāt), *v.t.* investigate. **-tion**, **-tor**, *n.* **-tive**, *adj.*

indenture (inden'tūr), *n.* written agreement, orig. torn or cut into two parts along a jagged line ; *pl.*, agreement between məster and apprentice ; *v.t.* notch ; wrinkle ; bind by contract.

Index Librorum Prohibitorum (in'-deks librōr'əm prəhibitor'əm), *Lat.*, "list of forbidden books" of the R.C. Church. **I. Expurgatorius** (-ekspəgətor'iəs), list of books allowed only in expurgated form.

indict (indīt'), *v.t.* accuse. **-ion** (-ik'shn), *n.* anct. Rom. tax ; property tax or assessment. **-ive** *adj.* **-ment**, *n.*

ə=*er* in *father* ; ə̄=*er* in *pert* ; th=*th* in *thin* ; dh=*th* in *then* ; zh.=*s* in *pleasure* ; k=*ch* in *loch* ; n̈=Fr. nasal *n* ; ü=Fr. *u*.

indigenous (indij'inəs), *adj.* native ; aboriginal ; inherent. **-nal,** *adj.* **-ne,** *n.* native. **-neity,** *n.*

indigent (in'dijənt), *adj.* poor ; destitute. **-nce,** *n.*

indigo (in'digō), *n.* dark blue colour and dye ; plant yielding it. **-ferous** (-gof'ərəs), *adj.* yielding i. **-tic** (-ot'ik), *adj.*

indite (indīt'), *v.t.* compose ; write down ; describe.

indoles (in'dəlēz), *n.* inherent disposition.

induciae (indū'shiē), Lat. *n.pl.* armistice.

inductance (induk'tənts), *n.* inertia-like property of elec. circuit causing time to elapse before full value of current is established, or before zero is reached when current is removed ; property of a circuit by virtue of which induction takes place.

induction (induk'shn), *n. Elec.,* production of electrified or magnetic state in body by the near presence of a charged or magnetised body ; production of a current in a circuit by a variation in the magnetic field linked with it or in current in an adjacent circuit ; *Log.,* reasoning from particular to general ; establishment of general rules from observation of individual cases. **-ive,** *adj.*

indue (indū'), *v.t.* put on ; assume ; endow ; supply.

induna (indoo'nə), Zulu *n.* chief.

indurate (in'dūr āt), *v.i.* & *t.* harden. **-tion,** *n.* **-tive,** *adj.*

ineffable (inef'əbl), *adj.* indescribable ; unspeakable.

ineluctable (iniluk'təbl), *adj.* irresistible ; unavoidable. **-bility,** *n.*

inept (inept'), *adj.* inappropriate ; weak ; silly.

inerm(ous) (inẽm', -əs), *adj. Bot.,* without prickles.

inert (inẽt'), *adj.* not capable of motion or action ; inactive, *espec.* chemically.

inertia (inẽ'shiə), *n.* matter's property of remaining at rest or of continuing to move in same straight line ; tendency to be inactive ; sluggishness.

in esse (in es'i), Lat., "in existence."

ineunt (in'iənt), *adj.* entering.

inexorable (ineks'ərəbl), *adj.* unalterable ; relentless. **-bility,** *n.*

in extenso (in eksten'sō), Lat., extended to full length.

in extremis (in ekstrē'mis), Lat., on point of death ; at last extremity.

in facie curiae (in fā'shiē kūr'iē), Lat., "in the presence of the court."

infand(ous) (infand', -əs), *adj.* unmentionable (in bad sense).

infanta (infan'tə), *n.* daughter of Sp. or Port. sovereign. **-te** (-tā), *n.* younger son of Sp. or Port. sovereign.

inferiae (infer'iē), Lat. *n.pl.* sacrifices to beings of underworld.

infeudation (infūdā'shn), *n.* granting of feoff ; transfer of tithes to layman.

in fieri (in fī'əri), *Lat.,* "pending."

in fine (in fī'ni), *Lat.,* "at the end" ; finally.

inflation (inflā'shn), *n. Econ.,* increase in purchasing power and means of exchange, causing fall in value of money and rise in prices. **-ary,** *adj.* **-ist,** *n.* advocate of i.

inflorescence (infləres'əns). *n.* flowering ; arrangement of flowers in a plant ; flower cluster or head. **-nt,** *adj.*

in forma pauperis (in faw'mə paw'pəris), *Lat.,* "in form of pauper" ; as a poor man.

in foro (in fōr'ō), *Lat.,* "in the forum" ; before the court.

infra (in'frə), Lat. *adv.,* "below", later ; afterwards. **i. dignitatem,** beneath one's dignity (*abbr.* **infra dig.**).

infra-red (infrə-red'), *adj.* signifying long (heat) waves beyond red end of spectrum.

infumate(d) (in'fūmāt, -id), *adj.* blackish ; smoky.

infundibular, -ate (infundib'ūlə, -ət), *adj.* funnel-shaped. **-liform,** *adj.*

infuscate(d) (infus'kāt, -id), *adj.* brownish ; obscured.

infusoria (infūzōr'iə), *n.pl.* class of protozoa found in water. **-l, -n,** *adj.* **-riform, -rioid,** *adj.* like i.

in genere (in jen'əri), *Lat.,* "in kind" ; in general.

ingénue (añzhänü'), Fr. *n.* guileless girl, *espec.* such stage rôle.

ingenuous (injen'ūəs), *adj.* innocent ; guileless. **-ness,** *n.*

ingest (injest'), *v.t.* take in as food ; digest. **-a**, *n.pl.* ingested matter. **-ion**, *n.* **-ive**, *adj.*

ingluvies (ingloo'viēz), *n.* bird's crop. **-vial**, *adj.*

ingrate (in'grāt), *n.* ungrateful person.

ingravescent (ingrəves'ənt), *adj.* continually becoming more severe.

inguinal (ing'gwinəl, -gwī'-), *adj.* pert. to or near the groin.

ingurgitate (ingəˈjitāt), *v.i.* & *t.* swallow up ; guzzle. **-tion**, *n.*

inhere (inhēr'), *v.i.* belong intimately and by nature ; be a part of. **-hesion**, **-nce**, *n.* **-nt**, *adj.* innate ; fixed ; settled ; constituting an inseparable part or attribute.

inhibit (inhib'it), *v.t.* restrain ; forbid. **-ion**, *n.* stopping ; check ; *Psych.*, restraint, *espec.* exercised by subconscious mind. **-ory**, *adj.*

in hoc (in hok), *Lat.*, "in this (respect)."

inhume (inhūm'), *v.t.* bury. **-mation**, *n.*

inimical (inim'ikl), *adj.* hostile ; unfavourable. **-ity**, *n.*

in initio (in inish'iō), *Lat.*, "in the beginning."

inkosi (inkō'si), Zulu *n.* chief ; king.

in loco (in lō'kō), *Lat.*, "in the (proper) place." i. l. **parentis** (-pərən'tis), in place or position of a parent.

in medias res (in mē'dias rēz), *Lat.*, "into the midst of things" ; beginning in the middle or at the most important part.

in memoriam (in mimōr'iam), *Lat.*, "in memory (of)."

innate (in'āt), *adj.* inborn ; forming natural or constitutional part ; inherited.

innocuous (inok'ūəs), *adj.* harmless.

innoxious (inoks'iəs), *adj.* harmless.

innuendo (inūen'dō), *n.* (*pl.* **-es**) allusion ; insinuation, *espec.* unpleasant.

inopinate (inop'ināt), *adj.* unexpected.

inosculate (inos'kūlāt), *v.i.* & *t.* unite ; combine ; blend. **-tion**, *n.*

in posse (in pos'i), *Lat.*, "in possibility."

in principio (in prinsip'iō), *Lat.*, "in the beginning."

in puris naturalibus (in pūr'is natūrā'libəs), *Lat.*, nu¹de.

inquiline (in'kwilīn, -in), *adj.* living in another's nest or dwelling ; *n.* such animal. **-nism**, **-nity**, *n.* **-nous**, *adj.*

inquinate (in'kwināt), *v.t.* corrupt. **-tion**, *n.*

in re (in rē), *Lat.* (*pl.* .....**rebus**) "in the thing" ; in reality ; concerning.

inscenation (insinā'shn), *n.* mise en scène.

insectivorous (insektiv'ərəs), *adj.* feeding on insects. **-re**, *n.* such animal.

inseminate (insem'ināt), *v.t.* sow ; impregnate. **-tion**, *n.* ; **artificial i.**, injection of sperm into female other than by natural means.

insidiate (insid'iāt), *v.i.* & *t.* conspire (against) ; ambush. **-ion**, *n.*

insidious (insid'iəs), *adj.* treacherous ; sly ; lying in wait to capture ; *Med.*, more serious than it appears.

insignia (insig'niə), *n.pl.* badges of office ; any distinctive emblems.

insipience (insip'iəns), *n.* stupidity. **-nt**, *adj.*

in situ (in sī'tū), *Lat.*, "on the site" ; in original position.

insolate (in'səlāt), *v.t.* expose to sunlight. **-tion**, *n.* such exposure ; sunstroke ; med. treatment by sun-bathing ; radiation from sun.

insouciance (insoo'siəns ; Fr., an-soos'iahns), *n.* indifference ; carefreeness.. **-nt**, *adj.*

inspissate (inspis'āt), *v.t.* thicken. **-ant**, *n.* & *adj.* thickening (substance). **-tion**, **-tor**, *n.*

in statu quo (ante) (in stā'tū kwō, an'ti), *Lat.*, "in same state (as before)."

instauration (instor ā'shn), *n.* restoration to former excellence. **-tor**, *n.*

insufflate (in'səflāt, -suf'-), *v.t.* blow on or into ; breathe upon. **-tion**, **-tor**, *n.*

insular (in'sūlə), *adi.* pert. to island ; narrow-minded. **-ity**, *n.*

insulin (in'sūlin), *n.* pancreatic hormone promoting absorption of sugar ; preparation from animal's pancreas injected as remedy for diabetes.

intaglio (intal'iō), *n.* engraved pattern in cavo relievo, *espec.* on gem ; gem bearing i. **-liate**, *v.t.* incise. **-liation**, *n.*

integer (in'tijə), *n.* whole number ; entity ; *adj.* whole. **-gral,** *adj.* essential ; constituent ; whole. **-grant,** *n.* & *adj.* component ; essential (part). **-grate,** *v.t.* complete ; unite into a harmonious whole ; indicate the total ; *adj.* composite. **-gration,** *n. Psych.,* harmonious union of mental processes and personality with each other and with environment. **-grity,** *n.* completeness ; purity ; honesty.

integument (integ'ūmənt), *n.* covering ; coating. **-al, -ary,** *adj.*

intellection (intelek'shn), *n.* superhuman knowledge ; act or exercise of intellect ; synecdoche.

intelligentsia (intelijent'siə), *n.* intellectual persons ; "highbrows."

intemerate (intem'ərət), *adj.* undefiled.

intempestive (intempes'tiv), *adj.* inopportune ; out of season. **-vity,** *n.*

intenerate (inten'ərāt), *v.t.* soften. **-tion,** *n.*

inter alia (in'tə ā'liə), *Lat.,* "among other (things)." **i.alios,** "among other (persons)."

interamnian (intəram'niən), *adj.* between rivers.

intercalary (intəkal'əri), *adj.* inserted in the calendar ; bissextile ; leap (year) ; interpolated. **-late** (-ā'kəlāt), *v.t.* **-lation,** *n.*

intercardinal (intəkah'dinəl), *n.* & *adj.* (point) half-way between two cardinal points of compass.

interciliary (intəsil'iəri), *adj.* between eyebrows.

intercolline (intəkol'īn, -in), *adj.* between hills.

intercosmic (intəkoz'mik), *adj.* between or among stars.

intercostal (intəkos'təl), *adj.* between ribs.

interdict (intədikt'), *v.t.* forbid ; (in'-), *n.* prohibition. **-ion, -or,** *n.* **-ive, -ory,** *adj.*

interdigitate (intədij'itāt), *v.t.* interlock ; intertwine. **-tion,** *n.*

interfenestral (intəfines'trəl), *adj.* between windows. **-ration,** *n.* such distance.

interferometer (intəfērom'itə), *n.* instr. measuring wavelengths of light and analysing spectra.

interfluvial (intəfloo'viəl), *adj.* between two rivers flowing in same direction. **-ve,** *n.* such area.

interjacent (intəjā'sənt), *adj.* situated between ; intervening. **-nce,** **-ncy,** *n.*

interlocutor (intəlok'ūtə), *n.* (*fem.* **-tress, -trice, -trix**) speaker in conversation ; interpreter ; member of minstrel show questioning others, announcing items, etc. **-tion,** *n.* conversation ; interruption. **-y,** *adj.* ; *Law,* done during action ; intermediate.

interlunar (intəloo'nə), *adj.* pert. to period between old and new moon. **-nation,** *n.* such period ; interval of darkness.

intern(e) (in'tən), *Amer. n.* hospital physician, surgeon or student.

internecine (intənē'sin, -nes'-), *adj.* causing death and destruction, *espec.* mutual.

internuncio (intənun'shiō), *n.* go-between ; papal emissary.

interosculate (intəros'kūlāt), *v.i.* intermix ; have common biol. characteristics. **-ant,** *adj.* intersecting. **-tion,** *n.*

interpellate (intəpel'āt), *v.t.* arraign or question for explanation. **-ant,** *adj.* interrupting ; *n.* person interpellating. **-tion,** *n.* interpellating ; interruption. **-tor,** *n.*

interregnum (intəreg'nəm), *n.* (*pl.* **-na**) interval, *espec.* between two successive reigns. **-rex,** *n.* (*pl.* **-reges**) ruler during i.

inter se (in'tə sē), *Lat.,* "among themselves."

intertessellation (intətesələ'shn), *n.* complicated inter-relationship.

intertonic (intəton'ik), *adj.* between accented sounds or syllables.

intertrigo (intətrī'gō), *n.* skin affection due to friction between moist surfaces. **-ginous** (-ij'inəs), *adj.*

intestate (intes'tət), *n.* & *adj.* (person dying) without having made a valid will. **-acy,** *n.*

in toto (in tō'tō), *Lat.,* "entirely."

intrados (intrā'dos), *n.* interior curve of arch.

intramural (intrəmūr'əl), *adj.* within the walls ; taking place within, or confined to, a college, institution, etc.

intransigent (intran'zijənt), *n.* & *adj.* uncompromising (person) ; radical. **-geant** (antrahńzēzhahń'), Fr. *n.* & *adj.* **-nce,** *n.*

intravasation (intravəsā'shn), *n.*

Med., entrance of externally formed matter into vessels.

intravenous (intrəvē'nəs), *adj.* into a vein.

intra-vitam (in'trə-vī'tam), *adj.* during life.

intrinsic (intrin'sik), *adj.* inward; inherent.

introit (intrō'it), *n.* psalm or hymn chanted at approach to altar of celebrant priest; first part of R.C. Mass.

introrse (intraws'), *adj.* inward-facing.

introspection (intrəspek'shn), *n.* looking inward; self-examination; intense, sometimes morbid, interest in one's own mental processes and emotions. **-tive,** *adj.*

introvert (in'trəvзt), *n.* person given to introspection, or able to find satisfaction in his own inner life.

intumesce (intūmes'), *v.i.* swell; bubble, *espec.* owing to heat. **-nce,** *n.* **-nt,** *adj.*

intussusception (intəsəsep'shn), *n.* movement or slipping of a part into another, *espec.* of small into large intestine. **-tive,** *adj.*

inula (in'ūle), *n.* elecampane. **-ceous,** **-loid,** *adj.* like i.

inunct (inungkt'), *v.t.* anoint. **-ion,** *n.* act of anointing; ointment; rubbing of ointment into skin. **-um,** *n.* lanolin ointment.

inustion (inus'chən), *n.* burning.

invaginate (invaj'ināt), *v.i. & t.* sheathe; infold; draw part of tube, etc., inside other part. **-tion,** *n.* act of invaginating; part invaginated; intussusception.

invenit (invē'nit), *Lat.,* "invented (it)."

invermination (invзminā'shn), *n.* infestation with intestinal worms.

inveterate (invet'ərət), *adj.* confirmed; long-established. **-racy,** *n.*

invictive (invik'tiv), *adj.* not defeatable.

invidious (invid'iəs), *adj.* tending to provoke envy or ill-will or give offence.

invigilate (invij'ilāt), *v.i.* supervise closely, *espec.* candidates in examination. **-tion,** **-tor,** *n.*

invination (invīnā'shn), *n.* inclusion or embodiment of blood of Christ in Communion wine.

inviscate (invis'kāt), *v.t.* make

sticky; entrap with sticky substance. **-tion,** *n.*

in vivo (in vī'vō), *Lat.,* "in living (creature)". **i.vitro** (-vī'trō), "in glass"; in test-tube or laboratory experiment.

involucre (in'vəlookə), *n.* covering, *espec.* whorl of bracts in plant. **-ral,** *adj.* like i. **-rate,** *adj.* having i.

involute (in'vəloot), *adj.* curved spirally inwards; complicated. **-tion,** *n.*

invultuation (invultū ā'shn), *n.* stabbing of wax image of person to be injured as form of witchcraft.

iodoform (ī ō'dəfawm, -od'-), *n.* antiseptic made from iodine and alcohol. **-dotherapy,** *n.* med. treatment with iodine.

ion (ī'ən), *n.* electrically charged particle or atom. **-isation,** *n.* **-ise,** *v.t.* convert into i.; make conductive by forming i. in. **-osphere** (ion'əsfēr), *n.* region of the atmosphere, from 25 miles up, in which air is ionised by sun's ultra-violet rays and reflects radio waves back to earth. **-tophoresis,** *n.* introduction of ions into body as med. treatment.

iota (ī ō'tə), *n.* ninth letter of Gr. alphabet (I, *ɩ,*); jot; atom.

ipecacuanha (ipikakūan'ə), *n.* dried roots of S. Amer. plant used as expectorant, etc. (*abbr.* **ipecac.**)

ipse dixit (ip'si diks'it), *Lat.,* "himself he said (it)"; dogmatic statement; dictum

ipseity (ipsē'iti), *n.* selfhood.

ipso facto (ip'sō fak'tō), *Lat.,* "by that fact"; by virtue of that very fact or case.

I.Q., *abbr.* of intelligence quotient, measure of intelligence arrived at by dividing mental age (ascertained by intelligence tests) by chronological age, and multiplying by 100.

irade (irah'di), *n.* Moham. edict, *espec.* sultan's decree.

irascent (iras'ənt, īr-), *adj.* becoming angry.

irenic(al), *see* **eirenic.**

iridescent (irides'ənt), *adj.* glittering with rainbow-like colours. **-nce,** **-ncy,** *n.*

iridisation (iridīzā'shn, -diz-), *n.* iridescence.

iridium (irid'iəm), *n.* rare, hard, platinum-like metal.

irisation (īrisā'shn), *n.* iridescence. **-scope,** *n.* apparatus producing iridescence.

iritis (īr ī'tis), *n.* inflammation of iris of eye. **-tic** (-it'ik), *adj.*

irredenta (iriden'tə), It. *adj.* "unredeemed"; app. to part of country under another's rule. **-tial,** *adj.* **-tism,** *n.* policy of attempting to recover i. region to country that has lost it. **-tist,** *n.*

irrefragable (iref'rəjəbl), *adj.* indisputable ; unbreakable.

irrefrangible (irifran'jibl), *adj.* unbreakable ; incapable of being refracted.

irremeable (irem'iəbl, -rē'-), *adj.* allowing of no return ; irrevocable.

irrevocable (irev'əkəbl), *adj.* incapable of being recalled or revoked ; unalterable.

isagoge (īsəgō'ji), *n.* introduction. **-gic(al)** (-oj'ik, -l), *adj.* **-gics,** *n.* introductory study of Bible.

isanemone (īsan'imōn), *n.* line on map connecting all places with same wind velocity.

ischaemia (iskē'miə), *n.* localised anaemia. **-mic,** *adj.*

ischialgia (iskial'jiə), *n.* sciatica. **-gic,** *adj.*

ischidrosis (iskidrō'sis), *n.* suppression of perspiration.

ischium (is'kiəm), *n.* seat bone.

ischuria, -ry (iskūr'iə, -i), *n.* retention of urine. **-retic** (-et'ik), *n. & adj.* (agent) causing i.

isinglass (ī'zingglahs), *n.* form of gelatine made from fishes' airbladders ; agar-agar.

ism (izm), *n.* doctrine, *espec.* a foolish one. **-al, -atic(al),** *adj.*

isobar (ī'səbah), *n.* line on map passing through all places with same barometric pressure. **-ic** (-ar'ik), *adj.*

isocheim (ī'səkīm), *n.* line on map passing through all places with same average winter temperature. **-al, -enal, -ic,** *adj.*

isochronous (īsok'rənəs), *adj.* lasting equal time ; recurring at equal intervals. **-nal, -nic(al),** *adj.* **-nise,** *v.t.* **-nism,** *n.* **-non,** *n.* chronometer.

isochroous (īsok'rōəs), *adj.* of uniform colour.

isoclinal (īsəklī'nəl), *n. & adj.* (line on map passing through all places) with same magnetic dip ;

having equal inclination. **-nic** (-in'ik), *adj.*

isocracy (īsok'rəsi), *n.* equal rule ; possession of equal power by all. **-crat,** *n.* **-cratic,** *adj.*

isocryme (ī'səkrīm), *n.* isotherm for coldest period of year. **-mal, -mic** (-im'ik), *adj.*

isodiabatic (īsədīəbāt'ik), *adj.* pert. to equal heat transmission.

isodynamic (īsədīnam'ik), *adj.* pert. to or having equal force. **-mia** (-ā'miə), *n.*

isogenesis (īsəjen'isis), *n.* sameness of origin. **-etic** (-jinet'ik), **-nic,** **-nous** (-oj'inəs), *adj.* **-ny,** *n.*

isoglossal (īsəglos'əl), *adj.* similar in speech.

isogonal (īsog'ənəl), *adj.* having equal angles. **-nic** (-on'ik), *adj.* ; *n.* line on map passing through all places with same magnetic declination.

isogram (ī'səgram), *n.* line on map passing through all places with same conditions or figures for the subject in question, as temperature, rainfall, etc.

isography (īsog'rəfi), *n.* imitation of other person's hand-writing. **-phic(al),** *adj.*

isohel (ī'səhel), *n.* line on map passing through all places with same hours of sunshine.

isohyet (īsəhī'et), *n.* line on map passing through all places with same rainfall. **-al,** *adj.*

isokeraunic (īsəkiraw'nik), *n. & adj.* (line on map connecting places) with equal or simultaneous occurrence of thunderstorms.

isomer (ī'səmə), *n.* compound of same elements in same proportions by weight as another, but having different structure and properties. **-ic** (-er'ik), *adj.* **-ise** (-om'ərīz), *v.t.* **-ism,** *n.* **-ous,** *adj.* having same number of parts, peculiarities, etc.

isomorphic (īsəmaw'fik), *adj.* of same or similar form. **-phism,** *n.* **-phous,** *adj.*

isonomy (īson'əmi), *n.* equality of legal rights. **-mic** (-om'ik), **-mous,** *adj.*

isonym (ī'sənim), *n.* word of same derivation or form as another; cognate word. **-ic,** *adj.* **-y** (-on'imi), *n.*

isopiestic (īsəpīes'tik), *n. & adj.* isobar(ic).

isopolity (īsəpol'iti), *n.* equality of political rights. **-tical,** *adj.*

isopsephic (īsopsef'ik, -sē'-), *adj.* numerically equal. **-phism,** *n.*

isopycnic (īsəpik'nik), *n. & adj.* (line passing through points) of equal density.

isorithm (ī'səridhm), *n.* line on map passing through places of same density of population.

isorropic (īsorop'ik), *adj.* of equal value.

isosceles (īsos'ilēz), *adj.* having two sides equal.

isoseismal (īsəsīs'məl), *n. & adj.* (line on map passing through places) of same intensity of earthquake shock. **-mic(al),** *adj.*

isostasy (īsos'təsi), *n.* state of equilibrium due to equal pressure on all sides. **-static,** *adj.*

isothere (ī'səthēr), *n.* isotherm for average summer temperature. **-ral** (-oth'ərəl), *adj.*

isotherm (ī'səthɜm), *n.* line on map passing through places with same temperature. **-al, -ic, -ous,** *adj.*

isotope (ī'sətōp), *n.* form of an element having same atomic number but different atomic weight and different radioactivity. **radioactive i.,** form of an element made radioactive and used in med. diagnosis and treatment, etc. **-pic** (-op'ik), *adj.*

isotropic (īsətrop'ik), *adj.* having same properties in every direction. **-pe,** *adj.* **-pism, -py** (-ot'rəpizm, -pi), *n.* **-pous,** *adj.*

iterate (it'ərāt), *v.t.* repeat. **-ant,** *adj.* repeating. **-ance, -ancy, -tion,** *n.* **-tive,** *adj.*

iterum (it'ərəm), Lat. *adv.* "again"; afresh.

ithyphallic (ithifal'ik), *adj.* indecent; pert. to verse line of three trochees.

itinerant (itin'ərənt, īt-), *adj.* journeying from place to place; *n.* wanderer; traveller. **-ncy,** *n.* **-rary,** *n.* journey; route; guidebook; *adj.* pert. to journey. **-rate,** *v.i.* journey from place to place, *espec.* preaching. **-ration,** *n.*

ixia (iks'iə), *n.* iris-like S. African plant; corn lily.

ixiodic (iksiod'ik), *adj.* pert. or due to ticks. **-dian** (-o'diən), **-did,** *n. & adj.* (pert. to a) tick.

J

jabot (zhab'ō), Fr. *n.* long frill in front of bodice.

jacamar (jak'əmah), *n.* long-billed brightly-coloured bird of tropical S. Amer.

jacinth (jā'sinth, jas'-), *n.* orange-coloured variety of the gem hyacinth. **-e,** *n.* orange colour.

Jacobin (jak'əbin), *n.* extreme revolutionary, *espec.* of Fr. revolution of 1789. **-ic(al),** *adj.* **-ise,** *v.t.* **ism,** *n.*

jaconet (jak'ənit), *n.* kind of thin cotton fabric, *espec.* with one side glazed.

Jacquerie (zhak'rē), Fr. *n.* peasant revolt, *espec.* of Fr. in 1358; peasant class.

jactancy (jak'tənsi), *n.* boasting. **-tation,** *n.* boasting; *Med.,* tossing or shaking of body.

jactitation (jaktitā'shn), *n.* jactation; false claim. **j. of marriage,** false claim to be married to a person.

jaculation (jakūlā'shn), *n.* hurling or darting, as of spears. **-liferous,** *adj.* with arrow-like prickles. **-tory,** *adj.*

j'adoube (zhadoob'), Fr., "I adjust"; call when merely adjusting, and not moving, a piece in chess, etc.

jaeger (yā'gə, jā'-), *n.* gull-like bird of prey, also called skua.

jagannath (jug'ənawt), *n.* juggernaut.

jai alai (hī ahlī'), Sp. *n.* rackets-like game of Spain and Sp. Amer.

jalap (jal'əp), *n.* root of Mex. plant used as purgative.

jalop(p)y (jəlop'i), *n.* worn-out motor-car or aircraft.

jalouse (jəlooz'), *v.t.* be jealous of; grudge; *Scot.,* suspect.

jalousie (zhaloozē'), Fr. *n.* blind or shutter with slats slanting upwards and inwards.

jambolan (jam'bələn), *n.* plum-like tree of Java with fruit used as astringent and drug. **-bool, -bul,** *n.* jambolan.

jampan (jam'pan), Anglo-Ind. n. kind of sedan chair. -ee, -i, n. bearer of j.

Janiform (jan'ifawm), adj. like the Rom. god Janus; two-faced.

janissary (jan'isəri), n. member of certain Turk. infantry corps.

janitor (jan'itə), n. door-keeper; caretaker.

janizary (jan'izəri), n. janissary.

jannock (jan'ək), dial. adj. pleasant; outspoken; honest; generous.

jardinière (zhahdēn'yār), Fr. n. ornamental flower stand.

jarrah (jah'rə), n. Austral. eucalyptus tree with mahogany-like timber; red gum tree of Austral.

jarvey (jah'vi), n. Irish car driver; hackney coachman.

jasper (jas'pə), n. green chalcedony; sev. mottled varieties of quartz, espec. bloodstone. -ated, -pé (zhas'pā), adj. mottled or streaked with colour. -pideous, -pidean, adj.

jecoral (jek'ərəl), adj. pert. to the liver. -rise, v.t. impregnate with ultra-violet rays; make similar in value to cod-liver oil.

jehad, ji- (jihahd'), n. Moham. religious war; crusade.

jejune (jijoon'), adj. empty; sterile; dry. -nity, n. -num, n. middle part of small intestine.

jellab (jilahb'), n. loose hooded cloak of Morocco, etc.

jelutong (zhelootong'), n. Malayan tree yielding rubbery resin; this resin.

jemadar (jem'ədah), Hind. n. sepoy lieutenant; any military or police leader.

je ne sais quoi (zhēn sā kwah'), Fr., "I do not know what"; indescribable attribute or quality; a "something."

jennet (jen'it), n. small Sp. horse; she-ass.

jentacular (jentak'ūlə), adj. pert. to breakfast.

jequirity (jikwir'iti), n. seed of Ind. liquorice used as weight, rosary-bead, etc.

jerboa (jəbō'ə), n. jumping rat, espec. of N. Africa.

jeremiad (jerimi'ad), n. mournful prophecy, story or complaint.

jerque (jěk), v.t. examine ship's papers for smuggling attempts,

etc. -r, n. customs officer who jerques ships.

jess (jes), n. ringed strap round hawk's leg.

jesuitry (jez'ūitri, jezh'-), n. casuistry. -tical, adj. cunning. -tism, n. jesuitry; quibble.

jetsam (jet'səm), n. goods thrown overboard, espec. when found cast up on shore.

jettison (jet'isən), v.t. throw overboard to lighten ship; cast off as nuisance; discard; n. such act; jetsam.

jeu d'esprit (zhö desprē'), Fr., "game of wit"; light, humorous work; witty sally.

jeune premier (zhön prəm'yā), Fr. (fem. -ière, -yār'), juvenile lead in musical play, etc.

jeunesse dorée (zhön'es dor'ā), Fr., "gilded youth"; rich young people.

jihad, see jehad.

jodhpurs (jöd'pōorz, -pəz), n.pl. riding breeches fitting lower leg tightly.

joie de vivre (zhwah də vē'vr), Fr., "joy of living"; zest.

jointure (join'tūr), n. settlement of estate on wife to become effective on death of husband; v.t. settle j. on. -tress, n. woman holding j.

jongleur (zhawnglēr'), Fr. n. medieval wandering minstrel; troubadour; juggler.

jorum (jōr'əm), n. large bowl containing drink; its contents.

joule (jōōl, jowl), n. unit of energy or work, equiv. of ten million ergs: energy expended by one watt in one second. -an, adj. pert. to heat arising from conversion of other form of energy.

juba (jōō'bə), Amer. negro n. ghost; negro dance.

judaise (jōō'dā īz), v.i. & t. make or become Jewish; keep Jewish observances; convert to Jewish beliefs. -aic, adj. -aism, n.

Judophobism (jōōdof'əbizm), n. anti-Semitism.

jugate (jōō'gāt), adj. in pairs; app. to two overlapping heads on coin. -tion, n.

juggernaut (jug'ənawt), Hind. n. huge Ind. idol of Vishnu, drawn at festivals on a cart beneath whose wheels worshippers were erron. believed to throw themselves to death ; any belief or object needing or receiving sacrifice of themselves by believers ; anything that crushes all in its path.

jugular (jug'ūlǝ), *adj.* pert. to neck or throat ; *n.* such vein. **-late,** *v.t.* kill by cutting throat or strangling.

julep (jōō'lip), *n.* sweet medicated beverage.

jumelle (jōōmel' ; Fr., zhümel'), *adj.* in or with pairs.

jumentous (jōōmen'tǝs), *adj.* like horse's.

juncaceous (jungkā'shǝs), *adj.* pert. to or like a rush ; belonging to rush family of plants.

juncture (jungk'tūr), *n.* junction ; joint ; critical moment of time.

Jungfrau (yoong'frow), Ger. *n.* young woman ; maiden.

Junker (yoong'kǝ), Ger. *n.* landed aristocrat, *espec.* of Prussia. **-dom, -ism,** *n.*

junta (jun'tǝ ; Sp., hōōn'tah), *n.* Sp. council ; any administrative body ; clique. **-to,** *n.* clique ; faction.

jural (jōōr'ǝl), *adj.* pert. to law or legal rights. **-amentum,** Lat. *n.* (*pl.* **-ta**) oath. **-ant,** *n.* & *adj.* (person) taking oath. **-ation,** *n.* swearing. **-atorial,** *adj.* pert. to jury. **-atory,** *adj.* pert. to oath.

jurisconsult (jōōriskǝnsult'), *n.* legal expert.

jurisdiction (jōōrisdik'shn), *n.* legal authority or administration ; extent or area of such authority. **-tive,** *adj.*

jurisprudence (jōōrisprōō'dǝns), *n.* science of law ; knowledge of law. **-nt,** *n.* & *adj.* (person) expert in j.

jurist (jōōr'ist), *n.* jurisconsult. **-ic,** *adj.* pert. to j. ; pert. to or permissible by law.

jus (jus), Lat. *n.* (*pl.* **jures**) law ; legal power or right. **j.gentium** (-jen'shiǝm), law of nations. **j. inter gentes** (-in'tǝ jen'tēz), international law. **j. primae noctis** (-prī'mē nok'tis), droit du seigneur. **jusqu'au bout** (zhūs'kō bōō'), Fr., "to the end." **-ist,** *n.* radical ; one willing to go to the bitter end.

jussive (jus'iv), *adj.* Gram., signifying command.

juvenescent (jōōvines'ǝnt), *adj.* becoming young. **-nce,** *n.*

juvenilia (jōōvinil'iǝ), Lat. *n.pl.* writer's or artist's youthful, early works.

juxtapose (juks'tǝpōs), *v.t.* place side by side or next to. **-sition,** *n.* **-sitize** (-poz'itiv), *adj.*

jyngine (jin'jīn, -in), *adj.* pert. to or like a wryneck ; belonging to wryneck subfamily of birds.

K

kadi, *see* **cadi.**

kaka (kah'kǝ), *n.* talking parrot of N.Z. **-po,** *n.* ground-owl-parrot of N.Z.

kakidrosis (kakidrō'sis), *n.* secretion of malodorous perspiration.

kakistocracy (kakistok'rǝsi), *n.* government by worst men.

kaleidoscope (kǝlī'dǝskōp), *n.* instr. containing fragments of coloured glass, etc., which are reflected in mirrors to produce a multitude of patterns ; any many-coloured, changing pattern or scene. **-pic** (-op'ik), *adj.*

kalends, *see* **calends.**

kamptulicon (kamptū'likǝn), *n.* kind of rubber and cork floorcloth.

kanaka (kan'ǝkǝ), *n.* native of S. Sea island.

kanya (kan'yǝ), *n.* shea tree and butter.

kaolin (kā'ǝlin), *n.* china clay, used in porcelain manufacture and in medicine.

Kapellmeister (kapel'mīstǝ), Ger. *n.* choirmaster.

kapok (kap'ok), *n.* soft fibre of silk-cotton tree, used to fill cushions, etc. ; the silk-cotton tree, its seeds and oil.

kappa (kap'ǝ), *n.* tenth letter of Gr. alphabet (K, κ).

karaka (kahrah'kah, krak'ǝ), *n.* N.Z. tree with edible seeds and fruit.

karakul (kar'ǝkul), *n.* sheep of Cent. Asia ; curled black fleece of its lambs.

karma (kah'mǝ), *n.* destiny ; in Buddhist belief, actions of one incarnation determining nature of next ; religious rite. **-mic,** *adj.*

karri (kar'i), *n.* W. Austral. giant gum tree, with red timber.

karroo (kərōō'), *n.* dry terrace-like plateau of S. Africa.

karyokinesis (kariəkinē'sis), *n.* cell division, *espec.* of nucleus. **-yoplasm,** *n.* protoplasm of cell nucleus. **-yotin** (-ō'tin), *n.* stainable matter of nucleus.

katabasis (kətab'əsis), *n.* (*pl.* **-ses**) descent; retreat; return, *espec.* to sea of Gr. soldiers of the anabasis. **-atic** (katəbat'ik), *adj.* descending.

katabothron (katəboth'rən), *n.* (*pl.* **-ra**) underground water channel.

katharometer (kathərom'itə), *n.* instr. measuring alterations in composition of gas mixture.

katipo (kah'tipō, kat'-), *n.* venomous black spider of Austral., N.Z., etc.

katydid (kā'tidid), *n.* large green grasshopper-like insect of Amer.

kauri (kow'ri), *n.* gum- and timber-yielding tree of N.Z.; its white timber; its resin found in lumps in ground.

kava (kah'vah), *n.* kind of pepper plant of Australasia, with root from which strong drink is made.

kayak (kī'ak), *n.* Eskimo canoe.

kazoo (kəzōō'), *n.* mus. toy with strip of catgut vibrating when hummed into.

kea (kā'ə, kē'ə), *n.* large green parrot of N.Z., said to kill sheep.

keddah (ked'ə), *n.* Ind. elephant trap.

kedge (kej), *n.* small anchor; *v.t.* move (ship) by hauling on anchor dropped ahead from boat.

keelhaul (kēl'hawl), *v.t.* haul under keel of ship as punishment.

keelson (kel'sən, kēl'-), *n.* wooden or steel structure lengthwise within ship's frame to bear and distribute stress.

kef (kāf), *Arab.* *n.* sleepiness, caused by drugs; hashish, etc.

kefir (kef'ə), *n.* koumiss-like liquor of Caucasus. **-ic** (-ir'ik), *adj.*

keloid (kē'loid), *n.* fibrous skin tumour, *espec.* over scar; raised scars forming pattern on body, in certain African tribes.

kelp (kelp), *n.* seaweed ashes, yielding iodine; sev. large brown seaweeds.

kelpie (kel'pi), *n.* water spirit in Gaelic myth.; *Austral.,* kind of sheep or cattle dog, derived partly from dingo.

kelson, *see* **keelson.**

kelt (kelt), *n.* salmon after spawning.

kenosis (kinō'sis), *n.* *Theol.,* action of Christ in humbling Himself, or divesting Himself of divine attributes, in becoming man. **-otic** (-ot'ik), *adj.*; *n.* believer in k. **-oticism** (-ot'isizm), **-otism** (ken'ətizm), *n.*

kepi, ké- (kep'i, kā'-), *n.* soldier's peaked cap with high and flat crown.

kerasine (ker'əsin), *adj.* horny.

keratin (ker'ətin), *n.* albuminoid from which horns, nails, hair and other like tissues develop. **-ise,** *v.i.* & *t.* make horny. **-ous** (-at'inəs), *adj.* horny.

keratogenic (kerətəjen'ik), *adj.* able to cause growth of horn, skin, hair, etc. **-nous** (-oj'inəs), *adj.* horn-producing. **-toid,** *adj.* horny. **-tode,** *n.* keratose substance. **-tose,** *n.* & *adj.* (substance) of horny fibres. **-tosis,** *n.* excessive growth of horny tissue of skin.

keraunograph (kəraw'nəgraf), *n.* instr. detecting distant thunderstorm; pattern made by lightning on struck object. **-noscopia, -noscopy,** *n.* divination by thunder.

kermes (kə'mēz), *n.* red cochineal-like dye made from dried bodies of certain female insects of Mediterranean; evergreen oak on which these insects feed. **-ic** (-es'ik), *adj.*

kerogen (ker'əjen), *n.* kind of bitumen found in oil shale. **-osene,** *n.* fuel oil also called paraffin.

kerygmatic (kerigmat'ik), *adj.* pert. to preaching, *espec.* of gospel. **-ystic,** *adj.* homiletic.

ketch (kech), *n.* two-masted fore-and-aft rigged sailing vessel.

ketone (kē'tōn), *n.* chem. compound of carbon, obtained by distilling salts of organic acids. **-naemia,** *n.* presence of k., *espec.* acetone, in blood. **-nic** (-on'ik), *adj.* **-nise,** *v.t.* convert into k. **-togenesis,** *n.* production of k., *espec.* in diabetes. **-tosis,** *n.* presence of excess of k. in body.

khalifa, -ate, *see* **caliph, -ate.**

khamsin, -seen (kam'sin, -sēn'), *Arab.* *n.* hot wind of Egypt blowing from Sahara; dust storm.

khan (kahn), *Turk.* *n.* prince; Tartar emperor; *Arab.,* cara-

---

hat, bah, hāte, hāre, crawl; pen, ēve, hēre; it, īce, fīre; on, bōne, boil, bōre, howl; foot, fōōd, bōōr, hull, tūbe, pūre.

vanserai. -ate, n. khan's office or jurisdiction. -jee, n. keeper of caravanserai.

Khedive (kidēv'), n. Turk. viceroy of Egypt. -val, adj.

khidmatgar (kid'mətgah), Hind. n. waiter.

khoja(h) (kaw'jah), Turk. n. title of respect; Moham. teacher.

kiang (kiang'), n. wild ass of Tibet.

kia ora (kē'ah ōr'ah), Maori, "be well"; good health!

kibe (kīb), n. chapped place on skin; ulcerated chilblain.

kibitzer (kib'itsə), Yid. n. giver of unwanted advice; interfering on-looker.

kieselguhr (kē'zelgoor), n. kind of porous diatomite.

kilderkin (kil'dəkin), n. measure of capacity, about 18 gallons; cask holding that amount.

killadar (kil'ədah), Ind. n. castle-governor.

kinesalgia (kinisal'jiə), n. muscular pain. -siatrics (-ēsiat'riks), n. med. treatment by muscular move-ments.

kinetic (kinet'ik), adj. pert. or due to movement. -esis (-ē'sis), n. movement. -s, n. study of changes of motion under forces. -togenic, adj. causing movement.

kinkajou (king'kəjoo), n. raccoon-like animal of Cent. and S. Amer.

kino (kē'nō), n. catechu-like gum obtained from sev. tropical trees. -fluous (-of'lūəs), adj. yielding k.

kippeen, -pin (kipēn', kip'in), Anglo-Ind. n. walking cane; match; any short stick.

Kirsch(wasser) (kirsh, -vas'ə), Ger. n. liqueur made from distilled fermented black cherry juice.

kismet (kiz'mit, kis'-), n. fate. -ic (-et'ik), adj.

kit-cat (kit'kat), n. & adj. not quite half-length (portrait).

klepht (kleft), n. Gr. brigand. -ic, adj. -ism, n.

kleptomania (kleptəmā'niə), n. un-controllable desire to steal. -c, n. -tic, adj. pert. to theft.

kloof (kloof), S. African n. ravine.

knout (nowt), n. whip with leather and wire thongs; v.t. scourge with k.

knur (nə), n. knob; knot in wood; hard ball. k. and spell, anct. game of hitting ball greatest dis-

tance in given number of strokes.

koala (kōah'lə), n. Austral. tree bear.

kobold (kō'bold, -ōld), n. sprite in Ger. folklore.

koftgari (koftgərē'), Hind. n. inlay-ing of gold on steel.

kohl (kōl), n. eye-shadow of Orient; Arab horse.

kohlrabi (kōlrah'bi), n. kind of cabbage with turnip-like stem.

kolkhos (kōlkawz'), Russ. n. collec-tive farm.

komatik (kəmat'ik), n. long Eskimo sledge.

kommetje (kom'etyi), utch n. circular hollow in ground of S. African veldt.

koniology (kōniol'əji), n. study of dust and germs in atmosphere. -nimeter, -niscope, n. instr. meas-uring amount of dust in air.

kookaburra (kookəbur'ə, -boor'-), n. laughing jackass of Austral.

kopek, -eck (kō'pek), n. Russ. coin worth one-hundredth part of rouble.

kopje (kop'i), S. African n. hillock.

Koran (korahn'), n. holy scriptures of Islam.

kosher (kō'shə), Heb. adj. permitted by, or prepared according to, Jewish relig. law; n. such food.

koumiss (koo'miss), n. intoxicating drink made from fermented mare's milk.

kourbash (koor'bash), n. whip of hide; v.t. scourge with k.

krait (krīt), n. venomous cobra-like Ind. snake.

krasis (krā'sis), n. addition of water to Communion wine.

kraurosis (kror ō'sis), n. shrivelling of skin. -otic (-ot'ik), adj.

Kriegspiel (krēg'shpēl), Ger. n. "war game," played by moving on a board pieces, flags, etc., representing armed forces.

kritarchy (krit'ahki), n. govern-ment, espec. of Jews, by judges.

kudos (kū'dos), n. glory; fame; reward.

kudu (koo'doo), n. larged curled-horned African antelope.

kukri (kook'ri), n. broad curved Gurkha knife.

kulak (koo'lak, koolahk'), Russ. n. rich peasant or farmer. -ism, n.

Kultur (kooltoor'), Ger. n. "culture," *espec.* representing civilisation of a nation.

kumiss, *see* **koumiss.**

kumquat (kum'kwot), *n.* round or oblong Chin. citrus fruit.

Kursaal (koor'zahl), Ger. *n.* entertainment hall, public room or hotel at spa or seaside resort.

kutcha (kuch'ə), Anglo-Ind. *adj.* makeshift ; crude.

kvas(s) (kvas), Russ. *n.* thin weak beer.

kymatology (kīmətol'əji), *n.* study of wave motion.

kymograph (kī'məgraf), *n.* instr. recording pressure curves, etc. **-ic,** *adj.*

kyphosis (kīfō'sis), *n.* hunchbacked condition. **-otic** (-ot'ik), *adj.*

kyrie eleison (kēr'ii ilā'ison), *Gr.,* "Lord, have mercy upon us" ; any response in, or mus. setting of, these words.

L

laager (lah'gə), S. African *n.* camp of wagons drawn into circle ; *v.i.* & *t.* make such camp.

laagte (lahg'tə), Dutch *n.* valley ; dry river bed.

labefact, -fy (lab'ifakt, -fī), *v.t.* weaken. **-ation, -ion,** *n.*

labellate (ləbel'ət), *adj.* lipped. **-loid,** *adj.* lip-like. **-lum,** *n.* (*pl.* **-la**) lip of flower's corolla.

labial (lā'biəl), *adj.* pert. to or pronounced with lips or with rounded lips ; *n.* such sound, as *p,* *oo.* **-iate,** *adj.* lipped ; *v.t.* labialise. **-ise,** *v.t.* make l. in pronunciation. **-ism,** *n.*

labidophorous (labidof'ərəs), *adj.* with a pair of pincer-like organs.

labile (lā'bīl, -il), *adj.* liable to err or change ; unstable. **-lise,** *v.t.* make l. **-lity,** *n.*

labiodental (lābiəden'təl), *adj.* pert. to or pronounced with lips and teeth ; *n.* such sound, as *f.* **-omancy,** *n.* lip-reading. **-onasal,** *n.* & *adj.* (sound) pronounced with lips and nasal passage, as *m.* **-ovelar,** *n.* & *adj.* (sound) pronounced with rounded lips and back of tongue raised, as *w.*

labret (lā'bret), *n.* savage's lip-ornament. **-ifery,** *n.* wearing of l.

labrose (lā'brōs), *adj.* thick-lipped.

labyrinth (lab'irinth), *n.* maze ; internal ear. **-al, -ian, -ic, -iform, -ine,** *adj.* **-itis,** *n.* inflammation of internal ear.

lac, *see* **lakh.**

lacerate (las'ərāt), *v.t.* tear ; mangle ; wound. **-tion,** *n.* **-tive,** *adj.*

lacertilian (lasətil'iən), *n.* & *adj.* (pert. to or like a) lizard. **-tian,** *n.* & *adj.* **-tiform,** *adj.* lizard-shaped. **-tine, -toid,** *adj.* lizard-like.

laches (lach'iz), *n.* negligence ; carelessness.

lachrymal (lak'riməl), *adj.* pert. to tears and weeping ; *n.pl.* organs secreting tears ; crying-fits. **-mary** *adj.* **-mation,** *n.* **-mator,** *n.* substance or gas causing tears. **-matory,** *n.* narrow-necked vase ; tear-bottle. **-miform,** *adj.* tear-shaped. **-mist,** *n.* weeper. **-mogenic,** *adj.* causing tears. **-mose,** *adj.* tearful.

laciniate (ləsin'iāt), *adj.* fringed. **-iform,** *adj.* like a fringe. **-iose,** *adj.* **-nulate,** *adj.* with fine or small fringe. **-tion,** *n.*

lacis (lā'sis), *n.* network ; filet lace.

laconic (ləkon'ik), *adj.* curt ; in few words ; unemotional. **-ism** (-sizm), **-nism,** *n.*

lactarium (laktār'iəm), *n.* dairy. **-ry,** *adj.* pert. to milk.

lactate (lak'tāt), *v.i.* secrete milk ; suckle young ; *n.* salt or ester of lactic acid. **-tion,** *n.*

lacteal (lak'tiəl), *adj.* pert. to milk ; *n.* & *adj.* (vessel) conveying chyle. **-tean,** *adj.* milky.

lactescent (laktes'ənt), *adj.* like milk ; secreting milk ; yielding milky substance. **-teous,** *adj.* milky. **-nce,** *n.*

lactic (lak'tik), *adj.* pert. to milk or sour milk. **-tiferous,** *adj.* yielding or conveying milk or milky substance. **-tific,** *adj.* producing milk. **-tifluous,** *adj.* full of milk. **-tiform,** *adj.* like milk.

lactometer (laktom'itə), *n.* instr. measuring the purity of milk. **-toscope,** *n.* instr. measuring amount of cream in milk.

lactose (lak'tōs), *n.* sugar occurring in milk.

lacuna (lakū'nə), n. (pl. -ae) gap; interval; hiatus. -l, -nose, -r, -ry, adj.

lacuscular (ləkus'kūlə), adj. pert. to pools.

lacustrine (ləkus'trīn, -in), adj. pert. to lakes. -ral, adj. -rian, adj.; n. lake-dweller.

Ladino (lahdē'nō), n. Spanish-speaking Sp. Amer. Indian or half-breed.

ladrone (lədrōn'), Sp. n. robber. -nism, n. brigandage.

laevoduction (lēvəduk'shn), n. movement leftwards. -ogyrate, -orotatory, adj. turning to left, espec. plane of polarised light. -oversion, n. turning of eyes to left. -vulose, n. kind of very sweet sugar obtained from sucrose.

lagan (lag'ən), n. goods sunk in sea at marked spot.

lagena (ləjē'nə), Lat. n. (pl. -ae) flask. -niform, adj. flask-shaped.

lagophthalmus, -mos (lagofthal'-məs), n. condition of incomplete closure of eye. -mic, adj.

lagostoma (ləgos'təmə), n. harelip.

laic (lā'ik), adj. not clerical or ecclesiastical; lay. -ise (-sīz), v.t. divest of eccl. nature; give over to lay control. -ism, n. anticlericalism.

laissez faire (lā'sā fār'), Fr., "let be" or "act"; policy of non-intervention by government in industry or industrial conditions.

lakh (lak), Hind. n. one hundred thousand (rupees).

lallation (lalā'shn), n. infant's talk, or speech similar to it; pronunciation of r as l.

laloplegia (laləplē'jiə), n. loss of speech caused by paralysis.

lama (lah'mə), n. Tibetan monk or priest. Dalai l., chief lama. -ic (ləmā'ik), -istic, adj. -ism, -ist, n. -sery (ləmah'səri, lah'məsəri), n. monastery of l.

lambda (lam'də), n. eleventh letter of Gr. alphabet (Λ, λ). -cism, n. undue use of l sound in speech, etc.; incorrect pronunciation of l; pronunciation of r as l. -doid, adj. shaped like Λ.

lambent (lam'bənt), adj. shining gently or playing about surface; flickering; gently radiant. -ncy, n.

lambert (lam'bət), n. unit of bright-ness: brightness of surface radiating one lumen per sq. cm.

lamella (ləmel'ə), n. (pl. -ae) thin plate or layer. -loid, adj. like l. -lose, -r, -ry, adj. -ted, adj. composed of l. -tion, n.

lamiaceous (lāmiā'shəs), adj. pert. to or like mint; belonging to mint family of plants.

lamina (lam'inə), n. (pl. -ae) thin plate or layer; flake. -l, -nose, -nous, -r, -ry, adj. -te, v.i. & t. split into l.; bond sev. l. together; plate with metal; adj. shaped like or composed of l. -tion, n.

lammergeier (lam'əgiə), n. eagle- and vulture-like bird of prey, largest of Europe; bearded vulture.

lampadedromy (lampəded'rəmi), n. foot race with lighted torches, espec. relay race in which torch is passed on. -dephore (-əd'ifor), n. torchbearer.

lampion (lam'piən), n. small crude lamp.

lampoon (lampōōn'), n. written satire on a person; v.t. satirise. -er, -ist, n. writer of l.

lamprey (lam'prā), n. slender eel-like fish with toothed sucking mouth.

lamprophony (lamprof'əni, lam'prəfōni), n. speaking in clear, loud voice.

lampyrid (lam'pirid), n. & adj. (pert. to) glow-worm or fire-fly. -rine, adj.

lanameter (lan'əmētə), n. mechanical means of determining quality of wool. -nate (lā'nāt), adj. woolly.

lanceolate (lahn'siəlāt), adj. having shape of lance head, espec. tapering at each end. -tion, n.

lancet (lahn'sit), n. pointed med. instr.; pointed window or arch.

lancinate (lahn'sināt), v.t. lacerate; pierce. -tion, n.

landau (lan'daw), n. four-wheeler carriage with folding hood and removable top. -lette, n. coupé with folding hood.

landes (lahnd), Fr. n.pl. desert or marshy lowlands beside sea.

landfall (land'fawl), n. the sighting of land from sea.

landgrave (land'grāv), n. kind of Ger. count. -viate, n. jurisdiction of l. -vine (-vēn), n. wife of l.; woman having position of l.

Landwehr (lahnt'vār), Ger. *n.* reserve of men who have completed conscription service in army.

languet(te) (lang'gwet), *n.* tonguelike appendage or outgrowth.

laniary (lā'niəri, lan'-), *adj.* canine (tooth). -**riform**, *adj.*

lanolin (lan'əlin), *n.* fat extracted from wool and used in ointments and cosmetics. -**nose**, *adj.* woolly.

lanugo (lənū'gō), *n.* woolly down. -**ginose, -ginous** (-ū'jinōs, -əs), *adj.* downy.

Laodicean (lāodisē'ən), *adj.* pert. to Laodicea and its "lukewarm" Christians (Rev. iii); zeal-less; *n.* such person.

lapactic (ləpak'tik), *n.* & *adj.* purgative. -**parectomy, -parotomy**, *n.* operation for removal of part of wall of abdomen.

lapicide (lap'isīd), *n.* stone-cutter.

lapidary (lap'idəri), *adj.* pert. to or engraved on stone; *n.* gem engraver. -**rian**, *adj.* pert. to or inscribed on stone. -**rist**, *n.* expert on gems and gem cutting.

lapidate (lap'idāt), *v.t.* stone to death. -**tion, -tor**, *n.*

lapideous (ləpid'iəs), *adj.* of or cut in stone. -**dicolous**, *adj.* living under stones. -**dific**, *adj.* forming stone. -**dify**, *v.t.* turn into stone.

lapillus (ləpil'əs), *n.* (*pl.* -**li**) small stone, *espec.* ejected by volcano. -**liform**, *adj.* like small stones.

lapis lazuli (lap'is laz'ūli), *n.* rich blue stone.

lappaceous (lapā'shəs), *adj.* prickly.

lapsus linguae (lap'səs ling'gwē), *Lat.* (*pl.* **lapsi**.....) "slip of the tongue." l.**calami** (-kal'əmī), slip of the pen. l.**memoriae** (-mimōr'iē), slip of memory.

Laputan (ləpū'tən), *adj.* pert. to Laputa, island of philosophers in Swift's *Gulliver's Travels*; absurd; fantastic.

lares (lah'rēz, lar'-), Lat. *n.pl.* local or tutelary gods. l. **and penates,** household gods.

largesse (lahjes'), *n.* bountiful gift of money; generosity. -**gitation**, *n.* giving of l.

larithmics (lərridh'miks), *n.* study of population statistics.

larmoyant (lahmoi'ənt; Fr., larmwayahn'), *adj.* tearful; weeping.

laroid (lar'oid), *adj.* pert. to or like gulls.

larva (lah'və), *n.* (*pl.* -**ae**) form of insect after hatching from egg and before pupation; earliest form of animal's young. -**l**, *adj.* -**te**, *adj.* hidden. -**viparous**, *adj.* bringing forth l. -**vivorous**, *adj.* feeding on l.

larynx (lar'ingks), *n.* (*pl.* -**nges**) upper part of windpipe; voice organ. -**ngal** (-ing'gəl), -**ngeal** (-in'jiəl), -**ngic**, *adj.* -**ngismus**, *n.* spasm closing l., with croup-like effect. -**ngitis**, *n.* inflammation of l. -**ngology** (-inggol'əji), *n.* study of l. -**ngoscope**, *n.* instr. for viewing l. -**ngotomy**, *n.* incision into l.

lascar (las'kə), *n.* E. Ind. native sailor or soldier.

lascivious (ləsiv'iəs), *adj.* lustful; lecherous.

lasher (lash'ə), *n.* weir; water in or pool below weir.

lashkar (lash'kah), Hind. *n.* army of Ind. tribesmen.

lassitude (las'itūd), *n.* tiredness.

latebricole (ləteb'rikōl), *adj.* living in holes.

lateen (latēn'), *adj.* app. to triangular sail rigged on spar forming angle of 45° with mast. -**er**, *n.* l.-rigged vessel.

latent (lā'tənt), *adj.* lying concealed or dormant. -**ncy**, *n.*

laterigrade (lat'ərigrād), *n.* & *adj.* (animal) moving sideways or crab-wise.

latescent (lates'ənt), *adj.* becoming latent.

latex (lā'teks), *n.* (*pl.* -**tices**) milky fluid, *espec.* yielding rubber, etc., secreted by certain trees. -**ticiferous**, *adj.* secreting l.

laticostate (latikos'tāt), *adj.* having broad ribs. -**identate**, *adj.* having broad teeth. -**ipennate**, *adj.* having broad wings. -**irostrate**, *adj.* having broad beak.

latitude (lat'itūd), *n.* width; freedom; *Geog.*, distance from equator; *Astron.*, angular distance from ecliptic. -**dinal**, *adj.* -**dinarian**, *n.* & *adj.* (person) having broad and free views, *espec.* religious. -**dinous**, *adj.* having breadth.

latrant (lā'trənt), *adj.* barking. -**ration**, *n.*

latrine (lətrēn'), *n.* place for evacuating excrements.

latticinio (lahtichē'nyō), It. *n.* kind of glass with white veins.

laud (lawd), *v.t.* & *n.* praise. **-ation,** *n.* **-atory, -ative,** *adj.* expressing praise.

laudanum (law'dənəm), *n.* tincture of opium.

laudator temporis acti (lawdā'tə tempŏr'is ak'ti), *Lat.*, "praiser of past time"; die-hard; Conservative.

laureate (lōr'iət), *adj.* crowned with laurel wreath as prize or sign of distinction; *n.* such person, *espec.* poet; (-iāt), *v.t.* bestow laurel wreath on. **-tion,** *n.*

laurustinus, -ne (lōrəstī'nəs, lōr'əstin), *n.* evergreen shrub, species of viburnum, with white or pink flowers.

lava (lah'və), *n.* fluid rock ejected by erupting volcano; this subsequently solidified.

lavabo (ləvā'bo), *n.* (*pl.* **-es**) *R.C.*, rite of washing hands by celebrant priest, while reciting Psalm xxvi, 6-12; towel or basin used in l.; wash-basin.

lavage (lav'ij), *n.* washing (out). **-vation,** *n.*

laverock (lav'rək), Scot. *n.* lark.

laxative (laks'ətiv), *n.* & *adj.* aperient. **-te,** *v.t.* loosen. **-tion,** *n.* act of loosening; state of being loosened.

layette (lāet'), *n.* clothing, bedding, etc., for new-born child.

lazar (lā'zə), *n.* leper; any plaguestricken person. **-etto** (laz'-), *n.* leper hospital.

lazarole (laz'ərol), *n.* medlar.

lazuli (laz'ūli), *n.* lapis lazuli. **-ne,** *adj.*

Lebensraum (lā'bnzrowm), Ger. *n.* "living space"; territory necessary for national self-sufficiency.

lecanomancy (lek'ənəmansi), *n.* divination by water in basin. **-noscopy,** *n.* staring at water in basin, as form of self-hypnotism.

lecher (lech'ə), *n.* sexually immoral person. **-ous,** *adj.* lustful **-y,** *n.*

lecithal (les'ithəl), *adj.* having yolk. **-ity,** *n.*

lectern (lek'tən), *n.* reading desk. **-tion,** *n.* reading; interpretation of text.

lectionary (lek'shənəri), *n.* list of parts of Scriptures ordered to be read in churches.

lectrice (lek'tris), *n.* female reader.

lectual (lek'tūəl), *adj.* necessitating confinement to bed.

legate (leg'ət), *n.* papal envoy; ambassador. **-tion** (ligā'shn), *n.* dispatch of l.; embassy.

legerdemain (lej'ədimān), *n.* sleight of hand.

leguleian (legūlē'ən), *adj.* like lawyer; pettifogging; *n.* lawyer. **-eious,** *adj.*

leguminous (ligū'minəs), *adj.* app. to plants with seeds in pods. **-me** (leg'ūm), *n.* vegetable; l. plant grown as forage; pod. **-miniform,** *adj.* pod-shaped. **-nose,** *adj.*

lei (lā'ē), Hawaiian *n.* garland of flowers.

leiotrichous (līot'rikəs), *adj.* smoothhaired. **-chy,** *n.* **-ophyllous,** *adj.* smooth-leaved.

leister (lē'stə), *adj.* trident for spearing fish.

leit-motif, -tiv (līt-mōtēf'), Ger. *n.* recurring mus. theme with definite association with a person, idea, event, etc.

lemma (lem'ə), *n.* (*pl.* **-mata**) *Log.*, major premise; (*pl.* **-s**) *Bot.*, flowering glume of grass.

lemming (lem'ing), *n.* rat of polar regions.

lemnaceous (lemnā'shəs), *adj.* pert. to or like duckweed; belonging to duckweed family of plants.

lemur (lē'mə), *n.* large-eyed, monkey-like animal of Madagascar, etc. **flying l.**, E. Ind. cat-like animal, with fold of skin on both sides of body enabling it to make long leaps. **-iform, -oid** (lem'ūroid), *adj.* like l.

lemures (lem'ūr ēz), Lat. *n.pl.* spirits of dead.

lenitive (len'itiv), *n.* & *adj.* soothing (drug); gentle laxative; palliative.

lenticular (lentik'ūlə), *adj.* shaped like lentil or convexo-convex lens; *n.* such lens. **-tiform,** *adj.*

lentigo (lenti'gō), *n.* (*pl.* **-gines**) freckle or freckle-like condition. **-ginous** (-ij'inəs), *adj.* freckly; scurfy.

lentiscus (lentis'kəs), *n.* mastic tree. **-cine,** *adj.*

lentisk (len'tisk), *n.* lentiscus.

lentitude (len'titūd), *n.* slowness; lethargy. **-dinous,** *adj.*

lentoid (len'toid), *adj.* lens-shaped.

leonine (lē'ənīn), *adj.* like a lion; *n.* Lat. verse line with internal rhyme; rhyming of last two or

three syllables in Fr. verse.
l. partnership, one in which partner
bears losses but receives no profits.

leontiasis (lionti'əsis), *n.* kind of
leprosy giving leonine appearance
to face. **Lossea,** hypertrophy of
facial bones.

leotard (lē'ətahd), *n.* acrobat's
low-cut sleeveless tights.

lepidopterous (lepidop'tərəs), *adj.*
having four scale-covered wings.
-ran, -ron, *n.* (*pl.* **-ra**) such insect,
as moth or butterfly.

lepidosis (lepidō'sis), *n.* scaly skin
disease. **-dote,** *adj.* scurf-covered.

leporine (lep'ərin), *adj.* pert. to or
like a hare. **-ride,** *n.* Belgian hare.
-riform, *adj.* like a hare.

lepra (lep'rə), *n. Med.,* leprosy.

leprechaun (lep'rikawn), *n.* fairy in
shape of old man, in Ir. folklore.

lepric (lep'rik), *adj.* pert. to leprosy.
-roid, *adj.* **-rology,** *n.* study of
leprosy. **-rose,** *adj.* scurfy.

leptocephalous (leptəsef'ələs), *adj.*
having very narrow head. **-lia**
(-sifā'liə), *n.* l. condition. **-lus,** *n.*
(*pl.* **-li**) larva of conger eel; conger
eel; l. person.

leptochrous (leptok'rəs), *adj.* having
very thin skin. **-roa,** *n.*

leptometer (leptom'itə), *n.* instr.
measuring viscosity of oil.

leptorrhinian (leptərin'iən), *n. & adj.*
(person) with long thin nose.
-nism, *n.*

Lesbian (lez'biən), *adj.* pert. to
Lesbos (Mytilene), and the im-
morality of its anct. inhabitants;
n. homosexual woman. **L.rule,**
rule or standard alterable to suit
circumstances. **-ism,** *n.* homosexuality between women.

lèse-majesté (lāz-mazh'estā), **lese-**
majesty, leze- (lēz-maj'isti), *n.*
treason; crime against sovereign's
person.

lesion (lē'zhn), *n.* injury, *espec.*
causing structural changes; injured area.

lethal (lē'thəl), *adj.* causing death;
n. such substance or agent. **-ity** *n.*

lethargy (leth'əji) *n.* sleepy state.
-gic (-ah'jik), *adj.* **-gise,** *v.t.* **-gus**
(-ah'gəs), *n.* sleeping sickness.

Lethe (lē'thi), *n.* river of Hades in
Gr. myth., whose waters grant
oblivion; forgetfulness of past;
peace of mind. **-an** (-ē'ən), *adj.*
-thiferous, *adj.* deadly.

lethologica (lēthəloj'ikə), *n.* forgetfulness of words.

lettre de cachet (let'r də kash'ā),
Fr. (*pl.* **lettres.....**), "sealed letter"; monarch's written edict;
order for imprisonment.

leucochroic (lūkəkrō'ik), *adj.* white;
pale.

leucocyte (lū'kəsīt), *n.* white corpuscle of blood. **-tic** (-it'ik), *adj.*
-toid, *adj.* like l. **-tolysis,** *n.* destruction of l. **-topoiesis,** *n.* formation of l. **-tosis,** *n.* excess of l.
in blood.

leucoma (lūkō'mə), *n.* whiteness
and thickening of cornea. **-tous**
(-om'ətəs), *adj.*

leucomelanous, -nic (lūkəmel'ənəs,
-milan'ik); *adj.* having dark hair
and eyes, and fair skin.

leucopenia (lūkəpē'niə), *n.* decrease
in number of leucocytes in blood.
-nic (-en'ik), *adj.*

leucophyllous (lūkəfil'əs), *adj.* with
white leaves.

leucorrhoea (lūkərē'ə), *n.* vaginal
discharge of whitish mucus; "the
whites." **-l,** *adj.*

leucotomy (lūkot'əmi), *n.* surgical
separation of white fibres in
prefrontal lobe of brain to relieve
mental illness.

leucous (lū'kəs), *adj.* white; fair;
albino.

leukaemia, -em- (lūkē'miə), *n.*
presence of excess leucocytes in
blood due to affection of organs
making blood. **-mic,** *adj.*

Levant (livant'), *n.* the East, *espec.*
the eastern end of Mediterranean.
-er, *n.* E. wind of Mediterranean.
-ine, *n. & adj.*

levant (livant'), *v.i.* flee from
creditors.

levator (livā'tə), *n.* (*pl.* **-es, -ōr'ēz**),
muscle raising limb or part.

levee (lev'i, livē'), *n.* monarch's
reception held for men; *Amer.,*
river embankment; quay.

leveret (lev'ərit), *n.* young hare.

leviathan (livī'əthən), *n.* sea monster mentioned in Bible; any
gigantic creature or work.

levigate (lev'igāt), *v.t.* make smooth;
polish; mix thoroughly; reduce
to powder or paste; *adj.* smooth.
-tion, -tor, *n.*

levitate (lev'itāt), *v.i. & t.* rise;
float; cause to rise or float. **-tion,**
n. raising of body without support,

---

espec. by spiritualistic means; illusion of floating. -tive, *adj.*

lewd (lūd, lōōd), *adj.* indecent; lecherous.

lewisite (lōō′isīt), *n. Chem.*, blistering liquid, derived from arsenic and acetylene, used in war; *Geol.*, yellow or brown mineral containing antimony.

lex (leks), Lat. *n.* (*pl.* leges, lē′jēz) law. l.fori, law of forum or law-court. l.mercatorum, -ria, mercantile law. l. non scripta, unwritten law. l.talionis, law of an eye for an eye; law of equal retaliation. l.terrae, law of the land.

lexicon (leks′ikən), *n.* dictionary. -cal, *adj.* pert. to l. or vocabulary. -cography, *n.* compilation of l. -cology, *n.* study of words, their meanings and origins.

lexigraphy (leksig′rəfi), *n.* art of definition of words; writing with characters each one representing a word. -phic(al), *adj.*

lexiphanic (leksifan′ik), *adj.* using many long words; bombastic. -ism (-sizm), *n.*

li (lē), Chin. *n.* unit of weight (equiv. of decigram) or measure (equiv. of millimetre, kilometre or centiare).

liaison (liā′zn; Fr., lē ā′zawṅ), *n.* illicit love affair; close connection; co-operation. l.officer, officer establishing close communication or co-operation between mil. or other units.

liana (liah′nə), *n.* climbing plant with roots in ground; vine.

lias (lī′əs), *n.* kind of fossiliferous limestone. -ssic (-as′ik), *adj.*

libanophorous (libanof′ərəs), *adj.* yielding incense. -niferous, -notophorous, *adj.*

libation (lībā′shn), *n.* offering of drink to gods; act of pouring out l. -ary, -tory, *adj.*

libeccio, -cchio (libech′ō), It. *n.* south-west wind.

liber (lī′bə), *n.* bast.

liberticide (libə′tisīd), *n.* destruction or destroyer of liberty. -dal, *adj.*

libertine (lib′ətēn, -ēn′), *n.* free-thinker; lecher; *adj.* freethinking; lecherous. -nage, -nism, *n.*

libido (libī′do, -bē′-), *n.* sexual desire; vital motive force deriving from sex or life instinct. -dinal (-id′inəl), *adj.* -dinous (-id′inəs), *adj.* lecherous.

librate (lī′brāt), *v.i.* oscillate before settling into equilibrium; be poised; balance. -tion, *n.*; *Astron.*, apparent swinging of moon's visible surface. -tory, *adj.*

libretto (libret′ō), *n.* (*pl.* -ti) book or words of opera, etc. -tist, *n.* writer of l.

libriform (lib′rifawm), *adj.* like liber.

licentiate (līsen′shiāt), *n.* certificated member; person with licence to practise. -tion, *n.*

licentious (līsen′shəs), *adj.* sexually immoral; unrestrained.

lichen (lī′kən), *n.* lowly grey-green flowerless plant encrusting rocks, trees, etc.; encrusting skin disease. -aceous, -ic (-en′ik), -oid, -ose, -ous, *adj.* -ography, *n.* description of or treatise on l. -ology, *n.* study of l.

lickerish (lik′ərish), *adj.* greedy; lecherous.

lictor (lik′tə), *n.* magistrate's attendant bearing fasces in anct. Rome. -ian (-ōr′iən), *adj.*

Lied (lēt), Ger. *n.* (*pl.* -er, -də) song, *espec.* short and expressing emotion.

lien (lē′ən), *n.* right over property or services.

lienal (lī ē′nəl), *adj.* pert. to spleen. -nic (-en′ik), *adj.* -nitis, *n.* inflammation of spleen.

lientery (lī′əntəri), *n.* diarrhoeal discharge of incompletely digested food. -ric (-er′ik), *adj.*

ligament (lig′əmənt), *n.* bond; bandage; band of tissue connecting bones, etc. -al, -ary, -ous, *adj.*

ligate (lī′gāt), *v.t.* tie. -gation, *n.* -gature, *n.* tie; link; bandage; two conjoined letters, as *fl.*

ligneous (lig′niəs), *adj.* wood-like; containing wood. -nescent, *adj.* rather woody. -nicolous, *adj.* living in wood. -nify, *v.i.* & *t.* become or make woody. -niperdous, *adj.* destroying wood. -nite, *n.* woody brown coal. -num vitae (lig′nəm vī′tē), *Lat.*, "wood of life"; sev. W. Ind. and other varieties of guaiacum tree.

ligule (lig′ūl), *n.* thin outgrowth at junction of leaf and leafstalk. -late, *adj.* having l.; strap-shaped. -loid, *adj.* like l.

Lilliputian (lilipū′shən), *adj.* pert. to Lilliput, a country of pygmies

---

in Swift's *Gulliver's Travels* ; small ; weak ; *n.* very small or puny person.

limacine (lim'əsīn, -ĭn ; II), *adj.* pert. to slugs. **-ceous,** *adj.* **-coid** (-koid), *adj.* slug-like.

limation (līmā'shn), *n.* polishing ; smoothing ; correction of astron. errors.

limbate (lim'bāt), *adj.* having border. **-bic, -biferous,** *adj.* **-tion,** *n.*

limbo (lim'bō), *n.* oblivion ; place for unwanted or neglected things ; dwelling-place of souls of persons excluded from heaven but not through sin, as unbaptized infants, etc.

limbus (lim'bəs), *n.* border.

limicolous (līmik'ələs), *adj.* living in mud. **-line,** *adj.* living on shore ; pert. to wading birds.

liminal (lim'inəl), *adj.* pert. to or at threshold.

limitrophe (lim'itrōf), *adj.* situated on border or along boundary ; adjacent.

limivorous (līmiv'ərəs), *adj.* swallowing mud.

limn (lim), *v.t.* portray ; paint ; delineate. **-er,** *n.*

limnetic (limnet'ik), *adj.* pert. to or inhabiting fresh water. **-nobiology,** *n.* study of freshwater life. **-nology,** *n.* general study of lakes and ponds. **-nophilous,** *adj.* inhabiting freshwater ponds.

limoniad (līmō'niad), *adj.* meadow nymph.

limpid (lim'pid), *adj.* pellucid. **-ity,** *n.*

limuloid (lim'ūloid), *n.* & *adj.* (pert. to) king crab.

linaceous (līnā'shəs), *adj.* pert. to or like flax ; belonging to the flax family of plants.

linctus (lingk'təs), *n.* medicated syrup for throat.

linden (lin'dən), *n.* lime tree.

lineal (lin'iəl), *n.* pert. to or composed of lines ; in direct line of descent. **-eage,** *n.* descent from ancestor ; family tree. **-ear,** *adj.* **-eate,** *v.t.* mark with lines. **-eation,** *n.* outline ; arrangement by or in lines. **-eolate,** *adj.* marked with fine lines.

lingua franca (ling'gwə frang'kə), *n.* hybrid universal language. **l. crioula,** creole speech. **l. geral,** lingua franca, *espec.* of Brazil.

l. vulgaris, common language ; vulgar Latin.

lingual (ling'gwəl), *adj.* pert. to tongue or speech ; pronounced with tongue, as *t* ; *n.* such sound. **-guiform,** *adj.* tongue-shaped. **-guist,** *n.* speaker of foreign languages. **-guistic,** *adj.* pert. to speech or linguistics. **-guistics,** *n.* study of speech and languages. **-gulate,** *adj.* tongue-shaped; ligulate.

liparian (lipār'iən), *n.* & *adj.* (pert. to a) sea-snail.

liparoid (lip'əroid), *adj.* fatty. **-pase,** *n.* enzyme hydrolysing fats. **-pogenous,** *adj.* fat-producing.

lipography (lipog'rəfi), *n.* accidental omission of a letter or syllable.

lipoid (lip'oid), *adj.* like fat. **-al, -ic,** *adj.* **-polysis,** *n.* disintegration of fat. **-poma,** *n.* (*pl.* -mata) fatty tumour. **-pomatosis,** *n.* presence of many lipomata ; obesity.

lipothymy, -mia (lipoth'imi, -əth'im'iə), *n.* swoon. **-mial, -mic,** *adj.*

lippitude (lip'itūd), *n.* soreness or bleariness of eyes.

lipsanographer (lipsənog'rəfə), *n.* writer about relics. **-notheca,** *n.* holder for relics.

liquescent (likwes'ənt), *adj.* melting. **-nce, -ncy,** *n.*

liquidate (lik'widāt), *v.i.* & *t.* pay a debt ; wind up a company by selling assets and paying debts ; *sl.* destroy, wipe out, murder. **-tion, -tor,** *n.*

liquifacient (likwifa'shənt), *n.* liquifying agent ; drug increasing liquid excretions. **-faction,** *n.*

lissotrichous (lisot'rikəs), *adj.* having straight hair. **-chan, -chian,** *adj.* **-chy,** *n.*

literate (lit'ərət), *adj.* able to read and write ; *n.* such person ; person in holy orders without university degree. **-acy,** *n.* **-ti** (-ā'ti, -ah'ti), *n.pl.* learned persons. **-tim,** Lat. *adv.* letter by or for letter ; literally.

litharge (lith'ahj, -ahj'), *n.* lead monoxide.

lithiasis (lithī'əsis), *n.* formation of calculi in body.

lithic (lith'ik), *adj.* pert. to stone, or stone in the bladder. **-thify,** *v.i.* & *t.* solidify into rock.

lithochromy (lith'əkrōmi), *n.* painting on stone. **-matics,** *n.* chromo-lithography.

lithoclase (lith'əklās), *n.* Geol., crack in rock. **-st,** *n.* stone breaker; stone-breaking instr.

lithogenesis (lithəjen'isis), *n.* study of rock formation ; calculi formation. **-netic** (-jinet'ik), *adj.* **-nous** (-oj'inəs), *adj.* producing stone.

lithoglyph (lith'əglif), *n.* engraving on stone or gem. **-er,** *n.* **-ic, -ptic,** *adj.* **-ptics,** *n.* gem engraving.

lithograph (lith'əgraf), *v.t.* draw or reproduce on stone or metal plate with greasy substance, from which impressions are taken ; *n.* impression so taken (*abbr.* **litho, lī'thō**). **-pher, -phy,** *n.* **-phic,** *adj.*

lithoid(al) (lith'oid, -əl), *adj.* stonelike. **-olatry,** *n.* worship of stones. **-ology,** *n.* study of rocks or calculi. **-ontrystic,** *n.* & *adj.* (substance) dissolving stones in bladder. **-ophagous** *adj.* swallowing, or burrowing in, stone. **-ophilous,** *adj.* growing among stones. **-ophyte,** *n.* plant growing on rock. **-opone,** *n.* mixture of zinc sulphide and barium sulphate used instead of white lead in paints, as filler in manufacture of rubber, linoleum, etc. **-osphere,** *adj.* solid region of earth. **-otomy,** *n.* cutting for stone in bladder. **-otrity,** *n.* breaking up stone in bladder. **-ous,** *adj.* calculus-like.

litigate (lit'igāt), *v.i.* & *t.* go to law (about). **-ant,** *n.* & *adj.* (person) engaged in lawsuit. **-gious** (-ij'əs), *adj.* habitually engaging in lawsuits ; quarrelsome ; involved in litigation. **-tion,** *n.*

litmus (lit'məs), *n.* dye obtained from lichens, used in chem. tests, being turned red by acid and blue by alkali.

litotes (lītō'tēz, lit-), *n.* rhet. device of understatement.

littérateur (lētārahtēr'), Fr. *n.* man of letters.

little go (lit'l gō), *n.* responsions.

littoral (lit'ərəl), *adj.* pert. to or on seashore ; *n.* such region.

liturate (lit'ūrāt), *adj.* spotted.

liturgy (lit'əji), *n.* body of church services and ritual. **-gical** (-ō'jikl), *adj.* **-gician,** *n.* student of l. **-gics,** *n.* study of l. and worship. **-giology,** *n.* study of or treatise on l. **-gism,** *n.* keeping strictly to l.

livedo (livē'dō, lī-), *n.* blueness of skin due to congestion.

lixiviate (liksiv'iāt), *v.t.* separate by washing with solvent ; treat with lye, etc. **-tion, -tor, -n.** **-vium,** *n.* solution resulting from lixiviation ; lye.

llanero (lyahnār'ō), Sp. *n.* cowboy ; plainsman.

loadstar, -stone, see **lodestar, -stone.**

lobate (lō'bāt), *adj.* having lobes. **-bal, -bar,** *adj.* lobe-like. **-botomy,** *n.* leucotomy, also called frontal or prefrontal l. **-bular** (lob'ūlə), *adj.* lobe-shaped. **-bulate,** *adj.* having lobules. **-bule,** *n.* small lobe.

locale (lokahl'), *n.* locality ; scene.

locative (lok'ətiv), *n.* & *adj.* Gram., (case) signifying place where.

locellus (ləsel'əs), *n.* (*pl.* **-li**) compartment of cell. **-late,** *adj.* divided into l.

lochetic (ləket'ik), *adj.* waiting for prey ; in ambush.

loco (lō'kō), Sp. *adj.* insane. **l.disease,** kind of nervous disease of cattle, sheep and horses, due to eating l. weed.

loco citato (lō'kō sītā'tō), Lat., "in the place (or passage) quoted" (*abbr.* **loc. cit.**).

locomobile (lōkəmō'bīl), *n.* & *adj.* self-propelling (machine).

loculus (lok'ūləs), *n.* (*pl.* **-li**) cell ; cavity ; compartment. **-lar, -late,** *adj.* having or divided into l. **-lation,** *n.*

locum tenens (lō'kəm ten'enz, tē'-), Lat., "holding place" ; deputy.

locus (lok'əs), *n.* (*pl.* **-ci**) place ; point ; Math., path of moving point or curve. **l.citatus,** see **loco citato. l.standi,** Lat., "place of standing" ; legal status ; right to be heard in law-court.

locution (lokū'shn), *n.* manner of speech ; phrase.

lode (lōd), *n.* vein of ore. **-star,** *n.* pole-star ; guiding star. **-stone,** *n.* magnetic iron oxide ; magnet.

loess (lō'es), *n.* deposit of rich loam soil occurring in belt in N. hemisphere. **-al, -ial, -ic,** *adj.*

logarithm (log'əridhm), *n.* math. device for simplifying calculation, being the power to which a fixed number, *espec.* 10, has to be raised to equal a given number (*abbr.* log). **-al, -ic,** *adj.*

loggia (loj'ə), *n.* verandah ; open arcade.

ə = er in *father* ; ə̄ = er in *pert* ; th = th in *thin* ; dh = th in *then* ; zh = s in *pleasure* ; k = ch in *loch* ; ñ = Fr. nasal *n*; ü = Fr. *u.*

logia (lō′jiə), Gr. *n.pl.* (*sing.* -ion) sayings, *espec.* of Christ.

logistics (ləjis′tiks), *n.* billeting, supply and transport of troops.

logogogue (log′əgog), *n.* person laying down law about words.

logogram, -graph (log′əgram, -graf), *n.* sign representing word. -mmatic, *adj.* -phy, *n.* reporting, as of speeches, etc., in long-hand by relays of writers.

logomachy (logom′əki), *n.* battle of words; dispute about words. -cher, -chist, *n.* -chic (-ak′ik), *adj.*

logopaedics, -dia (logəpē′diks, -diə), *n.* study of speech defects.

logos (log′os), Gr. *n.* divine rational principle; the Word of God.

logotype (log′ətīp), *n.* single body of type containing frequently occurring word or syllable. -py, *n.*

loimic (loi′mik), *adj.* pert. to plague. -mology, *n.* study of plagues.

longe (lunj), *n.* rope or place for training horses.

longéron (lon′jərən; Fr. lawn′zhārawn), *n.* structure running length of aeroplane fuselage.

longevity (lonjev′iti), *n.* long life; length of life. -vous (-ē′vəs), *adj.*

longiloquence (lonjil′əkwəns), *n.* long-winded speech.

longitude (lon′jitūd), *n.* *Geog.,* distance along equator between meridian of a place and the Greenwich meridian; *Astron.,* distance of foot of great circle passing through object and ecliptic pole from vernal equinox, measured along ecliptic. -dinal, *adj.* pert. to l. or length; lengthwise.

loquacious (ləkwā′shəs), *adj.* talkative. -city (-as′iti), *n.*

loquat (lō′kwat, -ot), *n.* plum-like fruit of evergreen tree of Asia.

loquitur (lok′witə), Lat. *v.i.* "he (she) speaks."

loranthaceous (lōranthā′shəs), *adj.* pert. to or like mistletoe; belonging to the mistletoe family of plants.

lorate (lōr′āt), *adj.* ligulate.

lorch(a) (lawch′, -ə), *n.* light Pacific vessel with two or three masts.

lordosis (lawdō′sis), *n.* forward spinal curvature; "duck's disease." -otic (-ot′ik), *adj.*

lore (lōr), *n.* *Zoo.,* space between eye and beak or snout. -ral, *adj.*

-real, *n.* & *adj.* (scale, etc.) situated on the l.

Lorelei (lōr′əlī), Ger. *n.* siren, *espec.* of the L. rock in the Rhine.

loricate (lor′ikāt), *v.t.* cover with protective layer; encrust; plate. -tion, *n.*

loris (lōr′is), *n.* lemur of Ind., E. Ind., and Ceylon. slender l., slow l., species of l.

lory (lōr′i), *n.* small Australasian parrot, feeding on flower nectar. -rikeet, -rilet, *n.* species of l.

lota(h) (lō′tə), Anglo-Ind. *n.* globular brass waterpot.

Lothario (ləthar′iō), *n.* seducer in Rowe's play *The Fair Penitent*; rake; seducer.

lotophagous (lətof′əgəs), *adj.* lotuseating; indolent. -gi (-jī), *n.pl* lotus-eaters; day-dreamers.

louchettes (lōoshets′), Fr. *n.pl.* blinker-like spectacles for squint.

louping-ill (lōo′ping-il), *n.* paralytic disease of sheep.

louvre, -ver (lōo′və), *n.* opening fitted with sloping or swivelling slats for ventilation; such slat.

loxodograph (loksod′əgraf), *n.* device for recording ship's course. -drome, *n.* line on globe equally oblique to all meridians. -dromics, *n.* sailing on loxodromes.

loxophthalmus (loksofthal′məs), *n.* squint.

loxotic (loksot′ik), *adj.* oblique; distorted. -tomy, *n.* oblique cut in amputation.

lubra (lōo′brə), *n.* Austral. aborigine woman or girl.

lubricity (lōobris′iti), *n.* slipperiness; wiliness; indecency. -cous (lōo′brikəs), *adj.*

lucarne (lūkahn′), *n.* dormer window.

lucent (lōo′sənt), *adj.* shining; clear. -nce, -ncy, *n.*

lucernal (lūsə′nəl), *adj.* pert. to lamp.

lucerne (lōosən′), *n.* alfalfa, also called purple medic.

luciferous (lōosif′ərəs), *adj.* illuminating. -form, *adj.* like light. -fugal, -fugous, *adj.* avoiding light. -imeter, *n.* instr. measuring intensity of light, or sunlight's power of evaporation.

lucre (lōo′kə), *n.* money; gain. -crative, -criferous, *adj.* yielding profit.

lucubrate (loo͞o'kūbrāt), *v.i.* study laboriously, *espec.* at night ; work by artificial light. **-tion,** *n.* act or result of lucubrating ; over-elaborated lit. work. **-tor,** *n.* **-tory,** *n.* pert. to night work ; laborious.

luculent (loo͞o'kūlənt), *adj.* lucid ; shining.

Lucullan, -lean, -lian (lookul'ən, -iən), *adj.* pert. to Lucullus, anct. Rom. consul, noted for his elaborate banquets.

lues (lū'ēz), *n.* syphilis ; any similar disease. **-etic** (-et'ik), *adj.*

Luftpost (looft'pōst), Ger. *n.* air mail. **L.-waffe** (-vahf'ə), Ger. *n.* air force.

lugubrious (loogū'briəs), *adj.* mournful.

lumbar (lum'bə), *adj.* pert. to or near the loins.

lumbrical (lum'brikl), *n. & adj.* (pert. to) small muscle of palm or sole.

lumbricine (lum'brisin, -īn), *adj.* pert. to or like an earthworm. **-ciform, -coid,** *adj.* like an earthworm. **-cosis,** *n.* infestation with intestinal round worms.

lumen (lū'mən), *n.* (*pl.* **-mina**) unit of light : luminous energy emitted per second in a unit solid angle by a source of one candlepower.

luminescence (loominnes'əns), *n.* any emission of light not due to incandescence. **-nt,** *adj.*

luminist (loo͞o'minist), *n.* impressionist.

lunate (loo͞o'nāt), *adj.* crescentshaped. **-tion,** *n.* changes of moon ; interval between successive new moons.

lunette (loonet'), *n.* crescent-shaped ornament or object ; opening or window in vault.

lunistice (loo͞o'nistis), *n.* time each month at which moon is farthest north or south. **-titial,** *adj.*

lunkah (lung'kə), *n.* Ind. cheroot.

lunule (loo͞o'nūl), *n.* crescent-shaped mark or organ ; "half-moon" on finger nail. **-late,** *adj.* bearing l. ; like a small crescent. **-t,** *n.* crescent-shaped spot.

lupanarian (loopənar'iən), *adj.* pert. to brothel.

lupine (loo͞o'pīn), *adj.* pert. to wolves. **-picide,** *n.* killing of wolf.

lupulin (loo͞o'pūlin), *n.* yellow powder on hop cones, used as sedative.

-e, -ous, *adj.* like a hop-cluster. **-ic,** *adj.* pert. to l. or hops.

lupus (loo͞o'pəs), *n.* tuberculous skin disease, with red patches or ulcers on face. **-piform, -poid,** *adj.* like l. **-pous,** *adj.*

lurdan(e) (lə'dən), *n. & adj.* dull and lazy (person). **-ism,** *n.*

lusory (loo͞o'səri), *adj.* playful.

lustration (lustrā'shn), *n.* purifying rite, *espec.* washing. **-ral, -rical** *adj.* used in l. **-rate,** *v.t.* purify.

lustrine (lus'trin), *n.* lustrous silk or cotton material. **-ng,** *n.* lustrous silk dress fabric.

lustrum (lus'trəm), Lat. *n.* (*pl.* **-ra**) period of five years ; purification of Rom. nation every five years ; census.

lutaceous (lootā'shəs), *adj.* pert. to or made of mud.

luteous (loo͞o'tiəs), *adj.* yellow ; yellowish. **-teolous,** *adj.* somewhat yellow. **-tescent,** *adj.* yellowish.

luthern (loo͞o'thən), *n.* lucarne.

lutose (loo͞o'tōs), *adj.* covered with mud or clay.

lutrine (loo͞o'trin, -in), *adj.* pert. to or like an otter ; belonging to the otter subfamily of animals.

lutulent (loo͞o'tūlənt), *adj.* thick ; muddy. **-nce,** *n.*

luxate (luks'āt), *v.t.* displace ; dislocate. **-tion,** *n.*

lycanthrope (lī'kənthrōp, -an'-), *n.* werewolf. **-pic** (-op'ik), **-pous** (-an'thrəpəs), *adj.* **-pise,** *v.i.* change from human to wolf's shape. **-py,** *n.* change to wolf's shape or characteristics ; form of insanity in which person believes himself to be a wolf.

lycée (lē'sā), Fr. *n.* secondary school. **-ceal,** *adj.* **-ceum** (lisē'əm), *n.* place of instruction, *espec.* in philosophy.

lycoperdon (līkəpə'dən), *n.* puff-ball fungus. **-daceous, -doid,** *adj.*

lycopod (lī'kəpod), *n.* club moss. **-iaceous,** *adj.*

lycosid (lī'kəsid), *n.* wolf spider.

lyddite (lid'īt), *n.* high explosive for shells, largely picric acid.

Lydian (lid'iən), *adj.* pert. to anct. Lydia, noted for its wealth and voluptuousness ; luxurious ; effeminate.

lye (lī), *n.* strong alkaline solution, *espec.* made from wood ashes ; lixiviation solution.

ə=*er* in *father* ; ē=*er* in *pert* ; th=*th* in *thin* ; dh=*th* in *then* ; zh=*s* in *pleasure* ; k=*ch* in *loch* ; ṅ=Fr. nasal *n* ; ü=Fr. *u.*

lymph (limf), *n.* colourless blood-like fluid containing leucocytes, conveying nourishment to, and collecting waste products from, tissues. **-adenia,** *n.* inflammation of l. glands. **-adenopathy,** *n.* disease of l. glands. **-agogue,** *n.* substance .increasing l. flow. **-angial,** *adj.* pert. to l. vessels. **-angitis,** *n.* inflammation of l. vessels. **-atic,** *adj.* pert. to or conveying l.; pale; lifeless; indolent; *n.* vessel conveying l. **-atism,** *n.* hypertrophy of l. tissues; lymphatic character. **-ocyte,** *n.* l. cell. **-odermia,** *n.* disease of l. vessels of skin. **-oid, -ous,** *adj.* like l. **-oma,** *n.* lymphoid tumour.

lyncean (linsē'ən), *adj.* pert. to or like a lynx; keen-sighted.
lypemania (lipimā'niə, lī-), *n.* intense nervous depression.
lypothymia (lipəthī'miə, lī-) *n.* lypemania.
lysis (lī'sis), *n. Chem.,* disintegration or destruction; *Med.,* gradual recovery from disease. **-sigenic, -sigenous,** *adj.* formed by l. **-sin,** *n.* substance causing l. **-sogen,** *n.* antigen increasing lysin production.
lyssa (lis'ə), *n.* rabies or hydrophobia. **-sic,** *adj.* **-sophobia,** *n.* dread of l.
lyterian (lītēr'ian), *adj. Med.,* pert. to lysis.
lytic (lit'ik), *adj. Chem.,* pert. to lysis.

M

macaco (məkā'kō), *n.* species of lemur and S. Amer. monkey. **m.worm,** parasitic larva of S. Amer. botfly.
macabre (məkah'bə, -br), *adj.* gruesome; pert. to death.
macaque (məkahk'), *n.* short-tailed monkey of Asia; Barbary ape.
macarism (mak'ərizm), *n.* pleasure in another's joy; a beatitude. **-rise,** *v.t.* pronounce blessed; praise; congratulate.
macaronic (makəron'ik), *adj.* like macaroni; muddled; mixed; *n.* kind of burlesque verses in pseudo-Latin and other mixed languages. **-ism** (-sizm), *n.*
macerate (mas'ərāt), *v.i.* & *t.* soften and separate by soaking; grow or make lean; torment; mortify. **-tion, -tor,** *n.*
machairodont (məkīr'ədont), *n.* & *adj.* sabre-toothed (animal).
machete (məshēt'; Sp., mahchā'tā; Fr., məshet'), *n.* long, heavy knife, with swordlike blade.
Machiavellian (makiəvel'iən), *adj.* pert. to Niccolo Machiavelli, 15th-cent. It. statesman; unscrupulously cunning. **-ism, -lism,** *n.*
machicolation (məchikəlā'shn), *n.* apertures in parapet or floor of gallery for firing upon persons below. **-te,** *v.t.* furnish with m.
machination (makinā'shn), *n.* device; plot. **-te,** *v.i.* & *t.* plot. **-tor,** *n.*

machinule (mak'inūl), *n.* surveyor's instr. for obtaining right angle.
Mach number (mak num'bə), *n.* measure of speed of aircraft, in which speed of sound (about 770 m.p.h.) is Mach One. **M. meter,** instrument showing speeds as fractions and multiples of speed of sound.
Machtpolitik (mahkt'pōletēk), Ger. *n.* doctrine of political unscrupulousness.
macies (mā'shiēz), *n.* atrophy.
maconochie (məkon'əki), *n.* army tinned stew.
macradenous (makrad'inəs), *adj.* with large glands.
macrencephalic, -lous (makrensifal'ik, -sef'ələs), *adj.* having large brain pan.
macrobian (makrō'biən), *adj.* longevous. **-biosis,** *n.* **-biote,** *n.* longevous person. **-biotic,** *adj.* longevous, or promoting longevity. **-biotics,** *n.* art of increasing length of life.
macrocephalous (makrəsef'ələs), *adj.* large-headed. **-lus,** *n.* (*pl.* -li) such person; wart-hog genus.
macrocosm (mak'rəkozm), *n.* universe; world; large entity. **-ic(al),** *adj.* **-ology,** *n.* description of m.
macrocyte (mak'rəsīt), *n.* abnormally large red blood corpuscle. **-thaemia,** *n.* presence of m. in blood. **-tosis,** *n.* production of m.
macrodont (mak'rədont), *adj.* large-toothed. **-ia, -ism,** *n.*

macrograph (mak'rəgraf), *n.* reproduction of object natural size or only slightly magnified. **-y,** *n.* large handwriting; viewing of object with naked eye.

macrology (makrol'əji), *n.* redundancy, *espec.* pleonasm.

macromania (makrəmā'niə), *n.* delusion in which things seem larger than natural size. **-cal** (-I'əkl), *adj.*

macrometer (makrom'itə), *n.* instr. for finding size and distance of distant objects.

macron (mā'kron, mak'-), *n.* mark (‾) placed over long vowels.

macrophotograph (makrəfō'təgraf), *n.* enlarged photograph. **-y,** *n.*

macropsia, -sy (makrop'siə, -si), *n.* disease of eye causing objects to seem very large.

macropterous (makrop'tərəs), *adj.* large-winged; large-finned.

macroscian (makrosh'iən), *n.* & *adj.* (person) casting long shadow; inhabitant of polar region.

macroscopic (makrəskop'ik), *adj.* observable with naked eye; seen as a whole or in the large.

macroseism (mak'rəsīzm), *n.* severe earthquake. **-mic,** *adj.* **-mograph,** *n.* instr. recording m.

macrotia (makrō'shiə), *n.* largeness of ears.

macrotome (mak'rətōm), *n.* instr. for making large sections for anatomical study.

macrotous (makrō'təs), *adj.* having large ears.

macrural (makroor'əl), *adj.* pert. to, like or belonging to the crustacean division including lobsters, prawns, etc. **-ran,** *n.* **-rous,** *adj.* having long tail.

mactation (maktā'shn), *n.* killing; *espec.* sacrificial.

macula (mak'ūlə), *n.* (*pl.* **-ae**) coloured spot. **-r,** *adj.* **-te(d),** *adj.* bearing m.; spotted; defiled. **-tion,** *n.*

macule (mak'ūl), *n.* macula. **-liferous,** *adj.* bearing m. **-lose,** *adj.* spotted.

madar, *see* **mudar.**

madarosis (madərō'sis), *n.* loss of eyelashes or eyebrows. **-otic** (-ot'ik), *adj.*

madescent (mədes'ənt), *adj.* growing damp.

madrasah (mədras'ə), *n.* Moham.

college, or school attached to mosque.

madrepore (mad'ripor), *n.* stony coral. **-rian, -ric, -riform,** *adj.*

madrigal (mad'rigəl), *n.* polyphonic part song, in five or six parts. **-ian** (-ā'liən), *adj.* **-ist,** *n.* composer of m.

madroña, -ño (mədrōn'yə, -yō), *n.* N. Amer. evergreen tree. **m. apples,** red berries of the m.

maelstrom (māl'strom), *n.* whirlpool, *espec.* off W. coast of Norway.

maenad (mē'nad), *n.* (*pl.* **-es**) bacchante; wildly excited woman. **-ic,** *adj.* **-ism,** *n.*

maestro (mī'strō), Sp. *n.* (*fem.* **-tra**) teacher; master, *espec.* of music. **m. di capella,** choirmaster.

mafia, -ffi- (mah'fiə), It. *n.* Sicilian secret society of criminals; antagonism towards law and police.

maffick (maf'ik), *v.i.* celebrate noisily and wildly. **-er,** *n.*

magas (mā'gas), *n.* bridge of stringed mus. instr.; monochord. **-gadis** (mag'ədis), *n.* monochord; anct. bridged instr. for playing octaves.

magi (mā'jī), *n.pl.* (*sing.* **-gus, -gəs**) anct. Pers. priests; the wise men present at Epiphany. **-an,** *n.* & *adj.*

magirics (məjir'iks), *n.* art of cookery. **-rology** (majirol'əji), *n.*

magistrand (maj'istrand), *n.* Scot. university student in fourth year.

magma (mag'mə), *n.* (*pl.* **-ta**) paste of mixed solid materials; *Geol.,* molten rock within the earth. **-tic** (-at'ik), *adj.*

magnanerie (manyan'rē), Fr. *n.* art or place of rearing silkworms.

magnanimous (magnan'iməs), *adj.* high-minded; noble; liberal. **-mity** (-ənim'iti), *n.*

magnesia (magnē'shə), *n.* magnesium oxide, used as antacid and insulating material. **m. alba,** a carbonate of magnesium, used as mild purge. **m. magma,** milk of m. **-n,** *adj.* **-sic,** *adj.* **-sium** (-ziəm), *n.* white metal used in alloys, signal lights and flashlights.

magneto (magnē'tō), *n.* small dynamo generating current producing spark that ignites fuel vapours in internal combustion engine.

magneton (mag'niton), *n.* unit of magnetic moment.

Magnificat (magnif′ikat), *n.* canticle beginning "My soul doth magnify the Lord" (Luke i), sung at Evensong ; any song of praise.

magniloquent (magnil′əkwənt), *adj.* using high-flown language ; bombastic. **-nce,** *n.*

magnum (mag′nəm), *n.* bottle holding half-gallon. **m.opus** (-ōpəs), *Lat.*, "great work" ; finest achievement, *espec.* literary.

mahajun, -jan (məhah′jən), Hind. *n.* moneylender.

mahalla, me- (məhal′ə), Arab. *n.* camp ; garrison ; district.

mahatma (məhat′mə), *n.* wise man ; person of noble intellect. **-ism,** *n.*

Mahdi (mah′di), *n.* Moham. Messiah.

mah-jongg (mah-jong′), *n.* anct. Chin. game played with domino-like pieces called "tiles."

mahout (məhowt′), *n.* driver of elephant.

mahseer, -sir, -sur (mah′sēr, -sə), *n.* Ind. freshwater food fish.

maidan (mīdahn′), Anglo-Ind. *n.* park ; parade ground ; market-place.

maieutic (mā ū′tik), *adj.* pert. to Socratic method. **-s,** *n.* Socratic method ; midwifery.

mainour (mā′nə), *n.* stolen property discovered on thief's person. **in** *or* **with the m.,** in the act ; red-handed.

maison (mā′zawn), Fr. *n.* house. **m. de santé** (-də sahn′tā), nursing home ; private asylum. **m.-dieu** (-dyə), hospital.

maître (mā′tr), Fr. *n.* master ; title of respect for barristers, etc. (*abbr.* **Mᵉ.**). **m. d'armes** (-dahrm), fencing master. **m. de danse** (də dahns), dancing master. **m. d'hôtel** (-dōtel′), major-domo.

majolica (majol′ika), *n.* elaborate, highly-coloured, glazed It. pottery ; faience. **-list,** *n.* maker of m.

majoon (məjoon′), Hind. *n.* narcotic mixture of drugs.

major-domo (mā′jə-dō′mō), *n.* steward ; head servant ; butler.

majuscule (məjus′kūl), *n.* (*pl.* **-lae, -s**) capital or other large letter. **-lar,** *adj.*

mako (mah′kō), *n.* large shark of Australasia, also called blue pointer. **m.-mako,** *n.* wineberry tree or bellbird of N.Z.

malachite (mal′əkīt), *n.* green ornamental stone, an ore of copper.

malacia (mala′shiə), *n.* softening of tissue ; craving for a certain food. **-codermous,** *adj.* having soft skin. **-coid,** *adj.* soft in substance. **-cology,** *n.* study of molluscs. **-cophonous,** *adj.* soft-voiced. **-lactic,** *adj.* emollient.

maladroit (mal′ədroit), *adj.* awkward ; gauche.

mala fide (mā′lə fī′dē), *Lat.*, "in bad faith." **m.fides** (-ēz), bad faith.

Malagasy (maləgas′i), *n.* native or language of Madagascar.

malagma (məlag′mə), *n.* (*pl.* **-ta**) emollient plaster.

malaise (malāz′), *n.* uneasiness ; indefinable feeling of illness or discomfort.

malapropos (maləpropō′), *adj.* & *adv.* not apropos ; inopportune(ly) ; *n.* such thing or remark. **-pism,** *n.* ludicrous misuse of long words, or such word misused, as by Mrs. Malaprop in Sheridan's *The Rivals*.

malax (mā′laks), *v.t.* soften by kneading or diluting. **-age** (mal′-), *n.* such softening of clay. **-ate,** *v.t.* **-ation, -ator,** *n.*

mal de mer (mal də mār), Fr. *n.* seasickness. **m. du pays** (-dü pā′ē), homesickness.

malediction (malidik′shn), *n.* curse. **-tive, -tory,** *adj.*

malefic(ent) (məlef′ik, -isənt), *adj.* evil ; harmful. **-cence,** *n.*

malfeasance (malfē′zəns), *n.* misconduct by official. **-nt,** *n.* & *adj.*

malgré (mal′grā), Fr. *prep.* in spite of. **m.lui** (-lwē), in spite of oneself ; against one's desires or beliefs.

maliferous (malif′ərəs), *adj.* harmful ; unhealthy.

malinger (məling′gə), *v.i.* feign illness, *espec.* to evade duty. **-er, -y,** *n.*

malism (mā′lizm), *n.* belief that world is bad or evil.

malison (mal′izn), *n.* curse.

mallard (mal′əd), *n.* common wild duck, *espec.* drake.

malleable (mal′iəbl), *adj.* capable of being hammered or pressed into shape ; pliable ; weak-willed. **-bility,** *n.* **-leation,** *n.* dent.

mallee (mal′ē), Austral. *n.* a eucalyptus shrub ; thick growth of such shrubs ; area covered by such growth.

---

hat, bah, hāte, hāre, crawl ; pen, ēve, hēre ; it, īce, fīre ; on, bōne, boil, bōre, howl ; foot, foōd, boōr, hull, tūbe, pūre.

malleiform (məlē'ifawm, mal'ii-), adj. hammer-shaped.

mallophagan (məlof'əgən), n. bird louse. -gous, adj.

malloseismic (maləsīz'mik), adj. frequently suffering from severe earthquakes.

malmsey (mahm'zi), n. sweet, scented wine.

malo animo (mā'lō an'imō), Lat., "with evil intent."

malvaceous (malvā'shəs), adj. pert. to or like a mallow; belonging to mallow family of plants.

malvasia (malvəsē'ə), n. grape from which malmsey is made. -n, adj.

malversation (malvəsā'shn), n. misconduct; corruption; misuse of public or other funds.

malvoisie (mal'voizi, -vəzi), n. malmsey.

mamba (mam'bah), n. venomous cobra-like snake of Africa; tree-cobra.

mameluke (mam'ilook), n. fighting slave, espec. of Egypt from 13th to 19th cent.; white slave.

mamma (mam'ə), n. (pl. -ae) milk-secreting gland; breast; teat.

mammal (mam'əl), n. (pl. -ia, -ā'liə; -s) any animal that suckles young. -ian (-ā'liən), n. & adj. -ogy (-al'əji), n. study of m.

mammary (mam'əri), adj. pert. to mamma. -te, adj. having mammae.

mammiferous (mamif'ərəs), adj. having breasts. -miform, adj. shaped like breast or nipple.

mammilla (mamil'ə), n. (pl. -ae) nipple. -liform, -loid, adj. like m. -r, -ry, adj. -te, adj. having m., or similar outgrowths. -tion, n.

mammon (mam'ən), n. riches; worship or god of riches; the wealthy classes. -iacal, -ic, adj. -ism, -ite, n. -olatry, n. worship of riches.

mana (mah'nah), n. spirit of nature as object of veneration.

manal (mā'nəl), adj. pert. to the hand.

mañana (mahnyah'nah), Sp. n. & adv. to-morrow.

manatee (manətē'), n. sea-cow. -tine (man'-), adj.

mancinism (man'sinizm), n. left-handedness.

manciple (man'sipl), n. college steward.

Mancunian (mankū'niən), n. & adj. (resident or native) of Manchester.

mandament (man'dəmənt), n. command.

mandamus (mandā'məs), Lat., "we command"; Law, Crown writ commanding performance of an action.

mandarin (man'dərin), n. higher public official of Chin. empire; chief dialect of China; small Chin. orange. -ate, n. office, rule or body of m. -ic, adj. -ism, n. rule by m.; bureaucracy.

mandat (mahn'dah), Fr. n. order; mandate; proxy; currency bill issued during Fr. revolution.

mandate (man'dāt), n. commission to perform act or rule for another; command; instruction, espec. to political representative. -d, adj. held or ruled under m. -tary, n. holder of m. -tive, adj. pert. to command. -tory, adj. obligatory.

M & B, abbr. of May and Baker, manufacturing chemists; pop. name for sulpha-drugs, espec. sulphanilamide (M & B 693).

mandible (man'dibl), n. lower jaw; either part of bird's beak or insect's mouth parts. -bular (-ib'ūlə), adj. -bulate, adj. having m. -buliform, adj. like m.

mandil (man'dil), Arab. n. turban.

mandorla (mahndor'lah), It. n. any almond-shaped object or ornament.

mandragora (mandrag'ərə), n. mandrake.

mandrake (man'drāk), n. S. Eur. plant with large forked root, believed to aid conception.

mandrel (man'drəl), n. spindle supporting work in lathe, etc.

mandriarch (man'driahk), n. founder or head of monastic order.

mandrill (man'dril), n. W. African baboon with blue markings on face and red posteriors.

manducate (man'dūkāt), v.t. masticate; eat. -tion, n. -tory, adj.

mane (mā'nē), Lat. adv. in the morning.

manège (mənāzh'), Fr. n. horsemanship; teaching or school of horsemanship.

manent (mā'nent), Lat. v. "they remain."

manes (mā'nēz), Lat. n.pl. spirits of dead; ghosts.

manet (mā'net), Lat. v. "he (she) remains."

---

mangel-wurzel (mang'gəl-wȯ'zəl), *n.* kind of large beet.

mango (mang'gō), *n.* (*pl.* -es) pearlike stoned tropical fruit. -steen, *n.* large reddish orange-like fruit of E. Ind.

mangold (mang'gold), *n.* mangelwurzel.

mangrove (mang'grōv), *n.* tropical swamp tree with aerial roots.

manicate (man'ikāt), *adj.* having dense woolly growth which can be peeled off.

manichord (man'ikawd), *n.* clavichord.

manifesto (manifes'tō), *n.* public declaration of policy.

maniform (man'ifawm), *adj.* handshaped.

manioc (man'iok, mā'-), *n.* cassava.

maniple (man'ipl), *n.* narrow embroidered band worn hanging from left arm by celebrant priest.

manism (mah'nizm), *n.* belief in mana.

manjak (man'jak), *n.* kind of asphalt of Barbados.

manometer (mənom'ltə), *n.* instr. measuring pressure of gases, or blood-pressure. -tric(al) (-et'rik, -l), *adj.* -try, *n.*

manqué (mahn'kā), Fr. *adj.* (*fem.* -ée) "lacking"; defective; having failed to achieve ambition; falling short of hopes or expectations.

manque (mahṅk), Fr. *n.* bet in roulette on low numbers, from 1 to 18.

mansard (man'sahd), *n.* kind of roof with two slopes, the upper being the less steep; garret formed within such roof.

mansuetude (man'switūd), *n.* sweetness of temper; tameness.

mantic (man'tik), *adj.* pert. to or having powers of prophecy or divination; divinely inspired. -ism (-sizm), *n.* divination.

manticore (man'tikōr), *n.* fabulous monster with man's head, lion's body and dragon's tail.

mantid (man'tid), *n.* & *adj.* (pert. to) mantis.

mantilla (mantil'ə), *n.* light cloak, cape or veil, *espec.* of Spain.

mantis (man'tis), *n.* (*pl.* -tes) grasshopper-like insect, having forelegs folded as if in prayer.

mantissa (mantis'ə), *n.* decimal part of logarithm.

mantistic (mantis'tik), *adj.* mantic.

manubrial (manū'briəl), *adj.* handleshaped.

manuduction (manūduk'shn), *n.* careful guidance; leading by the hand; introduction; guide. -tory, *adj.*

manuka (mah'nūkə), Maori *n.* bush with tea-like leaves; "tea-tree."

manumit (manūmit'), *v.t.* liberate (slave). -mission, *n.* -missive, *adj.*

manu propria (mā'nū prō'priə), *Lat.,* "with one's own hand."

manustupration (manūstūprā'shn), *n.* masturbation.

maquette (maket'), Fr. *n.* rough sketch or model.

maqui(s) (mak'ē), *n.* thicket of shrubs of Mediterranean coastland and central Corsica, refuge of outlaws; "underground" resistance movement in German-occupied France and Belgium (1940–45). -sard (-zahr), *n.* member of m.

marabou (mar'əbōō), *n.* stork-like bird; adjutant bird; its down used in millinery.

marabout (mar'əbōōt), *n.* Moham. monk, saint or hermit; thin, downy silk.

marantic (mər07an'tik), *adj.* marasmic.

marascha (məras'kə), *n.* bitter wild cherry. -chino (-əskē'nō), *n.* liqueur distilled from juice of m.

marasmus (məraz'məs), *n.* intense emaciation due to malnutrition. -mic, -mous, *adj.* -moid, *adj.* like m.

marcasite (mah'kəsēt), *n.* crystallised iron pyrites, used in jewelry. -tic (-it'ik), *adj.*

marcescent (mahses'ənt), *n.* & *adj.* (plant with leaves) withering but remaining on plant. -nce, *n.*

Märchen (mār'kən), Ger. *n.* fairy or folk tale.

marcor (mah'kōr), *n.* marasmus.

Mardi gras (mahr'di grah), *Fr.,* "fat Tuesday"; Shrove Tuesday, a carnival day.

mare clausum (mār'ē klaw'səm), *Lat.,* "closed sea"; territorial waters. **m. liberum** (-lib'ərəm, lī-), "open sea"; sea outside territorial waters.

maremma (mərem'ə), It. *n.* (*pl.* -me) marsh; landes; miasma. -tic, *adj.*

margaritaceous (mahgərita'shəs), *adj.* pearl-like. -tiferous, *adj.* yielding pearls.

margin (mah'jin), *n. Comm.*, deposit of cash held by broker as security or instalment of purchase price; amount remaining to, or to be paid by, client at termination of account; speculation partly financed by broker. -al, *adj.*; m.utility, *Econ.*, minimum usefulness that will cause production of commodity, etc., to continue.

marginalia (mahjinā'liə), Lat. *n.pl.* notes in margin.

margrave (mah'grāv), *n.* Ger. title of nobility, equiv. of marquess. -vial, *adj.* -viate, *n.* jurisdiction of m. -vine, *n.* m.'s wife or woman having power of m.

maricolous (mərik'ələs), *adj.* inhabiting the sea. -rigenous, *adj.* produced by or in sea. -rigraph (mar'-), *n.* tide gauge.

marijuana (mariwah'nə), *n.* dried leaves and flowers of cannabis (Indian hemp) smoked as narcotic drug in cigarettes.

marimba (mərim'bə), *n.* kind of xylophone.

marinate (mar'ināt), *v.t.* steep in brine. -nade, *n.* brine for steeping fish, etc.

Mariolater (mārriol'ətə), *n.* worshipper of the Virgin Mary. -trous, *adj.* -try, *n.*

marital (mar'itəl), *adj.* connubial; pert. to husband. -ity, *n.* excessive fondness for husband.

markhor (mah'kōr), *n.* wild goat of N.W. India.

marline (mah'lin), *n.* line of two loosely twisted strands. m.-spike, *n.* pointed tool for unravelling m. in splicing.

marmarise (mah'məriz), *v.t.* transform into marble. -rosis, *n.*

marmoreal (mahmōr'iəl), *adj.* pert. to or like marble. -raceous, *adj.* -rate, *adj.* veined like marble. -ric, *adj.* pert. to marble.

marmot (mah'mot), *n.* squirrel-like rodent of Pyrenees and Alps; woodchuck.

marque (mahk), *n.* taking possession of object as pledge or reprisal. letters of m., authorisation by Crown of seizure of foreign goods, etc., as reprisal; privateer's commission.

marquetry (mah'kitri), *n.* art of inlaying; inlaid work.

marrano (mərah'nō), Sp. *n.* Jew converted to Christianity, *espec.* merely to evade persecution. -nise, *v.t.* -nism, *n.*

marron (mar'awn), Fr. *n.* chestnut. -s glacés (-glas'ā), chestnuts preserved or coated with sugar.

marsala (mahsah'lə), *n.* sherry-like wine of Sicily.

marsupial (mahsū'piəl), *n.* & *adj.* (animal) carrying young in abdominal pouch. -pium, *n.* (*pl.* -ia) m.'s pouch of skin.

martello mahtel'ō), *adj.* app. to small round coastal defence fort.

marten (mah'tin, -tən), *n.* large weasel-like animal, with fine fur; its fur, called sable. pine-m., m. of Eur. pine woods; Amer. sable. stone-m., m. of Eur. beech woods.

martinet (mahtinet'), *n.* strict enforcer of discipline.

martingale (mah'tinggāl), *n.* check-rein holding horse's head down; betting system, *espec.* of doubling stakes.

martlet (máht'lit), *n.* martin (bird); *Her.*, footless, beakless bird, denoting fourth son.

martyrolatry (mahtərol'ətri), *n.* excessive veneration of martyrs. -ology, *n.* study of, treatise on, or list of, martyrs.

Marxian (mahks'iən), *adj.* pert. to 19th-cent. Ger. communist writer, Karl Marx, and his doctrines; communist. -xism, *n.* -xist, *n.* adherent of M. doctrine.

mascara (məskah'rə), *n.* dark dye for colouring eyelashes.

mascle (mas'kəl), *n.* diamond-shaped scale or plate. -d, *adj.* covered with m.

mashie (mash'i), *n.* broad-bladed iron golf club. m. niblick, club with head partaking of both m. and niblick.

masjid (mus'jid), *n.* Moham. mosque.

masochism (mas'əkizm), *n.* taking pleasure in suffering pain, *espec.* inflicted by sexual partner. -ist, *n.* -istic, *adj.*

masseter (məsē'tə), *n.* muscle raising lower jaw.

massif (mas'if; Fr., masēf'), *n.* main mountain group or region.

massotherapy (masəther'əpi), *n.* med. treatment by massage.

---

mastic (mas'tik), *n.* resin of S. Eur. tree, used in varnishes, etc.; any sticky paste.

mastigophoric (mastigəfor'ik), *adj.* carrying a whip.

mastitis (mastī'tis), *n.* inflammation of breast or milk gland.

mastodon (mas'tədən), *n.* extinct elephant-like animal. -toid, *adj.*

mastoid (mas'toid), *adj.* nipple- or breast-like; denoting such bony outgrowth behind ear. -ectomy, *n.* operation to remove m. bone. -itis, *n.* inflammation of m. cells. -otomy, *n.* surg. incision into m.

mastology (mastol'əji), *n.* mammalogy.

masturbate (mas'təbāt), *v.i.* practise masturbation. -tion, *n.* sexual self-abuse. -tional, -tic (-at'ik), -tory, *adj.* -tor, *n.*

matara(h) (mat'ərə), Arab. *n.* water-bottle or -skin.

maté (mah'tā, mat'-), *n.* Paraguay tea (plant and beverage).

matelassé (matlah'sā), Fr. *adj.* with quilting-like ornamentation.

Mater dolorosa (mā'tə dōlərō'sə, mah'-), *Lat.*, "sorrowing mother"; the Virgin Mary.

materia (mətēr'iə), Lat. *n.* matter. m. ex qua, material out of which (something is made). m. in qua, material in which (something subsists). m.medica, study of med. remedies.

mathesis (məthē'sis), *n.* learning; wisdom; mathematics. -etic (-et'ik), *adj.*

matin (mat'in), *adj.* pert. to morning. -al, *adj.* -s, *n.* morning prayer.

matrass, -ti- (mat'ras), *n.* long-necked round-bodied chem. flask; closed glass tube.

matriarch (mā'triahk), *n.* mother ruling family or group. -al, *adj.* -ate, *n.* -y, *n.* inheritance in female line.

matric(al) (mā'trik, mat'rikl), *adj.* pert. to matrix or womb.

matricide (mā'trisīd), *n.* killing or killer of own mother. -dal, *adj.*

matricular (matrik'ūlə), *adj.* matric.

matriculate (mətrik'ūlāt), *v.i.* & *t.* admit, or obtain admission by passing examination, to university as student. -lant, *n.* matriculating student. -tion, *n.* act of matriculating; examination necessary to m. -tory, *adj.*

matriherital (mātriher'itəl, mat'-), *adj.* pert. to inheritance in female line. -rilineal, *adj.* tracing descent in female line. --rilocal, *adj.* pert: to marriage in which husband goes to reside with wife and her family. -ripotestal, *adj.* pert. to mother's power.

matrix (mā'triks), *n.* (*pl.* -ices) womb; mould for casting; cement.

matroclinous (matrəklī'nəs, mat'-), *adj.* inheriting characteristics from mother. -ny, *n.*

mattock (mat'ək), *n.* pick-like digging tool.

mattoid (mat'oid), *n.* congenital idiot.

maturate (mat'ūr āt), *v.i.* & *t.* come mature or ripe; cause to suppurate. -tion, *n.* -tive, *adj.*

maturescent (matūres'ənt), *adj.* becoming mature. -nce, *n.*

matutinal (matūtī'nəl, -tū'tin-), *adj.* pert. to or occurring in morning.

maudlin (mawd'lin), *n.* sentimental; tearful, *espec.* when drunk.

maugre, -ger (maw'gə), *prep.* in spite of.

maulstick (mawl'stik), *n.* painter's stick for steadying the hand.

maund (mawnd), Anglo-Ind. *n.* measure of weight, equiv. of from 25 to 82 lbs.

maundy (mawn'di), *n. orig.*, ceremony of washing of feet of poor by sovereign; *mod.*, alms-giving by sovereign in its stead. m.money, such alms. m.Thursday, Thursday before Easter, on which m. ceremony was performed and m. money is distributed.

mausoleum (mawsəlē'əm), *n.* monumental tomb, *espec.* elaborate. -ean, *adj.*

mauvais (mō'vā), Fr. *adj.* (*fem.* -e) bad; wicked. m.sujet (-sü'zhā), "bad or wicked subject" or person.

mavis (mā'vis), *n.* song- or missel-thrush.

maxilla (maksil'ə), *n.* (*pl.* -ae) jaw-bone, *espec.* bearing upper molars and canines. -ry (maks'-), *adj.*

maximalism (maks'iməlizm), *n.* uncompromising adherence to maximum demands, as in trade dispute, etc. -ist, *n.* radical; extremist.

maxwell (maks'wəl), *n.* unit of magnetic flux.

maya (mah'yah), Hind. *n.* magic;

creative power of universe ; God's power of manifestation.

mayhem (mā'həm), *n. Law,* maiming.

mazarine (mazərēn'), *n.* & *adj.* (of) reddish-blue hue.

mazurka (məzē'kə), *n.* Polish dance in slow waltz time.

mazzard (maz'əd), *n.* wild sweet cherry.

meable (mē'əbl), *adj.* easily penetrable.

mea culpa (mē'ə kul'pə), *Lat.,* "my fault."

mead (mēd), *n.* strong drink of fermented honey and water.

meatus (miā'təs), *n.* passage of the body. **-tal,** *adj.*

mechanolater (mekənol'ətə), *n.* worshipper of machines. **-nomorphic,** *adj.* having form of machine. **-notherapy,** *n.* med. treatment by mechanical means.

mecometer (mikom'itə), *n.* length-measuring instr. **-try,** *n.*

meconology (mēkənol'əji), *n.* treatise on opium. **-nophagist,** *n.* consumer of opium.

meden agan (māden' ah'gahn, mē'den ag'än), *Gr.,* "nothing too much" ; the golden mean.

medianic (mēdian'ik), *adj.* pert. to spiritualist medium, or prophet. **-nimic,** *adj.* **-nimity, -nity,** *n.*

mediastinum (mēdiəstī'nəm), *n.* (*pl.* **-na**) chest cavity containing heart. **-nal,** *adj.* **-nitis,** *n.* inflammation of tissue enclosing organs in m.

medicaster (med'ikastə), *n.* quack doctor.

medieval, -iaeval (mediē'vəl), *adj.* pert. to the Middle Ages. **-ism,** *n.*

medlar (med'lə), *n.* crab-apple-like fruit and tree.

medresseh (medres'ā), *n.* madrasah.

medulla (midul'ə), *n.* marrow or pith. **m.oblongata,** posterior part of brain joining it to spinal cord. **m.spinalis,** spinal cord. **-lose, -ry,** *adj.*

meerkat (mēr'kat), S. African *n.* mongoose-like animal ; suricate.

meerschaum (mēr'shm), *n.* white fine clayey silicate of magnesium ; smoking pipe made or partly made of m.

megacephalic (megəsifal'ik), *adj.* having large head.

megaceros (migas'iros), *n.* extinct giant deer ; Irish elk. **-rine, -rotine** (-ser'ətin), *adj.*

megachiropteran (megəkīrop'tərən), *n.* & *adj.* (pert. to a) fruit bat. **-rous,** *adj.*

megadont (meg'ədont), *adj.* having large teeth.

megalith (meg'əlith), *n.* any large prehistoric stone monument. **-ic,** *adj.*

megalocyte (meg'ələsīt), *n.* macrocyte.

megalomania (megələmā'niə), *n.* form of insanity in which patient believes himself to be person of great importance ; mania for doing grand actions. **-c,** *n.* **-cal** (-ī'əkl), *adj.*

megalophonous (megəlof'ənəs), *adj.* high-sounding ; having loud voice. **-nic** (-əfon'ik), *adj.*

megalophthalmus (megəlofthal'məs), *n.* state of having large eyes. **-pic** (-op'ik), *adj.* large-eyed ; pert. to megalops.

megalopolis (megəlop'əlis), *n.* vast city. **-litan** (-ol'itən), *adj.*

megalops (meg'əlops), *n.* larval stage of crab.

megalosaur(us) (meg'ələsōr, -ōr'əs), *n.* huge carnivorous dinosaur. **-rian, -roid,** *adj.*

megameter (megam'itə), *n.* instr. for finding longitude from stellar observations.

megapod (meg'əpod), *adj.* having large feet ; *n.* such bird of Australasia, as jungle fowl, brush turkey, etc.

megaprosopous (megəpros'əpəs), *adj.* having large face.

megapterine (megap'tərin, -in), *n.* & *adj.* (pert. to a) humpback whale.

megascope (meg'əskōp), *n.* magnifying magic lantern. **-opic** (-op'ik), *adj.* magnified ; macroscopic.

megaseism (meg'əsizm), *n.* macroseism.

megatherium (megəthēr'iəm), *n.* fossil sloth-like animal. **-re,** *n.* **-rian, -rine, -rioid,** *adj.*

megatherm (meg'əthəm), *n.* plant thriving only in tropical heat and moisture. **-ic,** *adj.*

megaton (meg'ətun), *n.* measure of explosive force of atomic and hydrogen bombs, equal to that of 1 million tons of T.N.T.

megohm (meg'ōm), *n.*-elec. unit, equiv. of one million ohms.

megrim (mē'grim), *n.* neuralgic pain

over eyebrow. **-s,** *n.pl.* state of nervous depression; the "dumps"; staggers in horses.

mehari (məhah'ri), *n.* racing dromedary. **-st,** *n.* soldier riding m.

mehtar (mā'tə), Hind. *n.* houseservant; groom.

meiosis (mī ō'sis), *n.* litotes; misrepresentation of thing as being less than its actual size or importance; *Biol.,* nuclear division with halving of chromosome number. **-otic** (-ot'ik), *adj.*

mekometer (mikom'itə), *n.* kind of range-finder.

melaena (milē'nə), *n.* black vomit or bowel discharge. **-nic,** *adj.*

melalgia (milal'jiə), *n.* pain in limbs. **-agra,** *n.*

melampodium (melampō'diəm), *n.* Christmas rose.

mélange (mā'lahnzh), Fr. *n.* mixture.

melanin (mel'ənin), *n.* dark or black pigment of body. **-nian** (-ā'niən), **-nic** (-an'ik), *adj.* darkskinned. **-niferous,** *adj.* containing m. **-nism,** *n.* abnormal blackness of skin or plumage; extreme darkness of complexion and hair. **-no,** *n.* extremely dark person. **-nochrous, -nochroic,** *adj.* darkskinned. **-nocomous, -notrichous,** *adj.* dark-haired. **-noderma, -nodermia,** *n.* abnormal blackness of skin. **-noid,** *adj.* **-nopathy, -nosis,** *n.* disease marked by deposition of m. in tissues. **-nous,** *adj.* with black hair and skin.

melasma (milaz'mə), *n.* dark patch of skin.

meldometer (meldom'itə), *n.* instr. for finding melting points.

meleagrine (meliag'rīn, -in), *adj.* pert. to or like a turkey; belonging to turkey genus of birds.

mêlée (mel'ā, -lē; Fr., mālā'), *n.* confused fight; struggling crowd.

melic (mel'ik), *adj.* pert. to song; lyric; *n.* such poetry, *espec.* of anct. Greece.

meliceris, -ra (meliser'is, -ə), *n.* tumour or exudation of honeylike matter. **-ric, -rous,** *adj.*

melichrous (mel'ikrəs), *adj.* honeycoloured.

meline (mē'līn, -in), *adj.* canaryyellow.

melinite (mel'inīt), *n.* explosive resembling lyddite.

meliorism (mē'liərizm), *n.* belief that world and Man tend to grow better. **-ist,** *n.* **-istic,** *adj.* **-rity,** *n.* inproved state.

meliphagous (milif'əgəs), *adj.* feeding on honey.

melisma (miliz'mə), *n.* (*pl.* **-ta**) melody; song; melodic ornamentation. **-tic** (-at'ik), *adj.* in florid style, *espec.* of singing one syllable on a number of notes. **-tics,** *n.* such florid singing.

melitaemia, -thaem- (melitē'miə, -thē'-), *n.* presence of excess of sugar in blood. **-turia,** *n.* presence of sugar in urine.

melittology (melitol'əji), *n.* study of bees. **-gist,** *n.*

melituria (melitūr'iə), *n.* sugar diabetes. **-ric,** *adj.*

mellaginous (melaj'inəs), *adj.* pert. to or like honey. **-leous,** *adj.* like or containing honey.

mellifluent, -uous (melif'looənt, -əs), *adj.* sweet-sounding; flowing with honey. **-ferous,** *adj.* honeyproducing. **-lisonant,** *adj.* sweetsounding. **-lisugent,** *adj.* sucking or eating honey. **-livorous,** *adj.* eating honey.

melologue (mel'əlog), *n.* recitation with mus. accompaniment. **-omania,** *n.* mania for music.

melongena (melənjē'nə), *n.* eggplant.

melophonic (meləfon'ik), *adj.* pert. to music. **-poeia** (-pē'yə), *n.* composition of music.

melton (mel'tən), *n.* short-napped woollen tailoring material. **-ian** (-ō'niən), *adj.* pert. to Melton Mowbray, Leics., and its hunting; hunter.

memento mori (mimen'tō mōr'ī), *Lat.,* "remember to die"; reminder of death, or of shortness of life.

memorabilia (memərəbil'iə), Lat. *n.pl.* memorable things; records.

memoriter (memōr'itə), Lat. *adv.* from memory; by heart.

memsahib (mem'sahib), Ind. *n.* title of respect for white women; madam.

ménage (mā'nahzh), Fr. *n.* household; art of housekeeping.

menald (men'əld), *adj.* speckled.

mendacious (mendā'shəs), *adj.* telling lies, *espec.* habitually. **-city** (-as'iti), *n.*

Mendelian (mendē'lian), *adj.* pert. to Gregor Mendel, and his theory of inheritance ; *n.* believer in his theory. **-lism** (men'dəlizm), *n.*

mendicant (men'dikənt), *n.* beggar ; *adj.* begging. **-city** (-is'iti), **-ncy,** *n.*

menhir (men'hēr), *n.* upright monolith.

meninges (menin'jēz), *n.pl.* membranes enclosing brain. **-geal, -gic,** *adj.* **-gitis,** *n.* inflammation of m.

meniscus (minis'kəs), *n.* (*pl.* **-ci**) crescent-shaped object, *espec.* cartilage of knee ; concavo-convex lens ; curved surface of liquid in a tube. **-cal, -cate, -coid,** *adj.* **-ciform,** *adj.* shaped like m. **-citis,** *n.* inflammation of m. of knee.

menology (minol'əji), *n.* calendar of months ; calendar of saints' days.

menopause (men'əpawz), *n.* cessation of menstruation in middle age ; "change of life." **-sic,** *adj.*

mensal (men'səl), *adj.* pert. to or for table ; monthly.

menses (men'sēz), *n.pl.* monthly discharge of blood, etc., from womb.

menstrual (men'strooəl), *adj.* monthly ; lasting a month ; pert. to menses ; solvent. **-ate,** *v.i.* discharge menses. **-ation,** *n.* **-uous,** *adj.* pert. to or discharging menses. **-uum,** *n.* (*pl.* **-ua**) solvent.

mensual (men'sūəl), *adj.* pert. to month ; monthly.

mensuration (mensūrā'shn), *n.* calculation of measurements. **-rable,** *adj.* measurable ; *Mus.*, rhythmic ; composed in first anct. form of notation. **-tive,** *adj.* of use in measuring.

mentation (mentā'shn), *n.* cerebration. **-tiferous,** *adj.* telepathic.

mentor (men'tor), *n.* adviser ; teacher. **-ial,** *adj.*

mepacrine (mep'əkrēn, -in), *n.* synthetic anti-malarial drug formerly called atebrin.

mephitis (mifi'tis), *n.* foul exhalation from earth ; stink. **-tic** (-it'ik), *adj.* ; **m.air,** air devoid of oxygen. **-tism,** *n.* poisoning by m.

meralgia (miral'jiə), *n.* neuralgia of thigh.

mercantile (mɜ'kəntīl), *adj.* pert. to trading and merchants. **m.system,** economic or political system aiming at increase in national strength through trade. **-lism,** *n.* commer-

cial practice ; practice of m. system. **-lity,** *n.*

mercer (mɜ'sə), *n.* dealer in textiles. **-ise,** *v.t.* make stronger and lustrous by treating with caustic alkali. **-y,** *n.*

mercurial (məkūr'iəl), *adj.* pert. to or containing mercury ; lively in mind ; volatile. **-rous,** *adj.* pert. to mercury.

merdivorous (mədiv'ərəs), *adj.* eating dung.

meretricious (meritrish'əs), *adj.* superficially attractive or ornamented ; gaudy ; pert. to prostitution. **-rix,** *n.* (*pl.* **-rices**) prostitute.

merganser (məgan'sə), *n.* hookedbilled crested duck.

meridian (mərid'iən), *n.* highest point ; *Geog.,* circle passing through both poles and any given place ; *adj.* pert. to midday or zenith. **-dional,** *adj.* pert. to m. ; southern.

merino (mərē'nō), *n.* breed of heavy-fleeced white sheep, *espec.* of Australia.

merlon (mē'lən), *n.* narrow wall between embrasures in battlements.

merism (mer'izm), *n.* synecdoche using two contrasted parts, as high and low. **-atic,** *adj.* pert. to meristem. **-ristem,** *n.* embryonic tissue capable of growth by division. **-ristic,** *adj.* divided into segments. **-rogenesis,** *n.* segmentation. **-rogony,** *n.* growth of embryo from part of egg. **-romorphic,** *adj.* fractional **-ropia,** *n.* partial blindness. **-rotomy,** *n.* division into parts.

mesa (mē'sah), *n.* flat-topped steep-sided mountain.

mésalliance (māzalyahñs'), Fr. *n.* mistaken marriage ; marriage into lower social class.

mesaticephalic (mesətisifal'ik), *adj.* having medium-sized head. **-lus** (-sef'ələs), *n.* (*pl.* **-li**) such person.

mesencephalon (mesensef'əlon), *n.* midbrain. **-lic** (-sifal'ik), *adj.*

mesentery (mes'əntəri), *n.* membrane enclosing intestines. **-rial** (-ēr'iəl), **-ric** (-er'ik), *adj.* **-ritis,** *n.* inflammation of m.

mesial (mē'ziəl), *adj.* middle. **-ad,** *adv.* towards the middle.

mesobar (mes'əbah, mē'-), *n.* region or isobar of normal atmospheric pressure.

mesocardia (mesəkah'diə, mē-), *n.* placing of heart in middle of thorax.

mesochroic (mesəkrō'ik, mē-), *adj.* having colour of skin midway between light and dark races.

mesode (mes'ōd), *n.* part of ode between strophe and antistrophe.

mesodont (mes'ədont, mē'-), *adj.* with teeth of medium size.

mesognathism (mesog'nəthizm, mis-), *n.* state of having jaws of medium size. **-thic** (-ath'ik), **-thous,** *adj.*

mesology (mesol'əji, mē-), *n.* ecology.

meson (mē'son), *n.* positively or negatively charged particle, of about 200 times mass of electron, occurring in cosmic and other rays.

mesoprosopic (mesəprəsop'ik, mē-), *adj.* with face of medium width.

mesotherm (mes'əthəm, mē'-), *n.* plant thriving only in moderate temperature.

mesquite (meskēt'), *n.* prickly shrub, forming thickets, of Mexico and S.W. United States.

Messiah (mesī'ə), *n.* Christ as deliverer ; deliverer whose coming is awaited by Jews. **-anic** (-ian'ik), *adj.*

messuage (mes'ūij), *n.* house with its land and outbuildings.

mestizo (mestē'zō), Sp. *n.* half-breed.

metabasis (metab'əsis), *n.* transition ; transfer. **-atic** (-at'ik), *adj.*

metabiosis (metəbī ō'sis), *n.* reliance by an organism on another to produce favourable environment ; change due to external agency. **-otic** (-ot'ik), *adj.*

metabolism (metab'əlizm), *n.* continuous process of chem. change in cells, with assimilation of food-stuffs and release of energy. **-bular, -lic** (-ol'ik), *adj.* **-ise,** *v.i.* & *t.* perform or subject to m. **-ite,** *n.* product of m.

metacarpus (metəkah'pəs), *n.* hand between wrist and base of fingers. **-pal,** *adj.* ; *n.* bone of the m.

metachemistry (metəkem'istri), *n.* speculative or theoretical, or subatomic, chemistry.

metachromatism (metəkrō'mətizm), *n.* change of colour.

metachronism (metak'rənizm), *n.* anachronism dating thing later than its correct date.

metachrosis (metəkrō'sis), *n.* ability to change colour voluntarily.

metage (mē'tij), *n.* official measure-ment ; fee paid for this.

metagnomy (mitag'nəmi), *n.* divination.

metagnostic (metagnos'tik), *adj.* beyond understanding.

metagraphy (metag'rəfi), *n.* transliteration.

metalepsis (metəlep'sis), *n.* rhet. device of changing figurative sense by metonymy. **-ptic(al),** *adj.* ; *Med.,* app. to muscle associated with others in action.

metallogeny (metəloj'ini), *n.* study of origin of ores. **-genic** (-jen'ik), **-genetic** (-jinet'ik), *adj.*

metallography (metəlog'rəfi), *n.* study of structure of metals and alloys. **-phist,** *n.*

metallurgy (mital'əji), *n.* art of extracting and refining metals. **-gical** (-ə'jikl), *adj.* **-gist,** *n.*

metameric (metəmer'ik), *adj.* pert. to serial segmentation of body ; isomeric. **-rism** (-am'ərizm), **-ry,** *n.* **-rous** (-am'ərəs), *adj.*

metamorphic (metəmaw'fik), *adj.* changing in form ; *Geol.,* changing or changed in composition, *espec.* to more solid and crystalline form. **-phism,** *n.*

metamorphose (metəmaw'fōz), *v.i.* & *t.* transform or be transformed. **-photic, -phous, -sian, -sic(al),** *adj.* **-sis,** *n.* (*pl.* **-ses**) complete transformation.

metanomen (metənō'men), *n.* metaphorical name.

metaphony (mitaf'əni), *n.* umlaut. **-nic(al),** *adj.* **-nise,** *v.t.*

metaphor (met'əfor, -fə), *n.* word or phrase used figuratively in place of another to express idea more vividly by the comparison (as to *steer the ship of state,* i.e. *act as Prime Minister*). **-ical** (-or'ikl), *adj.* pert. to or like m. ; figurative.

metaphrase (met'əfrāz), *n.* translation ; *v.t.* translate ; paraphrase. **-st** (-ast), *n.* person putting verse into different metre, or prose into verse. **-stic(al),** *adj.*

metaphysics (metəfiz'iks), *n.* study of matters beyond, or unexplain-able by, the physical sciences ; phil. study of being, the nature of reality, etc. ; ontology ; any abstract or abstruse phil. study. -cal, adj. -cian, n.

metaphysis (mitaf'isis), n. metamorphosis. -seal (-iz'iəl), adj.

metaplasia (metəplā'zhiə), n. change of one kind of tissue into another.

metaplasm (met'əplazm), n. lifeless matter in cell; Gram., alteration in spelling of word. -stic, adj. pert. to m. or metaplasia.

metapolitics (metəpol'itiks), n. theoretical political study. -cal (-it'ikl), adj. -cian (-ish'ən), n.

metapsychical (metəsī'kikl), adj. beyond, or unexplainable by, psychology; spiritualistic. -chology, n. speculative psych. theory. -chosis, n. telepathy.

metasomatosis (metəsōmətō'sis), n. Geol., chemical metamorphism. -masis (-ō'məsis), -tism, n. -tic (-at'ik), adj.

metastasis (mitas'təsis), n. transformation; change of subject; metabolism; movement to another part of body of agent causing disease. -e, v.i. -tatic, adj.

metasthenic (metəsthen'ik), adj. having strong hindquarters.

metastrophe (metas'trəfi), n. mutual exchange. -phic (-of'ik), adj.

metatarsus (metətah'səs), n. foot between ankle and base of toes; instep. -sal, adj. ; n. bone of m.

metathesis (mitath'isis), n. (pl. -ses) transposition of letters or sounds in a word. -e, v.t. -stic(al) (-et'ik, -l), adj.

métayer (metā'yə; Fr., mātayā'), n. person doing agricultural work for a share of the yield. -yage (-ij; Fr., -yahzh'), n. such system.

metazoa (metəzō'ə), n.pl. (sing. -zoon) all animals except protozoa. -l, -oic, adj. -n, n. & adj.

metel (mē'tel), n. thorn apple.

metempiric (metempir'ik), adj. transcending but associated with empirical knowledge. -ism (-sizm), n. -s, n. study of m. ideas.

metempsychosis (metemsīkō'sis, -mp-), n. (pl. -ses) passage of soul into another body at death. -se, v.t. transfer such soul.

metemptosis (metemptō'sis), n. omission of day from calendar (as of intercalary day once in 134 years) to correct date of new moon.

metensomatosis (metensōmətō'sis),

n. passage into another body of soul after or before death.

meteor (mē'tiŏr, -ə), n. shooting star. -ic (-or'ik), adj. like a m.; brilliant but of short duration. -ise, v.i. shine like m.; vaporise. -ism, n. abdominal distension due to flatulence. -ite, n. stony concretion falling to earth from beyond atmosphere. -ology, n. study of atmospheric conditions and weather.

methane (meth'ān), n. marsh gas.

metheglin (mitheg'lin), n. mead.

métier (māt'yā), Fr. n. profession; vocation; forte.

métis (mātēs'), Fr. n. (fem. -sse) half-breed.

metochy (met'əki), n. harmless insect parasitism. -chous, adj.

metonymy (miton'imi), n. figurative use of a word for another closely associated with it, espec. of attribute for its subject (as the crown for the sovereign or monarchy). -mical (-im'ikl), -mous, adj.

metopic (mitop'ik, adj. pert. to forehead. -pomancy (met'-), n. divination by face or forehead.

metritis (mitrī'tis), n. inflammation of womb.

metrology (mitrol'əji), n. study of weights and measures. -gical, adj. -gist, -gue, n.

metromania (metrəmā'niə), n. mania for composing verse. -c, n.

metronome (met'rənōm), n. adjustable pendulum marking musical tempo. -mic (-om'ik), adj.

metronymic (metrənim'ik, mē'-), n. & adj. (name) derived from mother's or ancestress's name; pert. to descent in the female line. -my (-on'imi), n. m. usage.

metropolis (metrop'əlis), n. capital city; see of metropolitan. -litan (-ol'itən), adj. pert. to m.; n. archbishop or bishop of eccl. province. -litanate, n. jurisdiction or see of metropolitan. -lite (-op'əlīt), n. metropolitan.

meubles (mœ'bl), Fr. n.pl. "movables"; furniture. -lé (-lā), adj. furnished.

meum et tuum (mē'əm et tū'əm), Lat., "mine and thine."

meuse (mūz, -s), n. gap through which wild animal's track passes.

mezereon (mizēr'iən), n. small

---

purple-flowered shrub. **-eum,** *n.* m.'s bark used in medicine.

mezzanine (mez'ǝnēn, -in), *n.* storey between two others, *espec.* between ground and first floor; such storey not extending throughout building.

mezzo-relievo (met'zō-rilē'vo, -rilyā'vo), *n.* (carving in) relief between alto-relievo and bas-relief.

mezzotint (met'zǝtint), *n.* engraving on roughened metal, which is smoothed and polished to produce light and shade.

mho (mō), *n.* unit of elec. conductance, opp. of ohm.

miamia (mī'mī), *n.* Austral. aborigine's hut.

mian (mē'ahn), Ind. *n.* title of respect; sir.

miasma (mīaz'mǝ), *n.* (*pl.* **-ta**) noxious exhalation from swamps, etc.; any such exhalation or atmosphere. **-l, -mous, -tic, -tous,** *adj.*

mi-carême (mē-karām'), Fr. *n.* Sunday in mid-Lent, a festival day.

micrander (mīkran'dǝ), *n.* dwarf male plant. **-drous,** *adj.*

microbiota (mīkrǝbī ō'tǝ), *n.* microscopic life of a region. **-tic** (-ot'ik), *adj.*

microcephalic, -lous (mīkrǝsifal'ik, -sef'ǝlǝs), *adj.* small-headed. **-lia** (-ā'liǝ), **-lism, -ly,** *n.* **-lus,** *n.* (*pl.* **-li**) such person.

microcosm (mī'krǝkozm), *n.* miniature representation of something vast, *espec.* universe; man as epitome of universe. **-al, -ian, -ic(al),** *adj.*

microdont (mī'krǝdont), *adj.* with small teeth. **-ism,** *n.* **-ous,** *adj.*

micrograph (mī'krǝgraf), *n.* instr. for writing or engraving on microscopic scale; drawing or photograph of object as seen through microscope. **-ic,** *adj.* **-y** (-og'rǝn), *n.*

micrology (mīkrol'ǝji), *n.* excessive devotion to minute details; art of using the microscope.

micromania (mīkrǝmā'niǝ), *n.* form of insanity in which patient constantly depreciates himself, or imagines that he has become very small. **-c,** *n.*

micrometer (mīkrom'itǝ), *n.* instr.

for measuring minute distances. **-tric(al)** (-et'rik, -l), *adj.* **-try,** *n.*

micron (mī'krǝn), *n.* millionth part of a metre (symbol μ).

micronometer (mīkrǝnom'itǝ), *n.* instr. measuring minute intervals of time.

microphagous (mīkrof'ǝgǝs), *adj.* feeding on small objects. **-gy** (-ji), *n.*

microphotograph (mīkrǝfō'tǝgraf), *n.* minute photograph; *erron.,* photomicrograph.

microphyllous (mīkrǝfil'ǝs), *adj.* having minute leaves.

microphyte (mī'krǝfīt), *n.* microscopic vegetable organism. **-tal, -tic** (-it'ik), *adj.* **-tology,** *n.* study of m.

micropodal, -dous (mīkrop'ǝdǝl, -ǝs), *adj.* having extremely small feet.

micropsia (mīkrop'siǝ), *n.* optical defect causing objects to appear smaller than their real size.

micropterous (mīkrop'tǝrǝs), *adj.* having small wings or fins. **-rygious,** *adj.* having small fins.

micropyle (mī'krǝpīl), *n.* microscopic orifice. **-lar,** *adj.*

microseism (mī'krǝsizm), *n.* small earth tremor. **-ic(al),** *adj.* **-ology,** *n.* study of m. **-ometer,** *n.* instr. measuring m.

microsomatous (mīkrǝsō'mǝtǝs), *adj.* having small body.

microstomatous, -mous (mīkrǝstom'ǝtǝs, -os'tǝmǝs), *adj.* having small mouth. **-me,** *n.* small opening.

microtherm (mī'krǝthēm), *n.* plant thriving only in very low temperature. **-ic,** *adj.*

microtis (mīkrō'shiǝ), *n.* abnormal smallness of ear.

microtome (mī'krǝtōm), *n.* instr. for cutting minute sections. **-mic(al)** (-om'ik, -l), *adj.* **-my** (-ot'ǝmi), *n.*

microwave (mī'krǝwāv), *n.* very short radio wave, as used in radar.

micrurgy (mī'krǝji), *n.* art of dissecting, etc., under microscope. **-gic(al),** *a lj.* **-gist,** *n.*

micturition (miktūrish'n), *n.* urination, *espec.* abnormally frequent. **-rate,** *v.i.*

midden (mid'n), *n.* dung- or refuse-heap.

Midi (mē'dē), Fr. *n.* the South.

---

midinette (mēdēnet'), Fr. *n.* shop-girl.

migraine (mē'grān, -grān'), *n.* pain in one side of head ; sick or nervous headache ; any pain of nervous or allergic origin. **-noid,** *adj.* like m. **-nous,** *adj.*

miles gloriosus (mī'lēz glōriō'səs), *Lat.,* "braggart soldier."

miliaria (miliār'iə), *n.* inflammatory irritating skin disease. **-ry** (mil'iəri), *adj.* like millet seeds ; with such skin eruption.

milieu (mēl'yö), Fr. *n.* surroundings ; environment.

millefiori, -re (milifiōr'i), *n. & adj.* (ornamental glassware) of fused coloured glass rods embedded in clear glass.

millennium (milen'iəm), *n.* (*pl.* -ia) period of one thousand years ; thousandth anniversary ; future period of ideal happiness on earth, *espec.* that foretold in Rev. xx. **-narian,** *adj.* pert. to m. ; believing in the occurrence of m. in near future ; *n.* such believer. **-narianism,** *n.* such belief. **-nary** (mil'-), *adj.* pert. to or consisting of a thousand ; commanding a thousand men ; *n.* a thousand (years) ; thousandth anniversary. **-nial,** *adj.* pert. to m. ; *n.* thousandth anniversary. **-nian,** *adj.* pert. to m. ; *n.* millenarian. **-niary,** *adj.* pert. to m.

millepede, -lip- (mil'ipēd), *n.* long cylindrical many-legged insect.

millepore (mil'ipōr), *n.* kind of branching coral. **-rite,** *n.* fossil m.

millesimal (miles'iməl), *n. & adj.* (pert. to) thousandth part.

milliad (mil'iad), *n.* a thousand years.

milliard (mil'yahd), *n.* one thousand millions.

milliary (mil'iəri), *adj.* pert. to miles, *espec.* anct. Roman.

milt (milt), *n.* fish's spawn ; *v.t.* impregnate with m.

mimesis (mimē'sis), *n.* imitation, *espec.* by animal of its surroundings, etc. **-etic** (-et'ik), *adj.* **-etism** (mim'itizm, mī-), *n.* mimicry.

mimography (mīmog'rəfi), *n.* representation in writing of language of signs.

minatory (min'ətəri), *n.* threatening. **-rial,** *adj.*

Minenwerfer (mē'nənvārfə), Ger. *n.* trench gun ; mine-thrower.

miniaceous (miniā'shəs), *adj.* having colour of red lead. **-niate,** *v.t.* paint with red lead ; decorate with red letters or rubrics ; illuminate (MSS.). **-tor,** *n.*

minimalism (min'iməlizm), *n.* provisional acceptance of a minimum offer, in trade disputes, etc. **-ist,** *n.*

minimifidian (minimifid'iən), *adj.* having smallest possible degree of faith. **-ism,** *n.*

minimuscular (minimus'kūlə), *adj.* tiny.

minion (min'yən), *n.* size of type (7-point) ; favourite ; hanger-on.

ministerial (minister'iəl), *adj. Parl.,* belonging to or on side of Government. **-ist,** *n.* supporter of Government.

minium (min'iəm), *n.* vermilion ; red lead.

miniver (min'ivə), *n.* unspotted ermine fur ; any white fur.

minnesinger (min'isingə), *n.* troubadour-like poet of medieval Germany. **-elied** (-əlēt), Ger. *n.* love song. **-esong,** *n.* m.'s song.

minuend (min'ūend), *n.* number from which another has to be subtracted.

minuscule (minus'kūl), *n.* small simple handwriting, *espec.* of anct. times ; such letter ; lower case letter ; *adj.* small ; petty ; diminutive. **-lar,** *adj.*

minutia (minū'shiə), *n.* (*pl.* -ae) minute detail ; triviality. **-tiose, -tious,** *adj.* paying undue attention to m.

miothermic (miəthō'mik), *adj. Geol.,* pert. to present temperature conditions.

mirabile dictu (mirab'ili dik'tū, mirah'-), *Lat.,* "wonderful to relate." **-lia,** *n.pl.* wonders. **-liary,** *n.* miracle worker.

mirador (mirədōr'), *n.* watchtower, or other archit. feature with fine view.

mirific(al) (mirif'ik, -l), *adj.* wonder-working ; miraculous.

mirliton (mō'litən, mēr'-), *n.* reed pipe.

mirza (mō'zə, mēr'-), Pers. *n.* title of honour ; prince.

misandry (mis'andri), *n.* hatred of men by woman.

misanthrope (mis'ənthrōp), *n.* hater

of mankind. **-pic** (-op'ik), *adj.* **-py** (-an'thrəpi), *n.*

miscegenation (misijinā'shn), *n.* racial interbreeding, *espec.* between blacks and whites. **-netic**, *adj.* **-te** (mis'-), *v.i.* & *t.* practise or produce by m. ; *n.* half-caste. **-tor**, *n.*

misdemeanour (misdimē'nə), *n. Law*, illegal but not felonious act. **-nant**, **-nist**, *n.* person guilty of m.

mise en scène (mēz' ahn sen), *Fr.*, staging, scenery, etc., of play; setting; locality; surroundings.

misfeasance (misfē'zəns), *n.* misuse of legal power; illegal performance of legal act. **-sor**, *n.* person guilty of m.

misocapnic (misəkap'nik, mī-), *adj.* hating tobacco smoke. **-nist**, *n.*

misogallic (misogal'ik, mī-), *adj.* hating the French.

misogamy (misog'əmi, mī-), *n.* hatred of marriage. **-mic** (-am'ik), *adj.* **-mist**, *n.*

misogyny (misoj'ini, mī-), *n.* hatred of women by men. **-nic(al)** (-jin'ik, -l), **-nous**, *adj.* **-n st**, **-nism**, *n.*

misology (misol'əji, mī-), *n.* hatred of argument. **-gist**, *n.*

misoneism (misonē'izm, mī-), *n.* hatred of change or novelty. **-ist**, *n.*

misopaedia (misəpē'diə, mī-), *n.* hatred of children, *espec.* one's own. **-dism**, **-dist**, *n.*

misopolemical (misəpolem'ikl, mī-), *adj.* hating war.

misosophy (misos'əfi, mī-), *n.* hatred of wisdom. **-pher**, **-phist**, *n.*

misotheism (misəthē'izm, mī-), *n.* hatred of gods or God. **-ist**, *n.*

misprision (misprizh'n), *n.* error of omission or commission; misdemeanour. **-se** (-īz'), *v.t.* & *n.* scorn.

missa (mis'ə), *n. (pl.* **-ae**) *R.C.*, service of mass. **m.bassa**, low mass. **m.cantata**, **m.media**, sung mass, without deacon or high mass ceremonial. **m.privata**, low mass, or one at which only priest communicates. **m.publica**, mass at which all faithful may communicate. **m.solemnis**, high mass.

missal (mis'əl), *n.* R.C. service-book.

mistral (mistrahl'), *n.* strong cold north wind of S. France.

mithridatism (mith'ridātizm), *n.* immunity from poison obtained by

consuming series of small doses. **-tic** (-at'ik), *adj.* **-tise**, *v.t.*

mitosis (mitō'sis), *n.* cell division, with division of nucleus first. **-otic** (-ot'ik), *adj.*

mitraille (mētrah'ē), *Fr. n.* grape and other similar shot of cannon. **-ur** (-ōr'), *n.* machine-gunner. **-use** (-ōz'), *n.* machine-gun.

mitrate (mī'trāt), *adj.* mitre- or bonnet-shaped. **-riform**, *adj.* mitre-shaped.

mittimus (mit'iməs), *Lat.*, "we send"; writ for committing to prison or removing records to other court; congé.

mneme (nē'mi), *n. Psych.*, persisting effect of memory of past events. **-mic**, *adj.* **-mist**, *n.*

mnemonic (nimon'ik), *adj.* pert. to or aiding memory; *n.* device to aid memory. **-al**, *adj.* **-nise** (nē'-), *v.t.* make into a m. **-nism**, *n.* practice of mnemonics. **-s**, **-motechny**, *n.* system of improving memory.

mnesic (nē'sik), *adj.* pert. to memory. **-stic**, *adj.* pert. to memory or mneme.

moa (mō'ə), *n.* extinct ostrich-like flightless bird of N.Z.

mockado (məkah'dō), *n.* anct. woollen fabric; inferior material; tawdry.

modal (mō'dəl), *adj.* pert. to or having form rather than substance. **-ity**, *n.*

modicum (mod'ikəm), *n.* small or reasonable quantity; bare sufficiency.

module (mod'ūl), *n.* unit of measurement or means of measuring.

modus operandi (mō'dəs opəran'dī), *Lat.*, "method of operating or proceeding." **m.vivendi**, "method of living"; compromise adopted until final settlement is reached.

mofussil (mofus'il), Anglo-Ind. *n.* the country or countryside; rural districts.

mogadore (mog'ədōr), *n.* ribbed silk necktie material.

mogigraphia, **-phy** (mojigraf'iə, -ig'rəfi), *n.* writing only with difficulty. **-ilalia**, *n.* speaking only with difficulty.

mohur (mō'hə), *n.* Ind. gold coin worth 15 rupees.

moidore (moi'dōr), *n.* anct. Port. gold coin.

moiety (moi'iti), *n.* half; small portion.

moire (mwahr), Fr. *n.* watered silk or other fabric. **-ré** (-rā), *adj.* with watered pattern; *n.* such pattern.

molar (mō'lə), *n.* & *adj.* (tooth) used to grind or chew; "double"-tooth. **-iform** (-ar'ifawm), *adj.* shaped like a m. **-y**, *adj.*

molasses (məlas'iz), *n.* treacle obtained in sugar manuf.

molecule (mol'ikūl, mō'-), *n.* very small particle or portion; smallest portion chemically identifiable, consisting of a number of atoms. **-lar** (-ek'ūlə), *adj.* **-larity**, *n.*

molimen (məli'men), *n.* strenuous effort or labour.

molinary (mol'inəri, mō'-), *adj.* pert. to mills or grinding.

mollescent (məles'ənt), *adj.* softening. **-lify**, *v.t.* soften; appease. **-lipilose** (molipi'lōs), *adj.* downy. **-lities** (-lish'iēz), *n. Med.*, softness. **-litious**, *adj.* softening; voluptuous.

Moloch (mō'lok), *n.* deity mentioned in O.T., to whom children were sacrificed; anything requiring human sacrifice; Austral. spiny lizard.

molossus (məlos'əs), *n.* verse foot of three long syllables; kind of tropical bat.

molybdenum (məlib'dinəm, məlibdē'nəm), *n.* iron-like white metal used in steel manuf. and dyeing. **-dic, -dous, -nic, -nous**, *adj.* **-niferous**, *adj.* yielding m.

momentaneous (mōməntā'niəs), *adj. Gram.*, signifying action completed in a moment; *Phon.*, pronounced with lips and nasal passage closed, as *b.*

momentum (məmen'təm), *n.* (*pl.* **-ta**) quantity of motion of a moving body; impetus.

Momus (mō'məs), *n.* Gr. god of ridicule; carping critic; satirist. **disciple, son**, etc., of M., person continually poking fun.

monachal (mon'əkl), *adj.* monastic. **-chate**, *n.* period of monkhood. **-chise**, *v.i.* & *t.* become or cause to become a monk or monkish. **-chism**, *n.*

monad (mon'ad, mō'-), *n.* unit; atom; microcosmic element underlying reality; God. **-ic**, *adj.* **-ism**, *n.* phil. theory that universe is composed of such elements.

monandry (inənan'dri), *n.* marriage to only one man at a time. **-dric, -drous**, *adj.*

monanthous (mənan'thəs), *adj.* single-flowered.

monarticular (monahtik'ūlə), *adj.* of or affecting only one joint.

monatomic (monətom'ik), *adj.* having one atom, or only one atom in molecule; univalent. **-ity** (-is'iti), **-mism** (-at'əmizm), *n.*

monaural (monōr'əl), *adj.* pert. to, having or for one ear only.

monde (mawnd), Fr. *n.* "world," *espec.* of fashion; one's own little world.

monepic (monep'ik), *adj.* comprising one word, or single-worded sentences.

monetise (mun'itīz), *v.t.* convert into or adopt as currency, or as currency standard.

Mongolism (mong'gəlizm), *n.* congenital imbecility with Mongolian features, as slanting eyes, broad skull, etc. **-loid**, *n.* such person.

mongoose (mong'gōos), *n.* (*pl.* **-s**) ferret-like snake-killing animal of India.

monial (mō'niəl), *n.* nun.

moniliform (mənil'ifawm), *adj.* having narrow intervals or joints resembling a string of beads. **-lethrix**, *n.* disease causing hair to have that appearance. **-licorn**, *n.* & *adj.* (beetle) with such antennae. **-lioid**, *adj.*

monism (mon'izm, mō'-), *n.* phil. belief that matter, mind, etc., consist of one substance only, which is the only reality. **-ist, -istic**, *adj.*

monition (mənish'n), *n.* caution; warning, *espec.* legal. **-tory** (mon'itəri), *adj.*; *n.* letter containing a m.

monoblepsia, -sis (monəblep'siə, -sis), *n.* normality of vision with one eye, but confusion when both are used; colour-blindness for all but one colour.

monocarpic (monəkah'pik), *adj.* fruiting only once.

monoceros (inənos'ərəs), *n.* unicorn; swordfish. **-rous**, *adj.* having one horn only.

monochord (mon'əkawd), *n.* mus. instr. with one string; similar apparatus determining mus. intervals; clavichord.

monochrome (mon'əkrōm), *n.* work of art in one colour. -chroic, -matic, -mic(al), *adj.* -matism, *n.* complete colour-blindness. -mist, -my, *n.*

monochronic (monəkron'ik), *adj.* contemporaneous.

monocline (mon'əklīn), *n. Geol.* single upward band or fold. -nal, *adj.*

monocotyledon (monəkotilē'dən), *n.* plant having single cotyledon. -ous (-ed'ənəs), *adj.*

monocracy (mənok'rəsi), *n.* autocracy. -crat (mon'-), *n.* -cratic, *adj.*

monocular (mənok'ūlə), *adj.* having, pert. to, or for one eye only. -list, -lus, *n.* one-eyed person. -lous, *adj.*

monodont (mon'ədont), *adj.* one-toothed.

monodrama (mon'ədrahmə), *n.* play acted by one person only; dramatic account of thoughts of one person. -tic (-drəmat'ik), *adj.*

monodromic (monədrom'ik), *adj.* uniform in value. -my (-od'rəmi), *n.*

monody (mon'ədi), *n.* song on one note or by one voice; dirge; melody.

monodynamic (monədīnam'ik), *adj.* having only one power or ability. -mism, *n.* belief in one force causing all activity.

monoecious (mənē'shəs), *adj.* having male and female organs in same organism, *espec.* having male and female flowers on same plant. -cism, *n.*

monogamy (mənog'əmi), *n.* marriage to only one person at a time. -mic (-am'ik), -mous, *adj.* -mist, *n.*

monogenesis (monəjen'isis), *n.* singleness of origin; theory that all human beings derive from one man and woman, or that all life derives from a single cell; asexual reproduction; development without change of form. -neous (-jē'niəs), -netic (-jinet'ik), -nic, -nous (-oj'inəs), *adj.* -nism, -ny (-oj'inizm, -i), *n.*

monoglot (mon'əglot), *n.* & *adj.* (person)knowingonelanguage only.

monogoneutic (monəgənū'tik), *adj.* single-brooded.

monogony (mənog'əni), *n.* non-sexual reproduction.

monograph (mon'əgraf), *n.* treatise on one subject; any learned treatise. -ic, *adj.* -ist, *n.*

monogyny (mənoj'ini), *n.* marriage to only one woman at a time, or to one chief wife, with other consorts. -nic, -nious (-jin'ik, -iəs), -nous, *adj.*

mono-ideism (mon'ō-īdē'izm), *n.* obsession with one idea. -deic, -deistic, *adj.*

monolatry (mənol'ətri), *n.* worship of one god only. -ter, -trist, *n.* -trous, *adj.*

monolingual (monəling'gwəl), *adj.* monoglot. -guist, *n.*

monoliteral (monəlit'ərəl), *adj.* comprising one letter only.

monolith (mon'əlith), *n.* single monumental stone or pillar, *espec.* of prehistoric origin. -ic, *adj.*

monology (mənol'əji), *n.* soliloquy; monopoly of the conversation. -gian, -gist, *n.* -gic(al), *adj.* -gise, *v.i.*

monomachy (mənom'əki), *n.* duel. -chist, *n.*

monomania (monəmā'niə), *n.* insanity on one subject only; obsession to insane degree with one subject. -c, *n.* -cal (-ī'əkl), *adj.*

monometallism (monəmet'əlizm), *n.* use of one metal as currency standard; theory advocating m. -ist, *n.*

monomial (mənō'miəl), *n.* & *adj.* (name or expression) comprising one term only.

monomorphic (monəmaw'fik), *adj.* having same form throughout life. -phism, *n.* -phous, *adj.*

mononym (mon'ənim), *n.* monomial name or term. -ic, *adj.* -ise (-on'imīz), *v.t.* -y, *n.*

monoousian (monō ōō'siən, -ow'-), *adj.* having same substance.

monophagous (mənof'əgəs), *adj.* eating one kind of food only. -gia (-ā'jiə), -gism (-jizm), -gy (-ji), *n.*

monophobia (monəfō'biə), *n.* dread of solitude.

monophonous (mənof'ənəs), *adj.* representing same sound, as *f* and *ph*; giving tones singly.

monophthalmus (monofthal'məs), *n.* congenital absence of one eye. -mic, *adj.*

monophthong (mon'ofthong), *n.* single vowel sound. -al, *adj.* -ise, *v.t.* pronounce as m.

monophyletic (monəfilet'ik), *adj.* derived from one common parental stock. -ism (-sizm), *n.*

monoplasmatic (monəplazmat′ik), *adj.* of one substance. **-stic,** *adj.* of one form.

monoplegia (monəplē′jiə), *n.* paralysis of one part of body only, *espec.* one limb. **-gic,** *adj.*

monopode (mon′əpōd), *n. & adj.* (creature) with one foot, *espec.* such fabulous Ethiopian race. **-dial, -dic** (-od′ik), **-dous** (-op′ədəs), *adj.* **-dium,** *n.* (*pl.* **-dia**) main axis. **-dy** (-op′ədi), *n.* verse measure of one foot.

monopolylogue (monəpol′ilog), *n.* dramatic entertainment with interpretation of many rôles by one person. **-gist** (-lil′əjist), *n.*

monopsychism (monəsī′kizm), *n.* belief in one universal soul.

monopteral, -rous (mənop′tərəl, -əs), *adj.* having one wing, fin, or ring of columns.

monoptic(al) (mənop′tik, -l), *adj.* one-eyed.

monoptote (mon′əptōt), *n.* noun (or adjective) with one form for all cases. **-tic** (-ot′ik), *adj.*

monopyrenous (monəpīr′ē′nəs), *adj.* app. to single-stoned or single-kernelled fruit.

monoschemic (monəskē′mik), *adj.* using same metrical foot throughout.

monospermous, -mal (monəspɜ′məs, -əl), *adj.* single-seeded. **-my,** *n.* fertilisation of egg by one sperm cell only.

monostich (mon′əstik), *n.* one verse line; poem of one verse line. **-ous** (-os′tikəs), *adj.* in one line or row.

monostrophe (mənos′trəfi), *n.* poem with all stanzas of same form. **-phic** (-of′ik), *adj.*

monotheism (monəthē′izm), *n.* belief in one God only. **-ist,** *n.* **-istic,** *adj.*

monothelious (monəthē′liəs), *adj.* polyandrous.

monotic (mənot′ik), *adj.* affecting one ear only.

monotocous (mənot′əkəs), *adj.* laying one egg, or bringing forth one young, only.

monotrophic (monətrof′ik), *adj.* monophagous.

monozygotic (monəzīgot′ik), *adj.* developed from one zygote only.

monoxide (monoks′īd), *n.* oxide with one oxygen atom in molecule.

mons (monz), Lat. *n.* mountain.

m.pubis, hair-covered eminence in pubic region. **m.Veneris,** "mountain of Venus"; fatty eminence in female pubic region.

monsoon. (monsōōn′), *n.* periodic wind, *espec.* of S. Asia, from S.W. in summer and N.E. in winter; such S.W. wind of Ind.; rainy season. **-al,** *adj.*

monstrance (mon′strəns), *n. Eccl.,* vessel for exposing eucharist.

montage (mawn′tahzh), Fr. *n.* a composite picture made up of many pictures artistically blended or laid out; any similar blending of scenes, sounds, etc.; manner of constructing artistically sequence of scenes in film.

mont-de-piété (mawn-də-pyā′tā), *Fr.,* "mount, or bank, of piety"; public pawnbroker's.

montero (montār′ō), Sp. *n.* huntsman; his cap.

montgolfier (montgol′fiə; Fr., mawngawl′fyā), *n.* fire balloon.

monticle, -cule (mon′tikl, -kūl), *n.* hillock. **-culate, -culous,** *adj.* having m.

moolvee (mōōl′vē), *n.* doctor of Moham. law; title of respect for learned man or teacher.

moong, *see* mung.

moonshee (mōōn′shē), *n.* Ind. native teacher or secretary. **-sif,** *n.* Ind. native judge.

mootsuddy (mootsud′i), Anglo-Ind. *n.* native Ind. clerk.

mopoke (mō′pōk), *n.* morepork.

moquette (məket′), *n.* thick-piled upholstery fabric or carpet.

mora (mōr′ə), *n.* (*pl.* **-ae**) unit of metre in prosody, equiv. of one short syllable; *Law,* postponement; default.

moraine (mərān′), *n.* detritus deposited by glacier. **-nal, -nic,** *adj.*

moratorium (morətōr′iəm), *n.* (*pl.* **-ria**) lawful suspension of payment; period of such suspension. **-tory** (mor′ətəri), *adj.* pert. to m. or delay.

morbid (maw′bid), *adj. Med.,* unhealthy; diseased. **-bific,** *adj.* causing disease. **-biferal, -biferous,** *adj.* carrying disease. **-ezza** (-et′sə), It. *n.* softness in artistic representation of flesh. **-ity,** *n.*

morbilli (mawbil′i), *n.pl.* measles. **-lary, -liform,** *adj.* like measles. **-lous,** *adj.*

---

morbus (maw'bəs), Lat. *n.* disease. m.Gallicus, "French disease"; syphilis.

morcellate (maw'səlāt), *v.t.* divide into small portions. -tion, *n.*

mordant (maw'dənt), *adj.* biting; corrosive; caustic; stinging; *n.* corrosive substance; colour fixative. -dacious, *adj.* biting; caustic. -dacity, -ncy, *n.*

mordent (maw'dənt), *n.* mus. device of alternating quickly a tone with another a half-tone lower.

more (mōr'ē), Lat. *adv.* "in the manner or style." m.suo, "in his own manner or fashion."

morel (nərel'), *n.* kind of edible fungus; black night-shade. -llo, *n.* dark-coloured cultivated cherry.

morepork (maw'pawk), *n.* N.Z., kind of owl; *Tasmania*, nightjar; *Austral.*, sev. birds with cry sounding like "more pork."

mores (mōr'ēz), Lat. *n.pl.* manners and customs.

morganatic (mawgənat'ik), *adj.* pert. to or denoting marriage of person of royal blood to person of inferior rank, by which the latter does not receive the royal spouse's rank nor do the children inherit his or her titles or property. -al, *adj.*

morganise (maw'gənīz), *v.t.* do away with secretly; burke.

morgue (mawg), *n.* mortuary, *espec.* where bodies are exposed for identification.

moribund (mor'ibənd), *adj.* about to die; half-dead; *n.* such person. -ity, *n.*

moriform (mor'ifawm), *adj.* mulberry-shaped.

morigerous (mərij'ərəs), *adj.* obsequiously obedient.

morology (mərol'əji), *n.* nonsense. -gical, *adj.* -gist, *n.*

moron (mōr'on), *n.* feeble-minded person. -cy, -ism, -ity, -ry, *n.* -ic, *adj.*

morosis (mərō'sis), *n.* feeble-mindedness.

Morpheus (maw'fiəs, -fūs), *n.* Rom. god of dreams. -ean, *adj.* -etic, *adj.* pert. to sleep.

morphia, -phine (maw'fiə; -ēn, -in), *n.* opium alkaloid used as narcotic, etc. -nic (-in'ik), *adj.* -nise, *v.t.* treat with m. -nism, *n.* condition due to habitual use of m.

morphogenesis, -ny (mawfəjen'isis -oj'ini), *n.* development of morphological characteristics. -netic (-jinet'ik), -nic (-en'ik), *adj.*

morphography (mawfog'rəfi), *n.* morphological description or study. -pher, *n.* artist portraying forms. -phic(al), *adj.* -phist, *n.*

morphology (mawfol'əji), *n.* biol. or philol. study of forms and structures; form and structure of an organism, word, etc. -gical, *adj.* -gist, *n.*

morphometry (mawfom'itri), *n.* measurement of form. -tric(al) (-et'rik, -l), *adj.*

morphonomy (mawfon'əmi), *n.* morphological biol. laws. -mic (-om'ik), *adj.*

morphosis (mawfō'sis), *n.* manner of development. -otic (-ot'ik), *adj.* pert. to m. or formation.

morphous (maw'fəs), *adj.* having definite form.

morsal (maw'səl), *adj.* pert. to cutting edge.

morse (maws), *n.* walrus.

mortician (mawtish'n), Amer. *n.* funeral undertaker.

mortmain (mawt'mān), *n.* Law, state of being held by a corporation; *v.t.* alienate into corporation's possession.

mortorio (mawtōr'iō), It. *n.* sculpture of the dead Christ.

moschate (mos'kāt), *adj.* musk-like in odour. -chiferous, *adj.* producing musk. -chine, *adj.* pert. to musk deer.

mot (mō), Fr. *n.* "word"; pithy saying; bon mot. m.juste (-zhūst), word or phrase exactly expressing an idea.

motatory, -rious (mō'tətəri, -ōr'iəs), *adj.* continually moving.

motet (mōtet'), *n.* kind of unaccompanied part-song or anthem.

motif, -tiv (mōtēf'), *n.* recurrent or dominating feature or theme.

motile (mō'til, -il), *adj.* able to move spontaneously; causing motion; *n.* person whose mental processes emerge in, or are best stimulated by, motion or action. -lity, *n.*

motmot (mot'mot), *n.* jay-like S. Amer. bird.

motorium (mōtōr'iəm), *n.* division of nervous system concerned with movement.

motricity (mōtris'iti), *n.* function of movement, *espec.* muscular.

motu proprio (mō'tū prō'priō) *Lat.*, "by its or one's own motion"; by own desire or impulse.

moucharaby (moōoshar' əbi), *n.* projecting latticed window in Moham. archit.; such balcony of castle.

mouchard (moōoshahr'), Fr. *n.* police spy.

moue (moō), Fr. *n.* pout; grimace.

mouflon, -ffl- (moō'flon), *n.* horned wild sheep of Mediterranean islands.

mouillé (moō'yā), Fr. *adj.* "wet"; made soft or palatal in pronunciation, as *ll* in *mouillé*, *ñ* in *cañon*, etc. -lation, -lure, *n.*

moujik (moō'zhik), *n.* Russ. peasant; lady's loose fur cape.

mournival (mawn'ivəl), *n.* set of four.

moutonnée (moōton'ā), Fr. *adj.* app. to rocks with rounded outlines like backs of flock of sheep.

mu (mū), *n.* twelfth letter of Gr. alphabet (M, μ); symbol for micron; *Elec.*, factor of amplification.

mucago (mūkā'gō), *n.* mucilage; mucus.

mucedine (mū'sidin), *n.* mould or mildew fungus. -naceous, -neous, -nous (-sed'inəs), *adj.* mildew-like.

muchacha (moōchah'chah), Sp. *n.* girl; female servant. -cho, *n.* boy; manservant.

mucid (mū'sid), *adj.* slimy; mucous. -ciferous, -cific, -cigenous, *adj.* secreting or stimulating secretion of mucus.

mucilage (mū'silij), *n.* gummy or adhesive substance. -ginous (-aj'inəs), *adj.*

mucivore (mū'sivōr), *n.* insect feeding on plant juices. -rous (-iv'ərəs), *adj.*

muckna (muk'nə), Anglo-Ind. *n.* male elephant lacking, or having only rudimentary, tusks; spurless cock.

mucocele (mū'kəsēl), *n.* cyst containing mucus; swelling due to accumulation of mucus. -coid (al), *adj.* like mucus. -copus, *n.* mixture of mucus and pus. -corrhoea, *n.* abnormal discharge of mucus. -cosa, *n.* mucous membrane. -cous, *adj.* secreting, like, or covered with mucus.

mucronate (mū'krənāt), *adj.* terminating in sharp point. -niferous, *adj.* -niform, *adj.* like a sharp point. -nulate (-on'ūlāt), *adj.* terminating in small sharp point. -tion, *n.*

muculent (mū'kūlənt), *adj.* slimy; like mucus.

mucus (mū'kəs), *n.* viscous fluid secreted by membranes lining body cavities.

mudar (mədah'), E. Ind. *n.* fibre-yielding shrub with root and bark used in medicine.

mudir (moōdēr'), Arab. *n.* governor of Egyptian province. -ia, -ieh, *n.* jurisdiction of m.

muezzin (mūez'in), *n.* person calling Moham. faithful to prayer.

mufti (muf'ti), Arab. *n.* person learned in Moham. law; civilian dress.

mugger, -ar, -ur (mug'ə), *n.* Ind. crocodile.

mugient (mū'jiənt), *adj.* bellowing, *espec.* like cattle. -nce, -ncy, *n.*

mugiloid (mū'jiloid), *n.* & *adj.* (fish) like grey mullet, or belonging to grey mullet family of fishes. -liform, *adj.*

muktar (moōk'tah), Anglo-Ind. *n.* native solicitor or agent.

mulatto (mūlat'ō), *n.* (*pl.* -es) offspring of a pure negro and a white parent; *adj.* having yellowish-brown skin.

mulct (mulkt), *v.t.* rob of; deprive of; fine; *n.* fine. -ation, *n.* -ative, -atory, *adj.* -uary, *adj.* punishable by fine.

muliebrile (mūliē'brīl, -il), *adj.* feminine. -rity, *n.* womanliness; womanhood. -rous, *adj.* effeminate.

mulier (mū'liə), *n.* woman; wife; legitimate child. m.puisne (-pū'ni), younger legitimate son.

mullah (mul'ə), *n.* Moham. teacher of law and theology.

mullid (mul'id), *n.* & *adj.* (fish) like red mullet, or belonging to red mullet family of fishes.

mullion (mul'yən), *n.* upright division, *espec.* of stone, between panes of window.

mulse (muls), *n.* boiled wine with honey.

multeity (multē'iti), *n.* state of being, or thing comprising, many.

multifid (mul'tifid), *adj.* having many divisions.

multilateral (multilat'ərəl), *adj.* many-sided.

multilinguist (multiling'gwist), *n.* speaker of many languages.

multiliteral (multilit'ərəl), *adj.* having many letters or unknown quantities.

multilocation (multiləkā'shn), *n.* appearance in many places at the same time.

multiloquent (multil'əkwənt), *adj.* talkative. **-quious** (-ō'kwiəs), **-quous,** *adj.* **-nce, -quy,** *n.*

multinomial (multinō'miəl), *n.* & *adj.* (expression) containing three or more terms.

multipara (multip'ərə), *n.* mother of two or more children. **-rity** (-ar'iti), *n.* state of being m. ; act of giving birth to two or more offspring. **-rous,** *adj.*

multiplepoinding (multiplpoin'ding), *n. Scot. Law,* action by holder of property, etc., requiring claimants upon it to appear and settle claims in court.

multiplicand (multiplikand'), *n.* number or amount to be multiplied.

multipotent (multip'ətənt), *adj.* having many powers.

multisonous (multis'ənəs), *adj.* producing many or loud sounds. **-nant,** *adj.*

multitarian (multitār'iən), *adj.* having many forms but one essence.

multivalent (multiv'ələnt, -vā'lənt), *adj.* having valency of more than two ; having more than one valency. **-nce, -ncy,** *n.*

multivious (multiv'iəs), *adj.* leading in many directions ; having many ways.

multivocal (multiv'əkəl), *adj.* having many meanings.

multivolent (multiv'ələnt), *adj.* not in agreement ; not of one mind.

multivoltine (multivol'tīn, -in), *adj.* having many broods in one season.

multum in parvo (mul'təm in pah'vō), *Lat.,* "much in little" ; compression of much into little space ; summary.

multure (mul'tūr), *n.* miller's fee for grinding corn.

mundane (mun'dān), *adj.* worldly ; earthly ; everyday ; secular. **-nity** (-an'iti), *n.*

mundify (mun'difī), *v.t.* cleanse ; heal. **-ficant,** *n.* & *adj.* **-fication, -fier,** *n.*

mung (moong), *n.* Ind. fibre-yielding vetch. **m.bean,** bean-like food plant of Asia ; fram.

muniments (mū'nimənts), *n. pl.* legal records, as deeds, etc.

munj (moonj)), *n.* mung.

munjeet (munjēt'), *n.* dye-yielding madder plant of Bengal ; dye obtained from its roots.

munshi, -sif, *see* **moonshee, -sif.**

muntjak (munt'jak), *n.* small tusked deer of S.E. Asia ; barking deer.

murage (mūr'ij), *n.* rate levied for upkeep of city's walls.

mural (mūr'əl), *adj.* pert. to or on a wall ; *n.* wall-painting.

muriate (mūr'iāt), *n.* chloride, *espec.* of potassium. **-d,** *adj.* impregnated with chloride, *espec.* silver chloride ; pickled ; briny. **-tic** (-at'ik), *adj.* hydrochloric.

muricate (mūr'ikāt), *adj.* prickly. **-culate,** *adj.* having small prickles.

murid (mooręd'), Arab. *n.* Moham. disciple. **-ism,** *n.*

murine (mūr'īn, -in), *n.* & *adj.* (animal) belonging to rats and mice family of rodents. **-riform,** *adj.* like rat or mouse ; like courses of bricks.

murrain (mur'in), *n.* plague, *espec.* of cattle.

murre (mū̄), *n.* kind of guillemot or auk. **-let,** *n.* sev. small sea-birds of N. Pacific.

murrhine (mə'rīn, -in), *adj.* app. to transparent glassware containing pieces of coloured glass ; *n.* such vase, or one made of valuable stone or porcelain.

musal (mū'zəl), *adj.* pert. to poetry or the Muses.

musang (mūsang'), *n.* civet-like animal of E. Ind.

muscae volitantes (mus'ē volitan'-tēz), *Lat.,* "flying flies" ; spots, lines, etc., seen before the eyes, caused by particles in the vitreous humour of the eye.

muscari (muskār'i), *n.* grape hyacinth. **-form** (-ar'ifawm), *adj.* brush-shaped. **-ne** (mus'karēn), *n.* poisonous alkaloid in fly agaric.

muscicide (mus'isīd), *n.* substance killing flies.

muscology (muskol'əji), *n.* study of mosses. **-coid, -cose,** *adj.* moss-like. **-gic(al),** *adj.* **-gist,** *n.*

muscovado (muskəvā'dō), *n.* unrefined sugar.

museology (mūziol'əji), *n.* science of collecting and arranging objects for museums. **-gist,** *n.*

musette (mūzet'), *n.* small Fr. bagpipe ; air or dance performed on or to a m. ; soldier's provision wallet.

musicale (mūzikahl'), *n.* musical evening ; private concert.

mussitate (mus'itāt), *v.i.* mutter. **-tion,** *n.*

mussuck (mus'uk), Anglo-Ind. *n.* leather bag for carrying water.

mustang (mus'tang), *n.* wild horse of Mexico and Texas.

mustee (mustē'), *n.* octoroon ; half-breed.

musteline (mus'tilin, -in), *n.* & *adj.* (animal) belonging to family of animals including otters, badgers, weasels, mink, etc. **-nous,** *adj.*

mutable (mū'təbl), *adj.* capable of being changed, *espec.* for the worse ; fickle. **-bility,** *n.*

mutation (mūtā'shn), *n.* change ; *Biol.,* sudden variation from type, due to change in genes. **-al,** *adj.* **-ism,** *n.* belief that m. is important in evolution of species.

mutatis mutandis (mūtā'tis mūtan'-dis), *Lat.,* with suitable or necessary alterations.

mutative (mū'tətiv), *adj. Gram.,* expressing change of place or state.

mutic (mū'tik), *adj. Zoo.,* lacking normal defensive parts, as claws, etc. **-ous,** *adj.* lacking a point.

mutive (mū'tiv), *adj.* tending to alter. **-vity,** *n.*

muzhik, -jik, *see* **moujik.**

myalgia (mīal'jiə), *n.* muscular rheumatism.

myalism (mī'əlizm), *n.* W. Ind. negro magic cult.

myall (mī'əl), *n.* Austral. acacia tree ; uncivilised Austral. native.

mycelium (mīsē'liəm), *n.* (*pl.* **-ia**) web of spore-bearing filaments of fungi ; "spawn." **-lial, -lian, -lioid, -loid,** *adj.*

mycetism (mī'sitizm), *n.* fungus poisoning. **-toid, -tous,** *adj.* fungus-like. **-tophagous,** *adj.* eating fungi.

mycoderma (mīkədə'mə), *n.* membrane formed on fermenting liquid; "mother" ; kind of fungus forming scum on liquid. **-mic, -toid, -tous,** *adj.*

mycoid (mī'koid), *adj.* fungus-like.

mycology (mīkol'əji), *n.* study of fungi. **-gical,** *adj.* **-gist,** *n.*

mycophagous (mīkof'əgəs), *adj.* eating mushrooms. **-gist, -gy,** *n.*

mycorrhiza, -orh- (mīkərī'zə), *n.* association in symbiosis of certain fungi with roots of certain plants and trees. **-l,** *adj.*

mycosis (mīkō'sis), *n.* (*pl.* **-ses**) infestation with fungi. **-otic** (-ot'ik), *adj.*

mycteric (mik'tərik), *adj.* pert. to cavities of nose. **-rism,** *n.* sneering.

mydriatic (midriat'ik), *n.* & *adj.* (substance) causing dilatation of pupil of eye. **-riasis** (midrī'əsis), *n.* such excessive dilatation.

myectopy, -pia (mīek'təpi, -ōpiə), *n.* dislocation of muscle.

myelic (mīel'ik), *adj.* pert. to spinal cord. **-lencephalous,** *adj.* having brain and spinal cord. **-litis,** *n.* inflammation of spinal cord or marrow of bones. **-locyte,** *n.* nerve-cell of brain or spinal cord. **-loid,** *adj.* myelic. **-loma,** *n.* tumour of bone marrow. **-lon,** *n.* spinal cord.

myentasis (mien'təsis), *n.* surg. stretching of muscle.

mygale (mig'əli), *n.* shrew mouse.

myiasis (mī'yəsis), *n.* disease due to flies' larvae in body.

myograph (mī'əgraf), *n.* instr. recording strength of muscular contraction. **-y,** *n.* description of muscles.

myoid (mī'oid), *adj.* muscle-like.

myology (mīol'əji), *n.* study of muscles. **-logic(al),** *adj.* **-gist,** *n.*

myopia, -py (mī ō'piə, mī'əpi), *n.* short-sightedness. **-pe,** *n.* person suffering from m. **-pio** (-op'ik), *adj.*

myosis (mī ō'sis), *n.* excessive contraction of pupil of eye.

myositis (mīəsī'tis), *n.* inflammation of muscles. **-tic** (-it'ik), *adj.*

myosotis (mīəsō'tis), *n.* forget-me-not.

myothermic (mīəthə'mik), *adj.* pert. to heat due to muscular contraction.

myotic (mīot'ik), *n.* & *adj.* (substance) causing myosis.

myotonia, -nus, -ny (mīətō'niə ; -ot'ənəs, -ni), *n.* muscular spasm or tone.

myoxine (mīoks'īn, -in), *adj.* pert. to dormice.

---

myriacanthous (miriəkan'thəs), *adj.* having many prickles.

myriapod (mir'iəpod), *n.* millepede or centipede. **-an, -ous** (-ap'ədən, -əs), *adj.*

myringa (miring'gə), *n.* ear drum. **-gitis** (-jītis), *n.* inflammation of m.

myristicaceous (miristikā'shəs), *adj.* like or pert. to nutmeg tree; belonging to nutmeg family of plants. **-ticivorous** (-siv'ərəs), *adj.* feeding on nutmegs.

myrmecoid (mə'mikoid), *adj.* ant-like. **-cology,** *n.* study of ants. **-cophagous,** *adj.* ant-eating. **-cophyte,** *n.* plant living in symbiosis with ants.

myrmidon (mə'midən), *n.* follower; hireling.

myrobalan (mīrob'ələn), *n.* prune-like tannin-containing fruit, used in tanning and dyeing; Ind. tree bearing m.

myrtaceous (mətā'shəs), *adj.* belonging to myrtle family of plants. **-tiform,** *adj.* myrtle-like.

mysophobia (mīsəfō'biə), *n.* dread of dirt.

mystacial (mistā'shəl), *adj.* having moustache-like stripe. **-cal, -cine, -cinous** (-ī'nəs), *adj.* **-tax,** *n.* mouth-hairs of insects.

mysticete (mis'tisēt), *n.* Arctic right whale. **-tous,** *adj.*

mythoclast (mith'əklast), *n.* destroyer of myths. **-ic,** *adj.* **-thogony,** *n.* study of myths' origins. **-thography,** *n.* descriptive study, or artistic representation, of myths. **-thology,** *n.* study or body of myths. **-thomania,** *n.* desire or aptitude for telling lies. **-thopoesis,** *n.* composition of myths.

mytilid (mī'tilid), *n.* mussel. **-liform, -loid,** *adj.*

myxoedema (miksidē'mə), *n.* skin disease, marked by swelling and dryness, due to insufficient thyroid secretion. **-mic, -toid, -tous,** *adj.* **myxoid** (miks'oid), *adj.* mucoid. **-xoma,** *n.* soft mucoid tumour. **-xomatosis,** *n.* fatal contagious disease of rabbits.

N

nabob (nā'bob), *n.* Ind. or Mogul governor; wealthy person, *espec.* retired Anglo-Indian.

nacelle (nəsel'), *n.* airship car; structure on aircraft wing containing engine.

nachtmaal (nahkt'mahl), S. African *n.* evening meal; Lord's Supper.

nacre (nā'kə), *n.* mother-of-pearl; shellfish bearing it. **-ous, -rine,** *adj.*

nadir (nā'də, -ēr), *n.* point opposite zenith; lowest point. **-al,** *adj.*

naevus (nē'vəs), *n.* small mark on skin; birthmark; tumour of small blood vessel. **-void,** *n.* like n.

nagana (nagah'nə), *n.* tropical disease of cattle transmitted by tsetse fly.

nagor (nā'gaw), *n.* S. African reed-buck.

naiad (nī'ad, nā'-), *n.* (*pl.* **-es, -ēz**) water-nymph; fresh-water mussel.

naif (nah'ēf), *see* **naïve.**

nainsook (nān'sook), *n.* Ind. fabric of fine cotton.

naissant (nā'sənt), *adj.* nascent.

naïve (nah'ēv), Fr. *adj.* (*masc.* **-if**)

simple; innocent; guileless. **-té** (-ēv'tā), **-ty,** *n.*

namaqua (nəmah'kwə), *n.* kind of African dove.

nanism (nā'nizm), *n.* state of being a dwarf. **-nisation,** *n.* art of dwarfing (plants).

nannander (nanan'də), *n.* dwarf male plant. **-drous,** *adj.*

nanocephalous (nānəsef'ələs), *adj.* having abnormally small head. **-noid,** *adj.* dwarfish. **-nomalous,** *adj.* having abnormally short limbs.

naology (nāol'əji), *n.* study of eccl. buildings. **-gical,** *adj.*

napalm (nā'pahm), *n.* gelled petrol used in incendiary bombs.

napellus (nəpel'əs), *n.* aconite.

naphtha (naf'thə), *n.* volatile petroleum-like liquid. **-lic, -thous,** *adj.* **-line, -lene,** *n.* hydrocarbon obtained from coal tar and used in dyeing, etc.

napiform (nā'pifawm), *adj.* turnip-shaped.

naprapathy (nəprap'əthi), *n.* med. treatment by manipulation of spine, thorax or pelvis.

narceine (nah'sīēn, -in), *n.* narcotic alkaloid found in opium.

narcissism (nahsis'izm), *n.* sexual love of, or excitement aroused by, one's own body. -ist, *n.* -istic, *adj.*

narcohypnia (nahkəhip'niə), *n.* numb feeling experienced on awakening.

narcolepsy (nah'kəlepsi), *n.* condition marked by short fits of heavy sleep. -ptic, *adj.*

narcoma (nahkō'mə), *n.* coma caused by narcotics. -tous, *adj.*

narcosis (nahkō'sis), *n.* stupor induced by narcotics. -cose, *adj.*

narcotic (nahkot'ik), *n.* & *adj.* (drug) inducing sleep or stupor, soothing nerves, relieving pain, etc. -ism, -tism, *n.* narcosis; tendency to fall asleep; abuse of n. -tine, *n.* alkaloid found in opium. -tise, *v.t.* induce narcosis in.

narcous (nah'kəs), *adj.* narcose.

nard (nahd), *n.* spikenard; ointment made of it. -ine, *adj.*

nares (nār'ēz), *n.pl.* nostrils.

narghile (nah'gili), *n.* Oriental tobacco pipe in which smoke is drawn through water by a long tube; hookah; hubble-bubble.

narial, -ric (nār'iəl, nar'ik), *adj.* pert. to nostrils. -riform, *adj.* nostril-like. -rine, *adj.* pert. to nostrils.

narthex (nah'theks), *n.* church porch; vestibule. -thecal (-ē'kəl), *adj.*

narwhal (nah'wəl), *n.* kind of greyish dolphin with one long tusk; sea-unicorn.

nascent (nas'ənt), *adj.* being born; beginning to grow; having enhanced chem. activity at moment of liberation from compound. -ncy, *n.*

nasicorn (nā'zikawn), *adj.* having horn(s) on nose; *n.* rhinoceros. -ous, *adj.*

nasillate (nā'zilāt), *v.i.* speak or sing nasally. -tion, *n.*

nasitis (nāsī'tis), *n.* nasal inflammation.

nasology (nāzol'əji), *n.* study of noses.

nasute (nā'sūt, -sūt'), *adj.* having large nose. -tiform, *adj.* nose-like.

natable (nā'təbl), *adj.* able to float. -bility, *n.*

natal (nā'təl), *adj.* pert. to birth;

native; pert. to nates. -ity, *n.* birth-rate; birth.

natant (nā'tənt), *adj.* swimming or floating.

natation (nətā'shn), *n.* swimming. -tor, *n.* -torial, -tory, *adj.* -torium, *n.* (*pl.* -ia) swimming pool.

nates (nā'tēz), *n.pl.* buttocks. -tiform, *adj.* like n.

natricine (nat'risīn, -in), *adj.* belonging to genus of snakes including grass and water snakes; *n.* such snake.

natron (nā'tron), *n.* natural carbonate of soda.

natterjack (nat'əjak), *n.* yellowish-brown European toad.

natuary (nat'ūəri), Amer. *n.* maternity ward of hospital.

natura naturans (natūr'ə nat'-ūranz) *n.* creative nature; Creator; God. n.naturata, created nature.

naturopathy (nātūrop'əthi) *n.* med. treatment by methods believed to aid nature. -th, -thist, *n.*

naumachy, -chia (naw'məki -ā'kiə), *n.* mock sea-battle; arena for it.

naupathia (nawpath'iə), *n.* sea-sickness.

nauplius (naw'pliəs), *n.* (*pl.* -ii) first larval form of crustacean. -lial, -liform, -lioid, *adj.*

nausea (naw'siə), *n.* desire to vomit; disgust. -eous, *adj.* -nt, *n.* & *adj.* (substance) causing n. -te, *v.t.*

nautch (nawch), *n.* Ind. dancing performance.

nautics (naw'tiks), *n.* art of navigation; *n.pl.* water sports.

nautilus (naw'tiləs), *n.* kind of mollusc of Pacific. paper n., eight-tentacled mollusc with thin papery shell; argonaut. pearly n., n. with pearly inner shell.

navarch (nā'vahk), *n.* fleet-commander. -y, *n.*

navarin (nav'əraň), Fr. *n.* stew of mutton and vegetables.

navicular (nəvik'ūlə), *adj.* pert. to or like a boat; *n.* boat-shaped bone of wrist. -loid, -viform, *adj.* boat-shaped.

nawab (nəwawb'), *n.* Ind. nobleman or governor; nabob.

Nazi (nah'tsē), Ger. *n.* (*abbr.* of *Nationalsozialist*) adherent of Ger. party which formed government headed by Hitler (1933-45), with totalitarian principles and ruthless suppression of all opposition and minorities. **-sm**, *n*. principles of Nazi party.

nazim (nah'zim), Arab. *n*. Ind. military governor.

nasir (nah'zir), Arab. *n*. Ind. court treasurer ; Moham. official.

Neanderthal (nian'dətahl), *adj*. app. to European early Stone Age race, remains of which were discovered at N., a valley near Düsseldorf, Germany.

neanic (nian'ik), *adj*. young ; brephic.

neatherd (nēt'hōd), *n*. cow-herd.

nebula (neb'ūlə), *n*. (*pl*. **-ae**) vast gaseous area of universe. **spiral** n., a galaxy, or island universe. **-lise**, *v.t*. vaporise ; atomise. **-lose**, **-lous**, *adj*. cloudy ; vague. **-r**, *adj*.

necessitarian (nisesitār'ion), *n*. & *adj*. *Phil*., fatalist. **-ism**, *n*.

necrogenic, **-nous** (nekrəjen'ik, -oj'inəs), *adj*. pert. to or derived from dead animals.

necrolatry (nekrol'ətri), *n*. worship of the dead.

necrology (nekrol'əji), *n*. death-roll ; obituary. **-logic(al)**, *adj*. **-gist**, *n*. **-gue**, *n*. obituary.

necromancy (nek'rəmansi), *n*. black magic ; divination by communication with spirits. **-cer**, *n*. **-ntic**, *adj*.

necromorphous (nekrəmaw'fəs), *adj*. feigning death.

necropathy (nekrop'əthi), *n*. necrotic disease.

necrophagous (nekrof'əgəs), *adj*. feeding on dead bodies.

necrophilia (nekrəfil'iə), *n*. love of the dead. **-le**, *n*. **-lic**, *adj*. **-lous** (-of'iləs), *adj*. fond of dead creatures as food.

necrophobia (nekrəfōbiə), *n*. dread of dead bodies or death. **-bic**, *adj*.

necropolis (nekrop'əlis), *n*. large cemetery. **-litan** (-pol'itən), *adj*.

necropsy (nek'ropsi), *n*. post-mortem examination. **-roscopy**, *n*.

necrosis (nekrō'sis), *n*. mortification of tissue. **-otic** (-ot'ik), *adj*. **-otise**, **-rose**, *v.i*. & *t*. suffer or cause to suffer n.

necrotomy (nekrot'əmi), *n*. dissection of dead bodies ; removal of necrosed part. **-mic** (-om'ik), *adj*. **-mist**, *n*.

necrotype (nek'rətīp), *n*. extinct creature or species. **-pic** (-ip'ik), *adj*.

nectar (nek'tə), *n*. sugary liquid secreted by flowers ; divine drink. **-eal**, **-ean**, **-eous**, **-ial**, **-ian**, **-ine**, **-ous**, *adj*. **-iferous**, **-tiferous**, *adj*. yielding n. **-ium** (*pl*. **-ia**), **-y**, *n*. plant's gland secreting n. **-ivorous**, *adj*. feeding on n.

nectopod (nek'təpod), *n*. swimming limb.

née (nā), Fr. *adj*. (*masc*. **né**) "born" ; maiden name being .....

ne exeat (nē eks'iat), *Lat*., "let him not go out" ; writ forbidding person to leave country or court's jurisdiction.

nefandous (nifan'dəs), *adj*. unspeakable.

nefarious (nifār'iəs), *adj*. evil.

négligé(e) (neg'lizhā), Fr. *n*. easy, comfortable dress ; partly-undressed state ; loose robe.

negotiable (nigō'shiəbl), *adj*. *Comm*., transferable ; capable of being exchanged for cash.

negrillo (nigril'ō), *n*. African pygmy. **-rito** (-ē'tō), *n*.

negus (nē'gəs), *n*. drink of wine, hot water and spices ; title of Abyssinian ruler.

nek (nek), S. African *n*. mountain pass.

nekton (nek'ton), *n*. swimming creatures of open sea. **-ic**, *n*.

nemaline (nem'əlīn), *adj*. threadlike.

nematoceran (nemətos'ərən), *n*. & *adj*. (insect) belonging to the suborder of flies including mosquitoes. **-rous**, *adj*.

nematode (nem'ətōd), *n*. parasitic round-worm. **-diasis**, *n*. infestation with n. **-tocide**, *n*. substance killing n. **-tology**, *n*. study of n.

Nemesis (nem'isis), *n*. Gr. goddess of revenge ; retribution ; inevitable consequence. **-sic** (-es'ik), *adj*.

nemoral (nem'ərəl), *adj*. pert. to or living in a forest or wood. **-mophilous**, *adj*. fond of forests or woods. **-ricolous**, **-ricoline**, *adj*. living in forests or groves.

nenuphar (nen'ūfah), *n*. white or yellow water-lily.

neoblastic (nēəblas'tik), *adj*. pert. to new growth. **-ogenesis**, *n*. new formation.

neolatry (niol'ətri), *n*. worship of novelty. **-ter**, *n*.

neolithic (nēəlith'ik), *adj*. pert. to the later Stone Age.

neologism (niol'əjizm), *n.* use or coining of a new word ; such new word ; *Theol.*, new doctrine, *espec.* rationalism. **-gian** (-ō'jiən), *n. Theol.*, rationalist **-gic(al)**, *adj.* **-gise**, *v.t.* **-gist**, **-gy**, *n.*

neomenia (nēəmē'niə), *n.* time of new moon. **-n**, *adj.*

neomorphic (nēəmaw'fik), *adj.* developed suddenly and not inherited. **-ph**, **-phism**, *n.*

neon (nē'on), *n.* colourless gas glowing red in vacuum, used in advertising signs.

neonatus (nēənā'təs), *n.* (*pl.* **-ti**) new-born child. **-tal**, *adj.*

neonomian (nēənō'miən), *n.* adherent of new law, *espec.* of that of the New Testament. **-ism**, *n.*

neophilism (niof'ilizm), *n.* mania for novelty. **-ophobia**, *n.* dread of novelty.

neophrastic (nēəfras'tik), *adj.* pert. to use of neologisms.

neophyte (nē'əfīt), *n.* recent convert ; novice ; beginner. **-tic** (-it'ik), *adj.* **-tism**, *n.*

neoplasm (nē'əplazm), *n.* abnormal new growth, *espec.* of tumours. **-stic**, *adj.* **-sty**, *n.* formation of part afresh by plastic surgery.

neoprene (nē'əprēn), *n.* rubber-like synthetic plastic.

neorama (nēərah'mə), *n.* view of interior of building.

neossology (nēosol'əji), *n.* study of nestling birds. **-soptile**, *n.* newly hatched bird's downy feather.

neoteny (nēot'əni), **-nia**, **-einia** (niot'ini ; nēətē'niə, -ī'niə), *n.* arrested development at immature stage. **-nic**, *adj.*

neoteric (nēəter'ik), *adj.* new ; modern ; *n.* such thing. **-rism** (-ot'ərizm), *n.* neologism. **-rise**, *v.t.* **-rist**, *n.* **-ristic**, *adj.*

neotropical (nēətrop'ikl), *adj.* occurring in or pert. to tropical part of New World.

nepenthe (nipen'thi), *n.* drug destroying sorrow. **-s** (-ēz), *n.* pitcher-plant.

nephalism (nef'əlizm), *n.* teetotalism. **-ist**, *n.*

nepheligenous (nefəlij'inəs), *adj.* discharging smoke in clouds. **-lognosy**, *n.* observation of clouds. **-loid**, *adj.* cloudy. **-lometer**, *n.* instr. measuring cloudiness. **-loro-meter**, *n.* instr. measuring clouds'

direction and velocity. **-loscope**, *n.* instr. demonstrating formation of clouds.

nephology (nifol'əji), *n.* study of clouds. **-phogram**, *n.* cloud photograph. **-phoscope**, *n.* instr. measuring direction, velocity, etc., of clouds.

nephrectomy (nefrek'təmi), *n.* removal of kidney. **-mise**, *v.i.* & *t.*

nephria (nef'riə), *n.* Bright's disease. **-ric**, *adj.* pert. to kidneys. **-rism**, *n.* chronic kidney disease.

nephrite (nef'rīt), *n.* kind of jade used as charm against kidney disease ; kidney stone.

nephritis (nifrī'tis) *n.* inflammation of kidneys. **-tic** (-it'ik), *adj.* pert. to n. or kidneys ; *n.* person suffering from nephritis.

nephroid (nef'roid), *adj.* kidney-shaped. **-rolith**, *n.* stone of the kidney. **-rology**, *n.* study of kidneys. **-rolysis**, *n.* destruction of tissue of kidneys. **-ropathy**, *n.* kidney disease. **-ropexy**, *n.* surg. fixing of floating kidney. **-roptosis**, *n.* floating kidney. **-rosis**, *n.* degeneration of kidneys. **-rotomy**, *n.* incision into kidney. **-rotoxic**, *adj.* poisoning the kidneys.

nepionic (nepion'ik), *adj.* very young ; at stage immediately following embryo.

ne plus ultra (nē plus ul'trə), *Lat.*, "no more beyond" ; highest or furthest attainable.

nepotism (nep'ətizm), *n.* favouring of relatives in giving appointments and offices. **-tal**, *adj.* pert. to nephew. **-tic** (-ot'ik), *adj.* **-tist**, *n.*

neptunium (neptū'niəm), *n.* one of the transuranic elements.

nereid (nēr'iid), *n.* sea-nymph ; sea-centipede.

neritic (nirit'ik), *n.* pert. to shallow coastal waters.

Neronian (nirō'niən, -on'ik), *adj.* like Nero, Roman emperor infamous for cruelty and vice. **-nise**, *v.i.* & *t.*

nerval (nə'vəl), *adj.* neural ; *n.* ointment for sinews. **-vation**, *n.* arrangement of nerves or veins.

nervine (nə'vīn, -ēn), *n.* & *adj.* (drug) affecting, *espec.* soothing, nerves.

nescient (nesh'ənt), *adj.* lacking or disclaiming knowledge ; *n.* agnostic. **-nce**, *n.*

ə=*er* in *father* ; ɜ=*er* in *pert* ; th=*th* in *thin* ; dh=*th* in *then* ; zh=*s* in *pleasure* ; k=*ch* in *loch* ; ñ=Fr. nasal *n* ; ü=Fr. *u.*

nesiote (nē'siōt), adj. living on an island.

nestitherapy (nestither'əpi), n. med. treatment by reducing food taken.

netsuke (net'sookā), Jap. n. kind of carved button of wood, ivory, bone, etc.

neural (nūr'əl), adj. pert. to nerves; dorsal.

neuralgia (nūral'jiə), n. pain along nerve. -c, n. person suffering from n. -gic adj. -giform, adj. like n.

neurasthenia (nūrəsthēniə), n. nervous debility or breakdown. -nic (-en'ik), n. & adj.

neuration (nūr ā'shn), n. nervation.

neurergic (nūr ə'jik), adj. pert. to nerve action.

neuric (nūr'ik), adj. pert. to or having nerves.

neurilemma (nūrilem'ə), n. outer nerve sheath. -l, -tic, -tous, adj. -mitis, n. inflammation of n.

neurine (nūr'ēn, -in), n. poison arising in decaying flesh.

neuritis (nūr ī'tis), n. inflammation of nerve.

neurogram (nūr'əgram), n. modification in nerve structure to which memory is due. -mmic, adj. -rography, n. formation of n.; descriptive neurology.

neuroid (nūr'oid), n. nerve-like.

neurology (nūrol'əji), n. study of nerves and brain. -gical, adj. -gist, n.

neurolysis (nūrol'isis), n. disintegration of nerve substance; surg. liberation of nerve.

neuroma (nūr ō'mə), n. nerve tumour. -tous, adj. -tosis, n.

neuromimesis (nūrəmimē'sis), n. imitation of symptoms of disease by neurotic person. -etic (-et'ik), adj.

neuron(e) (nūr'on, -ōn), n. nerve cell. -nal, -nic, adj. -nism, n. theory that n. of brain are most important in mental processes.

neuropath (nūr'əpath), n. person believing that majority of diseases have nervous origin; sufferer from nervous disease. -ic, adj. -ology, n. pathology of nervous system. -y (-op'əthi), n. morbid condition of nerve.

neuropterous (nūrop'tərəs), adj. pert. or belonging to insect order including lace-wing flies. -ran, -ron (pl. -ra), n. such insect. -rist,

n. student of n. insects. -rology, n. study of n. insects.

neurosis (nūr ō'sis), n. (pl. -ses) activity of nervous system; disorder of nervous system. -otic, (-ot'ik), n. & adj. (person) suffering from nervous disease; (drug) acting on nerves.

neurotomy (nūrot'əmi), n. dissection of or incision into nerve. -mical (-om'ikl), adj. -mist, n.

neutrino (nūtrē'nō), n. uncharged atomic particle of less mass than neutron.

neutron (nū'tron), n. uncharged proton-like particle of atom.

newel (nū'əl), n. post at foot or head of stairs, or about which spiral staircase turns.

nexus (neks'əs), n. bond; tie; interconnected group.

niblick (nib'lik), n. iron-headed golf club with steeply angled face, for playing out of bunkers.

niccolic, -lous (nik'əlik, -əs), adj. nickel.

nichevo (nyechevav'), Russ. excl. "it doesn't matter."

nicolo, -icc- (nik'əlō), n. blue-black variety of onyx.

nicotian (nikō'shiən), n. tobacco-user.

nictate (nik'tāt), v.i. nictitate. -tion, n.

nictitate (nik'titāt), v.i. wink or blink. -tant, adj. winking. -ting membrane, membrane of certain animals and birds that can be drawn across eyeball; n.spasm, spasm of eyelid. -tion, n.

nidatory (nid'ətəri), adj. pert. to nests. -dicolous, adj. living in nests. -dificate, -dify, v.i. construct nest. -difugous, adj. leaving nest at early stage. -dology, n. study of nests. -dulant, adj. nestling. -dus (nī'dəs), n. (pl. -di) nest; place of breeding or origin.

niello (niel'ō), n. (pl. -li) black alloy used to fill engraved designs on metal; work or object decorated with n.; v.i. decorate with n. -list, n.

nigrescent (nigres'ənt), adj. becoming or somewhat black. -nce, n. -rine, adj. black. -rities, n. unusually dark colouring. -ritude, n. blackness. -rous (nī'grəs), adj.

nihilism (nī'ilizm), n. extreme anarchism; terrorism; Phil., denial that anything has real existence. **-ist,** *n.* **-lity,** *n.* nothingness ; thing of no worth.

nilgai (nil'gī), *n.* blue-grey short-horned Ind. antelope.

nimbus (nim'bəs), *n.* (*pl.* **-bi**) halo ; cloud of glory ; low, black rain-cloud. **-bose,** *adj.* cloudy.

nimiety (nimī'iti), *n.* excess.

nirvana (nəvah'nə), *n.* oblivion ; loss of identity at death by union with Brahma. **-nic,** *adj.*

nisi (nī'sī), Lat. *conj.* "unless." **decree n.,** order, *espec.* of divorce, to become effective at certain future time, unless reasons against it appear in the meantime. **n.prius** (-prī'əs), "unless before"; formerly, writ summoning jurors to Westminster unless in the meantime judges of assize had come to county in question ; now, trial by jury before a single judge, in London or at assizes.

nisus (nī'səs), *n.* effort, *espec.* to evacuate faeces ; desire, *espec.* sexual of birds.

nitchevo, *see* **nichevo.**

nitidous (nit'idəs), *adj.* shining.

nitre (nī'tə), *n.* saltpetre (potassium nitrate). **cubic n.,** sodium nitrate. **-rate,** *n.* salt of nitric acid ; *v.t.* treat with nitric acid. **-ric,** *adj.* **-rify,** *v.t.* **-rogen,** *n.* colourless inactive gas of atmosphere. **-ro-glycerine,** *n.* violent explosive liquid. **-rophilous,** *adj.* flourishing in soil rich in nitrogen. **-rophyte,** *n.* nitrophilous plant. **-rous,** *adj.*

nival (nī'vəl), *adj.* marked by, or living in, snow.

nivellate (niv'əlāt), *v.t.* level. **-tion,** **-tor,** *n.*

niveous (niv'iəs), *adj.* snowy. **-vosity,** *n.*

nix (niks), *n.* (*fem.* **-ie**) water sprite.

nizam (nī'zam ; nizam', -ahm'), Hind. *n.* title of former ruler of Hyderabad ; Turkish soldier.

Noachian, -ic (nō ā'kiən, -ik), *adj.* pert. to Noah and his period.

nobiliary (nəbil'iəri), *n.* pert. to nobility. **n.particle,** prep. indicating nobility, *e.g.* *de* (Fr.) or *von* (Ger.).

noblesse (nobles'), *n.* foreign nobility. **n.oblige** (-oblēzh'), *Fr.* "nobility obliges"; obligation upon persons of high birth to act nobly.

nocent (nō'sənt), *adj.* harmful ; criminal.

noctambulant (noktam'bulənt), *adj.* walking by night or in one's sleep. **-lation, -lism,** *n.* **-lous,** *adj.*

noctiflorous (noktiflor'əs), *adj.* flowering at night.

noctidiurnal (noktidī ē'nəl), *adj.* comprising one day and night.

noctilucan (noktilū'kən), *n.* luminescent sea creature. **-cal, -cent,** *adj.* luminescent (app. to living organisms only). **-cence,** *n.* **-cous,** *adj.* shining at night ; luminescent.

noctivagant (noktiv'əgənt), *adj.* wandering about at night. **-gation,** *n.* **-gous,** *adj.*

noctovision (nok'təvizhn), *n.* transmission by infra-red rays of image of object invisible through darkness.

noctuid (nok'tūid), *n.* night-flying moth.

nocturia (noktūr'iə), *n.* abnormal urination at night.

nocuous (nok'ūəs), *adj.* harmful.

nodus (nō'dəs), *n.* (*pl.* **-di**) crucial or difficult point ; knot.

noegenesis (nōijen'isis), *n.* production of knowledge. **-etic** (-jinet'ik), *adj.*

noesis (nō ē'sis), *n.* pure knowledge ; cognition. **-etic** (-et'ik), *n. & adj.* **-etics,** *n.* laws of logic.

Noetic (nōet'ik), *adj.* Noachian.

noggin (nog'in), *n.* small cup or quantity ; gill.

nolens volens (nō'lenz vō'lenz), *Lat.*, willy-nilly.

noli me tangere (nō'lī mē tan'jəri), *Lat.*, "touch me not."

nolition (nəlish'n), *n.* unwillingness.

nolle prosequi (nol'i pros'ikwī), *Lat.*, "to be unwilling to prosecute"; withdrawal of suit by plaintiff.

nom (nawn), F. *n.* "name." **n. de guerre** (də gār'), "name of war"; pseudonym. **n. de plume** (-də plüm), "name of pen"; writer's pseudonym.

nomenclature (nō'menklātūr, -men'-klət-), *n.* system or arrangement of names. **-tor,** *n.* lexicographer ; announcer or inventor of names. **-torial, -ural,** *adj.*

nomial (nō'miəl), *n.* single term.

nomic (nom'ik, nō'-), *adj.* customary ; conventional ; *n.* such non-phonetic spelling.

nominalism (nom'inəlizm), *n.* *Phil.*, doctrine that universal terms and abstractions are mere names and have no reality. **-ist,** *n.*

nominative (nom'inətiv), *n.* & *adj.* *Gram.*, (case) signifying subject of sentence.

nomism (nō'mizm), *n.* acceptance of moral law as basis of conduct. **-istic,** *adj.*

nomocracy (nəmok'rəsi), *n.* government based on legal system.

nomogenist (nəmoj'inist), *n.* believer in non-miraculous origin of life. **-nous,** *adj.* **-ny,** *n.*

nomography (nəmog'rəfi), *n.* drafting of laws ; treatise on n. **-pher,** *n.* **-phic(al),** *adj.*

nomology (nəmol'əji), *n.* science of law. **-gical,** *adj.* **-gist,** *n.*

nomothetic (nōməthet'ik), *adj.* legislative ; based on law. **-tes** (nəmoth'itēz), Gr. *n.* (*pl.* **-tai**) law-giver.

nonage (nō'nij), *n.* state of being under age.

nonagenarian (nōnəjinār'iən), *n.* & *adj.* (person) in from ninetieth to hundredth year. **-gesimal,** *adj.* ninetieth.

nonchalant (non'shələnt), *adj.* carefree ; at ease ; casual. **-nce,** *n.*

nones (nōnz), *n.pl.* ninth day before ides in anct. Rom. calendar ; *Eccl.*, office said at ninth hour.

non est (non est), *Lat.*, "(it) is not" ; non-existent ; lacking. **n. e. disputandum**, not to be disputed. **n.esse**, non-existence.

non-feasance (non-fē'zəns), *n.* failure to perform an act or obligation.

nonferrous (nonfer'əs), *adj.* not pert. to or including iron ; pert. to metals other than iron.

non grata (non grā'tə), *Lat.*, "not welcome" ; not acceptable to society or by authority.

nonillion (nənil'yən), *n.* a million octillions (10^{54}) ; *Fr.* & *Amer.*, a thousand octillions (10^{30}).

non-juror (non-jōōr'ə), *n.* person refusing to take oath, *espec.* of allegiance to William and Mary (1688). **-rant,** *adj.* **-rism,** *n.*

non libet (non lī'bet, lib'-), *Lat.*, "it is not pleasing." **n.licet** (-lī'set, lis'-), "it is not lawful." **n.liquet** (-lī'kwet, lik'-), "it is not clear."

non obstante (non obstan'ti), *Lat.*, notwithstanding (*abbr.* **non obst.**).

nonpareil (nonpərel'), *n.* size of type : 6-point ; *n.* & *adj.* unique (thing or person).

nonparous (nonpar'əs), *adj.* having not given birth to any offspring.

non placet (non plā'sit), *Lat.*, "(it) does not please" ; negative vote, *espec.* at university, etc.

non possumus (non pos'ūməs), *Lat.*, "we cannot" ; plea of inability ; refusal.

non prosequitur (non prōsek'witə), *Lat.*, "(he) does not prosecute" ; judgment against plaintiff on his non-appearance in court (*abbr.* **non pros.**).

non sequitur (non sek'witə), *Lat.*, "(it) does not follow" ; illogical deduction ; fallacy ; anacoluthon.

nonuple (non'ūpl), *adj.* ninefold ; consisting of, or in sets of, nine.

non-user (non-ū'zə), *n.* *Law*, failure to use, or exercise right.

noology (nōol'əji), *n.* study of intuition and reason. **-oscopic,** *adj.* pert. to examination of mind.

nopal (nō'pəl), *n.* prickly pear ; cochineal fig.

nordcaper (nawd'kāpə), *n.* right whale.

normocyte (naw'məsīt), *n.* red blood corpuscle.

nosism (nō'zizm), *n.* conceit on part of a group ; use of "we" in speaking of oneself.

nosology (nōzol'əji), *n.* classification of diseases. **-socomium,** *n.* hospital. **-sography,** *n.* descriptive n. **-somania,** *n.* delusion of suffering from imaginary disease.

nostalgia (nostal'jiə), *n.* homesickness. **-gic,** *adj.*

nostology (nostol'əji), *n.* study of senility. **-gic,** *adj.*

nostrification (nostrifikā'shn), *n.* acceptance of foreign university degrees as equal with native.

nostrum (nos'trəm), *n.* illusive remedy or scheme ; quack medicine.

nota bene (nō'tə bē'ni), *Lat.*, "note well" (*abbr.* **N.B.**).

notabilia (nōtəbil'iə), Lat. *n.pl.* things worth noting.

notacanthous (nōtəkan'thəs), *adj.* spiny-backed.

notal (nō'təl), *adj.* dorsal. **-gia,** *n.* pain in back.

notandum (nōtan'dəm), Lat. *n.* (*pl.* -da) thing to be noted.

notary (nō'təri), *n.* law officer certifying deeds, affidavits, etc.; in England, such eccl. official only. n.public, non-eccl. notary. -rial, *adj.*

nothosaur (nō'thəsor), *n.* plesiosaurus-like fossil reptile. -ian, *n. & adj.*

nothous (nō'thəs), *adj.* spurious; bastard.

notochord (nō'təkawd), *n.* backbone-like series of cells in lowest vertebrates. -al, *adj.*

notornis (nətaw'nis), *n.* extinct domestic-fowl-like bird of N.Z.

noumenon (nōō'minon), *n.* (*pl.* -mena) object perceived by intellect or reason alone. -nal, *adj.* -nalism, *n.* belief in existence of n. -nism, *n.* belief about n.

nous (nows, noos), *n.* pure intellect; reason; commonsense.

nouveau riche (nōō'vō rēsh'), *Fr.* (*pl.* nouveaux riches; *fem.* nouvelle.....) newly-rich person.

nova (nō'və), *n.* (*pl.* -ae) star suddenly increasing in brightness for short time.

novenary (nəvē'nəri, nov'-), *adj.* pert. to or consisting of nine; *n.* set of nine. -ndial, *n. & adj.* (festival) lasting nine days. -nnial, *adj.* happening every ninth year.

novercal (nəvē'kəl), *adj.* pert. to stepmother.

noxal (noks'əl), *adj.* noxious; pert. to damage.

noxious (nok'shəs), *adj.* harmful.

noyade (nwayad'), Fr. *n.* drowning, *espec.* of many persons together as form of execution.

nu (nū), *n.* thirteenth letter (N, *ν*) of Gr. alphabet; (nü) Fr. *adj.* naked.

nuance (nü'ahns), Fr. *n.* slight shade or difference.

nubia (nū'biə), *n.* cloud; lady's fleecy head-wrap. -bilate, *v.t.* obscure.

nubile (nūbīl, -il), *adj.* marriageable (app. to women only). -lity, *n.*

nubilous (nū'biləs), *adj.* cloudy; vague.

nucal (nū'kəl), *adj.* of nuts.

nuchal (nū'kəl), *adj.* pert. to nape of neck; *n.* such bone, etc. -gia (-al'jiə), *n.* pain in nape.

nuciferous (nūsif'ərəs), *adj.* yielding nuts. -ciform, *adj.* nut-shaped. -civorous, *adj.* nut-eating.

nucleus (nū'kliəs), *n.* (*pl.* nuclei, -klii) kernel, core, central part or body, *espec.* of atom, composed of protons and neutrons, round which electrons revolve. -lear, *adj.* pert. to, situated or comprised in, n.; n. energy, energy produced by splitting atom n.; n. fission, fusion, *see* fission, fusion; n. physics, study of atom n.; n. reactor, apparatus in which atom n. are split.

nudicaudate (nūdikaw'dāt), *adj.* with hairless tail. -caulous, *adj.* with leafless stems. -iflora, *adj.* flowering before leaves appear. -iflorous, *adj.* with naked flowers. -iped, *n. & adj.* (animal) with naked feet.

nugacious (nūgā'shəs), *adj.* unimportant. -city, *n.* triviality; futility. -gae (nū'jē), Lat. *n.pl.* trifles.

nugatory (nū'gətəri), *adj.* futile; powerless; null; nugacious.

nullah (nul'ə), Anglo-Ind. *n.* dry watercourse; gully; stream. n.-nullah, Austral. aborigine's club.

nullibist (nul'ibist), *n.* person denying soul's existence in space.

nullifidian (nulifid'iən), *n. & adj.* sceptic(al).

nulliparous (nulip'ərəs), *adj.* having borne no children. -ra, *n.* such woman. -rity (-ar'iti), *n.*

nullius filius (nul'iəs fil'iəs), Lat., "nobody's son"; bastard.

numen (nū'men), *n.* (*pl.* -mina) local or presiding divinity; god in human form. -minism, *n.* belief in n. -minous, *adj.* pert. to n.; awe-inspiring; supernatural.

numerology (nūmərol'əji), *n.* study of mystic meanings in numbers. -rist, *n.*

numismatic (nūmizmat'ik), *adj.* pert. to coins. -s, -tology, *n.* study and collection of coins and medals. -tician, -tist, *n.* -tography, *n.* description of coins.

nummary (num'əri), *adj.* pert. to coin. -miform, *adj.* coin-shaped.

nummular(y) (num'ūlər, -i), *adj.* nummary; nummiform. -lite, *n.* coin-like fossil shell.

Nunc Dimittis (nungk dimit'is), Lat., "now thou lettest depart"; canticle (Luke ii, 29–32) sung at

---

ə=*er* in *father*; ō=*er* in *pert*; th=*th* in *thin*; dh=*th* in *then*; zh=*s* in *pleasure*; k=*ch* in *loch*; ṅ=Fr. nasal *n*; ü=Fr. *u*.

Evensong ; permission to depart ; congé.

nuncio (nun'shiō), *n.* papal envoy. **-ciate,** *n.* messenger. **-ciative,** *adj.* bearing messages. **-ciature,** *n.* office of n.

nuncupate (nun'kūpāt), *v.t.* declare verbally ; dedicate. **-tion, -tor,** *n.* **-tive, -tory,** *adj.* oral ; not written down ; designative.

nundinal (nun'dinəl), *n.* one of first eight letters of alphabet, indicating day of week in anct. Rome ; *adj.* pert. to n. ; pert. to market or market-day. **-nation,** *n.* trading. **-ne,** *n.* market-day, held in anct. Rome every eighth day.

nuptial (nup'shəl), *adj.* pert. to wedding. **-ity,** *n.* wedding ; marriage-rate. **-s,** *n.pl.* wedding.

nuque (nūk ; Fr., nük), *n.* nape.

nutation (nūtā'shn), *n.* nodding ; such motion of earth's axis. **-tant,** *adj.* nodding or drooping. **-al,** *adj.*

nutria (nū'triə), *n.* coypu.

nutrice (nū'tris), *n.* nurse. **-cial,** *adj.*

nux vomica (nuks vom'ikə), *n.*

strychnine-containing seed of Asiatic tree.

nychthemer(on) (nik'thimə, -thē'-məron), *n.* period of one night and day. **-ral,** *adj.*

nyctalopia (niktəlō'piə), *n.* condition of seeing poorly at night or in partial darkness, while day sight is normal ; *erron.,* the opposite condition. **-pic** (-op'ik), *adj.* person suffering from n. **-pic** (-op'ik), *adj.*

nyctophobia (niktəfō'biə), *n.* dread of darkness.

nycturia (niktūr'iə), *n.* nocturia.

nylghau, -ai (nil'gaw, -gī), *n.* nilgai.

nylon (nī'lon), *n.* synthetic material made from coal, air, and water, obtainable as textile filaments, bristles, etc.

nymphitis (nimfī'tis), *n.* inflammation of inner lips of vulva. **-pho-lepsy,** *n.* emotional frenzy ; *Med.,* removal of inner lips of vulva. **-phomania,** *n.* sexual mania in female.

nystagmus (nistag'məs), *n.* involuntary oscillation of the eyeballs. **-mic,** *adj.*

O

oakum (ō'kəm), *n.* fibre of old untwisted ropes.

oast (ōst), *n.* hop-kiln.

obbligato (obligah'tō), *adj.* & *n. Mus.,* accompanying, or accompaniment by solo instr. other than piano.

obdormition (obdawmish'n), *n.* numbness or "going to sleep" of a limb, etc.

obdurate (ob'dūrət), *adj.* obstinate ; hard-hearted. **-racy,** *n.*

obeah (ō'biə), *n.* W. African magic cult ; magical spell.

obeisance (ōbā'səns), *n.* bow or curtsey ; paying of homage. **-nt,** *adj.*

obeism (ō'biizm), *n.* practice of obeah.

obelise (ob'ilīz), *v.t.* mark with obelus ; denounce as spurious.

obelisk (ob'ilisk), *n.* tapering rectangular stone pillar. **-oid,** *adj.*

obelus (ob'iləs), *n.* (*pl.* **-li**) mark of reference (†) ; mark (— or ÷) signifying spurious passage in MS., etc.

obtuscate (obfus'kāt), *v.t.* make

dark or obscure ; confuse. **-cous,** *adj.* **-tion, -tor,** *n.*

obi (ō'bi), Jap., *n.* wide Jap. girdle.

obiit (ob'iit), *Lat.,* "died" (*abbr.* **ob.**). **o. sine prole** (-sī'nē prō'lē), "died without issue."

obit (ō'bit), *n.* death ; funeral or memorial service ; obituary.

obiter dictum (ob'itə dik'təm), *Lat.* (*pl.* ..... **dicta**) "thing said in passing" ; casual or incidental remark or opinion.

obituary (ōbit'ūəri), *n.* death-record or roll ; biographical notice of recently dead person ; *adj.* pert. to person's death. **-rian,** *n.* & *adj.* **-rist,** *n.* writer of o.

objet d'art (ob'zhä dahr'), *Fr.* (*pl.* **objets** .....) thing of artistic value.

objicient (objish'ənt), *n.* objector.

objurgate (ob'jəgāt), *v.t.* rebuke ; scold. **-tion,** *n.* **-tive, -tory,** *adj.*

oblate (ob'lāt), *n.* & *adj.* dedicated (person) ; *adj. Geom.,* flattened at poles. **-tion,** *n.* offering ; sacrifice. **-tional, -tory,** *adj.*

oblique (oblēk'), *adj.* slanting ; indirect ; underhand. **-quity**

---

hat, bah, hāte, hāre, crawl ; pen, ēve, hēre ; it, īce, fīre ;
on, bōne, boil, bōre, howl ; foot, fōōd, bōōr, hull, tūbe, pūre.

(-ik'witi), *n*. deviation from straight line or moral code.

oblivion (obliv'iən), *n*. complete forgetfulness or forgottenness. **-vescence,** *n*. act of forgetting. **-vial, -vious,** *adj*. **-viscence,** *n*. forgetfulness.

obloquy (ob'ləkwi), *n*. abuse ; disgrace. **-locutor** (-lok'ūtə), *n*. one who denies or disputes.

obreption (obrep'shn), *n*. attempt to obtain eccl. dispensation, etc., fraudulently. **-titious,** *adj*. performed in underhand fashion.

obrogate (ob'rəgāt), *v.t*. alter (law) by passing new law. **-tion,** *n*.

obscurantism (obskūr'əntizm), *n*. prevention of enlightenment. **-tic** (-an'tik), *adj*. **-tist,** *n*.

obsecrate (ob'sikrāt), *v.t*. beseech. **-tion,** *n*.

obsequies (ob'sikwiz), *n.pl*. funeral. **-quious** (-ē'kwiəs), *adj*. servile.

obsidian (obsid'iən), *n*. dark-coloured volcanic glass.

obsidional, -ary (obsid'iənəl, -əri), *adj*. pert. to siege.

obsolescent (obsəles'ənt), *adj*. becoming obsolete. **-nce,** *n*. **-lete,** *adj*. disused ; out-of-date. **-letism,** *n*. obsolete thing.

obstetric(al) (obstet'rik, -l), *adj*. pert. to childbirth or midwifery. **-cate,** *v.i*. & *t*. assist at childbirth. **-cian, -rist,** *n*. expert in obstetrics. **-rix,** *n*. midwife. **-s,** *n*. midwifery.

obstipation (obstipā'shn), *n*. complete constipation.

obstriction (obstrik'shn), *n*. obligation.

obstruent (ob'strooənt), *n*. & *adj*. (medicine) blocking up body passage.

obtenebrate (obten'ibrāt), *v.t*. darken ; cast shadow over.

obtest (obtest'), *v.t*. beseech ; invoke ; adjure. **-ation,** *n*.

obtruncate (obtrung'kāt), *v.t*. behead. **-tion, -tor,** *n*.

obtund (obtund'), *v.t*. blunt ; dull. **-ent** *n*. & *adj*. (drug) dulling pain. **-ity,** *n*.

obturate (ob'tūr āt), *v.t*. seal up. **-tion, -tor,** *n*.

obumbrate (obum'brət), *adj*. darkened ; hidden under a projection. **-rant,** *adj*. over-hanging.

obvallate (obval'āt), *adj*. walled in.

obvention (obven'shn), *n*. casual or occasional happening or gift.

obverse (ob'vəs), *n*. front or top side ; "head" of coin ; counterpart ; *adj*. facing observer ; with top wider than base.

obvert (obvət'), *v.t*. turn ; alter. **-rsion,** *n*.

obvolute (ob'vəloot), *adj*. over-lapping ; twisted. **-tion,** *n*. **-tive,** *adj*.

ocarina (okərē'nə), *n*. egg-shaped whistle-like mus. instr.

occamy (ok'əmy), *n*. alloy imitating silver or gold.

occident (ok'sidənt), *n*. the west. **-al,** *adj*.

occiput (ok'sipət), *n*. back of head. **-pital** (-ip'itəl), *adj*. ; *n*. such bone.

occlude (oklood'), *v.t*. shut up, in or out ; *v.i*. shut mouth so that teeth meet. **-nt,** *n*. & *adj*. **-usal,** *adj*. pert. to cutting edge of tooth. **-usion, -usor,** *n*. **-usive,** *adj*. ; *n*. sound (as *t*) made by stopping breath.

occult (ok'ult), *adj*. mysterious ; hidden ; magical ; supernatural ; *v.t*. *Astron*., obscure (object) by passing between it and observer. **-ation,** *n*.

ocellus (ōsel'əs), *n*. (*pl*. **-li**) small eye ; eye-like coloured spot. **-lar,** *adj*. **-late(d),** *adj*. bearing o. **-lation,** *n*. **-liferous, -ligerous,** *adj*. bearing o.

ocelot (ō'silot), *n*. yellow, spotted, wild cat of S. and Cent. Amer., and its fur. **-loid,** *adj*. like o.

ochlesis (oklē'sis), *n*. unhealthy condition due to over-crowding. **-etic** (-et'ik), **-sitic,** *adj*.

ochlocracy (oklok'rəsi), *n*. mob rule. **-crat,** *n*. **-cratic,** *adj*. **-lophobia,** *n*. dread of crowds.

ochre (ō'kə), *n*. red or yellow iron-containing earth used as pigment ; yellowish - brown hue. **-ous, -raceous, -rous,** *adj*. **-roid,** *adj*. like o.

ocracy (ok'rəsi), *n*. government.

ocreate (ō'kriāt, ok'-), *adj*. wearing boots or leggings.

octactinal (oktak'tinəl), *adj*. eight-rayed.

octad (ok'tad), *n*. group of eight.

octagon (ok'təgən), *n*. 8-sided plane figure. **-al** (-ag'ənəl), *adj*.

octahedron (oktəhē'drən), *n*. 8-sided solid figure. **-ral,** *adj*.

octamerous (oktam'ərəs), *adj*. having its parts in eights. **-rism,** *n*.

---

octameter (oktam'itə), *n.* verse-line of eight feet.

octan (ok'tən), *adj.* happening or recurring every eight days.

octane (ok'tān), *n.* liquid hydrocarbon of paraffin series. o. number, number representing antiknock property of a motor spirit, being the percentage of a certain octane in a mixture used for testing by comparison. high o., denoting a motor spirit of high o. number, *i.e.*, having high anti-knock properties.

octant (ok'tənt), *n.* eighth part of circle (45°); angle-measuring instr. with that arc. -al, *adj.*

octapla (ok'təplə), *n.* multi-lingual book in eight texts.

octaploid (ok'təploid), *adj.* eightfold; having eight times haploid number; *n.* such cell. -ic, *adj.*

octapody (oktap'ədi), *n.* octameter. -dic (-od'ik), *adj.*

octarchy (ok'tahki), *n.* government by eight persons; alliance of eight independent governments.

octarius (oktār'iəs), *n.* pint.

octastich (ok'təstik), *n.* poem or stanza of eight lines. -on (-as'ti-kon), *n.*

octateuch (ok'tatūk), *n.* series of eight books; first eight books of Old Testament.

octave (ok'tiv), *n.* group of eight; *Eccl.*, week following feast day; eighth day (including feast day) after feast day; *Mus.*, interval comprising eight tones; *Lit.*, first eight lines of sonnet; eight-line stanza.

octavo (oktā'vō), *n.* book size: foolscap o., $6\frac{3}{4}'' \times 4\frac{1}{4}''$; crown o., $7\frac{1}{2}'' \times 5''$; large crown o., $8'' \times 5\frac{1}{4}''$; demy o., $8\frac{3}{4}'' \times 5\frac{5}{8}''$; medium o., $9\frac{1}{2}'' \times 6''$; royal o., $10'' \times 6\frac{1}{4}''$; super royal o., $10\frac{1}{4}'' \times 6\frac{3}{4}''$; imperial o., $11'' \times 7\frac{1}{2}''$ (*abbr.* 8vo.).

octennial (okten'iəl), *adj.* happening in every eighth year; lasting eight years.

octillion (oktil'yən), *n.* a million septillions (10^{48}); *Fr. & Amer.*, a thousand septillions (10^{27}).

octodecimo (oktədes'imō), *n.* book size: demy o., $5\frac{3}{4}'' \times 3\frac{3}{4}''$ (*abbr.* 18mo.).

octogenarian (oktəjinār'iən), *n. & adj.* (person) in from eightieth to ninetieth year.

octonarian (oktənār'iən), *n. & adj.* (verse-line) of eight feet.

octonary (ok'tənəri), *adj.* pert. to or consisting of eight; in groups of eight; *n.* stanza of eight lines.

octopod (ok'təpod), *n. & adj.* (mollusc) belonging to the order of cephalopods having eight arms. -an, -ous (-op'ədən, -əs), *adj.*

octoroon (oktəroōn'), *n.* child of quadroon and white.

octosyllable (ok'təsiləbl), *n.* verse line or word of eight syllables. -bic (-ab'ik), *adj.*

octroi (oktrwah'), *Fr. n.* trading privilege; concession; monopoly; tax on goods imported into town, and place where it is collected.

octuple (ok'tūpl), *adj.* in groups of eight; eightfold; *v.i. & t.* multiply eightfold. -x, *adj.* pert. to telegraphic system whereby eight messages can be sent by one wire.

ocular (ok'ūlə), *adj.* pert. to eyes; visual. -late, *adj.* having eyes. -liform, *adj.* eye-shaped. -list, *n.* med. expert on eyes. -lus, *n. Archit.*, any eye-like feature, *espec.* window.

odalisque (ō'dəlisk), *n.* woman of harem.

odium (ō'diəm), *n.* hatred; reproach. -ious, *adj.*

odograph (ō'dəgraf), *n.* instr. recording distance travelled, *espec.* by pedestrian. -ometer, *n.*

odontology (ōdontol'əji), *n.* study of teeth. -tiasis, *n.* teething. -tic, *adj.* dental. -tocate, *n.* toothed whale. -tognathous, *adj.* pert. to extinct toothed birds. -tography, *n.* description of or treatise on teeth. -toid, *adj.* tooth-like. -tolith, *n.* dental tartar. -toloxia, *n.* irregularity of teeth. -toma, *n.* dental tumour. -torrhagia, *n.* haemorrhage from tooth socket. -tosis, *n.* dentition. -totomy, *n.* incision into tooth. -totrypy, *n.* drilling into a tooth.

odorivector (ōdor'ivektə), *n.* substance causing odour.

odyssey (od'isi), *n.* protracted, wandering journey.

oecist (ē'sist), *n.* colonist.

oecodomic (ēkədom'ik), *adj.* pert. to architecture.

oecumenical, *see* ecumenical.

Oedipus (ē'dipəs), *n.* prince of

Thebes in Gr. legend, who unknowingly murdered his father and married his mother, and who answered the riddle of the Sphinx; one who solves riddles. **O.complex,** *Psych.,* fixation on one's mother, *espec.* with hatred of father.

oeil-de-boeuf (ōi-də-bōf'), Fr. *n.* (*pl.* **oeils** .....) round or oval window.

oeillade (ēyahd'), Fr. *n.* glance, ogle.

oenology (ēnol'əji), *n.* study of wines. **-gical,** *adj.* **-gist,** *n.* **-nometer,** *n.* instr. testing alcoholic strength of wines. **-nophilist,** *n.* wine-lover. **-nophobist,** *n.* wine-hater. **-nopoetic,** *adj.* pert. to wine-making.

oersted (ō'sted), *n.* unit of magnetic field strength or intensity.

oesophagus (ēsof'əgəs), *n.* food passage between mouth and stomach.

oestrum, -us (ē'strəm, -əs), *n.* period of sexual heat; frenzy. **-rous, -rual,** *adj.* **-ruate,** *v.i.* be on heat. **-ruation,** *n.*

offal (of'əl), *n.* refuse; garbage; edible animal entrails and organs.

officinal (ofis'inəl), *adj.* used in med., art or industry; stocked by pharmacists; *n.* such drug.

Oflag (of'lahg), Ger. *n.* (*abbr.* of *Offizierlager*) prisoner-of-war camp for officers.

ogam, *see* **ogham.**

ogdoad (og'dōad), *n.* eight; group of eight.

ogee (ō'jē), *n.* moulding with S-shaped section; *adj.* S-shaped. **o.arch,** pointed arch with o. curve on either side.

ogham (og'əm), *n.* anct. Brit. alphabet of notches; character of o. **-ic,** *adj.*

ogive (ō'jīv, -jiv'), *n.* pointed arch; vault's diagonal rib. **-val,** *adj.*

ohm (ōm), *n.* unit of elec. resistance; resistance of circuit in which current of one amp. is produced by one volt. **-age,** *n.* **-ic,** *adj.* **-mmeter,** *n.* instr. measuring resistance in o.

oikology (oikol'əji), *n.* domestic economy.

okapi (ōkah'pi), *n.* African animal like short-necked giraffe, with whitish face and black-striped whitish legs.

oleaginous (ōliaj'inəs), *adj.* oily.

oleander (ō'liandə), *n.* poisonous white- or red-flowered evergreen shrub of E. Ind.

oleaster (ō'liastə), *n.* yellow-flowered, olive-like shrub of S. Eur.; *erron.,* wild olive.

olecranon (ōlek'rənon, -ā'non), *n.* projecting bone of elbow; "funnybone." **-nal,** *adj.*

oleic (ōlē'ik), *adj.* pert. to or derived from oil. **-iferous,** *adj.* oil-producing.

olent (ō'lənt), *adj.* fragrant.

oleoduct (ō'liədukt), *n.* channel conveying oil.

oleograph (ō'liəgraf), *n.* lithographic reproduction of oil painting. **-y,** *n.*

oleometer (ōliom'itə), *n.* oil hydrometer; instr. measuring amount of oil in substance.

oleraceous (olərā'shəs), *adj.* potherb-like; edible. **-riculture** (ol'-), *n.* vegetable-growing.

olfactory (olfak'təri), *adj.* pert. to sense of smell. **-tible,** *adj.* capable of being smelt. **-tion,** *n.* act or sense of smelling. **-tology,** *n.* study of smells. **-tometer,** *n.* instr. measuring keenness of sense of smell, and olfactibility of odours.

olid (ol'id), *adj.* evil-smelling.

oligarch (ol'igahk), *n.* member of oligarchy. **-ic(al),** *adj.* **-y,** *n.* government by the few.

oligidria (olijid'riə), *n.* insufficient perspiration.

oligist (ol'ijist), *n.* haematite.

oligochrome (ol'igəkrōm), *n. & adj.* (work of art) done in few colours. **-chronometer,** *n.* instr. measuring very short time intervals. **-cythaemia,** *n.* deficiency of red corpuscles in blood. **-odontous,** *adj.* having few teeth. **-odynamic,** *adj.* pert. to effect of small quantities; having effect in small quantities only. **-ophagous,** *adj.* eating a few sorts of food only. **-ophrenia,** *n.* feeble-mindedness. **-osyllable,** *n.* word of few syllables.

olio (ō'liō), *n.* miscellany; hotchpotch.

olitory (ol'itəri), *adj.* pert. to potherbs or kitchen garden.

oliver (ol'ivə), *n.* treadle-hammer.

olivet (ol'ivet), *n.* artificial pearl; olive grove; Mount of Olives.

olla-podrida (ol'ə-pədrē'də), *n.* olio.

---

olympiad (əlim'piad), *n.* interval of four years between Gr. Olympic games ; *mod.*, Olympic games.

Olympian (əlim'piən), *adj.* pert. to Olympus, abode of Gr. gods ; divine ; magnificent ; magnanimous.

omasum (ōmā'səm), *n.* (*pl.* -a) third stomach of ruminants. **-sitis**, *n.* inflammation of o.

ombre (om'bə), *n.* Sp. card game for three persons.

ombré (awn'brā), Fr. *n.* & *adj.* shaded (fabric). **-s chinoises** (-shēnwahz'), "Chinese shadows" ; shadow-play.

ombrology (ombrol'əji), *n.* study of rain. **-rograph**, *n.* recording ombrometer. **-rometer**, *n.* rain gauge. **-rophile**, *n.* plant flourishing in extremely rainy conditions. **-rophobe**, *n.* plant thriving only in desert conditions.

omega (ō'migə), *n.* last (twenty-fourth) letter (Ω, ω) of Gr. alphabet ; ending. **-goid**, *adj.* Ω-shaped.

omentum (ōmen'təm), *n.* (*pl.* -ta) fold of the peritoneum. **great o.**, fat-filled sac covering small intestines. **lesser o.**, o. joining stomach with liver.

omicron (ōmī'kron, om'-), *n.* fifteenth letter (O, ο) of Gr. alphabet ; short o.

omlah (om'lə), Anglo-Ind. *n.* body of N. Ind. court officers.

omneity (omnē'iti), *n.* state of including all things. **-nes** (-ēz), Lat. *n.pl.* "all (persons)". **-niana**, *n.* ana of every kind.

omnicompetent (omnikom'pitənt), *adj.* legally competent in all matters. **-corporeal**, *adj.* including all bodies. **-ifarious**, *adj.* of all kinds. **-ify**, *v.t.* make large or universal. **-igenous** (-nij'inəs), *adj.* of all kinds. **-imodous** (-nim'ədəs), *adj.* of all kinds. **-ipotent** (-nip'ə-tənt), *adj.* all-powerful. **-ipresent**, *adj.* present everywhere. **-iscient** (-nis'iənt), *adj.* knowing everything. **-ium**, *n.* Comm., total of parts of fund or stock ; **o. gatherum**, *n.* miscellaneous collection, *espec.* of persons. **-ivorous** (-niv'ərəs), *adj.* feeding on all kinds of food.

omodynia (ōmədin'iə), *n.* pain in shoulder.

omophagy, **-gia** (ōmof'əji, -ā'jiə), *n.* eating of raw flesh. **-gic** (-aj'ik), **-gous** (-gəs), *adj.*

omphalos (om'fələs), Gr. *n.* (*pl.* -li) navel ; central point. **-kepsis**, *n.* meditation while gazing at one's navel. **-lic** (-al'ik), *adj.* **-loid**, *adj.* like a navel.

omrah (om'rə), *n.* Moham.court lord.

onager (on'əjə), *n.* (*pl.* -gri) wild ass of Asia. **-graceous**, *adj.* belonging to evening primrose family of plants.

onanism (ō'nənizm), *n.* masturbation. **-ist**, *n.* **-istic**, *adj.*

oncology (ongkol'əji), *n.* study of tumours. **-gic(al)**, *adj.* **-ometer**, *n.* instr. measuring changes in internal organs' size. **-osis**, *n.* development of tumours. **-otomy**, *n.* incision into tumour.

ondatra (ondat'rə), *n.* musk-rat.

on dit (awn dē'), *Fr.*, "one says" ; rumour ; hearsay.

ondograph (on'dəgraf), *n.* instr. measuring variations in wave formation of elec. current. **-gram**, *n.* record of o. **-oscope**, *n.* instr. showing such wave form.

ondoyant (awndway'ahn), Fr. *adj.* wavy.

oneiric (ōnī'ik), *adj.* pert. to dreams. **-rocritic**, *n.* interpreter of dreams. **-rotic**, *adj.*

onerous (on'ərəs), *adj.* burdensome ; weighty.

oniomania (ōniəmā'niə), *n.* mania for making purchases. **-c**, *n.*

onolatry (ōnol'ətri), *n.* ass-worship.

onomastic (onəmas'tik), *adj.* pert. to or consisting of names ; pert. to autograph signature to document written by another. **-mancy**, *n.* divination from names. **-matology**, *n.* science of names. **-matomania**, *n.* irresistible desire to repeat certain words continually, *espec.* words of something to be remembered. **-on**, *n.* vocabulary of proper names.

onomatopoeia (onomatəpē'ə), *n.* lit. device of using to describe a thing words whose sound suggests the thing described ; formation of names for things from latters' sound ; name so formed. **-ial**, **-ian**, **-ic**, **-oetic**, *adj.* **-plasm**, *n.* word formed by o.

onomatous (onom'ətəs), *adj.* bearing author's name.

ontal (on'təl), *adj.* pert. to reality or noumena.

ontogeny, -nesis (ontoj'ini, -jen'-isis), *n.* individual life history. -netic (-jinet'ik), -nic (-jer'ik), *adj.* -ocycle, *n.* cycle-like development with return in old age to infantile character.

ontology (ontol'əji), *n.* branch of philosophy dealing with the ultimate nature of reality or being. -gic(al), *adj.* -gism, *n.* ontological doctrine. -tography, *n.* description of reality or being.

onus (ō'nəs), *n.* burden ; responsibility ; obligation. o.probandi, obligation to prove.

onychia (ōnik'iə), *n.* inflammation of root of nail. -chauxis, *n.* hypertrophy of nails. -chitis, *n.* inflammation at side or base of nail. -choid, *adj.* fingernail-like. -chosis, *n.* disease of nail.

onym (on'im), *n.* scientific name. -al, -atic, *adj.* -ise, *v.i.* -y, *n.* scientific nomenclature.

onyxis (ōniks'is), *n.* ingrowing nail.

oögamete (ōəgamēt'), *n.* female gamete. -genesis, *n.* egg-formation. -mous, *adj.* heterogamous.

oöid(al) (ō'oid, -l), *adj.* egg-shaped.

oölite (ō'əlīt), *n.* limestone comprising small egg-like grains. -tic (-it'ik), *adj.*

oölogy (ōōl'əji), *n.* collection and study of birds' eggs. -gic(al), *adj.* -gise, *v.i.* search for birds' eggs. -gist, *n.*

oom (ōōm), Dutch *n.* uncle.

oömeter (ōōm'itə), *n.* egg-measuring instr. -tric (-et'rik), *adj.* -try, *n.*

oont (oont), Anglo-Ind. *n. sl.* camel.

oöscope (ō'əskōp), *n.* instr. for examining interior of egg.

oösperm (ō'əspəm), *n.* fertilised egg. -spore, *n.* spore arising from fertilised egg cell.

oötocous (ōōt'əkəs), *adj.* oviparous.

opacity (ōpas'iti), *n.* quality or state of being opaque. -cify, *v.t.* make opaque.

opah (ō'pə), *n.* large brightly-coloured fish.

opalescent (ōpəles'ənt), *adj.* iridescent. -nce, *n.*

opaque (ōpāk'), *adj.* not transparent ; dark ; stupid.

ope et consilio (ō'pē et konsil'iō), *Lat.*, "with aid and advice."

opeidoscope (ōpī'dəskōp), *n.* instr.

showing sound vibrations by vibrating mirror.

operculum (ōpə'kūləm), *n.* (*pl.* -la) lid-like organ, as of moss capsule and mollusc shell ; fish's gill cover. -cle, *n.* -cular, *adj.* -culate, -culiferous, -culigerous, *adj.* having o.

opere citato (op'ərē sītā'tō), *Lat.*, "in the work quoted" (*abbr.* o.c.).

operose (op'ərōs), *adj.* needing labour ; working hard.

ophelimity (ōfəlim'iti), *n.* ability to satisfy.

ophiasis (ōfī'əsis), *n.* baldness in wavy bands.

ophic (of'ik), *adj.* pert. to serpents. -phism, *n.* snake-worship.

ophicleide (of'iklīd), *n.* bass bugle-like keyed brass mus. instr. -an, *adj.* -dist, *n.*

ophidian (ofid'iən), *n.* & *adj.* (reptile) belonging to order of reptiles including snakes. -diophobia, *n.* dread of snakes. -phioid, *adj.* snake-like. -phiomorphic, *adj.* snake-shaped.

ophiuran (ōfiūr'ən, of-), *n.* brittle star.

ophthalmia (ofthal'miə), *n.* inflammation of eye. -mic, *adj.* pert. to eye or o. -mious, *adj.* -mology, *n.* study of eye and its diseases. -mometer, *n.* instr. for measuring eye, *espec.* for astigmatism. -moplegia, *n.* paralysis of ocular muscles.

opiate (ō'piāt), *n.* & *adj.* (drug or thing) inducing sleep or soothing pain ; *v.t.* impregnate with opium ; treat with o. ; soothe or dull. -tic (-at'ik), *adj.*

opiniâtre (ōpēnyah'tr), Fr. *adj.* opinionated.

opisometer (opisom'itə), *n.* instr. measuring curved lines.

opisthenar (opis'thinah), *n.* back of hand. -thognathous, *adj.* with receding jaws. -thograph, *n.* thing bearing writing on both sides. -thoporeia, *n.* walking backwards involuntarily. -thosomal, *adj.* pert. to posteriors.

opopanax (opop'ənaks), *n.* aromatic gum resin used in perfumery.

opossum (əpos'əm), *n.* small grey Amer. marsupial, and its fur. playing o. or 'possum, feigning death ; remaining silent or concealed.

oppidan (op'idən), *adj.* pert. to town; *n.* town-dweller; student at Eton boarding in the town.

oppilate (op'ilāt), *v.t.* stop up. **-tion,** *n.* **-tive,** *adj.*

opprobrium (oprō'briəm), *n.* reproach; abuse; disgrace. **-rious,** *adj.*

oppugn (opūn'), *v.i.* & *t.* deny; resist; conflict with. **-ate** (-ug'nāt), *v.i.* & *t.*

opsonin (op'sənin), *n.* substance of blood serum making bacteria vulnerable to phagocytic action. **-nic** (-on'ik), *adj.*; **o.index,** ratio of phagocytic index to normal. **-niferous,** *adj.* producing o. **-nify,** *v.t.* **-noid,** *adj.* like o. **-nology,** *n.* study of o.

optative (optā'tiv), *n.* & *adj. Gram.,* (mood) expressing wish.

optician (optish'n), *n.* maker or seller of optical instr., eye-glasses, etc. **-cs,** *n.* study of light. **-tigraph,** *n.* telescopic instr. for copying distant objects.

optimate (op'timāt), *n.* & *adj.* (member) of the nobility or aristocracy.

optimum (op'timəm), *n.* (*pl.* **-ma**) the best; *adj.* best; producing best result.

optogram (op'təgram), *n.* image fixed on retina. **-tology,** *n.* eye-testing. **-tometry,** *n.* measuring range of vision; eye-testing. **-tophone,** *n.* instr. enabling blind to read by transforming light into sound. **-totypes,** *n.pl.* varying-sized print for eye-testing.

opulent (op'ūlənt), *adj.* rich. **-nce,** *n.*

opus (ō'pəs, op'-), *Lat. n.* (*pl.* **opera**) "work"; mus. work or set of works (*abbr.* **op.**). **magnum o.,** *see* **magnum.**

opuscule, -lum (opus'kūl, -əm), *n.* (*pl.* **-la**) minor composition or work. **-lar,** *adj.*

oracular (orak'ūlə), *adj.* like an oracle; sententious; prophetic; ambiguous.

orant (or'ənt), *n.* representation of a praying figure.

ora pro nobis (ōr'ā prō nō'bis), *Lat.,* "pray for us."

orarian (ōr ār'iən), *n.* & *adj.* (dweller) of the seashore.

oratio recta (orā'shiō rek'tə), *Lat.,* "direct speech." **o.obliqua,** indirect speech.

orbicular (awbik'ūlə), *adj.* spherical; circular. **-late,** *adj.* **-lation,** *n.*

orbific (awbif'ik), *adj.* world-creating.

orbis terrarum (aw'bis terār'əm), *Lat.,* "orb of lands"; world; globe.

orc (awk), *n.* grampus. **-a,** *n.* killer whale.

orchesis (awkē'sis), *n.* art of dancing. **-stic,** *adj.* **-stics,** *n.* dancing.

orchidaceous (awkidā'shəs), *adj.* pert. to or like an orchid; exceptionally beautiful; ostentatious; gaudy.

orchil (aw'kil, -chil), *n.* archil.

orchitis (awkī'tis), *n.* inflammation of testicles. **-chotomy,** *n.* incision into testicles.

ordinal (aw'dinəl), *n.* & *adj.* (number) signifying position in series, as *third;* ordination service book; R.C. service book.

ordinance (aw'dinəns), *n.* decree.

ordinate (aw'dinət), *adj.* in rows.

ordnance (awd'nəns), *n.* military stores or supplies; artillery.

ordure (aw'dūr), *n.* dung; filth.

oread (ōr'iad), *n.* mountain nymph.

orectic (orek'tik), *adj.* pert. to desires and their satisfaction. **-rexis,** *n.* desire; effort. **-tive,** *adj.*

orfe (awf), *n.* kind of yellow fish.

organic (awgan'ik), *adj.* structural; of or derived from living organisms; *Med.,* of or affecting organ of body; *Chem.,* of carbon compounds. **-nogenesis, -nogeny,** *n.* development of organs. **-nogenic,** *adj.* derived from organic substance. **-noleptic,** *adj.* affecting whole organ or organism. **-nonomy,** *n.* laws of organic life. **-nopathy,** *n.* disease of an organ. **-notherapy,** *n.* med. treatment with animal organs.

organum, -non (aw'gənəm, -ən), *n.* logical system or method.

orgasm (aw'gazm), *n.* emotional paroxysm, *espec.* at completion of coitus. **-ic, -stic,** *adj.*

oriel (ōr'iəl), *n.* projecting window or part of building containing window.

orient (ōr'iənt), *n.* the East; pearl's lustre; *adj.* app. to rising sun; being born; lustrous; brilliant; (-ent'), *v.t.* point towards east; discover compass-bearings of; adjust to suit situation. **-al,** *adj.* **-ate,** *v.t.* to orient. **-ation,** *n.*

oriflamme (or'iflam), *n.* royal Fr. red banner ; battle standard.

oriform (or'ifawm), *adj.* mouth-shaped.

oriole (ōr'iōl), *n.* yellow black-winged bird also called golden o.

orismology (ōrizmol'əji), *n.* technical definition or terminology. -gic(al), *adj.*

orison (or'izn), *n.* prayer.

orlop (aw'lop), *n.* ship's lowest deck.

ormolu (aw'məlōō), *n.* gilt metal ; gold-like brass ornament of furniture.

ornis (aw'nis), *n.* avifauna.

ornithology (awnithol'əji), *n.* study of birds. -gical, *adj.* -gist, *n.* -thic, *adj.* pert. to birds. -thocopros, *n.* guano. -thoid, *adj.* bird-like. -thomancy, *n.* divination from flight of birds. -thomyzous, *adj.* parasitic on birds. -thon, *n.* aviary. -thophilous, *adj.* app. to flowers pollinated by birds. -thorhyncus, *n.* duck-bill. -thoscopy, *n.* bird-watching ; ornithomancy. -thotomy, *n.* anatomy of birds.

orobathymetric (ōrəbathimet'rik), *adj.* pert. to map showing sea depths or submerged heights.

orogen (or'əjen), *n.* mountain pass. -ic, *adj.* -esis (-en'isis), -y (-oj'ini), *n.* formation of mountains.

orograph (ōr'əgraf), *n.* machine recording heights and distances traversed. -ic, *adj.* showing heights. -y, *n.* study of mountains.

orology (ōrol'əji), *n.* study of mountains. -ometer, *n.* barometer showing height above sea-level.

orotund (ōr'ətund), *adj.* using high-flown language ; speaking or singing clearly and strongly. -ity, *n.*

orphrey (aw'fri), *n.* gold-embroidered band on eccl. robes.

orpiment (aw'pimənt), *n.* yellow compound of arsenic, used as pigment, etc.

orpine (aw'pin), *n.* kind of stonecrop ; live-forever.

orrery (or'əri), *n.* moving model of solar system.

orris (or'is), *n.* kind of iris, and its rootstock used in perfumery, medicine, etc.

ort (awt), *n.* morsel ; crumb.

orthobiosis (awthəbiō'sis), *n.* correct or moral living.

orthoclase (aw'thəklāz), *n.* feldspar.

orthodontia, -tics (awthədon'shiə, -tiə ; -tiks), *n.* correction of irregularity of teeth. -tic, *adj.* -tist, *n.*

orthodox (aw'thədoks), *adj.* having correct or accepted opinions ; approved ; in accordance with standard or authorised practice. -al, -ical, *adj.* -y, *n.*

orthodromy, -mics (awthod'rəmi, -drom'iks), *n.* navigation by great circle. -mic, *adj.*

orthoëpy (awthō'ipi), *n.* correct pronunciation ; study of pronunciation. -pic (-ep'ik), *adj.* -pist, *n.*

orthogenesis (awthəjen'isis), *n.* recurring biol. variation resulting in new species ; belief that the development of civilisation always proceeds in same way. -etic (-jinet'ik), *adj.* -nic, *adj.* pert. to correction of children's mental defects.

orthognathism (awthog'nəthizm), *n.* state of having straight jaws. -thic (-ath'ik), -thous, *adj.* -thy, *n.*

orthogonal (awthog'ənəl), *adj.* right-angled. -ity, *n.*

orthography (awthog'rəfi), *n.* correct spelling. -pher, -phist, *n.* -phic(al), *adj.* -phise, *v.i.*

ortholøgy (awthol'əji), *n.* correct use of words. -ger, -gian, *n.* -gical, *adj.*

orthometopic (awthəmitop'ik), *adj.* having vertical forehead.

orthopaedic (awthəpē'dik), *adj.* correcting physical deformities, *orig.* of children. -dist, *n.* -s, *n.*

orthopathy (awthop'əthi), *n.* drugless med. treatment. -th, -thist, *n.* -thic (-ath'ik), *adj.*

orthophony (awthof'əni), *n.* correct voice production. -nic (-on'ik), *adj.*

orthopnoea (awthopnē'ə), *n.* ability to breathe in upright position only. -oeic, *n.* & *adj.*

orthopraxy, -xis (aw'thəpraksi, -praks'is), *n.* correct action ; orthopaedic surgery.

orthopter (awthop'tə), *n.* bird-like flying machine propelled by moving wings.

orthopterous (awthop'tərəs), *adj.* pert. or belonging to insect order including grasshoppers, crickets, etc. -ran, *n.* & *adj.* -rist, *n.* student of o. insects. -rology, *n.* study of o. insects. -ron, *n.* (*pl.* -ra) such insect.

orthoptic (awthop'tik), *adj.* pert. to correct vision.

orthoscope (aw'thəskōp), *n.* instr. for examining exterior of eye, or measuring cranial surfaces. -pic (-op'ik), *adj.* producing normal image.

orthosis (awthō'sis), *n.* correction of neurotic state.

orthostatic (awthəstat'ik), *adj.* pert. to erect or standing position. -thotic (-ot'ik), *adj.*

orthotomic (awthətom'ik), *adj.* cutting at right angles.

orthotonus (awthot'ənəs), n. spasmic bodily rigidity due to tetanus.

orthotropism (awthot'rəpizm), *n.* vertical growth. -pic (-op'ik), *adj.*

ortolan (aw'tələn), *n.* kind of bunting (bird) esteemed as food; *Amer.*, bobolink.

oryctognosy (oriktog'nəsi), *n.* mineralogy. -stic(al) (-os'tik, -l), *adj.* -tology, *n.* mineralogy or palaeontology.

oryx (ōr'iks, or'-), *n.* large straight-horned African antelope.

oryzivorous (oriziv'ərəs), *adj.* rice-eating.

os (os), Lat. *n.* (*pl.* ossa) bone; (ōs ; *pl.* ora) mouth.

oscheal (os'kiəl), *adj.* scrotal.

oscillograph (əsil'əgraf), *n.* instr. recording elec. oscillations, *e.g.* A.C. current wave forms.

oscillometer (osilom'itə), *n.* instr. measuring ship's rollings, etc.; instr. measuring blood pressure variations. -tric(-et'rik),*adj.* -try,*n.*

oscilloscope (əsil'əskōp), *n.* instr. showing variations in elec. potential, on a fluorescent screen by means of deflection of a beam of electrons.

oscine (os'in, -īn), *n.* & *adj.* (bird) belonging to sub-order of birds including singing birds. -nine, *adj.*

oscitance, -cy (os'itəns, -i), *n.* yawning; sleepiness; dullness. -nt, *adj.* -tate, *v.i.* yawn. -tation, *n.*

osculate (os'kūlāt), *v.s.* & *t.* make contact; coincide; kiss. -ant, -tory, *adj.* -lar, *adj.* pert. to mouth or kissing. -tion, *n.*

Osmanli (ozman'li), *adj.* of Turkish Empire; Ottoman; *n.* Western Turk.

osmatic (ozmat'ik), *adj.* having olfactory organs. -mesis, *n.* act of smelling. -midrosis, *n.* secretion of strong-smelling perspiration. -mology, *n.* study of smells and olfactory process. -mometry, *n.* measurement of smells.

osmosis (ozmō'sis), *n.* passage of solvent through a separating membrane between two solutions of different strengths. -otic (-ot'ik), *adj.*

osophy (os'əfi), *n.* belief or doctrine ; ism.

osphresis (osfrē'sis), *n.* sense of smell. -etic (-et'ik), *adj.*

osphyalgia (osfial'jiə), *n.* pain in loin. -gic, *adj.*

osprey (os'prā), *n.* large fish-eating hawk ; *erron.*, egret feather.

osseous (os'iəs), *adj.* bony. -sicle, *n.* small bone, *espec.* of ear. -sifluent, *adj.* derived from softened bone.

ossifrage (os'ifrij), *n.* lammergeier.

ossuary (os'ūəri), *n.* charnel-house.

osteal (os'tiəl), *adj.* pert. to or like bone. -eitis, *n.* inflammation of bone.

osteology (ostiol'əji), *n.* study of bones ; bony structure. -oblastic, *adj.* pert. to formation of bone. -ochondrous, *adj.* pert. to bone and cartilage. -oclasis, *n.* surg. breaking of bone. -odermatous, *adj.* having bone-like skin. -ogen, *n.* bone-forming tissue. -ogenesis, *n.* bone formation. -ography, *n.* descriptive o. -oid, *adj.* bone-like. -oma, *n.* bone tumour. -ometry, *n.* measurement of bones or skeleton. -opath, *n.* one who treats disease by osteopathy. -opathy, *n.* med. treatment by manipulation of bones. -ophone, *n.* apparatus enabling deaf to hear sounds transmitted through cranial bones. -ophyte, *n.* bony process. -osclerosis, *n.* hardening of bone. -otomy, *n.* surg. cutting into, or removal of a piece of, bone.

ostiary (os'tiari), *n.* door-keeper, *espec.* of church.

ostosis (ostō'sis), *n.* bone formation.

ostracise (os'trəsiz), *v.t.* exile from society. -ism, *n.*

ostreiform (os'treifawm, -trē'-), *adj.* oyster-shaped or -like. -eiculture, *n.* oyster-breeding. **-eoid**, *adj.* oyster-like. **-eophagous**, *adj.* oyster-eating.

otacoustic (ōtəkōō'stik), *n.* & *adj.* (instr.) aiding hearing.

otalgia, **-y** (ōtal'jiə, -ji), *n.* earache. **-gic**, *n.* & *adj.* (curative) of earache.

otiant (ō'shiənt), *adj.* idle ; resting.

otic (ō'tik, ot'-), *adj.* pert. to the ear. **-odinia**, *n.* dizziness caused by otic disease.

otidine (ō'tidīn, -in), *adj.* pert. to a bustard. **-diform**, *adj.* bustard-like.

otiose (ō'shiōs), *adj.* idle ; useless ; futile. **-sity**, *n.*

otocleisis (ōtəklī'sis), *n.* obstruction of auditory passage. **-olith**, *n.* concretion or "stone" of ear. **-ology**, *n.* study of ear and its diseases. **-orhino-laryngology**, *n.* study of ear, nose and throat. **-oscope**, *n.* instr. for examining ear. **-osis**, *n.* mishearing of speech.

otto (ot'ō), *n.* attar.

Ottoman (ot'əmən), *adj.* pert. to Turks or Turkish Empire.

oubliette (ōōbliet'), *n.* dungeon with entrance in roof.

ounce (owns), *n.* Zoo., snow-leopard of Tibet and Siberia.

ousel (ōō'zəl), *n.* blackbird. **ring o.**, Eur. thrush with white collar.

outrance, *see* à outrance.

outré (ōōt'rā), Fr. *adj.* (*fem.* **-ée**) unconventional ; exaggerated.

outspan (owt'span), S. African *v.i.* & *t.* remove harness (from) ; *n.* halting- or camping-place.

ousel, *see* ousel.

ovary (ō'vəri), *n.* female egg-producing organ. **-rian**, *adj.* **-riotomy**, *n.* removal of o. **-ritis**, *n.* inflammation of o.

overt (ō'vət), *adj.* unconcealed.

ovicide (ō'visīd), *n.* substance killing eggs, *espec.* of insects ; killing of sheep. **-dal**, *adj.*

oviduct (ō'vidukt), *n.* passage conveying eggs to exterior or place of fertilisation ; Fallopian tube. **-al**, **-cal**, *adj.*

ovine (ō'vīn), *adj.* pert. to or like sheep ; *n.* such animal. **-viform**, *adj.* sheep- or egg-like.

oviparous (ōvip'ərəs), *adj.* producing offspring in eggs. **-positor**, *n.* insect's tube-like organ for depositing eggs. **-rity** (-ar'iti), *n.*

ovopyriform (ōvəpir'ifawm), *adj.* between pear-shaped and egg-shaped.

ovoviviparous (ōvəvivip'ərəs), *adj.* producing offspring in eggs that hatch within parent's body. **-rism**, **-rity** (-ar'iti), *n.*

ovum (ō'vəm), *n.* (*pl.* **-va**) female's germ-cell from which, after fertilisation, embryo develops. **-ule**, *n.* unfertilised seed.

oxalidaceous (oksalidā'shəs), *adj.* pert. to or like sorrel (plant) ; belonging to sorrel family of plants. **-lic**, *adj.* of or from sorrel ; **o.acid**, poisonous acid used in dyeing, etc.

oxide (oks'īd), *n.* compound of oxygen. **-dise**, *v.i.* & *t.* combine or cause to combine with oxygen ; coat with oxide ; rust or make rusty ; give (metal) dull lustre or aged appearance by treating with chemicals.

oxyacanthous (oksiəkan'thəs), *adj.* with sharp thorns. **-yaesthesia**, *n.* extreme acuteness of sensation. **-yaphia**, *n.* sensitivity of touch sense. **-yblepsia**, *n.* keen-sightedness. **-ygeusia**, *n.* extreme sensitivity of taste sense.

oxymoron (oksimōr'ən), *n.* rhet. device of conjoining contradictory words.

oxyopia (oksiō'piə), *n.* abnormal keen-sightedness. **-yosphresia**, *n.* extreme sensitivity of smell sense. **-yphonia**, *n.* shrillness of voice. **-yrhine**, *adj.* sharp-nosed ; keen-scented. **-yrhyncous**, *adj.* sharp-nosed. **-ytocia**, *n.* quickness of child-birth.

oxytone (oks'itōn), *adj.* bearing acute accent on last syllable ; *n.* such word ; *v.t.* pronounce as o. **-sis**, *n.* such pronunciation.

ozocerite (ōzō'kərit, -sər-, -sēr'-), *n.* kind of waxy mineral.

ozone (ō'zōn), *n.* form of oxygen present in atmosphere, with refreshing odour. **-nic** (-on'ik), **-nous**, *adj.* **-niferous**, *adj.* producing o.

ozostomia (ōzostō'miə), *n.* evil-smelling breath.

ə=*er* in *father* ; ē=*er* in *pert* ; th=*th* in *thin* ; dh=*th* in *then* ; zh=*s* in *pleasure* ; k=*ch* in *loch* ; ñ=Fr. nasal *n* ; ü=Fr. *u*.

P

paauw (pah'ōō, pow), S. African *n.* bustard.

pabulum (pab'ūləm), *n.* food.

pacable (pak'əbl), *adj.* capable of being pacified.

pace (pā'si), Lat. *prep.* "by permission of"; in spite of.

pachisi (pahchē'zi), *n.* back-gammon-like Ind. game.

pachyderm (pak'idəm), *n.* thick-skinned animal, *espec.* elephant. -al, -atous, -ic, -ous, *adj.* -ia, *n.* elephantiasis. -ydactyl(ous), *adj.* thick-toed. -yglossal, *adj.* thick-tongued. -ylosis, *n.* thickening and dryness of skin. -ymenia, *n.* thickening of skin or membrane. -ymeninx, *n.* dura mater. -ymeter, *n.* thickness-measuring instr. -ynsis, *n.* thickening.

paddymelon (pad'imelən), Austral. *n.* small wallaby.

padishah (pad'ishah), Pers. *n.* emperor; Shah of Persia; *Ind.*, Emperor of India.

padmasana (pudmah'sənə), *n.* Buddhə-like manner of sitting cross-legged.

padre (pah'drā), *n.* minister of religion, *espec.* chaplain of forces.

padrone (pahdrō'nā), It. *n.* (*pl.* -ni) master; inn-keeper; employment agent. -nism, *n.* system of obtaining labour through such agents.

paean (pē'ən), *n.* thanksgiving song.

paedarchy (pē'dahki), *n.* government by children. -derasty, *n.* unnatural sexual intercourse with a boy. -diatrics, *n.* study of children's diseases. -dobaptism, *n.* infant baptism. -dodontia, *n.* care of children's teeth. -dology, *n.* child study. -domorphism, *n.* continuance of infantile characteristics in adult. -donymic *n.* name taken from one's child. -dophilia, *n.* love of children. -dopsychologist, *n.* expert on child psychology. -dotrophy, *n.* correct rearing of children.

paeon (pē'ən), *n.* metrical foot of one long and three short syllables. first, second, etc., p., p. in which long syllable is the first, second, etc. -ic (-on'ik), *n.* & *adj.*

paginate (paj'ināt), *v.t.* arrange and number pages of (book). -nal, *adj.* pert. to or consisting of pages; page for page. -nary, *adj.* -tion, *n.*

pagurian (pagūr'iən), *n.* & *adj.* (crab) belonging to hermit crab family. -rid, *n.* -rine, -roid, *adj.*

pah (pah), Maori *n.* village, *espec.* fortified.

paideutic(s) (pādū'tik, -s), *n.* art of teaching. -donosology, *n.* study of children's diseases.

paillasse (pal'yas), *n.* palliasse.

pakeha (pah'kihə, pak'iə), Maori *n.* white man; foreigner.

palaceous (pəlā'shəs), *adj.* spade-shaped.

paladin (pal'ədin), *n.* medieval champion or knight, *espec.* of court of Charlemagne; hero.

palaeoanthropic (paliōanthrop'ik, pā'-), *adj.* pert. to earliest form of Man. -obiology, *n.* study of fossil life. -obotany, *n.* study of fossil plants. -odendrology, *n.* study of fossil trees. -oethnic, *adj.* pert. to earliest races of Man. -ogenetic, *adj.* of past origin. -ography, *n.* study of anct. writings. -olithic, *adj.* pert. to early Stone Age. -ology, *n.* study of antiquities. -ontography, *n.* description of fossils. -ontology, *n.* study of past life and fossils. -ophile, *n.* antiquarian. -ophytic, *adj.* pert. to palaeobotany. -ornithology, *n.* study of fossil birds. -osophy, *n.* anct. learning. -otechnic, *adj.* pert. to anct. art. -ozoology, *n.* study of fossil animals.

palaestra, -les- (pəles'trə), *n.* wrestling; gymnasium. -l, -rian, -ric, *adj.*

palamate (pal'əmāt), *adj.* web-footed.

palatine (pal'ətīn), *adj.* having royal authority over a certain locality. count p., such count. county p., jurisdiction of count p. -nate (-at'inət), *n.* jurisdiction of count p.

paleaceous (pālia'shəs), *adj.* chaff-like. -eate, *adj.*

paletot (pal'itō), *n.* loose outer garment; overcoat.

palfrey (pawl'fri), *n.* quiet-moving saddle horse.

palilogy, **-gia** (pəlil'əji, palilō'jiə), *n.* emphatic repetition of word. **-getic**, *adj.*

palimpsest (pal'impsest), *n.* parchment, etc., of which first writing has been erased to enable it to be used again. **-ic**, *adj.*

palindrome (pal'indrōm), *n.* word, phrase, etc., reading the same backwards or forwards. **-mic** (-om'ik), *adj.* **-mist** (-in'drəmist), *n.*

palingenesis (palinjen'isis), *n.* resuscitation; rebirth; metempsychosis; exact reproduction of ancestral characteristics. **-esian** (-jinē'zion), **-etic** (-jinet'ik), *adj.* **-nist**, **-t**, *n.*

palinode (pal'inōd), *n.* recantation, *espec.* in verse. **-dist**, *n.*

Palladian (pəlā'diən), *adj.* pert. to or like classical archit. style of Andrea Palladio, 16th-cent. It. architect; pert. to Pallas Athena, Gr. goddess of wisdom; wise; learned. **-dium**, *n.* (*pl.* **-ia**) safeguard; protection.

pallaesthesia (palesthē'zhiə), *n.* sense of vibration.

palliasse (pal'ias), *n.* hard straw mattress.

palliate (pal'iāt), *v.t.* mitigate; ease; relieve but not cure; excuse. **-tion**, **-tor**, *n.* **-tive**, *n.* & *adj.* **-tory**, *adj.*

pallium (pal'iəm), *n.* (*pl.* **-ia**) R.C., white woollen band symbol of archbishop's power; *Med.*, cerebral cortex.

pallograph (pal'əgraf), *n.* instr. measuring ship's vibration. **-ic**, *adj.*

palma Christi (pal'mə kris'ti), *Lat.*, "hand of Christ"; palmcrist.

palmary (pal'məri), *adj.* meriting highest prize; principal.

palmate (pal'māt), *adj.* like hand, *espec.* with fingers spread; webfooted. **-tion**, *n.*

palmcrist (pahm'krist), *n.* castor-oil plant.

palmetto (palmet'ō), *n.* fan palm and its leaves.

palmiped (pal'miped), *n.* & *adj.* web-footed (animal).

palmus (pal'məs), *n.* palpitation; twitching; nervous tic. **-modic**, *adj.* **-moscopy**, *n.* observation of pulse.

palmyra (palmīr'ə), *n.* tall African palm, yielding timber, thatching leaves, edible fruit, sugar and wine.

palpable (pal'pəbl), *adj.* tangible; provable; obvious. **-bility**, *n.* **-pate**, *v.t.* examine by touching. **-pation**, *n.* **-patory**, *adj.*

palpebra (pal'pibrə), *n.* (*pl.* **-ae**) eyelid. **-l**, *adj.* **-ritis**, *n.* inflammation of p. **-te**, *adj.* having p.; *v.i.* wink. **-tion**, *n.* wink.

palpi (pal'l i), *n.pl.* (*sing.* **-pus**) insect's or crustacean's feelers.

paludal (pəlū'dəl, pal'-), *adj.* pert. to marshes. **-dic**, *adj.* **-dicolous** (pal-), *adj.* inhabiting marshes. **-dinal**, **-dine** (pal'-), **-dinous**, *adj.* marshy. **-dism** (pal'-), *n.* marsh fever; malaria. **-dose**, **-dous** (pal'-), *adj.* marshy; living in marshes; malarial. **-drine**, *n.* synthetic anti-malarial drug.

pampas (pam'pəs), *n.pl.* grassy plains of Argentine. **-pean**, *n.* & *adj.* (inhabitant) of the p. **-pero**, *n.* cold west wind of the p.

pampiniform (pampin'ifawm), *adj.* like a tendril.

pan (pahn), Hind. *n.* betel-nut.

panacea (panəsē'ə), *n.* universal cure. **-ceist**, *n.* believer in p. **-n**, *adj.*

panache (pənash'), *n.* plume on helmet; swaggering air. **-d**, *adj.* having coloured stripes.

panarchy (pan'ahki), *n.* universal rule.

panaris (pənār'is), *n.* whitlow.

panarthritis (panahthrī'tis), *n.* arthritis of all joints of body, or of whole of one joint.

panary (pan'əri), *adj.* pert. to bread and baking.

panchromatic (pankrəmat'ik), *adj.* sensitive to light of every colour; *n.* such photog. film. **-tise** (-ō'mətīz), *v.t.* **-tism**, *n.*

pancosmism (pankoz'mizm), *n.* belief that nothing exists beyond the material universe. **-mic**, *adj.* pert. to p., or to universe in its entirety.

pancratic (pankrat'ik), *adj.* athletic; pert. to or having ability in all matters. **-tian**, *adj.* **-tism**, *n.* panarchy.

pancreas (pang'kriəs), *n.* large digestive gland behind stomach; sweetbread. **-eatic** (-at'ik), *adj.* **-eatitis**, *n.* inflammation of p.

pancyclopaedic (pansĭklǝpē'dik), *adj.* encyclopaedic.

panda (pan'dǝ), *n.* raccoon-like animal of Himalayas. **giant** *or* **great p.,** rare bear-like Tibetan animal.

pandal (pan'dal), Anglo-Ind. *n.* shed ; summerhouse.

pandects (pan'dekts), *n.pl.* complete summary of anct. Rom. legal decisions ; legal code ; any summary of or treatise on whole of subject.

pandemic (pandem'ik), *adj.* universal ; affecting majority of people of an area ; epidemic everywhere. **-mia** (-ē'miǝ), *n.* p. disease.

pandemoniac (pandimō'niak), *adj.* pert. to all deities, or to general tumult. **-nism** (-dē'mǝnizm), *n.* worship of spirits dwelling in all forms of nature. **-nium,** *n.* riotous uproar or place.

pandiculation (pandikūlā'shn), *n.* act of stretching oneself.

panegyric (panijir'ik), *n.* eulogy. **-al,** *adj.* **-rise** (pan'-), *v.t.* praise highly. **-rist,** *n.*

paneity (panē'iti), *n.* state of being merely bread.

panentheism (panen'thiizm), *n.* belief that world is part of God.

pangamy (pang'gǝmi), *n.* marriage without limitation as to spouses. **-mic** (-am'ik), **-mous,** *adj.*

pangenesis (panjen'isis), *n.* theory that reproductive cells contain particles from all parts of parents. **-etic** (-jinet'ik), **-nic,** *adj.*

Panglossian (panglos'iǝn), *adj.* pert. to Pangloss, character in Voltaire's *Candide,* and his optimism.

pangolin (panggō'lin), *n.* scaly anteater of Asia and Africa.

pangrammatist (pangram'ǝtist), *n.* person composing sentences, verses, etc., containing all letters of alphabet.

panhygrous (panhī'grǝs), *adj.* moist in all parts.

panicle (pan'ikl), *n.* loose much-branched flower-head, *espec.* of grasses ; compound raceme. **-cular** (-ik'ūlǝ), *adj.* **-culate,** *adj.* having or arranged in p.

panification (panifikā'shn), *n.* transformation into bread.

panivorous (pǝniv'ǝrǝs), *adj.* bread-eating.

panmixy, -xia (pan'miksi, -miks'iǝ), *n.* interbreeding without limitation.

panmnesia (pannē'zhiǝ), *n.* belief that every mental impression continues in memory.

pannage (pan'ij), *n.* pigs' food in woods, as nuts, etc. ; right to, or fee paid for, feeding pigs in woods.

pannicular (panik'ūlǝ), *adj.* pert. to or like a sheet or thin layer.

pannose (pan'ōs), *adj.* felt-like.

panoptic(al) (panop'tik, -l), *adj.* giving view of whole at once. **-con,** *n.* such optical instr. ; exhibition ; building, as prison, whole of interior of which can be watched from one point.

panorpid (pǝnaw'pid), *n.* scorpion fly. **-pian,** *n.* & *adj.* **-pine,** *adj.*

pansexualism (panseks'ūǝlizm), *n.* obsession with sex in all activities ; belief that sexual instinct is basis of all activity. **-ist,** *n.* **-lity,** *n.*

pansophism (pan'sǝfizm), *n.* claim to know everything. **-phist,** *n.* **-phy,** *n.* knowledge of everything.

panstereorama (panstēriǝrah'mǝ), *n.* geographical model in relief.

pantagamy (pantag'ǝmi), *n.* marriage in which all spouses are held in common ; free love.

pantarchy (pan'tahki), *n.* government by all.

pantechnic (pantek'nik), *adj.* pert. to all arts. **-on,** *n.* removal van.

pantheism (pan'thiizm), *n.* belief that universe is God ; worship of many or all gods. **-ist,** *n.* **-istic,** *adj.* **-theology,** *n.* theology including all gods.

pantheon (pan'thiǝn), *n.* temple to all gods ; body of a nation's gods ; temple of fame containing remains of nation's great men. **-ic** (-on'ik), *adj.*

pantisocracy (pantisok'rǝsi), *n.* anarchistic community. **-crat** (-is'ǝkrat, -ī'-), *n.* **-cratic,** *adj.*

pantochronometer (pantǝkrǝnom'-itǝ), · *n.* combined sundial and compass, showing time in all parts of world.

pantoglot (pan'tǝglot), *n.* speaker of all languages. **-ttism,** *n.*

pantograph (pan'tǝgraf), *n.* instr. for copying maps, etc., on any scale. **-ic,** *adj.*

pantology (pantol'ǝji), *n.* system of universal knowledge. **-gic(al),** *adj.* **-gist,** *n.*

pantomnesia (pantomnē'zhiə), *n.* remembrance for ever of everything learnt. **-sic,** *adj.*

pantomorphic (pantəmaw'fik), *adj.* taking on all shapes. **-phia,** *n.* state of being p.; complete symmetry.

pantothenic (pantəthen'ik), *adj.* denoting an acid which is a growth-promoting vitamin of vitamin B complex.

panurgic (panə'jik), *adj.* adept at all kinds of work.

Panzer (pan'tsə), Ger. *n.* "armour"; armoured vehicle or division; tank.

panzoism (panzō'izm), *n.* vital energy; life force; belief that Man and animals are kin. **-zootic,** *adj.* app. to disease attacking animals of many kinds.

paparchy (pā'pahki), *n.* government by pope. **-chical,** *adj.*

papaveraceous (papavərā'shəs), *adj.* pert. to or like a poppy; belonging to the poppy family of plants. **-rous** (-av'ərəs), *adj.* pert. to or like a poppy.

papilionaceous (papilyənā'shəs), *adj.* shaped like a butterfly.

papilla (pəpil'ə), *n.* (*pl.* -ae) nipple; projection shaped like nipple. **-liform,** *adj.* nipple-shaped. **-loma,** *n.* small tumour, *e.g.* wart. **-ry** (pap'-), *adj.* **-te, -lose,** *adj.* having p.

papolatry (pāpol'ətri), *n.* excessive reverence paid to pope. **-ter,** *n.* **-trous,** *adj.*

papoose (pəpōos'), *n.* Red Ind. baby.

pappus (pap'əs), *n.* (*pl.* -pi) downy tuft on plant seed; down. **-pescent,** *adj.* producing p. **-pose, -pous,** *adj.* having or like p.

paprika (pap'rikə, -ē'kə), *n.* kind of pepper.

papule (pap'ūl), *n.* pimple. **-lar, -late, -liferous,** *adj.* pert. to or bearing p. **-lose, -lous,** *adj.* pimply.

papyrus (pəpīr'əs), *n.* (*pl.* -ri) kind of sedge from which paper-like material was made; writing on p. **-raceous, -ral, -rian, -rine, -ritious,** *adj.* like or pert. to p. or paper. **-rine,** *n.* parchment paper. **-rology,** *n.* study of p. **-rotamia,** *n.* manuf. of paper flowers.

parablepsy, -sia, -sis (pərəblep'si, -siə, -sis), *n.* false vision. **-ptic,** *adj.*

parabola (pərab'ələ), *n.* curve formed by cutting of cone by plane parallel to its side. **-lic** (-ol'ik), *adj.* pert. to p.; like or described in a parable. **-liform** (-ol'ifawm), *adj.* like a p. **-list,** *n.* teller of parables.

paracentesis (parəsentē'sis), *n.* tapping of body fluid.

paracentral (parəsen'trəl), *adj.* situated near centre. **-ric,** *adj.* not circular.

parachroma (parəkrō'mə), *n.* discoloration. **-tism,** *n.* colour-blindness. **-topsia,** *n.* abnormality of colour sense.

parachronism (parak'rənizm), *n.* error of chronology, *espec.* placing event at date later than it actually happened. **-stic,** *adj.*

paraclete (par'əklēt), *n.* advocate; Holy Ghost.

paracme (parak'mi), *n.* stage following acme; decline.

paracusia, -sis (parəkū'siə, -sis), *n.* abnormality of hearing. **-sic,** *adj.*

paradigm (par'ədīm, -im), *n.* example, *espec.* of gram. inflections. **-atic(al)** (-igmat'ik, -l), *adj.*

paradox (par'ədoks), *n.* apparently self-contradictory statement; heterodox statement. **-ical,** *adj.* **-ician, -ist, -ographer,** *n.* **-ology,** *n.* use of p.

paradromic (parədrom'ik), *adj.* adjacent; side by side.

paraenesis (pərən'isis, -rē'-), *n.* advice; exhortation. **-e,** *v.t.* **-etic** (-inet'ik), *adj.*

paraesthesia (paresthē'zhiə), *n.* tingling sensation on skin. **-etic** (-et'ik), *adj.*

parageusia, -sis (parəgū'siə, -sis), *n.* abnormality in taste sense. **-sic,** *adj.*

paragnosia (paragnō'siə), *n.* misunderstanding.

paragoge (parəgō'ji), *n.* addition of sound at end of word. **-gic(al)** (-oj'ik, -l), *adj.*

paragon (par'əgən), *n.* model of perfection; *v.t.* compare; act as p.

paragraphia (parəgraf'iə), *n.* writing of unintended words or letters.

parakinesis, -sia (parəkinē'sis, -iə), *n.* abnormality of nervous control over movement; production of movements by spiritualist medium. **-etic** (-et'ik), *n.*

---

paralalia (parəlā'liə), *n.* abnormality of speech sounds.

paraldehyde (pəral'dihīd), *n.* sleep-inducing drug.

paraleipsis, -ep-, -ip- (parəlīp'sis, -ep'-, -ip'-), *n.* rhet. device of emphasising thing by omitting it or mentioning it only cursorily.

parallax (par'əlaks), *n.* apparent difference in object's position or direction as viewed from different points. -lactic, *adj.*

parallelepiped (parəlelipī'ped), *n.* solid figure with every side a parallelogram. -al, -ic, -onal, -ous (-pip'-), *adj.*

paralogism (paral'əjizm), *n.* illogical or fallacious deduction. -gical, -gistic, *adj.* -gise, *v.i.* be illogical; draw unwarranted conclusions. -gy, *n.*

paramatta (parəmat'ə), *n.* cotton and worsted dress material.

paramedian (parəmē'diən), *adj.* near middle line.

paramenia (parəmē'niə), *n.* abnormality of menstruation.

parametric (parəmet'rik), *adj. Med.*, adjacent to womb.

paramnesia (paramnē'zhiə), *n.* abnormality of memory, *espec.* forgetting of meaning of words, or illusion of having before experienced events which are being experienced for the first time.

paramour (par'əmoor), *n.* illicit lover; mistress.

paranephric (parənef'rik), *adj.* near kidney; suprarenal.

parang (pah'rang, -rahng'), *n.* large Malay or Dyak sheath-knife.

paranoia (parənoi'ə), *n.* form of insanity in which patient believes himself to be a person of great importance, or thinks himself persecuted by everyone. -c, *n.* & *adj.* -oid, *adj.* like p.

paranosic (parənō'sik), *adj.* connected with disease.

paranymph (par'ənimf), *n.* best man; bridesmaid; advocate.

paraparesis (parəpərē'sis, -par'isis), *n.* paralysis of lower limbs. -etic (-et'ik), *adj.*

paraphasia (parəfā'zhiə), *n.* mental disorder marked by constant talking with misuse of words. -sic, *adj.*

paraphrase (par'əfrāz), *v.t.* restate in different words; *n.* such re-

statement. -sia, *n.* incoherence. -stic (as'tik), *adj.*

paraphrenia (parəfrē'niə), *n.* dementia praecox. -nic (-en'ik), *adj.*

paraplegia (parəplē'jiə), *n.* paralysis of lower half of body. -gic, -lectic, *adj.*

parapraxis (parəpraks'is), *n.* blunder. -xia, *n.* committing of blunders.

pararthria (parah'thriə), *n.* incoherence.

parasigmatism(us) (parəsig'mətizm, -iz'məs), *n.* inability to pronounce sound of *s.*

parastatic (parəstat'ik), *adj.* pert. to protective mimicry of animals.

parasynesis (parəsin'isis), *n.* corruption of form of words. -etic (-et'ik), *adj.*

parataxis (parətaks'is), *n.* unconnected arrangement; *Gram.*, omission of connectives between related sentences; *Psych.*, disorder of emotions. -tactic, *adj.*

parathesis (pərath'isis), *n.* (*pl.* -ses) prayer commending new converts, etc., to God. -etic (-et'ik), *adj.*

parathyroid (parəthir'oid), *adj.* near thyroid gland, *espec.* app. to such small glands whose hormone controls calcium content of body; *n.* such gland. -al, *adj.* -roprival, *adj.* due to deficiency of p. hormone.

paratonic (parəton'ik), *adj.* arresting growth; due to external impulse.

paratriptic (parətrip'tik), *n.* & *adj.* (substance) preventing wasting of tissue.

paratyphoid (parətī'foid), *n.* & *adj.* (fever) resembling typhoid but caused by different bacillus.

paravane (par'əvān), *n.* knife-bearing torpedo-like device for cutting mines adrift.

paravent (par'əvent), *n.* windscreen.

parcener (pah'sinə), *n.* co-parcener.

parciloquy (pahsil'əkwi), *n.* laconism.

pardine (pah'dīn, -in), *adj.* pert. to or like a leopard; spotted.

paregoric (parigor'ik), *n.* & *adj.* (drug) soothing pain, *espec.* tincture of opium.

parenchyma (pəreng'kimə), *n.* fundamental or essential tissue of organ or plant. **-l**, **-tic** (-at'ik), **-tous** (-kim'ətəs), *adj.*

parentelic (parəntē'lik, -el'ik), *adj.* related by blood.

parenthesis (pəren'thisis), *n.* (*pl.* **-ses**) word, statement, etc., inserted incidentally into sentence ; round bracket ( ), containing such word, etc. **-etic(al)** (-et'ik, -l), *adj.*

parergon (parə'gon), *n.* subordinate work ; accessory.

paresis (pərē'sis, par'isis), *n.* partial paralysis ; omission of element of word. **-etic** (-et'ik, -ē'tik), *n.* & *adj.*

pareunia (pəroo̅'niə), *n.* coïtus.

parget (pah'jit), *n.* & *v.t.* plaster, whitewash, rough-cast, etc.

parhelion (pahhēl'yən), *n.* (*pl.* **-ia**) halo-like light seen at point opposite sun ; mock sun. **-lic**, *adj.*

pariah (par'iə, pərī'ə), *n.* low caste Ind. ; outcast ; mongrel stray dog of streets.

paridrosis (paridrō'sis), *n.* abnormality of perspiration.

parietal (pərī'itəl), *adj.* pert. to wall of cavity or body. **p.bone**, bone of top and sides of cranium.

parietary (par'iətəri, -rī'-), *n.* pellitory.

pari mutuel (par'ē mütüel'), *Fr.*, "mutual bet" ; form of betting whereby winners receive share of all stakes placed ; totalisator or pool betting.

parine (pār'in, -in), *adj.* like or pert. to titmouse.

pari passu (par'i pas'ū), *Lat.* "at equal pace" ; in equal degree, proportion, etc.

paristhmion (paris'thmiən), *n.* tonsil. **-mic**, *adj.*

parisyllabic (parisilab'ik), *n.* & *adj.* (word) having same number of syllables in all forms.

Parnassian (pahnas'iən), *adj.* pert. to Gr. mountain sacred to Muses and Apollo ; poetic ; member of 19th-cent. Fr. school of classical poets.

parodinia (parədin'iə), *n.* difficult childbirth.

paroemia (pərē'miə), *n.* proverb. **-c**, *adj.* **-iography**, *n.* composition of proverbs. **-iology**, *n.* study of proverbs.

paromoeon (parəmē'ən), *n.* alliteration.

paromology (parəmol'əji), *n.* appa-

rent concession of opponent's point which in reality strengthens one's own argument. **-getic**, *adj.*

paronomasia (parənəmā'zhiə), *n.* pun ; punning. **-l**, **-mastic**, **-n**, **-siastic**, *adj.*

paronychia (parənik'iə), *n.* whitlow. **-l**, *adj.*

paronym (par'ənim), *n.* word having same derivation as another, or formed from foreign word, or having same form as cognate foreign word. **-ic** (-im'ik), **-ous** (-on'iməs), *adj.* **-y**, *n.*

paropsis (parop'sis), *n.* abnormality of vision.

parorexia (parəreks'iə), *n.* desire to eat strange foods.

parosmia (paroz'miə), *n.* desire for strange scents. **-mic**, *adj.*

parotic (pərot'ik), *adj.* adjacent to ear. **-tid**, *adj.* pert. to salivary gland below ear ; *n.* such gland. **-titis**, *n.* mumps.

parous (par'əs), *adj.* bringing forth, or having borne, offspring.

parousia (paroo̅'zhiə), *n.* coming, *espec.* second coming of Christ.

paroxysm (par'oksizm), *n.* sudden convulsion or fit. **-al**, **-ic**, *adj.*

paroxytone (paroks'itōn), *n.* & *adj.* (word) having acute accent on last syllable but one.

parr (pah), *n.* young salmon.

parrhesia (pərē'zhiə), *n.* outspokenness.

parricide (par'isīd), *n.* killer or killing of parent, close relative, or king, etc. **-dal**, *adj.*

parsec (pah'sek), *n.* astron. measure of distance, approx. equiv. of 19.5 billion miles.

parsimony (pah'siməni), *n.* stinginess ; economy. **-nious** (-ō'niəs), *adj.*

parthenian (pahthē'niən), *adj.* pert. to virgin. **-nic** (-en'ik), *adj.* **-nocarpy** (-thin-), *n.* bearing of fruit without fertilisation. **-nogenesis**, *n.* reproduction without fertilisation ; virgin birth. **-nolatry**, *n.* worship of Virgin Mary. **-nology**, *n.* med. study of virginity. **-noparous**, *adj.* bearing offspring without fertilisation.

particeps criminis (pah'tiseps krim'-inis), *Lat.*, "participant in the crime" ; accomplice.

participle (pah'tisipl), *n.* verbal adjective. **-pial** (-ip'iəl), *adj.*

ə=*er* in *father* ; ē=*er* in *pert* ; th=*th* in *thin* ; dh=*th* in *then* ; zh=*s* in *pleasure* ; k=*ch* in *loch* ; ñ=Fr. nasal *n* ; ü=Fr. *u*.

parti pris (pahr'tē prē'), *Fr.*, "side taken"; prejudice; preconception.

partisan (pahtizan'), *n.* adherent or follower of a party, person, or principle; member of armed resistance group in enemy-occupied country; *adj.* devotedly adhering to a party, etc., strongly biassed.

parturition (pahtūrish'n), *n.* bringing forth of young. **-rient,** *adj.* **-rifacient,** *n.* & *adj.* (drug) inducing p. **-tive,** *adj.* pert. to p.

parulis (pərōō'lis), *n.* gumboil.

parure (parūr'), *Fr. n.* set of jewels or other ornaments.

paruria (parōōr'iə), *n.* disorder of urination.

parvenu (pah'vənū), *n.* vulgar newly-rich person; upstart.

parvipotent (pahvip'ətənt), *adj.* having little power. **-iflorous,** *adj.* having small flowers. **-iscient,** *adj.* having little knowledge.

parvule (pah'vūl), *n.* minute pill.

parwannah, *see* purwannah.

P.A.S., *abbr.* of para-aminosalicylic acid, used with streptomycin to treat tuberculosis.

pas (pah), *Fr. n.* "step"; dance step or figure. **p. de deux** (-də dē'), dance (figure) for two. **p.seul** (-sēl'), solo dance (figure).

paschal (pas'kəl), *adj.* pert. to Easter, or Passover. **p.letter,** bishop's letter of anct. Church concerning next Easter date. **p.moon,** new moon of vernal equinox.

pascual (pas'kūəl), *adj.* pert. to pasture. **-uous,** *adj.*

pasha (pəshah'), *n.* Turk. title of high mil. rank. **-lik,** *n.* jurisdiction of p.

pasigraphy (pəsig'rəfi), *n.* universal written language, *espec.* using symbols for ideas rather than words. **-phic(al),** *adj.*

pasque-flower (pask-flow'ə), *n.* white- or purple-flowered anemone-like plant.

pasquinade (paskwinād), *n.* lampoon, *espec.* exhibited in public place.

passacaglia (pasakahl'yah), *n.* old slow It. or Sp. dance.

passado (pəsah'dō), *n.* forward thrust in fencing.

passé (pas'ā), *Fr. adj.* (*fem.* **-ée**) "past"; worn out; out of date; antiquated.

passementerie (pasmahn'trē), *Fr. n.* bright trimmings of gilt, tinsel, etc.

passe partout (pas pahtōō', pahs), *n.* picture-frame, *espec.* of adhesive cloth holding together glass, picture and back; universal passport; master-key.

passerine (pas'ərīn, -in), *n.* & *adj.* (bird) belonging to the bird order including perching birds. **-riform,** *adj.*

passim (pas'im), Lat. *adv.* "everywhere": recurring frequently or here and there.

passometer (pasom'itə), *n.* pedometer.

passulate (pas'ūlāt), *v.t.* dry (grapes). **-tion,** *n.*

passus (pas'əs), *n.* canto of poem.

pastel (pas'təl, -tel'), *n.* crayon; crayon-drawing; light lit. work; *adj.* delicately coloured.

pastern (pas'tən), *n.* part of horse's foot between fetlock joint and upper edge of hoof.

pasteurise (pah'stūr īz, pas'-), *v.t.* sterilise partially, by heating to, and maintaining at, a high temperature. **-sation,** *n.*

pasticcio (pahstē'chō), It. *n.* (*pl.* **-ci**) olio; medley; pot-pourri.

pastiche (pastēsh'), *n.* work of art or lit. in imitation of, or satirising, another's style. **-ur** (-ēr'), *n.* maker of p.

pastose (pas'tōs), *adj.* painted thickly.

patamar, patt- (pat'əmah), *n.* Ind. messenger or mail-boat; W. Ind. lateen-rigged boat.

patavinity (patəvin'iti), *n.* dialectal term; use of such terms.

patchouli (pach'ooli), *n.* kind of E. Ind. mint, and strong perfume obtained from it.

pâté de fois gras (pah'tā də fwah grah), *Fr.,* paste made of fattened goose's liver.

patella (patel'ə), *n.* kneecap. **-liform,** *adj.* limpet-shaped. **-r,** *adj.* **-te,** *adj.* having p.

paten (pat'n), *n.* Communion bread plate.

pateriform (pat'ərifawm), *adj.* saucer-shaped.

paternoster (pat'ənostə, pā'-), *n.* Lord's Prayer, or recital of it; rosary bead on which p. is said; curse or spell; bead-like moulding.

pathema (pəthē'mə), *n. Med.,* disease. **-tic,** *adj.* **-tology,** *n.* physiological study of emotions.

pathodontia (pathədon'shiə), *n.* study of dental diseases.

pathogenesis (pathəjen'isis), *n.* origin or development of disease. **-etic** (-jinet'ik), *adj.* **-nic,** *adj.* causing disease.

pathognomy (pəthog'nəmi), *n.* diagnosis. **-mic** (-om'ik), **-monic,** *adj.* aiding p. ; distinctive.

pathology (pəthol'əji),· *n.* study of disease ; condition due to disease. **-gical,** *adj.* **-gist,** *n.*

pathomania (pathəmā'niə), *n.* moral insanity.

pathopoeia (pathəpē'ə), *n.* excitation of passion, *espec.* by rhetoric.

pathy (path'i), *n.* med. treatment ; nostrum.

patibulate (pətib'ūlāt), *v.t.* execute by hanging.

patina (pat'inə), *n.* film formed on exposed metals, etc., *espec.* green film on copper or bronze ; any such sign of mellowing or old age. **-nise,** *v.t.* coat with p. ; make bronze-like. **-nous,** *adj.* bearing p. **-te,** *v.i.* & *t.*

patisserie (patēs'rē) Fr. *n.* pastry shop.

patois (pat'wah), *n.* dialect ; jargon.

patrial (pā'triəl), *adj.* pert. to, derived from, or signifying native country.

patriarch (pā'triahk) *n.* tribal elder, ruler or father ; any venerable ancient man ; *R.C.*, bishop ; metropolitan ; bishop next below pope in rank. **-al,** *adj.* **-ate,** *n.* office of p. **-y,** *n.* government by p.

patrician (pətrish'n), *n.* & *adj.* (person) of noble birth. **-ciate,** *n.* position of p. ; nobility.

patricide (pat'risīd), *n.* killing or killer of own father ; traitor or act of treason. **-dal,** *adj.*

patrilineal (patrilin'iəl), *adj.* pert. to or descending in male line.

patrimony (pat'riməni), *n.* inherited property. **-nial** (-ō'niəl), *adj.*

patriolatry (patriol'ətri), *n.* excessive devotion to native country.

patristic (patris'tik), *adj.* pert. to the Fathers of the Church. **-ism** (-sizm), *n.* p. theology. **-s,** *n.* study of the Fathers' lives and works.

patrix (pā'triks), *n.* die from which matrix is made.

patroclinous (patrəklī'nəs), *adj.* pert.

to, or having, inherited paternal characteristics. **-ny** (pat'-), *n.*

patrology (pətrol'əji), *n.* patristics. **-gic(al),** *adj.*

patronymic (patrənim'ik), *n.* & *adj.* (name) derived from father or ancestors ; surname, *espec.* formed by addition of suffix (as *-son,* etc.) to father's name. **-nomatology,** *n.* study of p.

patruity (patrōō'iti), *n.* degree of relationship of paternal uncle.

patten (pat'n), *n.* wooden sole, or clog, for raising foot above wet.

pattu (pat'ōō), *n.* woollen cloth or shawl of Kashmir.

patulous (pat'ūləs), *adj.* widespreading or -open.

pauca verba (paw'kə və̄'bə), *Lat.,* "few words." **paucis verbis** (paw'-sis-), "in few words."

pauciloquy (pawsil'əkwi), *n.* brevity in speech.

paucity (paw'siti), *n.* state of being few or small ; scarcity ; lack.

paulopast (paw'ləpahst), *adj.* just finished or past. **-post,** *adj.* just after.

pavane (pavahn'), *n.* slow stately dance.

paviour (pā'vyə), *n.* labourer doing, or tool for, paving work.

pavonated (pav'ənātid), *adj.* peacock blue. **-nian** (-ō'niən), **-nine,** *adj.* like or coloured like a peacock.

pavor nocturnus (pā'vor noktə̄'nəs), *Lat.,* "night fear."

pawky (paw'ki), *adj.* sly ; coy ; dry.

pawnee (pawnē'), Anglo-Ind. *n.* water. **whisky-p.,** whisky and water.

pax (paks), Lat. *n.* "peace." **p.regis,** king's peace. **p.vobiscum,** "peace (be) with you."

paynim (pā'nim), *n.* pagan.

paysage (pāēzahzh'), Fr. *n.* landscape. **-gist** (pā'zəjist), *n.* painter of p.

pearl (pə̄l), *n.* size of type : 5-point.

peccable (pek'əbl), *adj.* liable to sin. **-adillo,** *n.* (*pl.* **-es**) minor sin. **-ant,** *adj.* sinning. *n.* sinner.

peccary (pek'əri), *n.* Amer. wild pig.

peccavi (pekā'vī), *Lat.,* "I have sinned" ; confession of sin. **-cation,** *n.* sinning.

pecten (pek'ten), *n.* (*pl.* **-tines**) scallop ; pubic bone ; comb-like membrane of eye of birds and reptiles.

pectin (pek'tin), *n.* principle in fruit causing jam, etc., to set. -aceous, *adj.*

pectinal (pek'tinəl), *adj.* pert. to or like a comb. -tinate, *adj.* comb-shaped; toothed. -tineal, *adj.* pert. to pubic bone. -tiniform, *adj.* like a comb or a scallop shell.

pectinous (pek'tinəs), *adj.* pert. to pectin. -tise, *v.t.* cause to set.

pectoral (pek'tərəl), *adj.* pert. to or worn on breast or chest; *n.* breast-plate; muscle of breast. -gia (-al'jiə), *n.* pain in chest. -riloquy, *n.* clear hearing of patient's voice in auscultation.

peculate (pek'ūlāt), *v.i. & t.* embezzle. -tion, -tor, *n.*

pedagogue (ped'əgog), *n.* schoolmaster; pedant. -gic(al) (-oj'ik, -l), *adj.* -gics (-oj'iks), -gy (-ogi), *n.* art of teaching; instruction in such art. -gism (-ogizm), *n.* p.'s character or occupation.

pedant (ped'ənt), *n.* person making display of his learning; learned person paying excessive attention to details; precisian. -ic (-an'tik), *adj.* -icism, -ism, -ry, *n.* -ocracy, *n.* government by p.

pedary (ped'əri), *adj.* pert. to walking or feet. -date, *adj.* like a foot; having feet.

pedesis (pidē'sis), *n.* Brownian movement.

pedialgia (pedial'jiə), *n.* pain in foot.

pedicel (ped'isəl), *adj.* short, thin stalk; footstalk. -cle, *n.* -llar, *adj.* -llate, *adj.* having p. -lliform, *adj.* like a p.

pedicular (pidik'ūlə), *adj.* pert. to or having lice. -late, *adj.* pedicellate. -licide, *n.* substance destroying lice. -losis, *n.* infestation with lice. -lous, *adj.*

pedicure (ped'ikūr), *n.* chiropody. -rist, *n.*

pediform (ped'ifawm), *adj.* foot-shaped. -digerous, *adj.* having feet. -diluvium, *n.* foot-bath.

pediment (ped'imənt), *n.* triangular space at end of gable, *espec.* ornamented; such space over door, window, etc. -al, *adj.*

pedipulate (pedip'ūlāt), *v.t.* work with the feet. -tion, -tor, *n.*

pedometer (pidom'itə), *n.* instr. measuring distance traversed by walker by recording number of his steps. -dograph, *n.* instr.

recording nature of ground passed over.

peduncle (pidung'kl), *n.* flower st-lk; stem. -cular, *adj.* -culate, *adj.* having p.

peepul (pē'pool), *n.* holy Ind. fig-tree; bo-tree.

pegamoid (peg'əmoid), *n.* kind of artificial leather.

peignoir (pānwahr'), Fr. *n.* loose dress; negligée.

peine (pān), Fr. *n.* "pain." **p. forte et dure** (-fort ā dūr'), "pain strong and hard"; execution by crushing to death under heavy weights.

pejorate (pē'jərāt), *v.t.* depreciate; worsen. -rism, *n.* extreme pessimism. -rity (-or'iti), *n.* being worse. -tion, *n.* -tive, *n. & adj.* disparaging (word or suffix, etc.).

pekoe (pē'kō), *n.* sort of black tea.

pelage (pel'ij), *n.* animal's coat.

pelagic (pilaj'ik), *adj.* pert. to or found in open sea, or near surface of sea. -gial (-ā'jiəl), *adj.* -gian (-ā'jiən), *n. & adj.* pelagic (animal).

pelargic (pilah'jik), *adj.* like or pert. to a stork.

pelargonium (pelahgō'niəm), *n.* geranium.

pelasgic (pilaz'jik), *adj.* Zoo., nomadic.

pelerine (pel'ərin, -ēn), *n.* fur cape with tippets in front.

pelioma (pēliō'mə, pel-), *n.* livid spot. -iosis, *n.* disease marked by p.

pelisse (pilēs'), *n.* long outer mantle.

pellagra (pəlag'rə, -ā'grə), *n.* nervous and digestive disease due to deficiency of nicotinic acid in diet. -ragenic, *adj.* causing p. -rin, *n.* person suffering from p. -rose, -rous, *adj.*

pellate (pel'āt), *v.i.* separate. -tion, *n.*

pellicle (pel'ikl), *n.* membrane; film. -cular, *adj.* -culate, *adj.* covered with p.

pellitory (pel'itəri), *n.* yarrow-like plant with root used in dentifrices.

pellucid (peloo'sid), *adj.* clear; transparent. -ity, *n.*

pelma (pel'mə), *n.* sole of foot. -tic (-at'ik), *adj.* -togram, *n.* impression showing shape of sole.

pelota (pelō'tə), Sp. *n.* "ball"; sev. tennis-like Sp. games, and fives-like Basque game.

pelotherapy (pēlōther'əpi, pel-), *n.* med. treatment by mud baths.

peltast (pel'tast), *n.* anct. Gr. soldier with light shield. **-tate, -tiform,** *adj.* shield-shaped. **-tiferous,** *adj.* bearing a shield.

pelvis (pel'vis), *n.* (*pl.* **-ves**) bony structure forming frame of abdominal cavity. **-vic,** *adj.* **-viform,** *adj.* basin-shaped.

pemmican (pem'ikən), *n.* pounded, pressed, dried meat.

penates (pinā'tēɩ, -ah'-), Lat. *n.pl.* household gods.

penchant (pen'chənt; *Fr.,* pahň'-shahň), *n.* inclination; liking.

pendente lite (penden'ti līꞌtē), *Lat.,* "during the lawsuit"; until completion of litigation.

peneplain (pē'niplān), *n.* land reduced to plain level by erosion. **-planation,** *n.*

penetralia (penitrā'liə), Lat. *n.pl.* private places; secrets. **-n,** *adj.*

penghulu (penghoo'loo), Malay *n.* village chieftain.

penial (pē'niəl), *adj.* pert. to penis.

penicillate (penisil'ət), *adj.* terminating in tuft of hairs. **-liform,** *adj.*

penicillin (penisil'in), *n.* antibiotic of wide use, produced by species of penicillium mould.

penis (pē'nis), *n.* (*pl.* **-nes**) male copulative organ. **-nile,** *adj.*

pennate (pen'āt), *adj.* having or like wings or feathers. **-niferous, -nigerous,** *adj.* feather-bearing. **-niform,** *adj.* feather-like.

penology (pēnol'əji), *n.* study of criminal punishment. **-gic(al),** *adj.* **-gist,** *n.*

pensile (pen'sīl, -il), *adj.* hanging; building a hanging nest. **-lity,** *n.*

pentachord (pen'təkawd), *n.* 5-stringed mus. instr.; series of five tones.

pentacle (pen'təkl), *n.* five-pointed star, *espec.* as talisman. **-cular** (-ak'ūlə), *adj.*

pentad (pen'tad), *n.* five; group of five.

pentadactyl (pentədak'til), *adj.* having five fingers or toes to each hand or foot. **-late, -loid,** *adj.* **-l'sm,** *n.*

pentadecagon (pentədek'əgən), *n.* 15-sided plane figure.

pentagamist (pentag'əmist), *n.* person who has, or has had, five spouses.

pentaglot (pen'təglot), *n.* & *adj.* (book, speaker, etc.), in or of five languages.

pentagon (pen'təgən), *n.* five-sided plane figure. **-al** (-ag'ənəl), *adj.*

pentagram (pen'təgram), *n.* pentacle. **-mmatic,** *adj.*

pentahedron (pentəhē'drən), *n.* five-sided solid figure. **-dral,** *adj.*

pentalogy (pental'əji), *n.* state of being fivefold or in five parts.

pentalpha (pental'fə), *n.* pentacle.

pentamerous (pentam'ərəs), *adj.* in five parts; *Bot.,* having its parts in fives. **-ral,** *adj.* **-rism,** *n.*

pentameter (pentam'itə), *n.* verseline of five feet. **-trist** (-et'rist), *n.*

pentangle (pen'tanggl), *n.* pentagon. **-gular,** *adj.*

pentapody (pentap'ədi), *n.* verseline of five feet.

pentapolis (pentap'əlis), *n.* group or alliance of five cities. **-litan** (-ol'itən), *adj.*

pentaptote (pen'taptōt), *n.* noun with five case forms.

pentarch (pen'tahk), *n.* member of pentarchy. **-y,** *n.* government by five persons; alliance between five powers.

pentastich (pen'təstik), *n.* stanza of five lines. **-ous** (-as'tikəs), *adj.* arranged in five rows. **-y,** *n.*

pentasyllable (pen'təsilabl), *n.* word, verse-line, etc., of five syllables. **-bic** (-ab'ik), *adj.*

pentateuch (pen'tətūk), *n.* first five books of Old Testament; books of Moses. **-al,** *adj.*

pentecost (pen'tikost), *n.* Jewish festival, like harvest thanksgiving, on fiftieth day after second day of Passover; *mod.,* Whitsunday, or the event which it commemorates. **-al,** *adj.* **-alism,** *n.* religious ecstasy.

pentothal (pen'təthal), *n.* anaesthetic injected into a vein, properly sodium pentothal.

penult (penult'), *n.* last but one, *espec.* such syllable. **-imate,** *n.* & *adj.*

penumbra (penum'brə), *n.* partly light margin surrounding complete shadow. **-l, -rous,** *adj.*

penurious (penūr'iəs), *adj.* poor; mean. **-y** (pen'-), *n.* poverty.

peon (pē'ən), *n.* agricultural labourer, or person bound to service for debt, of Sp. Amer.; *Ind.,* infantryman; native policeman. **-age, -ism,** *n.*

peotomy (piot'əmi), *n.* surg. removal of penis.

pepsin (pep'sin), *n.* gastric digestive juice. **-ate,** *v.t.* treat or mix with p. **-iferous,** *adj.* yielding p. **-ptic,** *adj.* pert. to p. or digestion ; aiding or capable of digestion ; pert. to, or in, stomach and duodenum ; *n.* aid to digestion. **-ptone,** *n.* substance resulting from digestion of protein by p. **-ptonise,** *v.t.* convert into peptone ; pre-digest. **-sis,** *n.* digestion.

peracute (pā'rəkūt), *adj.* very acute.

per capita (pē kap'itə), *Lat.,* "by heads" ; shared or sharing equally among individuals.

percheron (pā'shərən), *n.* kind of dappled or black cart horse.

perciform (pā'sifawm), *adj.* like a perch (fish).

percurrent (pəkur'ənt), *adj.* extending whole length.

percuss (pəkus'), *v.i.* & *t.* strike, tap, *espec.* part of body in med. diagnosis. **-ion,** *n.* act of striking violently ; impact of violent sound on ear ; mus. instr. as drums, etc., sounded by being struck. **-ive,** *adj.* **-or,** *n.*

percutaneous (pəkūtā'niəs), *adj.* taking effect through the skin.

percutient (pəkū'shiənt), *adj.* percussive ; *n.* percussor.

perdricide (pā'drisīd), *n.* killer of partridges.

perdu (pā'dū), *adj.* (*fem.* **-e**) out of sight ; lost ; reckless.

peregrinate (per'igrināt), *v.i.* & *t.* wander (through). **-tion, -tor,** *n.* **-tory,** *adj.*

peregrine (per'igrin, -īn), *n.* kind of falcon used in sport.

peremptory (per'əmptəri), *adj.* commanding ; allowing no denial, refusal, or delay ; arrogant.

perennial (pəren'iəl), *adj.* everlasting ; *n.* plant flowering every year.

perequitate (pərek'witāt), *v.t.* ride through on horse.

perfidy (pā'fidi), *n.* treachery ; breaking of promise. **-dious,** *adj.*

perfuse (pəfūz'), *v.t.* cover or sprinkle with ; pour over. **-sion,** *n.* **-sive,** *adj.*

pergameneous (pəgəmē'niəs), *adj.* resembling parchment. **-ntaceous,** *adj.*

per gradus (pā grā'dəs), *Lat.,* "(step) by step."

pergunnah (pəgun'ə), *n.* group of Ind. villages.

peri (pēr'i), *n.* Pers. fairy, *espec.* excluded from paradise ; beautiful woman.

perianth (per'ianth), *n.* external part of flower, including corolla and calyx. **-ial,** *adj.*

periapt (per'iapt), *n.* amulet.

pericardium (perikah'diəm), *n.* (*pl.* **-ia**) membranous sac containing heart. **-diac, -dial,** *adj.* **-ditis,** *n.* inflammation of p.

pericarp (per'ikahp), *n.* seed-vessel of plant. **-ial, -ic,** *adj.*

periclitate (pərik'litāt), *v.t.* jeopardise. **-tion,** *n.*

pericope (pərik'əpi), *n.* selection or quotation from book. **-pal, -pic** (-op'ik), *adj.*

pericranium (perikrā'niəm), *n.* membrane investing skull. **-nial,** *adj.*

periegesis (periijē'sis), *n.* description or tour of an area. **-etic** (-et'ik), *adj.*

perigee (per'ijē), *n.* point in orbit nearest earth. **-geal, -gean,** *adj.*

perigraph (per'igraph), *n.* marking round ; rough outline.

perihelion (perihēl'yən), *n.* point in orbit nearest sun. **-ial, -ian,** *adj.*

perimeter (pərim'itə), *n.* outer boundary, and its length. **-tric** (perimet'rik), *adj.* **-trium** (-et'-riəm), *n.* part of peritoneum round uterus.

periodontal (periədon'təl), *adj.* round tooth or teeth. **-tia, -tology,** *n.* study of diseases of such tissues.

perioeci (periē'si), *n.pl.* (*sing.* **-cus**) persons living in same latitude on opposite sides of earth. **-c,** *adj.*

periosteal (perios'tiəl), *adj.* round a bone. **-eum,** *n.* such membranous tissue.

periotic (periot'ik, -ō'tik), *adj.* round the ear.

peripatetic (peripətet'ik), *adj.* walking about or from place to place ; belonging to Aristotle's school of philosophy ; *n.* such person.

peripety, -tia, -teia (pərip'iti, peripē'tiə, -itē'ə), *n.* sudden and violent change in circumstances, *espec.* in drama.

periphery (pərif'əri), *n.* perimeter, *espec.* of round object or surface ; area of termination of nerves. **-ral, -ric** (-er'ik), *adj.*

periphrasis (perif'resis), *n.* (*pl.* -ses) circumlocution. -stic (-as'tik), *adj.*; *Gram.*, formed with auxiliaries, prepositions, etc.

periplus (per'iplos), *n.* tour round.

peripteral (perip'terel), *adj.* with row of columns on every side; pert. to air about moving body.

periscian (perish'ien, -is'-), *n.* person living in polar circle.

perispheric (perisfer'ik), *adj.* spherical.

peristalith (piris'telith), *n.* prehistoric stone circle.

peristalsis (peristal'sis), *n.* (*pl.* -ses) wave-like movement of intestines forcing contents onward. -ltic, *adj.*

peristeronic (peristeron'ik), *adj.* pert. to pigeons.

peristole (piris'teli), *n.* peristalsis.

peristrephic(al) (peristref'ik, -l), *adj.* rotating.

peristyle (per'istīl), *n.* row of columns, *espec.* on all sides of court, etc.; area enclosed by it.

peritomy (perit'emi), *n.* circumcision.

peritoneum (peritene'em), *n.* membranous sac lining abdominal cavity. -neal, *adj.* -nitis, *n.* inflammation of p.

perityphlic (peritif'lik), *adj.* round caecum. -litis, *n.* inflammation of p. tissue.

perlaceous (pelā'shes), *adj.* pearly. -ligenous, *adj.* producing pearls.

perlustrate (pelus'trāt), *v.t.* inspect with care. -tion, -tor, *n.*

permutation (pēmūtā'shn), *n.* transformation; change in order of objects, etc., or number of such possible changes. -te (-mūt'), *v.t.* arrange in different order.

pernancy (pē'nensi), *n. Law,* receiving.

pernine (pē'nīn, -in), *adj.* pert. to honey buzzard.

pernoctation (pēnoktā'shn), *n.* act of spending the night.

pernor (pē'ne), *n.* person taking or receiving.

peroneal (perenē'el), *adj.* pert. to fibula.

peroral (peror'el), *adj.* through the mouth.

perorate (per'erāt), *v.i.* make grandiloquent speech; bring speech to close. -tion, *n.* final passage of speech. -tive, -tory, (-or'eteri), *adj.*

peroxide (peroks'id), *n.* oxide containing large proportion of oxygen, *espec.* p. of hydrogen.

per procurationem (pē prokūr āshio'nem), *Lat.,* "by agency"; by agent or proxy (*abbr.* p.p. *or* per pro.).

perry (per'i), *n.* cider-like drink made from pears.

per se (pē sē), *Lat.,* "by itself"; of or in itself; essentially; by virtue of its own essence. -ity, *n.* self-sufficiency.

perseverate (pesev'erāt), *v.i.* repeat action, etc., continually; recur persistently. -tion, *n.*

persiennes (pēsienz'), *n.pl.* kind of Venetian blinds; outside shutters with movable slats.

persiflage (pē'siflahzh), *n.* raillery; idle chatter.

persimmon (pesim'en), *n.* dateplum.

persona grata (peso'ne grā'te), *Lat.,* "welcome or acceptable person." p. non g., unwelcome or unacceptable person.

personalia (pesenā'lie), Lat. *n.pl.* personal details or anecdotes; personal belongings.

personalty (pē'senelti), *n.* personal property.

perspicacious (pēspikā'shes), *adj.* clear-sighted; having discernment. -city (-as'iti), *n.*

perspicuous (pespik'ūes), *adj.* easily understood; clearly expressed. -uity, *n.*

pertinacity (pōtinas'iti), *n.* persistence; tenacity. -cious, *adj.*

pertussis (petus'is), *n.* whooping-cough. -sal, *adj.*

peruke (perōok'), *n.* wig.

perulate (per'oolāt), *adj.* having scales.

pervigilium (pōvijil'iem), *n.* (*pl.* -ia) night vigil; insomnia.

perwitsky (pewit'ski), *n.* pole-cat of N. Asia and its fur.

pes planus (pēz plā'nes), *Lat.,* "flat foot"; flatfootedness. p.valgus, kind of clubfoot.

pessary (pes'eri), *n.* supporting instr. or suppository introduced into vagina.

pestiferous (pestif'eres), *adj.* carrying infection or plague; noxious. -ticide, *n.* pest-killing substance. -tology, *n.* scientific study of pests.

petard (pitahd'), *n.* bomb attached to, and for bursting open, gates,

---

etc. **hoist with own p.**, blown up by own bomb; damaged by own devices to injure others.

petiole (pet'iōl), *n*. leaf-stalk. **-lar,** *adj.* **-late,** *adj.* having p. **-lule,** *n*. p. of a leaflet.

petitio principii (pitish'iō prinsip'ii), *Lat.*, "begging the question."

petrean (pitrē'ən), *adj.* pert. to or of rock.

petrel (pet'rəl), *n*. small dark seabird. **stormy p.,** such bird of the Atlantic and Mediterranean; person fond of, or whose presence heralds, strife.

petricolous (petrik'ələs), *adj.* inhabiting rocks.

pétrissage (pā'trēsahzh), *Fr. n.* kneading (in massage).

petrogenesis (petrəjen'isis), *n*. origin or development of rocks. **-nic,** *adj.* forming rock. **-roglyph,** *n*. anct. rock-carving. **-rography,** *n*. description and classification of rocks. **-rolithic,** *adj.* as hard as rock, app. to road surface. **-rology,** *n*. geol. study of rocks. **-rophilous,** *adj.* living on rocks. **-rous,** *adj.* rocky; hard as stone.

pettitoes (pet'itōz), *n.pl.* pig's trotters.

petto (pet'ō), *It. n*. breast. **in p.,** in mind; in secret thoughts.

phacochoere (fak'əkēr), *n*. wart-hog. **-rine,** *adj.*

phacoid (fā'koid, fak'-), *adj.* lenticular. **-cometer,** *n*. lens-measuring instr.

phaeton (fā'itən), *n*. light twohorse four-wheeled open carriage.

phagedaena (fajidē'nə), *n*. gangrene; extensive ulceration. **-nic(al), -nous,** *adj.*

phagocyte (fag'əsīt), *n*. leucocyte destroying harmful bacteria, etc. **-tal, -tic** (-it'ik), *adj.* **-tosis,** *n*. destruction of harmful elements by p.

phagomania (fagəmā'niə), *n*. insane mania for food.

phalacrosis (faləkrō'sis), *n*. baldness.

phalanger (fələn'jə), *n*. sev. kinds of long-tailed Austral. marsupial. **-ine,** *adj.*

phalanges (fələn'jēz), *n.pl.* (*sing.* **-nx**) bones of finger or toe. **-geal,** *adj.* **-gigrade,** *adj.* walking on p.

phalanx (fal'angks), *n*. closely-

ranked infantry formation; any such closely packed or organised body.

phalarope (fal'ərōp), *n*. small sandpiper-like shore bird.

phallus (fal'əs), *n*. (*pl.* **-li**) representation of penis, symbol of generative power, as object of worship. **-lephoric,** *adj.* carrying the p. **-lic,** *adj.* **-licism, -lism,** *n*. p.-worship.

phanerogam (fan'ərəgam), *n*. flowering plant. **-ic, -ous** (-og'əməs), *adj.* **-y,** *n*.

phaneromania (fanərəmā'niə), *n*. habit of biting nails, picking at scars, etc.

phanerosis (fanərō'sis), *n*. becoming visible.

phanic (fan'ik), *adj.* visible; obvious.

phantasmagoria (fantazməgōr'iə), *n*. crowd of phantoms; series of shifting images or scenes. **-rial, -rian, -ric,** *adj.*

pharisee (far'isē), *n*. Jewish religious adherent to ritual formalities; person ostentatiously religious, or self-righteous; hypocrite. **-saic(al)** (-sā'ik, -l), *adj.* **-saism** (far'-), *n.*

pharmaceutical (fahməsū'tikl), *adj.* pert. to pharmacy; *n*. drug used in med. **-macal, -macic,** *adj.* **-macist,** *n*. practiser of pharmacy. **-macite,** *n*. mineral used in med. **-macognosy,** *n*. study of med. drugs. **-macology,** *n*. study of med. drugs and their properties. **-macometer,** *n*. instr. measuring drugs. **-macon,** *n*. drug; poison. **-macopaedics,** *n*. study of drugs. **-macopoeia,** *n*. official list of drugs. **-macopolist,** *n*. seller of drugs. **-macy,** *n*. preparation, dispensing and selling of drugs; chemist's shop.

pharos (fār'os), *n*. lighthouse. **-rology,** *n*. study of lighthouses.

pharynx (far'ingks), *n*. (*pl.* **-nges**) part of throat between mouth and oesophagus. **-ngeal,** *adj.* **-ngismus,** *n*. spasm of p. **-ngitis,** *n*. inflammation of p. **-ngology** (-gol'əji), *n*. med. study of p. **-ngoscope** (-gəskōp), *n*. instr. for viewing p.

phellem (fel'em), *n*. cork. **-logen,** *n*. tissue producing cork. **-loplastics,** *n*. cork-modelling.

phemic (fē'mik), *adj.* like or pert. to speech.

---

hat, bah, hāte, hāre, crawl; pen, ēve, hēre; it, īce, fīre; on, bōne, boil, bōre, howl; foot, fōod, bōor, hull, tūbe, pūre.

phenakistoscope (fenəkis'təskōp), *n.* apparatus or instr. in which figures on a moving dial, etc., seem to move when viewed through a slit ; earliest form of cinematograph.

phenobarbitone (fēnōbah'bitōn), *n.* sedative and sleep-inducing drug, also called luminal.

phenogenesis (fēnəjen'isis), *n.* origin of races. **-etic** (-jinet'ik), *adj.* **-nology,** *n.* study of relations between recurring biol. activities and climate.

phenomenon (finom'inən), *n.* (*pl.* **-mena**) any fact or happening ; anything perceived by the senses ; *pop.,* remarkable thing or person, or rare event. **-menal,** *adj.* **-menology,** *n.* description and classification of p.

pheretrer (fer'itrə), *n.* keeper of a shrine.

philabeg, *see* filibeg.

philadelphian (filədel'fiən), *adj.* pert. to or exercising brotherly love.

philalethist (filəlē'thist), *n.* truth-lover.

philately (filat'ili), *n.* stamp-collecting. **-lic** (-el'ik), *adj.* **-list,** *n.*

philematology (filēmətol'əji), *n.* art or science of kissing.

philhellene (fil'əlēn, -hel'-), *n.* lover of Greece or things Greek. **-nic,** *adj.* **-nism** (-hel'inizm), **-nist,** *n.*

philhippic (filhip'ik), *adj.* horse-loving.

philippic (filip'ik), *n.* diatribe ; abusive speech.

philippine (fil'ipēn), *n.* double-kernelled nut.

philocaly (filok'əli), *n.* love of beauty. **-lic** (-al'ik), *adj.* **-list,** *n.*

philodemic (filədem'ik), *adj.* fond of the common people.

philodox (fil'ədoks), *n.* dogmatic person ; person fond of opinions, *espec.* his own.

philogynist (filoj'inist), *n.* lover of women. **-nous,** *adj.* **-ny,** *n.*

philology (filol'əji), *n.* study of language. **-gical,** *adj.* **-gist,** *n.*

philomathy (filom'əthi), *n.* fondness for learning. **-thic(al)** (-ath'ik, -l), *adj.*

philonoist (filon'ōist), *n.* one seeking knowledge.

philoprogenitive (filəprəjen'itiv), *adj.* desirous of having children ; fond of children.

philotechnic(al) (filətek'nik, -l), *adj.* devoted to the arts. **-nist,** *n.*

philotheism (filəthē'izm), *n.* love of God. **-ist,** *n.*

philotherian (filəthēr'iən), *n.* animal-lover. **-ism,** *n.*

philtre (fil'tə), *n.* love potion.

phlebitis (flibi'tis), *n.* inflammation of vein. **-tic** (-it'ik), *adj.*

phlebotomy (flibot'əmi), *n.* blood-letting. **-mic** (-om'ik), *adj.* **-mise,** *v.i. & t.* **-mist,** *n.*

phlegmagogue (fleg'məgog), *n.* phlegm-expelling drug. **-masia,** *n.* inflammation. **-mon,** *n.* boil.

phloem (flō'em), *n.* bast tissue. **-oeophagous,** *adj.* feeding on bark of trees.

phlogiston (fləjis'tən), *n.* principle of combustibility once supposed to exist in all inflammable substances. **-gogenetic,** **-genic** (flog-), *adj.* causing inflammation. **-gosis,** *n.* inflammation. **-gotic,** **-tic,** *adj.* pert. to inflammation.

phobia (fō'biə), *n.* fear ; dread. **-bic,** *adj.* **-bist,** **-o,** *n.*

phocine (fō'sīn, -in), *adj.* pert. to seals (animals). **-cacean,** **-caceous** (-kā'shn, -shəs), **-cal** (-kəl), *adj.* **-ciform** (-sif-), **-coid** (-koid), *adj.* seal-like.

phoenicopter, **phe-** (fē'nikoptə, fen-), *n.* flamingo. **-ourous,** *adj.* having red tail.

phon (fon), *n.* unit of loudness of sound.

phonal (fō'nəl), *adj.* vocal ; phonetic. **-nate,** *v.i.* speak or sing **-nation,** *n.*

phoneme (fō'nēm), *n.* collective variations of a sound pronounced with slight differences in differing circumstances. **-mic,** *adj.*

phonesis (fonē'sis), *n.* phonation.

phonetic (fənet'ik), *adj.* pert. to or showing speech sound. **-s,** *n.* study of vocal sounds and their representation ; the speech sounds of a language collectively. **-ian,** **-ist,** **-tist,** *n.* **-ise,** *v.t.* spell in phonetic alphabet.

phonic (fon'ik, fō'-), *adj.* phonetic ; acoustic. **-niatrics,** *n.* study and correction of speech defects. **-s,** *n.* phonetics ; acoustics ; study of phonetic method of teaching reading.

phonogram (fō'nəgram), *n.* symbol representing sound, syllable or word. **-graph**, *Amer. n.* gramophone. **-graphy**, *n.* description and representation of speech sounds ; Pitman's shorthand system.

phonology (fənol'əji), *n.* study of speech sounds and their development. **-gical**, *adj.* **-gist**, *n.*

phonometry (fənom'itri), *n.* measurement of intensity, etc., of sounds. **-ter**, *n.* instr. used in p. **-tric** (-et'rik), *adj.*

phonophorous (fənof'ərəs), *adj.* transmitting sound waves. **-re**, *n.* system of hearing for the deaf conducting sounds to the teeth ; device for sending telephonic and telegraphic messages over same line simultaneously.

phonotype (fō'nətīp), *n.* printing type of phonetic alphabet ; a character of p. **-pic** (-ip'ik), *adj.* **-py**, *t.* phonetic spelling advocated for ordinary use.

phorometry (fōrom'itri), *n.* study and correction of abnormalities of muscles of eye. **-ter**, *n.* instr. used in p.

phosgene (fos'jēn), *n.* colourless poison gas made from chlorine and carbon monoxide.

phosphate (fos'fāt), *n.* salt of phosphoric acid ; drink of aerated water with phosphoric acid, flavouring, etc. ; fertiliser containing phosphorus. **-tic** (-at'ik), *adj.*

phosphene (fos'fēn), *n.* sensation of seeing lights in darkness or when lids are closed.

phossy (phos'i), *adj.* caused by phosphorus. **p.jaw**, necrosis of jaw among workers handling phosphorus.

phot (fot), *n.* unit of illumination of a surface.

photaesthesia, -sis (fōtesthē'zhiə, -sis), *n.* sense of vision. **-etic** (-et'ik), *adj.*

photic (fō'tik), *adj.* pert. to or penetrated by light. **-s**, *n.* study of light.

photobathic (fōtəbath'ik), *adj.* pert. to sea depths penetrated by sunlight. **-biotic**, *adj.* thriving only in light.

photochromy (fō'təkrōmi), *n.* colour photography. **-matic, -mic**, *adj.*

photodromy (fətod'rəmi), *n.* motion towards light.

photoelectric (fōtōilek'trik), *adj.*

pert. to discharge of electrons by, or decrease in resistance in, certain substances when exposed to light. **-ity**, *n.*

photogenic (fōtəjen'ik), *adj.* generating light ; suitable for being photographed.

photogrammetry (fōtəgram'itri), *n.* photographical surveying.

photogravure (fōtəgrəvūr′), *n.* printing from engraved plates photographically prepared.

photogyric (fōtəjīr'ik), *adj.* turning towards light.

photokinesis (fōtəkinē'sis), *n.* activity caused by light. **-etic** (-et'ik), *adj.*

photology (fətol'əji), *n.* study of light. **-gic(al)**, *adj.* **-gist**, *n.*

photolysis (fətol'isis), *n.* decomposition caused by light. **-ytic** (-it'ik), *adj.*

photometer (fətom'itə), *n.* instr. measuring intensity, etc., of light. **-tric** (-et'rik), *adj.* **-try**, *n.*

photomicrograph (fōtəmī'krəgraf), *n.* enlarged photograph of minute object ; photograph taken through microscope.

photonasty (fō'tənasti), *n. Bot.*, adoption of certain position due to effect of light on growth. **-tic**, *adj.*

photonosus (fəton'əsəs), *n.* morbid condition due to exposure to light. **-topathy**, *n.* any such disease.

photophile (fō'təfil, -īl), *n. & adj.* (organism) loving light. **-lous** (-of'iləs), *adj.* **-ly** (-of'ili), *n.* **-phobia**, *n.* dislike or dread of light. **-phobic, -phobous** (-of'əbəs), *adj.* **-phygous** (-of'igəs), *adj.* avoiding or disliking light.

photoscope (fō'təskōp), *n.* apparatus for observing light, *espec.* changes in its intensity, or magnifying photographs. **-pic** (-op'ik), *adj.*

photosensitive (fōtəsen'sitiv), *adj.* sensitive to light, espec. sunlight.

photosphere (fō'təsfēr), *n.* sun's luminous envelope. **-ric** (-er'ik), *adj.*

photostat (fō'təstat), *n.* photographic copy of document, etc. **-ic**, *adj.*

photosynthesis (fōtəsin'thisis), *n.* formation of carbohydrates by chlorophyll-containing cells of plant exposed to light. -e, v.i. & t. -etic (-et'ik), adj.

phototachometry (fōtətakom'itri), n. measurement of speed of light. -ter, n. instr. used in p. -tric (-et'rik), adj.

phototaxis (fōtətaks'is), n. growth or movement directed by light. -tactic, adj.

phototherapy (fōtəther'əpi), n. med. treatment by means of light. -peutic, -pic (-thirap'ik), adj.

photothermic (fōtəthə'mik), adj. pert. to heat and light.

phototonus (fətot'ənəs), n. sensitivity to light. -nic (-on'ik), adj.

phototropism (fətot'rəpizm), n. movement directed by light; heliotropism. -pic (-op'ik), adj.

phratry (frā'tri), n. clan; tribe. -tor, n. member of p. -triac, -trial, -tric, adj.

phreatic (friat'ik), adj. pert. to wells and subterranean water.

phrenetic, see frenetic.

phrenic (fren'ik), adj. pert. to diaphragm, or mind. -nitis, n. brain fever. -nograph, n. instr. recording motions of diaphragm in breathing.

phrenology (frenol'əji), n. study of outline of skull giving supposed indication of mental ability and characteristics. -gical, adj. -gist, n. -nopathy, n. mental disease. -noplegia, n. sudden loss of brain power.

phrontistery (fron'tistəri), n. place for study.

phthinoid (thī'noid, thin'-), adj. pert. to phthisis.

phthiriasis (thīrī'əsis), n. infestation with lice. -rophagous, adj. eating lice.

phthisis (thī'sis, tī-, fthī'-), n. tuberculosis of lungs. -sical, adj. -siogenesis, n. development of p. -siology, n. study of p. -siophobia, n. dread of contracting p. -siotherapy, n. med. treatment of p.

phycology (fīkol'əji), n. study of seaweeds or algae. -cography, n. description of seaweeds or algae.

phygogalactic (fīgəgəlak'tik), n. & adj. (substance) stopping milk secretion.

phylactery (filak'təri), n. small leather box containing scriptural extracts worn by Jews at prayer on head and arm; relic-con-

tainer; amulet; reminder; record; words in a balloon-like circle drawn issuing from mouth. -ric(al) (-er'ik, -l), adj.

phylactic (filak'tik), adj. defending against disease.

phylliform (fil'ifawm), adj. leaf-shaped. -line, adj. leaf-like. -logenetic, adj. pert. to production of, or producing, leaves. -loid, adj. phylline. -lomania, n. abnormal leaf-production. -lomorph, n. artistic leaf-like detail. -lophagous, adj. leaf-eating. -lophorous, adj. bearing leaves. -lotaxy, n. arrangement of leaves of plant.

phylloxera (filoksēr'ə, -loks'ərə), n. plant-louse harmful to vines.

phylogeny (fīloj'ini), n. history or development of a race, species, etc. -netic(al) (-jinet'ik, -l), -nic (-jen'-ik), adj. -nist, n.

phylum (fī'ləm), n. (pl. -la) largest subdivision of natural kingdom.

phyma (fī'mə), n. (pl. -ta) skin tumour. -tic (-at'ik), adj. -toid, adj. like p. -tosis, n. disease characterised by p.

physagogue (fī'səgog, fis'-), n. & adj. (drug) expelling wind.

physeterine (fisē'tərin, -in), adj. pert. to or like a sperm whale.

physiatrics (fiziat'riks), n. use of natural healing agents.

physiocracy (fiziok'rəsi), n. government that does not interfere with the operation of natural laws. -crat, n. advocate (espec. Fr., 18th-cent.) of p. -cratic, adj.

physiognomy (fiziog'nəmi, -on'əmi), n. face; facial expression; divination of character or fortune from face. -mic (-om'ik), -monic (-on'ik), adj.

physiography (fiziog'rəfi), n. physical geography; topography; description of natural phenomena. -pher, n. -phical, adj.

physiolatry (fiziol'ətri), n. nature worship. -ter, n. -trous, adj.

physiology (fiziol'əji), n. study of functions of healthy living organism; such functions collectively. -gical, adj. -gist, n.

physiotherapy (fiziōther'əpi), n. med. treatment by physical means: massage, exercises, electricity, etc. -pist, n.

physitheism (fizithē'izm), n. nature worship; ascription to God of

ə=er in father; ē=er in pert; th=th in thin; dh=th in then; zh=s in pleasure; k=ch in loch; ṅ=Fr. nasal n; ü=Fr. w.

physical shape. **-tism**, *n.* nature worship.

physiurgic (fiziэ'jik), *adj.* due to natural causes.

phytivorous (fītiv'эrэs), *adj.* feeding on plants.

phytogamy (fītog'эmi), *n. Bot.*, cross-fertilisation. **-genesis**, *n.* development and origin of plants. **-genic**, *adj.* derived from plants. **-graphy**, *n.* descriptive botany. **-oid**, *adj.* plant-like. **-olithology**, *n.* palaeobotany. **-ology**, *n.* botany. **-ophagic**, **-ophagous**, *adj.* phytivorous. **-ophilous**, *adj.* fond of plants. **-osis**, *n.* infestation with plant parasites. **-otomy**, *n.* anatomy of plants.

pi (pī), sixteenth letter (Π, π) of Gr. alphabet ; *Math.*, ratio (3.1416) of circumference to diameter of circle.

piacle (pī'эkl), *n.* sin ; crime. **-cular** (-ak'ūlэ), *adj.* expiatory ; sinful. **-cularity**, *n.*

pia mater (pī'э mā'tэ), *n.* inner membrane enclosing brain.

piarhaemia (pīэrē'miэ), *n.* existence of fat in blood. **-mic**, *adj.*

piazza (piat'sэ), *n.* open square in city ; courtyard ; gallery round p. **-zian**, *adj.*

pibroch (pē'brok), *n.* piece of music for bagpipe.

pica (pī'kэ), *n.* size of type : 12-point. **small p.**, 11-point. **double p.**, 22-point.

picador (pik'эdōr), *n.* mounted bull-fighter with lance.

picaro (pikah'rō), Sp. *n.* (*fem.* **-ra**) rogue. **-resque**, *adj.* pert. to rogues, *espec.* app. to literature about rogues and vagabonds. **-roon**, *n.* rogue ; thief ; pirate.

pice (pīs), *n.* E. Ind. coin, value of one-quarter anna.

piceous (pī'siэs, pis'-), *adj.* like pitch ; inflammable.

piciform (pī'sifawm, pis'-), *adj.* like a woodpecker. **-cine**, *adj.* pert. to woodpeckers.

pickerel (pik'эrэl), *n.* young pike (fish).

picric (pik'rik), *adj.* app. to yellow, bitter, poisonous acid used as dye and disinfectant and in manuf. of explosives.

pidan (pēdahn'), *n.* preserved Chin. duck's eggs.

piddock (pid'эk), *n.* rough-shelled, boring, marine bivalve.

pidgin (pij'in), *n. & adj.* business. **p.English**, broken English of Far East natives.

pièce de résistance (pē ās' dэ rāzē'stahns), *Fr.*, "piece of resistance ;" culminating or main item. **p. d'occasion** (-dokah'-zyawn), piece written or composed for a special occasion ; bargain.

pied-à-terre (pyād'-ah-tār'), *Fr.*, "foot on the ground" ; temporary or subsidiary home.

Pierian (pī ēr'iэn), *adj.* pert. to Pieria, Macedonia, where the Muses were worshipped ; pert. to the Muses or poetry.

pierid (pī'эrid), *n. & adj.* (butterfly) belonging to the family including cabbage and other butterflies. **-ine** (-er'idīn), **-rine**, *adj.*

pietà (pyā'tah), It. *n.* "piety" ; representation of the dead Christ held and mourned by the Virgin Mary.

pietism (pī'itizm), *n.* unquestioning religious devotion ; priggishness. **-ist**, *n.*

piezochemistry (pī ēzэkem'istri), *n.* study of chem. effects of pressure. **-zo-electricity**, *n.* production of elec. charges on certain crystals when under pressure ; slight change in shape of crystal when in elec. field. **-zometer**, *n.* instr. measuring compressibility of liquids.

pignorate (pig'nэrāt), *v.t.* pawn ; take in pawn. **-tion**, *n.* **-titious**, *adj.*

pilaster (pilas'tэ), *n.* rectangular pillar projecting from and supporting wall. **-trade**, *n.* row of p. **-tric**, *adj.*

pileus (pī'liэs, pil-), *n.* (*pl.* **-ei**) cap- or umbrella-like top of mushroom. **-eate(d)**, *adj.* having p. ; with crest on pileum. **-eiform**, *adj.* shaped like p. **-eolus**, *n.* (*pl.* **-li**) small p. **-eum**, *n.* top of bird's head.

pilose (pī'lōs), *adj.* hairy. **-liferous**, *adj.* bearing hair. **-sis**, *n.* overgrowth of hair. **-sity**, *n.* hairiness.

pilular (pil'ūlэ), *adj.* pert. to or like a pill.

pimelitis (pimэli'tis), *n.* inflammation of fatty tissue.

pimento (pimen'tō), *n.* Sp. pepper; allspice.

pinaceous (pīnā'shəs), *adj.* pert. to or like a pine tree; belonging to the pine family of trees.

Pinakothek (pinakōtāk'), Ger. *n.* picture gallery.

pinaster (pīnas'tə, pin-), *n.* cluster pine.

pinchbeck (pinch'bek), *n.* gold-like alloy of copper and zinc; tawdry jewellery; *adj.* spurious; trashy.

pineal (pin'iəl), *adj.* pert. to or like a pine cone. **p.body** *or* **gland**, small gland-like process of brain cavity.

pinguefy (ping'gwifī), *v.i.* & *t.* become or make fat or rich. **-faction,** *n.* **-guedinous,** *adj.* fatty. **-guid,** *adj.* fatty; oily; rich.

pinnate (pin'āt), *adj.* like a feather; with leaflets on either side of a leafstalk. **-tifid,** divided pinnately. **-tion,** *n.*

pinochle (pin'okl, pē'nukl), *n.* bezique-like Amer. card game.

pinxit (pingks'it), *Lat.,* "painted (it)."

pipal, *see* peepul.

pip emma (pip em'ə), *adj.* & *adv.* signaller's sl. for post meridiem.

piperaceous (pī'pərā'shəs), *adj.* pert. to or like pepper plant; belonging to pepper family of plants.

pipette (pipet'), *n. Chem.,* narrow tube into which liquids are sucked for measurement, etc.

pipistrelle (pipistrel'), *n.* brown bat.

pipit (pip'it), *n.* sev. lark-like singing birds; titlark.

pipkin (pip'kin), *n.* small pot.

pis aller (pēz al'ā), *Fr.,* "go worst"; last resort; something done or accepted for lack of anything better; less desirable alternative.

piscary (pis'kəri), *n.* fishing rights or place.

piscatology (piskətol'əji), *n.* art or science of fishing. **-tor** (-ā'tə), *n.* angler. **-torial, -torious, -tory,** *adj.* pert. to fishing.

piscine (pis'īn, -in), *adj.* pert. to fish. **-ciculture,** *n.* fish breeding. **-cifauna,** *n.* fish life of a region. **-ciform,** *adj.* fish-shaped. **-civorous,** *adj.* fish-eating. **-na** (-ē'nə), *n.* small tank; fishpond; water basin in church sanctuary. **-nity,** *n.*

pisiform (pī'sifawm), *adj.* like pea(s).

pismire (pis'mīr), *n.* ant. **-rism,** *n.* hoarding of small things.

pisteology (pistiol'əji), *n.* science of faith. **-tic,** *adj.* pert. to faith; pure.

pistil (pis'til), *n.* plant's ovary with style and stigma. **-llar, -lline,** *adj.* **-llate,** *adj.* having p. **-lloid,** *adj.* like a p.

pistiology (pistiol'əji), *n.* doctrine about faith. **-tology,** *n.* division of theology dealing with faith.

Pithecanthropus (pithikanthrō'pəs, -kan'-), *n.* genus of ape like men; "missing link." **P.erectus,** such creature whose remains were discovered in Java: "Java man." **-pe,** *n.* **-pic, -poid,** *adj.*

pithecoid (pith'ikoid, -thē'-), *adj.* pert. to anthropoid apes. **-cism,** *n.* p. characters in Man. **-comorphic,** *adj.* like anthropoid apes.

pituitary (pitū'itəri), *adj.* denoting or pert. to ductless gland at base of brain secreting a hormone controlling bone growth and activity of thyroid and reproductive glands, and another controlling blood pressure and activity of involuntary muscles. **-te** (pit'ū īt), *n.* mucus. **-tous,** *adj.* mucous.

pityriasis (pitiri'əsis), *n.* scaly skin infection. **-sic** (-as'ik), *adj.* **-yroid,** *adj.* bran-like.

pixilated (piks'ilātid), *adj.* as if bewitched by fairies; slightly crazy.

place aux dames (plas ō dahm'), *Fr.,* "(make) room for the ladies."

placebo (pləsē'bō), *Lat.,* "I will please"; *R.C.,* first word of Vespers for dead; such Vespers; something given to please or quiet, *espec.* medicine given merely to please patient; dummy medicine given to "controls" in med. experiment.

placenta (pləsen'tə), *n.* (*pl.* **-ae**) mammal's organ attached to and nourishing foetus in womb; afterbirth. **-l, -ry,** *adj.* ; *n.* mammal having p. **-te,** *adj.* having p. **-tion,** *n.* structure or attachment of p. **-tiferous, -tigerous,** *adj.* bearing p. **-tiform, -toid,** *adj.* like p.

placer (plā'sə), *n.* gold deposit other than vein, *e.g.* where it is obtained by washing.

placet (plā'sit), *Lat.,* "it pleases"; assenting vote or expression.

placoid (plak'oid), *adj.* pert. to or like teeth-like scales.

plage (plahzh), Fr. *n.* sea beach; seaside resort.

plagiarism (plā'jiərizm), *n.* copying another's words, ideas, etc., and publishing them as one's own. **-rise,** *v.i.* & *t.* **-rist, -ry,** *n.*

plagiograph (plā'jiograf), *n.* kind of pentograph.

planarian (plənār'iən), *n.* kind of flatworm. **-riform, -rioid,** *adj.* like p.

planchette (plahnshet'), Fr. *n.* board supported on two wheels and a pencil, which is supposed to write "spirit messages."

planetarium (planitār'iəm), *n.* (*pl.* **-ia**) model of solar system. **-tesimal,** *adj.* pert. to minute bodies moving in space, supposed by some to have joined to form planets, etc. **-togeny,** *n.* theory of origin of planets. **-tography,** *n.* description of planets. **-tology,** *n.* study of planets' surface.

plangent (plan'jənt), *n.* deep- or loud-sounding. **-gorous,** *adj.* mournful. **-ncy,** *n.*

planigraph (plan'igraf, plā'-), *n.* instr. for copying drawings on different scale. **-nimeter,** *n.* instr. measuring plane figure's area. **-nimetry,** *n.* such measurement.

planipennate (plānipen'āt), *adj.* having flat, broad wings. **-irostral,** *adj.* having such beak. **-isphere,** *n.* map of heavens on plane surface.

plankton (plangk'tən), *n.* floating or minute swimming organisms of ocean. **-ic,** *adj.* **-t,** *n.* organism included in p. **-tology,** *n.* study of p.

planography (planog'rəfi), *n.* cartography; printing from flat surface. **-ometry,** *n.* gauging of plane surface.

plantaginaceous (plantajinā'shəs), *adj.* pert. to or like plantain; belonging to plantain family of plants.

plantigrade (plan'tigrād, plahn'-), *n.* & *adj.* (animal) walking on sole of foot, as Man. **-dy,** *n.*

plantivorous (plahntiv'ərəs), *n.* plant-eating.

plasma (plaz'mə), *n.* fluid part of blood, etc. **-matic** (-mat'ik), **-mic,** *adj.* **-mocyte,** *n.* white blood corpuscle. **-mophagous,** *adj.* consuming p.

plastic (plas'tik), *adj.* moulding; forming; capable of being moulded; *n.* such synthetic organic substance. **p.surgery,** surgery remedying defects by transferring tissue from another part of body or from another body.

plastid (plas'tid), *n.* minute mass of protoplasm in cell.

plastron (plas'tron), *n.* breast-pad or -cloth for defence or ornament.

plataleiform (platəlē'ifawm), *adj.* spoonbilled.

plateasm (plat'iazm), *n.* broad speech.

platen (plat'n), *n.* plate pressing paper against type in printing machine; roller of typewriter.

platitude (plat'itūd), *n.* trite statement. **-dinarian,** *n.* & *adj.* (person) making p. **-dinism,** *n.* **-dinise,** *v.s.* utter p. **-dinous,** *adj.*

Platonic (plətoń'ik), *adj.* pert. to Plato, Gr. philosopher, and his doctrines; ideal; spiritual; theoretical; harmless.

platurous (plətūr'əs), *adj.* flat-tailed.

platycephaly (platisef'əli), *n.* flatness of crown of head. **-lic** (-sifal'ik), **-lous,** *adj.* **-ycoria,** *n.* abnormal dilatation of pupil of eye. **-ydactyl,** *adj.* having flat digits. **-ypod,** *adj.* having broad, flat feet. **-ypodia,** *n.* flat-footedness. **-ypus,** *n.* duckbill. **-yrrhinian,** *n.* & *adj.* (person) with short, flat nose.

plebeian (plibē'ən), *n.* & *adj.* (person) of common people or lower classes; vulgar. **-biscite** (pleb'isit), *n.* nation's or district's direct vote on a specific measure. **-bs** (plebs), Lat. *n.* the common people.

plectrum (plek'trəm), *n.* (*pl.* **-ra**) instr. for plucking strings of mus. instr. **-tridial,** *adj.* drumstick-shaped.

pledget (plej'it), *n.* small wound dressing.

plegometer (pligom'itə), *n.* instr. measuring strength of a blow.

pleiobar (plī'əbah), *n.* isobar or area of high atmospheric pressure. **-ophylly,** *n.* abnormal increase in number of leaves.

plenary (plē'nəri), *adj.* full; entire; unlimited.

plenilunar (plēnilōō'nə), *adj.* like or pert. to full moon.

plenipotentiary (plenipəten'shəri), *n.* & *adj.* (envoy) having full power.

plenitude (plen'itūd), *n.* fullness; sufficiency; abundance; entirety.

plenum (plē'nəm), *n.* (*pl.* -na) space full of matter; plenary meeting.

pleochroic (plēəkrō'ik), *adj.* showing different colours when viewed in different directions. -roitic, -romatic, -roous, *adj.* -roism, -romatism, *n.*

pleonasm (plē'ənazm), *n.* use of unnecessary words; redundancy. -stic, *adj.*

pleonectic (plēənek'tik), *adj.* covetous. -nexia, *n.*

plerosis (plirō'sis), *n. Med.*, restoration of weight lost during illness. -otic (-ot'ik), *n.* & *adj.*

plesiosaurus (plēziəsōr'əs), *n.* extinct long-necked swimming reptile.

plethora (pleth'ərə), *n.* excess, *espec.* of blood in body. -ric, -rous, *adj.*

pleura (plŏŏr'ə), *n.* (*pl.* -ae) membrane lining half of thorax. -l, -ric, *adj.* -risy, *n.* inflammation of p. -ritic, *adj.* -rocentesis, *n.* surg. puncturing of p. -rogenic, *adj.* formed in p. -rolith, *n.* stone in p. -ronectid, *n.* & *adj.* (pert. to) flatfish. -rotomy, *n.* incision into p. -rotropous, *adj.* laterally flattened.

plexus (pleks'əs), *n.* network. -xal, *adj.* -xicose, -xiform, *adj.* like p. -xure, *n.* inter-weaving.

plicate (plī'kāt), *v.t.* pleat; plait; fold; *adj.* pleated; plaited. -tite (plik'-), *adj.* foldable. -tion, *n.*

plinth (plinth), *n.* rectangular base of column, pedestal, etc.

pliofilm (plī'əfilm), *n.* thin transparent waterproof sheet used for packaging, etc.

pliosaurus (plīəsōr'əs), *n.* shorternecked plesiosaurus.

pliothermic (plīəthā'mik), *adj.* pert. to periods of temperature above average.

plosive (plō'siv), *n.* & *adj. Phon.*, explosive (sound), as *p.* -sion, *n.*

plumbago (plumbā'gō), *n.* graphite; *Bot.*, leadwort. -ginous (-aj'inəs), *adj.*

plumbeous (plum'biəs), *adj.* leaden. -bic, -bous, -ean, *adj.* -bism, *n.* lead-poisoning.

plumeopicean (plŏŏmiəpī'siən), *adj.* of tar and feathers.

pluperfect (plŏŏ'pəfekt), *n.* & *adj.*

(gram. tense) signifying completion of action before a certain point in past time.

pluralism (plŏŏr'əlizm), *n. Phil.*, belief that ultimate reality is of several kinds, or consists of several entities; holding of more than one office. -ist, *n.*

plurennial (plooren'iəl), *n.* & *adj.* (plant) lasting many years. -rilateral, *adj.* of more than two sides or parties. -riliteral, *adj.* of more than three letters. -rinominal, *adj.* of more than one name. -riparous, *adj.* bringing forth more than one at a birth. -risyllable, *n.* word of more than one syllable.

plutocracy (plŏŏtok'rəsi), *n.* government by wealthy class. -crat, *n.* -cratic, *adj.* -tolatry, *n.* worship of riches. -tology, *n.* study of wealth.

plutonic (plŏŏton'ik), *adj.* of volcanic or deep-seated origin.

plutonium (plŏŏtō'niəm), *n.* one of the transuranic elements, product of decay of neptunium, used in the atomic bomb.

plutonomy (plŏŏton'əmi), *n.* economics.

pluvial (plŏŏ'viəl), *adj.* pert. or due to rain; having much rain. -vian, -vine, *adj.* -viography, *n.* recording of rainfall. -viometer, *n.* rain gauge. -vious, -viose, *adj.* rainy.

pneumatic (nūmat'ik), *adj.* pert. to, using or worked by air. -s, *n.* study of mechanics of gases. -tograph, *n.* instr. measuring thoracic movements in breathing. -tographer, *n.* person receiving and writing spirit messages. -tology, *n.* pneumatics; doctrine about spirits or Holy Ghost. -tomachy, *n.* denial of Holy Ghost's divinity. -tomorphic, *adj.* spirit-like. -tophany, *n.* appearance of spirit or Holy Ghost. -tophony, *n.* sound caused by spirit. -tosis, *n.* presence of gas in body.

pneumonia (nūmō'niə), *n.* inflammation of lungs. -nic (-on'ik), *adj.* -ocentesis, *n.* surg. puncturing of lung. -oconiosis, *n.* lung disease due to inhaling metallic, etc., particles. -ography, *n.* description of lungs. -olith, *n.* stone in the lung. -ology, *n.* study of lungs. -onography, *n.* taking of X-ray photographs of lungs. -orrhagia, *n.* haemorrhage from lungs. **-otherapy**, *n.* treatment of lung diseases. **-othorax**, *n.* presence or introduction of air in thorax, causing collapse of lung. **-otomy**, *n.* incision into lung.

poaceous (pō ā'shəs), *adj.* pert. to or like grass ; belonging to the grass family of plants.

pochard (pō'cəd), *n.* kind of red-headed duck.

pococurante (pōkōkūran'ti), *n.* & *adj.* (person) lacking interest ; indifferent ; apathetic. **-tism**, *n.*

poculation (pokūlā'shn), *n.* drinking of alcoholic liquors. **-liform**, *adj.* cup-shaped.

podagra (pod'əgrə, pədag'-), *n.* gout. **-ral**, **-ric**, **-rous**, *adj.*

podalic (pədal'ik), *adj.* pert. to feet.

podesta (pədes'tə ; It., pōdestah'), *n.* It. mayor or chief magistrate. **-terate**, *n.* office of p.

podex (pō'deks), *n.* (*pl.* **-dices**) posterior.

podiatry (pədī'ətri), *n.* med. study of abnormalities of feet. **-dical** (pod'-), *adj.* pert. to podex. **-dology**, *n.* physiological study of feet. **-doscaph** (pod'-), *n.* boat-shaped boot for walking on water ; boat with bicycle mechanism.

poecilonym (pē'silənim), *n.* synonym. **-y** (-on'imi), *n.* use of synonyms.

poetaster (pō'itastə), *n.* poor or unimportant poet. **-tric**, *adj.*

pogoniasis (pōgəni'əsis), *n.* overgrowth of beard ; growth of beard in woman. **-nology**, *n.* book on beards. **-notrophy**, *n.* growing of a beard.

pogrom (pogrom'), *n.* wholesale massacre of a class or race, *espec.* of Jews in Russia.

poiesis (poiē'sis), *n.* creation. **-etic** (-et'ik), *adj.*

poikilothermic (poikiləthə'mik), *adj.* cold-blooded. **-mism**, *n.* **-mous**, *adj.*

poilu (pwal'ü), Fr. *adj.* "hairy" ; *n. sl.* infantry soldier.

poimenic (poimen'ik), *adj.* pastoral. **-s**, *n.* p. theology.

point (point), *n.* measure of depth of letter in printing : one seventy-second of an inch.

point d'appui (pwan dapwē'), *Fr.*, "point of support" ; fulcrum ; mil. basis.

pointillism (pwan'tilizm), *n.* method of painting in dots of colour. **-ist**, *n.*

polacca (pəlah'kə), *n.* square-sailed, two- or three-masted Mediterranean vessel.

polarimeter (pōlərim'itə), *n.* instr. measuring amount of polarised light or rotation of plane of polarised light. **-iscope** (-ar'iskōp), *n.* instr. for studying polarised light or objects in it. **-ise**, *v.t.* modify normally transverse light vibrations so that they are confined to one plane.

polder (pōl'də), Dutch *n.* piece of land reclaimed from sea.

polemic (pəlem'ik), *adj.* disputatious ; abusive ; *n.* dispute ; abusive language. **-ian** (-ish'n), **-ist** (-sist), *n.* **-s**, *n.* controversy.

policlinic (poliklin'ik), *n.* outpatient department of hospital.

poligar (pol'igah), *n.* village chieftain of S. Ind. ; follower of p. **p.-dog**, large S. Ind. dog.

poliomyelitis (pōliōmīəli'tis), *n.* virus disease of the spinal cord, often causing paralysis ; infantile paralysis (*abbr.* polio).

poliosis (poliō'sis), *n.* greyness of hair.

politicaster (pəlit'ikastə), *n.* minor or petty politician ; dabbler in politics.

pollack (pol'ak), *n.* cod-like food fish.

pollam (pol'am), *n.* jurisdiction of poligar.

pollard (pol'ahd), *v.t.* cut off top of (tree) ; *n.* pollarded tree ; harmless animal.

pollen (pol'ən), *n.* yellowish dust, each grain containing male reproductive element, of plants.

pollex (pol'eks), *n.* (*pl.* **-lices**) thumb. **-lical**, *adj.* **-lice verso**, *Lat.*, "with thumb turned down," indicating condemnation, *espec.* to death. **-licitation**, *n.* offer not accepted.

pollinate (pol'ināt), *v.t.* fertilise with pollen. **-lination**, *n.* **-linic**, *adj.* **-liniferous**, **-linigerous**, *adj.* p.-bearing. **-linosis**, *n.* hay fever.

polonaise (polənāz'), *n.* stately Polish dance ; dress-like garment worn over skirt.

polony (pəlō'ni), *n.* sort of sausage.

poltergeist (pol'tərgīst), *n.* active

manifestation of spirit in rappings, moving of furniture, etc.; such manifested spirit.

poltophagy (poltof'əji), *n.* lengthy mastication of food reducing it to semi-liquid state. **-gic** (-aj'ik), *adj.* **-gist,** *n.*

polyacoustic (poliəkōō'stik), *adj.* amplifying sounds.

polysaemia (poliē'miə), *n.* plethora.

polyandry (pol'iandri), *n.* marriage of one woman to two or more men at same time. **-ric, -rous,** *adj.* **-rist,** *n.*

polyarchy (pol'iahki), *n.* government by many persons.

polychaete (pol'ikēt), *n. & adj.* (pert. to) marine worm. **-tous,** *adj.*

polychotomy (polikot'əmi), *n.* division into many parts. **-mous,** *adj.*

polychrest (pol'ikrest), *n.* remedy for several diseases. **-ic(al),** *adj.* **-y,** *n.*

polychrome (pol'ikrōm), *n.* work of art in many colours. **-matic** (-əmat'ik), **-mic, -mous,** *adj.* many-coloured. **-mia,** *n., Med.,* excessive coloration. **-my,** *n.*

polyclinic (poliklin'ik), *n.* general hospital.

polydemic (polidem'ik), *adj.* native to several countries.

polydipsia (polidip'siə), *n.* abnormal thirst.

polyeidic (polii'dik), *adi.* app. to insects with conspicuous metamorphosis. **-dism,** *n.*

polyergic (poliē'jik), *adj.* many-functioned.

polyethnic (polieth'nik), *adj.* derived from or containing many races.

polygamy (pəlig'əmi), *n.* marriage to more than one spouse at same time. **-mic** (-am'ik), **-mous,** *adj.* **-mist,** *n.*

polygenesis (polijen'isis), *n.* derivation from many origins. **-esic, -etic, -nic,** *adj.* **-nism** (-ij'inizm), *n.* theory of p. of Man.

polyglot (pol'iglot), *adj.* in or pert. to several languages; *n.* person speaking or book printed in several languages. **-ttal, -ttic, -ttous,** *adj.*

polygon (pol'igən), *n.* many-sided plane figure. **-al** (-ig'ənəl), *adj.*

polygoneutic (poligənū'tik) *adj.* having several broods in a season. **-tism,** *n.*

polygram (pol'igram), *n.* many-sided figure. **-mmatic,** *adj.*

polygraph (pol'igraf), *n.* kind of copying machine. **-phic,** *adj.* pert. to p. or polygraphy. **-y,** *n.* large or diverse literary output.

polygyny (pəlij'ini), *n.* marriage of man to several wives at once. **-nist,** *n.* **-nous,** *adj.*

polyhedron (polihē'drən), *n.* many-sided solid figure. **-ral, -ric,** *adj.*

polyhidrosis (polihidrō'sis), *n.* excessive perspiration.

polyhistor (polihis'tə), *n.* person of exceptionally wide knowledge. **-ian** (-ōr'iən), *n.* **-ic** (-or'ik), *adj.*

polylith (pol'ilith), *n.* prehistoric monument of many stones. **-ic,** *adj.*

polymath (pol'imath), *n. & adj.* polyhistor(ic). **-y** (-im'əthi), *n.*

polymicrian (polimī'kriən), *adj.* compressed into little space.

polymorphous, -phic (polimaw'fəs, -ik), *adj.* having many forms or functions. **-phism, -phy,** *n.*

polymythy (pol'imithi), *n.* use of many plots in one story. **-thic,** *adj.*

polynesic (polinē'sik, -nes'-), *adj.* in many different spots.

polyneuritis (polinūrī'tis), *n.* neuritis of many nerves simultaneously. **-tic** (-it'ik), *adj.*

polynomial (polinō'miəl), *n. & adj. Math.,* (expression) of more than one term; *Biol.,* (name) of more than three terms. **-ism,** *n.* **-mic** (-om'ik), *adj.*

polyommatous (poliom'ətəs), *adj.* many-eyed.

polyonymy (polion'imi), *n.* use of many names for same thing; use of polynomial term or name. **-mal, -mic, -mous,** *adj.*

polyopia (poliō'piə), *n.* multiple vision. **-pic** (-op'ik), *adj.*

polyp (pol'ip), *n.* hollow-bodied, tentacled marine invertebrate, as coral, sea-anemone, etc. **-ean,** *adj.*

polyphagia (polifā'jiə), *n.* eating of excessive amount, or many different kinds, of food. **-gic** (-aj'ik), **-gous** (-if'əgəs), *adj.* **-gist** (-if'əjist), **-n,** *n.* **-gy** (-if'əji), *n.*

polypharmacy (polifah'məsi), *n.* treatment with many medicines, or with medicine containing many ingredients. **-cist,** *n.* **-con,** *n.* such medicine. **-mic,** *adj.*

polyphony (pəlif'əni), *n. Mus.,* composition in separate, but simultaneous and harmonising, parts; counterpoint; *Phon.*, use of one symbol for several sounds. -nic (-on'ik), *adj.* -nist (-ō'nist), *n.* composer of p.; ventriloquist.

polyphyletic (polifīlet'ik), *adj.* having more than one original type. -lesis (-ē'sis), *n.* such descent.

polypnoea (polipnē'ə), *n.* rapid breathing. -oeic, *adj.*

polypod (pol'ipod), *n.* & *adj.* many-legged (animal).

polypragmatist (poliprag'mətist), *n.* busybody. -ism, *n.*

polypsychic (polisī'kik), *adj.* having several souls. -chism, *n.*

polypus (pol'ipəs), *n.* (*pl.* -i) swollen mucous membrane.

polysarcous (polisah'kəs), *adj.* obese. -cia (-shiə), *n.*

polysemant (polisē'mant), *n.* word with many meanings. -ic, *adj.* -mia, -my, *n.*

polystachious (polistak'iəs), *adj.* many-spiked.

polystichous (pəlis'tikəs), *adj.* in several rows.

polystomatous (polistom'ətəs, -stō'-), *adj.* many-mouthed.

polystyle (pol'istīl), *n.* & *adj.* (building) with many columns.

polystyrene (polistīr'ēn), *n.* a transparent colourless plastic.

polysyllable (pol'isiləbl), *n.* many-syllabled word. -bic (-ab'ik), *adj.* pert. to or using p.

polysyndeton (polisin'diton), *n.* rhet. device of repeating conjunction for emphasis. -tic (-et'ik), *adj.*

polythalamous (polithal'əməs), *adj.* having many chambers.

polytheism (polithē'izm), *n.* belief in several gods. -ist, *n.* -istic, *adj.*

polythene (pol'ithēn), *n.* a flexible tough translucent plastic.

polytocous (pəlit'əkəs), *adj.* bringing forth many young at once.

polytomous (pəlit'əməs), *adj.* divided into several parts. -my, *n.*

polyuria (poliūr'iə), *n.* excessive urination. -ric, *adj.*

polyvinyl (polivī'nil), *adj.* denoting a group of plastics used as adhesives, for waterproofing, insulating, etc.

polyvoltine (polivol'tīn, -in), *adj.* polygoneutic.

pomace (pum'is), *n.* crushed apples in cider-making. -ous (-ā'shəs), *adj.*

pomatum (pomā'təm), *n.* hair pomade.

pomfret (pom'frit), *n.* large black marine food fish.

pomiculture (pō'mikultūr), *n.* fruit growing. -iform, *adj.* apple-shaped. -mology, *n.* science of fruit growing.

poncho (pon'chō), Sp. *n.* simple kind of cloak with slit for head.

ponderable (pon'dərəbl), *adj.* having weight; tangible; *n.* tangible thing. -bility, *n.* -ral, *adj.* pert. to weight. -rous, *adj.* weighty; heavy.

pone (pōn), *n.* card player on dealer's right, who cuts the cards.

ponerology (ponərol'əji), *n.* division of theology dealing with evil.

pons (ponz), Lat. *n.* (*pl.* -ntes) "bridge". p.asinorum (-asinōr'əm), "bridge of asses"; test of ignorant person's ability. -ntine, *adj.* -ntist, *n.* bridge-builder.

pood (pōōd), *n.* Russ. weight, equiv. of 36 lb.

pooja (pōō'jah), *n.* Hindu religious rite or ritual.

pookoo, see puku.

poonah (pōō'nə), *adj.* app. to style of painting, and brush, thin paper, etc., used in it, imitating Oriental art.

poöphyte (pō'əfīt), *n.* meadow plant. -tic (-it'ik), *adj.*

poort (pōōrt), S. African *n.* mountain pass.

popliteal (poplit'iəl, -tē'əl), *adj.* pert. to the back of the knee.

porbeagle (paw'bēgəl), *n.* voracious N. Atlantic and Pacific shark.

porcine (paw'sīn, -in), *adj.* pert. to or like pigs.

porism (pōr'izm), *n.* geom. proposition that it is possible, in certain conditions, for a problem to have any number of solutions. -atic, -stic, *adj.*

pornography (pawnog'rəfi), *n.* indecent writing or pictorial work. -nerastic, *adj.* lewd; lecherous. -nocracy, *n.* government by harlots. -pher, -phist, *n.* -phic, *adj.*

porogamy (pōrog'əmi), *n.* fertilisation of seed plants. -mic (-am'ik), -mous, *adj.*

porphyry (paw'firi), *n.* rock composed of crystals in purple-coloured matrix; any rock of like composition. -ritic, *adj.* -rogenitic, *adj.* royal-born. **-rogenitism,** *n.* succession to throne of son born after his father's accession in preference to elder son not so born.

porraceous (pərā'shəs), *adj.* like leek in colour.

porrect (pərekt'), *adj.* stretched at length.

porrigo (pərī'gō), *n.* scalp disease causing baldness. **-ginous (-ij'-inəs),** *adj.*

portfolio (pawtfō'liō), *n.* case for carrying papers ; office of cabinet minister. **minister without p.,** cabinet minister not having charge of a state department.

portière (paw'tyār), *n.* curtain covering door or across doorway.

portreeve (pawt'rēv), *n.* mayor.

poseur (pōzēr'), Fr. *n.* (fem. **-euse,** **-ōz'**) person who poses or pretends; affected person.

positivism (poz'itivizm), *n.* *Phil.,* doctrine excluding everything not an observable natural phenomenon.

positron (poz'itron), *n.* positively charged atomic particle of same mass as electron, emitted by transuranic elements and found in cosmic rays.

posology (pəsol'əji), *n.* study of med. doses. **-gist,** *n.*

posset (pos'it), *n.* hot spiced drink of milk and wine.

'possum (pos'əm), *see* **opossum.**

post (pōst), Lat. *prep.* "after." **p.bellum,** after the war. **p.diem,** after the appointed day. **p.factum,** after the event ; late ; retrospective. **p.hoc,** after this. **p. hoc ergo propter hoc,** after this therefore on account of this ; fallacy that because one event follows another the second must be caused by the first. **p.meridiem,** after noon (*abbr.* **p.m.**). **p.-mortem,** after death ; examination of dead body to determine cause of death. **p.-obit,** following death ; becoming effective after death ; **p.-mortem. p.partum,** after childbirth. **p.rem,** after the thing or matter.

postament (pōs'təment), *n.* pedestal ; frame.

postcenal (pōstsē'nəl), *adj.* post-prandial.

postcibal (pōstsī'bəl), *adj.* after a meal.

postconnubial (pōstkənū'biəl), *adj.* after marriage.

postdiluvian (pōstdilōō'viən), *adj.* after the Flood.

posteen (postēn'), Anglo-Ind. *n.* Afghan leather jacket.

poste restante (pōst rest'ahṅt), Fr., department of post office holding letters until called for.

posterity (poster'iti), *n.* later generati n(s) ; one's descendants.

postern (pos'təu, pō'-), *n.* back-door.

postexilic (pōstegzil'ik), *adj.* after exile, *espec.* after Babylonian captivity of Jews.

posthumous (pos'tūməs), *adj.* after person's death ; born after father's death ; published after author's death. **-ma,** *n. pl.* p. writings.

postiche (pōstēsh'), Fr. *n.* & *adj.* artificial or spurious (thing) ; false (hair) ; (ornament) added, *espec.* inappropriately, to finished thing.

postil (pos'til), *n.* note in margin ; comment.

postjacent (pōstjā'sənt), *adj.* posterior.

postmundane (pōstmun'dān), *adj.* after the (end of the) world.

postnatal (pōstnā'təl), *adj.* after birth. **-ti,** *n.pl.(sing.* **-tus)** persons born after a certain event.

postprandial (pōstpran'diəl), *adj.* after dinner.

posttonic (pōstton'ik), *adj.* after accent or accented syllable.

postulate (pos'tūlāt), *v.t.* require or assume as necessary or true ; *n.* assumption ; necessary condition ; axiom. **-lant,** *n.* candidate for religious order. **-tion,** *n.* **-tory,** *adj.*

postvocalic (pōstvəkal'ik), *adj.* after a vowel.

potable (pō'təbl), *adj.* drinkable ; *n.* beverage.

potamic (pətam'ik), *adj.* pert. to rivers. **-mology,** *n.* study of rivers.

potation (pōtā'shn), *n.* act of drinking ; drinking bout ; thing drunk. **-tatory,** *adj.*

pot-au-feu (pot-ō-fə'), Fr., "pot on fire" ; stew of vegetables and meat.

poteen, -th- (potēn'), *n.* illicitly distilled Ir. whisky.

potential (pəten'shəl), *adj.* possible ; latent ; having power to become ; *n. Elec.,* degree of electrification

.work done in bringing a unit positive charge to a point from infinity. **p. difference**, voltage. **-ity,** *n.* **-tiate,** *v.t.* make possible.

potomania (potəmā′niə), *n.* dipsomania.

pottah (pot′ə), Anglo-Ind. *n.* lease.

pottle (pot′l), *n.* half-gallon (pot).

poulard (pōōlahd′), *n.* sterilized or fat pullet.

poult (pōlt), *n.* young fowl, *espec.* turkey.

pounce (powns), *n.* fine powder formerly spread on writing paper to arrest running of ink; powder for tracing perforated design, or such design.

poundal (pown′dəl), *n.* unit of force : force imparting to one pound mass acceleration of one foot per sec. per sec.

pour ainsi dire (pōōr an̄′se dēr), *Fr.*, "so to speak."

pourboire (pōōr′bwahr), Fr. *n.* tip; gratuity.

pourparler (pōōr′pahrlā), Fr. *n.* preliminary or informal discussion.

pour rire (pōōr rēr′), *Fr.*, "for laughing"; not serious.

pou sto (pōō stō, pow-), *Gr.*, "where I may stand"; place to stand; basis; locus standi.

praepostor (pripos′tə), *n.* school prefect. **-rial,** *adj.*

praetor (prē′tōr), *n,* anct. Rom. magistrate of high rank. **-ian,** *adj.* pert. to p.; belonging to or forming Rom. emperor's bodyguard.

pragmatic(al) (pragmat′ik, -l), *adj.* interfering; conceited; matter-of-fact; practical; dogmatic. **p.sanction,** decree of head of state having force of law. **-tise,** *v.t.* materialise; represent as factual. **-tism,** *n.* *Phil.*, doctrine emphasising practical bearing or value of philosophy. **-tist,** *n.*

praline (prah′lēn), *n.* sweetmeat made of sugar and nuts.

prandial (pran′diəl), *adj.* pert. to or at dinner.

pratincolous (prəting′kələs), *adj.* inhabiting meadows.

praxinoscope (praksin′əskōp), *n.* instr. with mirrors in which a series of moving drawings appear as a continuously moving picture; early form of cinematograph.

preadamic (prēadam′ik), *adj.* before Adam. **-mite** (-ad′əmīt), *n.*

preagonal (prēag′ənəl), *adj.* immediately preceding death throes. **-ny,** *n.* such period.

preamble (prē′ambl), *n.* preface; introduction. **-bulation,** *n.* making a p. **-bulatory,** *adj.*

prebend (preb′end), *n.* *Eccl.*, stipend of member of chapter. **-al,** *adj.* **-ary,** *n.* holder of p.

precative, -tory (prek′ətiv, -təri), *adj.* beseeching.

precentor (prisen′tə), *n.* (*fem.* **-tress, -trix**) leader of singing. **-ial,** *adj.*

precept (prē′sept), *n.* rule of conduct; law; command. **-ive,** *adj.* **-or,** *n.* (*fem.* **-ress**) teacher. **-ual,** *adj.* conveying p.

precession (prisesh′n), *n.* preceding. **p. of equinoxes,** westward movement of equinoctial points, bringing equinox to meridian earlier every day. **-al,** *adj.*

preciation (prēshiā′shn), *n.* determination of value or price.

precinct (prē′singkt), *n.* ground belonging to eccl. or other building; surroundings; *Amer.*, police-district.

preciosity (prēshios′iti), *n.* excessive elegance, *espec.* of lit. style.

précis (prā′si), *n.* summary; *v.t.* summarise.

precisian (prisizh′n), *n.* person excessively devoted to minute observance of rules. **-ism,** *n.* **-sive** (-ī′siv), *adj.* separating; defining; exact.

precocial (prikō′shəl), *adj.* app. to birds having downy young able to run immediately they are hatched.

preconise (prē′kəniz), *v.t.* proclaim; publish publicly. **-sation,** *n.*

predaceous, -ious (pridā′shəs), *adj.* pert. to preying; living on prey. **-cean,** *n.* such animal. **-city,** *n.*

predatory (pred′ətəri), *adj.* pert. to or living by plundering; destructive. **-tism, -tor,** *n.* **-tive,** *adj.*

predella (pridel′ə), *n.* (*pl.* **-le**) platform for altar; work of art on p.; portable altar or decoration on it; shelf behind altar.

predicable (pred′ikəbl), *n.* & *adj.* affirmable (thing); attribute. **-bility,** *n.*

predicate (pred′ikāt), *v.t.* affirm; preach; state; (-ət), *n.* attribute affirmed; *Gram.*, part of sentence containing statement about subject. **-ant**, *n.* & *adj.* preaching (friar). **-tion**, **-tor**, *n.* **-tive** (-ik'ətiv), **-tory**, *adj.*

predilection (prēdilek'shn), *n.* preference.

pre-emption (pri-emp'shn), *n.* first right to purchase; appropriation. **-tive**, *adj.* pert. to p.; seizing for oneself by preventing others from acting. **-tor**, *n.* **-tory**, *adj.*

pre-exilian (prē-egzil'iən), *adj.* before exile, *espec.* Babylonian captivity of Jews.

prefabricated (prēfab'rikātid), *adj.* composed of components manufactured elsewhere and put together on site (*abbr.* **prefab**, *n.* a prefabricated house).

prehensile (prihen'sīl, -il), *adj.* capable of or adapted for grasping. **-lity**, **-sion**, **-sor**, *n.* **-sive**, **-sorial**, **-sory**, *adj.*

prelapsarian (prēlapsār'iən), *adj.* pert. to time before Man's fall.

prelect (prilekt'), *v.i.* deliver lecture. **-ion**, *n.* lecture. **-or**, *n.* lecturer.

premiate (prē'miāt), *v.t.* give prize or premium for.

première (prəm'yār), Fr. *n.* first performance. **p.danseuse** (-dahṅ-sēz'), first or leading dancer (female).

premise (prem'is), *n.* proposition, condition or statement from which conclusion is drawn; thing previously stated; *v.t.* (primīz'), set out before, or as preface; presuppose.

premolar (prēmō'lə), *n.* & *adj.* (tooth) in front of molars, or between molars and canines.

premorse (primaws'), *adj.* bitten off short; as if bitten off.

premundane (prēmun'dān), *adj.* before creation of world.

prenarial (prēnār'iəl), *adj.* pert. to or in front of nostrils.

prenatal (prēnā'təl), *adj.* before birth.

prepense (pripens'), *adj.* deliberate; premeditated.

prepollent (pripol'ənt), *adj.* predominant.

prepotent (pripō'tənt), *adj.* very or more powerful; predominant. **-ncy**, *n.*; *Biol.*, propensity for transmitting certain heritable characteristics.

prepuce (prē'pūs), *n.* foreskin. **-utial**, *adj.*

prerupt (prirupt'), *adj.* abrupt; steep.

prerogative (prirog'ətiv), *n.* right or power peculiar to a person or office.

presbycousis (prezbikoo'sis), *n.* hardness of hearing in old age. **-yophrenia**, *n.* loss of memory in old age. **-yopia**, **-ytia**, *n.* long-sightedness in old age.

prescience (presh'yəns), *n.* foreknowledge; foresight. **-nt**, *adj.*

prescind (prisind'), *v.i.* & *t.* abstract or separate (oneself). **-cission**, *n.*

prescribe (priskrīb'), *v.t.* ordain; direct; order; confine; outlaw. **-ript** (prē'-), *n.* & *adj.* (thing) prescribed. **-ription**, *n.* act of prescribing; thing prescribed; establishment of claim by proof of long use or exercise of right. **-riptive**, *adj.* prescribing; based on long use; customary; traditional.

preseminal, **-nary** (prēsem'inəl, -əri), *adj.* before development of fertility.

presentient (prēsen'shənt), *adj.* having premonition.

presidial (prisid'iəl), *adj.* presidential.

presimian (prēsim'iən), *adj.* before occurrence of anthropoid apes.

prestidigitator (prestidij'itātə), *n.* juggler; conjuror. **-gital**, *adj.* light-fingered. **-gitate**, *v.i.* perform juggling or conjuring tricks. **-tion**, *n.*

preterite (pret'ərit), *adj. Gram.*, signifying past time; aorist; *n.* such tense. **-rist**, *n.* lover of the past. **-tion**, *n.* passing over.

preterlabent (prētələ'bənt), *adj.* flowing by.

pretermit (prētəmit'), *v.t.* omit; neglect; interrupt. **-mission**, *n.*

pretone (prē'tōn), *n.* syllable or vowel before accented syllable. **-nic** (-on'ik), *adj.*

pretzel (pret'səl), *n.* a dry, salted biscuit of figure-8 or similar shape; a chocolate of this shape.

prevenient (privē'niənt), *adj.* preceding; anticipating; having foresight; preventing. **-nce**, *n.*

prevernal (prēvā'nəl), *adj.* flowering or foliating early.

prevocalic (prēvəkal'ik), *adj.* before a vowel.

prevoyant (privoi'ənt), *adj.* having foresight. **-nce**, *n.*

ə=*er* in *father*; ō=*er* in *pert*; th=*th* in *thin*; dh=*th* in *then*; zh=s in *pleasure*; k=ch in *loch*; ṅ=Fr. nasal *n*; ü=Fr. *u*.

Priapean (prīəpē'ən), *adj.* pert. to Priapus, Gr. god of male reproductive power ; phallic. **-pism** (prī'-), *n.* obscenity ; obscene act ; persistent erection of penis.

prie-dieu (prē'-dyə), Fr. *n.* praying-desk.

prima facie (prī'mə fā'shiē), *Lat.,* "at first sight" ; on the face of it ; enough to cause fact to be presumed true.

primate (prī'māt), *n.* Eccl., archbishop ; Zoo., member of highest order of mammals. **-tial,** *adj.*

primavera (prēmahvār'ah), It. *n.* spring (season).

primer (prī'mə), *n.* size of type : **long p.,** 10-point ; **great p.,** 18-point.

primigenial (prīmijē'niəl), *adj.* first to be formed ; original.

primipara (prīmip'ərə), *n.* woman bearing first child, or having borne only one child. **-rous,** *adj.* **-rity** (-ar'iti), *n.*

primitiae (primish'iē), Lat. *n.pl.* first fruits ; annates. **-tial,** *adj.*

primogeniture (prīmōjen'itūr), *n.* principle of inheritance by eldest child ; state of being eldest child. **-nial** (-jē'niəl), **-tal, -tary,** *adj.* **-nous** (-oj'inəs), *adj.* pert. to first stage in development. **-tor,** *n.* ancestor.

primordial (prīmaw'diəl), *adj.* pert. to, or having existed from, beginning ; in original form ; first ; primary. **-ity,** *n.*

primum mobile (prī'məm mob'ili), *Lat.,* in anct. astron., outermost sphere of heaven bearing fixed stars.

primus inter pares (prī'məs in'tə pār'ēz), *Lat. (fem.* **prima** .....), "first among his equals."

princeps (prin'seps), Lat. *adj.* first, *espec.* edition of book.

pristine (pris'tīn), *adj.* primitive ; ancient ; unspoiled.

privateer (prīvətēr'), *n.* privately owned ship commissioned by government to attack enemy vessels ; captain or seaman of p.

privative (priv'ətiv), *adj.* depriving ; signifying negation or deprivation ; *n.* such prefix (as *un-*) or suffix (as *-less*.).

privity (priv'iti), *n.* private knowledge ; connivance.

proa (prō'ə), *n.* kind of Malay sailing boat.

proairesis, -aer- (prō ār'isis, -ēr'-), *n.* deliberate choice.

probate (prō'bāt), *n.* proving of a will.

probity (prō'biti), *n.* integrity of character.

proboscis (prəbos'is), *n.* (*pl.* **-ses**) long snout ; prominent nasal organ. **-cidal, -cidiform, -ciform,** *adj.* like a p. **-cidate, -cidial, -cidiferous,** *adj.* having a p. **-cidean, -cidian,** *n.* & *adj.* (animal) with p.

probouleutic (prōbōōlū'tik), *adj.* pert. to prior discussion and deliberation.

procacious (prəkā'shəs), *adj.* insolent. **-city,** *n.*

procatalectic (prōkatəlek'tik), *adj.* with unaccented part of first metrical foot lacking.

procathedral (prō'kəthēdrəl), *n.* parish church used as cathedral.

proceleusmatic (prōsilūsmat'ik), *adj.* exhorting ; encouraging ; *n.* metrical foot of four short syllables.

procellous (prəsel'əs), *adj.* stormy.

procephalic (prōsifal'ik), *adj.* pert. to front of head.

procès-verbal (prō'sā-vār'bahl), Fr. *n.* official report or memorandum ; minutes of meeting.

prochronism (prō'krənizm), *n.* error of assigning to an event a date before its real date.

procidence (prō'sidəns, pros'-), *n.* prolapse. **-nt,** *adj.*

proclitic (prəklit'ik), *adj.* app. to naturally unaccented words dependent for pronunciation and accent on following word ; *n.* such word. **-clisis** (prō'-, prok'-), *n.* such pronunciation.

proclivity (prəkliv'iti), *n.* tendency ; natural bent. **-tous,** *adj.* steep. **-vous** (-ī'vəs), *adj.* bending forward at an angle.

procrastinate (prəkras'tināt), *v.i.* delay or defer action ; be dilatory. **-tion, -tor,** *n.* **-tive, -tory,** *adj.*

procreate (prō'kriāt), *v.i.* & *t.* produce young. **-ant, -tion, -tor,** *n.* **-tive, -tory,** *adj.*

procryptic (prəkrip'tik), *adj.* pert. to or having protective coloration. **-psis,** *n.*

proctal (prok'təl), *adj.* pert. to or near anus or rectum. **-toclysis,** *n.* injection of fluid into rectum.

-tology, n. med. study of anus and rectum. -toptosis, n. rectal prolapse.

proctor (prok'tə), n. disciplinary officer of university. -age, n. -al, -ial, adj.

procumbent (prəkum'bənt), adj. lying flat; trailing along ground.

procurator (prok'ūrātə), n. (fem. -trix) governor of territory; agent; manager of another's affairs. -ial, adj.

procuress (prəkūr'es), n. (masc. -rer) woman supplying women to brothels, etc.

procursive (prōkə'siv), adj. running forward. -rrent, adj.

prodigal (prod'igəl), adj. wasteful; extravagant; lavish; generous; n. such person; spendthrift. -ism, -ity, n.

prodigy (prod'iji), n. marvel; extraordinary thing or person. -gious (-ij'əs), adj. extraordinary, espec. in size.

prodrome (prō'drōm), n. symptom appearing before setting in of disease. -mal (prod'rəməl), adj. -mus (prod'-), n. prefatory work.

proem (prō'im), n. preface. -ial (-ē'miəl), adj.

proemptosis (prōempto'sis), n. addition once in every three centuries of one day to lunar calendar.

proethnic (prōeth'nik), adj. pert. to primitive races.

profligate (prof'ligət), adj. immoral; dissolute; n. such person. -gacy, n.

profluent (prof'looənt), adj. abundant; exuberant. -nce, n.

prog (prog). n. sl. proctor; food.

progamic (prōgam'ik), adj. before fertilisation. -mete, n. germ or sperm cell.

progenitive (prəjen'itiv), n. reproductive. -tal, adj. -tor, n. (fem. -tress, -trix) ancestor.

progeny (proj'ini), n. offspring.

progeria (prəjēr'iə), n. second childhood, espec. premature.

prognathism (prog'nəthizm), n. state of having projecting jaws. -thic (-ath'ik), -thous, adj. -thus, n. (pl. -thi) such person. -thy, n.

prognosis (prognō'sis), n. (pl. -ses) forecast, espec. of development of disease. -se, v.t. -stic (-os'tik), adj. -sticate, v.i. & t. prophesy.

projacient (prōjā'shənt), adj. jutting forward. -jicient, adj. projecting; communicating between organism and its surroundings.

prolapse, -sus (prō'laps, -lap'səs), n. falling (of bodily organ) forward or downward.

prolate (prō'lāt), adj. having flattened sides due to lengthwise elongation.

prolegomena (prōligom'inə), n.pl. (sing. -non) introductory remarks. -nist, n. -nous, -ry, adj.

prolepsis (prōlep'sis, -ep'-), n. (pl. -ses) rhet. device of weakening objections by anticipating them; use of adjective that anticipates result of verb; prochronism; assumption. -ptic, adj.; Med., recurring at decreasing intervals. -ptical, adj. prehistoric. -ptics, n. prognosis.

proletariat (prōlitār'iət), n. working classes. -rian, n. & adj. (member) of p.

prolicide (prō'lisīd), n. killing or killer of own offspring. -dal, adj.

proliferate (prəlif'ərāt), v.i. & t. produce (offspring, cells or buds) in large numbers at short intervals; grow by such reproduction of parts. -tion, n. -tive, adj.

proligerous (prōlij'ərəs), adj. bearing offspring.

prolix (prō'liks), adj. long-winded; verbose. -ity, n.

prolocutor (prōlok'ūtə), n. (fem. -trix) spokesman; speaker of House of Lords or convocation.

prolusion (prōlōō'zhn), n. preliminary performance; preface. -sory, adj.

Promethean (prōmē'thiən), adj. pert. to Prometheus, Gr. god who created Man or founded civilisation; creative; giving life; n. such person.

promiscuous (prəmis'kūəs), adj. mixed in haphazard fashion; indiscriminate. -cuity (promiskū'iti), n. such mixing or mixture, espec. sexual union.

promissory (prom'isəri), adj. promising. p.note, written promise to pay sum of money; I.O.U.

promulgate (prom'oolgāt), v.t. publish; announce; put into action. -tion, -tor, n.

promuscis (prəmus'is), n. proboscis, espec. insect's. -cidate, adj. having p.

pronation (prōnā'shn), *n.* turning of hand and forearm so that palm is downward ; procumbency. **-tor**, *n.* muscle used in p.

pronograde (prō'nəgrād), *adj.* walking with body parallel to ground.

pronominal (prənom'inəl), *adj.* pert. to a pronoun.

prooemium (prō ē'miəm), *n.* proem. **-miac**, *adj.*

propaedeutic(al) (prōpidū'tik, -l), *adj.* preliminary, *espec.* of instruction ; *n.* introductory part of science or art ; preliminary course of study. **-cs**, *n.* preliminary instruction.

propensity (prəpen'siti), *n.* natural inclination or tendency.

prophylactic (profilak'tik), *n.* & *adj.* preventive against disease ; protective. **-laxis**, *n.* such knowledge, act or treatment.

propinquity (prəping'kwiti), *n.* nearness.

proplasm (prō'plazm), *n.* mould ; preliminary model. **-stic**, *n.* & *adj.*

propolis (prop'əlis), *n.* resin of tree buds collected by bees ; bee glue. **-e**, *v.t.* cement with p.

proponent (prəpō'nənt), *n.* proposer, *espec.* of beatification.

proprio motu (prō'priō mō'tū), *Lat.*, "by (his) own motion" ; of own initiative. **p.jure**, 'by (his) own right." **p.vigore**, "by (its) own force."

proptosis (proptō'sis) *n.* prolapse of eyeball.

propugnation (prōpugnā'shn) *n.* defence.

pro rata (prō rah'tə, rā'tə) *Lat.*, "in proportion."

pro re nata (prō rē nā'tə), *Lat.*, "for the thing born" ; to meet an emergency.

proreption (prōrep'shn), *n.* slow secret advance ; creeping attack.

prorogue (prərōg'), *v.t.* end session (of Parl.) ; postpone (meeting). **-gation** (prōragā'shn), *n.*

prorrhesis (prərē'sis), *n.* preface.

proscenium (prōsē'niəm), *n.* part of stage before curtain.

proscribe (prōskrīb'), *v.t.* outlaw ; prohibit ; condemn. **-ription**, *n.* **-riptive**, *adj.*

proselyte (pros'ilīt), *n.* convert, *espec.* to Jewish faith. **-tical** (-it'ikl), *adj.* **-tise**, *v.i.* & *t.* **-tism**, *n.*

prosenchyma (proseng'kimə), *n.*

supporting plant tissue containing little protoplasm. **-atous**, *adj.*

prosilient (prōsil'iənt), *adj.* jumping forth ; conspicuous. **-ncy**, *n.*

prosit (prō'sit), *Lat.*, "may it do good" ; good health !

prosodemic (prosədem'ik), *adj.* contagious or infectious.

prosody (pros'ədi), *n.* study or art of versifying, *espec.* of metre, rhyme and stanza-form ; method of versifying. **-dial** (-ō'diəl), **-dic** (-od'ik), *adj.*

prosopic (prəsop'ik, -sō'-), *adj.* pert. to face. **-pography**, *n.* description of face. **-popoeia**, *n.* personification.

prospice (pros'pisē), *Lat.*, "look forward."

prostate (pros'tāt), *adj.* app. to gland at head of urethra in man, discharging mucoid fluid. **-tic** (-at'ik), *adj.* **-tism**, *n.* disease of p. gland.

prosthesis (pros'thisis), *n.* replacement of lost part of body with artificial substitute ; addition of sound at beginning of word. **-etic** (-et'ik), *adj.* **-etist**, *n.* **-thodontia**, *n.* provision of artificial teeth.

prostitute (pros'titūt), *n.* woman hiring herself for sexual purposes ; *v.t.* debase for gain ; make bad use of. **-tion**, **-tor**, *n.*

prostyle (prō'stīl), *n.* & *adj.* (building) with columns in front only.

protactic (prətak'tik), *adj.* preliminarily explanatory ; prefatory.

protagonist (prətag'ənist), *n.* chief character in play ; supporter ; spokesman. **-nism**, *n.*

protandry (prətan'dri), *n.* development of male organs before female to avoid self-fertilisation. **-dric**, **-drous**, *adj.* **-drism**, *n.*

protanopia (prōtanō'piə), *n.* colour blindness towards red. **-pe**, *n.* **-pic** (-op'ik), *adj.*

protasis (prot'əsis), *n.* introductory and explanatory part of drama. **-tatic** (-at'ik), *adj.*

protean (prō'tiən), *adj.* pert. to or like Rom. god Proteus, who was able to assume any shape ; versatile ; *n.* actor taking, or able to take, many parts.

protégé (prot'ezhā), *n.* (*fem.* **-ée**) person under another's protection, or in whose career another takes an interest.

protein, **-eid** (prō'tēn, -ēd), *n.* organic compound of carbon, hydrogen, oxygen and nitrogen, with other elements, essential to life in food and as part of every living cell. **-aceous, -eic, -ous,** *adj.*

pro tempore (prō tem'pəri), *Lat.*, "for the time (being)" (*abbr.* **pro tem.**).

protensive (prəten'siv), *adj.* extensive in time or lengthwise. **-sity,** *n.*

proteogenous (prōtioj'inəs), *adj.* derived from protein. **-olysis,** *n.* disintegration of protein. **-opexis,** *n.* incorporation of protein in tissues. **-ose,** *n.* substance derived from protein in digestion.

proteranthous (prōteran'thəs), *adj.* with flowers appearing before leaves.

protervity (prətə̄'viti), *n.* petulance.

prothalamion, **-mium** (prōthəlā'-miən, -əm), *n.* song in honour of a marriage.

prothonotary (prəthon'ətəri, prō-thənō'-), *n. R.C.*, official keeper of canonisation records and signatory to papal bull.

protocanonical (prōtəkənon'ikl), *adj.* pert. to the first canon.

protocol (prō'təkol), *n.* preliminary draft of treaty; collection of formulae; rules of procedure and etiquette of state ceremonies, diplomatic exchanges, etc.

protogenic (prōtəjen'ik), *adj.* formed at beginning. **-nist** (-oj'inist), *n.* inventor.

protograph (prō'təgraf), *n.* holograph.

protogyny (prətoj'ini), *n.* development of female organs before male to avoid self-fertilisation. **-nous,** *adj.*

protolithic (prōtəlith'ik), *adj.* pert. to earliest Stone Age.

protomartyr (prō'təmahtə), *n.* first martyr.

protomorphic (prōtəmaw'fik), *adj.* primitive.

proton (prō'ton), *n.* positively charged particle of atom nucleus.

protopathy (prōtop'əthi), *n.* first or direct experience.

protophyte (prō'təfīt), *n.* unicellular plant. **-tic** (-it'ik), *adj.*

protoplasm (prō'təplazm), *n.* essential semi-fluid living substance of cells. **-al, -atic, -ic,** *adj.* **-st,** *n.* first formed person or thing;

original ancestor; protoplasmic content of cell.

prototrophic (prōtətrof'ik), *adj.* feeding directly on uncombined elements.

prototype (prō'tətīp), *n.* original model or type. **-pal, -pic(al)** (-ip'ik, -l), *adj.*

protozoa (prōtəzō'ə), *n.pl.* (*sing.* **-zoon**) the microscopic unicellular animals. **-l,** *adj.* **-n,** *n.* **-oology,** *n.* study of p.

protreptic (prətrep'tik), *adj.* hortatory; doctrinal.

provection (prəvek'shn), *n.* carrying forward of sound at end of word to beginning of next (as *a newt* from orig. *an ewt*).

proveditor (prəved'itə), *n.* purveyor of supplies.

provenance (prov'inəns), *n.* source; origin. **-nience** (-vē'niəns), *n.* **-nient,** *adj.* issuing forth.

providore (prov'idōr), *n.* proveditor; steward.

proviso (prəvī'zō), *n.* stipulation. **-ry,** *adj.*

provost (prov'əst), *n.* Scot. mayor; head of cathedral or college. **p.marshal** (prəvō'-), head of military police.

proxenete (proks'inēt), *n.* procurer; marriage broker. **-tism,** *n.*

proxime accessit (proks'imi akses'it), *Lat.*, "(he) came nearest"; competitor next to prize-winner.

proximo (proks'imō), *adj.* of next month (*abbr.* **prox.**).

proxysm (proks'izm), *n.* near relationship.

pruinose (prōō'inōs), *adj.* bearing whitish dust; hoary. **-nescence,** *n.* **-nous,** *adj.*

prurient (prōōr'iənt), *adj.* having indecent desires; lascivious; curious about lewd subjects. **-nce,** *n.*

prurigo (prōōr ī'gō), *n.* skin disease with small itching pustules. **-ginous** (-ij'inəs), *adj.*

pruritus (prōōr ī'təs), *n.* itching of skin. **-tic** (-it'ik), *adj.*

psaltery (sawl'təri), *n.* anct. zither-like mus. instr.

psammophyte (sam'əfīt), *n.* plant of arid, sandy soil. **-tic** (-it'ik), *adj.*

psammous (sam'əs), *adj.* sandy.

psellism (sel'izm), *n.* defective pronunciation.

pseudacusis (sūdəkū′sis), *n.* false or mistaken hearing.

pseudaesthesia (sūdesthē′zhiə), *n.* imaginary feeling, as of pain, etc.

pseudandry (sū′dandri), *n.* use by woman of man's name as assumed name.

pseudaphia (sūdā′fiə), *n.* pseud-aesthesia.

pseudaposematic (sūdəpəsimat′ik), *adj.* imitating in colour, etc., a dangerous animal.

pseudepigrapha (sūdepig′rəfə), *n.pl.* spurious books supposed to be written by or about Biblical persons but not contained in Apocrypha. -**l**, *adj.* -**phic** (-af′ik), *adj.* pert. to p. or pseudepigraphy. -**phous**, *adj.* bearing wrong name ; wrongly attributed. -**phy**, *n.* mistaken attribution of works to wrong authors.

pseudoblepsis, -**sia** (sūdəblep′sis, -siə), *n.* false or imaginary vision.

pseudocarp (sū′dəkahp), *n.* fruit, as apple, comprising more than mere seeds. -**ous**, *adj.*

pseudochromaesthesia (sūdəkrōmesthē′zhiə), *n.* mental association of sounds with colours. -**mia**, *n.* false colour perception.

pseudochronism (sūdok′rənizm), *n.* error in date. -**nologist**, *n.* person making p.

pseudodox (sū′dədoks), *n.* & *adj.* false (doctrine or opinion). -**al**, *adj.*

pseudogeusia, -**stia** (sūdəgū′ziə, -stiə), *n.* false taste perception.

pseudograph (sū′dəgraf), *n.* spurious writing ; forgery. -**er**, *n.* -**ia**, *n.* false or meaningless writing. -**y** (-og′rəfi), *n.* incorrect writing or spelling.

pseudogyny (sūdoj′ini), *n.* use by man of woman's name as assumed name.

pseudolalia (sūdəlā′liə), *n.* incoherence or nonsense of speech.

pseudolatry (sūdol′ətri), *n.* false worship.

pseudology (sūdol′əji), *n.* telling of lies. -**gical**, *adj.* wildly exaggerated or untrue. -**gue**, *n.* mythomaniac.

pseudomania (sūdəmā′niə), *n.* mania for lying. -**c**, *n.*

pseudomorph (sū′dəmawf), *n.* false or abnormal form. -**ic**, -**ous**, *adj.* -**ism**, *n.* -**ose**, *v.t.* make into p. -**osis**, *n.*

pseudonym (sū′dənim), *n.* assumed name. -**al** (-on′iməl), -**ic**, -**ous** (-on′iməs), *adj.* -**ity**, *n.*

pseudopia (sūdop′siə), *n.* optical illusion. -**ptics**, *n.* psych. study of p.

pseudoscope (sū′dəskōp), *n.* instr. producing images in reversed relief. -**pic** (-op′ik), *adj.* -**py** (-os′kəpi), *n.*

pseudosmia (sūdoz′miə), *n.* false smell perception.

pseudosoph(er) (sū′dəsof, -os′əfə), *n.* pretender to wisdom. -**phical**, *adj.* -**phist**, -**phy**, *n.*

pseudovum (sūdō′vəm), *n.* (*pl.* -**va**) parthenogenetic egg.

psi (psī, sī, psē), *n.* 23rd letter (Ψ, ψ) of Gr. alphabet.

psilanthropy (sīlan′thrəpi), *n.* denial of divinity of Christ. -**pic** (-op′ik), *adj.* -**pism**, -**pist**, *n.*

psilosis (sīlō′sis), *n.* falling of hair ; sprue. -**othrum**, *n.* depilatory. -**otic** (-ot′ik), *adj.*

psittaceous (sitā′shəs), *adj.* like or pert. to parrot; belonging to parrot family of birds. -**cine** (sit′-), *adj.* -**cism**, *n.* parrot-like repetition in speech. -**cosis**, *n.* contagious parrot disease, causing fever and pneumonia in man.

psoas (sō′əs), *n.* loin muscle ; tenderloin. -**oitis**, *n.* inflammation of p.

psomophagy (səmof′əji), *n.* bolting of food. -**gic** (-aj′ik), *adj.* -**gist**, *n.*

psora (sōr′ə), *n.* sev. itching skin diseases.

psoriasis (sōrī′əsis), *n.* skin disease with white-scaled red eruptions. -**atic** (-iat′ik), *n.* & *adj.* (person) suffering from p. -**siform** (-ias′i-fawm), *adj.* like p.

psoroptic (sōrop′tik), *adj.* pert. to scab mite.

psorophthalmia (sōrofthal′miə), *n.* ulcerative blepharitis. -**mic**, *adj.*

psychaesthesia (sīkesthē′zhiə), *n.* sensation in relation to feeling and thought. -**etic** (-et′ik), *adj.*

psychagogic (sīkəgoj′ik), *adj.* attractive ; encouraging. -**gy** (sī′kəgōji), *n.* psych. treatment by persuading patient to adopt an absorbing interest or life work.

psychalgia (sīkal′jiə), *n.* mental pain or distress.

psychasthenia (sīkasthē′niə), *n.* acute apathetic neurasthenic condition. -**nic** (-en′ik), *adj.*

psyche (si'ki), *n.* soul ; ego ; mind.

psychiasis (sīkī'əsis), *n.* healing of the soul.

psychiatry (sīkī'ətri, sī'kiatri), *n.* med. study and treatment of mental disorders. **-ter** (-ī'ətə), **-trist,** *n.* expert in p. **-tric** (-at'rik), *adj.*

psychic (sī'kik), *adj.* pert. to spirit or mind ; having mediumistic powers. **-al,** *adj.* mental ; spiritualistic. **-ism** (-sizm), *n.* research on spiritualistic subjects ; mentality.

psychoanalysis (sīkōənal'isis), *n.* treatment of neurotic persons by the analysis of their neuroses and revelation of their origins ; system of such treatment, and body of theories related to it. **-yse** (-an'əlīz), *v.t.* treat patient by p. **-yst,** *n.* expert in p. **-ytic(al)** (-it'ik, -l), *adj.*

psycho-asthenics (sīkōasthen'iks), *n.* study of mental deficiency.

psychodynamic (sīkədīnam'ik), *adj.* pert. to psych. motives and causation.

psychofugal (sīkof'ūgəl), *adj.* proceeding outwards from mental state.

psychogalvanic (sīkəgalvan'ik), *adj.* pert. to change in elec. resistance of skin resulting from mental processes which cause alterations in secretion of perspiration. **-nometer,** *n.* instr. measuring such elec. change ; lie detector.

psychogenesis (sīkəjen'isis), *n.* origin in internal or mental state. **-etic(al)** (-jinet'ik, -l), *adj.* **-etics,** *n.* study of p. **-nic,** *adj.* derived from the mind.

psychognosis, **-sy** (sīkognō'sis, -og'nəsi), *n.* study of mentality or character. **-stic** (-os'tik), *adj.*

psychogram (sī'kəgram), *n.* spirit message ; psych. description of person ; mental picture. **-graph,** *n.* instr. recording spirit messages ; photog. plate recording spirit image ; psych. biography. **-grapher,** *n.* writer of psychograph. **-graphist,** *n.* medium through whom written spirit messages are received. **-graphy,** *n.*

psychokinesia (sīkəkinē'zhiə), *n.* maniacal fit due to inhibitions. **-sis,** *n.* psychical production of physical motion.

psycholepsy (sī'kəlepsi), *n.* period of intense nervous depression and apathy.

psychology (sīkol'əji), *n.* study of the mind ; mental equipment or state of a person, etc. **-gical,** *adj.* **-gise,** *v.i.* & *t.* study or dabble in p. ; hypnotise. **-gism,** *n.* doctrine applying p. to other subject ; psychological term. **-gist,** *n.* expert in p.

psychomachy (sīkom'əki), *n.* conflict between body and soul.

psychometry (sīkom'itri), *n.* measurement of mental aptitudes and intelligence. **-trist,** *n.*

psychomorphism (sīkəmaw'fizm), *n.* attribution of human mentality to inanimate objects. **-phic,** *adj.*

psychomotor (sīkəmō'tə), *adj.* pert. to physical action as immediate result of mental act.

psychonomics (sīkənom'iks), *n.* psychology. **-mic,** *adj.*

psychopannychism (sīkəpan'ikizm), *n.* belief in sleep of souls from death to bodily resurrection. **-ist, -ite,** *n.*

psychopathy (sīkop'əthi), *n.* mental disorder, *espec.* minor. **-thic** (-ath'ik), *adj.* pert. to p. ; marked by abnormal religious sensitiveness. **-thist,** *n.* expert on p. **-thology,** *n.* psych. study of p.

psychopetal (sīkop'itəl), *adj.* proceeding inwards to the mind.

psychophysics (sīkəfiz'iks), *n.* study of relationship between mental and physical processes. **-cal,** *adj.* **-cist** (-sist), *n.*

psychorealism (sīkərē'əlizm), *n.* realistic representation of mental life. **-ist,** *n.*

psychorhythmia (sīkəridh'miə), *n.* mental state marked by involuntary repetition of mental actions. **-mic(al),** *adj.*

psychorrhagy (sīkor'əji), *n.* separation of soul from body. **-gic** (-aj'ik), *adj.*

psychosis (sī'kō'sis), *n.* (*pl.* **-ses**) major mental disorder or disease.

psychosomatic (sīkəsəmat'ik), *adj.* pert. to mind and body as a whole ; pert. to med. study of interaction between mind and body. **-me** (sī'kəsōm), *n.* unit formed by mind and body.

psychosophy (sīkos'əfi), *n.* doctrine concerning the soul.

psychotaxis (sīkətaks'is), n. involuntary alteration of mental outlook for the satisfaction of the personality.

psychotechnology (sīkəteknol'əji), n. practical use of psychology. -gical, adj.

psychotheism (sīkəthē'izm), n. belief in pure spirituality of God.

psychotherapy (sīkəther'əpi), n. treatment of mental disease. -peutic(al), adj. -peutics, n. science of p.

psychotic (sīkot'ik), n. & adj. (person) affected with psychosis; insane (person).

psychroaesthesia (sīkrōesthē'zhiə), n. feeling of cold in part of body actually warm.

psychrometer (sīkrom'itə), n. wet and dry bulb hygrometer. -rograph, n. recording p. -try, n.

psychrophile (sī'krəfīl), n. plant thriving in cold. -lic (-il'ik), adj.

psychrophobia (sīkrəfō'biə), n. dread of cold.

psychrophyte (sī'krəfīt), n. alpine or arctic plant.

psychurgy (sī'kəji), n. mental energy or function.

ptarmic (tah'mik), n. & adj. (substance) causing sneezing.

ptarmigan (tah'migən), n. kind of northern grouse with white winter plumage and feathered feet.

pteric (ter'ik), adj. alar.

pteridium (terid'iəm), n. (pl. -ia) samara; bracken. -dography, n. description of ferns. -dology, n. study of ferns. -dophyte, n. fern.

pterocarpous (terəkah'pəs), adj. with winged fruits.

pterodactyl (terədak'til), n. extinct featherless flying reptile. -ian, -ic, -id, -ous, adj. -oid, adj. like a p.

pterography (terog'rəfi), n. treatise on or description of feathers. -phic(al), adj. -ropaedes, n.pl. birds capable of flying soon after hatching.

pteropid (ter'əpid), n. & adj. (pert. to) fruit bat.

pteropod (ter'əpod), n. small swimming mollusc, often shell-less. -al, -an (-op'ədəl, -ən), -ial (-ō'diəl), adj.

pterospermous (terəspə'məs), adj. with winged seeds.

pterygium (terij'iəm), n. (pl. -ia) fleshy growth over inner corner of eyeball, common in old age; overgrowth of cuticle. -ial, adj.

pterygoid (ter'igoid), adj. wing-like.

pterylosis (terilō'sis), n. arrangement of bird's feathers. -lology, n. study of p.

ptilosis (tilō'sis), n. plumage; loss of eyelashes.

ptisan (tizan', tiz'-), n. kind of barley-water; tisane.

ptochocracy (təkok'rəsi), n. government by the poor.

ptomaine (tō'mān), n. poisonous alkaloid in decaying matter. -nic, adj.

ptosis (tō'sis), n. prolapse; drooping of eyelid. -otic (tot'ik), adj.

ptyalin (tī'əlin), n. enzyme, acting on starch, of saliva. -lagogue (-al'əgog), n. substance promoting salivation. -lism, n. salivation, espec. excessive.

puberty (pū'bəti), n. time of reaching sexual maturity. -ral, -tic, adj.

puberulent (pūber'oolənt), adj. covered with minute down.

pubes (pū'bēz), n. lower abdominal region; hair growing in that region. -bian, -bic, adj. -bigerous, adj. hairy. -bis, n. (pl. -bes) fore-bone of pelvis. -cent (-es'ənt), adj. reaching or having reached puberty; covered with soft down; n. youth at puberty. -cence, -ncy, n.

publicist (pub'lisist), n. writer on political and economic subjects.

pucka, see **pukka**.

pudency (pū'dənsi), n. modesty; prudery. -dibund, adj. bashful; prudish. -dic, adj. pudendal. -dicity, n. modesty; chastity. -ndal (-en'dəl), adj. pert. to reproductive organs. -ndum, n. (pl. -da) external reproductive organ, espec. of female. -nt, adj. bashful.

pueblo (pweb'lō), Sp. n. town; native tenement house of New Mexico.

puerile (pū'əril), adj. childish. -lism, n. childish conduct. -lity, n. -riculture, n. bringing up of children; antenatal care.

puerperal (pū ə'pərəl), adj. pert. to childbirth. -ism, n. morbid condition related to childbirth. -rium (-ēr'iəm), n. condition immediately following childbirth.

puisne (pū'ni), *adj.* later ; inferior ; junior.

puissant (pwis'ənt), *adj.* powerful. -nce, *n.*

pukka (puk'ə), Anglo-Ind. *adj.* good ; sound ; reliable ; genuine.

puku (pōō'kōō), *n.* red Cent. African antelope.

pulchritude (pulk'ritūd), *n.* physical beauty. -dinous, *adj.*

pulicine (pū'lisīn, -in), *adj.* pert. to fleas. -cene, -cose, -cous, *adj.* infested with fleas. -cosity, *n.* such infestation. -cid, *n.* & *adj.* -cide, *n.* substance killing fleas. -coid, *adj.* flea-like.

pullulate (pul'ūlāt), *v.i.* sprout forth; bud ; teem. -lant, *adj.* -tion, *n.*

pulmogastric (pulmøgas'trik), *adj.* pert. to lungs and stomach.

pulmometry (pulmom'itri), *n.* measurement of lungs' capacity.

pulmonar (pul'mənə), *adj.* having lungs.

pulmonary (pul'mənəri), *adj.* pert. to or like lungs ; having lungs. -nate, *adj.* pulmonar. -nic (-on'ik), *adj.* pulmonary ; affecting lungs ; pneumonic ; *n.* medicine for, or person with, lung disease. -nitis, *n.* pneumonia.

pulque (pōōl'kā), Sp. *n.* Mex. fermented drink made from agave.

pulsatile (pul'sətīl, -il), *adj.* vibrating ; pulsating ; *Mus.,* percussive ; *n.* percussion instr. -lity, *n.*

pulsatilla (pulsətil'ə), *n.* pasqueflower.

pulsimeter (pulsim'itə), *n.* pulsemeasuring instr.

pultaceous (pultā'shəs), *adj.* pulpy ; like porridge.

pultun, -an (pul'tən), *n.* Ind. native infantry regiment.

pulverise (pul'vərīz), *v.t.* reduce to powder or fragments ; grind ; smash. -raceous, -reous (-ār'iəs), -rous, -rulent (-er'oolənt), *adj.* covered with dust ; dusty ; crumbling into dust. -rulence, *n.*

pulvillar (pul'vilə), *adj.* like a cushion or pad. -lliform, *adj.*

pulvinar (pulvī'nə), *adj.* pulvillar. -nate (pul'vinət), *adj.* swelling ; pulvillar. -nation, *n.* swelling ; bulge. -niform (-in'ifawm), *adj.*

pulwar (pul'wah), *n.* light flat-bottomed Ind. river boat.

pumpernickel (pum'pənikl ; Ger., poom'-), *n.* kind of rye bread.

punaluan (pōōnahlōō'ən), *adj.* pert. to primitive group marriage of a number of brothers to a number of sisters.

puncheon (pun'chən), *n.* large cask, with capacity of seventy galls. ; engraved punch or die.

punctate (pungk'tāt), *adj.* like or ending in a point ; like a dot ; bearing spots ; pitted. -tal, *adj.* like a point. -tatim, Lat. *adv.* "point for point." -tation, *n.* -ticular, -ticulate, -ticulose, *adj.* bearing small spots. -tiform, *adj.* point-like.

punctilio (pungktil'iō), *n.* small point or detail of conduct ; close observance of such points. -liar, -lious, *adj.*

punctulate (pungk'tūlət), *adj.* bearing small spots. -le, *n.* small spot. -tion, *n.*

pundigrion (pundig'riən), *n.* play on words ; pun.

pundit (pun'dit), *n.* (*fem.* -a) learned man, *espec.* Hindu. -ic, *adj.* -ry, *n.*

puniceous (pūnish'əs), *adj.* bright or purplish red.

punitive (pū'nitiv), *adj.* pert. to or inflicting punishment. -tional, -tory, *adj.*

punk (pungk), *n.* decayed wood ; tinder made from dried fungus impregnated with saltpetre.

punkah (pung'kə), *n.* large fan, *espec.* moved by rope. -wallah, *n.* servant moving p.

punnet (pun'it), *n.* shallow fruit basket.

punto (pun'tō), It. *n.* stroke, as in fencing. p. diritto, direct stroke, as in fencing. p. reverso, back-handed stroke.

pupa (pū'pə), *n.* (*pl.* -ae) quiescent stage of insect's development between larval and adult stages ; chrysalis. -l, *adj.* -piform, *adj.* like a p. -te, *v.i.* pass chrysalis stage. -tion, *n.*

pupillage (pū'pilij), *n.* state of being a pupil or under age. -lary, *adj.* pert. to pupil or guardianship ; pert. to pupil of eye.

purblind (pə'blīnd), *adj.* half-blind ; dull-witted ; obtuse.

purdah (pə'də), *n.* curtain concealing Ind. women of high birth ; system of concealing such women from public gaze.

purée (pūr'ā), Fr. *n.* pulpy mixture; boiled and sieved food; thick soup.

purfle (pə̄'fl), *v.t.* ornament edges of, *espec.* with embroidery; *n.* such edge or trimming. -ling, *n.*

purgatory (pə̄'gətəri), *n.* place of suffering or purification; *R.C.*, state intermediate between death and Heaven where sin is punished. -rial, *adj.*

puriform (pūr'ifawm), *adj.* like pus.

Purim (pūr'im; Heb., poor ēm'), *n.* Jewish festival (15th day of Adar) celebrating deliverance of Jews from Haman.

purlicue (pə̄'likū), Scot. *n.* space between extended thumb and index finger; curl or flourish in writing; summary of speeches; peroration; *pl.* caprices.

purlieus (pə̄'lūz), *n.pl.* neighbourhood; suburb(s).

purpresture (pəpres'tūr), *n.* wrongful seizing of, or encroachment on, other's or common land.

purpura (pə̄'pūrə), *n.* peliosis. p. haemorrhagica, p. with severe haemorrhage; similar fever of horses.

purpureal, -eous (pəpūr'iəl, -əs). *adj.* purple. -escent, *n.* becoming or somewhat purple. -rogenous, *adj.* causing purple colour.

pur sang (pūr sahn'), *Fr.*, "pure blood"; *adj.* pure-blooded.

pursuivant (pə̄'swivənt), *n.* official of College of Heralds inferior to herald.

purulent (pūr'oolənt), *adj.* pert. to, containing or discharging pus. -loid, *adj.* like pus. -nce, *n.*

purwannah (pəwah'nə), Anglo-Ind. *n.* official letter of permission, etc.

pusillanimity (pūsilanim'iti), *n.* cowardice; mean-spiritedness. -mous (-an'iməs), *adj.*

pustule (pus'tūl), *n.* pus-containing pimple. -lant, *n.* & *adj.* (medicine) producing p. -lar, -latous, -lose, -lous, *adj.* -late, *v.i.* & *t.*

putamen (pūtā'men), *n.* fruit stone; membrane lining eggshell. -minous (-am'inəs), *adj.*

putanism (pū'tənizm), *n.* lewdness in woman; prostitution.

putative (pū'tətiv), *adj.* supposed; believed. -tion, *n.*

putid (pū'tid), *adj.* decayed; worthless; fetid.

putrefy (pū'trifi), *v.i.* & *t.* rot; decay; fester. -facient, -factive,

adj. pert. to or causing putrefaction; *n.* such thing. -faction, *n.* -resce, *v.i.* & *t.* -rescent, *adj.* decaying; tending to decay. -rescence, *n.* -rilage, *n.* thing decaying; products of decay. -rilaginous, *adj.*

Putsch (pooch), Ger. *n.* rebellion; rising.

putti (poo'tē), It. *n.pl.* (*sing.* -to) figures of naked children or cherubs in art.

puttoo, *see* pattu.

pyaemia (pī ē'miə), *n.* blood-poisoning accompanied by widespread abscesses. -mic, *adj.*

pyal (pī'əl), Ind. *n.* verandah.

pyarthrosis (pīahthrō'sis), *n.* suppuration in joint.

pycnometer (piknom'itə), *n.* kind of bottle for measuring specific gravities or densities. -morphic, -morphous, *adj.* compact. -nosis, *n.* thickening.

pyedog (pī'dog), Anglo-Ind. *n.* stray or pariah dog.

pyemesis (pīem'isis), *n.* vomiting of pus.

pygal (pī'gəl), *adj.* pert. to rump. -gia (-al'jiə), *n.* pain in rump.

pyic (pī'ik), *adj.* pert. to or discharging pus.

pyknic (pik'nik), *adj.* fat (person).

pylon (pī'lən), *n.* towered gateway; any tower-like erection.

pylorus (pīlor'əs), *n.* opening from stomach into intestine. -ric (-or'ik), *adj.*

pyoid (pī'oid), *adj.* pus-like. -orrhoea, *n.* discharge of pus, *espec.* in inflammation of tooth sockets. -osis, *n.* suppuration.

pyracanth(a) (pīr'əkanth, -an'thə), *n.* small white-flowered red-berried evergreen shrub; firethorn.

pyranometer (pīranom'itə), *n.* instr. measuring solar radiation.

pyrenocarp (pīr ē'nəkahp), *n.* drupe. -nodean, -nodeous (-nō'diən, -əs), -noid, *adj.* like a p. or a wart.

pyrethrum (pīrē'thrəm, -eth'-), *n.* chrysanthemum-like garden plant; kind of insect powder.

pyretic (pīret'ik), *adj.* pert. to fever. -osis, *n.* fever. -togenesis, *n.* origin of fever. -tology, *n.* med. study of fevers. -totherapy, *n.* med. treatment by causing fever.

pyrexia (pīreks'iə), *n.* fever. -l, -xic(al), *adj.*

pyrgeometer (pīrjiom'itə), *n.* instr. measuring radiation from earth.

pyrgology (pəgol'əji), *n.* study of towers. **-gist,** *n.* **-goidal,** *adj.* tower-shaped.

pyrheliometer (pīrhēliom'itə), *n.* instr. measuring sun's heat. **-tric** (-et'rik), *adj.* **-try,** *n.*

pyridine (pir'idēn, -in), *n.* nitrogenous base used as antiseptic, etc. **-dic** (pīrid'ik), *adj.*

pyriform (pir'ifawm), *adj.* pear-shaped.

pyrite(s) (pīr'īt, -s), *n.* sulphide of a metal with metallic appearance. **-tic(al)** (-it'ik, -l), *adj.* **-tiferous,** *adj.* yielding p. **-tise** (pir'-), *v.t.* convert into p. **-toid,** *adj.* like p. **-tology,** *n.* blowpipe analysis.

pyroelectricity (pīr'ōilektris'iti), *n.* elec. charge produced in some crystals by temperature changes.

pyrogenation (pīrəjinā'shn), *n.* subjection to heat. **-genesis** (-jen'isis), *n.* production of heat. **-genic** (-jen'ik), **-genous** (-oj'inəs), *adj.* due to heat or fever.

pyrognomic (pīrognom'ik), *adj.* easily made incandescent. **-gnostic,** *adj.* pert. to, or shown by, blowpipe analysis.

pyrography (pīrog'rəfi), *n.* tracing of designs by burning; "poker work." **-pher,** *n.* **-phic,** *adj.* **-ravure,** *n.* design traced by p.

pyrolatry (pīrol'ətri), *n.* fire-worship. **-ter,** *n.*

pyrology (pīrol'əji), *n.* study of heat or fever and its effects. **-gical,** *adj.* **-gist,** *n.*

pyrolysis (pīrol'isis), *n.* decomposition due to heat. **-ytic** (-it'ik), *adj.*

pyromachy (pīrom'əki), *n.* use of fire in fighting.

pyromancy (pīr'əmansi), *n.* divination by flames or fire. **-cer,** *n.* **-ntic,** *adj.*

pyromania (pīrəmā'niə), *n.* mania for setting fire to things. **-c,** *n.* **-cal** (-ī'əkl), *adj.*

pyrometer (pīrom'itə), *n.* instr. measuring very high temperatures. **-tric** (-et'rik), *adj.* **-try,** *n.*

pyrophanous (pīrof'ənəs), *adj.* becoming transparent when heated.

pyrophobia (pīrəfō'biə), *n.* dread of fire.

pyrophorus (pīrof'ərəs), *n.* (*pl.* **-ri**) substance igniting when exposed to air. **-ric** (-or'ik), **-rous,** *adj.*

pyroscope (pīr'əskōp), *n.* kind of optical thermometer or pyrometer.

pyrosis (pīrō'sis), *n.* heartburn.

pyrostat (pīr'əstat), *n.* automatic fire-alarm and extinguisher; thermostat.

pyrotechnics, -ny (pīrətek'niks, -ni), *n.* manufacture or display of fireworks. **-nic(al),** *adj.* **-nist,** *n.*

pyrotic (pīrot'ik, *n.* & *adj.* caustic (medicine); pert. to pyrosis.

pyrrhic (pir'ik), *n.* anct. Greek war dance; metrical foot of two short syllables; *adj.* pert. to such dance or foot, or to Pyrrhus, king of Epirus. **P.victory,** victory like that of Pyrrhus of Epirus over Romans in 279 B.C., when his army sustained tremendous losses; fruitless victory. **-hian,** *adj.* app. to verse composed of p. feet. **-cist** (-sist), *n.* dancer of p. dance.

Pyrrhonian (pirō'niən), *adj.* pert. to Pyrrho, Gr. sceptic philosopher of 4th cent. B.C.; extremely sceptical. **-nism** (pir'ənizm), *n.*

pyrrhotism (pir'ətizm), *n.* red-hairedness. **-hous,** *adj.* ruddy.

pythogenic (pīthəjen'ik, pith-), *adj.* due to or causing dirt- or decay. **-nesis,** *n.* **-netic** (-jinet'ik), *adj.*

pythonic (pīthon'ik), *adj.* like a python; like an oracle. **-nism** (pī'thənizm, pith-), *n.* possession by oracular spirit; prophecy. **-nist,** *n.*

pyx (piks), *n.* vessel for reservation of Eucharist; box containing specimens of newly-minted coins. **trial of the p.,** test for weight, etc., of newly-minted coins.

Q

qua (kwā), Lat. *conj.* "as"; in capacity of.

quad (kwod), *n. abbr.* of quadrat; *v.t.* fill with quadrats.

quadra (kwod'rə), *n.* plinth; square frame.

quadragenerian (kwodrəjinār'iən), *n.* & *adj.* (person) in from fortieth to fiftieth year.

quadragesima (kwodrəjəs'imə), *n.* first Sunday of Lent. **-l,** *adj.* pert. to Lent; consisting of forty, *espec.* consisting of, or lasting, forty days.

quadragintesimal (kwodrəjintes'- iməl), *adj.* in forty parts; forty-fold.

quadral (kwod'rəl), *adj.* in four parts.

quadrant (kwod'rənt), *n.* quarter of circumference of circle; instr. for measuring altitudes. -al (-an'təl), *adj.*

quadrat (kwod'rət), *n.* small square area or block, *espec.* used as space in printing (*abbr.* quad).

quadrate (kwodrāt'), *v.i. & t.* square; agree; make to agree; *n. & adj.* (kwod'rət), square; oblong; *Astron.*, distant 90° from each other. -tic (-at'ik), *adj.* square; app. to algebraic expression containing square but no higher power of unknown quantity; *n.* such equation. -tics, *n.* algebra dealing with quadratic equations. -ture (kwod'rətūr), *n.* problem or act of finding square with area equal of another known figure; act of determining areas; *Astron.*, relation of quadrate heavenly bodies.

quadrennial (kwodren'iəl), *adj.* lasting four years; occurring every fourth year; *n.* fourth anniversary. -nium, *n.* (*pl.* -nia) period of four years.

quadricentennial (kwodrisenten'iəl), *n. & adj.* (pert. to) four hundredth anniversary.

quadriceps (kwod'riseps), *n.* thigh muscle extending leg.

quadricinium (kwodrisin'iəm), *n.* mus. composition for four voices.

quadrifid (kwod'rifid), *adj.* divided into four portions.

quadriform (kwod'rifawm), *adj.* having fourfold form; square.

quadriga (kwodrī'gə), *n.* (*pl.* -ae) four-horse chariot.

quadrigamist (kwodrig'əmist), *n.* person married four times, *espec.* having four spouses at once.

quadrigeminal (kwodrijem'inəl) *adj.* in four similar or equal parts; having two parts, each equally or similarly divided. -nous, *adj.*

quadrigenarious (kwodrijinār'iəs), *adj.* comprising four hundred.

quadrilateral (kwodrilat'ərəl), *n. & adj.* four-sided (figure).

quadrilingual (kwodriling'gwəl), *adj.* in or speaking four languages.

quadriliteral (kwodrilit'ərəl), *n. & adj.* (form) of four letters or consonants.

quadrillion (kwodril'yən), *n.* a million trillions (10^{24}); *Amer. & Fr.,* a thousand trillions (10^{15}).

quadrimum (kwodrī'məm), *n.* best or oldest wine. q.merum, *Lat.,* four-years-old wine.

quadrinomial (kwodrinō'miəl), *n. & adj.* (expression) consisting of four terms. -minal (-nom'inəl), *adj.*

quadripartite (kwodripah'tīt), *adj.* pert. to or for four parts or parties. -tion, *n.*

quadrisect (kwod'risekt), *v.t.* divide into four equal parts. -ion, *n.*

quadrisyllable (kwod'risiləbl), *n.* word of four syllables. -bic (-ab'ik), *adj.*

quadrivalent (kwodriv'ələnt, -vā'-), *adj.* having valency of four.

quadrivial (kwodriv'iəl), *adj.* leading in four directions; pert. to meeting of four ways.

quadrivoltine (kwodrivol'tin), *adj.* having four broods in one year; *n.* such creature.

quadroon (kwodrŏŏn'), *n.* child of white and mulatto parents, having one-quarter negro blood.

quadrual (kwod'rooəl), *n. & adj.* (number) denoting four.

quadruped (kwod'rooped), *n. & adj.* four-footed (mammal). -al (-roo'pidl), -antic(al), *adj.* -ism, *n.*

quaestor (kwē'stə), *n.* anct. Rom. public treasurer or assistant mil. commander. -ial, *adj.*

quaestuary (kwē'stūəri, kwes'-), *n. & adj.* (person) in business for profit, or having profit as sole aim.

quagga (kwag'ə), *n.* extinct zebra-like wild ass of S. Africa.

quale (kwā'lē), *n.* (*pl.* -lia) thing having quality; sensation considered in virtue of its own quality alone; quality having independent existence.

quant (kwont), *n.* punting pole; *v.t.* propel with q.

quantulum (kwon'tūləm), *n.* small quantity.

quantum (kwon'təm), *n.* (*pl.* -ta) large, necessary or allotted amount; share; unit of energy in q. theory. q.theory, theory that atoms emit or absorb energy by steps, each of which is emission or absorption of an amount of energy (the quantum) found by multiplying the appropriate frequency of the atom by Planck's constant.

quaquaversal (kwăkwəvə'sal), *adj.* dipping in all directions; dome-like.

quarantine (kwor'əntēn), *n.* time for which, and place where, ships, persons or animals suspected of infection are isolated ; *v.t.* place in q.

quarender, -den (kwor'əndə, -n), *n.* kind of dark red apple.

quartan (kwaw'tən), *n.* & *adj.* (fever) recurring after four days (*i.e.* every third day).

quarto (kwaw'tō), *n.* book size made by folding sheet into four leaves : **foolscap q.**, 8½″ × 6¾″ ; **crown q.**, 10″ × 7½″ ; **demy q.**, 11¼″ × 8½″ ; **royal q.**, 12½″ × 10″ ; **imperial q.**, 15″ × 11″ (*abbr.* 4to).

quasi (kwā'si, -sī ; kwah'si), *adj.* & *adv.* as if ; seemingly ; in a manner.

quassia (kwosh'ə), *n.* drug obtained from certain tropical Amer. trees, used as tonic, insecticide, etc.

quatercentenary (kwatəsentē'nəri, kwā-), *n.* four hundredth anniversary.

quaternary (kwətə'nəri), *n.* four ; set f four ; *adj.* in four parts ; in sets of four ; *Geol.*, app. to period following Tertiary. **-nion,** *n.* set of four ; *Math.*, quotient of two vectors, or factor changing (by multiplication) one vector into another. **-nity,** *n.* state of being fourfold.

quatorzain (kətaw'zān, kat'ə-), *n.* 14-line poem ; sonnet.

quatrain (kwot'rān), *n.* stanza of four lines.

quatral (kwot'rəl), *n.* & *adj.* quadrual.

quatrefoil (kat'rifoil), *n.* any figure like leaf or flower with four leaflets. **-foliated,** *adj.*

quattrocento (kwahtrochen'tō), It. *n.* & *adj.* 15th century.

quean (kwēn), *n.* virago ; lewd woman ; hussy.

quebracho (kābrah'chō), *n.* sev. tropical Amer. trees and their timber or bark.

quenelle (kənel'), *n.* fish or meat forcemeat ball.

quenouille (kənwē'), Fr. *adj.* app. to training of trees, etc., into cone-like outline.

quercetum (kwəsē'təm), *n.* oak plantation.

querimony (kwer'iməni), *n.* complaint. **-nious** (-ō'niəs), *adj.*

quern (kwən), *n.* hand-power grinding mill.

querulent (kwer'ūlənt), *n.* & *adj.* habitually and abnormally suspicious (person). **-lous,** *adj.* peevish ; fretful ; complaining.

question extraordinaire (kest'yawn ekstrahōr̄dēnā̄r'), *Fr.*, final or severest torture.

quidam (kwī'dam), Lat. *pron.* somebody ; unknown person.

quiddity (kwid'iti), *n.* quintessence ; equivocation ; triviality. **-dative,** *adj.*

quidnunc (kwid'nungk), *n.* gossiper ; inquisitive person.

quid pro quo (kwid prō kwō), *Lat.*, "what for which" ; equivalent ; thing given in return.

quiescent (kwīes'ənt), *adj.* resting ; dormant ; not pronounced. **-nce, -ncy,** *n.*

quietism (kwī'itizm), *n.* kind of mysticism in which indifference to world is obtained by passive contemplation of divinity ; passivity. **-ist,** *n.*

quietus (kwī ē'təs), *n.* receipt ; release ; act of dispatching or disposing of ; knock-out or fatal blow ; death.

qui-hi (kwī'hī), Anglo-Ind. call for a servant ; Ind. *n. sl.* Anglo-Indian.

quillet (kwil'it), *n.* quibble ; small tube.

quinary (kwī'nəri), *adj.* pert. to or comprising five ; in fives ; *Math.*, having five as base.

quincentenary (kwinsentē'nəri), *n.* & *adj.* (pert. to) five hundredth anniversary.

quincunx (kwing'kungks), *n.* four corners and centre of rectangle ; arrangement of five things in those positions. **-ial, -ncial** (-un'shəl), *adj.*

quindecagon (kwindek'əgən), *n.* 15-sided plane figure. **-casyllabic,** *adj.* having 15 syllables. **-cennial,** *adj.* pert. to 15 years.

quinquagenarian (kwingkwəjinā̄r'-iən), *n.* & *adj.* (person) in from fiftieth to sixtieth year. **-ry** (-aj'inəri), *adj.* fifty-year-old ; *n.* 50th anniversary.

ə=*er* in *father* ; ə̄=*er* in *pert* ; th=*th* in *thin* ; dh=*th* in *then* ; zh=*s* in *pleasure* ; k=*ch* in *loch* ; n̄=Fr. nasal *n* ; ū=Fr. *u.*

Quinquagesima (kwingkwəjes'imə), *n.* Sunday before Lent. **-l**, *adj.* pert. to fifty days.

quinquennial (kwingkwen'iəl), *adj.* lasting five years; occurring every fifth year. **-nium**, *n.* (*pl.* **-nia**) period of five years.

quintain (kwin'tin), *n.* object, or target, tilted at; tilting at q.

quintal (kwin'təl), *adj.* hundredweight; 100 lb.

quintan (kwin'tən), *n.* & *adj.* (fever) recurring after five days (*i.e.* every fourth day).

quintant (kwin'tənt), *n.* fifth part of circumference of circle; instr. having that arc for taking altitudes.

quintary (kwin'təri), *adj.* fifth.

quintessence (kwintes'əns), *n.* purest essence. **-ntial** (-en'shəl), *adj.*

quintillion (kwintil'yən), *n.* a million quadrillions (10^{30}); *Amer.* & *Fr.*, a thousand quadrillions (10^{18}).

quintroon (kwintrōōn'), *n.* child of white and octoroon.

quire (kwīr), *n.* two dozen sheets of paper.

Quirinal (kwir'inəl), *adj.* It. Court.

quisling (kwiz'ling), *n.* traitor collaborating with enemy occupiers of his country.

quitrent (kwit'rent), *n.* small nominal rent commuting feudal services.

qui vive (kē vēv'), *Fr.*, who goes there? **on the q.v.**, on the alert.

quixotic (kwiksot'ik), *adj.* idealistic; altruistic; unpractical. **-tism, -try**, *n.*

quod erat demonstrandum (kwod er'at demənstran'dəm), *Lat.*, "which was to be demonstrated" (*abbr.* Q.E.D.). **q.e. faciendum** (-fāshien'dəm), "which was to be done" (*abbr.* Q.E.F.).

quodlibet (kwod'libet), *Lat.*, "what you like"; moot or subtle point; fruitless or pedantic argument. **-arian**, *n.* **-ic(al)**, *adj.*

quod vide (kwod vī'di), *Lat.* (*pl.* **quae .....**, *abbr.* **qq.v.**) "which see" (*abbr.* q.v.).

quoin (kwoin) *n.* angle; wedge; cornerstone.

quondam (kwon'dam) Lat. *adv.* "formerly"; *adj.* former.

quorum (kwōr'əm), *n.* minimum number of members whose presence is necessary at a meeting; select body of persons.

quota (kwō'tə), *n.* due share; amount allowed to be imported from a certain country.

quotidian (kwətid'iən), *adj.* daily; *n.* fever recurring daily.

quotient (kwō'shənt), *n.* answer of division sum.

quotiety (kwətī'iti), *n.* number; numerical relationship.

quo vadis (kwō vā'dis, vah'-), *Lat.*, "whither goest thou?"

R

rabbet (rab'it), *n.* groove into which projection fits; frame against which door, etc., closes; *v.t.* cut such groove; join with a r.

rabbinical (rabin'ikl), *adj.* pert. to rabbis and Talmud; denoting a kind of simplified Heb. alphabet. **-nism**, *n.* teaching of rabbis and Talmud.

rabboni (rabō'nī, -i), Heb. *n.* "my great master," as title of respect.

Rabelaisian (rabəlā'ziən), *adj.* pert. to or like the coarse, uproarious humour of François Rabelais (16th cent.).

rabic (rab'ik), *adj.* pert. to rabies.

rabid (rab'id), *adj.* furious; fanatical; mad; pert. to rabies. **-ity**, *n.*

rabies (rā'bēz), *n.* infectious madness in dogs; hydrophobia. **-etic**

(-iet'ik), *adj.* **-ific, -igenic**, *adj.* causing r. **-iform**, *adj.* like r.

raccoon (rakōōn'), *n.* squirrel-like animal of N. Amer. and Mexico, and its fur.

raceme (rasēm'), *n.* kind of inflorescence with flowers borne on footstalks up a central stem, as in lily of valley. **-miferous**, *adj.* bearing r. **-miform**, *adj.* like r. **-mose, -mous** (ras'-), *adj.* **-mule**, *n.* small raceme.

rach(e) (rach), *n.* dog hunting by scent.

rachis (rā'kis), *n.* (*pl.* **-ides**) spine; central axis. **-chialgia**, *n.* pain in spine. **-chidian**, *adj.* **-chiform**, *adj.* like r. **-chiometer**, *n.* instr. measuring spine.

rachitis (rəki'tis), *n.* inflammation of spine; rickets. **-tic** (-it'ik), *adj.* pert. to or having r. **-tism** (rā'kitizm, rak'-), *n.* tendency towards r. **-togenie,** *adj.* causing r.

rackrent (rak'rent), *n.* reasonable rent, equiv. of two-thirds or more of annual value of building for which it is paid ; *pop.* excessive rent.

raconteur (rakawn̄tō̄r') Fr. *n.* (*fem.* **-euse, -ō̄z'**) anecdote-teller.

racoon, *see* raccoon.

radar (rā'dah), *n.* detection and location of objects, stationary or moving, by measuring the direction and time-lag of "echoes" of very short radio waves reflected by them ; formerly called radio-location.

radectomy (rədek'təmi) *n.* removal of part of tooth root.

radical (rad'ikl) *adj.* pert. to, like, deriving from or striking at root ; fundamental ; extreme ; *Math.,* pert. to radix ; *n.* root ; fundamental principle ; advocate of radical, *espec.* socialistic, policy ; basic constituent of chemical compound ; group of atoms replaceable by single atom. **r.sign,** *Math.,* sign (√) indicating extraction of root.

radicle (rad'ikl) *n.* rootlike organ or part ; *Bot.,* portion of seed developing into root ; *Chem.,* radical. **-colous,** *adj.* living on roots. **-cular,** *adj.* **-culitis,** *n.* inflammation of nerve root. **-culose,** *adj.* having many rootlets.

radioactive (rādiōak'tiv), *adj.* emitting radiant energy, *i.e.* energy in form of alpha-, beta-, etc., rays due to disintegration of atomic nuclei. **-vate,** *v.t.* make r. **-vity,** *n.*

radiodontia (rādiədon'shiə), *n.* making and study of X-ray photographs of teeth. **-tic,** *adj.* **-tist,** *n.*

radiogoniometer (rādiəgōniom'itə), *n.* radio direction-finding apparatus. **-try,** *n.*

radiogram (rā'diəgram), *n.* telegram transmitted by radio ; combined gramophone and radio receiver.

radiography (rādiog'rəfi), *n.* making and study of X-ray photographs. **-pher,** *n.* **-phic(al),** *adj.*

radiology (rādiol'əji), *n.* science of X-rays and their med. application. **-gical,** *adj.* **-gist,** *n.*

radiolucent (rādiəloo'sənt), *adj.* penetrable by X-rays.

radiometer (rādiom'itə), *n.* instr. measuring energy emitted by radioactive substance, or sun's radioactivity. **-tric** (-et'rik), *adj.* **-try,** *n.*

radiomicrometer (rādiəmīkrom'itə), *n.* instr. measuring intensity of radioactivity.

radiopraxis (rādiəpraks'is), *n.* med. use of radioactivity.

radioscope (rā'diəskōp), *n.* instr. detecting radioactivity. **-py** (-os'kəpi), *n.* examination of opaque bodies by X-rays.

radiosonde (rā'diōsond), *n.* radio transmitter, borne into and from upper atmosphere by balloon and parachute, sending out information on atmospheric conditions.

radiotherapy (rādiəther'əpi), *n.* med. treatment by X-rays. **-peutics,** *n.* **-pist,** *n.*

radiotropism (rādiot'rəpizm), *n.* direction of growth by radio-activity. **-pic** (-ətrop'ik), *adj.*

radium (rā'diəm), *n.* rare radio-active metallic element found in pitchblende, etc. **-therapy,** *n.* med. treatment by r.

radix (rā'diks), *n.* (*pl.* **-dices**) root ; *Math.,* base of a numerical system, as 10 is of decimal system.

radon (rā'don), *n.* gaseous emanation of radium.

radula (rad'ūlə), *n.* (*pl.* **-ae**) rasp-like toothed band of tissue in mollusc's mouth. **-r,** *adj.* **-te,** *adj.* having r. **-uliform,** *adj.* rasp-like.

ragout (ragoo'), *n.* highly seasoned stew of vegetables and meat.

rahdar (rah'dah), Hind. *n.* road toll-keeper. **-ee, -i,** *n.* road tolls.

rail (rāl), *n. Ornith.,* kind of small crane-like wading bird. **land r.,** corncrake.

rais (rīs), Arab. *n.* chief ; captain.

raison d'être (rā'zawn̄ dā'tr), *Fr.,* "reason for being" ; justification for existence. **r. d'état** (-dātah'), "reason of state."

raj (rahj), Hind. *n.* rule. **-ah,** *n.* prince ; king ; ruler. **-put,** *n.* member of N. Ind. ruling caste.

rale (rahl), *n.* sound symptomatic of disease heard in auscultation.

ralliform (ral'ifawm), *adj.* like the rails (birds). **-line,** *adj.* pert. to rails.

ramage (ram'ij), *n.* boughs of tree. **-mal, -meal** (rā'-), *adj.* pert. to branch.

ə=*er* in *father* ; ō̄=*er* in *pert* ; th=*th* in *thin* ; dh=*th* in *then* ; zh=*s* in *pleasure* ; k=*ch* in *loch* ; n̄=Fr. nasal *n* ; ü=Fr. *u.*

ramellose (ram'ǝlōs), *adj.* having small branches.

ramentaceous (ramǝntā'shǝs), *adj.* bearing, like or consisting of small shavings or chaffy scales. **-tal** (-en'tǝl), *adj.* **-tiferous**, *adj.* bearing such scales. **-tum**, *n.* (*pl.* -ta) shaving; chaffy scale on young ferns.

rameous (rā'miǝs), *adj.* ramal.

ramex (rā'meks), *n.* hernia.

ramie (ram'i), *n.* fibre-yielding E. Asiatic plant; its fibre, used in manuf. of gas-mantles, etc.; China grass.

ramiferous (rǝmif'ǝrǝs), *adj.* bearing branches. **-form** (ram'-), *adj.* branch-like.

ramify (ram'ifī), *v.i.* & *t.* branch out; make complex. **-fication**, *n.*

ramoneur (ramōnēr'), Fr. *n.* chimney-sweep.

ramose (ramōs'), *adj.* branched. **-mous** (rā'mǝs), *adj.* ramose; ramiform.

rampant (ram'pǝnt), *adj.* rearing up on hind legs; fierce; dominating; exuberant; rank; *Archit.*, having one abutment higher than other. **-ncy**, *n.*

rampion (ram'piǝn), *n.* kind of campanula with root used in salad

ramsons (ram'zǝnz), *n.pl.* kind of garlic with root used in salad.

ramulus (ram'ūlǝs), *n.* (*pl.* -li) small branch. **-lar**, *adj.* **-liferous**, *adj.* bearing r. **-lose**, **-lous**, *adj.* having many r.

rana (rah'nah), Hind. *n.* prince.

ranarium (rǝnār'iǝm), *n.* (*pl.* -ia) place for rearing frogs.

rand (rand), S. African *n.* mountains flanking river valley. **The R.**, gold-mining district about Johannesburg.

randan (ran'dan, -dan'), *n.* boat for three oarsmen, *viz.* one sculler with two oars in middle and an oarsman with one oar fore and aft; such style of rowing. **-dem**, *adv.* with three horses in single file.

ranee (rah'nē), Hindu *n.* queen or princess; wife of rajah.

rangiferine (ranjif'ǝrin, -in), *adj.* pert. to or like reindeer; belonging to animal genus containing reindeer.

rani, *see* **ranee.**

ranine (rā'nīn, -in), *adj.* pert. to or like frogs; belonging to subfamily

of amphibians including frogs. **-iform**, *adj.* frog-like.

ranula (ran'ūlǝ), *n.* (*pl.* -ae) small cyst on tongue. **-r**, *adj.*

ranunculaceous (rǝnungkūlā'shǝs), *adj.* pert. to or like buttercups; belonging to buttercup family of plants. **-lus**, *n.* (*pl.* -li) buttercup, *espec.* cultivated.

rapaceus (rǝpā'siǝs), *adj.* shaped like turnip.

rapacious (rǝpā'shǝs), *adj.* greedy; obtaining by extortion; predacious; ravenous. **-city** (-as'iti), *n.*

rape (rāp), *v.t.* carry off; assault sexually; ravish; *n.* act of raping; *Bot.*, cabbage-like forage plant with oil-containing seeds. **-pine** (rap'in), *n.* pillaging.

rapparee (rapǝrē'), Ir. *n.* irregular soldier; vagabond.

rappee (rapē'), *n.* kind of strong snuff.

rapport (rapawt'; Fr., rapōr'), *n.* relationship, *espec.* harmonious. **en r.** (ahn-), Fr., "in rapport."

rapprochement (rapros'mahn), Fr. *n.* resumption of or improvement in relations between countries or persons.

raptatorial (raptǝtōr'iǝl), *adj.* raptorial. **-ry** (rap'-), *adj.*

raptorial (raptōr'iǝl), *adj.* predacious; pert. to birds of prey.

raptus (rap'tǝs), *n.* trance; rapture; seizure.

rara avis (rār'ǝ ā'vis), *Lat.* (*pl.* **rarae aves**) "rare bird"; any unusual person or thing, *espec.* of excellence.

rarefy (rār'ifī), *v.t.* make thin, rare or tenuous. **-faction**, *n.*

ras (rahs), *n.* headland; Abyssinian prince.

rasorial (rǝsōr'iǝl), *adj.* scratching ground for food; pert. to domestic fowls.

ratafia (ratǝfē'ǝ), *n.* almond-flavoured liqueur or biscuit.

ratel (rah'tǝl), *n.* badger-like S. African and Ind. animal.

Rathaus (raht'hows), Ger. *n.* (*pl.* **-häuser**, **-hoi'zǝ**) town hall.

ratify (rat'ifī), *v.t.* confirm, approve formally. **-fication**, *n.*

ratihabition (ratihǝbish'n), *n.* ratification.

ratiocinate (ratios'ināt), *v.i.* reason; argue logically. **-ant**, *adj.* reasoning. **-tion**, **-tor**, *n.* **-tive**, *adj.*

rationale (rashənah'li, -ā'li), *n.* fundamental principles or reasons ; logical basis.

rationalise (rash'ənəlīz), *v.t.* make reasonable, scientific or logical ; give reasonable or natural explanation of ; free from supernatural, illogical or prejudiced elements ; *Comm.,* conduct in scientifically efficient manner, *espec.* with avoidance of waste, unnecessary competition, etc. **-ism,** *n.* belief in truth and supreme power of reason ; phil. theory of reason as source of knowledge ; deductive method. **-ist,** *n.* **-istic,** *adj.*

ratite (rat'īt), *adj.* having flat breastbone ; *n.* such flightless bird, as ostrich, emu, etc.

ratline (rat'lin), *n.* small rope forming rung of rope ladder.

rattan (ratan'), *n.* kind of palm with long jointed stems used for walking-sticks, etc.

ratten (rat'ən), *v.t.* compel to obey trade union by damaging or depriving of machinery, tools, etc.

ravelin (rav'lin), *n.* projecting outwork in fortification, having two embankments forming salient angle ; "half-moon."

ravissant (ravēsahṅ'), Fr. *adj.* (*fem.* **-e,** *-ahṅt'*) ravishing ; causing rapture.

reagent (rē ā'jənt), *n. Chem.,* substance used in detecting, measuring, etc., other substances by their reaction with it.

realism (rē'əlizm), *n.* rationalism ; acceptance of existing positions and things, and repudiation of idealism ; truth to real life ; *Phil.,* doctrine of the separate and real existence of universal qualities, or of objects of cognition. **-ist,** *n.* **-istic,** *adj.*

Realpolitik (rāahl'pōlitēk'), Ger. *n.* practical politics, *espec.* belief that might is right. **-er,** believer in R.

realty (rē'əlti), *n.* real estate, *i.e.* houses and land. **-tor,** Amer. *n.* dealer in r.

rebarbative (ribah'bətiv), *adj.* repulsive.

rebec(k) (rē'bek), *n.* anct. three-stringed violin.

reboant(ic) (reb'ōənt, -an'tik), *adj.* reverberating.

rebus (rē'bəs) *n.* picture puzzle representing word.

recalcitrant (rikal'sitrənt) *n. & adj.* disobedient or stubborn (person). **-nce, -ration,** *n.*

recalesce (rēkəles') *v.i.* liberate heat suddenly when cooling through certain temperature. **-nt,** *adj.* **-nce,** *n.*

recapitulate (rēkəpit'ūlāt) *v.i. & t.* repeat ; summarise. **-tion,** *n.* ; **r.theory,** theory that in its development an individual organism passes through all the stages of the history of the race to which it belongs. **-tive, -tory,** *adj.*

recension (risen'shn), *n.* revision ; revised text. **-nse,** *v.t.* make r. of.

recessional (risesh'ənəl) *n. & adj.* (hymn) sung during withdrawal of clergy and choir at end of service ; concluding voluntary.

réchauffé (rāshō'fā). Fr. *n. & adj.* warmed-up (dish) ; rehash.

recherché (rəshār'shā), Fr. *adj.* refined ; carefully done ; curious ; far-fetched ; extravagant.

recidivism (risid'ivizm), *n.* state of returning habitually to crime. **-ist,** *n.* **-ve** (res'idiv), *v.i.* relapse ; recur. **-vous,** *adj.*

reciprocal (risip'rəkl), *adj.* mutual ; complementary ; interchangeable ; *n. Math.,* expression the product of which and another is 1. **-cate,** *v.i. & t.* return equally ; interchange ; alternate ; move backwards and forwards. **-cation, -cator, -city** (resipros'iti) *n.*

recision (risizh'n) *n.* rescission.

réclame (rāklahm') Fr. *n.* publicity.

recitative (resitətēv'), *n.* speech-like declamatory song in opera, oratorio, etc.

recoct (rēkokt'), *v.t.* cook again ; concoct ; improvise.

recognisance (rekon'izəns), *n.* sum of money as pledge of person's promise to court or magistrate.

recondite (rek'əndīt), *adj.* concealed ; abstruse ; erudite.

reconnaissance (rikon'isəns), *n.* mil. survey of country, disposition of forces, etc. ; act of spying out land. **-noitre** (rekənoit'ə), *v.i. & t.* make r. (of).

recreant (rek'riənt), *n. & adj.* cowardly or renegade (person). **-ncy,** *n.*

recrement (rek'rimənt), *n.* redundant matter ; dross ; *Med.,* se-

---

ə=*er* in *father* ; ē=*er* in *pert* ; th=*th* in *thin* ; dh=*th* in *then* ; zh=*s* in *pleasure* ; k=*ch* in *loch* ; ṅ=Fr. nasal *n* ; ü=Fr. *u*.

cretion of body absorbed again by body. -al, -itial, adj.

recriminate (rikrim′ināt), v.s. make countercharge; make mutual accusations or abuse. -tion, -tor, n. -tive, -tory, adj.

recrudesce (rēkroōdes′), v.i. grow up or break out again. -nce, -ncy, n. -nt, adj.

rectal (rek′təl), adj. pert. to rectum.

rectigrade (rek′tigrād), adj. moving in straight line.

rectilinear (rektilin′iə), adj. pert. to or bounded by straight lines; rectigrade. -neal, adj. -ity, n.

rectirostral (rektiros′trəl), adj. having straight beak.

rectiserial (rektisēr′iəl), adj. in vertical ranks.

recto (rek′tō), n. right-hand page, or front cover of book.

rectrices (rek′trisēz), n.pl. (sing. -rix) quill feathers of bird's tail. -cial (-ish′əl), adj.

rectum (rek′təm), n. last part of large intestine, leading to anus.

recumbent (rikum′bənt), adj. lying at ease. -ncy, n.

recusant (rek′ūzənt), n. person refusing to obey command, espec. to attend Anglican Church service; adj. disobedient; nonconformist. -nce, -ncy, n.

redaction (ridak′shn), n. preparing for publication; editing; new edition. -tor, n. -torial, adj.

redan (ridan′), n. fieldwork in fortification, with two parapets making salient angle.

redhibition (redhibish′n), n. cancellation of sale of defective article with its return to vendor. -tory (-hib′-), adj.

redintegrate (ridin′tigrāt), v.t. make whole again; restore. -tion, n.; Psych., revival of mental state at recurrence of part of it. -tive, adj.

redivivus (redivi′vəs), adj. living again.

redolent (red′ələnt), adj. smelling or smacking (of). -nce, -ncy, n.

redoubt (ridout′), n. fortification within an outwork, espec. such rough and temporary work.

reductio ad absurdum (riduk′shiō ad absō′dəm), Lat., "reduction to absurdity"; proving a proposition by showing that its opposite is absurd; disproving a proposi-

tion by deducing from it an absurd conclusion; such conclusion.

redundant (ridun′dənt), adj. excessive to requirements; superfluous. -ncy, n.

reeve (rēv), n. chief magistrate; bailiff; Can., rural council's president; Ornith., female ruff (bird); v.t. pass (rope) through ring; fasten by reeving.

refection (rifek′shn), n. light meal; refreshment. -tory, n. dining room of monastery, college, etc.

referendum (referen′dəm), n. (pl. -da) direct vote on an issue by whole electorate.

reflex (rē′fleks), adj. turned back; reflected; resulting from reaction; Psych., resulting directly, without conscious will, from a stimulus; n. reflected light, etc.; image; involuntary act. **conditioned r.**, Psych., r. transferred to new or different stimulus. -ive, adj. reflex; reflective; Gram., signifying action directed or done to subject; n. Gram., such verb or pronoun. -ology, n. psych. theory of the reflex nature of all behaviour.

refluent (ref′looənt), adj. flowing back or backward. -ux, n.

refract (rifrakt′), v.t. deflect (ray of light, etc.) on its passage from a medium to another of different density, with, usually, dispersion or splitting up of the ray; distort. -ion, -or, n. -ional, -ive, adj. -ometer, n. instr. measuring amount of r.

refractory (rifrak′təri), adj. stubborn; disobedient; immune; n. material resistant to heat, corrosion, fusion, etc.

refrangible (rifran′jibl), adj. capable of being refracted. -gent, adj. refracting.

refringent (rifrin′jənt), adj. refracting. -nce, -ncy, n.

refulgent (riful′jənt), adj. brightly shining. -nce, n.

refute (rifūt′), v.t. prove to be false or wrong. -tation (ref-), n. -tative, -tatory, adj.

regalism (rē′gəlizm), n. doctrine of supremacy of sovereign, espec. in eccl. matters.

regardant (rigah′dənt), adj. Her., in profile and looking to rear.

regicide (rej′isīd), n. killing or

killer of king ; person who signed death-warrant of Charles I of England, or Louis XVI of France. -dal, *adj.*

régime (rā'zhēm), Fr. *n.* system, *espec.* of government.

regimen (rej'imen), *n.* system, *espec.* of diet or way of life ; gram. government. -minal (-im'inəl), *adj.*

regina (rijī'inə), Lat. *n.* queen. -l, *adj.*

regius (rē'jiəs), *adj.* royal. **r. professor**, one holding professorship founded by royalty.

reglementation (reglimentā'shn), *n.* regulation.

regnal (reg'nəl), *adj.* pert. to reign. -nancy, *n.* rule. -nant, *adj.* reigning.

regurgitate (rigə'jitāt), *v.i. & t.* throw or pour back, or be thrown or poured back, *espec.* from crop or stomach into mouth ; vomit. -ant, *adj.* -tion, *n.*

rehabilitate (rēhabil'itāt), *v.t.* restore to former position, rights, ability to earn living, etc. -tion, *n.*

Reichstag (rīks'tahk), Ger. *n.* Ger. parliament and parliament building. -swehr (-vār), *n.* standing army.

reify (rē'ifī), *v.t.* make concrete ; materialise. -fication, *n.*

reimburse (rēimbəs'), *v.t.* repay. -ment, *n.*

re infecta (rē infek'tə), Lat., "the matter being not completed."

reis, *see* rais.

reiterate (rēit'ərāt), *v.t.* repeat many times. -ant, *adj.* -tion, *n.* -tive, *adj.* ; *n.* word signifying repetition of action.

reive (rēv), *v.i. & t.* rob ; plunder ; carry off. -r, *n.*

rejectamenta (rijektəmen'tə), *n.pl.* rejected things ; excrements.

rejuvenate (rijoo'vināt), *v.i. & t.* become or make young again. -nescence, -tion, -tor, *n.*

relativity (relətiv'iti), *n. Phys.*, principle, formulated by Einstein, and based primarily on the constancy of the velocity of light, denying the absoluteness of space and time and establishing time as a "fourth dimension." **special theory of r.**, as above. **general theory of r.**, conclusions from special theory as it affects gravitation, which is

identified with inertia and interpreted by the varying geometrical structure of the space in which masses are moving. **r. of knowledge,** *Phil.*, doctrine that knowledge is limited by nature of mind, which is unable to perceive the reality of, but only the relations between, objects.

relegate (rel'igāt), *v.t.* banish ; assign. *espec.* to less important place or person. -tion, *n.*

relict (rel'ikt), *n.* widow ; survivor ; *adj.* pert. to land bared by reliction. -ion, *n.* recession of sea leaving land bare ; land so left.

religate (rel'igāt), *v.t.* tie together ; restrain. -tion, *n.*

religieuse (rəlē'zhēz), Fr. *n.* (*masc.* -eux, -ē) nun.

reliquary (rel'ikwəri), *n.* container for holy relics.

reliquiae (relik'wiē), Lat. *n.pl.* "remains." -ian, *adj.* -ism (rel'-), *n.* worship of relics.

relucent (riloo'sənt), *adj.* reflecting ; refulgent.

reluctance (riluk'təns), *n. Elec.*, magnetic resistance. -tivity, *n.* amount of r.

remanent (rem'ənənt), *adj.* remaining ; residual. -nce, *n.*

remiform (rem'ifawm), *adj.* oar-shaped. -igate, *v.i.* row. -iges, *n.pl.* (*sing.* -mex) quill feathers of bird's wing. -iped, *n. & adj.* (creature) having legs or feet adapted for propelling it through water.

remontant (rimon'tənt), *n. & adj.* (rose) flowering more than once in season.

remount (rimount', rē'-), *v.i. & t. Mil.*, provide (with) fresh horses ; *n.* horse replacing one lost or wounded.

renaissance (rinā'səns), *n.* revival, *espec.* of art, architecture and literature in 14th-16th centuries in Europe.

renal (rē'nəl), *adj.* pert. to kidneys.

renascence (rinas'əns), *n.* re-birth ; revival ; renaissance. -nt, *adj.*

rencontre (renkon'tə), Fr., rahn-kawn'tr), *n.* meeting ; encounter ; duel.

rendezvous (ron'divoo ; Fr., rahn'-dāvoo), *n.* meeting or meeting-place ; assignation ; *v.i.* meet by arrangement.

ə=*er* in *father* ; ō=*er* in *pert* ; th=*th* in *thin* ; dh=*th* in *then* ; zh=*s* in *pleasure* ; k=*ch* in *loch* ; ń=Fr. nasal *n* ; ü=Fr. *u.*

rendition (rendish'n), *n.* surrender ; *pop.* manner of, or item in, performance.

renegade (ren'igād), *n.* deserter ; turn-coat ; *adj.* pert. to r. or traitor ; *v.i.* become r.

renege (rineg', -ig'), Amer. *v.i.* revoke (in card-playing) ; break promise.

reniform (rē'nifawm, ren'-), *adj.* kidney-shaped.

renitent (ren'itənt, rinī'-), *adj.* resisting ; refractory. **-nce, -ncy,** *n.*

rennet (ren'it), *n.* contents or part of stomach, or preparation therefrom, of young animal, used to curdle milk. **-nin,** *n.* gastric enzyme curdling milk.

renography (rinog'rəfi), *n.* treatise on or description of kidneys.

rentes (rahnt), Fr. *n.pl.* government stock, bonds, etc. **-tier** (-tyā), *n.* owner of r. ; one living on income from investments ; one living on fixed income.

reparation (repərā'shn), *n.* compensation. **-able, -tive,** *adj.*

repatriate (ripā'triāt), *v.t.* restore to, or re-establish in, native land ; *n.* repatriated person. **-tion,** *n.*

repertoire (rep'ətwah), *n.* list of plays, pieces, etc., which company or person can perform. **-torial,** *adj.* **-tory,** *adj.* pert. to or having a permanent acting company which plays through and continually adds to its r. ; *n.* repertoire.

repetend (rep'itend), *n.* digit(s) repeated in recurring decimal ; repetition of same or similar word in sentence ; refrain.

replete (riplēt'), *adj.* full. **-tion,** *n.* **-tive,** *adj.*

replevin (riplev'in), *n. Law,* repossession of goods wrongfully taken with pledge to return them if defeated in lawsuit on the matter. **-visor,** *n.* **-vy,** *v.t.*

replica (rep'likə), *n.* exact copy, *espec.* made by artist who made the original. **-te,** *adj.* folded back ; repeated ; *v.t.* fold back or repeat. **-tion,** *n.* making of r. ; reply ; echo ; *Law,* reply of plaintiff to defendant's plea. **-tive,** *adj.*

répondez s'il vous plait (rāpawn'dā sēl vōō plā), Fr., "reply, if you please" (*abbr.* R.S.V.P.).

repoussé (rəpōō'sā), Fr. *adj.* shaped

in relief by being beaten up from under or reverse side ; *n.* such artistic work. **-sage** (-sahzh'), *n.* art of doing r. work.

reprehend (reprihend'), *v.t.* rebuke. **-nsible,** *adj.* **-nsion,** *n.*

reprisal (riprī'zəl), *n.* securing of redress or compensation by violent measure ; act of retaliation in same kind or to same degree as offence.

reprobate (rep'rəbāt), *v.t.* rebuke ; disapprove of ; reject ; abandon ; *adj.* sinful ; depraved ; *n.* hardened sinner. **-tion,** *n.* **-tive,** *-tory, adj.*

reptant (rep'tənt), *adj.* creeping. **-tation,** *n.* **-tatorial, -tatory,** *adj.*

requiem (rek'wiem), *n.* Mass or dirge for the dead.

requiescat (rekwies'kat), *Lat.* "may he (or she) rest" ; *n.* prayer for dead. **r. in pace,** "may he (or she) rest in peace" (*abbr.* R.I.P.).

reredos (rēr'dos), *n.* screen behind altar ; *erron.*, choir screen.

rerum cognoscere causas (rēr'əm kognos'əri kaw'sas), *Lat.*, "to know the causes of things."

rescind (risind'), *v.t.* cancel ; revoke. **-cission,** *n.* **-cissory,** *adj.*

rescript (rē'skript), *n.* decree ; rewriting or rewritten thing. **-ive,** *adj.*

réseau (rā'zō), Fr. *n.* network, *esprc.* of lines on astron. photograph.

resect (risekt'), *v.t. Surg.,* remove part of organ. **-ion,** *n.* such surg. operation ; determination of position by drawing lines on map from two or more known objects.

res gestae (rēz jes'tē), *Lat.,* "things done" ; matters incident to question in lawsuit.

residue (rez'idū), *n.* remainder. **-ual, -uary** (rizid'uəl, -əri), *adj.* pert. to or receiving r. **-uent,** *n.* by-product. **-uum,** *n.* (*pl.* **-ua**).

resile (rizīl'), *v.i.* draw back ; return to first position or shape. **-lient** (-il'iənt), *adj.* elastic. **-lience,** *n.*

resipiscent (resipis'ənt), *adj.* returning to one's senses, or to wiser course ; reforming. **-nce, -ncy,** *n.*

resorb (risawb'), *v.t.* reabsorb. **-ent, -rptive,** *adj.* **-ence, -rption,** *n.*

responsions (rispon'shnz), *n.pl.* first examination for B.A. degree at

Oxford University; "little go"; "smalls."

ressala(h) (risah'lə), *n.* Ind. native cavalry squadron. **-ldar,** *n.* Ind. native cavalry captain.

restaurateur (restōrahtēr'), Fr. *n.* restaurant-keeper.

résumé (rā'sümā), Fr. *n.* summary; *v.t.* summarise.

resupinate (risū'pinət), *adj.* upside down. **-ne,** *adj.* supine. **-tion,** *n.*

resurgam (risə'gam), *Lat.,* "I shall rise again."

resurgent (risə'jənt), *adj.* rising again. **-nce,** *n.*

resuscitate (risus'itāt), *v.i.* & *t.* restore, or return, to life. **-tion, -tor,** *n.* **-tive,** *adj.*

rete (rē'ti), *n.* (*pl.* -tia, -shiə) network; net. **-cious** (rītē'shəs), **-tial, -tiary,** *adj.*

reticulate (ritik'ūlāt), *v.t.* mark with network-like lines; *adj.* like network. **-lar,** *adj.* net-like; intricate. **-le** (ret'ikūl), *n.* handbag, *espec.* of net. **-lose,** *adj.* reticulated. **-tion,** *n.* reticulate marking.

retina (ret'inə), *n.* (*pl.* -ae) membrane at back of eye receiving image. **-l,** *adj.* **-nise,** *v.i.* read mechanically, with eye alone. **-nitis,** *n.* inflammation of r.

retinoid (ret'inoid), *adj.* like resin.

retortion (ritaw'shn), *n.* turning or twisting back; retaliation.

retrad (rē'trad, ret'-), *adv.* backwards. **-rahent,** *adj.* drawing back. **-ral,** *adj.* backward; at the back.

retrench (ritrench'), *v.i.* & *t.* reduce; economise. **-ment,** *n.*

retribution (retribū'shn), *n.* just punishment or reward; requital. **-tive, -tory** (-ib'ūtiv, -əri), *adj.*

retro (rē'trō), Lat. *adv.* backwards.

retroact (retrōakt'), *v.i.* act backwards or opposite; react. **-ion,** *n.* **-ive,** *adj.* taking effect as from a previous date.

retrocede (retrəsēd'), *v.i.* & *t.* go back or inwards; cede back. **-cession,** *n.* **-cessive,** *adj.*

retrochoir (ret'rəkwīr, rē'-), *n.* space in choir behind high altar.

retrograde (ret'rəgrād), *adj.* moving or directed backwards; deteriorating; *v.i.* move backwards; revert. **-gress,** *v.i.* retrograde; degenerate. **-gression,** *n.* **-gressive,** *adj.*

retroject (ret'rəjekt), *v.t.* throw back. **-ion,** *n.*; *Med.,* washing of cavity from within.

retromingent (retrəmin'jənt), *n.* & *adj.* (animal) urinating rearwards.

retromorphosis (retrəmawfō'sis), *n.* degenerative metamorphosis; change for the worse.

retrospect (ret'rəspekt), *n.* act of, or view seen on, looking back. **-ion,** *n.* act of looking back to past. **-ive,** *adj.* pert. to r.; retroactive.

retrostalsis (retrəstal'sis), *n.* reversed peristalsis. **-ltic,** *adj.*

retrousse (rətrōō'sā), *adj.* turned up (app. to nose only).

retrovert (retrəvēt'), *v.t.* turn back. **-rse,** *adj.* turned back. **-rsion,** *n.*

revalescent (revələs'ənt), *adj.* convalescent. **-nce,** *n.*

revalorise (rēval'əriz), *v.t.* restore to original value, *espec.* such monetary unit. **-sation,** *n.*

revanche (rəvahnsh'), Fr. *n.* revenge; desire to regain lost territory; favour done in return.

revehent (rev'ihənt, rivē'-), *adj.* carrying back.

revenant (rev'ənənt), *n.* person returning after supposed death or long absence; ghost.

revenons à nos moutons (rəv'nawn ah nō mōō'tawn), *Fr.,* "let us return to our sheep"; let us return to the subject in hand.

revetment (rivet'mənt), *n.* facing of embankment or trench.

revirescent (revires'ənt), *adj.* growing young or strong again. **-nce,** *n.*

reviviscent (revivis'ənt), *adj.* capable of causing revival. **-nce,** *n.*

revolute (rev'əlōōt), *adj.* rolled back, *espec.* at edges.

rhabdomancy (rab'dəmansi), *n.* divination by means of rod; water-divining. **-dos,** *n.* magic wand.

Rhadamanthus (radəman'thəs), *n.* in Gr. myth. a judge of the souls of the dead; stern judge. **-thine,** *adj.*

rhaebosis (ribō'sis), *n.* curvature; bandiness.

rhamphoid (ram'foid), *adj.* beak-shaped.

rhapontic (rəpon'tik), *n.* knapweed; rhubarb.

rhea (rē'ə), *n.* Amer. ostrich.

rhema (rē'mə), Gr. *n.* word; verb. **-me,** *n.* speech element expressing an idea. **-tic** (-at'ik), *adj.* pert. to formation of words; derived from verbs. **-tology,** *n.* study of rhemes.

ə=*er* in *father*; ō̄=*er* in *pert*; th=*th* in *thin*; dh=*th* in *then*; zh=s in *pleasure*; k=*ch* in *loch*; ṅ=Fr. nasal *n*; ü=Fr. *u.*

rheology (riol'əji), n. study of flow of matter. -ometer, n. instr. measuring or controlling currents. -ophile (rē'-), adj. living in running water. -ophore, n. wire connection of elec. apparatus. -oscope, n. galvanoscope. -ostat, n. variable elec. resistance. -otaxis, n. direction of movement by water. -otrope, n. commutator reversing elec. current. -otropism, n. direction of growth by water.

rhetoric (ret'ərik), n. art of effective expression in words ; oratory ; bombastic language. -al (-or'ikl), adj. pert. to r. ; r.question, question used merely for effect and not expecting an answer. -ian (-ish'ən), n.

rheum (rōōm), n. watery discharge from eyes and nose. -ic, -y, adj. pert. to or causing r. ; damp.

rhexis (reks'is), n. rupture.

rhigosis (rigō'sis), n. sensation of cold ; ability to feel cold. -otic (-ot'ik), adj.

rhinal (rī'nəl), adj. nasal. -gia (-al'jiə), n. pain in nose. -nenchysis (rīnənki'sis), n. injection into nose. -nitis, n. inflammation of nose or its mucous membrane. -nodynia, n. rhinalgia. -nogenous, adj. deriving from nose. -nolalia, n. nasal speech. -nology, n. med. study of the nose. -nophyma, n. acne of the nose. -norrhagia, n. nose-bleeding. -norrhoea, n. continuous nasal catarrh. -noscopy, n. med. examination of nose.

rhipidate (rip'idāt), adj. fan-shaped.

rhizanthous (rīzan'thəs), adj. with flowers emerging from root.

rhizocarpous (rīzəkah'pəs), adj. with perennial root, etc., but annual foliage and stems.

rhizogenic (rīzəjen'ik), adj. root-producing. -nous (-oj'inəs), adj.

rhizoid (rī'zoid), n. thin root-like filament of fern, etc. ; adj. root-like.

rhizome, -ma (rī'zōm, -ō'mə), n. root-like underground stem ; rootstock. -matic (-at'ik), -matous (-om'ətəs, -ō'-), -mic, adj. -morphous, adj. root-like.

rhodocyte (rō'dəsīt), n. red blood corpuscle.

rhomb(us) (rom, rom'bəs), n. equilateral oblique-angled parallelogram. -bic(al), -biform, adj.

-bohedron, n. (pl. -dra) six-sided prism with each face a parallelogram. -boid, n. oblique-angled and non-equilateral parallelogram ; adj. like r. or rhomboid.

rhonchus (rong'kəs), n. whistling sound heard in auscultation. -chial, adj.

rhotacism (rō'təsizm), n. mis-pronunciation or overuse of sound r. -cise, v.i. -cistic, adj.

rhumb (rum), n. point of compass ; loxodrome.

rhyparography (rīpərog'rəfi), n. painting or description of mean or sordid things ; still-life or genre painting. -pher, -phist, n. -phic, adj.

rhysimeter (rīsim'itə), n. instr. measuring speed of current or ship.

ria (rē'ah), Sp. n. long, wide creek.

riant (rī'ənt), adj. laughing ; gay.

ribald (rib'əld), adj. low ; indecent. -ry, n.

ricochet (rik'əshā), n. glancing rebound ; v.i. move in or like r.

rictus (rik'təs), n. orifice ; mouth, espec. gaping. -tal, adj.

rideau (rē'dō), n. ridge or mound of earth, espec. as protection.

ridel, -dd- (rid'l), n. altar-curtain.

ridibund (rid'ibund), adj. easily moved to laughter.

rigadoon (rigədōōn'), n. anct. lively skipping dance.

rigescent (rijes'ənt), adj. becoming. numb or stiff. -nce, n.

rigor (rī'gor, rig'-), n. shiver ; chill ; rigidity ; abbr. of r. mortis. r.mortis, stiffening of body for period shortly after death.

rima (rī'mə), n. (pl. -ae) narrow fissure. r.oris, space between lips. -l, adj. -mose, -mous, adj. having many r. -mulose, adj. having many small r. -te, adj. having r.

rinderpest (rin'dəpest), n. cattle plague.

riparian (rīpār'iən, rip-), adj. pert. to or on river bank or lake shore ; n. person living on or owning river bank. -ial, -ious, -picolous, adj. living on river banks.

riposte (ripōst'), n. quick return thrust or reply ; v.i. make a r.

risible (riz'ibl), adj. pert. to or capable of laughter ; used in laughing ; laughable. -s, n.pl. sense of humour ; inclination to laugh. -bility, n.

risorgimento (rēsōrjēmen'tō), It. *n.* revival; It. renaissance; 19th-cent. It. liberal and national political movement.

risorial (rīsōr'iəl), *adj.* pert. to or causing laughter.

risqué (ris'kā; Fr., rēs'kā), Fr. *adj.* improper; mildly indecent.

ritornel(le), -llo (ritənel', -ō), *n.* short prelude or interlude for mus. instr. in song or opera.

Ritter (rit'ə), Ger. *n.* knight.

riverain, -rine (riv'ərān, -īn), *n.* & *adj.* riparian.

rivose (rī'vōs), *adj.* bearing winding furrows. -vulation, *n.* having irregular marks of colour. -vulose, *adj.* bearing winding and haphazard lines.

riziform (riz'ifawm), *adj.* like a rice grain.

robinet (rob'inet), *n.* chaffinch; robin; anct. light cannon.

roble (rō'blā), *n.* sev. kinds of New World oak, or other hard-timbered tree.

roborant (rob'ərənt), *n.* & *adj.* tonic. -rate, *v.t.* strengthen; corroborate. -rative, *adj.*

roborean (rəbōr'iən), *adj.* like an oak; strong. -eous, *adj.*

roc (rok), *n.* myth. Arab. bird of great size. r.'s egg, unattainable object.

rocaille (rokī'), Fr. *n.* florid shell-like 18th-cent. ornamentation; rococo scroll ornamentation.

roche moutonnée (rosh mōōton'ā), Fr., (*pl.* roches moutonnées) "sheep-like rock"; rock rounded by glacial action.

rochet (roch'it), *n.* bishop's or abbot's vestment resembling surplice; red gurnard.

rococo (rokō'kō), *n.* & *adj.* (pert. to or like) 18th-cent. style of ornamentation with florid, unsymmetrical curves and shell-work; showy; fantastic.

rodent (rō'dənt), *n.* & *adj.* gnawing (animal). -ian (-en'shən), *adj.*

rodomontade (rodəmon'tād), *n.* bragging talk; rigmarole; *v.i.* brag. -dist, -dor, *n.*

rogation (rəgā'shn), *n.* special prayer for r. days. r. days, three days before Ascension Day.

roi (rwah), Fr. *n.* king. le r. le veult (lə rwah lə vö), "the king wills it"; signification of royal assent

to Act of Parl. le r. s'amuse (-samüz'), "the king is being amused." r.fainéant (-fānāahn'), powerless king.

roinek (roi'nek), S. African *n.* "red neck"; new immigrant, *espec.* British; greenhorn.

rojo (rō'hō), Sp. *adj.* red; *n.* Mex. Indian.

rolley (rol'i), *n.* lorry; trolley.

romal (rōmahl'), Ind. *n.* silk or cotton fabric; handkerchief of r.

roman (rō'mahn), Fr. *n.* anct. Fr. saga-like poem; novel; romance. r.policier (-pōlēs'yā), detective story.

romaunt (rōmawnt', -ahnt'), *n.* anct. romance in verse.

rondeau (ron'dō), *n.* thirteen-lined poem with two rhymes and refrain. -del, *n.* such poem of fourteen lines.

rondo (ron'dō), *n.* mus. composition with main theme occurring three or more times, interspersed with minor themes.

Röntgen-rays (rönt'yən-rāz), *n.pl.* X-rays. -nogram, -nograph, *n.* X-ray photograph. -nology, *n.* radiology. -noscopy, *n.* X-ray examination.

rood (rōōd), *n.* crucifix or cross; one-quarter of acre; seven or eight yards. r.screen, screen bearing crucifix.

rooinek (rōō'inek), S. African *n.* roinek. -ibok, *n.* impala.

roomaul (rōōmahl'), *n.* romal.

roric (rōr'ik), *adj.* dewy.

rorqual (raw'kwəl), *n.* large whalebone whale; finback.

rorulent (rōr'oolənt), *adj.* covered with dew.

rosarium (rəzār'iəm), *n.* rose garden.

Roscius (rosh'iəs), *n.* famous anct. Rom. actor; great actor.

roseola (rōziō'lə), *n.* rash of rose-coloured patches; rose rash. -liform, -lous, -r, *adj.*

rosin (roz'in), *n.* solid resin; *v.t.* rub with r.

rosmarine (roz'mərēn, -īn), *n.* walrus; myth. walrus-like sea animal believed to feed on dew; sea dew.

rosorial (rəsōr'iəl), *adj.* rodential.

rostel(lum) (ros'təl, -el'əm), *n.* small beak, or beak-like outgrowth. -llar, *adj.* -llate, *adj.* having r. -lliform, *adj.* like r.

---

roster (ros'tə, rō'-), *n.* list of persons showing their times of duty.

rostrum (ros'trəm), *n.* (*pl.* -ra) beak; prow of anct. warship; platform or pulpit for speaking; mus. conductor's dais; any beak-like part or thing. -ral, *adj.* -rate, *adj.* beaked. -riform, -roid, *adj.* beak-like. -rulum, *n.* (*pl.* -la) small r.

rosular, -ate (roz'ūlə, -ət; rō'-), *adj.* in rosettes.

rota (rō'tə), *n.* roster; R.C. tribunal; *Mus.*, round. -meter, *n.* instr. measuring length of curved lines.

rotacism, *see* rhotacism.

rotifer (rō'tifə), *n.* microscopic multicellular fresh-water creature with rotating cilia at one end. -al, -ous, *adj.* -form, *adj.* wheel-shaped.

rotisserie (rōtēs'rē), Fr. *n.* shop selling roast meat, *espec.* restaurant where meat is roasted in view of diners.

rotograph (rō'təgraf), *n.* photograph of MS., etc., made direct on bromide paper, without negative.

rotor (rō'tə), *n.* rotating part of machine, *espec.* of elec. generating machine; rotating wing of helicopter.

rotula (rot'ūlə), *n.* kneecap. -lian, -r, *adj.* -liform, *adj.* like r.

rotunda (rətun'də), *n.* circular domed building or room. -te, *adj.* rounded.

roué (rōō'ā), Fr. *n.* debauched man; lecher. -rie, *n.*

rouge-et-noir (rōōzh-ā-nwahr'), *Fr.*, "red-and-black"; gambling game of betting on those colours; trente et quarante.

roughage (ruf'ij), *n. Med.*, coarse fibrous food, or such element in food, stimulating peristalsis.

roulade (rōōlahd'), *n.* arpeggio-like mus. figure sung to one syllable.

rounceval (rown'sivəl), *adj.* large; *n.* marrowfat pea.

roundel (rown'dl), *n.* rondeau; any round thing; badge on aircraft, of concentric coloured rings.

roup (rōōp), *n.* poultry disease with mucous discharge and hoarseness. -y, *adj.*

rouseabout, -oust- (rowz'əbowt, rowst'-), Austral. *n.* odd-job man, *espec.* helping sheep-shearers.

rowan (rō'ən, row'-), Scot. *n.* mountain ash, and its fruit.

rubedinous (rōōbed'inəs), *adj.* ruddy. -dity, *n.*

rubefacient (rōōbifā'shənt), *n.* & *adj.* (substance) causing redness of skin. -faction, *n.*

rubella (rōōbel'ə), *n.* German measles.

rubeola (rōōbē'ələ), *n.* measles; German measles. -loid, *adj.* like r. -r, *adj.*

rubescent (rōōbes'ənt), *adj.* reddening; flushing. -nce, *n.*

rubiaceous (rōōbiā'shəs), *adj.* like or pert. to madder plant; belonging to madder family of plants.

rubican (rōō'bikən), *adj.* red bay; sorrel.

Rubicon (rōō'bikon), *n.* river between Italy and Cisalpine Gaul, the crossing of which by Julius Caesar began civil war and made him dictator. **to cross the R.**, make a fateful and irrevocable decision.

rubific (rōōbif'ik), *n.* & *adj.* rubefacient. -ation, *n.* -ative, *adj.*

rubiginous (rōōbij'inəs), *adj.* rust-coloured; rusty. -nose, *adj.*

rubineous (rōōbin'iəs), *adj.* ruby-coloured.

rubor (rōō'bor), *n.* redness due to excess of blood in part.

rubric (rōō'brik), *n.* passage in book printed in red or other distinctive type, *espec.* such direction in service book; any direction as to conduct or ceremony; title; heading. -al, *adj.* -ality, *n.* ceremony. -ate, *v.t.* mark in red; fix like a ritual. -ation, *n.* -ian (-ish'ən), *n.* student of r. -ism, -ity, *n.* strict adherence to r.; formalism. -ose, *adj.* ruddy.

rubrific (rōōbrif'ik), *adj.* rubefacient.

rucervine (rōōsə'vīn, -in), *adj.* pert. to or like Ind. swamp deer.

ruderal (rōō'dərəl), *adj. Bot.*, growing in refuse or waste ground.

rudiment (rōō'dimənt), *n.* elementary principle; undeveloped part or organ. -al, -ary, *adj.*

rufescent (rōōfes'ənt), *adj.* ruddy; bronzy. -nce, *n.*

ruff (ruf), *n. Ornith.*, sandpiper.

rufous (rōō'fəs), *adj.* reddish; tawny; red-haired. -fulous, *adj.* somewhat r.

rugose (rōōgōs'), *adj.* ridged; wrinkled. -gate, -gous, *adj.*

---

hat, bah, hāte, hāre, crawl; pen, ēve, hēre; it, īce, fīre; on, bōne, boil, bōre, howl; foot, fōōd, bōōr, hull, tūbe, pūre.

-gulose, adj. having small or fine wrinkles. -sity, n.

rumal (rōōmahl'), n. romal.

rumchunder (rumchun'de), n. fine Ind. silk.

rumen (rōō'men), n. (pl. -mina) first stomach of ruminant; cud. -itis, n. inflammation of r. -otomy, n. incision into r.

ruminate (rōō'mināt), v.i. chew the cud; ponder. -ant, n. & adj. (animal) that chews the cud; pondering. -tion, n. -tive, adj.

runcinate (run'sinət), adj. pinnate with lobes pointing downwards.

rune (rōōn), n. character of simple anct. Teutonic alphabet; magical mark or sign; magic. -nic, adj. -niform, adj. like r. -nology, n. study of r.

runt (runt), n. small cattle; any small animal or person.

rupestrian (rōōpes'trian), n. made of, or written on, rock. -ral, adj. -rine, adj. living on or in rocks.

rupicoline, -lous (rōōpik'əlīn, -in; -əs), adj. rupestrine.

ruridecanal (rōōridīkā'nəl), adj. pert. to rural dean and his jurisdiction.

rus in urbe (rus in ə'bi), Lat., "countryside in the town."

rusine (rōō'sīn, -in), adj. pert. to E. Ind. maned deer.

rusticate (rus'tikāt), v.i. & t. live in country; make rustic; punish by expelling from university for a period. -tion, n.

rut (rut), n. period of sexual excitement in deer, cattle, etc.; v.s. & t. have r., or sexual intercourse (with).

rutidosis (rōōtidō'sis), n. wrinkling.

rutilant (rōō'tilənt), adj. shining red, -lous, adj.

rynchosporous (ringkəspōr'əs), adj. having beaked fruit.

ryot (rī'ot), n. Ind. peasant. -war, adj. pert. to system of rent- or tax-collecting with direct settlement between government and r. -wary, n. & adj.

S

sabbatarian (sabətār'iən), n. & adj. (person) devoted to strict keeping of sabbath. -ism, n.

sabbatic(al) (səbat'ik, -l), adj. pert. to or suitable for sabbath. s.year, every seventh year when anct. Jews ceased tilling; leave taken by professor, etc., every seventh year. -tism, n. freedom from work on sabbath; sabbatarianism.

sabicu (sab'ikōō, -kū), n. mahogany-like W. Ind. tree and timber.

sabot (sab'ō), n. wooden shoe; clog. -age (-ətahzh), n. damage to machinery, etc., and obstruction of work by workers; any destructive or obstructive activity by spies, resistance workers, etc., in a country at war; v.t. perform s. upon. -eur (-ər'), n. person performing sabotage.

sabretache (sā'bətash), n. satchel suspended by straps from cavalry officer's belt.

sabulous, -ose (sab'ūləs, -ōs), adj. sandy. -line, adj. -losity, n.

saburra (səbur'ə), n. Med., foulness of mouth. -l, adj. -tion (sab-), n. Med., arenation.

sac (sak), n. any membranous bag or cavity.

sacatra (sak'ətrə), n. person of one-eighth white and seven-eighths negro blood.

saccadic (səkad'ik), adj. twitching.

saccate (sak'āt), adj. sac-like.

saccharin (sak'ərin), n. substitute for sugar obtained from coal-tar. -e, adj. very sweet; cloying; pert. to sugar. -ric (-ar'ik), adj. pert. to saccharine substances. -riferous, adj. containing sugar. -rify, -rise, v.t. transform into, or impregnate with, sugar. -rimeter, n. polarimeter measuring amount, and kind, of sugar in a solution. -roid, adj. sugary; granular. -rometer, n. hydrometer measuring amount of sugar in a solution.

sacciferous (sakif'ərəs), adj. bearing sac(s). -form, adj. sac-shaped.

saccular (sak'ūlə), adj. sac-like. -late (-ət), adj. having sacs; v.t. (-āt) enclose in sac. -le, -lus, n. little sac.

sacerdotal (sasədō'təl), adj. pert. to priest, espec. sacrificial; granting or believing in mysterious or miraculous priestly powers. -docy, *n.* priesthood. -ism, *n.*

sachem (sā'chəm), *n.* Amer. Ind. chieftain ; boss. -ic (-em'ik), *adj.*

sackbut (sak'but), *n.* anct. trombone-like mus. instr.

sacral (sā'krəl), *adj.* pert. to sacrum. -gia (-al'jiə), *n.* pain in sacrum.

sacrilege (sak'rilij), *n.* violation of sacred place or object ; stealing from a church. -gious (-ē'jəs), *adj.*

sacring (sā'kring), *n.* hallowing ; consecration ; ordination. s.bell, bell rung at moment of elevation of the Host.

sacristan (sak'ristən), *n.* eccl. official having care of sacred objects ; sexton. -ty, *n.* s.'s room in church ; vestry.

sacrum (sā'krəm), *n.* (*pl.* -ra) flat triangular bone at base of spine.

sadhu (sah'dōō), *n.* Hind. holy man.

sadism (sā'dizm), *n.* finding of sexual pleasure in, or associated with, infliction of pain upon another ; inhuman cruelty. -ist, *n.* -istic, *adj.*

saeculum (sek'ūləm), Lat. *n.* (*pl.* -la) "generation" ; age ; aeon.

safari (safah'ri), Arab. *n.* hunting expedition.

saffian (saf'iən), *n.* brightly-coloured goatskin or sheepskin leather.

saga (sah'gə), *n.* story, *espec.* in verse, of anct. Scandinavian gods or heroes ; any heroic story or recital.

sagacious (səgā'shəs), *adj.* wise ; perspicacious. -city (-as'iti), *n.*

sagamore (sag'əmōr), *n.* sachem.

sagittal (saj'itəl), *adj.* pert. to or like an arrow. -tate, *adj.* arrowhead-shaped.

sainfoin (san'foin), *n.* pink-flowered forage plant ; "French clover."

sake (sah'ki, sak'-), Jap. *n.* Jap. beer made from rice.

saki (sah'ki), *n.* white-bearded and -ruffed S. Amer. monkey.

sakia, -ieh, -iyeh (sah'kiə), *n.* bucket-bearing wheel used in Egypt for raising water.

salacious (səlā'shəs), *n.* obscene ; lascivious. -city (-as'iti), *n.*

salamander (sal'əmandə), *n.* lizardlike amphibian animal, fabled to live in fire ; utensil for browning pastry, etc. ; portable stove. -driform, *adj.* s.-shaped. -drine, -droid, *adj.* like s. ; able to withstand fire.

salame (səlah'mi), *n.* (*pl.* -mi) It. salted sausage.

salep (sal'ep), *n.* dried root of species of orchid, used as food, etc.

salic (sal'ik), *adj.* Frankish. s.law, exclusion of women from succession to throne.

salicaceous (salikā'shəs), *adj.* pert. to or like a willow ; belonging to the willow family of plants.

salient (sā'liənt), *adj.* leaping ; outstanding ; pointing outwards ; *n.* such angle or curve, *espec.* in battle-line. -nce, *n.*

saliferous (səlif'ərəs), *adj.* containing salt. -fy, *v.t.* form salt with ; transform into salt.

saline (sā'līn), *adj.* salty ; *n.* metallic salt ; soluble salt ; solution of salt and water. -niform, *adj.* like salt. -nity (-in'iti), *n.* -nometer, *n.* hydrometer measuring amount of salt in a solution.

salivant (sal'ivənt), *n.* & *adj.* (substance) promoting secretion of saliva. -vate, *v.i.* & *t.* secrete saliva ; cause excessive saliva in. -vous (səli'vəs), *adj.*

salle (sal), Fr. *n.* "room." s. à manger (-ah mahn'zhā) "diningroom."

salmagundi (salməgun'di), *n.* highly seasoned mixed dish of meat, eggs, etc. ; olio.

salmi (sal'mē), *n.* ragout, *espec.* of game.

salon (sal'awn), Fr. *n.* "drawingroom" ; reception at which famous persons are present ; hostess's circle of fashionable or famous acquaintances.

saloop (səlōōp'), *n.* salep ; sassafras ; drink made of salep and milk. -lopian, *adj.*

salpinx (sal'pingks), *n.* (*pl.* -nges) Eustachian or Fallopian tube. -ngian, *adj.* -ngitis, *n.* inflammation of s. -ngotomy, *n.* incision into s.

salsify (sal'sifi), *n.* purple-flowered plant, with root (called "oyster plant") boiled as vegetable.

salsuginous, -ose (salsū'jinəs, -ōs), *adj. Bot.* thriving in salt-impregnated soil.

saltant (sal'tənt), *adj.* leaping ; dancing. -tation, *n.* act of leaping or dancing ; spurt ; sudden metamorphosis ; mutation. -tative-ness, *n.* ability to jump. -tatorial,

-tatory, *adj.* pert. to leaping or dancing; taking place by leaps and bounds.

saltire (sal'tīr), *n.* X-shaped cross. -wise, *adj.*

saltigrade (sal'tigrād), *adj.* having leaping legs; *n.* such spider.

saltpetre (sawltpē'tə), *n.* potassium nitrate; nitre. -trous, *adj.*

salubrious (səloo'briəs), *adj.* health-giving. -rify, *v.t.* make s. -rity, *n.*

saluki (səloo'ki), *n.* greyhound-like Arab dog; gazelle hound.

salutary (sal'ūtəri), *adj.* having good results; healthy; wholesome.

salvific(al)(salvif'ik,-l), *adj.* tending to save.

salvo (sal'vō), *n.* (*pl.* -es) firing of large number of guns; any simultaneous discharge; (*pl.* -s) proviso.

sal volatile (sal vəlat'ili), *n.* ammonium carbonate as smelling-bottle.

samara (sam'ərə, -ār'ə, -ah'rə), *n.* propeller-like winged fruit, as of ash; key fruit. -riform (-ar'i-fawm), -roid, *adj.* like s. in shape.

sambuke (sam'būk), *n.* sackbut; hurdy-gurdy, etc.

sambur (sam'būr), *n.* Ind. elk and its hide.

samiel (sam'yel), Turk. *n.* simoom.

samisen (sam'isen), *n.* Jap. banjo-like instr.

samite (sam'īt), *n.* anct. rich silk fabric.

samlet (sam'lit), *n.* young salmon.

samogon (sahmōgōn'), Russ. *n.* illicitly-distilled vodka.

samovar (saməvah', sam'-), *n.* Russ. tea-urn.

samoyed(e) (samōyed'), Russ. *n.* white sledge-dog.

sampan (sam'pan), *n.* small Chin. river boat.

samphire (sam'fīr), *n.* fleshy sea-coast plant; glasswort.

samshu (sam'shoo), *n.* Chin. liquor distilled from rice.

samurai (sam'oorī), *n.* (member of) anct. Jap. mil. caste; mil. officer.

sanative (san'ətiv), *adj.* healing. -torium, *n.* (*pl.* -ria) hospital, *espec.* for tuberculosis. -tory, *adj.* producing health.

sanction (sangk'shn), *n.* ratification; permission; penalty incurred or reward lost by breaking law; *v.t.* permit. -ative, *adj.*

sanctum (sangk'təm), *n.* (*pl.* -ta) holy or private place. s.sanctorum

(-sangktōr'əm), "holy of holies"; holiest, innermost or most private room.

sanctus (sangk'təs), *n.* part of Communion service beginning "Holy, Holy, Holy." s.bell, bell rung as s. is said.

sangaree (sanggərē'), *n.* drink of spiced wine and water.

sang-froid (sahńfrwah'), *Fr.,* "cold blood"; calmness in danger; levelheadedness.

sanguinary (sang'gwinəri), *adj.* bloody; bloodthirsty; causing bloodshed. -naceous, -ne, *adj.* hopeful; optimistic; blood-red. -neous, *adj.* bloody; pert. to, containing or having blood; full-blooded; blood-red. -nolent, *adj.* containing blood; bloodthirsty. -uisuguous, *adj.* blood-sucking.

sanhedrin (san'idrin), *n.* highest court of anct. Jerusalem. -rist, *n.* member of s.

sanies (sā'niēz), *n. Med.,* discharge from ulcers, etc. -nious, *adj.*

sanitarium (sanitār'iəm), *n.* (*pl.* -ria) sanatorium. -ry, *adj.* pert. to or causing health; pert. to disposal of waste or sewage; hygienic.

sanjak (sanjak'), *n.* division of a vilayet. -beg, -bey, *n.* governor of s.

sannup (san'up), *n.* Amer. Ind. warrior, *espec.* married.

sans (sanz) *Fr.,* sahn), Fr. *prep.* "without." s.-culotte, "without trousers"; violent or low class Fr. revolutionary. s.gêne, "without trouble"; unembarrassed; familiarity. s. peur et s. reproche, "without fear and without reproach," app. to perfect knight of chivalry. s.serif, "without serif." s.souci, "without worry"; condition of indifference or carefreeness.

santonin(e) (san'tənin), *n.* anthelmintic extracted from wormwood or derived from naphthalene.

sapajou (sap'əjoo; *Fr.,* -zhoo') Fr. *n.* capuchin or spider monkey.

saphena (səfē'nə), *n.* one of two main superficial veins of leg. -nous, *adj.*

sapid (sap'id), *adj.* pleasantly-flavoured; having flavour; agreeable. -ity, *n.*

sapient (sā'piənt, sap'-), *adj.* wise; pretending to be wise. -ial (-en'shəl), *adj.* providing wisdom. -nce, *n.*

ə=*er* in *father*; ə̄=*er* in *pert*; th=*th* in *thin*; dh=*th* in *then*; zh=*s* in *pleasure*; k=*ch* in *loch*; ń=Fr. nasal *n*; ü=Fr. *u*.

sapodilla (sapədil'ə), *n.* large tropical evergreen chicle-yielding tree ; naseberry.

saponaceous (sapənā'shəs), *adj.* soapy ; slippery. **-nification,** *n.* act of making (into) soap ; hydrolysis of a fat.

sapour (sā'pə), *n.* flavour. **-porific,** *adj.* having flavour. **-porous,** *adj.* tasty ; pleasant in taste.

sapota (səpō'tə), *n.* sapodilla. **-ceous,** *adj.* pert. to or like s. ; belonging to s. family of trees.

Sapphic (saf'ik), *adj.* pert. to Sappho, anct. Gr. poetess of Lesbos, and her love poems ; erotic. **-phism,** *n.* homosexuality in women. **-s,** *n.* verses by, or like in form those of, Sappho.

sapraemia (saprē'miə), *n.* bloodpoisoning with bacterial products in blood. **-mic,** *adj.*

saprodontia (saprədon'shiə), *n.* decay of teeth.

saprogenic (saprəjen'ik), *adj.* causing decay ; produced in decaying matter. **-nous** (-oj'inəs), *adj.*

sapropel (sap'rəpel), *n.* ooze composed mainly of decaying organic matter. **-ic,** *adj.* living in s. **-ite,** *n.* coal formed of s.

saprophagous (saprof'əgəs), *adj.* feeding on decaying matter. **-philous,** *adj.* flourishing in decaying matter.

saprophyte (sap'rəfīt), *n.* plant living on dead or decaying matter. **-tic** (-it'ik), *adj.* **-tism,** *n.*

saprostomous (sapros'təməs), *adj.* having foul breath.

saprozoic (saprəzō'ik), *adj.* app. to animals living on dead or decaying matter.

sapsago (sap'səgō), *n.* hard green Swiss cheese.

sapwood (sap'wood), *n.* soft tissues immediately beneath bark of tree.

saraband(e) (sar'əband), *n.* stately Sp. dance.

sarafan (sar'əfahn), *n.* national dress of Russ. peasant woman.

sarangousty (sarəngōō'sti), *n.* waterproof stucco.

sarcenet (sah'snit), *n.* soft lining silk fabric ; *adj.* soft ; gentle.

sarcoid (sah'koid), *adj.* flesh-like ; *n.* formation of nodules in skin, leaving scars. **-ooline,** *adj.* fleshcoloured. **-cology,** *n.* anatomy of flesh.

sarcoma (sahkō'mə), *n.* (*pl.* **-ta**) fleshy tumour. **-toid,** *adj.* like s. **-tosis,** *n.* condition of having s. **-tous,** *adj.*

sarcophagus (sahkof'əgəs), *n.* (*pl.* **-gi**) coffin of stone. **-gal,** *adj.* **-gous,** *adj.* feeding on flesh ; like a s. **-gic** (-aj'ik), *adj.* feeding on flesh. **-philous,** *adj.* fond of flesh.

sarcoptid (sahkop'tid), *n.* itch mite. **-tic,** *adj.*

sarcotic (sahkot'ik), *n.* & *adj.* (medicine) promoting growth of flesh.

sarcous (sah'kəs), *adj.* pert. to flesh or muscle.

sard (sahd), *n.* deep orangecoloured kind of chalcedony.

sardonic (sahdon'ik), *adj.* bitterly or evilly humorous ; grimly mocking. **-ism** (-sizm), *n.*

sardonyx (sahdon'iks), *n.* onyx with alternate layers of sard and other mineral.

sargasso (sahgas'ō), *n.* kind of floating seaweed ; gulfweed. **S.Sea,** area of N. Atlantic covered with mass of s.

sari (sah'ri), *n.* Hindu women's robe.

sarmentum (sahmen'təm), *n.* (*pl.* **-ta**) *Bot.* runner. **-taceous,** **-tiferous, -tose, -tous,** *adj.* producing s.

sarong (sarong'), *n.* Malayan skirtlike garment, of long strip cloth wound round body.

sarrusophone (sarus'əfōn), *n.* double-reeded bassoon-like mus. instr.

sarsaparilla (sahspəril'ə), *n.* kind of smilax ; drink made from its root or with its flavour.

sarsenet, *see* sarcenet.

sartorial (sahtor'iəl), *adj.* pert. to tailoring or men's clothes.

sassafras (sas'əfras), *n.* kind of laurel and its root-bark, used medicinally.

sassenach (sas'ənak), Scot. *n.* Saxon; Englishman; Lowland Scot.

satiate (sā'shiāt), *v.t.* fill to brim; cloy ; glut ; *adj.* surfeited. **-tient,** *adj.* causing satiety. **-tiety** (sətī'iti), **-tion,** *n.*

satisdation (satisdā'shn), *n.* Law, security, or the giving of it.

satrap (sat'rap), *n.* anct. Pers. ruler of province ; despot, *espec.* in petty position. **-al,** *adj.* **-y,** *n.*

saturnalia (satənā'liə), *n.pl.* anct. Rom. festival in honour of Saturn ; orgy. **-n,** *adj.*

saturnine (sat'ənīn), *adj.* melancholy ; *Med.,* pert. to lead poisoning. **-ninity,** *n.* **-nism,** *n.* lead poisoning.

satyr (sat'ə), *n.* half-animal follower of Bacchus, in anct. myth. ; obscene or bestial man. **-esque,** *adj.* **-ess,** *n.* female s. **-iasis,** *n.* insatiable sexual desire in male. **-io** (-ir'ik), *adj.* **-ism,** *n.* uncontrolled licentiousness.

sauerkraut (sow'əkrowt), Ger. *n.* pickled salted cabbage.

saurian (sōr'iən), *n. & adj.* (animal) belonging to order including crocodiles, lizards, etc. **-rophagous,** *adj.* eating lizards.

sauterelle (sōtərel'), Fr. *n.* mason's angle-making instr.

sauve qui peut (sōv kē pə'), Fr. "(let him) save (himself) who can" ; every man for himself ; rout.

savannah (səvan'ə), *n.* open grassy plain of tropical Amer.

savant (sav'ahn), Fr. *n.* learned man.

savarin (sav'ərań), Fr. *n.* ring-shaped cake tin.

savoir faire (sav'wahr fār'), Fr., "to know how to do" ; knowledge of correct action ; tact ; adroitness. **s.vivre** (-vē'vr), "to know how to live" ; good behaviour or breeding.

saxatile (saks'ətīl), *adj.* pert. to or living in rocks. **-xicavous,** *adj.* boring into rocks. **-xicole, -xicoline, -xigenous,** *adj.* growing in rocks. **-xifrage,** *n.* kind of rock plant. **-xifragous,** *adj.* breaking stone.

scaberulous (skəber'ūləs), *adj.* bearing small raised roughnesses.

scabies (skā'bēz), *n.* the itch ; mange. **-etic** (-iet'ik), *-ious, adj.* pert. to s. or scabs.

scabrous (skrā'brəs), *adj.* having rough or scurfy surface ; scaly ; full of difficulties ; risqué ; obscene. **-rate,** *adj.* **-rescent,** *adj.*

scaberulous. **-rid,** *adj.* somewhat s. **-rities,** *n.* scabby skin condition.

scacchic (skak'ik), *adj.* like or pert. to chess.

scagliola (skalyō'lə), It. *n.* stone-like plasterwork for interior decoration. **-list,** *n.*

scalar (skā'lə), *adj.* like a ladder ; denotable by a number. **-iform** (-ar'ifawm), *adj.* like a ladder.

scalene (skalēn', skā'-), *adj. Geom.,* not equilateral ; *n.* such triangle. **-nous,** *adj.*

scallion (skal'yən), *n.* shallot ; leek.

scalpel (skal'pəl), *n.* thin-bladed surg. knife. **-llic** (-el'ik), *adj.*

scalpriform (skal'prifawm), *adj.* like chisel in shape.

scammony (skam'əni), *n.* kind of convolvulus of Near East, with root yielding resin used as purge. **-niate** (-ō'niət), *adj.*

scanderoon (skandərōōn'), *n.* kind of homing pigeon.

scandent (skan'dənt), *adj.* climbing.

scansion (skan'shn), *n.* determination of metre of verse ; prosody.

scansorial (skansōr'iəl), *adj.* climbing ; used for climbing.

scantling (skant'ling), *n.* small amount ; small beam ; trestle.

scaphion (skā'fiən), *n.* kind of sundial. **-phism** (skaf'-), *n.* mode of execution by smearing criminals with honey and exposing them to insects.

scaphoid (skaf'oid), *adj.* boat-shaped ; such bone of carpus or tarsus.

scapiform (skā'pifawm), *adj.* like a stalk. **-poid,** *adj.* **-pose,** *adj.* bearing stalks.

scapula (skap'ūlə), *n.* (*pl.* **-ae**) shoulder-blade. **-r,** *adj.* ; *n.* bandage for s. ; cowl-bearing part of monk's habit ; badge, worn over shoulders, of monastic order ; feather on bird's shoulder. **-ry,** *n. & adj.* scapular ; shoulder strap.

scarab(aeus) (skar'ab, -ē'əs), *n.* large black Mediterranean dung beetle, held sacred by anct. Egyptians ; gem cut in shape of s. **-aeiform,** *adj.* like s. **-aeoid,** *n.* image of s. **-boid,** *n. & adj.* (gem) like s.

scaramouch (skar'əmōōsh, -owch), *n.* ne'er-do-well.

scarify (skar'ifī), *v.t.* scratch ; cut ; scar. **-fication, -ficator, -fier,** *n.*

scarious (skār'iəs), *adj.* thin and tough ; bract-like. **-iose,** *adj.*

scaroid (skār'oid), *n. & adj.* (fish) like parrot fish, or belonging to parrot fish family of fishes.

scarp (skahp), *n.* steep drop ; cliff ; *v.t.* make steep.

scarpetti (skahpet'i), It. *n.pl.* hemp-soled climbing shoes.

scatology (skatol'əji), *n.* study of excrement or obscenity. **-gic(al),** *adj.* **-tophagous,** *adj.* eating dung. **-toscopy** *n.* examination of faeces.

scaturient(skətūr'iənt), *adj.* gushing.

scaurie (skōr'i, -ah'ri), Scot. *n.* young gull.

scazon (skā'zon), *n.* limping verse; choliamb. **-tic,** *adj.*

scelalgia (selal'jiə), *n.* pain in leg. **-lotyrbe** (-tə'bi), *n.* hesitation in walking; paralysis of legs.

scenario (sinär'iō), *n.* outline or description of scenes, characters, etc., *espec.* of film-play. **-rist,** *n.*

scenography (sinog'rəfi), *n.* representation of object in perspective. **-ph, -pher,** *n.* **-phic(al),** *adj.*

Schadenfreude (shah'dnfroidə), Ger. *n.* glee at others' misfortunes.

schapska (shap'skə), *n.* flat-topped cavalry helmet.

schediasm (shē'diazm), *n.* impromptu action. **-stic,** *adj.*

schematograph (skimat'əgraf), *n.* instr. tracing reduced outline of person. **-tonics,** *n.* art of gesture expressing tones, etc.

schesis (skē'sis), *n.* rhet. device of weakening force of opponent's arguments by reference to his habit of thought.

schiller (shil'ə), *n.* & *adj.* (having) bronzy lustre. **-ise,** *v.t.*

schipperke (ship'əki, sk-), *n.* small black Belgian canal-boat dog.

schism (sizm), *n.* division, *espec.* of church, into two parties. **-atic(al),** *adj.* pert. to or causing s. **-atise,** *v.i.* & *t.* **-atism,** *n.*

schist (shist), *n.* foliated metamorphic crystalline rock. **-aceous,** *adj.* slate-coloured. **-ic, -ose,** *adj.* **-oid,** *adj.* like s.

schizocarp (skiz'əkahp), *n.* compound fruit splitting into several one-seeded ones. **-ic, -ous,** *adj.* **-zogenesis, -zogony,** *n.* reproduction by division. **-zoid,** *adj.* pert. to, like or suffering from schizophrenia. **-zophrenia,** *n.* mental disorder with "splitting" of personality and separation from environment. **-zothymia,** *n.* schizophrenia-like mental disorder. **-zotrichia,** *n.* splitting of hair. **-stic,** *adj.* pert. to or marked by splitting.

schlenter (shlen'tə), S. African *n.* & *adj.* imitation (diamond).

Schloss (shlos), Ger. *n.* (*pl.* Schlösser) castle.

schnapps (shnaps), *n.* strong Hollands gin.

schnauzer (shnow'zə), *n.* blackish Ger. terrier.

Schnörkel (shnaw'kl; Ger., shnə̄'-), Ger. *n.* wide tube for taking in air and expelling exhaust gases, projected above surface from submerged submarine.

schoenabatic (skēnəbat'ik), *adj.* pert. to rope-walking. **-tist** (-ob'ətist), *n.*

scholium (skō'liəm), *n.* (*pl.* **-ia**) marginal note, *espec.* by anct. grammarian. **-liast,** *n.* writer of s.

schooner (skōō'nə), *n.* two-masted fore-and-aft rigged vessel; large beer-measure.

schorl (shawl), *n.* tourmaline. **-aceous, -ous, -y,** *adj.*

schottische (shotēsh'), *n.* polka-like 19th-cent. dance.

scialytic (sīəlit'ik), *adj.* dispelling shadows. **-iagraphy,** *n.* art of shading; X-ray photography. **-iamachy,** *n.* mock battle; fighting with shadows or imaginary enemies. **-iapodous,** *adj.* with large feet. **-iatheric,** *adj.* pert. to measurement of time by shadow, as in sundial.

sciatic (sīat'ik), *adj.* pert. to hip. **-a,** *n.* neuralgia of hip and thigh.

scibile (sib'ili), *n.* thing which it is possible to know.

scientia (sien'shiə), Lat. *n.* science; knowledge. **s. scientiarum,** "science of sciences"; philosophy.

scilicet (skī'liset), Lat. *adv.* "that is to say"; namely (*abbr.* **sc.**).

scintilla (sintil'ə), *n.* (*pl.* **-ae**) spark; atom. **-ant,** *adj.* sparkling. **-lescent,** *adj.* twinkling. **-lometer,** *n.* instr. measuring scintillation of star. **-te,** *v.i.* sparkle. **-tion,** *n.*

sciolism (sīəlizm), *n.* pretence to wisdom; conceit due to it. **-ist,** *n.* **-istic,** *adj.*

sciomancy (sī'əmansi), *n.* divination by reference to spirits of dead. **-ntic,** *adj.*

scion (sī'ən), *n.* young member of family; shoot of plant, *espec.* taken for grafting.

sciophilous (sīof'iləs), *adj.* app. to

shade-loving plants. **-phyte**, *n.* such plant.

scioptic (sīop'tik), *adj.* pert. to formation of images in darkened room, as in camera obscura. **-s**, *n.* **-tric**, *adj.*

scirrhus (skir'əs), *n.* (*pl.* **-hi**) hard tumour. **-hoid**, *adj.* like s. **-hous**, *adj.*

scissile (sis'īl), *adj.* easily cut or split. **-sion**, *n.* act of cutting or dividing; schism.

scissure, **-ra** (sish'ə, -izh'ə; -sūr'ə), *n.* cleft; fissure; scission.

sciuroid (sī ūr'oid), *adj.* like a squirrel or a squirrel's tail. **-romorphic**, *adj.* like or pert. to squirrels; belonging to squirrel division of rodents.

sclera (sklēr'ə), *n.* dense white coat of eyeball. **-l**, *adj.* **-rectomy**, *n.* removal of s. **-rema**, *n.* induration. **-renchyma**, *n.* thickened and woody tissue of plants. **-riasis**, *n.* induration, *espec.* of edge of eyelid.

scleroderma (sklerədə'mə, sklēr-), *n.* disease marked by hardening of skin. **-mic**, **-mous**, **-tous**, *adj.* hard-skinned; having bony armour.

sclerogenous (skliroj'inəs), *adj.* producing hard tissue. **-nic** (-jen'ik), *adj.* **-roid** (sklēr'-), *adj.* indurated. **-roma**, *n.* induration. **-rometer**, *n.* instr. measuring hardness. **-ronychia**, *n.* hardening of nails.

sclerosis (sklerō'sis), *n.* (*pl.* **-ses**) hardening. **-rotic** (-ot'ik), *adj.* hard; pert. to sclera; *n.* sclera. **-rotitis**, *adj.* inflammation of sclera. **-rotomy**, *n.* incision into sclera. **-rous** (sklēr'-), *adj.* hard.

scobiform (skō'bifawm, skob'-), *adj.* like sawdust.

scolex (skō'leks), *n.* (*pl.* **-leces**) head of tapeworm. **-leciasis**, *n.* infestation with tape-worms. **-lecid**, *adj.* **-leciform**, *adj.* like s.

scoliometer (skōliom'itə), *n.* instr. measuring curvature. **-ographic**, *adj.* marked by oblique lines. **-osis**, *n.* lateral spinal curvature.

scolopaceous (skoləpā'shəs), *adj.* snipe-like. **-cine**, *adj.* belonging to snipe family of birds.

scombriform (skom'brifawm), *adj.* like mackerel; belonging to mackerel division of fishes. **-broid**, *n.* & *adj.* (fish) like mackerel.

scopate (skō'pāt), *adj.* brush-like.

scopic (skop'ik), *adj.* visual.

scopolamine (skəpol'əmēn, -lam'in, -mēn'), *n.* sleep-inducing drug obtained from nightshade family of plants.

scopulate (skop'ūlət), *adj.* brush-like.

scorbutic (skawbū'tik), *n.* & *adj.* (person) suffering from scurvy; pert. to or like scurvy.

scoria (skor'iə), *n.* (*pl.* **-ae**) slag; slag-like mass of lava. **-c**, **-ceous**, **-rious**, *adj.* **-riform**, *adj.* like s. **-rify**, *v.t.* reduce to s.

scorpioid (skaw'pioid), *adj.* scorpion-like; curved at end.

scortation (skawtā'shn), *n.* fornication. **-tory**, *adj.*

scoter (skō'tə), *n.* black sea duck; coot.

scotodinia (skotədin'iə, skō'-), *n.* dizziness together with headache and loss of vision. **-tograph**, *n.* instr. for writing without seeing; X-ray photograph. **-toma**, *n.* (*pl.* **-tomata**) blind spot. **-tophobia**, *n.* dread of darkness. **-topia**, *n.* seeing in dark. **-toscope**, *n.* instr. detecting objects in darkness.

scow (skow), *n.* large blunt-ended, flat-bottomed boat; refuse lighter.

scrannel (skran'əl), *adj.* weak; thin; harsh-sounding.

scree (skrē), *n.* steep slope with loose soil and stones.

scriniary (skrin'iəri), *n.* keeper of archives.

scrip (skrip), *n.* *Comm.*, document showing entitlement to receive something; share certificate, *espec.* preliminary issued on payment of first instalment; certificate transferable into share issued as dividend.

scriptitious (skriptish'əs), *adj.* like handwriting. **-tory**, *adj.*

scriptorium (skriptor'iəm), *n.* (*pl.* **-ia**) writing room, *espec.* of scribes in medieval monastery. **-ry**, *n.*

scripturient (skriptūr'iənt), *n.* having violent desire to write. **-ncy**, *n.*

scrivello (skrivel'ō), *n.* elephant's tusk.

scrivener (skriv'inə), *n.* writer-out of documents; lawyer. **s.'s palsy**, writer's cramp. **-y**, *n.*

scrobiculate (skrəbik'ūlət), *adj.* pitted. **-le**, **-lus**, *n.* small depression. **-lus cordis**, pit of stomach.

scrofula (skrof'ūlə), *n.* tuberculous condition, *espec.* of children, with enlargement of lymphatic glands of neck; king's evil. **-lism, -losis,** *n.* **-litic, -lous,** *adj.*

scrophulariaceous (skrofūlāriā'shəs), *adj.* pert. to or like figwort: belonging to figwort family of plants, which includes veronica, antirrhinum, etc.

scrotum (skrō'təm), *n.* (*pl.* **-ta**) bag of flesh containing testicles. **-tal,** *adj.* **-tiform,** *adj.* pouch-shaped.

scrutator (skrōōtā'tə), *n.* one who scrutinises or investigates. **-tineer,** *n.* person scrutinising votes. **-tinise,** *v.t.* examine carefully. **-tiny,** *n.* such examination.

scullion (skul'yən), *n.* scullery servant; washer of dishes; *adj.* menial; wretched.

sculpsit (skulp'sit), *Lat.,* "carved (it)"; "engraved (it)."

scupper (skup'ə), *n.* gap in ship's bulwarks for drainage of water.

scurrilous (skur'iləs), *adj.* abusive; ribald; obscene. **-lity,** *n.*

scurvy (skə'vi), *n.* disease, due to deficiency of vitamin C, marked by skin haemorrhage, anaemia, spongy gums, etc.

scutal (skū'təl), *adj.* pert. to shield. **-tate,** *adj.* shield- or buckler-shaped; having horny scales. **-te, -tum,** *n.* large scale, as of reptile's head. **-tella,** *n.* (*pl.* **-ae**) small scute. **-tellate, -tulate,** *adj.* shaped like platter; covered with scutellae. **-telligerous,** *adj.* bearing scutellae. **-tiferous,** *adj.* bearing a shield or scutes. **-tiform,** *adj.* shield-shaped. **-tigerous,** *adj.* bearing scutes.

scyphate (sī'fāt), *adj.* cup-shaped. **-phiform,** *adj.*

scytodepsic (sītədep'sik), *adj.* pert. to tanning of leather.

séance (sā'ahns), Fr. *n.* meeting; session; gathering of spiritualists and medium, to receive spirit messages.

sebaceous (sibā'shəs), *adj.* fatty; greasy; secreting oily substance. **-borrhagia, -borrhoea** (seb-), *n.* excessive secretion of sebaceous glands. **-bum** (sē'-), *n.* fatty substance secreted by sebaceous glands.

sebundy (sibun'di), *n.* irregular Ind. soldier(s).

secant (sē'kənt, sek-), *n.* & *adj.* cutting (line), *espec.* one cutting curve at two points; radius produced through one end of arc to meet tangent drawn to other end; ratio of this line to radius (*abbr.* **sec.**).

secateurs (sekətēz'), *n.pl.* pruning shears; wire-cutters.

secco (sek'ō), It. *n.* painting on dry plaster.

secern (sisən'), *v.i.* & *t.* secrete; separate; discriminate. **-ent,** *n.* & *adj.* (thing) secreting or causing secretion. **-ment,** *n.*

secodont (sek'ədont), *adj.* having cutting teeth.

secque (sek), *n.* light sabot; clog.

secreta (sikrē'tə), *n.pl.* products of secretion. **-gogue,** *n.* stimulant of secretion.

secretaire (sekritār'), *n.* writing desk.

secrete (sikrēt'), *v.t.* conceal; discharge; emit. **-tion,** *n.* act of secreting; thing or substance secreted, *espec.* from bodily glands. **-tional, -tionary, -tory,** *adj.*

secretum (sikrē'təm), *n.* (*pl.* **-ta**) private seal.

sectarian (sektār'iən), *n.* & *adj.* (person) belonging to religious sect; bigot(ed). **-ry,** *n.*

sectile (sek'til, -il), *adj.* capable of being cut, *espec.* cleanly; cut into small divisions. **-lity,** *n.*

sector (sek'tə), *n. Geom.* figure bounded by two radii and the arc which they include; math. instr. of two rulers jointed together; astron. angle-measuring instrument; *Mil.,* area of operations. **-ial,** *adj.* pert. to s.; adapted for cutting; *n.* such tooth.

secular (sek'ūlə), *adj.* worldly; non-religious; not belonging to religious order; lasting for centuries; occurring once in a century. **-ise,** *v.t.* makes s. **-ity,** *n.*

secund (sē'kənd), *adj.* on one side only. **-iflorous,** *adj.* having such flowers.

secundipara (sekəndip'ərə), *n.* woman having had two child-deliveries. **-rous,** *adj.* **-rity** (-ar'iti), *n.*

secundogeniture (sikundəjen'itūr), *n.* state of being second eldest child; custom whereby such child inherits parent's property.

---

hat, bah, hāte, hāre, crawl; pen, ēve, hēre; it, īce, fīre; on, bōne, boil, bōre, howl; foot, fōōd, bōōr, hull, tūbe, pūre.

secundum (sikun'dəm), Lat. *prep.*, "according to". **s.legem**, according to law.

securiform (sikūr'ifawm), *adj.* axe-shaped. **-rigerous**, *adj.* bearing an axe.

secus (sē'kəs), Lat. *adv.* "otherwise."

sedative (sed'ətiv), *n. & adj.* soothing (drug). **-tion**, *n.*

sedent (sē'dənt), *adj.* in sitting position.

sedentary (sed'əntəri), *adj.* habitually sitting; done while sitting; stationary. **-tation**, *n.*

sederunt (sidēr'ənt), *Lat.*, "they sit"; session of court; gathering; long discussion.

sedilia (sidī'liə), *n.pl.* (*sing.* **-le**) clergy's stone seats in chancel wall.

sedition (sidish'n), *n.* incitement to rebellion. **-ary, -tious**, *adj.*

seduce (sidūs'), *v.t.* lead away or astray; entice; violate chastity of. **-ction**, *n.* **-ctive**, *adj.*

sedulous (sed'ūləs), *adj.* taking great care; assiduous. **-lity**, *n.*

seersucker (sēr'sukə), *n.* light puckered linen or cotton fabric.

segregate (seg'rigāt), *v.t.* separate from fellows; set or place apart; *n. & adj.* segregated (species). **-tion**, *n.*

seiche (sāsh), *n.* rocking movement of surface of lake or inland sea.

seichento (sāchen'tō), It. *n. & adj.* 17th century.

Seidel (zī'dl), Ger. *n.* large beer mug with lid.

seigneur (sānyər'), *n.* lord, *espec.* of manor. **-ial, -niorial, -norial**, *adj.* **-niorage, -nioralty, -niory, -y**, *n.* lordship; dominion; brassage; mining royalty.

seine (sān), *n.* large vertical fishing net; *v.i. & t.* catch (fish) with s.

seisin (sē'zin), *n.* freehold possession of land.

seismic (sīz'mik, sīs'-), *adj.* pert. to earthquakes. **-ity**, *n.* **-mal, -matical, -metic**, *adj.* **-mism**, *n.* s. phenomena. **-mograph**, *n.* instr. recording earthquakes. **-mology**, *n.* study of earthquakes. **-mometer**, *n.* sort of seismograph measuring movements of ground in earthquake. **-moscope**, *n.* instr. merely showing occurrence of earthquake. **-motectonic**, *adj.* pert. to geol. features related to

earthquakes. **-motherapy**, *n.* med. treatments by vibrations. **-motic**, *adj.* causing earthquakes.

seity (sē'iti), *n.* personality; "self-ness."

seizin, *see* seisin.

sejant (sē'jənt), *adj. Her.*, sitting.

sejugate (sej'oogāt, -jōō'-), *v.t.* separate.

selachian (silā'kiən), *n. & adj.* (fish) like shark or ray; belonging to shark family of fishes; a shark or ray

selah (sē'lə), Heb. *n.* pause; kind of mus. sign of Psalms.

selenian (silē'niən), *adj.* lunar. **-nic** (-en'ik), *adj.* like the moon. **-nite** (sel'-), *n.* dweller on moon; kind of gypsum. **-nitic**, *adj.* pert. to or affected by moon. **-nocentric**, *adj.* pert. to moon's centre; having moon as centre. **-nography**, *n.* study of moon's surface. **-nology**, *n.* study of moon. **-nomancy**, *n.* divination by the moon. **-noscope**, *n.* instr. for viewing moon.

selliform (sel'ifawm), *adj.* saddle-shaped. **-late**, *adj.* having saddle.

sememe (siman'tēm), *n.* word expressing an idea, as a noun. **-tic**, *adj.* pert. to meaning. **-tics, -tology**, *n.* science of meanings of words.

semasiology (simāsiol'əji), *n.* semantics. **-gical**, *adj.* **-gist**, *n.*

sematic (simat'ik), *adj.* warning. **-tography**, *n.* writing in signs and not letters. **-tology**, *n.* semantics.

sematrope (sem'ətrōp), *n.* heliograph.

semeiography, -mio- (sēmīog'rəfi), *n.* description of signs or symptoms. **-ology**, *n.* study or art of signs or symptoms. **-on**, Gr. *n.* (*pl.* **-eia**) either division of metrical foot. **-otic**, *adj.* pert. to signs or symptoms.

semelincident (seməlin'sidənt), *adj.* occurring only once in same person.

semen (sē'men), *n.* (*pl.* **-mina**, sem'inə) seed; whitish fluid carrying sperms, in reproduction.

semester (simes'tə), Amer. *n.* academic half-year.

semibreve (sem'ibrēv), *n. Mus.*, longest generally used note, having twice length of minim and half that of breve.

---

semic (sē'mik), *adj.* pert. to a sign.
seminal (sē'minəl, sem'-), *adj.* pert.
to semen ; pert. to first thing or
basic principle ; reproductive ;
pregnant. -nar, *Amer. n.* class of
post-graduate students ; tutorial
session. -nary, *n.* school, *espec.*
for training R.C. priests ; place of
origin. -nation, *n.* sowing of seed.
-native, *adj.* producing growth.
-niferal, -niferous, -nific(al), *adj.*
producing seed or semen. -ni-
vorous, *adj.* seed-eating. -nule, *n.*
small seed ; spore.
semioviparous (semiōvip'ərəs), *adj.*
bringing forth young in incompletely developed state.
semiped (sem'iped), *n.* half a
metrical foot. -al, *adj.*
semiquote (sem'ikwōt), *n.* single
quotation mark or inverted comma (' ').
semitaur (sem'itōr), *n.* myth. creature, half-man and half-bull.
semper (sem'pə), *Lat. adv.*
"always." **s.**fidelis, "always
faithful." **s.**idem (*fem.* **s.**eadem),
"always the same."
sempiternal (sempitə'nəl), *adj.*
eternal. -nity, *n.*
senary (sē'nəri), *adj.* having six as
base ; six-fold. -rius, *n.* (*pl.* -rii)
verse of six feet.
senectitude, -ctude (sinek'titūd,
-tūd), *n.* old age. -ctuous, *adj.* old.
senescent (sines'ənt), *adj.* growing
old. -nce, *n.*
seneschal (sen'ishəl), *adj.* steward,
espec. of anct. palace or manor.
senicide (sē'nisīd), *n.* killing off of
old men.
senile (sē'nīl), *adj.* pert. to, or
characteristic of, old age. -lism,
-lity (-il'iti), *n.*
sennight (sen'īt), *n.* week.
sennit (sen'it), *n.* plaited rope,
straw, etc.
senocular (sinok'ūlə), *adj.* having
six eyes.
sententia (senten'shiə), *n.* (*pl.* -ae)
aphorism ; opinion. -ry, *n.*
speaker of s. -tious, *adj.* aphoristic ; full of aphorisms ; pom-
pously moralising.
sentient (sen'shiənt), *adj.* capable
of feeling. -nce, *n.*
sentisection (sentisek'shn), *n.* vivisection without use of anaesthetic.
sepal (sep'əl, sē'-), *n.* portion of
calyx. -ine, -oid, *adj.* like s.

sepia (sē'piə), *n.* cuttle-fish; inky
secretion of cuttle-fish ; rich brown
pigment obtained from s. -pic
(sē'-, sep'-), *adj.* done in s. colour.
-rian, -ry, *n.* & *adj.* (pert. to)
cuttle-fish.
sepicolous (sipik'ələs), *adj.* dwelling in hedges. -piment (sep'-), *n.*
hedge.
sepoy (sē'poi), *n.* Ind. native soldier
or policeman.
sepsis (sep'sis), *n.* state of poisoning
in part of body or blood stream.
sept (sept), *n.* division of tribe ; clan.
septaemia (septē'miə), *n.* septicaemia.
septal (sep'tal), *adj.* pert. to sept.
septan (sep'tən), *n.* & *adj.* (fever)
recurring after seven days (*i.e.*
every sixth day).
septate (sep'tāt), *adj.* having septum. -tion, *n.*
septave (sep'tiv), *n.* seven-tone mus.
scale.
septemfluous (septem'flooəs), *adj.*
in seven streams. -foliate, *adj.*
having seven leaves.
septemplicate (septem'plikət), *n.*
one of seven copies.
septemvir (septem'və), *n.* member
of septemvirate. -ate, *n.* government by, or group of, seven men.
septenary (septē'nəri, sep'tin-), *adj.*
pert. to seven ; *n.* seven ; set of
seven. -nate, *adj.* divided into
seven portions.
septendecimal (septendes'iməl), *adj.*
pert. to seventeen.
septennary (septen'əri, -iəl),
adj. lasting for seven years ;
occurring every seven years. -nate,
-nium (*pl.* -nia), *n.* period of
seven years.
septentrional (septen'triənəl), *adj.*
pert. to north.-ity, *n.* -nic (-on'ik),
adj.
septic (sep'tik), *adj.* pert. or due to
decay, poisoning, or sepsis. -aemia
(-sē'miə), *n.* blood-poisoning with
presence of bacteria and their
toxins in blood. -ity (-is'iti), *n.*
-opyaemia, *n.* combination of
septicaemia and pyaemia.
septilateral (septilat'ərəl), *adj.* having seven sides.
septillion (septil'yən), *n.* a million
sextillions (10⁴⁸) ; *Amer. & Fr.*, a
thousand sextillions (10²⁴).
septimal (sep'timəl), *adj.* pert. to
seven.

---

septimanal (septimā'nəl), *adj.* weekly.

septisyllable (sep'tisiləbl), *n.* word of seven syllables. **-bic** (-ab'ik), *adj.*

septuagenarian, -ry (septūəjinār'iən, -jē'nəri), *n.* & *adj.* (person) in from seventieth to eightieth year.

Septuagesima (septūəjes'imə), *n.* third Sunday before Lent ; period of seventy days. **-l,** *adj.*

septuagint (sep'tūəjint), *n.* Greek version of Old Testament, supposedly translated by seventy scholars.

septum (sep'təm), *n.* (*pl.* **-ta**) partition. **-tulum,** *n.* (*pl.* **-la**) small s.

sepulchre (sep'oolkə), *n.* tomb. whited s., hypocrite ; seemingly holy but really evil person or thing. **-ral** (-ul'krəl), *adj.* pert. to s. ; gloomy ; hollow.

sepulture (sep'ooltūr), *n.* interment. **-ral** (-ul'tūrəl), *adj.*

sequacious (sikwā'shəs), *adj.* easily led or moulded ; servile ; logical. **-city** (-as'iti), *n.*

sequela (sikwē'lə), *n.* (*pl.* **-ae**) thing or person following ; consequence. **-lant,** *n.*

sequent (sē'kwənt), *adj.* following in sequence or as consequence. **-ial** (-en'shəl), *adj.*

sequester (sikwes'tə), *v.t.* set apart ; seclude. **-trate** (sē'-), *v.t.* confiscate ; set apart income of estate to meet claims. **-tration, -trator,** *n.*

sequitur (sek'witə), *Lat.,* "(it) follows" ; natural or logical consequence or deduction.

sequoia (sikwoi'ə), *n.* gigantic redwood or "big tree" of California.

sérac (serak'), *Fr. n.* ice pinnacle among glacier crevasses.

seraglio (serah'lyō), *n.* (*pl.* **-li,** -yē) harem ; palace of sultan.

serai (serī'), *n.* caravanserai ; seraglio ; *Anglo-Ind.,* long-necked water bottle.

serang (serang'), Anglo-Ind. *n.* boatswain of Lascar crew.

serape (serah'pi), *n.* Sp.-Amer. shawl.

seraph (ser'əf), *n.* (*pl.* **-im**) kind of angel. **-ic** (-af'ik), *adj.* angelic.

serendipity (serəndip'iti), *n.* propensity for finding things by chance or in unexpected places.

seriatim (seriā'tim), Lat. *adv.* in series ; point by point.

sericate, -ceous (ser'ikət, sirish'əs),

adj. silky ; bearing silky hairs. **-ctery,** *n.* caterpillar's silk-producing gland. **-culture,** *n.* breeding of silk-worms for silk production.

serif (ser'if), *n.* minute fine line, *espec.* horizontal, of a letter, as at top and bottom of verticals in "h".

serific (sirif'ik), *adj.* silk-producing. **-igraph, -imeter,** *n.* instr. for testing silk.

serin (ser'in), *n.* small finch.

serment (sē'mənt), *n.* oath.

sermuncle (sē'mungkl), *n.* short sermon.

serology (sirol'əji), *n.* study of serums. **-gic(al),** *adj.* **-gist,** *n.*

serositis (sērəsī'tis), *n.* inflammation of serous membrane. **-ty** (-os'iti), *n.* state of being serous ; serous fluid.

serotine (ser'ətin, -in), *n.* brown bat ; *adj.* serotinous.

serotinous (sirot'inəs), *adj.* flowering late.

serous (sēr'əs), *adj.* pert. to or like serum ; thin and watery ; producing such fluid.

serpette (sēpet'), Fr. *n.* kind of pruning knife.

serpiginous (səpij'inəs), *adj. Med.,* spreading by creeping. **-go** (-ī'gō), *n.* such disease ; ringworm.

serpivolant (səpiv'ələnt), *n.* flying serpent.

serpolet (sē'pəlit), *n.* wild thyme.

serrate (ser'āt), *adj.* having notched or toothed edge. **-dentate,** *adj.* having serrations which are themselves serrate. **-tic** (-at'ik), *adj.* like a saw. **-tion, -ture,** *n.*

serriferous (serif'ərəs), *adj.* having a saw-like organ. **-form,** *adj.* like a saw.

serrulate (ser'oolāt), *adj.* finely serrate. **-tion,** *n.*

serrurerie (serūr'ərē), Fr. *n.* wrought-iron work.

sertule, -lum (sē'tūl, -əm), *n.* umbel ; scientific collection of plants. **-tum,** *n.* treatise on such a collection.

serum (sēr'əm), *n.* (*pl.* **-s, -ra**) watery part of bodily fluid, *espec.* blood, separated in coagulation ; such fluid containing antibodies.

serval (sē'vəl), *n.* African wild cat and its fur. **-ine,** *adj.*

servile (sē'vīl), *adj.* pert. to or like a slave ; slavish ; cringing. **-lism,**

ə=*er* in *father* ; ẽ=*er* in *pert* ; th=*th* in *thin* ; dh=*th* in *then* ; zh=*s* in *pleasure* ; k=*ch* in *loch* ; ñ=Fr. nasal *n* ; ü=Fr. *u.*

n. slavery ; advocation of slavery. -lity (-il'iti), *n.*

servo-motor (sŏ'vŏmōtə), *n.* small auxiliary elec. motor operating a control, or carrying out subsidiary operation in a machine. **s.-mechanism**, *n.* machine having s.

sesame (ses'əmi), *n.* E. Ind. seed-yielding plant. **open s.**, spell opening door in story of Ali Baba and the Forty Thieves ; any master-key or magical command. **-moid**, *adj.* pert. to mass of bone or cartilage in a tendon, as knee-cap.

sesquialteral (seskwial'tərəl), *adj.* one and a half times as big ; having ratio 3 : 2. **-ran, -rate, -rous,** *adj.*

sesquicentennial (seskwisenten'iəl), *adj.* pert. to 150 years ; *n.* 150th anniversary.

sesquiduplicate (seskwidū'plikət), *adj.* having ratio of 2½ : 1. **-quinonal,** *adj.* having ratio 10 : 9. **-quioctaval,** *adj.* having ratio 9 : 8.

sesquipedalian (seskwipidā'liən), *adj.* a foot and a half long ; using very long words ; *n.* such thing or word. **-ism, -lity,** *n.*

sesquiquartal (seskwikwaw'təl), *adj.* having ratio 5 : 4. **-quintal,** *adj.* having ratio 6 : 5.

sesquiseptimal (seskwisep'timəl), *adj.* having ratio 8 : 7. **-sextal,** *adj.* having ratio 7 : 6.

sesquitertian (seskwitə'shən), *adj.* having ratio 4 : 3.

sessile (ses'īl, -il), *adj.* attached by base without a stalk ; attached permanently. **-lity,** *n.*

sestet (sestet'), *n.* sextet ; six-lined stanza ; final six lines of sonnet.

sestina (sestē'nə), *n.* (*pl.* -ne) poem of six-lined stanzas with six end-words repeated in each stanza and in the envoi.

seta (sē'tə), *n.* (*pl.* -ae) bristle ; any bristle-like organ. **-ceous** (sitā'shəs), *adj.* bristly. **-l,** *adj.* **-rious,** *adj.* like a bristle. **-tiferous,** *adj.* bearing bristles ; pert. to swine.

seton (sē'tən), *n.* thread passed under skin acting as channel for discharge.

setose (sē'tōs), *adj.* bristly.

settecento (setāchen'tō), It. *n.* & *adj.* 18th century.

setula (set'ūlə), *n.* (*pl.* -ae) small

seta. **-le,** *n.* **-liform,** *adj.* like s. **-lose, -lous,** *adj.* having s.

sève (sāv), Fr. *n.* wine's distinctive bouquet ; sap.

severy (sev'əri), *n.* compartment of vaulted ceiling.

sevum (sē'vəm), *n.* tallow.

sexadecimal (seksədes'iməl), *adj.* pert. to sixteen ; sixteenth.

sexagenarian (seksəjinār'iən), *n.* & *adj.* (person) in from sixtieth to seventieth year. **-ry** (-aj'inəri), *n.* ; *adj.* pert. to sixty ; proceeding by sets of sixty.

Sexagesima (seksəjes'imə), *n.* second Sunday before Lent. **-l,** *adj.* pert. to sixty.

sexcentenary (sekssentē'nəri), *adj.* pert. to six hundred (years) ; *n.* six hundredth anniversary.

sexenary (seks'inəri), *adj.* six-fold. **-xennial,** *adj.* lasting six years ; occurring every six years ; *n.* such occurrence. **-xennium,** *n.* (*pl.* -nia) period of six years.

sexipara (seksip'ərə), *n.* woman having had six child-deliveries. **-rous,** *adj.* **-rity** (-ar'iti), *n.*

sextain (seks'tān), *n.* sestina ; sestet.

sextan (seks'tən), *n.* & *adj.* (fever) recurring after six days (*i.e.* every fifth day).

sextant (seks'tənt), *n.* sixth part of circle ; naut. instr. with that arc for measuring altitudes.

sextennial (seksten'iəl), *adj.* sexennial.

sextern (seks'tən), *n.* quire of six sheets.

sextillion (sekstil'yən), *n.* a million quintillions (10³⁶) ; *Amer.* & *Fr.*, a thousand quintillions (10²¹).

sextodecimo (sekstədes'imō), *n.* book size : 5⅞ × 4¾ ins. (*abbr.* 16mo.).

sextumvirate (sekstum'virət), *n.* government by six men.

sforzando (sfortsan'dō), It. *adj.* *Mus.*, accented (*abbr.* **sf, sfz**).

sfumato (sfōomah'to), It. *adj.* misty.

sgraffito (zgrahfē'tō), It. *n.* pottery decoration by scratching through surface to reveal a differently-coloured ground.

shabash (shah'bahsh), Pers. *excl.* bravo !

shabrack (shab'rak), *n.* saddle-cloth.

shad (shad), *n.* deep-bodied herring-like marine fish, spawning in rivers.

---

shaddock (shad'ək), *n.* grape-fruit-like tree and fruit.

shadoof, -duf (shahdoof'), *n.* method of raising water in Egypt in a counterpoised bucket at end of a long pole.

shagreen (shəgrēn'), *n.* untanned leather bearing many small round protuberances, *espec.* dyed green ; shark-skin.

shagroon (shəgroon'), N.Z. *n.* original Eng. settler.

shahin (shahhēn'), Pers. *n.* kind of Ind. falcon.

shahzada(h) (shahzah'də), Hind. *n.* king's son.

shaitan (shātahn'), Arab. *n.* the Devil ; evil spirit ; *Ind.*, dust-storm.

shako (shəkō'), *n.* soldier's high crowned peaked cap.

shaksheer (shakshēr'), *n.* Oriental women's loose trousers.

shale (shāl), *n.* laminated rock of consolidated clay or mud.

shallop (shal'əp), *n.* light river boat with sail and oars.

shalom (shahlōm', shaw'-), Heb. *n.* peace (Jewish greeting). **a. alekhem** (-ahlā'kem), "peace be unto you."

shalwar, *see* **shulwar.**

shama (shah'mə), *n.* Ind. millet-like cereal ; Ind. song-bird.

shaman (shah'mən, sham'-), *n.* medicine man ; witch doctor. **-ess,** *n.* female s. **-ic,** *adj.* **-ism,** *n.* primitive religion in which s. are much venerated as having power to communicate with gods and spirits. **-istic,** *adj.*

shandrydan (shan'dridan), *n.* Irish two-wheeled cart ; any worn-out antique vehicle.

shanghai (shanghī'), *v.t.* drug and ship aboard a vessel as a sailor.

Shangri-La (shanggrēlah'), *n.* never-never land offering escape from world and daily anxieties ; the hidden Tibetan valley of James Hilton's novel *Lost Horizon.*

shard (shahd), *n.* piece of broken pottery ; elytrum.

shawm (shawm), *n.* anct. oboe-like mus. instr.

shea (shē), *n.* African tree with seeds yielding a white fat. **a. butter,** such fat.

sheading (shē'ding), *n.* administrative division of Isle of Man.

shearling (shēr'ling), *n.* one-year-old sheep, from which one crop of wool has been taken.

shearwater (shēr'wawtə), *n.* gull-like oceanic bird of the petrel family.

shebang (shibang'), Amer. *n.* hut ; outfit ; contrivance ; business.

shebeen (shibēn'), Ir. *n.* unlicensed liquor-selling place.

Sheol (shē'ol), Heb. *n.* Hell ; the underworld ; the grave. **-ic,** *adj.*

sherardise (sher'ədīz), *v.t.* coat with zinc by process invented by Sherard Cowper-Coles.

sherd (shēd), *n.* shard.

sherif (sherēf'), *n.* Arab prince ; Moham. ruler. **-ate,** *n.* s.'s jurisdiction or office. **-ian,** *adj.*

shibah (shib'ah), Heb. *n.* seven days' mourning.

shibboleth (shib'əleth), *n.* slogan ; watchword ; anything forming test of loyalty, nationality, etc., or distinguishing a party or denomination ; linguistic peculiarity. **-ic,** *adj.*

shikar (shikahr'), Anglo-Ind. *n.* hunting ; game ; *v.i.* & *t.* hunt (animal) as sport. **-ee, -i, -y,** *n.* native attendant on sportsmen.

shillelagh (shilā'lə), Ir. *n.* cudgel.

shingles (shing'glz), *n.* skin disease with clustering vesicles, due to nervous disorder or to chicken-pox virus.

shirakashi (shērəkah'shi), Jap. *n.* Jap. evergreen oak.

shogun (shō'goon), Jap. *n.* one of a series of Jap. mil. governors exercising imperial powers until 19th century. **-al,** *adj.* **-ate,** *n.*

shola (shō'lə), *n.* jungle of S. Ind.

shooldarry (shooldar'i), Anglo-Ind. *n.* small steep-roofed tent.

shrievalty (shrē'vəlti), *n.* sheriff's office or jurisdiction.

shrive (shrīv), *v.t.* give absolution to after confession.

shulwar (shulwahr'), *n.pl.* loose Oriental trousers.

shyster (shī'stə), Amer. *n.* dishonest lawyer ; swindler.

sial (sī'əl), *n.* siliceous rock ; outer part of earth's surface.

sialagogic (sīələgoj'ik), *n.* & *adj.* (substance) promoting salivation. **-gue,** *n.* **-lic,** *adj.* pert. to saliva. **-loid,** *adj.* like saliva.

sib (sib), *n.* kindred ; kinsman ;

brother or sister; descendants from a common ancestor; *adj.* blood-related.

sibilant (sib'ilənt), *n.* & *adj.* hissing (sound). **-late,** *v.i.* & *t.* pronounce like s. **-lation,** **-nce,** **-ncy,** *n.* **-latory, -lous,** *adj.*

sibling (sib'ling), *n.* one of several children of the same parents; brother or sister.

sic (sik), Lat. *adv.* "thus"; appearing thus in the original.

sicarian (sikar'iən), *n.* murderer.

siccation (sikā'shn), *n.* act of drying. **-tive,** *adj.*

siccimeter (siksim'itə), *n.* instr. measuring evaporation from liquid surface.

sice (sīs), Anglo-Ind. *n.* groom; horseman's foot attendant.

sideration (sidərā'shn), *n.* use of green manure.

sidereal (sīdēr'iəl), *adj.* pert. or according to stars; measured by stellar motion. **-ean,** *adj.* **-rism** (sid'-), *n.* belief in influence of stars on human affairs.

siderognost (sid'ərognost), *n.* instr. measuring magnetic intensity. **-graphy,** *n.* art of steel engraving, or copying such engravings.

sideromancy (sid'ərəmansi), *n.* divination by the stars.

sideroscope (sid'ərəskōp), *n.* instr. detecting presence of iron magnetically. **-rose,** *adj.* like or containing iron. **-rous,** *adj.* like iron. **-rurgy,** *n.* metallurgy of iron.

sidi (sē'di), *n.* African negro; African Moham. titie of respect.

sierra (sēer'ə), *n.* rugged mountain chain. **-n,** *adj.*

siesta (sēes'tə), Sp. *n.* short rest, *espec.* at midday.

sifflate (sif'ilāt), *v.t.* whisper.

siffleur (sēflēr'), Fr. *n.* (*fem.* **-euse,** -ēz') whistler.

sigil (sij'il), *n.* seal; image. **-llary, -llistic,** *adj.* **-llate,** *adj.* bearing seal-like marks; *v.t.* seal. **-llation,** *n.* **-llative,** *adj.* causing or tending to scar-formation. **-llography,** *n.* study of seals. **-llum,** *n.* (*pl.* **-lla**) seal, *espec.* of confession.

sigla (sig'lə), *n.pl.* signs representing words.

sigma (sig'mə), *n.* eighteenth letter (Σ, σ, s) of Gr. alphabet; thousandth part of second. **-te,** *adj.*

having shape of Σ or S; *v.t.* add -s in tense formation.

sigmoid (sig'moid), *adj.* S-shaped. **s.flexure,** such portion of intestine between descending colon and rectum.

signate (sig'nāt), *adj.* distinct; distinguished; having letter-like marks. **-tion,** *n.* act of signing. **-tory,** *n.* & *adj.* (person or state) who has signed a treaty, etc.

silage (sī'lij), *n.* green fodder preserved for winter in silo by fermentation.

silentiary (sīlen'shiəri), *n.* person maintaining or bound to silence; confidant; privy councillor.

silenus (sīlē'nəs), *n.* (*pl.* **-ni**) satyrlike woodland god; attendant of Bacchus; tipsy person.

silica (sil'ikə), *n.* pure flint. **-iceous** (-ish'əs), **-icic** (-is'ik), *adj.* **-icicolous,** *adj.* growing in flinty soil. **-iciferous,** *adj.* producing s. **-icify,** *v.t.* convert into s. **-icon,** *n.* very common non-metallic element, obtained from s. **-icone,** *n.* oily or plastic compound of silicon used in lubricants, polishes, paints, waterproofing, etc. **-icosis,** *n.* lung disease due to inhaling s. dust. **-te,** *v.t.* combine or coat with s.; *n.* salt of silicic acid.

sillabub (sil'əbub) *n.* cream, etc., curdled with wine, or whipped to stiff froth; frothy language or thing.

silladar (silədah'), Anglo-Ind. *n.* irregular cavalryman.

sillograph (sil'əgraf), *n.* writer of satires. **-er,** *n.*

sillometer (silom'itə), *n.* instr. measuring ship's speed.

silo (sī'lō), *n.* storage pit or building for silage.

silva, *see* **sylva.**

silvics (sil'viks), *n.* study of tree's life. **-cal,** *adj.* **-colous,** *adj.* living in woods. **-culture,** *n.* forestry.

sima (sī'mə), *n.* basic igneous rock.

simian (sim'iən), *n.* & *adj.* (like) ape or monkey. **-ity,** *n.* **-miad, -mial,** *adj.*

simile (sim'ili), *n.* lit. device of comparing one thing with another, using *like* or *as.* **-lia,** *n.pl.* similar things. **-liter,** Lat. *adv.* in similar manner.

simioid, -ious (sim'ioid, -əs), *adj.* simian.

simony (sī'məni), n. buying and selling of eccl. preferments. -niac (simō'niak), n. -niacal (-ənī'əkl), adj. -nism, -nist, n.

simoom (simōōm'), n. dry hot dusty wind of deserts.

simous (sī'məs), adj. having flat, upturned nose.

simulacrum (simūlā'krəm), n. (pl. -ra) image ; semblance ; vague likeness ; sham. -cral, adj.

simulate (sim'ūlāt), v.i. & t. pretend ; imitate. -tion, -tor, n. -tive, -tory, adj.

sinal (sī'nəl), adj. pert. to sinus.

sinapise (sin'əpīz), v.t. sprinkle ; powder. -ism, n. mustard-plaster.

sinciput (sin'sipoot), n. forehead ; part of head from crown to forehead. -pital (-sip'ital), adj.

sindon (sin'dən), n. fine linen fabric ; thing made of it, as altar frontal, winding-sheet, etc.

sine (sī'ni), Lat. prep. "without." s.die (-dī'ē), "without a day or date" ; indefinitely. s.mora, "without delay." s. qua non, "without which not" ; essential adjunct or condition.

sinecure (sī'nikūr), n. office involving no toil or duties. -ral, adj. -rist, n.

singhara (singgah'rə), n. Ind. water chestnut and edible nut.

singillatim (sinjilā'tim), Lat. adv. "singly."

singultus (singgul'təs), n. Med., hiccup(s). -tous, adj.

Sinicism (sin'isizm), n. Chinese peculiarity, etc. -cise, -nify, v.t. make Chinese. -nism, n.

sinistrad (sin'istrad), adv. towards left. -ral, adj. pert. to left ; left-handed ; illegitimate. -ration, n. -rogyrate, -rogyric, adj. moving to left. -romanual, adj. left-handed. -trorse, adj. turning spirally from right to left.

Sino- (sī'nō-, sin'-), prefix, Chinese. -gram, n. character in Chin. alphabet. -logy, n. study of Chin. history, literature, etc. -phile, n. lover or supporter of China.

sinter (sin'tə), n. iron dross ; Geol., deposit of hot siliceous springs ; v.i. & t. agglomerate by heating.

sinuate (sin'ūāt), adj. wavy ; v.i. curve. -tion, n.

sinus (sī'nəs), n. cavity, espec. of skull bone. -al, adj. -itis, -nitis, n. inflammation of s.

siphonogam (sī'fənəgam, -fon'-) n. seed plant. -ic, -ous (-og'əməs), adj.

sipid (sip'id), adj. sapid. -ity, n.

sircar (sə'kah), Anglo-Ind. n. Ind. Government or its head ; steward of house ; native accountant.

sirdar (sə'dah), n. Brit. general commanding Egyptian army.

siren (sīr'ən), n. sweet-singing female deity in Gr. myth., carrying off souls of sailors ; seductive or enticing woman ; hooter. -ian (-ē'niən), -ic(al) (-en'ik, -l), adj.

siriasis (sirī'əsis), n. sunstroke. -riometer, n. Astron., unit of distance, equiv. of one million times mean distance of earth from sun.

sirocco (sirok'ō), n. hot wet, or dry dusty, southerly wind of Italy, etc., blowing from N. Africa.

sisal (sī'səl), n. fibre of Amer. aloe. s.-kraft, board made of compressed s. fibre.

sise (sīs), n. six, espec. on dice.

siskin (sis'kin), n. small green-yellow Eur. finch.

sissoo (sis'ōō), n. E. Ind. tree with hard timber and leaves used as fodder.

Sisyphean (sisife'ən), adj. pert. to Sisyphus, in Gr. myth. king of Corinth, condemned in underworld to roll huge stone to top of hill from which it constantly fell back ; laborious and fruitless ; endless.

sitology (sītol'əji), n. treatise on food or diet ; science of diet. -otoxism, n. vegetable-food poisoning.

sitringee (sitrin'jē), Anglo-Ind. n. striped cotton carpet.

sittine (sit'īn, -in), adj. pert. to or like a nuthatch ; belonging to nuthatch family of birds.

sitz (sits), adj. app. to bath in which one bathes sitting.

siwash (sī'wosh), n. Alaskan dog like Eskimo dog.

sizar (sī'zə), n. Cambridge under-graduate receiving allowance for expenses from college. -ship, n.

sjambok (sham'bok), S. African n. heavy whip ; v.t. flog with it.

skald (skawld), n. anct. Scand. bard.

skat (skat), n. card game for three persons, resembling solo whist.

skatology, *see* **scatology.**

skean (shkēn), Gael. *n.* dagger.

s.dhu (-dhōō), Scot. Highlander's dagger.

skelic (skel'ik), *adj.* pert. to skeleton. **s.index,** figure resulting from division of length of leg by length of trunk.

skeuomorph (skū'əmawf), *n.* ornament representing vessel or tool. **-ic,** *adj.*

skewbald (skū'bawld), *adj.* bearing patches of white and some colour not black.

skijoring (skējōr'ing, shē-), *n.* sport of being drawn on skis over snow by horse or motor.

skoal (skōl), Nor. *n.* "cup"; good health!

skua (skū'ə), *n.* jaeger.

sloid, -yd (sloid), *n.* Swed. system of manual training, *espec.* in wood-carving.

smalt (smawlt), *n.* deep-blue pigment.

smalto (zmahl'tō), It. *n.* (*pl.* **-ti**) piece of coloured glass in mosaic.

smaragd (smar'agd), *n.* emerald. **-ine,** *adj.*

smectic (smek'tik), *adj.* purifying.

smegma (smeg'mə), *n.* soapy matter of sebaceous gland. **-tic,** *adj.* like soap; cleansing.

smew (smū), *n.* smallest merganser.

smilax (smī'laks), *n.* green-brier; *erron.,* S. African greenhouse plant with bright green leaves.

smithsonite (smith'sənīt), *n.* natural zinc carbonate; calamine.

smörgåsbord (smä'gosbōōrd), Swed. *n.* large variety of hors d'oeuvres, meat, fish, etc., served from buffet.

snaffle (snaf'l), *n.* light bridle bit.

snell (snel), *n.* short line with which fish-hook is fastened to line.

snood (snōōd), *n.* snell; hair net.

soboles (sob'əlēz), *n. Bot.,* sucker; shoot. **-liferous,** *adj.* producing s.

sobriquet, soub- (sō'brikā, sōō'-), *n.* nickname.

sociology (sōsiol'əji), *n.* study of human society. **-ocracy,** *n.* government by society as a whole. **-ogenesis,** *n.* evolution or origin of human societies.

socius (sō'shiəs), *n.* (*pl.* **-ii**) member; companion; associate; individual. **s.criminis,** accomplice in crime.

socle (sok'l), *n. Archit.,* moulded

member at base of plinth or pedestal.

Socratic (səkrat'ik), *adj.* pert. to Socrates, Gr. philosopher, and his method of argument. **S.irony,** method of argument by pretending ignorance and asking seemingly simple questions in order to draw opponent into making errors or rash statements. **S.method,** instruction by asking questions.

sodality (sədal'iti), *n.* association; union; brotherhood. **-list** (sō'-), *n.* member of s.

sodomy (sod'əmi), *n.* unnatural sexual intercourse. **-mite,** *n.* **-mitical,** *adj.*

soffit (sof'it), *n. Archit.,* underside of auxiliary part of building, as arch, staircase, etc.

soi-disant (swah'dēzahn'), *Fr.,* "calling himself"; self-styled; would-be.

soigné (swah'nyā), Fr. *adj.* (*fem.* **-ée**) "carefully done"; well-groomed.

soirée (swah'rā), Fr. *n.* "evening"; evening party.

soka (sō'kə), Hind. *n.* blight; drought.

sola (sō'lə), *n.* Ind. plant with stems containing pith. **s.topi** (-tō'pi), sun-helmet made of s. pith.

solan (sō'lən), *n.* gannet.

solanaceous (solənā'shəs), *adj.* pert. to or like a potato or nightshade plant; belonging to the potato or nightshade family of plants. **-neous,** *adj.*

solano (səlah'nō), *n.* hot East wind of Mediterranean Sp. coast.

solarise (sō'lərīz), *v.i.* & *t.* expose to sunlight; subject to or be affected by solarisation. **-sation,** *n.* reversal of gradation sequence in photog. image after very long or intense exposure.

solaristics (sōləris'tiks), *n.* study of relation between sun and its radiation and earth.

solarium (səlār'iəm), *n.* (*pl.* **-ia**) room, porch, etc., exposed to sunshine.

solatium (səlā'shiəm), *n.* (*pl.* **-ia**) compensation, *espec.* for hurt feelings.

soldan (sol'dən), *n.* sultan; Moham. ruler.

solecism (sol'isizm), *n.* ignorant

error. **-ise,** *v.i.* **-ist,** *n.* **-istic(al),** *adj.*

soleiform (sələ'ifawnɪ), *adj.* shaped like a slipper.

solenitis (solinī'tis), *n.* inflammation of duct.

solenium (sələ'niəm), *n.* stolon. **-ial,** *adj.*

solenoid (sō'linoid), *n.* tubular coil of wire producing magnetic field. **-al,** *adj.* pert. to s. or tube.

solfatara (solfahtah'rah), It. *n.* vent for sulphurous volcanic gases. **-ric,** *adj.*

solfeggio (soltej'ō), *n.* (*pl.* **-gi**) tonic sol-fa system or scale.

solidago (solidā'go), *n.* golden rod plant.

solidum (sol'idəm), *n.* total ; pedestal's dado.

solidungular, -late, -lous (solidung'-gūlə, -ət, -əs), *adj.* having single hoof on each foot.

solidus (sol'idəs), *n.* (*pl.* **-di**) oblique line (/) used to separate shillings and pence, or in fractions (as 3/4 for ¾).

solifidian (solifid'iən), *n.* believer that faith alone will ensure salvation. **-ism,** *n.*

soliform (sō'lifawm), *adj.* sun-like.

soliloquy (səlil'əkwi), *n.* act of talking to oneself ; speech made thus. **-quise,** *v.i.* **-quist,** *n.*

soliped (sol'iped), *n.* & *adj.* solidungular (animal). **-al, -ous** (-ip'idəl, -əs), *adj.*

solipsism (sol'ipsizm), *n.* belief that all reality is subjective, or that the self can know no more than its own states. **-al,** *adj.* **-sist,** *n.*

soliterraneous (soliterā'niəs), *adj.* pert. to sun and earth, *espec.* their joint meteorological effect. **-tidal,** *adj.* pert. to tides caused by sun.

solivagant, -gous (səliv'əgənt, -əs), *adj.* wandering alone.

solmisate (sol'mizāt), *v.i.* & *t.* sing or set to sol-fa notation. **-tion,** *n.*

solonist (sō'lənist), *n.* wise man.

solstice (sol'stis), *n.* point or time when sun is furthest from Equator. **summer s.,** such time in summer in N. lats. (about June 22). **winter s.,** such time in winter (about Dec. 22). **-titial,** *adj.*

solus (sō'ləs), Lat. *adj.* "alone."

solute (sol'ūt), *n.* in a solution, the substance which is dissolved.

solvent (sol'vənt), *adj.* Comm.,

able to pay debts ; *Chem.,* dissolving ; *n.* such substance. **-ncy,** *n.* **-volysis,** *n.* decomposition of dissolved substance.

soma (sō'mə), *n.* E. Ind. vine with milky juice ; anct. Ind. drink made from it ; *Anat.,* (*pl.* **-ta**) whole of body excluding limbs. **-l, -tic,** *adj.* pert. to body or trunk. **-tasthenia,** *n.* bodily weakness. **-tism,** *n.* materialism. **-tognosis,** *n.* diagnosis of bodily conditions. **-tology,** *n.* study or doctrine of properties of substances ; anthropological study of structure, etc., of human body. **-topsychic,** *adj.* pert. to person's ideas of or attitude towards his own body.

sommelier (som'əlyā), Fr. *n.* butler ; wine waiter ; cellarman.

somnambulate (somnam'būlāt), *v.i.* walk in one's sleep. **-lic, -listic,** *adj.* **-lism, -list,** *n.*

somnifacient (somnifā'shənt), *n.* & *adj.* soporific. **-ferous,** *adj.* inducing sleep. **-niloquence, -niloquy,** *n.* talking in one's sleep. **-nipathy,** *n.* hypnotic sleep.

somnolent (som'nələnt), *adj.* sleepy ; causing, or resembling, sleep. **-lescent,** *adj.* becoming s. **-nce,** *n.* **-norific,** *adj.* soporific.

sonant (sō'nənt), *adj.* sounding ; *Phon.,* voiced. **-al, -ic,** *adj.* **-nable,** *adj.* capable of being sounded. **-nce,** *n.*

sonata (sənah'tə), *n.* instr. composition in three or more movements. **s. da camera,** chamber s. **s. da chiesa,** church s. **-tina,** *n.* short s.

sonation (sənā'shn), *n.* sounding. **-ndation,** *n.* sounding, *espec.* by boring, of the earth.

sonderclass (son'dəklahs), *n.* class of small yachts.

soneri (son'əri, sō'-), Anglo-Ind. *n.* cloth of gold.

sonic (son'ik), *adj.* pert. to sound waves. **-niferous,** *adj.* producing sound. **-nification,** *. n.* act of producing sound.

sonorescent (sonəres'ənt), *adj.* emitting sound under influence of some radiation. **-nce,** *n.*

soojee (sōō'jē), *n.* flour from Ind. wheat.

sophiology (sofiol'əji), *n.* science of ideas. **-gic,** *adj.*

sophism (sof'izm), *n.* deceptive or fallacious argument. **-ist,** *n.* fallacious arguer. **-istic(al)**, *adj.* **-isticate**, *v.i.* make artificial or worldly; corrupt. **-istry**, *n.* s., or use of s.; mere empty argument.

sophomore (sof'əmōr), Amer. *n.* college student in second year. **-ic**, *adj.* adolescent; immature; pompous.

soporific (sopərif'ik), *n.* & *adj.* (drug) inducing sleep. **-ferous**, *adj.* **-rose**, *adj.* sleepy.

soral (sōr'əl), *adj.* pert. to sorus.

sorbefacient (sawbifā'shənt), *n.* & *adj.* (substance) promoting absorption.

sorbile (saw'bīl), *adj.* that can be sipped or drunk.

sordes (saw'dēz), *n.* foul or excreted matter. **-dor**, *n.* refuse; sordidness.

sorghum (saw'gəm), *n.* kind of tropical forage grass, yielding syrup. **-go**, *n.* sweet s.

soricid (sor'isid), *n.* & *adj.* (pert. to) shrew (animal). **-cine**, *adj.* pert. to or like a shrew. **-ent** (-is'idənt), *adj.* having teeth like shrew's.

sorites (səri'tēz), *n.* series of syllogisms following one from another, with the first and last closely linked; collection of facts, things, etc.; heap. **-tic(al)** (-it'ik, -l), *adj.*

sororal (sərōr'əl), *adj.* pert. to sisters. **-ricide**, *n.* killing or killer of own sister. **-rity**, *n.* sisterhood; *Amer.*, club of college girls.

sorosis (sərō'sis), *n.* kind of fruit in which many flowers are united, as in pineapple.

sortes (saw'tēz), Lat. *n.pl.* (*sing.* **sors**) lot; drawing lots. **s. Vergilianae**, divination by reference to book of Virgil's poems opened at random.

sortie (saw'tē), *n.* sally by beleaguered troops.

sortilege (saw'tilej, -ij), *n.* divination by casting lots; witchcraft; enchantment. **-gic, -gious** (-lē'jik, -əs), *adj.* **-r**, *n.*

sortition (sawtish'n), *n.* casting of, or assignment by, lots.

sorus (sōr'əs), *n.* cluster of spore cases on fern fronds; "fruit dots."

soterial (sətēr'iəl), *adj.* pert. to salvation. **-riology**, *n.* theol. study of salvation; treatise on hygiene.

sottise (sotēz'), Fr. *n.* stupid or blundering act.

sotto voce (sot'ō vō'chi), *It.*, "under the voice"; in a whisper or undertone; secretly.

sou (soo), *n.* former Fr. coin, one-twentieth part of franc.

soubise (soobēz'), *n.* onion sauce.

soubrette (soobret'), *n.* role of light-hearted or coquettish girl in drama; actress playing such part.

soubriquet, *see* **sobriquet**.

soucar (sow'kah), *n.* Hindu usurer or banker.

souchong (soo'shong), *n.* high grade black Chin. tea; coarse Ind. or Ceylon tea.

soufflé (soo'flā), *adj.* decorated with scattered spots of colour; puffed out by cooking; *n.* such light dish; any light, delicate mixture.

soupçon (soop'sawn), Fr. *n.* "suspicion"; faint flavour or trace.

sousaphone (soo'zəfōn), *n.* large-bellied, bass brass instr. with circular horn placed round player's body.

soutane (sootahn'), *n.* R.C. priest's cassock.

soviet (sov'iet), *n.* Russ. workers' council. **-ic**, *adj.* **-ise**, *v.t.* **-ism, -ist**, *n.*

sovkhoz (sov'koz), *n.* Russ. co-operative farm.

sowar (sowahr'), Anglo-Ind. *n.* native cavalryman or mounted policeman, etc. **-rry**, *n.* high official's mounted follower; mounted guard or retinue.

soya (soi'ə), *n.* kind of Asiatic bean, yielding meal, flour and oil, and used as forage.

spadassin (spad'əsin; Fr., spadasan'), Fr. *n.* swordsman; fighter.

spadiceous (spədish'əs), *adj.* chestnut-coloured; pert. to spadix. **-cifloral, -ciflorous**, *adj.* having flowers in a spadix. **-cose**, *adj.* **-dix**, *n.* (*pl.* **-dices**) flower-spike covered by large leaf, as of arum plant.

spado (spā'dō), *n.* (*pl.* **-nes**) impotent person; castrated animal.

spahi (spah'hē), *n.* Algerian cavalryman in Fr. army.

spanaemia (spənē'miə), *n.* anaemia. **-mic**, *adj.*

spandrel (span'drəl), *n.* triangular space between curve of arch and right angle enclosing it; design in corner of postage stamp.

---

hat, bah, hāte, hāre, crawl; pen, ēve, hēre; it, īce, fīre; on, bōne, boil, bōre, howl; foot, food, boor, hull, tūbe, pūre.

spanopnoea (spanopnē'ə), *n.* slow deep breathing as a morbid condition.

sparadrap (spar'ədrap; Fr., spa-radra'), *n.* med. plaster.

spargosis (spahgō'sis), *n. Med.*, swelling.

sparoid (spar'oid), *adj.* pert. to or like sea bream.

sparsim (spah'sim), Lat. *adv.* "here and there."

Spartacist (spah'təsist), *n.* member of Ger. socialist party formed in 1918; any extreme socialist. -ism, *n.*

Spartan (spah'tən), *adj.* pert. to anct. Sparta, famous for its severity and discipline; hardy; harsh; fearless.

spastic (spas'tik), *adj. Med.*, pert. to or marked by spasms; *n.* person, *espec.* child, suffering from s. paralysis. -ity, *n.*

spatchcock (spach'kok), *n.* roughly prepared and cooked fowl; *v.t.* prepare and cook as a s.; interpolate unnecessarily or inappropriately; patch in or together.

spathe (spādh), *n.* large sheath-like bract or leaf, as of arum plant. -thaceous, -thal, -those, -thous, *adj.*

spatiate (spā'shiāt), *v.i.* ramble; saunter. -tion, *n.*

spatiotemporal (spāshiōtem'pərəl), *adj.* pert. to or having space and time.

spatula (spat'ūlə), *n.* broad thin flexible knife. -liform, -lose, -r, -te, *adj.* like s.

spavin (spav'in), *n.* tumour on horse's leg. bog-s., s. on hock. bone-s., bony outgrowth on hock.

spay (spā), *v.t.* render (female animal) sterile.

specie (spē'shiē), *n.* coined money.

specific (spisif'ik), *adj.* definite; distinct; special; pert. to or characterising a species; *n.* remedy for a certain disease. s.gravity, ratio of weight of a substance to weight of equal volume of water. s.heat, ratio of amount of heat required to raise temperature of substance or body one degree to that required to raise temperature of equal mass of water one degree; amount of heat required to raise one gram of a substance one degree Centigrade.

specious (spē'shəs), *adj.* plausible; superficial. -ciosity, *n.*

spectrum (spek'trəm), *n.* (*pl.* -ra) series of images, colours, etc., formed when ray of radiant energy is dispersed into its component parts. -robolograph, *n.* photog. record of lines of infra-red s. -rogram, *n.* representation of a s. -rograph, *n.* instr. showing s. -roheliogram, *n.* photograph of sun. -rohelioscope, *n.* instr. for making observations or spectro-heliograms of sun. -rology, *n.* chem. analysis by means of s. -rometer, *n.* instr. measuring refractive indices, and wavelengths of rays of a s. -roscope, *n.* instr. for forming s. by dispersing ray. -roscopy, *n.* production and study of s.

speculum (spek'ūləm), *n.* (*pl.* -la) mirror; reflector; instr. for examining body passages; coloured patch on bird's wing. -lae, *adj.*

Speisekarte (ɛ̄hpī'zəkahrtə), Ger. *n.* menu.

spelaean, -lean (spilē'ən), *adj.* pert. to or living in caves. -leology (spēliol'əji), *n.* study and exploration of caves. -leologist, *n.*

spelt (spelt), *n.* kind of wheat.

spelter (spel'tə), *n.* zinc.

speluncar, -cean (spilung'kə, -un'siən), *adj.* pert. to or like a cave.

sperm (spəm), *n.* seed; male reproductive element or fluid; spermatozoon or semen.

spermaceti (spəməsē'ti), *n.* wax-like substance used in candles, ointments, etc., obtained from oil of sperm-whale, etc.

spermatic (spəmat'ik), *adj.* pert. to or like sperm. -tise, *v.t.* impregnate with sperm. -tism, *n.* emission of sperm. -toblast, *n.* sperm-producing cell. -tocyte, *n.* cell producing spermatozoa. -to-genesis, *n.* formation of spermatozoa. -toid, *adj.* like sperm. -torrhoea, *n.* involuntary and frequent spermatism. -tozoon, *n.* (*pl.* -oa) male sexual cell, which fertilises egg.

spermology (spəmol'əji), *n.* bot. study of seeds. -gical, *adj.* -gist, *n.*

spermophile (spē'məfīl), *n.* gopher.

sphacel (sfas'əl), *n.* gangrene. **-ate**, *v.i.* & *t.* affect with gangrene; mortify; *adj.* gangrenous. **-ation**, **-ism**, *n.* **-oderma**, *n.* s. of skin. **-ous**, *adj.* **-us**, *n.* gangrene; necrosis.

sphagnum (sfag'nəm), *n.* (*pl.* **-na**) peat or bog moss. **-nicolous**, *adj.* growing in s. **-nology**, *n.* study of s. **-nous**, *adj.*

sphenic (sfen'ik), *adj.* wedge-shaped; *Math.*, having three different prime numbers as its factors. **-nocephaly**, *n.* state of having s. head. **-nogram** (sfē'-), *n.* cuneiform character. **-nography**, *n.* art of using or interpreting sphenograms. **-noid** (sfē'-), *adj.*

spheroid (sfēr'oid), *n.* sphere-like figure. **-al**, **-ic**, *adj.* **-rometer**, *n.* instr. measuring curvature. **-rule** (sfer'ool), *n.* small sphere or s.

sphincter (sfingk'tə), *n.* ring-like muscle closing body passage. **-al**, **-ial**, **-ic**, *adj.* **-ate**, *adj.* having s.; contracted as if by s.

sphingal (sfing'gəl), *adj.* like sphinx.

sphingid (sfin'jid), *n.* hawk moth. **-giform**, **-gine**, *adj.* like s. or sphinx.

sphragistic (sfrəjis'tik), *adj.* pert. to or like a seal. **-s**, *n* study of seals.

sphygmic (sfig'mik), *adj.* pert. to pulse (of heart). **-mochronograph**, *n.* instr. recording pulse. **-modic**, *adj.* pulsating. **-mograph**, *n.* instr. recording pulse of artery. **-moid**, *adj.* like a pulse. **-mology**, *n.* study of pulse. **-momanometer**, *n.* instr. registering blood pressure. **-mophone**, *n.* instr. for hearing the pulse. **-mus**, *n.* *Med.*, the pulse.

spicate (spī'kāt), *adj.* having, like or in a spike. **-cal**, **-cant**, **-ciferous**, **-ciform**, **-cigerous**, **-cose**, **-cous**, *adj.* having spikes. **-cula**, **-cule** (spik'-), *n.* small spike; small spiky body in sponges and similar creatures.

spigot (spig'ət), *n.* bung; plug of a tap; end of smaller pipe when inserted into larger one to form a junction.

spikenard (spīk'nahd), *n.* anct. sweetly scented ointment; Ind. plant yielding it.

spiloma (spīlō'mə), *n.* birthmark; naevus. **-lus**, *n.* (*pl.* **-li**) naevus.

spinaceous (spinā'shəs), *adj.* pert. to or like spinach; belonging to spinach family of plants.

spindrift (spin'drift), *n.* sea spray.

spinel (spin'əl), *n.* ruby-like precious stone.

spinescent (spines'ənt), *adj.* becoming or tending to be spiny; tapering. **-nce**, *n.*

spinnaker (spin'əkə), *n.* large triangular sail on side opposite mainsail.

spinneret (spin'əret), *n.* insect's or spider's silk-spinning organ.

spinthariscope (spinthar'iskōp), *n.* instr. demonstrating the emission of alpha rays by radium compound.

spintherism (spin'thərizm), *n.* seeing of sparks before the eyes.

spiracle (spīr'əkl), *n.* air-hole. **-cular** (-ak'ūlə), *adj.* **-culate**, **-culiferous**, *adj.* having s.

spirant (spīr'ənt), *n.* & *adj.* (consonant) pronounced with friction of breath against part of mouth, as *f* or *s.* **-rate**, *adj.* voiceless. **-ration**, *n.* act of breathing.

spirochaete (spīr'ōkēt), *n.* spirally-moving, disease-producing organism. **-taemia**, *n.* presence of s. in blood. **-ticide**, *n.* substance killing s. **-tosis**, *n.* infection by s.

spirograph (spīr'əgraf), *n.* instr. recording movements of breathing. **-gram**, *n.* record made by s. **-rometer**, *n.* instr. recording volume of air taken in by lungs, or volume of gas.

spirulate (spir'ūlət), *adj.* spirally arranged.

spissated (spis'ātid), *adj.* thickened. **-situde**, *n.*

splanchnic (splangk'nik), *adj.* visceral. **-nology**, *n.* study of viscera. **-nopathy**, *n.* disease of viscera. **-notomy**, *n.* incision into viscera.

spleen (splēn), *n.* gland-like organ near stomach, concerned in blood-cell production; malice; anger. **-lenetic** (-inet'ik), *adj.* ill-tempered; crabbed. **-lenic** (-en'ik), *adj.* pert. to s. **-lenisation**, *n.* congestion of tissue which becomes spleen-like. **-lenitive** (-en'itiv), *adj.* fiery; splenetic.

spodium (spō'diəm), *n.* bone charcoal. **-dogenic**, **-dogenous**, *adj.* pert. to or due to waste matter. **-domancy**, *n.* divination by study of ashes.

spokeshave (spōk'shāv), *n.* plane or knife for rounding spokes or spoke-like objects.

spoliation (spōliā'shn), *n.* pillage. -tive, *adj.* robbing; diminishing. -tor, *n.* robber. -tory, *adj.*

spondee (spon'dē), *n.* metrical foot of two long syllables. -daic (-ā'ik), -dean, *adj.*

spondyl(e) (spon'dil), *n.* vertebra. -lexarthrosis, *n.* displacement of s. -lic, -lous, *adj.* -litis, *n.* inflammation of s. -lotherapeutics, *n.* med. treatment by manipulating spine.

sponsion (spon'shn), *n.* act of taking pledge or becoming surety for a person.

sponson (spon'sən), *n.* projection from side of ship, as protection, gun platform, etc.

spontaneous (spontā'niəs), *n.* occurring without external impulse; unconstrained; natural. -neity (-ənē'iti), *n.*

sporadic (spərad'ik), *adj.* occurring in isolated and scattered instances. -dism (spōr'ədizm), -ity, *n.*

sporangium (spəran'jiəm), *n.* (*pl.* -gia) spore case or receptacle of ferns, fungi, etc. -gial, *adj.* -giferous, *adj.* having s. -giform, *adj.* like s. -giophore, *n.* stalk bearing s.

spore (spōr), *n.* plant's or protozoan's reproductive body. -riferous, *adj.* producing s. -rocarp, *n.* body producing s. -rogenesis, *n.* reproduction by, or production of, s. -rogony, *n.* reproduction by spores. -rophorous, *adj.* sporiferous. -rophyll, *adj.* sporiferous leaf. -rophyte, *n.* spore-bearing phase of plant. -rozoan, *n.* parasitic spore-producing kind of protozoan.

sporulate (spōr'oolāt), *v.i.* & *t.* form (into) spores. -le, *n.* small spore. -liferous, *adj.* producing sporules. -loid, *adj.* like a sporule. -tion, *n.*

sprew, -eeuw (sprōō, -ā'ōō), S. African *n.* African starling.

springbok (spring'bok), S. African *n.* white-striped and -rumped S. African gazelle.

sprue (sprōō), *n.* tropical inflammatory disease of digestive tract.

spruit (sprōō'it, sprīt), S. African *n.* small stream flowing only in wet season.

spumescent (spūmes'ənt), *adj.* foaming; foamy. -nce, *n.*

sputum (spū'təm), *n.* saliva or mucus spat out. -tative, *adj.* habitually spitting.

squab (skwob), *n.* young pigeon; nestling.

squadrism (skwod'rizm), *n.* government by armed squadrons of supporters or party members.

squaliform (skwā'lifawm), *adj.* shark-shaped. -loid, *adj.* like a shark.

squamaceous (skwəmā'shəs), *adj.* scaly. -mate, -meous, -mose, -mous, *adj.* like, having or covered with scales. -mellate, -melliferous, -mulate, -mulose, *adj.* having small scales. -moid (skwā'moid), *adj.* like a scale.

squatinid (skwat'inid), *n.* & *adj.* (pert. to an) angelfish.

squill (skwil), *n.* sea onion, used as expectorant, etc.

squinancy (skwin'ənsi), *n.* wild plant believed to cure quinsy.

squinch (skwinch), *n.* arch, etc., across corner of room.

Stabat Mater (stah'bat mah'tə, stā'bat mā'tə), Lat., "the mother stood"; hymn describing the Virgin Mary at the Cross.

stabile (stā'bil, stab'-), *adj.* stationary. -lise, -litate, *v.t.* make stable.

staccato (stakah'tō), *adv.* & *adj.* Mus., with notes sharply separated.

stactometer (staktom'itə), *n.* glass for measuring drops.

stadimeter (stədim'itə), *n.* kind of sextant. -diometer, *n.* kind of theodolite; wheel by which length of line is measured.

stagiary (stā'jiəri), *n.* resident canon; law student.

Stagirite (staj'irīt), *n.* native or inhabitant of anct. Stagira, Macedonia; Aristotle. -tic (-it'ik), *adj.*

stagmometer (stagmom'itə), *n.* device for measuring number of drops in certain volume of liquid.

stagnicolous (stagnik'ələs), *adj.* living in stagnant water.

Stakhanovism (stəkah'nəvizm), *n.* Russ. voluntary system of increasing production through hard work, efficiency, teamwork, and competition. -vite, *n.* worker honoured for success in the system.

stalactite (stal'əktīt), *n*. icicle-like lime deposit hanging from roof of cave. **-tic, -tital, -titic,** *adj.* **-tiform, -tiliform,** *adj.* like a s. **-tilious,** *adj.* with s.

Stalag (stal'ahg), Ger. *n.* (*abbr.* of *Stammlager*) prisoner-of-war camp for non-commissioned officers and men.

stalagmite (stal'əgmīt), *n.* lime deposit rising from floor of cave. **-mometer,** *n.* drop-measuring instr. **-itic(al)** (-it'ik, -l), *adj.*

stamen (stā'mən), *n.* (*pl.* **-mina**) flower's pollen-bearing organ, comprising filament and anther. **-minal,** *adj.* **-minate,** *adj.* having s. **-mineal, -mineous,** *adj.* pert. to or having s.

stanchion (stahn'shən), *n.* upright support or post.

stanhope (stan'əp), *n.* high four-wheeled driving carriage.

stannary (stan'əri), *n.* tin-mine or -works. **-nic,** *adj.* pert. to tin ; *Chem.*, in which tin has valency of four. **-nous,** *adj.* pert. to tin ; *Chem.*, in which tin has valency of two.

stapes (stā'pēz), *n.* innermost bone of ear ; stirrup bone. **-pedectomy,** *n.* removal of s. **-pedial,** *adj.* pert. to s. **-pediform,** *adj.* like a s. or stirrup.

staphylic (stəfil'ik), *adj.* pert. to alveolar arch. **-lorrhaphy,** *n.* surg. union of cleft palate.

stasis (stā'sis), *n.* (*pl.* **-ses**) stoppage in circulation ; stagnation.

static (stat'ik), *adj.* motionless ; in equilibrium ; Amer. atmospherics. **-s,** *n.* study of bodies and forces in equilibrium.

statist (stā'tist), *n.* statistician.

statistics (stətis'tiks), *n.* compilation or study of classified facts or figures. **-cal,** *adj.* **-cian** (statistish'ən), *n.* student of s.

stator (stā'tə), *n.* stationary part of motor.

statoscope (stat'əskōp), *n.* kind of aneroid barometer recording minute barometric changes.

status quo (ante), *see* in statu quo (ante).

staurolatry (storol'ətri), *n.* worship of the cross or crucifix.

stavesacre (stāv'zākə), *n.* kind of larkspur, from which ointment for lice is obtained.

staxis (staks'is), *n.* haemorrhage.

stearin (stē'ərin), *n.* hard fat. **-ric** (-ar'ik), *adj.* **-riform,** *adj.* like s. **-rrhoea,** *n.* seborrhoea.

steatite (stē'ətīt), soapstone. **-tic** (-tit'ik), *adj.* **-togenous,** *adj.* fat-producing. **-topathic,** *adj.* pert. to disease of sebaceous glands. **-topygic** (-əpij'ik), **-topygous** (-əpī'gəs), *adj.* having excessively fat buttocks. **-tosis,** *n.* adiposity.

stechados (stek'ədos), *n.* Fr. lavender.

steganography (steganog'rəfi) *n.* cryptography.

stegnosis (stegnō'sis), *n.* constipation. **-notic** (-ot'ik), *n.* & *adj.* (medicine) causing c.

stein (stīn), Ger. *n.* large earthenware beer-mug.

steinbok (stīn'bok), *n.* small S. African antelope.

stele (stē'li), *n.* (*pl.* **-lae**) carved or painted stone pillar or slab ; central part of plant's stem. **-lar,** *adj.*

stella (stel'ə), Lat. *n.* "star." s.maris, "star of the sea" ; Virgin Mary. s.polaris, Pole Star. **-liferous,** *adj.* having many stars. **-lify,** *v.t.* place among stars ; glorify. **-lular,** *adj.* like a star ; having star-like spots. **-r,** *adj.* **-te,** *adj.* star-like.

stenocardia (stenəkah'diə), *n.* angina pectoris. **-c,** *adj.* **-cephaly,** *n.* narrowness of head. **-chromy,** *n.* printing of many-coloured pattern at one impression.

stenography (stenog'rəfi), *n.* shorthand. **-pher,** *n.* **-phic,** *adj.*

stenometer (stenom'itə), *n.* distance-measuring instr.

stenopaic, -paeic (stenəpā'ik, -pē'ik), *adj.* with narrow aperture. **-petalous,** *adj.* with narrow petals. **-phyllous,** *adj.* with narrow leaves.

stenosis (stinō'sis), *n.* narrowing of an orifice. **-notic** (-ot'ik), *adj.* **-otypy,** *n.* phonetic script in ordinary characters.

stentor (sten'tor), *n.* loud-voiced person. **-ian, -ious, -ophonic,** *adj.*

stercoraceous (stəkerā'shəs), *adj.* pert. to dung. **-ral, -rous,** *adj.* **-rary** (stə'kərəri), *n.* place for dung. **-ricolous,** *adj.* living in dung.

stereobate (ster'iəbāt), *n.* basement, etc., of building above ground. **-tic** (-at'ik), *adj.*

---

stereochemistry (stēriəkem'istri), *n.* chem. study of arrangement of molecules and atoms.

stereochromy (stēr'iəkrōmi), *n.* kind of wall painting. **-me**, *n.* **-mic**, *adj.*

stereognosis (stēriəgnō'sis), *n.* ability to perceive weight, form, etc., of a body. **-stic**, *adj.*

stereography (stēriog'rəfi), *n.* representation of solid bodies on plane surface. **-gram**, *n.* representation giving impression of solidity of object. **-ph**, *n.* picture used in stereoscope. **-phic**, *adj.*

stereometry (stēriom'itri), *n.* measurement of volumes, etc., of solid figures. **-tric(al)** (-et'rik, -l), *n.*

stereomonoscope (stēriəmon'əskōp), *n.* instr. projecting image with appearance of solidity, by means of two lenses.

stereophonic (stēriəfon'ik); *adj.* denoting system of sound recording and reproduction of life-like fidelity, using several separate loudspeakers, etc.

stereoplasm (stēr'iəplazm), *n.* solid protoplasm.

stereopsis (stēriop'sis), *n.* stereoscopic vision.

stereoscope (stēr'iəskōp), *n.* instr. with two lenses combining images of two almost identical pictures to give effect of solidity and distance. **-pic** (-op'ik), *adj.* pert. to s. or stereoscopy. **-py** (-os'kəpi), *n.* use of the s.; seeing or representation of objects with the effect of solidity and distance.

stereostatic (stēriəstat'ik), *adj.* geostatic. **-s**, *n.* statics of solids.

stereotomy (stēriot'əmi), *n.* cutting of solids, *espec.* stone. **-mical** (-om'ikl), *adj.* **-mist**, *n.*

stereotype (stēr'iətīp), *n.* metal printing plate cast from a mould of the set-up type ; *v.t.* make s. of ; fix permanently; make trite; repeat without alteration. **-pic** (-ip'ik), *adj.* **-py**, *n.*

steric(al) (ster'ik, -l), *adj.* stereochemical.

sterlet (stē'lit), *n.* small sturgeon yielding best caviare.

sternum (stē'nəm), *n.* (*pl.* **-na**) breastbone. **-nal**, *adj.*

sternutation (stēnūtā'shn), *n.* sneezing. **-tive**, **-tory**, *n.* & *adj.* (substance) causing s.

sterol (ster'ol), *n.* organic solid alcohol.

stertor (stē'tə), *n.* *Med.*, snoring. **-ous**, *adj.* breathing loudly or hoarsely; snoring.

stet (stet), *Lat.*, "let it stand"; direction to ignore alteration; *v.t.* mark with such direction.

stethoscope (steth'əskōp), *n.* instr. for hearing sounds inside body. **-ometer**, *n.* instr. measuring chest expansion in breathing. **-pic** (-op'ik), *adj.* **-py** (-os'kəpi), *n.* examination with a s. **-spasm**, *n.* spasm of chest muscles.

stevedore (stē'vədor), *n.* dock labourer loading or unloading ship. **-rage**, *n.*

sthenia (sthē'niə), *n.* strength. **-nic** (-en'ik), *adj.* strong.

stibial (stib'iəl), *adj.* pert. to antimony. **-iated**, *adj.* containing antimony. **-ism**, *n.* antimony poisoning.

stibnite (stib'nīt), *n.* natural compound of antimony from which it is obtained.

stich (stik), *n.* line of verse. **-ic**, *adj.* **-ometry**, *n.* measurement by counting lines, *espec.* of books or documents; division of written or printed matter into lines, *espec.* in accordance with the sense. **-omythy**, *n.* dialogue ; repartee.

stifle (stī'fl), *n.* joint above hock of horse, equiv. of human knee.

stigma (stig'mə), *n.* (*pl.* **-ta**) mark ; spot ; stain ; disgrace ; mark representing wound of Christ ; *Bot.*, part of pistil, *espec.* end of style, on which pollen germinates. **-l**, **-tic**, **-tiform**, *adj.* **-tise**, *v.t.* mark with a spot or stain ; brand as infamous or evil. **-tism**, *n.* correct focusing power of lens or eye.

stimie (stī'mi), *n.* obstruction of golfer's putt by opponent's ball. **-d**, *adj.* so obstructed.

stimulus (stim'ūləs), *n.* (*pl.* **-li**) thing or influence causing activity ; incentive.

stipe (stīp), *n.* *Bot.*, short stalk.

stipend (stī'pend), *n.* salary. **-iary**, *n.* & *adj.* (person) receiving s.

stipes (stī'pēz), *n.* stock ; stalk. **-piform**, *adj.* like a stalk. **-pitate**, *adj.* borne on a stipe.

stipulate (stip'ūlāt), *v.i.* & *t.* bargain; guarantee ; demand as a condition. **-tion**, **-tor**, *n.* **-tory**, *adj.*

stipule (stip′ūl), *n.* one of a pair of leaf-like appendages at base of leaf. **-liferous,** *adj.* producing s. **-liform,** *adj.* like s.

stirpiculture (stŭ′pikultūr), *n.* breeding of special stocks.

stithy (stidh′i), *n.* blacksmith's anvil or forge.

stiver (stī′və), *n.* Dutch coin worth about one penny; thing of little or no value.

stochastic (stəkas′tik), *adj.* hypothetical; pert. to conjecture.

stoep (stōōp), S. African *n.* verandah.

stogy (stō′gi), *n.* cheap cigar.

stoichiology (stoikiol′əji), *n.* phys. study of composition of animal tissues. **-ometry,** *n.* *Chem.,* calculation of elements′ combining weights; study of chem. composition and combination.

stolon (stō′lon), *n.* runner of plant. **-ate,** *adj.* having s. **-iferous,** *adj.* producing s.

stoma (stō′mə), *n.* (*pl.* **-ta**) mouth; orifice; breathing pore of plants. **-tal,** *adj.* **-tic,** *adj.* pert. to s.; *n.* & *adj.* (medicine) used for disorders of mouth. **-tiferous,** *adj.* having s. **-titis,** *n.* inflammation of mouth. **-tology,** *n.* med. study of mouth. **-tose, -tous,** *adj.* having s.

storge (stor′jē, -gē), *n.* parental instinct.

storiate (stor′iāt), *v.t.* ornament with historical designs. **-tion,** *n.*

storiology (stōriol′əji), *n.* study of folk-lore. **-gical,** *adj.* **-gist,** *n.*

stovaine (stō′vān), *n.* anaesthetic cocaine-substitute, chiefly injected into spine.

strabismus (strəbiz′məs), *n.* squint. **-mal, -mic(al),** *adj.* **-mometer,** *n.* instr. measuring degree of s.

strafe (strahf), *v.t.* punish; damage; annihilate; *n.* punishment; damage; annihilating attack.

stramineous (strəmin′iəs), *adj.* like straw or its colour; worthless.

stramonium (strəmō′niəm), *n.* thorn apple, and its leaves used in med.

strandlooper (strand′lōōpə), S. African *n.* Bushman; native beach-comber.

strappado (strapā′dō), *n.* form of torture in which victim was let fall the length of a rope tied to his wrists, etc.

strata, *see* **stratum.**

stratagem (strat′əjim), *n.* ruse; trick, *espec.* mil. **-atic, -ical,** *adj.* **-tegic(al)** (-ē′jik, -l), *adj.* pert. to strategy. **-tegist,** *n.* expert in strategy. **-tegy,** *n.* art of war, *espec.* general direction and long-term planning for ultimate victory.

strath (strahth, -ath), Scot. *n.* wide river valley. **-spey,** *n.* reel-like Scot. dance.

stratification (stratifikā′shn), *n.* arrangement in layers or strata. **-form,** *adj.* like a stratum.

stratigraphy (stratig′rəfi), *n.* study of geol. strata; stratification. **-pher, -phist,** *n.* **-phic,** *adj.*

stratocracy (stratok′rəsi), *n.* military rule. **-crat,** *n.* **-cratic,** *adj.* **-tography,** *n.* art of directing an army.

stratosphere (strat′əsfēr, strah′-), *n.* upper atmosphere, from about 7 miles up. **-ric(al),** *adj.*

stratum (strah′təm, strā′-), *n.* (*pl.* **-ta**) layer, *espec.* of earth's crust. **-tose,** *adj.* in s. **-tous,** *adj.* in s.; like stratus.

stratus (strah′təs, strā′-), *n.* (*pl.* **-ti**) sheet of cloud covering sky at height of 2,000 to 7,000 ft.

strepor (strep′ə), *n.* noise. **-pent, -pitant, -pitous,** *adj.*

strepsis (strep′sis), *n.* twisting.

streptococcus (streptəkok′əs), *n.* (*pl.* **-ci**) harmful bacterium occurring in chains. **-cal,** *adj.*

streptomycin (streptəmī′sin), *n.* antibiotic produced by a soil fungus, used chiefly against tuberculosis.

stretcher (strech′ə), *n.* brick placed lengthwise in brick-laying.

stria (strī′ə), *n.* (*pl.* **-ae**) line; small groove; scratch; strip. **-te,** *v.t.* mark with s. **-tion,** *n.*

strickle (strik′l), *n.* scythe-sharpening instr.; template.

stricture (strik′tūr), *n.* harsh criticism; *Med.,* contraction; constriction of body passage; constricted passage.

stridor (strī′də), *n.* harsh noise; whistling sound in breathing. **-dulate** (-id′ūlāt), *v.i.* make a shrill or harsh noise. **-dulation, -dulator,** *n.* **-dulous,** *adj.* squeaky.

striga (strī′gə), *n.* (*pl.* **-ae**) stria; flute of column; plant's stiff bristle. **-l,** *adj.* **-te,** *adj.* having s.

strigilation (strigilā′shn), *n.* scraping.

strigine (strī'jin, -ĭn), *adj.* pert. to or like an owl.

strigose (strī'gōs), *adj.* having strigae.

stringent (strin'jənt), *adj.* strict; tight; cogent. -ncy, *n.*

striola (strī'ələ), *n.* (*pl.* -ae) small or weak stria. -te, *adj.* having s.

strobic (strob'ik), *adj.* spinning; like a top.

strobile (strob'il, -īl), *n.* cone-like inflorescence, *espec.* of hop. -laceous, -line, -loid, *adj.* like s.

stroboscope (strob'əskōp), *n.* instr. for studying periodic motion by illuminating object with flashes at same frequency as that of its motion. -pic (-op'ik), *adj.* -py (-os'kəpi), *n.*

strombuliform (strombū'lifawm), *adj.* like a spinning top or screw.

strongyle (stron'jil), *n.* parasitic roundworm; spicule. -late, *adj.* having s. -lidosis, -losis, *n.* infestation with s.

strophe (strō'fi), *n.* section of Gr. ode sung by chorus when moving from right to left; stanza. -phic (-of'ik), *adj.* -phosis, *n.* twist; turn.

strudel (shtrōō'dl), Ger. *n.* kind of tart with fruit between layers of very thin pastry. apfel-s., s. containing apple.

struma (strōō'mə), *n.* (*pl.* -ae) goitre. -mectomy, *n.* surgical removal of s. -mose, -mous, -tic, *adj.*

strumpet (strum'pit), *n.* prostitute.

struthian (strōō'thiən), *adj.* ratite. -thiform, *adj.* like an ostrich. -thionine, -thious, *adj.*

stucco (stuk'ō), *n.* (*pl.* -es) kind of plaster for exteriors of buildings, *espec.* highly ornamented.

stulm (stulm), *n.* adit.

stultify (stul'tifī), *v.t.* make to seem foolish; frustrate; make futile. -fication, *n.*

stupa (stōō'pə), *n.* dome-like Buddhist shrine.

stupe (stūp), *n.* flannel for fomentation; pledget.

stupefacient (stūpifā'shənt), *adj.* stupefying; *n.* narcotic. -fy, *v.t.* make stupid; daze.

stupeous (stū'piəs) *adj.* tow-like. -pose, *adj.* having tow-like tufts.

stupration (stūprā'shn), *n.* rape.

stupulose (stū'pūlōs), *adj.* downy.

Sturm und Drang (shtoorm oont drahng'), *Ger.*, "storm and stress"; nationalist literary movement of 18th-cent. Ger.

sturnine (stə'nīn), *adj.* pert. to starlings. -noid, *adj.* like a starling.

Stygian (stij'iən), *adj.* pert. to Styx, river of the myth. underworld; murky; app. to solemn, unbreakable vow.

style (stīl), *n.* anct. writing instr. with one sharp and one blunt end; *Bot.* stalk-like outgrowth of ovary bearing stigma. -late, -liferous, *adj.* bearing a s. -liform, *adj.* like s. -line, *adj.* -lite, *n.* ascetic saint living on top of pillar.

stylobate (stī'ləbāt) *n.* coping, etc., supporting colonnade.

stylography (stīlog'rəfi) *n.* writing with a style on wax tablet, etc. -phic, *adj.* app. to fountain pens with needle-like point.

stylometer (stīlom'itə) *n.* column-measuring instr.

stylus (stī'ləs) *n.* style; gramophone needle; any pointed tracer or indicator.

styptic (stip'tik) *n.* & *adj.* (substance) checking bleeding by constricting blood vessels. -psis, *n.* use of s.

stythe (stīdh), *n.* choke-damp.

suasion (swā'zhn), *n.* persuasion; advice.

sub (sub), Lat. *prep.* "under." s.judice (-jōō'disi), still under consideration. s.plumbo, "under lead"; under the Pope's seal. s.rosa, in confidence; secret. s.sigillo, "under seal"; in strict confidence. s.silentio (-silen'shiō), secret; tacit. s.specie, "under appearance" (of). s.voce, under that word; in the place where that subject is considered (*abbr.* s.v.).

subacid (subas'id), *adj.* slightly acid.

subacute (subəkūt'), *adj.* app. to diseases between acute and chronic.

subaerial (subā'riəl, -ā ēr'-), *adj.* in open air; on surface of ground.

subahdar (sōōbədah'), Anglo-Ind. *n.* viceroy; provincial governor; sepoy company commander.

subalary (subal'əri), *adj.* beneath wings.

subalpine (subal'pīn), *adj.* of higher mountain slopes below timber line.

subangular, -late (subang'gūlə, -t), *adj.* somewhat angular.

subarid (subar'id), *adj.* slightly arid.

subarrhation (subərā'shn), *n.* betrothal, with gift from man to woman.

subastral (subas'trəl), *adj.* sublunary.

subaudition (subawdish'n), *n.* understanding of something not expressed ; thing so understood. **-dible,** *adj.* hardly audible. **-ditur,** *n.* thing understood ; implication.

subbifid (subbi'fid), *adj.* somewhat bifid.

subboreal (subbōr'iəl), *adj.* very cold.

subcentral (subsen'trəl), *adj.* beneath the centre ; not exactly central.

subcontinent (sub'kontinənt), *n.* mass of land almost as large as a continent. **-al,** *adj.*

subcutaneous (subkūtā'niəs), *adj.* beneath the skin.

subdecimal (subdes'iməl), *adj.* app. to quotient of division by a multiple of ten. **-cuple,** *adj.* containing one part of ten.

subduplicate (subdū'plikət), *adj.* expressed by square root.

subereous (subēr'iəs), *adj.* pert. to or like cork. **-rise,** *v.t.* convert into corky tissue. **-rose,** *adj.* like cork.

subfluvial (subflōō'viəl), *adj.* beneath, or at bottom of, a river.

subfocal (subfō'kəl), *adj.* of which one is not entirely conscious.

subfusc(ous) (subfusk', -əs), *adj.* dusky.

subglacial (subglā'shəl), *adj.* beneath, or at bottom of, a glacier.

subinfeudate (subinfū'dāt), *v.i.* & *t.* grant to another land held from feudal lord ; sublet. **-tion, -tory,** *n.*

subitaneous (subitā'niəs), *adj.* sudden.

subito (sōō'bitō), Lat. & It. *adv.* "at once" ; immediately ; suddenly.

subjacent (subjā'sənt), *adj.* lying or situated below.

subjective (subjek'tiv), *adj.* pert. to subject or self ; individual ; pert. to or expressing one's personal conceptions or emotions ; resulting from state of mind ; not reliable. **-vism,** *n.* phil. doctrine that all knowledge is merely subjective, or that attaches great importance to subjective experiences.

subjunctive (subjungk'tiv), *n.* & *adj. Gram.,* (pert. to) mood of verb expressing possibility, desire, etc., and not actuality or fact.

sublate (sublāt'), *v.t.* deny ; cancel ; reduce, *espec.* an idea to subordinate part of a greater unity. **-tion,** *n.* **-tive,** *adj.* tending to remove.

sublethal (sublē'thəl), *adj.* not quite fatal.

sublimate (sub'limāt), *v.t.* vaporise substance and allow to solidify ; *Psych.,* direct instinctive energy to higher plane ; *adj.* refined ; *n.* product of sublimating. **-tion,** *n.* **-tory,** *adj.*

subliminal (sublim'inəl), *adj. Psych.,* present though unknown to conscious mind ; too weak, small, or rapid to be consciously noticed.

sublineation (subliniā'shn), *n.* act of underlining.

subluvary (sublōō'nəri), *adj.* of the world ; terrestrial.

subluxation (subluksā'shn), *n.* state of being almost dislocated.

submaxillary (submaks'iləri, -il'əri), *adj.* beneath lower jaw. **s.gland,** salivary gland discharging beneath tongue.

submicron (submī'kron), *n.* ultramicroscopic particle.

submiliary (submil'iəri), *adj.* smaller than a millet seed.

subminimal (submin'iməl), *adj.* less than minimum necessary ; subliminal.

submontane (submon'tān), *adj.* at foot of mountain.

submultiple (submul'tipl), *n.* & *adj.* (quantity) dividing into another exactly.

subnubilar (subnū'bilə), *adj.* under clouds. **-nuvolar,** *adj.*

suboctuple (subok'tūpl), *adj.* containing one part of eight ; related as 1 is to 8.

suborn (subawn'), *v.t.* induce, *espec.* to commit crime ; procure. **-ation,** *n.* **-ative,** *adj.* **-er,** *n.*

subpoena (subpē'nə, sup-), *n.* writ calling person to attend at court ; *v.t.* serve s. on. **-l,** *adj.* under penalty.

subquintuple (subkwin'tūpl), *adj.* having ratio of 1 to 5.

subreptary (subrep'təri), *adj.* adapted to crawling. **-tion,** *n.* false or unfair deduction or representation

due to suppression of truth.
-titious, adj. pert. to subreption.
subrident (subrī'dənt), adj. smiling.
-rision, n.
subrogate (sub'rəgāt), v.t. substitute. **-tion,** n.
subserve (subsə̄v'), v.t. be useful to; promote. **-vient,** adj. servile.
subsextuple (subseks'tūpl), adj. related as 1 is to 6.
subsidy (sub'sidi), n. assistance; grant of money. **-dise,** v.t. aid or support by s.
subsist (subsist'), v.i. & t. continue to exist; abide; feed and clothe. **-ence,** n. **-ent(ial),** adj.
subsolar (subsō'lə), adj. beneath the sun; sublunary; between tropics.
substantive (sub'stəntiv), adj. pert. to or like a substance or entity; existing alone; independent; substantial; solid; essential; real, actual; Gram., expressing existence; n. noun or pronoun. **-val** (-ī'vəl), adj.
substituent (substit'ūənt), n. thing, espec. atom, substituted for another.
substratum (sub'strahtəm, -strā-), n. (pl. **-ta**) underneath layer; foundation. **-tal, -tive,** adj. **-te,** n. **-tose,** adj. imperfectly stratified.
subsultus (subsul'təs), n. convulsive movement. **-tory,** adj. leaping.
subsume (subsūm'), v.t. include. **-mption,** n. **-mptive,** adj.
subtend (subtend'), v.t. extend beneath or opposite to. **-nse,** adj. pert. to object of known length by which distances are measured.
subterfuge (sub'təfūj), n. means of evading; trick.
subtrahend (sub'trəhend), n. amount to be subtracted.
subtrist (subtrist'), adj. rather sad.
subturbary (subtə̄'bəri), adj. beneath turf.
subulate (sū'būlət), adj. long and tapering; awl-shaped. **-licorn,** adj. having such horns or antennae. **-liform,** adj.
subungual, -uial (subung'gwəl, -iəl), adj. beneath a nail or hoof.
suburbicarian (subəbikār'iən), adj. pert. to suburbs, espec. of Rome.
subvention (subven'shn), n. subsidy. **-ne,** v.t. support; aid; happen to help.
subvert (subvə̄t'), v.t. overthrow; pervert; destroy. **-rsion,** n. **-rsive,** adj. tending to overthrow existing order.

subvocal (subvō'kəl), adj. put into words but not spoken.
succedaneum (suksidā'niəm), n. (pl. **-ea**) substitute; remedy. **-eous,** adj.
succent (suksent'), v.t. sing second part. **-or,** n.
succès d'estime (sük'sā destēm'), Fr., "success of esteem"; state of being highly praised or respected but not a financial success.
succinct (suksingkt'), adj. concise; curt.
succiniferous (suksinif'ərəs), adj. producing amber.
succise (suksīs'), adj. having appearance of having lower part cut off.
succorrhoea (sukərē'ə), n. excessive secretion.
succory (suk'əri), n. chicory.
succubus (suk'ūbəs), n. (pl. **-bi**) demon, espec. one taking on female form to have sexual intercourse with man in his sleep; harlot. **-bine,** adj.
succursal (səkə̄'səl), adj. like a branch or outgrowth; subordinate.
succus (suk'əs), n. (pl. **-ci**) juice. **s.entericus,** digestive secretion of small intestine.
succuss (səkus'), v.t. shake violently. **-ation, -ion,** n. **-atory, -ive,** adj.
sucrose (sū'krōs), n. cane or beet sugar.
suctorial (suktōr'iəl), adj. pert. to, or for, sucking; having such organs. **-ian,** n. such animal.
sudamen (sūdā'mən), n. (pl. **-mina**) eruption due to retention of sweat under skin.
sudarium (sūdār'iəm), n. (pl. **-ia**) handkerchief or cloth for wiping away sweat, espec. St. Veronica's, on which portrait of Christ is supposed to have been impressed. **-datorium,** n. (pl. **-ia**) sweating room of a bath.
sudatory (sū'dətəri), adj. sweating; sudorific; n. sudatorium; sudarium.
sudd (sud), n. mass of floating weed blocking the Nile.
sudiform (sū'difawm), adj. having shape of stake.
sudor (sū'dōr), Lat. n. sweat. **-al, -ic,** adj. **-esis,** n. copious sweating. **-iferous, -iparous,** adj. sweat-producing. **-ific,** n. & adj. (drug) promoting perspiration.

Suecism (swē'sizm), *n.* Swedish peculiarity of speech, thought, life, etc.

suffaminate (su flam'ĭnāt), *v.t.* check; obstruct. **-tion**, *n.*

sufflation (sufla'shn), *n.* afflatus.

suffragan (suf'rəgən), *adj. Eccl.*, subordinate ; *n.* assistant bishop. **-al, -eous**, *adj.* **-ate, -cy**, *n.* office or jurisdiction of s.

suffrage (suf'rij), *n.* vote ; right to vote ; supplication. **-gial** (ā'jiəl), *adj.* **-gist**, *n.* believer in extension of s. **-tte**, *n.* woman actively working for women's s.

suffrutescent (sufrōotes'ənt), *adj.* having woody base. **-ticose, -ticous**, *adj.* app. to such perennial plant, remaining herbaceous in upper part.

suffuse (sufūz'), *v.t.* spread from within ; fill with fluid. **-sion**, *n.* **-sive**, *adj.*

sugent (sū'jənt), *adj.* suctorial. **-gescent**, *adj.*

suggilate (suj'ilāt, sug'j-), *v.t.* beat black and blue ; slander. **-tion**, *n.*

sui generis (sū'ī jen'əris), *Lat.* "of its, his or her own kind" ; unique. **s.juris**, "in his or her own right" ; having full legal rights.

suilline (sū'ilīn, -in), *n.* & *adj.* (person or animal) like a pig.

suint (swint), *n.* sheep's dried perspiration in wool.

sulcate (sul'kāt), *adj.* having grooves ; furrowed ; *v.t.* furrow. **-tion**, *n.*

sullage (sul'ij), *n.* refuse ; sewage ; pollution ; silt.

sulpha-drugs (sul'fə-drugz), *n.pl.* group of synthetic chem. drugs also called sulphonamides, including **sulphadiazine** (-dī'əzēn) for pneumonia ; **sulphaguanidine** (-gwah'nidēn) for intestinal infections ; **sulphanilamide** (-nil'əmĭd) for throat infections, blood-poisoning, etc. ; and others.

sulphate (sul'fāt), *n.* salt of sulphuric acid. **-phide**, *n.* compound of sulphur. **-phite**, *n.* salt of sulphurous acid.

sulphonal (sul'fənəl), *n.* kind of sedative drug. **-ism**, *n.* condition due to abuse of s.

sulphonamide (sulfon'əmĭd), *n.* sulpha-drug.

sulphurate (sul'fūr āt), *v.t.* impregnate with sulphur. **-reous**, *adj.*

pert. to or like sulphur. **-retted**, *adj.* impregnated with sulphur. **-ric**, *adj.* containing sulphur in higher valency. **-rous**, *adj.* containing sulphur in lower valency.

summa (sum'ə), *n.* (*pl.* **-ae**) comprehensive treatise. **s.rerum**, "sum of things" ; great public interest. **s.summarum**, "sum of sums" ; consummation.

summation (sumā'shn), *n.* total ; addition ; summing up. **-tive, -tory**, *adj.*

summum bonum (sum'əm bō'nəm), *Lat.*, "highest good." **s.jus**, exact legal right.

sumpitan (sum'pitən), *n.* E. Ind. poisoned-arrow blow-pipe.

sumpter (sump'tə), *n.* pack ; pack horse ; beast of burden.

sumptuary (sump'tūəri), *adj.* regulating expenditure.

sunn (sun), *n.* E. Ind. plant yielding hemp-like fibre.

sunnud (sun'ood), Anglo-Ind. *n.* grant ; charter.

Suomic (swō'mik), *adj.* Finnish.

supari (sōopah'rē), Hind. *n.* betel nut.

superannuate (sōopəran'ū āt, sūp-), *v.t.* discharge as too old ; pension off. **-tion**, *n.* retirement pension.

supercargo (sōo'pəkahgō, sū'-), *n.* (*pl.* **-es**) ship's official in charge of business affairs.

superciliary (sōopəsil'iəri, sūp-), *adj.* pert. to brows or eyebrows. **-lious**, *adj.* haughty ; contemptuous.

supercrescent (sōopəkres'ənt, sūp-), *adj.* parasitic.

supererogate (sōopərer'əgāt, sūp-), *v.i.* do more than necessary. **-tion, -tor**, *n.* **-tive, -tory** (-rog'ətiv, -təri), *adj.*

superfetate (sōopəfē'tāt, sūp-), *v.i.* conceive during pregnancy. **-tion**, *n.* such conception ; cumulative growth by accretion ; overproduction.

superficies (sōopəfish'iēz, sūp-), *n.* surface ; surface area. **-cial**, *adj.* pert. to or on surface only. **-ciary**, *adj.* built on another's land.

superheterodyne (sōopəhet'ərədīn, sūp-), *adj. Rad.*, app. to reception in which oscillations of slightly different frequency are imposed on the received oscillations, producing beats of a frequency above audio-frequency which are easily amplified.

superhumeral (sōōpəhū'mərəl, sŭp-), *n.* garment, *espec.* eccl., worn over shoulders.

superinduce (sōōpərindūs', sŭp'-), *v.t.* bring as addition. -otion, *n.*

superjacent (sōōpəjā'sənt, sŭp-), *adj.* lying over or above.

superlative (sōōpə'lətiv, sŭp-), *n. & adj.* (of) the highest degree.

superlunary (sōōpəlōō'nəri, sŭp-), *adj.* above the moon ; other-worldly.

supermaxillary (sōōpəmaks'iləri, -il'əri ; sŭp-), *adj.* pert. to the upper jaw.

supernal (sōōpə'nəl, sŭp-), *adj.* heavenly.

supernatant (sōōpənā'tənt, sŭp-), *adj.* floating on surface. -tation, *n.*

supernumerary (sōōpənū'mərəri, sŭp-), *n. & adj.* (person) in addition to usual or necessary number.

superphosphate (sōōpəfos'fāt, sŭp-), *n.* acid phosphate.

superscribe (sōōpəskrīb', sŭp-), *v.t.* write on top or at head. -ript, *adj.* written above. -ription, *n.*

supersensible (sōōpəsen'sibl, sŭp-), *adj.* beyond physical perception ; spiritual.

supersolid (sōō'pəsolid, sŭ'-), *n.* magnitude of more than three dimensions.

supersonic (sōōpəson'ik, sŭp-), *adj.* denoting speed greater than speed of sound ; pert. to vibrations above the audible limit.

superstratum (sōōpəstrah'təm, -trā'-; sŭp-), *n.* (*pl.* -ta) over-lying layer.

superterranean, -eous (sōōpəterā'-niən, -iəs ; sŭp-), *adj.* above or on surface of earth. -rene, *adj.*

supervene (sōōpəvēn', sŭp-), *v.i.* occur in addition or unexpectedly ; follow close upon. -nient, *adj.* -nience, -ntion, *n.*

supinate (sōō'pināt, sū'-), *v.i. & t.* lie or make lie on back ; turn arm so that palm is upward. -tion, *n.* -tor, *n.* muscle producing supination.

supine (sūpīn'), *adj.* lying flat on back ; sluggish ; lazy ; (sū'-), *n. Gram.,* kind of Lat. verbal noun.

suppedaneum (supidā'niəm), *n.* (*pl.* -ea) support for feet, *espec.* on cross for crucifixion. -eous, *adj.*

suppliant (sup'liənt), *n. & adj.* beseeching (person). -licate, *v.i. & t.* beseech ; beg. -lication, *n.*

suppository (səpoz'itəri), *n.* soluble med. remedy introduced into orifice.

suppressio veri (səpres'iō vēr'ī), *Lat.,* "suppression of truth."

suppurate (sup'ūr̄āt), *v.i.* fester ; discharge pus. -tion, *n.* -tive, *adj.*

supra (sū'prə), Lat. *adv.* "above" ; previously. vide s., "see above" (*abbr.* v.s.).

supraliminal (sōōprəlim'inəl, sŭp-), *adj.* conscious.

supraorbital (sōōpraaw'bitəl, sŭp-), *adj.* above the eye socket.

suprarenal (sōōprərē'nəl, sŭp-), *adj.* above the kidneys ; adrenal.

surah (soor'ə, sūr'-), *n.* soft silk fabric.

sural (sūr'əl), *adj.* pert. to calf of leg.

surcease (sə'sēs), *v.i. & t.* cease ; stop ; *n.* cessation.

surcingle (sə'singgəl), *n.* band fastening anything on horse's back.

surculose (sə'kūlōs), *adj.* producing suckers. -lous, *adj.* -lus, *n.* (*pl.* -li) sucker.

surd (səd), *adj.* deaf ; senseless ; *Phon.,* unvoiced ; *n. Math.,* irrational number, as π. -imutism, *n.* -omute, *n.* deaf and dumb person.

suricate (sūr'ikət), *n.* mongoose-like animal of S. Africa.

surma (soor'mə), *n.* Ind. eye-shadow.

surmullet (səmul'it), *n.* red mullet.

surnominal (sənom'inəl), *adj.* pert. to surnames.

surrealism (sərē'əlizm), *n.* form of art expressing dream-like unconnected images. -ist, *n.* -istic, *adj.*

surrogate (sur'əgət), *n.* deputy, *espec.* for bishop ; *adj.* deputising. -tion, *n.*

sursum corda (sə'səm kaw'də), *Lat.,* "lift up your hearts" ; versicle in church service.

surveillance (səvā'ləns), *n.* observation ; watch. -nt, *n. & adj.*

surwan (sə'wan), Anglo-Ind. *n.* camel driver.

suscept (səsept'), *n.* parasite's host.

suscitate (sus'itāt), *v.t.* stimulate. -tion, *n.*

suspensus per collum (səspen'səs pə kol'əm), *Lat.,* "hung by the neck" ; executed (*abbr.* sus. per coll.).

suspire (səspīr'), *v.i.* sigh. -ration, *n.* -rative, *adj.*

susurrate (sūsə′rāt), *v.i.* whisper. **-rant,** *adj.* **-rous,** *adj.* rustling. **-rus,** *n.* whispering sound. **-tion,** *n.*

sutler (sut′lə), *n.* camp-follower vending provisions. **-y,** *n.*

suttee (sute′), *n.* Hindu woman, or custom of women, committing suicide on husband's funeral pyre. **-ism,** *n.*

suture (sōō′tūr, sū′-), *n.* stitching up of wound; seam-like joint between parts; connection; *v.t.* stitch up. **-ral,** *adj.* **-ration,** *n.*

suum cuique (sū′əm kwī′kwi), *Lat.,* "to each his own."

suzerain (sōō′zərin, sū′-), *n.* & *adj.* sovereign. **-ty,** *n.*

swage (swāj), *n.* groove; metal-worker's grooved shaping tool; *v.t.* shape with s.

swale (swāl), *n.* meadow; marshy hollow.

swami (swah′mi), Hind. *n.* lord; learned master.

swaraj (swarahj′), Hind. *n.* self-government. **-ist,** *n.*

sybarite (sib′ərīt), *n.* inhabitant of Sybaris, S. Italy; person excessively fond of luxury. **-tic** (-iʻik), *adj.*

sybil (sib′il), *n.* prophetess; hag. **-llic, -lline,** *adj.* like s. or oracle; mysterious. **-llism,** *n.* prophecy by s.

sybotic (sībot′ik), *adj.* pert. to swineherd. **-tism,** *n.*

syce, *see* **sice.**

syconium (sīkō′niəm), *n.* form of fruit with ovaries on enlarged receptacle, as fig.

sycophant (sik′əfant), *n.* flatterer; parasite. **-ic,** *adj.* **-ncy, -ry,** *n.*

sycosis (sīkō′sis), *n.* inflammatory pustular disease of facial hair follicles. **-siform,** *adj.*

syllabary (sil′əbəri), *n.* set of symbols for syllables. **-batim** (-bā′tim), Lat. *adv.* syllable by syllable.

syllabus (sil′əbəs), *n.* programme, *espec.* educational.

syllepsis (silep′sis), *n.* (*pl.* **-ses**) use of word agreeing with only one of them to govern two or more words; use of word in figurative and literal senses in same phrase. **-ptic(al),** *adj.*

syllogism (sil′əjizm), *n.* argument in which conclusion is deduced from two premises. **-ise,** *v.i.* & *t.* **-istic(al),** *adj.*

sylph (silf), *n.* spirit of air; slim girl. **-ic, -id,** *adj.*

sylva (sil′və), *n.* tree of a region; treatise on trees; anthology. **-n, -vestral,** *adj.*

symbiosis (simbiō′sis), *n.* living together of two organisms of different kinds, *espec.* to their mutual benefit. **-on, -ont, -ote,** *n.* such organism. **-otic** (-ot′ik), *adj.* **-otics,** *n.* study of s.

symbolaeography (simbəleog′rəfi), *n.* drawing up of legal documents.

symbolofideism (simbələfī′diizm), *n.* having faith in symbols. **-lolatry,** *n.* worship of symbols.

symphily (sim′fili), *n.* living together to their mutual benefit of insects and other organisms. **-lic, -lous,** *adj.*

symphonious (simfō′niəs), *adj.* harmonious.

symphysis (sim′fisis), *n.* (*pl.* **-ses**) fixed articulation of two bones, *espec.* by cartilaginous pad. **s. menti,** s. of two lower jawbones at chin. **s.pubis,** s. of two pubic bones. **-ytic** (-it′ik), *adj.*

symploce (simpləsi), *n.* repetition of initial and concluding phrases or words of a sentence at beginning and end of following sentence.

symposium (simpō′ziəm), *n.* (*pl.* **-ia**) collection of opinions; discussion. **-siac(al)** (-iak, -ī′əkl), *adj.* **-siast,** *n.* contributor to s.

symptosis (simptō′sis), *n.* emaciation.

synactic (sinak′tik), *adj.* acting in addition or together; cumulative.

synaeresis (siner′isis, -ēr′-), *n.* pronunciation as one of two vowels usually pronounced separately.

synaesthesia (sinesthē′zhiə), *n.* sensation occurring in part distant from part stimulated; association of sensation, as colour, etc., with other sensation. **-etic** (-et′ik), *adj.*

synallagmatic (sinəlagmat′ik), *adj.* bilateral; reciprocal.

synaloepha (sinəlē′fə), *n.* contraction of two syllables into one by omission of vowel.

synanthesis (sinan′thisis), *n.* synchronous maturity of male and female elements of plant. **-etic** (-et′ik), *adj.* **-thy,** *n.* growing together of two flowers.

synapse (sinaps′), *n.* place of

passage of impulse from one neurone to next.

synarchy (sin'ahki), *n.* joint rule. -chical, *adj.*

synartesis (sinahtē'sis), *n.* close junction. -throsis, *n.* (*pl.* -ses) fixed articulation of bones.

synastry (sinas'tri, sin'-), *n.* conjunction of stellar influences on person.

syncategorematic (sinkatigorimat'-ik), *adj.* having meaning only in conjunction with another word.

synchoresis (sinkərē'sis), *n.* rhet. device of apparently conceding point to strengthen argument.

synchronous (sing'krənəs), *adj.* pert. to or happening at same time. -nal, -nic, *adj.* -nise, *v.i.* & *t.* occur or make occur simultaneously. -nism, *n.*

synchrotron (sing'krətron), *n.* apparatus, combination of betatron and cyclotron, for accelerating charged particles for atomic fission experiments.

synchysis (sing'kisis), *n.* confusion.

synclastic (sinklas'tik), *adj.* curved in all directions towards same point.

syncline (sin'klīn), *n. Geol.*, downward fold. -nal, -nical, *adj.*

syncopate (sing'kəpāt), *v.t.* omit part from interior of ; *Mus.*, begin rhythm on unaccented beat. -pe (-pi), *n.* omission of sound from word ; *Med.*, fainting. -tion, *n.*

syncrasy (sing'krəsi), *n.* combination.

syncretism (sing'kritizm), *n.* combination of different religious beliefs ; eclecticism ; compromise. -ise, *v.i.* & *t.* become or cause to become fused. -ist, *n.* -istic, *adj.*

syndactyl(e) (sindak'til), *n.* & *adj.* (animal) with digits joined together. -lia, -lism, -ly, *n.* -lic, -lous, *adj.*

syndetic(al) (sindet'ik, -l), *adj.* connective.

syndic (sin'dik), *n.* magistrate ; member of committee. -al, *adj.* -alism, *n.* theory of obtaining control of means of production by workers' organisations.

syndrome (sin'drōm), *n.* group of things, *espec.* med. symptoms, happening together.

synecdoche (sinek'dəki), *n.* lit.

device of signifying thing by its part, or part by whole, etc. -chic(al) (-ok'ik, -l), *adj.* -chism, *n.*

synechiology (sinekiol'əji), *n.* doctrine of the continuity or union of things. -gical, *adj.*

synechthry (sin'ekthri), *n.* living together of hostile species.

synecphonesis (sinekfənē'sis), *n.* synaeresis.

synergetic (sinəjet'ik), *adj.* cooperating. -gise, *v.i.* -gism, -gy, *n.*

synesis (sin'isis), *n. Gram.*, construction in which gram. agreement is according to sense rather than syntax.

synethnic (sineth'nik), *adj.* of same race or country.

syngamy (sing'gəmi), *n.* conjunction of gametes, etc. -mic (-am'ik), -mous, *adj.*

syngenesis (sinjen'isis), *n.* sexual reproduction. -etic (-jinet'ik), *adj.*

synizesis (sinizē'sis), *n.* contraction of two syllables by combining pronunciation of successive vowels.

synkinesis (singkinē'sis), *n.* movement of part when another is moved.

synod (sin'əd), *n.* assembly or council, *espec.* of Church. -al, -ic(al), *adj.* ; *Astron.*, between two conjunctions with sun.

synoecious (sinē'shəs), *adj.* having male and female flowers in same inflorescence. -cise, *v.t.* join together. -cism *n.* -cy, *n.* association of species with benefit to one and neither harm nor benefit to other.

synonym (sin'ənim), *n.* word having same meaning as another. -ic, -ous (-on'iməs), *adj.* -y (-on'imi), *n.* use for emphasis of several s.

synopsis (sinop'sis), *n.* (*pl.* -ses) summary ; outline. -ptic(al), *adj.* giving or pert. to s. ; taking the same view ; *s.Gospels*, those according to Matthew, Mark and Luke. -ptist, *n.* writer of synoptic Gospel.

synorthographic (sinawthəgraf'ik), *adj.* spelt alike.

synovia (sīnō'viə), *n.* lubricating fluid secreted by certain membranes. -l, *adj.* -viparous, *adj.* producing s. -vitis, *n.* inflammation of synovial membrane.

syntax (sin'taks), *n.* sentence-construction; systematic arrangement. **-tactic(al)**, *adj.*

syntectic (sintek'tik), *adj.* pert. to syntexis.

synteresis (sintərē'sis), *n.* intuitive knowledge of right and wrong; "divine spark" of the soul.

syntexis (sinteks'is), *n.* wasting or melting away.

synthermal (sinthə'məl), *adj.* having same temperature.

synthesis (sin'thisis), *n.* (*pl.* **-ses**) combination of parts into a uniform whole. **-e,** *v.t.* make by s.; build up (a chem. compound); make artificial equivalent of (a natural substance). **-etic** (-et'ik), *adj.* pert. to or resulting from s.; artificially compounded; not natural or genuine.

syntony (sin'təni), *n.* tuning wireless instr. to same wavelength. **-nic** (-on'ik), **-nous**, *adj.* **-nise**, *v.t.*

syphilis (sif'ilis), *n.* contagious venereal disease; pox. **-litic** (-it'ik), *n.* & *adj.* **-loid**, *adj.* like s. **-loma**, *n.* tumour occurring in s. **-losis**, *n.*

syringadenous (siringad'inəs), *adj.* pert. to sweat glands.

syrinx (sir'ingks), *n.* (*pl.* **-nges**) tubular object; bird's vocal organ; Pan's pipes.

systaltic (sistal'tik), *adj.* pulsatory.

systatic (sistat'ik), *adj.* bringing together.

systole (sis'təli), *n.* contraction, alternating with diastole, in pulsation of heart; shortening of long syllable. **-lic** (-ol'ik), *adj.*

syzygy (siz'iji), *n.* point in orbit when planet is in conjunction or opposition; verse group of two feet. **-getic, -gial**, *adj.*

T

Taal (tahl), S. African *n.* S. African Dutch language; Afrikaans.

tabacosis (tabəkō'sis), *n.* tobacco-poisoning.

tabagie (tabazhē'), Fr. *n.* smoking-room or -party.

tabard (tab'ahd), *n.* herald's sleeveless tunic; coat worn over armour.

tabaret (tab'ərit), *n.* striped material of watered silk and satin.

tabasco (təbas'kō), *n.* kind of pepper sauce.

tabasheer (tabashēr'), *n.* hard substance extracted from bamboo joints and used medicinally; sugar of bamboo.

tabefaction (tabifak'shn), *n.* emaciation.

tabellion (təbel'yən), *n.* scrivener.

tabes (dorsalis) (tā'bēz, dorsā'lis), *n.* locomotor ataxia. **-betic** (-et'ik), **-bid** (tab'id), *adj.* **-cent** (-es'ənt), *adj.* wasting away. **-cence,** *n.*

tabinet (tab'init), *n.* silk-and-wool watered material.

tabitude (tab'itūd), *n.* tabes.

tablature (tab'lətūr), *n.* mental image; description; picture; any plate-like surface or object.

tableau (tab'lō), *n.* (*pl.* **-x**) artistic or dramatic scene. **t.vivant,** "living picture"; t. in dumb show.

table d'hôte (tah'bl dōt'), *Fr.*, "table of the host"; meal of limited choice of dishes at fixed price.

taboo (təbōō'), *n.* consecration or prohibition of thing or person, which must not be touched or spoken of; *v.t.* & *adj.* put under t.

tabor (tā'bor), *n.* small drum.

tabouret (tab'ərit), *n.* low stool; small tabor; embroidery frame.

tabu, *see* **taboo.**

tabula rasa (tab'ūlə rā'sə), *Lat.,* "smoothed tablet"; condition of mind free from ideas or impressions.

tace (tā'si), *Lat.,* "be silent." **-t,** "it, he or she is silent."

tach (tach), *n.* link.

tacheography (takiog'rəfi), *n.* tachygraphy.

tachometer (təkom'itə), *n.* speedometer. **-try,** *n.* measurement of speed.

tachygraphy (takig'rəfi), *n.* shorthand; shortened cursive writing. **-pher, -phist,** *n.* **-phical,** *adj.* **-ymeter,** *n.* speedometer; instr. for making quick surveys. **-yscope,** *n.* early cinematograph.

tacit (tas'it), *n.* silent; unspoken; merely implied. **-urn,** *adj.* silent; morose. **-urnity,** *n.*

tactile (tak'til, -il), *adj.* pert. to sense of touch; tangible; *n.* person whose mental processes arc stimulated most by sense of touch. **-lity,** *n.* **-tion,** *n.* touching. **-tometer,** *n.* instr. measuring sense of touch. **-tual,** *adj.* **-tus,** *n.* sense of touch.

taenia (tē'niə), *n. (pl.* **-ae**) band ; fillet ; tapeworm. **-cide, -nicide,** *n.* substance destroying tapeworms. **-fuge, -nifuge,** *n.* substance expelling tapeworms. **-l,** *adj.* **-niform, -te,** *adj.* ribbon-like. **-nioid,** *adj.* like a ribbon or tapeworm. **-sis** (-i'əsis), *n.* infestation with tapeworms.

taffrail (taf'rāl), *n.* rail round ship's stern.

tahsil (təsēl'), Arab. *n.* revenue-collection. **-dar,** *n.* tax-collector.

taipan (tī'pan), Chin. *n.* rich merchant.

taj (tahj), Arab. *n.* cap, *espec.* of dervish.

talalgia (təlal'jiə), *n.* pain in heel or ankle.

talapoin (tal'əpoin), *n.* Buddhist monk ; species of monkey of W. Africa.

talar (tā'lə), *n.* ankle-length robe. **-ic** (təlar'ik), *adj.* pert. or reaching to ankles.

talc (talk), *n.* kind of mica ; soapstone-like mineral. **-ous,** *adj.* **-um,** *n.*

taligrade (tal'igrād), *n. & adj.* (animal) walking on outer side of foot.

talionic (talion'ik), *adj.* retaliatory.

talipes (tal'ipēz), *n.* clubfoot. **-ped,** *n.* person with t.

talipot (tal'ipot), *n.* S. Ind. palm tree with huge leaves.

talisman (tal'izmən), *n.* thing believed to have magical power. **-ic(al)** (-an'ik, -l), *adj.*

talliate (tal'iāt), *v.t.* tax.

tallith (tal'ith), *n.* Jewish prayer-shawl.

Talmud (tal'mud), *n.* Jewish scriptures. **-ic,** *adj.*

talpa (tal'pə), *n. Med.,* mole.

taluk (tah'look), *n.* Ind. estate. **-dar,** *n.* owner of t.

talus (tā'ləs), *n. (pl.* **-li**) ankle bone ; slope ; *Geol.,* rock detritus at base of slope.

tamandu(a) (tam'əndoo, tamand-wah'), *n.* small anteater of Cent. and S. America. **-noir,** *n.* ant bear.

tamaricaceous (tamərikā'shəs), *adj.*

pert. to or like tamarisk ; belonging to tamarisk family of trees.

tamarind (tam'ərind), *n.* cultivated tropical tree, with edible leaves and flowers, and fruit used as medicine, flour and in preserves. **-risk,** *n.* heathlike shrub or tree of warm regions.

tamasha (təmah'shə), Anglo-Ind. *n.* show ; important occasion ; commotion.

tambour (tam'boor), *n.* drum; embroidery frame ; sloping buttress or fortification.

tamis (tam'is), *n.* woollen cloth for straining.

tampan (tam'pən), *n.* venomous S. African tick.

tampon (tam'pən), *n.* surg. plug of cotton-wool ; double-headed drumstick. **-age,** *n.* use of t.

tanager (tan'əjə), *n.* finch-like Amer. bird.

tanagra (tan'əgrə), *n.* brown madder ; terra-cotta statuette, *espec.* found at T., Greece.

tangent (tan'jənt), *adj.* touching ; meeting but not cutting a curve at a point ; *n.* such line. **-ial** (-en'shəl), *adj.* **-nce, -ncy,** *n.*

tangible (tan'jibl), *n.* that can be touched ; real. **-bility,** *n.*

tangram (tang'gram), *n.* puzzle or toy made by cutting square into seven pieces, which are fitted together to form other shapes.

tannin (tan'in), *n.* highly astringent substance obtained from many plants. **-nic,** *adj.* **-niferous,** *adj.* yielding t. **-noid,** *adj.* like t.

tantalus (tan'tələs), *n.* case or stand, fitted with a lock, for wine or spirit bottles.

taphephobia (tafifō'biə), *n.* dread of being buried alive.

tapinosis (tapinō'sis), *n.* use of degrading diction about a subject.

tapir (tā'pə), *n.* ant-eater with short proboscis.

tapis (tap'is ; Fr., -ē), Fr. *n.* "carpet." **on the t.,** under discussion.

tapotement (tapot'mahṅ), Fr. *n.* use of percussion in massage.

tappal (təpawl'), Anglo-Ind. *n.* mail ; post, *espec.* by relays of runners.

tarantas(s) (tarəntas'), Russ. *n.* low four-wheeled Russ. carriage.

tarantella (tarəntel'ə), *n.* fast violent

ə=*er* in *father* ; ə̄=*er* in *pert* ; th=*th* in *thin* ; dh=*th* in *then* ; zh=*s* in *pleasure* ; k=*ch* in *loch* ; ṅ=Fr. nasal *n* ; ü=Fr. *u.*

S. It. dance. **-tism,** *n.* nervous disease marked by desire to dance.

tarantula (təran′tūlə), *n.* poisonous spider of S. Europe. **-lous, -r,** *adj.*

tarassis (təras′is), *n.* male hysteria.

taraxacum (təraks′əkəm), *n.* dandelion, and its dried roots used in med.

tarboosh (tah′boōsh), *n.* fez.

tardigrade (tah′digrād), *adj.* slow-moving. **-diloquous,** *adj.* slow in speech. **-dive,** *adj.* unpunctual.

tarlatan, -let- (tah′lətən), *n.* kind of thin stiff muslin.

tarpon (tah′pon), *n.* large Amer. marine game fish.

tarsal (tah′səl), *adj.* pert. to tarsus. **-sectomy,** *n.* removal of tarsal bone.

tarsier (tah′siə), *n.* large-eyed squirrel-like E. Ind. animal.

tarsus (tah′səs), *n.* (*pl.* **-si**) ankle and bones supporting it.

tartar (tah′tə), *n.* crust-like deposit of grape juice on wine casks ; incrustation on teeth. **-eous** (-ār′iəs), **-ic** (-ar′ik), *adj.*

tartarology (tahtərol′əji), *n.* doctrine about Hell.

tartrate (tah′trāt), *n.* salt of tartaric acid.

tashrif (tashrēf′), Anglo-Ind. *n.* respect ; honour ; compliment.

tasimetry (təsim′itri), *n.* measurement of pressures. **-ter,** *n.* instr. measuring temperature changes by responding to minute changes of air pressure due to expansion and contraction of solid bodies.

tassie (tas′i), Scot. *n.* small cup.

tatou (tatoō′), *n.* armadillo. **-ay,** *n.* large S. Amer. armadillo.

tau (tow), *n.* nineteenth letter (T, τ) of Gr. alphabet ; any T-shaped thing.

taupe (tōp), *n.* mole-colour.

taurian (tor′iən), *adj.* pert. to bull. **-ricide,** *n.* killing or killer of bull. **-riform,** *adj.* bull-like. **-rine,** *adj.* **-rodont,** *adj.* having teeth like bull's. **-romachy,** *n.* bullfight. **-romorphic,** *adj.* bull-shaped.

tautology (tawtol′əji), *n.* repetition of sense of word(s) in other unnecessary words. **-gical,** *adj.* **-gise,** *v.i.* **-tochronous,** *adj.* lasting same time. **-tomerism,** *n.* possession by a substance of more than one structure. **-tometric,** *adj.* same metrically. **-tophony,** *n.* repetition of same sound.

taws(e) (tawz), *n.* thong for punishment.

taxaceous (taksā′shəs), *adj.* pert. to or like yew ; belonging to the yew family of trees.

taxidermy (taks′idəmi), *n.* art of curing and stuffing animal skins. **-mal, -mic,** *adj.* **-mist,** *n.* expert in t.

taxine (taks′in, -īn), *adj.* taxaceous.

taxis (taks′is), *n.* movement of organisms to or from a stimulus.

taxonomy (takson′əmi), *n.* classification, *espec.* of animals and plants. **-mic(al)** (-om′ik, -l), *adj.* **-mist,** *n.*

tazza (taht′zə), *n.* cup with saucer-shaped bowl on a pedestal.

tebbad (teb′ad), *n.* simoom of Cent. Asia.

technocracy (teknok′rəsi), *n.* government by technical experts. **-nography,** *n.* description of arts and crafts. **-nolithic,** *n.* pert. to implements of stone. **-nology,** *n.* application of science to industry ; scientific nomenclature. **-nonomy,** *n.* laws of industrial arts.

tecnology (teknol′əji), *n.* teaching of children.

tectiform (tek′tifawm), *adj.* rooflike.

tectonic (tekton′ik), *adj.* structural. **-s,** *n.* science of design and structure.

tectorial (tektōr′iəl), *adj.* acting as covering.

tectrix (tek′triks), *n.* (*pl.* **-rices**) bird's wing or tail covert. **-ricial,** *adj.*

ted (ted), *v.t.* spread out for drying.

tedesco (tedes′kō), It. *adj.* (*fem.* **-ca**) German. **-can,** *adj.*

Te Deum (tē dē′əm), *Lat.,* *abbr.* of t. d. laudamus, "we praise thee, O God" ; anct. Christian hymn sung at morning service ; any song of praise or thanks.

tedium (tē′diəm), *n.* tiredness ; boredom.

teg (teg), *n.* sheep, and fleece, in second year.

tegmen (teg′men), *n.* (*pl.* **-mina**) covering. **-minal, -tal,** *adj.*

tegula (teg′ūlə), *n.* (*pl.* **-ae**) tile. **-r,** *adj.* **-ted,** *adj.* made of overlapping plates.

tegument (teg′ūmənt), *n.* integument. **-al, -ary,** *adj.*

te igitur (tē. ij′itə), *Lat.,* "thee

---

therefore"; first words of Canon of Roman Mass ; binding oath.

teil (tēl), *n.* lime tree.

teinoscope (tī'nəskōp), *n.* prism telescope.

telacoustic (teləkōō'stik), *adj.* pert. to telaesthesia by sound.

telaesthesia (telesthē'zhiə), *n.* perception of events or objects not actually present or near, *e.g.* clairvoyance.

telamon (tel'əmon), *n.* atlantis.

telarian (tilar'iən), *n.* & *adj.* (spider) spinning web. **-ry** (tel'əri, tē'-), *adj.* web-spinning.

telecommunication (telikəmūnikā'-shn), *n.* transmission of messages over great distances by telegraph, telephone, or radio.

teledu (tel'idōō), *n.* Javanese skunk.

telegenic (teligen'ik), *adj.* suitable for being televised.

telegnosis (telegnō'sis), *n.* clairvoyance. **-stic** (-os'tik), *adj.*

telegony (teleg'əni), *n.* supposed influence of female's first mate on offspring of her later matings with other males. **-nic** (-on'ik), **-nous**, *adj.*

telekinesis (telikinē'sis), *n.* causing objects to move by spiritualistic means. **-etic** (-et'ik), *adj.*

telelectric (telilek'trik), *adj.* pert. to elec. transmission over long distance. **-trograph**, *n.* instr. transmitting a picture electrically.

telemark (tel'imahk), *n.* method of turning in ski-ing.

telemechanics (telimikan'iks), *n.* transmission of power, or control of machinery, over a distance, *espec.* by radio.

telemeter (tilem'itə), *n.* distance- or strain-measuring instr. ; instr. recording a measurement of quantity and transmitting it over a distance. **-tric** (-et'rik), *adj.* **-trograph**, *n.* telescopic instr. for measuring and drawing distant objects. **-try**, *n.*

telenergy (telen'əji), *n.* application of spiritualistic energy at a distance. **-gic** (-ə'jik), *adj.*

teleology (teliol'əji, tē-), *n.* fact of being directed to an end, as by Providence ; doctrine as to the purposes of nature ; explanation of a phenomenon by reference to its purpose. **-gical**, *adj.* **-gist**, *n.*

teleorganic (teliawgan'ik), *adj.* vital.

teleost(ean) (tel'iost, -os'tiən), *adj.* pert. to the bony fishes.

telepathy (tilep'əthi), *n.* communication between minds without aid of senses. **-thic** (-ath'ik), *adj.* **-thist**, *n.* •

telephotography (telifətog'rəfi), *n.* photography of distant objects with telescopic lens ; elec. transmission of photographs.

teleplasm (tel'iplazm), *n.* ectoplasm. **-mic**, **-stic**, *adj.*

telergy (tel'əji), *n.* force that effects telepathy. **-gic** (-ə'jik), *adj.* effective at a distance.

teleseism (tel'isīsm), *n.* tremor due to distant earthquake. **-ic**, *adj.* **-ology**, *n.* study of t.

telestich (tel'istik, -es'-), *n.* acrostic-like poem, etc., in which last letters of lines spell a name.

teletactor (telitak'tə), *n.* instr. enabling deaf to feel sound vibrations with finger tips. **-tile**, *adj.*

teletherapy (telither'əpi), *n.* med. treatment by telepathy.

telic (tel'ik), *adj.* purposive ; *Gram.,* signifying intention.

tellurian (telūr'iən), *adj.* pert. to the earth ; *n.* dweller on the earth. **-ric**, *adj.* **-rism**, *n.* disease production by the soil.

telmatology (telmətol'əji), *n.* study of swamps. **-gical**, *adj.*

telodynamic (telədīnam'ik), *adj.* pert. to transmission of power to a distance.

telopsis (telop'sis), *n.* visual telaesthesia. **-ptic**, *adj.*

teloteropathy (telətirop'əthi), *n.* telepathy between living persons. **-thic**, *adj.*

telpher (tel'fə), *n.* electrically propelled light car on overhead cable. **-age**, *n.* transportation by t.

telson (tel'sən), *n.* last segment of crustacean, etc.

telurgy (tel'əji), *n.* telepathy.

temerity (timer'iti), *n.* boldness.

tempera (tem'pərə), *n.* painting with white of egg or similar medium replacing oil.

temperative (tem'pərətiv), *adj.* moderating ; soothing.

template (tem'plit), *n.* bezel ; supporting beam, etc. ; shaped plate used as gauge or pattern.

temporal (tem'pərəl), *adj.* pert. to time ; earthly ; secular ; pert.

to temples of head. **-ity,** *n.* earthly possession of relig. body.

tempore (tem'pəri), Lat. *adv.* "in the time of."

temporise (tem'pəriz), *v.i.* procrastinate ; delay ; comply with circumstances.

tempus fugit (tem'pəs fū'jit), *Lat.,* "time is fleeting."

tenable (ten'əbl), *adj.* that can be held or maintained. **-bility,** *n.*

tenacious (tinā'shəs), *adj.* grasping firmly ; clinging closely ; not quickly relinquishing or forgetting. **-city** (-as'iti), *n.*

tendentious (tenden'shəs), *adj.* tending to uphold or advance a cause ; not impartial. **-tial,** *adj.*

tendinous (ten'dinəs), *adj.* pert. to or like a tendon ; sinewy.

tendresse (tahndres'), Fr. *n.* tender feeling ; care ; delicacy.

tenebra (ten'ibrə), Lat. *n.* (*pl.* -ae) "darkness" ; *pl.,* R.C. matins and lauds for last three days of Holy Week. **-brific,** *adj.* making dark. **-brious, -brose, -brous,** *adj.* dark ; gloomy. **-brity, -brosity,** *n.*

tenesmus (tinez'məs), *n. Med.,* urgent desire to evacuate but without effect ; straining to evacuate. **-mic,** *adj.*

tenet (ten'it), *n.* doctrine ; dogma.

tenon (ten'ən), *n.* projecting part of joint for inserting into mortise.

tenonectomy (tenənek'təmi), *n.* surg. removal of tendon. **-nitis, -nositis,** *n.* inflammation of tendon. **-notomy,** *n.*

tensile (ten'sīl, -il), *adj.* pert. to tension ; that can be stretched. **t. strength,** ability to endure lengthwise pull without breaking. **-sible,** *adj.* **-sive,** *adj.* causing tension. **-sor,** *n.* stretching muscle.

tentamen (tentā'men), Lat. *n.* experiment ; attempt. **-tation,** *n.* experiment by trial and error. **-tative,** *adj.* experimental ; provisional ; not firm or definite.

tenue (tənü'), Fr. *n.* general appearance or manner.

tenuous (ten'ūəs), *adj.* thin ; sparse ; rarefied. **-uity,** *n.*

tepary (tep'əri), *n.* kind of hardy bean of southern U.S.A. and Mexico.

tepee (tē'pē), *n.* Red Ind. tent.

tepefy (tep'ifī), *v.t.* make tepid. **-faction,** *n.*

tephrosis (tifrō'sis), *n.* incineration.

tepor (tē'pə, tep'-), *n.* tepidness.

teramorphous (terəmaw'fəs), *adj.* monstrous ; of abnormal form.

teraph (ter'əf), *n.* (*pl.* **-im**) anct. Jewish household god.

teratism (ter'ətizm), *n.* monstrosity ; love of monsters or marvels. **-tical** (-at'ikl), *adj.* **-toid,** *adj.* abnormal. **-tology,** *n.* composition of fantastic stories ; study or description of, or doctrine about, miracles ; study of freaks, monsters, and physical abnormalities. **-tosis,** *n.*

tercel (tə'səl), *n.* male hawk.

tercentenary (təsentē'nəri), *adj.* pert. to or lasting 300 years ; *n.* 300th anniversary. **-nnial** (-en'iəl), **-rian,** *adj.*

tercet (tə'sit), *n.* set of three rhyming verse-lines.

terdiurnal (tədī ə'nəl), *adj.* three times per day.

terebinth (ter'ibinth), *n.* tree yielding turpentine. **-ine,** *adj.*

terebrant (ter'ibrənt), *adj.* boring (hole in) ; pert. to long thin sharp sea-shell. **-brate,** *v.t.* bore. **-bration,** *n.*

teredo (terē'do), *n.* ship worm.

terek (ter'ek), *n.* kind of sandpiper.

terephah (tarā'fah), Heb. *n.* unclean or forbidden meat.

terete (ter'ēt), *adj.* round and tapering.

tergal (tə'gəl), *adj.* pert. to back.

tergiversation (təjivəsā'shn), *n.* act or state of being apostate or renegade ; equivocation. **-tor,** *n.* **-tory,** *adj.*

termagant (tə'məgənt), *n.* virago.

terminology (təminol'əji), *n.* nomenclature ; set of words special to an art or science, etc. **-gical,** *adj.*

terminus (tə'minəs), Lat. *n.* (*pl.* **-ni**) boundary ; end. **t. ad quem,** "end to which" ; termination. **t. a quo,** "end from which" ; starting point.

termite (tə'mīt), *n.* destructive ant-like insect, called *erron.* "white ant". **-tal, -tic** (-it'ik), *adj.* **-tary,** *n.* nest of t.

ternary (tə'nəri), *adj.* triple ; pert. to or consisting of three(s) ; in threes ; having three as base ; *n.* set of three. **-nion,** *n.* three ; set of three.

Terpsichore (təpsik'əri), *n.* muse presiding over the dance. **-al,**

-an (-ē′əl, -n), *adj.* pert. to T. or dancing.

terra (ter′ə), Lat. & It. *n.* "earth." **t.alba**, "white earth"; gypsum, kaolin, magnesia, etc. **t.cotta**, glazed earthenware and its reddish colour. **t.firma**, dry land. **t.incognita**, unknown land.

terraceous (terā′shəs), *adj.* earthen.

terrain (terān′, ter′-), *n.* area of land, *espec.* as scene of event or limiting certain activity.

terramara (terəmah′rə), *n.* kind of earthy fertiliser; neolithic pile dwelling.

terramycin (terəmī′sin), *n.* antibiotic produced by a soil fungus.

terrane (ter′ān), *n.* geol. formation; area covered by certain rock. **-an, -ous,** *adj.* pert. to earth.

terrapin (ter′əpin), *n.* kind of edible N. Amer. turtle.

terraqueous (terā′kwiəs), *adj.* amphibious ; consisting of land and water.

terrazzo (terat′zo), *n.* flooring of marble chips.

terrene (ter′ēn), *adj.* pert. to or consisting of earth ; mundane.

terricolous (terik′ələs), *adj.* living in or on ground.

terrigenous (terij′inəs), *adj.* produced by earth ; indigenous.

terrine (terēn′), *n.* earthenware jar or dish ; tureen ; ragout.

territelarian (territilār′iən), *n.* & *adj.* (pert. to) trap-door spider.

terry (ter′i), *n.* & *adj.* (cloth) with pile of uncut loops.

tertian (tə̄′shn), *n.* & *adj.* (fever) recurring after three (*i.e.*, every two) days. **-iary,** *adj.* of third degree ; *n.* member of third monastic order. **-ium quid,** *n.* "third something," not included in simple classification ; anomalous thing. **-ius,** *n.* third of the name ; "minimus."

Terylene (ter′ilēn), *n.* synthetic material of the nylon type.

terza rima (tāt′sah rē′mah), *It.,* "third rhyme"; rhyming scheme of linked tercets. **-zet, -zetto,** *n.* trio.

tessara (tes′ərə), *n.pl.* quadrilaterals. **-glot,** *adj.* pert. to, in or speaking four languages.

tesselated (tes′əlātid), *adj.* chequered ; pert. to or like mosaic. **-tion,** *n.*

tessera (tes′ərə), *n.* (*pl.* **-ae**) small block of stone, tile, etc., used in mosaic ; password. **-l, -sular,** *adj.* **-tomy,** *n.* division into four parts.

test (test), *n. Zoo.,* shell of invertebrate. **-acean,** *n.* shell-fish. **-aceous,** *adj.* pert. to, like or bearing a t.

testacy (tes′təsi), *n.* dying testate.

testamur (testā′mə), *n.* certificate of passing university examination.

testate (tes′tāt), *n.* & *adj.* (person) dying leaving a valid will. **-tion,** *n.* **-tor, -trix,** *n.* **-tory,** *adj.*

tester (tes′tə), *n.* bed canopy.

testicle (tes′tikl), *n.* male reproductive gland. **-cular,** *adj.* **-culate,** *adj.* like t. in shape.

testis (tes′tis), *n.* (*pl.* **-tes**) testicle.

testudinal (testū′dinəl), *adj.* pert. to or like tortoise or tortoiseshell. **-narious,** *adj.* **-nate,** *adj.* like tortoiseshell ; arched ; *n.* turtle. **-neal, -neous** (-in′iəl, -əs), **-nous,** *adj.*

tetanus (tet′ənəs), *n.* muscular spasm due to a soil bacillus ; lockjaw. **-nic(al)** (-an′ik, -l), *adj.* **-nise,** *v.t.* cause t. in. **-noid,** *adj.* like t. **-ny,** *n.* state resembling t.

tête-à-tête (tāt-ah-tāt′), *Fr.,* "head to head"; (meeting or conversation) of two persons ; private; confidential.

tethydan (tithī′dən), *n.* ascidian.

tetrabrach (tet′rəbrak), *n.* metrical foot, or word, of four short syllables.

tetrachord (tet′rəkawd), *n.* mus. scale of four tones, or instr. with four strings. **-al,** *adj.*

tetrachotomous (tetrəkot′əməs), *adj.* divided into fours.

tetrachromatic (tetrəkrəmat′ik), *adj.* having four colours ; denoting or pert. to theory that there are four primary colours.

tetrad (tet′rad), *n.* four ; set of four.

tetradactyl(e) (tetrədak′til), *n.* & *adj.* (animal) with four digits. **-lous,** *adj.*

tetraglot (tet′rəglot), *adj.* in four languages. **-ttic(al),** *adj.*

tetragon (tet′rəgən), *n.* four -sided plane figure. **-al** (-ag′ənəl), *adj.*

tetragram (tet′rəgram), *n.* word of four letters ; quadrilateral. **-mmaton,** *n.* four Heb. consonants (JHWH) forming name of Creator (Jahweh, or Jehovah).

tetrahedron (tetrəhē'drən), *n.* four-sided solid figure. **-ral,** *adj.*

tetralemma (tetrəlem'ə), *n.* dilemma-like position with four alternatives.

tetralogy (tetral'əji), *n.* set of four connected works of literature or music.

tetramerous (tetram'ərəs), *adj.* having four parts; *Bot.,* having parts in fours. **-ral, -ric** (-er'ik), *adj.*

tetrameter (tetram'itə), *n.* verse line of four feet.

tetrapla (tet'rəplə), *n.* edition of book, *espec.* Old Testament, with four texts.

tetraplegia (tetrəplē'jiə), *n.* paralysis of all four limbs.

tetrapod (tet'rəpod), *n.* & *adj.* quadruped.

tetrapody (tetrap'ədi), *n.* verse of four feet. **-dic** (-od'ik), *adj.*

tetrapolis (tetrap'əlis), *n.* group of four cities. **-litan** (-ol'itən), *adj.*

tetrapous (tet'rəpəs), *adj.* four-footed.

tetrapteran (tetrap'tərən), *adj.* four-winged. **-ron,** *n.* (*pl.* **-ra**) such insect. **-rous,** *adj.*

tetraptych (tetrap'tik), *n.* painting in four parts, *espec.* hinged.

tetrarch (tet'rahk, tē'-), *n.* ruler of quarter of a province; member of tetrarchy. **-ic,** *adj.* **-y,** *n.* jurisdiction or office of t.; rule by four persons.

tetrastich (tet'rəstik), *n.* four-lined poem or stanza. **-al** (-as'tikl), **-ic,** *adj.* **-ous** (-as'tikəs), *adj.* in four rows.

tetrasyllable (tet'rəsiləbl), *n.* word of four syllables. **-bic** (-ab'ik), *adj.*

tetravalent (tetrav'ələnt, -vā'), *adj.* quadrivalent.

tetter (tet'ə), *n.* kinds of skin disease, as eczema, etc. **-ous,** *adj.*

thalamus (thal'əməs), *n.* (*pl.* **-mi**) part of between-brain receiving sense perception. **-mic** (-am'ik), *adj.*

thalassa (thəlas'ə), Gr. *n.* "the sea," *espec.* exclamation of the Gr. soldiers on seeing the Black Sea in the Anabasis. **-l, -sic,** *adj.* **-sian,** *n.* sea turtle. **-siophyte,** *adj.* seaweed. **-socracy,** *n.* supremacy at sea. **-sography,** *n.* study and mapping of the seas. **-someter,** *n.* tide gauge. **-sophilous,** *adj.* living

in or fond of the sea. **-sophobia,** *n.* dread of the sea. **-sotherapy,** *n.* med. treatment by sea baths, etc.

Thalian (thəli'ən), *adj.* pert. to Thalia, muse of comedy.

thallus (thal'əs), *n.* (*pl.* **-li**) frond-like body of lower plants, as lichens, algae, etc. **-liform,** *adj.,* shaped like t. **-line, -lodal** (-ō'dəl), **-lodic** (-od'ik), **-loid, -lose,** *adj.* **-logen, -lophyte,** *n.* plant having t.

thalposis (thalpō'sis), *n.* sensation of warmth. **-potic** (-ot'ik), *adj.*

thamuria (thəmūr'iə), *n.* abnormally frequent micturition.

thanatography (thanətog'rəfi), *n.* description of person's death. **-gnomonic** (-tōnəmon'ik), *adj.* indicating death. **-toid,** *adj.* deathly; deadly. **-tology,** *n.* study, description or theory of death. **-tophidian,** *n.* venomous snake. **-tosis,** *n.* necrosis; state imitating death. **-tousia,** *n.* funeral rites.

thaumaturgy (thaw'mətəji), *n.* miracle-working; magic. **-ge, -gist, -gus,** *n.* miracle-worker; saint. **-gic,** *adj.* **-gics, -gism,** *n.* **-tology,** *n.* study of t.

theaceous (thiā'shəs), *adj.* pert. to or like tea-plant; belonging to tea family of plants.

theandric (thian'drik), *adj.* pert. to combination of divine and human; Christ-like. **-nthropic,** *adj.* pert. to god-like human being; theandric. **-nthropism,** *n.* state of being both God and man; anthropomorphism. **-nthropos,** *n.* god-man; Christ.

thearchy (thē'ahki), *n.* government by or power of God; theocracy.

theca (thē'kə), *n.* (*pl.* **-ae**) spore-case; capsule; sheath. **-l,** *adj.* **-te,** *adj.* having t.

thé dansant (tā dahṅ'sahṅ), *Fr.* (*pl.* **thés dansants**) "tea dance."

theiform (thē'ifawm), *adj.* like tea or tea plant. **-ine,** *n.* caffeine.

theism (thē'izm), *n.* belief in God, *espec.* one God; *Med.,* condition due to excessive tea-drinking. **-istic,** *adj.*

thelemite (telem'īt), *n.* libertine.

thelyotoky (theliot'əki), *n.* production of females parthenogenetically. **-kous,** *adj.*

thematic (thimat'ik), *adj.* pert. to theme or topic; *Gram.,* pert. to stem of word.

theobromine (thēəbrō'mēn), *n.* caffeine-like alkaloid in cocoa beans.

theocentric (thēəsen'trik), *adj.* having God or divine being as central fact. -ism (-sizm), *n.*

theocracy (thiok'rəsi), *n.* government of a state by priests or according to religious law. -cratic, *adj.* -rasy, *n.* worship of a mixture of gods.

theodicy (thiod'isi), *n.* proof of God's justice ; theol. study of God's government, *espec.* over the soul. -cean, *adj.*

theodolite (thiod'əlīt), *n.* surveyor's angle-measuring swivel-telescope. -tic (-it'ik), *adj.*

theody (thē'ədi), *n.* hymn in praise of God.

theogamy (thiog'əmi), *n.* marriage of gods.

theogony (thiog'əni), *n.* doctrine of origin of gods. -nal, -nic (-on'ik), *adj.* -nism, *n.* belief in a t.

theoktony (thiok'təni), *n.* death of gods. -nic (-on'ik), *adj.*

theology (thiol'əji), *n.* study of God and his revelations of himself to Man ; system of religious knowledge or belief. -gian (-ō'jiən), *n.* -gical, *adj.* -goumenon (-gōō'-minon), *n.* way of speaking of, or opinion about, God.

theomachy (thiom'əki), *n.* battle between or against gods. -chist, *n.*

theomancy (thē'əmansi), *n.* divination by divinely inspired oracles. -ntic (-an'tik), *adj.*

theomania (thēəmā'niə), *n.* delusion that one is God or inspired.

theomastix (thēəmas'tiks), *n.* punishment, or punisher, of mortals sent by God.

theomicrist (thiom'ikrist), *n.* person belittling God.

theomorphic (thēəmaw'fik), *adj.* god-like. -phism, *n.*

theonomy (thion'əmi), *n.* government by God.

theopantism (thēəpan'tizm), *n.* belief that God is the only reality.

theopathy (thiop'əthi), *n.* mystical religious experience ; entire devotion to religion. -thetic, -thic (-ath'ik), *adj.*

theophagy (thiof'əji), *n.* eating of god, or of thing symbolising god, as a sacrament. -gic (-aj'ik), -gous, *adj.* -gite, *n.*

theophany (thiof'əni), *n.* manifesta-

tion of a god. -nic (-an'ik), -nous, *adj.* -nism, *n.*

theophilanthropism (thēəfilan'thrəpizm), *n.* love of God and Man. -pic (-op'ik), *adj.* -pist, -py, *n.*

theophile (thē'əfīl, -il), *n.* person loving, or loved by, God.

theophorous (thiof'ərəs), *adj.* having name of a god ; derived from god's name. -ric (-or'ik), *adj.*

theopneustic (thēəpnū'stik), *adj.* divinely inspired. -ty, *n.*

theorbo (thiaw'bō) *n.* 17th-cent. double-necked lute.

theorem (thē'ərəm), *n.* proved proposition ; rule. -atic, -ic (-em'ik), *adj.*

theosophy (thios'əfi), *n.* supposed mystical or philosophical knowledge of God, *espec.* of a Buddhist-like sect, "The Theosophical Society." -phical, *adj.* -phist, *n.*

theotechny (thē'ətekni), *n.* world in which gods interfere in human affairs. -nic, *adj.*

theotherapy (thēəther'əpi), *n.* faith-healing.

therapeutic (therəpū'tik), *adj.* remedial ; pert. to healing ; *n.* prophylactic. -s, *n.* med. study of remedies. -tist, *n.*

therapy (ther'əpi), *n.* therapeutics ; system of healing ; healing quality.

thereoid (ther'ioid), *adj.* bestial ; savage.

thereology (theriol'əji), *n.* therapeutics.

theriac(a) (ther'iak, thirī'əkə), *n.* antidote to poison ; treacle. -cal, -rial, *adj.* medicinal.

therianthropic (therianthrop'ik), *adj.* half-man half-animal ; pert. to such gods. -pism (-an'thrəpizm), *n.*

theriatrics (theriat'riks), *n.* veterinary medicine.

theriodic (theriod'ik), *adj.* malignant.

theriomorphic (theriəmaw'fik), *adj.* having form of an animal. -phism, *n.* such representation of a god. -phous, *adj.*

thermae (thə'mē), Lat. *n.pl.* warm baths ; public baths. -sthesia, *n.* sensitiveness to heat.

thermal (thə'məl), *adj.* pert. to heat or temperature ; *n.* rising current of warm air.

thermantidote (thəman'tidōt), *n.* air-cooling apparatus.

ʋ=*er* in *father* ; ə̄=*er* in *pert* ; th=*th* in *thin* ; dh=*th* in *then* ; zh=*s* in *pleasure* ; k=*ch* in *loch* ; ṅ=Fr. nasal *n* ; ü=Fr. *u.*

thermatology (thə̄mətol'əji), *n.* study of heat as med. remedy. **-gic,** *adj.* **-gist,** *n.*

hermic (thə̄'mik), *adj.* thermal; due to heat.

thermion (thə̄'mīon), *n.* ion emitted by incandescent object or substance. **-ic** (-on'ik), *adj.* ; **t.valve,** vacuum tube with sev. electrodes —cathode, anode, and grid(s)— the heated cathode emitting electrons.

thermit(e) (thə̄'mit, -mīt), *n.* heat-producing mixture of powdered aluminium and iron oxide, used in welding and incendiary bombs.

thermodynamics (thə̄mədīnam'iks), *n.* study of relationships of heat and mechanical energy.

thermoelectricity (thə̄mōilektris'iti), *n.* electricity due directly to action of heat.

thermogenesis (thə̄məjen'isis), *n.* production of heat ; spontaneous combustion. **-netic** (-jinet'ik), **-nic, -nous** (-oj'inəs), *adj.*

thermograph (thə̄'məgraf), *n.* recording thermometer. **-y,** *n.* writing or printing process in which heat is used.

thermokinematics (thə̄məkinimat'-iks), *n.* study of motion of heat.

thermology (thəmol'əji), *n.* study of heat. **-gical,** *adj.*

thermolysis (thəmol'isis), *n.* disintegration by heat ; loss of body heat. **-yse,** *v.t.* **-ytic** (-it'ik), *adj.*

thermonasty (thə̄'mənasti), *n.* abnormality in position of plant organs due to heat. **-tic,** *adj.*

thermonous (thə̄'mənəs), *adj.* pert. to stimulation by heat.

thermonuclear (thə̄mənū'kliə), *adj.* pert. to fusion of atomic nuclei brought about by, and producing, intense heat, as in hydrogen bomb.

thermophile (thə̄'məfil, -il), *n.* organism thriving in great heat. **-lic** (-il'ik), **-lous** (-of'iləs), *adj.*

thermophore (thə̄'məfōr), *n.* heat-conveying apparatus.

thermopile (thə̄'məpīl), *n.* thermo-electric instr. measuring minute changes in temperature.

thermoplastic (thə̄məplas'tik), *n.* & *adj.* (substance) becoming soft and mouldable when heated.

thermopolypnoea (thə̄məpolipnē'ə), *n.* rapid respiration due to heat. **-oeic,** *adj.*

thermoscope (thə̄'məskōp), *n.* instr. indicating, but not measuring, changes of temperature. **-pic** (-op'ik), *adj.*

thermosetting (thə̄məset'ing), *adj.* becoming permanently hard and rigid when heated.

thermostat (thə̄'məstat), *n.* automatic apparatus for regulating temperature, or for actuating a mechanism at a pre-set temperature. **-ic,** *adj.* **-ics,** *n.* study of thermal equilibrium.

thermotaxis (thə̄mətaks'is), *n.* movement controlled or influenced by heat. **-tactic,** *adj.*

thermotherapy (thə̄məther'əpi), *n.* med. treatment by heat. **-peutics,** *n.*

thermotic(al) (thəmot'ik, -l), *adj.* thermal. **-s,** *n.* thermology.

thermotropism (thəmot'rəpizm), *n.* growth influenced by temperature. **-pic** (trop'ik), *adj.*

theroid (ther'oid), *adj.* feral. **-rology,** *n.* study of wild mammals. **-romorphism,** *n.* reversion to animal type in human being.

thersitical (thəsit'ikl), *adj.* like Thersites, an ugly and scurrilous Greek in Gr. legend ; scurrilous ; violent in speech.

thesaurus (thisōr'əs), *n.* (*pl.* **-ri**) treasure-house, *espec.* of information ; kind of dictionary.

thesis (thē'sis), *n.* (*pl.* **-ses**) theme ; proposition ; essay ; stressed part of metrical foot, *erron.* unstressed part.

thesmothete(s) (thes'məthēt,-moth'-itēz), Gr. *n.* (*pl.* **-tae**) lawgiver.

Thespian (thes'piən), *adj.* pert. to Thespis, supposed founder of Gr. drama ; pert. to drama ; *n.* actor or actress.

theta (thē'tə), *n.* eighth letter (Θ, *θ*) of Gr. alphabet.

thetic (thet'ik), *adj.* prescribed ; pert. to thesis.

theurgy (thē'əji), *n.* miracle ; magical act ; art of persuading divinity to perform desired act. **-gic,** *adj.* **-gist,** *n.*

thionate (thī'ənāt), *v.t.* combine with sulphur. **-nic** (-on'ik), *adj.* pert. to or containing sulphur.

thlipsis (thlip'sis), *n.* *Med.,* compression.

thole (thōl), *n.* upright peg in boat's gunwale against which oar is worked ; *dial.* *v.i.* & *t.* endure.

thooid (thō'oid), *adj.* like a wolf.

thorax (thōr'aks), *n.* (*pl.* -races) cavity between neck and abdomen, containing lungs, heart, etc.; chest. **-racic** (-as'ik), *adj.* **-racoscope,** *n.* stethoscope; instr. for viewing t.

thranite (thrā'nīt), *n.* anct. galley (ship). **-tic** (thrənit'ik), *adj.*

thrasonical (thrəson'ikl), *adj.* boasting.

thremmatology (thremətol'əji), *n.* science of breeding domesticated animals and plants.

threnetic(al) (thrinet'ik, -l), *adj.* mournful.

threnody (thren'ədi), *n.* lament; dirge. **-dial** (-ō'diəl), **-dic** (-od'ik), *adj.* **-dist,** *n.*

threpsology (threpsol'əji), *n.* science of nutrition. **-ptic,** *adj.* pert. to rearing of young.

thrombin (throm'bin), *n.* substance in blood helping to form fibrin in clotting. **-bogen,** *n.* substance from which t. is derived.

thrombus (throm'bəs), *n.* (*pl.* -bi) clot of blood; tumour in blood vessel. **-bogenic,** *adj.* producing t. **-boid,** *adj.* like t. **-bosis,** *n.* formation of t.

Thule (thū'li), *n.* northernmost region in anct. geog. **ultima T.,** furthest T.; any very distant or unknown region; distant objective or end.

Thummim (thum'im), *n.* one of the sacred instruments (Urim and T.) of anct. Jews, worn by high priest in breastplate in some ceremonies.

thurible (thūr'ibl), *n.* censer. **-rifer,** *n.* carrier of c. **-riferous,** *adj.* yielding frankincense. **-rify,** *v.t.*

Thyestean (thīes'tiən), *adj.* pert. to Thyestes, in Gr. legend, whose sons were killed and served to him at a banquet by his brother. **T. banquet,** one at which human flesh is eaten.

thylacitis (thīləsī'tis), *n.* inflammation of skin glands secreting oil.

thymus (thī'məs), *n.* lymphoid gland in lower part of throat, disappearing in adult. **-mic,** *adj.* **-mogenic,** *adj.* due to emotion. **-mopathy,** *n.* mental disorder; disease of t.

thyroid (thīr'oid), *adj.* denoting, or pert. to, large ductless gland of the neck, the hormone of which

influences growth, etc. **-ism,** *n.* deficient t. action. **-rocele,** *n.* goitre. **-rogenic,** *adj.* due to t. action. **-rotherapy,** *n.* med. treatment by t. extract. **-roxine,** *n.* hormone of t. gland.

thyrsus (thə'səs), *n.* (*pl.* -si) ornamented staff carried by Bacchus; *Bot.*, mixed cymose and racemose inflorescence, as of lilac. **-soid,** *adj.* like t.

tibia (tib'iə), *n.* shin-bone; kind of anct. flute. **-l,** *adj.*

tic (tik), *n.* involuntary nervous movement. **t.douloureux** (-dōō-lōōrə'), neuralgia with t. of facial muscles.

ticca (tik'ə), Ind. *adj.* hired. **t.garry,** such carriage.

tichorrhine (tik'ərīn), *n.* woolly rhinoceros.

ticpolonga (tikpəlong'gə), *n.* venomous Ind. snake; Russell's viper.

tierce (tērs), *n.* three or third; sequence of three playing cards of same suit; eccl. service sung at third hour (9 a.m.).

tiercel (tēr'səl), *n.* tercel.

Tiergarten (tēr'gahrtən), Ger. *n.* zoological garden.

tiffany (tif'əni), *n.* light gauzy material.

tiffin (tif'in), Anglo-Ind. *n.* light meal; lunch.

tigella (tijel'ə), *n. Bot.*, short stem. **-te,** *adj.*

til (til, tēl), Hind. *n.* sesame.

tilbury (til'bəri), *n.* kind of two-wheeled carriage.

tilde (til'dā), *n.* wavy mark (~) indicating *ny* sound of Sp. ñ (as in *cañon* or *canyon*).

tileaceous (tiliā'shəs), *adj.* pert. to or like linden tree; belonging to linden family of trees.

tilka (til'kə), *n.* Hindu caste-mark on forehead.

timbal (tim'bəl), *n.* kettledrum.

timbre (tam'bə; Fr., tañ'br), *n.* distinctive quality of a sound.

timbrel (tim'brəl), *n.* tambourine.

timocracy (timok'rəsi), *n.* ideal state in which love of honour is ruling principle. **-cratic,** *adj.*

timpani (tim'pəni), It. *n.pl.* (*sing.* -no) set of kettledrums. **-st,** *n.* player of t.

tinction (tingk'shən), *n.* act of dyeing. **-torial,** *adj.* pert. to t. or colours. **-tumutation,** *n.* change of colour.

tincture (tingk'tūr), *n.* colour ; dye ; slight amount ; extract of medicinal principle of a plant ; *v.t.* stain ; imbue.

tine (tīn), *n.* prong.

tinea (tin'iə), *n.* ringworm, or similar disease. **-l,** *adj.*

tinnitus (tinī'təs), *n.* ringing sound in the head.

tintinnabulate (tintinab'ūlāt), *v.i.* ring ; tinkle. **-lant, -lar(y), -lous,** *adj.* **-lism,** *n.* bell-ringing. **-tion,** *n.*

tiqueur (tēkēr'), *n.* person suffering from tics.

tirade (tīr ād'), *n.* long, violent speech.

tirailleur (tēr āyēr'), Fr. *n.* infantry soldier.

tiro (tīr'ō), *n.* beginner. **-cinium,** *n.* (*pl.* **-ia**) first experience.

tisane (tizan'), *n.* medicinal beverage of barley, camomile, etc. ; ptisan.

Titan (tī'tən), *n.* one of a race of giants in Gr. myth. ; giant ; genius. **-ic** (-an'ik), *adj.*

tithe (tīdh), *n.* tenth part ; tax payable to church.

Titian (tish'ən), *adj.* reddish-brown.

titillate (tit'ilāt), *v.t.* tickle ; stimulate. **-ant,** *adj.* **-tion, -tor,** *n.* **-tive, -tory,** *adj.*

titrate (tit'rāt, tī'-), *v.t. Chem.,* determine strength of, or analyse, etc., by finding the smallest amount of the substance that will produce a given effect with another known quantity. **-re,** *n.* such smallest amount. **-rimetry,** *n.* measuring by such means. **-tion,** *n.*

titubant (tit'ūbənt), *adj.* staggering. **-ncy,** *n.*

titular (tit'ūlə), *n.* pert. to or acting as title ; in name only ; patronal ; *n.* nominal representative or holder. **-y,** *n.* & *adj.*

tmesis (tmē'sis), *n.* introduction of word, etc., between parts of a compound word.

toadstone (tōd'stōn), *n.* any stone or stone-like concretion believed to be formed in a toad and to have magic powers.

toccata (təkah'tə), It. *n.* brilliant, quick, fantasia-like mus. composition.

tocology (təkol'əji), *n.* midwifery. **-gical,** *adj.* **-gist,** *n.*

tocsin (tok'sin), *n.* alarm bell.

tody (tō'di), *n.* very small, long-billed W. Ind. bird.

toga (tō'gə), *n.* common garment, draped round whole body, of anct. Rome. **t. praetexta,** t. with broad purple border, worn by magistrates, etc. **-ted,** *adj.* wearing t. ; dignified.

tohubohu (tō'hōobō'hōo), Heb. *n.* chaos.

toison (twah'zawṅ), Fr. *n.* sheep's fleece. **t. d'or,** Golden Fleece.

toluene (tol'ū ēn), *n.* light liquid hydrocarbon, obtained from coal tar and used in dye manufacture.

tombac (tom'bak), *n.* alloy of zinc and copper used for cheap jewelry, etc. ; Dutch gold.

tombola (tom'bələ), *n.* kinds of lottery, *gen.* in which each entrant must win a prize.

tomentose, -tous (təmen'tōs, -təs), *adj.* bearing thickly matted hairs. **-tulose,** *adj.* slightly t.

tomography (təmog'rəfi), *n.* X-ray photography in which parts of body in front of, or behind, the part under examination are not shown. **-gram,** *n.* such photograph. **-phic(al),** *adj.*

tomosis (təmō'sis), *n.* disease of cotton plant.

tonant (tō'nənt), *adj.* making loud, deep noise.

tonetics (tənet'iks), *n.* study of intonation in languages. **-cian** (tōnetish'ən, ton-), *n.*

tonga (tong'gə), *n.* light Ind. two-wheeled carriage ; tonka.

tonic (ton'ik), *adj. Med.,* pert. to tension, *espec.* muscular ; improving muscular condition ; invigorating ; *Mus.,* pert. to keynote ; *n. Med.,* t. medicine ; *Mus.,* keynote. **-ity,** *n.*

tonitruous (tənit'rooəs), *adj.* thundering. **-uone,** *n.* mus. instr. imitating thunder.

tonka (tong'kə), *n.* Amer. bean-like tree and seed, used in perfumes, vanilla extract, etc.

tonneau (ton'ō), *n.* rear extension of motor-car body.

tonometer (tənom'itə), *n.* instr. measuring pitch of tones ; *Med.,* instr. measuring tension or pressure. **-ograph** (ton'-), *n.* recording t.

tonsillectomy (tonsilek'təmi), *n.*

surg. removal of tonsils. **-llitis,** *n.* inflammation of tonsils. **-llotomy,** *n.* removal of part or all of tonsils.

tonsure (ton´sūr), shaving of a circular patch on crown of head, symbolic of monkhood. **-sorial,** *adj.* pert. to barber.

tontine (tontēn´), *n.* allocation of certain benefits, as annuities, etc., among a group of persons such that at the death of one member the remainder share his portion; annuity, etc., so shared.

tonus (tō´nəs), *n.* normal response to stimuli; muscular spasm.

topaesthesia (topesthē´zhiə), *n.* determining place by sense of touch.

toparch (top´ahk, tō´-), *n.* ruler, *espec.* of toparchy. **-y,** *n.* petty state under a t.

tope (tōp), *n.* small shark.

topee, *see* topi.

tophaceous (təfā´shəs), *adj.* gritty. **-phus** (tō´fəs), *n.* (*pl.* **-phi**) tufa; bodily concretion.

topi, -pee (tō´pi), *n.* sola topi. **t.wallah,** European.

topiary (tō´piəri), *n.* & *adj.* (pert. to) art of clipping shrubs, etc., into ornamental shapes. **-rian,** *adj.* **-rist,** *n.* expert in t.

topography (təpog´rəfi), *n.* geography of a locality; configuration of a land surface; arrangement of physical features. **-pher,** *n.* **-phic(al),** *adj.* **-pology,** *n.* topographical study of one place; regional anatomy.

toponym (top´ənim), *n.* name of, or designating, a place. **-ic,** *adj.* **-ics,** *n.* study of place-names. **-y** (-on´imi), *n.* region's place-names.

topophobia (topəfō´biə), *n.* dread of certain places.

toque (tōk), *n.* woman's turban-like brimless hat.

torah (tōr´ah), Heb. *n.* law; revelation; Pentateuch.

torchon (tōr´shn), *n.* kind of coarse lace or paper.

torcular (taw´kūlə), *n.* tourniquet.

tore (tōr), *n.* surface described by rotation of a conic section about straight line of its own plane.

toreador (tor´iədōr), Sp. *n.* mounted bullfighter.

toreutic (tərōō´tik), *adj.* pert. to metal ornamented with small engraved patterns; chased. **-s,** *n.* art of doing such work.

toric (tor´ik), *adj.* pert. to or like a tore.

torii (tōr´iē), *n.* Jap. gateway of curved posts and lintel only.

tormentum (tawmen´təm), *n.* (*pl.* **-ta**) anct. catapult-like war machine.

tormina (taw´minə), Lat. *n.pl.* gripes. **-l, -nous,** *adj.*

tornote (taw´nōt), *adj.* with blunt extremities.

torose (tōr´ōs), *adj.* bulging knobbly; muscular. **-rous,** *adj.* **-sity** (-os´iti), *n.*

torpid (taw´pid), *n.* numb; sleepy; dull. **-ity,** *n.* **-pify,** *v.t.* make t. **-por,** *n.* torpid state; apathy. **-porific,** *adj.* torpifying.

torrid (tor´id), *n.* dried up; very hot; tropical. **-refy, -rify,** *v.t.* scorch; parch.

torsade (tawsād´, -ahd´), *n.* twisted cord.

torsion (taw´shn), *n.* act of twisting; state of being twisted. **-sibility,** *n.* tendency to untwist. **-sile,** *adj.* **-sive,** *adj.* spirally twisted.

torso (taw´sō), *n.* (*pl.* **-si**) trunk of body.

tort (tawt), *n.* wrongful deed. **t.-feasor,** person committing t.

torticollis (tawtikol´is), *n.* stiff neck.

tortile (taw´tīl, -il), *adj.* twisted; capable of being twisted. **-lity,** *n.*

tortious (taw´shəs), *adj.* causing or committing tort.

torulose, -lous (tor´ūlōs, -əs) *adj.* slightly torose.

torus (tōr´əs), *n.* (*pl.* **-ri**) rounded swelling; *Archit.,* such lowest moulding of column; *Bot.,* receptacle.

torvous (taw´vəs), *adj.* stern. **-vity,** *n.*

totalisator (tō´təlizātə), *n.* parimutuel, *espec.* at a racecourse (*abbr.* tote).

totalitarian (tōtalitar´iən), *adj.* pert. to single-party political system, as Communism and Fascism, in which minority views are ruthlessly suppressed; *n.* adherent of this. **-ism,** *n.*

totara (tō´tərə, -ah´rə), *n.* timber tree, with reddish wood, of N.Z.; mahogany pine.

totem (tō'təm), *n.* animal or plant adopted as ancestor by savage tribe, and held in great veneration. **t.pole,** carved pole bearing totemic symbols. **-ic** (-em'ik), *adj.* **-ism,** *n.*

toties quoties (tō'shiēz kwō'shiēz), *Lat.,* "as often as"; repeatedly; *R.C.,* indulgence obtainable as often as desired.

toty (tō'ti), Anglo-Ind. *n.* low caste odd-job man.

touché (tōo'shā), Fr. *adj.* "touched" by opponent's rapier in fencing; hit; defeated in argument.

toupee (tōopē', -pā'), *n.* small patch of false hair.

tourbillion (toorbil'yən; Fr., tōor-bēyawn'), *n.* whirlwind; whirlpool; any whirling object.

tourmaline (tōor'məlin), *n.* kind of black, blue, red and green silicate cut as gem.

tourniquet (tōor'nikā), *n.* device to stop bleeding, as a bandage twisted tight by a stick, etc.

tournure (tōornūr'), Fr. *n.* grace; poise; expressive phrase.

tout (tōo), Fr. *n. & adj.* "all." **t. à fait** (tōot ah fā'), "entirely." **t. à l'heure** (tōot ah lèr'), "in a moment"; "a moment ago." **t.court** (-kōor'), "quite short"; simply; without any addition. **t. de suite** (tōot swēt'), "immediately." **t.ensemble** (tōot ahn-sahn'bl), "all together"; general effect; outfit.

tovarish, -isch (təvah'rish), Russ. *n.* "comrade."

toxic (toks'ik), *adj.* poisoning; pert. to or due to poison. **-ogenic,** *adj.* producing or produced by poison. **-ology,** *n.* study of poisons. **-opathy,** *n.* disease due to poison. **-ophagy,** *n.* eating of poisons. **-osis,** *n.* condition due to poisoning. **-xaemia,** *n.* blood poisoning due to toxins in blood. **-xiferous,** *adj.* producing poison. **-xin,** *n.* disease-causing poison produced by living organism. **-xiphobia,** *n.* dread of being poisoned.

toxophily (toksof'ili), *n.* archery. **-lite,** *n.* person fond of t. **-lous,** *adj.*

trabeate(d) (trā'biāt, -id), *adj.* constructed of horizontal beams. **-tion,** *adj.*

trabecula (trəbek'ūlə), *n.* (*pl.* -ae) small bar, rod, etc. **-r,** *adj.* **-te,** *adj.* crossbarred.

trachea (trəkē'ə, trā'kiə), *n.* (*pl.* -ae) windpipe. **-eitis** (trak-, trā-), *n.* inflammation of t. **-eotomy,** *n.* making of incision into t. **-l, -ry,** *adj.*

trachoma (trəkō'mə), *n.* chronic form of conjunctivitis. **-tous,** *adj.*

trachycarpous (trakikah'pəs, trā-), *adj.* rough-fruited. **-yglossate,** *adj.* rough-tongued. **-yphonia,** *n.* roughness of voice. **-yspermous,** *adj.* rough-seeded.

tractable (trak'təbl), *n.* easily managed or led; obedient; malleable. **-bility,** *n.*

tractarian (traktār'iən), *n.* writer of tracts; Anglo-Catholic, *espec.* member of Tractarian movement at Oxford in 1833-41.

tractile (trak'til), *adj.* ductile. **-lity** (-il'iti), *n.*

tractive (trak'tiv), *adj.* pulling.

traduce (trədūs'), *v.t.* slander. **-ction, -ment,** *n.*

tragacanth (trag'əkanth), *n.* valuable gum exuded by Ind. tree, used in med.

tragopan (trag'əpan), *n.* kind of bright-hued Asiatic pheasant.

tragus (trā'gəs), *n.* (*pl.* -gi) prominence in front of opening of ear.

trajectory (traj'iktəri), *n.* curved path taken by body moving in space.

tralatition (tralətish'n), *n.* metaphor. **-tious,** *adj.* metaphorical; handed down from father to son.

trammel (tram'əl), *n.* net to catch fish, birds, etc.; shackle on horse's leg; check; obstacle; instr. for drawing ellipses; *v.t.* restrain; hamper.

tramontane (trəmon'tān), *adj.* (from) across the mountains; trans-alpine.

tranquilliser (trang'kwilīzə), *n.* sedative drug.

transalpine (tranzal'pīn), *adj.* on the other (*i.e.* the north) side of the Alps; pert. to France, Germany and England; ultramontane.

transcalent (tranzkā'lənt), *adj.* pervious to heat. **-lescent,** *adj.* **-ncy,** *n.*

transcend (transend'), *v.t.* pass beyond or over; surpass; lie outside; excel. **-ence, -ency,** *n.* **-ent,** *adj.* **-ental,** *adj.* beyond human understanding; supernatural; not founded on experience; theoretical. **-entalism,** *n.* phil. theory emphasising that which transcends knowledge or sense perception, or the importance of spiritual over material things.

transcribe (transkrīb'), *v.t.* make a written or typewritten copy of; *Mus.,* arrange for other instrument(s) or voice(s); *Rad.,* prerecord for sound broadcasting. **-ript,** *n.* such copy, arrangement, or recording. **-ription,** *n.*

transect (transekt'), *v.t.* cut across; *n.* cross section. **-ion,** *n.*

transept (tran'sept), *n.* transverse part of church at right angles to and between nave and choir. **-al,** *adj.*

transfluent (tranz'flooənt), *adj.* flowing across. **-flux,** *n.*

transforation (tranzfərā'shn), *n.* perforation.

transhume (tranzum'), *v.t.* move (cattle) to summer pastures or winter quarters. **-mance,** *n.*

transient (tran'siənt), *adj.* fleeting. **-nce,** *n.*

transilient (transil'iənt), *adj.* leaping across; abruptly discontinuous. **-nce,** *n.*

transire (transīr'i), *n.* ship's document for customs declaration, showing cargo, etc.

transistor (tranzis'tə), *n.* elec. semiconductor, *espec.* a crystal of germanium, etc., performing function of thermionic valve.

transition (tranzish'n), *n.* act or state of passing from one condition or time to another. **-al,** *adj.* **-tive,** *adj.* *Gram.,* requiring direct object. **-tory,** *adj.* transient.

transliterate (tranzlit'ərāt), *v.t.* write in letters of another alphabet. **-tion, -tor,** *n.*

translucent (tranzloo'sənt), *adj.* shining through; permitting the passage of light but not transparent. **-cid,** *adj.* **-nce,** *n.*

translunary (tranzloo'nəri), *adj.* beyond the moon; spiritual; unearthly.

transmarine (tranzmərēn'), *adj.* across or beyond the sea.

transmigrate (tranz'mīgrāt, -mī'-), *v.i.* & *t.* pass from one body or place into another; transfer. **-tion,** *n.* **-tive,** *adj.*

transmogrify (tranzmog'rif̄), *v.t.* transform. **-fication,** *n.*

transmute (tranzmūt'), *v.t.* change into another substance or species. **-tation,** *n.* **-tative,** *adj.*

transom (tran'səm), *n.* horizontal or transverse beam or bar.

transpadane (tranz'pədān), *adj.* on the other (*i.e.* the north) side of the river Po.

transpicuous (transpik'ūəs), *adj.* easily seen through or understood. **-uity,** *n.*

transpire (transpīr'), *v.i.* & *t.* exhale; give off or escape as vapour; *erron.,* become known; happen. **-ration,** *n.* **-ratory,** *adj.*

transpontine (tranzpon'tīn), *adj.* on the other (*i.e.* the south) side of the bridges over the Thames; pert. to or like the lurid melodrama formerly played in theatres there.

transrhenane (tranzrē'nān), *adj.* on the other (*i.e.* the east) side of the river Rhine; German.

transubstantiate (transubstan'-shiāt), *v.t.* transmute. **-tion,** *n.*; *Theol.,* conversion of Communion bread and wine into body and blood of Christ.

transude (transūd'), *v.i.* be exuded. **-date,** *n.* such substance. **-dation,** *n.* **-dative, -datory,** *adj.*

transumptive (transump'tiv), *adj.* transferred; metaphorical.

transuranic (tranzūrā'nik), *adj.* denoting any chem. element having atomic number beyond uranium (92), not occurring in nature but artificially produced by bombardment of atoms.

transverbate (tranzvə'bāt), *v.t.* translate word for word. **-tion,** *n.*

transverberate (tranzvə'bərāt), *v.t.* pierce. **-tion,** *n.*

transvest (tranzvest'), *v.i.* & *t.* disguise; wear clothes of another, *espec.* of other sex. **-ism,** *n.* **-ite,** *n.* & *adj.*

transvolation (tranzvəlā'shn), *n* flying higher than normal.

trapezium (trəpē'ziəm), *n.* (*pl.* **-ia**) quadrilateral with two parallel sides; any irregular quadrilateral; *Amer.,* trapezoid. **-zial, -ziform,** *adj.* **-zoid** (trap'-), *n.* quadrilateral with no sides parallel; *Amer.,* trapezium.

traulism (traw'lizm), *n.* stammering.

trauma (traw'mə), *n.* (*pl.* **-ta**) injury; shock, *espec.* mental. **-tic** (-at'ik), *adj.* **-tology,** *n.* description of wounds. **-tropism,** *n.* alteration in direction of growth due to wound.

trave (trāv), *n.* crossbeam; space between crossbeams. **-vated,** *adj.*

travertine (trav'ətin, -ēn), *n.* crystalline calcium carbonate, deposit of hot springs; onyx marble.

travesty (trav'isti), *n.* & *v.t.* burlesque.

trebuchet (treb'ūshet), *n.* large sling-like medieval engine for hurling stones.

trecento (trāchen'tō), It. *n.* & *adj.* thirteenth century. **-tist,** *n.* writer or artist of that period.

trefoil (trē'foil), *n.* clover, or other plants with leaf divided into three lobes; archit. ornament of that shape.

trematode (trem'ətōd, trē'-), *n.* kind of parasitic flatworm.

tremallose (trem'əlōs), *adj.* gelatinous.

trenchant (tren'chənt), *adj.* sharp; cutting.

trente et quarante (trahnt ā karahnt), *Fr.,* "thirty and forty"; gambling card game with betting on red and black.

trepan (tripan'), *n.* surg. saw for incision into skull; *v.t.* use t. on; decoy; swindle. **-ation** (trep-), *n.*

trepang (tripang'), *n.* bêche-de-mer.

trephine (trifēn'), *n.* form of trepan; *v.t.* use t. on. **-nation** (tref-), *n.*

tressilate (tres'ilāt), *v.i.* quiver. **-tion,** *n.*

trey (trā), *n.* card, domino, etc., bearing three pips.

triad (trī'ad), *n.* group of three; *Mus.,* chord of three notes. **-ic,** *adj.*

triagonal (trīag'ənəl), *adj.* triangular.

triarch (trī'ahk) *n.* triumvir. **-y,** *n.*

tribade (trib'əd) *n.* homosexual woman. **-dism,** *n.*

tribometer (trībom'itə), *n.* instr. measuring sliding friction.

tribrach (trī'brak), *n.* verse foot of three syllables; object, etc., with three branches. **-ial** (-ā'kiəl), **-ic,** *adj.*

tribuloid (trib'ūloid), *adj.* yielding prickly fruit.

tribune (trib'ūn), *n.* tribal chief; representative of a section of people; demagogue; platform; dais. **-nitian,** *adj.*

tricenary (trīsē'nəri), *adj.* pert. to or consisting of thirty; lasting thirty days. **-ntennial,** *n.* & *adj.* tercentenary.

tricephalous (trīsef'ələs), *adj.* having three heads. **-lus,** *n.* (*pl.* **-li**) such monster.

triceps (trīseps), *n.* muscle of back of upper arm with three points of attachment.

trichinosis (trikinō'sis), *n.* disease due to eating pork infested with certain kind of nematode worms. **-nise,** *v.t.* infest with such worms. **-notic** (-ot'ik), **-nous,** *adj.*

trichocarpous (trikəkah'pəs), *adj.* hairy-fruited.

trichoclasis (trikok'ləsis), *n.* brittleness of hair. **-ogenous,** *adj.* producing hair. **-oid,** *adj.* hair-like. **-ology,** *n.* study of hair. **-omatosis,** *n.* disease causing matting of hair. **-omycosis,** *n.* fungal disease of hair. **-opathy, -osis,** *n.* any disease of hair. **-ophytosis,** *n.* ringworm. **-oschisis,** *n.* splitting of hair.

trichotomy (trikot'əmi), *n.* division into three parts or categories. **-mic** (-om'ik), **-mous,** *adj.*

trichromatic (trīkrəmat'ik), *adj.* pert. to or in three colours.

tricipital (trisip'itəl), *adj.* pert. to triceps; tricephalous.

triclinic (trīklin'ik), *adj.* having three unequal axes meeting at oblique angles.

tricorn (trī'kawn), *adj.* having three corners or horns. **-e,** *n.* three-cornered hat.

tricot (trē'kō), *n.* silk, rayon, nylon or woollen fabric resembling knitting. **-ine** (trikətēn'), *n.* double-twilled worsted fabric.

tridactyl (trīdak'til), *n.* having three fingers or toes. **-dentate,** *adj.* having three teeth. **-digitate,** *adj.* tridactyl.

tridiurnal (trīdī ə'nəl), *adj.* lasting three days; happening every three days.

triennial (trīen'iəl), *adj.* happening every three years; lasting three years; *n.* such plant; third anniversary.

trieteric (trīiter'ik), *n.* & *adj.* (festival) occurring each third year (*i.e.* in alternate years).

trifarious (trīfār'iəs), *adj.* facing three ways.

---

trifid (trī'fid), *adj.* divided into three parts.

triforium (trīfōr'iəm), *n.* gallery over nave and choir. **-rial,** *adj.*

trifurcate (trīfɜ'kāt), *v.t.* divide into three forks; *adj.* so dividing. **-tion,** *n.*

trigamy (trig'əmi), *n.* state of being married to three living spouses. **-mist,** *n.* **-mous,** *adj.*

trigeminal (trījem'inəl), *adj.* pert. to pair of nerves from cranium to jaw. **-nous,** *adj.* (one of) three born together; threefold.

trigeneric (trījiner'ik), *adj.* belonging to three kinds or genera; having three genders.

triglot (trī'glot), *n.* & *adj.* (book) in three languages.

triglyph (trig'lif), *n.* archit. ornament of tablet bearing two V-shaped channels. **-al, -ic,** *adj.*

trigonal (trig'ɔnəl), *adj.* pert. to or having three angles.

trigoneutic (trīgɔnū'tik), *adj.* three-brooded.

trigonic (trīgon'ik), *adj.* trigonal.

trigonometry (trigɔnom'itri), *n.* math. study of triangles and measurement by deducing unknown from known sides and angles. **-tric** (-et'rik), *adj.*

trigonous (trig'ɔnəs), *adj.* having three angles.

trigram (trī'gram), *n.* figure of three lines; inscription of three letters. **-mmatic,** *adj.*

trigraph (trī'graf), *n.* three letters having one sound, as *eau.* **-ic,** *adj.*

trihedron (trīhē'drən), *n.* solid figure of three planes. **-ral,** *adj.*

trihoral (trihōr'əl), *adj.* happening every three hours.

trijugate (trī'joogāt), *adj.* with three pairs of leaflets.

trilabiate (trīlā'biāt), *adj.* having three lips. **-laminar,** *adj.* having three layers.

trilateral (trīlat'ərəl), *n.& adj.* three-sided (figure).

trilemma (trīlem'ə), *n.* dilemma-like position offering three choices.

trilinear (trīlin'iə), *adj.* pert. to, having or bounded by three lines.

trilingual (trīling'gwəl), *adj.* pert. to, in or speaking three languages.

triliteral (trīlit'ərəl), *n.* & *adj.* (word) of three letters.

trilith(on) (trī'lith, trīl'ithən), *n.*

anct. monument of two upright stones bearing one transverse stone.

trillion (tril'yən), *n.* a million billions (10^{18}); *Amer.* & *Fr.*, a thousand billions (10^{12}).

trilobite (trī'ləbīt), *n.* oval, flattened fossil with trifid body. **-tic** (-it'ik) *adj.*

trilocular (trīlok'ūlə), *adj.* having three cells. **-late,** *adj.*

trilogy (tril'əji), *n.* series of three connected literary or musical works. **-gical,** *adj.* **-gist,** *n.*

trimacer (trim'əsə), *n.* metrical foot of three long syllables.

trimacular, -late (trīmak'ūlə, -ət), *adj.* bearing three spots.

trimensual (trīmen'sūəl), *adj.* happening every three months.

trimerous (trim'ərəs), *adj.* *Bot.,* having its parts in threes.

trimester (trīmes'tə), *n.* period of three months. **-tral,-trial,** *adj.*

trimeter (trim'itə), *n.* verse-line of three feet. **-tric** (trīmet'rik), *adj.*

trimorph (trī'mawf), *n.* substance crystallising into three forms. **-ism,** *n.* **-ous,** *adj.*

trin (trin), *n.* triplet. **-al** (trī'nəl), **-e** (trīn), *adj.* threefold. **-ary** (trīnəri), *n.* group of three.

tringoid (tring'goid), *adj.* pert. to sandpipers.

trinitrotoluene (trinitrōtol'ūen), *n.* high explosive obtained from toluene (*abbr.* **T.N.T.**).

Trinkgeld (tringk'gelt), Ger. *n.* "drink money"; tip; gratuity. **-klied** (-lēt), *n.* "drinking song."

trinoctial (trīnok'shəl), *adj.* lasting three nights.

trinomial (trīnō'miəl), *adj.* pert. to or using three names; having name of three terms; pert. to such scientific nomenclature; *n.* math. expression of three terms joined by + or —. **-minal** (-om'-inəl), *adj.*

trioecious (trīē'shəs), *adj.* having male, female and hermaphrodite flowers on different plants. **-cism,** *n.*

triolet (trī'ɔlit), *n.* eight-lined poem, with repetition of first line as fourth and seventh, and of second line as eighth; and with first, third, fourth, fifth and seventh lines, and second, sixth and eighth lines, rhyming.

trionym (trī'ənim), *n.* trinomial expression. **-al** (-on'iməl), *adj.*

tripara (trip'ərə), *n.* woman who has had three childbirths.

tripartite (trĭpah'tīt), *adj.* in three parts ; between three parties or States. **-tient** (-ah'shiənt), *adj.* dividing into three parts. **-tion,** *n.*

tripedal (trī'pidəl, trip'-), *adj.* having three feet.

triphthong (trif'thong), *n.* three vowel sounds pronounced as one.

triphyllous (trīfil'əs), *adj.* three-leaved.

triplegia (trīplē'jiə), *n.* hemiplegia with paralysis of a part on the other side.

triplopia (triplō'piə), *n.* triple vision.

tripody (trip'ədi), *n.* verse measure of three feet.

tripos (trī'pos), *n.* honours examination at Cambridge University.

tripsis (trip'sis), *n.* act of rubbing or grinding ; massage.

triptote (trip'tōt), *n. & adj. Gram.,* (noun) with three cases only.

triptych (trip'tik), *n.* painting in three parts, *espec.* altar piece with one central and two hinged side panels.

triptyque (trēptēk'), Fr. *n.* customs pass for importing motor car.

triquetra (trīkwet'rə, -kwē'-), *n.* triangular-shaped pattern, object, etc. **-l, -ric, -rous,** *adj.*

trireme (trīr'ēm),. *n.* anct. galley with three banks of oars.

trisect (trīsekt'), *v.t.* cut into three equal parts. **-ion, -or,** *n.*

triskelion (triskel'yən), *n.* pattern of three curved branches, *espec.* of three bent legs as badge of Isle of Man.

trismus (triz'məs), *n.* lockjaw. **-mic,** *adj.*

tristachyous (trīstā'kiəs), *adj.* three-spiked.

triste (trēst), Fr. *adj.* "sad." **-sse,** *n.* sadness.

tristich (tris'tik), *n.* stanza of three lines. **-ic,** *adj.* **-ous,** *adj.* in three rows.

tristiloquy (tristil'əkwi), *n.* mournful manner of speech. **-tisonous,** *adj.* mournful-sounding.

trisulcate (trīsul'kāt), *adj.* with three ridges, forks or furrows.

trisyllable (tris'iləbl), *n.* word of three syllables. **-bic** (-ab'ik), *adj.*

tritheism (trī'thēizm), *n.* belief that members of Trinity are three separate gods. **-ist,** *n.*

triticism (trit'isizm), *n.* trite remark.

triticoid (trit'ikoid), *adj.* like wheat.

tritium (trit'iəm), *n.* isotope of hydrogen of mass number 3.

triturate (trit'ūrat), *v.t.* rub ; bruise ; grind to powder. **-ral,** *adj.* of use in grinding. **-tion, -tor,** *n.*

triumvir (trium'və), *n. (pl. -i)* member of triumvirate. **-ate,** *n.* ruling body of three men.

triune (trī'ūn), *adj.* three in one. **-nity,** *n.*

trivalent (triv'ələnt, trīvā'-), *adj.* having valency of three.

trivia (triv'iə), Lat. *n.* cross-roads ; *n.pl.* trivial matters

trivirgate (trīvā'gāt), *adj.* bearing three linear markings.

trivoltine (trīvol'tīn), *adj.* three-brooded.

trochaic (trəkā'ik), *adj.* pert. to or consisting of trochees ; *n.* such verse line.

troche (trō'ki), *n.* circular lozenge, *espec.* for throat affection. **-ameter,** *n.* instr. counting wheel's revolutions. **-chal, -chate,** *adj.* circular ; wheel-like.

trochee (trō'ki), *n.* verse foot of one long and one short syllable.

trochilic (trəkil'ik), *adj.* rotary ; able to turn. **-s,** *n.* study of rotary motion.

trochiline, -lidine (trok'ilīn, -il'idīn), *adj.* pert. to or like a humming-bird ; belonging to humming-bird family of birds. **-lus,** *n.* humming-bird ; crocodile bird ; gold-crest.

trochiscus (trəkis'kəs), *n. (pl. -ci)* troche. **-cation,** *n.* making of t.

trochlea (trok'liə), *n.* pulley-like structure of shoulder, thigh, or orbit of eye. **-leiform, -r, -riform, -te,** *adj.* like a pulley.

trochocephalic (trokəsifal'ik), *adj.* having abnormally round head. **-lia** (-ā'liə), **-lus, -ly** (-sef'ələs, -li), *n.* such condition.

troglodyte (trog'lədīt), *n.* cave-dweller. **-tal, -tic** (-it'ik), *adj.*

trogon (trō'gon), *n.* brightly-coloured bird of Amer., African and Ind. jungle.

troika (troi'kə), Russ. *n.* carriage drawn by three horses abreast.

troll (trol), *n.* cave-dwelling dwarf or giant of Ger. and Scand. myth.

tronc (trawn), Fr. *n.* "alms-box" ;

---

hat, bah, hāte, hāre, crawl ; pen, ēve, hēre ; it, īce, fīre ; on, bōne, boil, bōre, howl ; foot, fōōd, bōōr, hull, tūbe, pūre.

system of pooling tips among waiters.

trope (trōp), *n.* figure of speech; heading; *Mus.*, melodic phrase occurring frequently as kind of formula. **-ic** (-ē'ik), *adj.* keel-like.

trophic (trof'ik), *adj.* pert. to nutrition. **-phesy,** *n.* disease due to fault in such nerves. **-phism,** *n.* nutrition. **-phogenic,** *adj.* due to differences in food. **-phology,** *n.* science of nutrition. **-phopathy,** *n.* disorder of nutritional processes. **-phoplasm,** *n.* nutritive substance of cell. **-photherapy,** *n.* med. treatment by dieting. **-photropism,** *n.* growth direction by nutritional factors.

tropism (trō'pizm), *n.* movement of an organism, *espec.* direction of growth of plant, in response to a stimulus; innate inclination. **-atic, -pistic,** *adj.*

tropology (trəpol'əji), *n.* figurative style of writing; interpretation of Bible stressing figurative nature of language.

tropometer (trəpom'itə), *n.* instr. measuring rotation.

tropopause (trop'əpawz), *n.* level where troposphere ends and stratosphere begins.

tropophilous (trəpof'iləs), *adj.* flourishing in seasonal extremes of climate. **-phyte** (trop'əfīt), *n.* such plant.

troposphere (trop'əsfēr), *n.* all the atmosphere below the stratosphere.

trotyl (trō'til), *n.* trinitrotoluene.

troubadour (trōō'bədoor), *n.* medieval romantic poet; wandering minstrel.

trousseau (trōō'sō), *n.* (*pl.* **-x**) bridal outfit.

trouvère (trōōvar'), Fr. *n.* troubadour of N. France.

trovatore (trōvahtōr'ā), It. *n.* (*pl.* **-ri**) troubadour.

trucidation (trōōsidā'shn), *n.* slaughter.

truculent (truk'ūlənt), *adj.* bellicose; cruel; savage. **-nce,** *n.*

truffle (truf'l), *n.* kind of underground fungus or its fruit, considered a delicacy.

truism (trōō'izm), *n.* obvious truth. **-atic, -stic(al),** *adj.*

truncate (trung'kāt), *v.t. & adj.* cut off. **-tion, -tor,** *n.*

trunnion (trun'yən), *n.* one of a pair of pivots.

truttaceous (trutā'shəs), *adj.* pert. to or like trout.

tryma (trī'mə), *n.* kind of nut-like fruit, as walnut.

trypanosome (trip'ənəsōm), *n.* parasitic protozoan, *espec.* causing sleeping sickness. **-miasis** (-səmī'əsis), *n.* infestation with t.

trypsin (trip'sin), *n.* pancreatic enzyme digesting protein. **-ptic,** *adj.*

tsetse (set'si), *n.* African fly carrying trypanosome that causes sleeping sickness.

tsiology (tsiol'əji), *n.* treatise on tea.

tuan (tooəhn'), Malay *n.* sir.

tuba (tū'bə), *n.* large bass saxhorn; bombardon; sousaphone.

tuber (tū'bə), *n.* fleshy underground stem, as potato. **-aceous,** *adj.* pert. to fungus family having t. **-ation,** *n.* formation of t.

tubercle (tū'bəkl), *n.* small knob or outgrowth; small tuber; *Med.,* small diseased nodule, *espec.* of tuberculosis. **-cular** (-ā'kulə), *adj.* pert. to t. or tuberculosis. **-culation,** *n.* formation of t. **-culin,** *n.* culture of products of tubercular bacilli used as test for tuberculosis. **-culosis,** *n.* a destructive disease, *espec.* of lungs. **-culous,** *adj.*

tubicinate (tūbis'ināt), *v.i.* blow a trumpet. **-tion,** *n.*

tubicolous (tubik'ələs), *adj.* spinning or living in a tubular web.

tubicorn(ous) (tū'bikawn, -kaw'nəs), *adj.* hollow-horned. **-ifacient,** *adj.* constructing a tube. **-ifer,** *n.* tubifacient animal. **-iform,** *adj.* tube-like. **-inarial,** *adj.* with tubular nostrils. **-iparous,** *adj.* secreting matter used in making tube.

tubulure (tū'būloor), *n.* tubular opening.

tucket (tuk'it), *n.* flourish on trumpet.

tucuma (tū'kūmə, tōōkōōmah'), *n.* fibre-yielding Brazilian palm.

tufa (tū'fə), *n.* porous calcareous rock deposited by springs, etc.; rock composed of fine volcanic detritus. **-ceous,** *adj.*

tufthunter (tuft'huntə), *n.* toady.

tuism (tū'izm), *n.* use of second person (*thou, you*); phil. theory stressing existence of a second, or other, self.

tulwar (tul'wah), *n*. Ind. sabre.

tumbak(i), -bek(i) (tumbak', -i; -bek', -i), *n*. kind of coarse tobacco of Persia.

tumbrel (tum'bril), *n*. farm-cart, *espec.* as used to carry condemned persons to the guillotine in Fr. revolution.

tumid (tū'mid), *adj.* swollen; bombastic. **-ity,** *n*. **-mefacient,** *adj.* producing swelling. **-mefy,** *v.t.* swell. **-mescent,** *adj.* somewhat t.

tumtum (tum'tum), Anglo-Ind. *n*. dog-cart.

tumulus (tū'mūləs), *n*. (*pl.* -li) mound over ancient grave; barrow. **-lar,** *adj.* **-lose,** *adj.* having many small mounds.

tuna (tū'nə), Amer. *n*. tunny fish; kind of prickly pear.

tundra (tun'drə), *n*. arctic plain with mosses, shrubs, etc.

tungsten (tung'stən), *n*. white metal, also called wolfram, with highest melting point of all metals, used in filaments of electric lamps, steel alloys, etc. **-ic** (-en'ik), **-stic,** *adj.*

tunicate (tū'nikāt), *n*. one of a class of marine animals, including ascidians; *adj.* covered with layers.

tup (tup), *n*. ram; cuckold.

tuque (tūk), *n*. kind of knitted winter cap.

tu quoque (tū kwō'kwi), *Lat.,* "thou also"; act of imputing to one's accuser the same fault as that with which one is charged.

turbellarian (təbəlar'iən), *n*. kind of flatworm.

turbid (tɜ'bid), *adj.* muddy; not clear. **-bescency,** *n*. growing turbid. **-ity,** *n*.

turbinate (tɜ'binət), *adj.* spirally rolled; like a peg-top in shape; *v.t.* spin; whirl. **-nal,** *adj.* **-tion,** *n*.

turbit (tɜ'bit), *n*. kind of fancy pigeon.

turdiform (tɜ'difawm), *adj.* like a thrush. **-doid,** *adj.*

turgid (tɜ'jid), *adj.* swollen; inflated; bombastic. **-gescent,** *adj.* becoming t. **-gor,** **-ity,** *n*.

turmeric (tɜ'mərik), *n*. E. Ind. plant with rootstock yielding dye, or used ground as condiment.

turpeth (tɜ'pith), *n*. root of tropical plant used as purge; Indian jalap.

turpitude (tɜ'pitūd), *n*. depraved state.

turrical (tur'ikl), *adj.* turret-like. **-cular,** **-culate,** *adj.* **-riferous,** *adj.* bearing towers.

tussis (tus'is), *n*. *Med.,* cough. **-sal,** **-sive,** *adj.* **-sicular,** *adj.* pert. to slight cough.

tutelage (tū'tilij), *n*. guardianship. **-lary,** *adj.* protecting.

tutti-frutti (tōō'ti-frōō'ti), *It.,* "all fruits"; mixture of, or flavoured with, fruits of many kinds.

tuxedo (tuksē'dō), Amer. *n*. dinner-jacket.

twabylade (twā'blād), *n*. kind of orchid with pair of leaves.

tychism (tī'kizm), *n*. theory based on chance, *espec.* such theory of evolution.

tyloma (tīlō'mə), *n*. callus. **-losis,** *n*. hardening of cells. **-lotic** (-ot'ik), *adj.*

tympanum (tim'pənəm), *n*. (*pl.* -na) ear-drum; *Archit.,* triangular face of pediment; space within arch. **-nal,** **-nic** (-an'ik), *adj.* **-ni,** *n.pl.* (*sing.* -no) timpani. **-niform,** *adj.* like t. **-nist,** *n*. timpanist. **-nites** (-ī'tēz), *n*. distention of abdomen by flatulence. **-nitis,** *n*. inflammation of t. **-ny,** *n*. inflation; turgidity.

Tynwald (tin'wold), *n*. legislature of Isle of Man.

typhlitis (tiflī'tis), *n*. appendicitis. **-lology,** *n*. study of blindness. **-lophile,** *n*. person kind to the blind. **-losis,** *n*. blindness.

typhoid (tī'foid), *adj.* pert. to or resembling typhus. **t. fever,** infectious fever, often fatal, due to contaminated water or food. **-phogenic,** *adj.* causing t. fever or typhus.

typhoon (tīfōōn'), *n*. tropical cyclone. **-phonic** (-on'ik), *adj.*

typhus (tī'fəs), *n*. severe contagious fever carried by body lice; spotted, or jail, fever. **-phose,** *adj.* like typhoid fever. **-phosis,** *n*. state of being typhoid. **-phous,** *adj.*

typography (tīpog'rəfi), *n*. art of printing; style and layout of printed matter. **-pher,** *n*. **-phic(al)** *adj.*

typology (tīpol'əji), *n*. study of human types; theol. doctrine of symbolisation of New Testament events in the Old Testament. -gist, n.

typtology (tiptol′əji), n. theory concerning rappings by spirits. -gical, adj. -gist, n.

tyrannicide (tiran′isīd, tīr-), n. killing or killer of tyrant.

tyremesis (tīrem′isis), n. vomiting of curd-like matter.

tyriasis (tirī′əsis), n. alopecia; elephantiasis.

tyro, see tiro.

tyroma (tīr ō′mə), n. (pl. -ta) cheese-like matter. -tous (-om′ətəs), adj.

U

uberous (ū′bərəs), adj. abundant; fruitful. -rty, n.

ubiety (ūbī′iti), n. state of being in a place; "thereness"; position.

ubiquity (ūbik′witi), n. state of being everywhere. -tarian, adj.: n. believer that Christ is present everywhere. -tous, adj.

udometer (ūdom′itə), n. rain gauge. -mograph, n. recording u. -tric (-et′rik), adj. -try, n.

uhlan (ū′lən; Ger., ōō′lahn), Ger. n. kind of lancer.

uitlander (oit′landə), S. African n. "foreigner"; British resident in Boer state.

ukase (ū′kās, -kās′), n. Russ. decree; proclamation.

ulatrophy (ūlat′rəfi), n. atrophy of gums. -laemorrhagia, n. bleeding from gums. -letic, adj. pert. to gums.

uliginose, -nous (ūlij′inōs, -nəs), adj. marshy; muddy.

ulitis (ūlī′tis), n. inflammation of gums.

ullage (ul′ij), n. lack; deficiency; amount by which a quantity, espec. of liquor, is short of full measure; dregs. -d, adj. not full measure.

ulna (ul′nə), n. (pl. -ae) inner of two bones of forearm. -d, adv. towards the u. -r, adj.

uloid (ū′loid), adj. like a scar.

ulotrichous (ūlot′rikəs), adj. having woolly hair. -chan, n. such person. -chy, n. state of being u.

ulterior (ultēr′iə), adj. further; beyond; not seen or avowed; secret.

ultimate (ul′timət), adj. furthest; last; final; basic. -macy, n. -mo, adv. of last month (abbr. ult.). -mogeniture, n. inheritance by the youngest son. -tum (-ā′təm), n. final declaration of terms, threatening serious consequences if not accepted.

ultracrepidarian (ultrəkrepidār′iən), adj. venturing beyond one's province; presuming. -date, v.i.

ultrafidian (ultrəfid′iən), adj. going beyond faith.

ultramarine (ultrəmərēn′), adj. beyond the sea; n. kind of greenish-blue colour or pigment.

ultramicroscope (ultrəmī′krəskōp), n. instr. for viewing particles too small to be seen by ordinary microscope. -pic (-op′ik), adj. pert. to u.; visible only with u. -py (-os′kəpi), n.

ultramontane (ultrəmon′tān), adj. beyond (i.e. south of) the Alps; supporting the supremacy of the Pope; n. such person. -nism, n.

ultramundane (ultrəmun′dān), adj. beyond the world; spiritual.

ultrasonic (ultrəson′ik), adj. denoting air-waves or vibrations with frequencies higher than those audible to the human ear, i.e. more than about 20,000 cycles per second. -s, n. study and use of such waves.

ultra vires (ul′trə vīr′ēz), Lat., "beyond strength"; beyond or exceeding the authority of a person, court, etc.

ultroneous (ultrō′niəs), adj. spontaneous.

ululate (ū′lūlāt), v.i. howl. -lant, -tory, adj. howling. -tion, n.

umbel (um′bel), n. umbrella-like inflorescence with stalks of equal length springing from one point, as in carrot. -llar, -llate, -lliferous, adj. having flowers in u. -llifer, n. plant having u., or belonging to carrot family.

umber (um′bə), n. reddish-brown pigment.

umbilicus (umbilī′kəs, -bil′i-), n. (pl. -ci) navel; navel-like growth. -cal, adj. pert. to u.; central; related on mother's side. -car, *adj.* **-cate, -ciform, -liform,** *adj.* navel-like.

umbo (um'bō), *n.* (*pl.* **-nes**) boss of shield ; any rounded projection. **-nal, -nic** (-bon'ik), *adj.* **-nate,** *adj.* having u.

umbrage (um'brij), *n.* offence ; shade ; foliage. **-ous** (-ā'jəs), *adj.* shady ; offended. **-ratile,** *adj.* shadowy ; unreal ; secluded ; giving shade. **-riferous,** *adj.* giving shade. **-rous.** *adj.* shady.

umiak (ōō'miak), *n.* Eskimo woman's light kayak.

umlaut (um'lowt), Ger. *n.* vowel changes due to following sound ; diaeresis marking such changed vowel in Ger.

unanimous (ūnan'iməs), *adj.* of one mind. **-mity** (-im'iti), *n.*

unasinous (ūnas'inəs), *adj.* being equally stupid.

uncate (ung'kāt), *adj.* hooked.

uncial (un'shəl), *n.* & *adj.* (letter or manuscript) written in large rounded script of before 10th cent. A.D. ; majuscule ; capital. **-ciatim,** Lat. *adv.* ounce by ounce.

unciform (un'sifawm), *adj.* hooklike. **-cinate,** *adj.* hooked.

unco (ung'kō), Scot. *adj.* strange ; foreign ; extraordinary. **u.guid** (-gid), strictly moral.

unconscionable (unkon'shənəbl), *adj.* unreasonable ; against the conscience.

unction (ungk'shn), *n.* act of, or oil used in, anointing ; fervour ; oiliness ; simulated emotion. **-al, -tious,** *adj.* **-tuous,** *adj.* oily ; greasy ; soothing ; suave ; smug.

undecagon (undek'əgon), *n.* 11-sided plane figure.

undecennial (undisen'iəl), *adj.* happening every, or lasting, eleven years.

undecillion (undisil'yən), *n.* a million decillions (10⁶⁶) ; *Amer.* & *Fr.*, a thousand decillions (10³⁶).

undecimal (undes'iməl), *adj.* in eleven parts.

underwrite (un'dərīt), *v.t.* insure, *espec.* marine risks ; agree to buy unsold balance of share issue on date and at price named ; guarantee against loss ; subscribe to. **-r,** *n.*

undine (un'dēn), *n.* water spirit marrying mortal.

und so weiter (oont zō vī'tə), *Ger.*,

"and so forth" ; et cetera (*abbr.* usw).

ungual (ung'gwəl), *adj.* pert. to or like nail, hoof or talon.

unguent (ung'gwənt), *n.* soothing ointment. **-ary, -ous,** *adj.*

unguiculate (unggwik'ūlāt), *adj.* having claws or nails.

unguinous (ung'gwinəs), *adj.* oily ; fatty.

ungulate (ung'gūlāt), *n.* & *adj.* hoofed (mammal). **-ligrade,** *adj.* walking on hoofs.

unicameral (ūnikam'ərəl), *adj.* having one chamber. **-city** (-is'iti), *n.* one-ness ; state of being unique. **-idextral,** *adj.* using one hand more deftly than other. **-ifarious,** *adj.* in one row or series. **-iflar,** *adj.* having or using one thread or wire. **-ifoliate,** *adj.* with one leaf only. **-igenesis,** *n.* non-sexual reproduction. **-igenital,** *adj.* only-begotten. **-igenous,** *adj.* of same kind. **-ilateral,** *adj.* one-sided ; done by one of two or more contracting parties. **-lingual,** *adj.* in one language only. **-iliteral,** *adj.* having one letter only. **-inominal,** *adj.* pert. to or consisting of one name only. **-ipara,** *n.* woman having had one childbirth only. **-iparous,** *adj.* producing only one at a birth. **-iped,** *n.* & *adj.* one-legged or one-footed (person). **-ipotent,** *adj.* powerful in one direction only. **-ireme,** *n.* & *adj.* (galley) with one bank of oars. **-isonous,** *adj.* in unison ; agreeing. **-itarian,** *n.* & *adj.* (person) denying doctrine of Trinity. **-ivalent,** *adj.* single ; having valency of one. **-ivocal,** *adj.* unmistakable ; pert. to things of same kind. **-ivoltine,** *adj.* single-brooded. **-ivorous,** *adj.* app. to parasites living on one host only.

Unterseeboot (oontəzā'bōt), Ger. *n.* submarine.

untoward (untō'əd), *adj.* unlucky ; awkward ; inconvenient ; improper.

upas (ū'pas), *n.* poison-yielding tree of Java.

upher (ū'fə), *n.* rough scaffolding pole of fir.

upsilon (upsī'lən), *n.* twentieth letter (ϒ, υ) of Gr. alphabet.

uraemia (ūr ē'miə), *n.* poisoning of

blood due to urinary products not excreted.

uranism (ūr'ənizm), *n.* homosexuality in males. **-ist,** *n.*

uranography (ūrənog'rəfi), *n.* description or mapping of heaven(s). **-olatry,** *n.* worship of heavenly bodies. **-ology,** *n.* treatise on or study of heavens. **-ometry,** *n.* chart or measurement of heavenly bodies. **-oscopy,** *n.* star-watching.

urbacity (ūbas'iti), *n.* excessive civic pride.

urbane (ūbān'), *adj.* refined ; courteous ; genial. **-nist** (ū'bən-), *n.* expert on town-planning. **-nite,** *n.* town-dweller. **-nity** (-an'iti), *n.*

urbarial (ūbār'iəl), *adj.* founded on landed property register. **-bicolous,** *adj.* city-dwelling.

urceus (ō'siəs), *n.* single-handed jug ; urn. **-ceiform, -ceolar, -ceolate,** *adj.* shaped like u.

ure (ūr), *n.* custom ; use.

urea (ūr ē'ə), *n.* crystalline constituent of urine. **-l,** *adj.*

uredinous (ūred'inəs), *adj.* pert. or belonging to rusts (fungus) ; *Med.,* pert. to or like uredo. **-noid,** *adj.* like rusts. **-nology,** *n.* study of rusts.

uredo (ūr ē'dō), *n.* burning feeling of skin.

ureic (ūr ē'ik), *adj.* pert. to urea. **-resis,** *n.* urination.

ureter (ūr'itə), *n.* duct through which urine enters bladder. **-al, -ic,** *adj.* **-thra,** *n.* duct through which urine leaves bladder. **-thral,** *adj.*

uretic (ūret'ik), *n.* & *adj.* (medicine) affecting urination.

Urgrund (ōōr'groont), Ger. *n.* basis ; primary principle, cause or factor.

uric (ūr'ik), *adj.* pert. to or contained in urine. **-ridrosis,** *n.* excretion of perspiration containing urinary products.

Urim (ūr'im), *see* Thummim.

urine (ūr'in), *n.* liquid excretion from kidneys. **-nal,** *n.* vessel for holding u. ; place for excreting u. **-nary,** *adj.* **-nate,** *v.i.* discharge u. **-nogenous,** *adj.* produced by u. **-nose, -nous,** *adj.* like u.

urocyst (ūr'əsist), *n.* the bladder. **-odynia,** *n.* painful urination. **-ogenital,** *adj.* pert. to organs used for urination and reproduction.

-ogenous, *adj.* producing, or produced by, urine. **-ology,** *n.* med. study of urinary organs. **-oscopy,** *n.* examination of urine in diagnosis. **-osis,** *n.* disease of urinary organs.

ursal (ō'səl), *n.* fur seal.

ursine (ō'sīn, -in), *adj.* pert. to or like a bear. **-niform,** *adj.* bearshaped. **-noid,** *adj.* like a bear.

urticaceous (ōtikā'shəs), *adj.* pert. to or like nettles ; belonging to nettle family of plants. **-cant,** *n.* & *adj.* stinging (substance). **-caria,** *n.* nettle-rash. **-cate,** *v.t.* sting ; cause wheals ; flog. **-cose,** *adj.* full of nettles.

user (ū'zə), *n. Law,* continued use ; right to use.

usine (üzēn'), Fr. *n.* factory.

usitative (ū'zitətiv), *adj.* signifying usual act.

usquebaugh (us'kwibaw), *n.* whiskey ; kind of Ir. cordial.

ustulate (us'tūlāt), *v.t.* give burned appearance to. **-tion,** *n.* roasting ; lust.

usufruct (ū'zūfrukt), *n.* right to enjoy property. **-uary,** *n.* & *adj.*

usurer (ū'zūrə), *n.* moneylender, *espec.* one demanding very high interest. **-rious,** *adj.* **-ry,** *n.*

ut (ut), Lat. *conj.* "as." **u.infra,** as below. **u.supra,** as above.

uterus (ū'tərəs), *n.* womb. **-rine,** *adj.*

utility (ūtil'iti), *n.* usefulness. public u., organisation providing public service, as transport, watersupply, etc. **u.car,** motor car adaptable for carrying goods. **-lise,** *v.t.* make use of. **-tarian,** *adj.* serving or aiming at useful purpose only ; *n.* person believing that true test of morality is the usefulness of an action.

Utopian (ūtō'piən), *adj.* pert. to or like Utopia, imaginary country where life is perfect ; ideal ; impracticable.

utraquist (ū'trəkwist), *n.* person speaking two or both languages, or believing that both kinds of Sacrament should be administered.

utricle (ū'trikl), *n.* small cavity or sac. **-cular, -culate,** *adj.* **-culiferous,** *adj.* producing u. **-culiform, -culoid,** *adj.* like a u.

utriform (ū'trifawm), *adj.* like a leather bottle.

---

uvula (ū'vūlə), *n.* (*pl.* -ae) fleshy outgrowth at back of soft palate. **-litis**, *n.* inflammation of u. **-r**, *adj.*

uxorious (uksōr'iəs), *adj.* loving wife to excess ; submitting to wife. **-rial**, *adj.* wifely. **-ricide**, *n.* killing or killer of own wife.

V

vaccine (vak'sin, -ēn), *n.* preparation of weakened or killed disease germs injected to produce immunity, *espec.* of cow-pox against smallpox. **-nate**, *v.t.* inoculate with v. **-nation**, **-nator**, *n.* **-nia**, *n.* cow-pox.

vacillate (vas'ilāt), *v.i.* waver ; fluctuate. **-tion**, **-tor**, *n.* **-tory**, *adj.*

vacuum (vak'ūəm), *n.* (*pl.* -ua) completely empty space, exhausted of air. **-uity**, *n.* emptiness. **-uole**, *n.* small air- or fluid-containing cavity. **-uous**, *adj.* empty.

vade-mecum (vā'di-mē'kəm), *Lat.*, "come with me" ; guide-book ; manual. **v. retro**, "go behind" ; "get thee behind me."

vagina (vəjī'nə), *n.* (*pl.* -ae) sheath ; tube ; passage from uterus to exterior. **-l** (vaj'inəl), *adj.* **-niferous**, *adj.* having a v. **-te**, *adj.* sheathed.

vagitus (vəjī'təs), *n.* new-born child's cry.

vale (vā'li), *Lat.*, "farewell." **-diction**, *n.* bidding farewell. **-dictory**, *adj.*

valency (vā'lənsi), *n.* element's power to combine, measured by number of atomic weights of other elements with which the atomic weight of the element will combine. **-nce**, *n.* **-nt**, *adj.* having v.

valetudinarian (valitūdinār'iən), *n.* hypochondriac ; sickly person. **-ism**, *n.* **-ry**, *adj.*

valgus (val'gəs), *n.* & *adj.* clubfoot ; bow-legged or knock-kneed (condition). **-goid**, *adj.* like v.

valid (val'id), *adj.* sound ; provable; effective ; legal. **-ate**, *v.t.* make v. **-ation**, **-ity**, *n.* **-atory**, *adj.*

vallate (val'āt), *adj.* having a raised rim. **-d**, *adj.* having a rampart. **-tion**, *n.* rampart.

vallecular (vəlek'ūlə), *adj.* pert. to or like a groove. **-late**, *adj.* bearing grooves.

valorise (val'əriz), *v.t.* fix arbitrary price of. **-sation**, *n.*

vandal (van'dəl), *n.* ignorant savage, *espec.* destroying artistic work. **-ism**, *n.*

vapid (vap'id), *adj.* dull ; uninteresting ; insipid. **-ity**, *n.*

vaquero (vahkār'ō), Sp. *n.* cowboy.

varec (var'ek) *n.* seaweed ; kelp.

varia (vār'iə), Lat. *n.pl.* miscellany.

varication (varikā'shn), *n.* varicose state.

varicella (vərisel'ə), *n.* chicker-pox. **-lous**, *adj.*

varicose (var'ikōs), *adj.* swollen, *espec.* in irregular lumps and twists. **-cotomy**, *n.* incision into v. vein. **-sis**, *n.* state of being v. **-sity**, *n.*

varietal (vərīitəl), *adj.* pert. to a variety. **-tist**, *n.* abnormal person.

variola (vərī'ələ), *n.* smallpox. **-lic**, **-lous**, **-r**, *adj.* **-liform**, *adj.* like v. **-litic**, *adj.* spotted. **-loid**, *adj.* like v. ; *n.* mild form of v. **-te**, *v.t.* inoculate with v.

variorum (vārīor'əm), *n.* & *adj.* (edition) with comments by various critics, or containing various versions of text.

varsovienne (vahsōv'yen), *n.* polka-like Polish dance.

varus (vār'əs), *n.* & *adj.* pigeon-toed (person or condition).

vas (vas), *n.* (*pl.* -a) *Med.*, duct ; vessel. **v.deferens**, spermatic duct. **-al**, *adj.* **-cular**, **-culose**, **-culous**, *adj.* pert. to fluid-conveying vessels ; hot-blooded. **-culature**, *n.* arrangement of blood vessels. **-culiform**, *adj.* flowerpot-shaped. **-iferous**, *adj.* bearing a v.

vasoconstriction (vasōkənstrik'shn), *n.* constriction of blood vessels. **-odilatation**, *n.* dilatation of blood vessels. **-omotor**, *adj.* app. to nerves controlling constriction and dilatation of blood vessels. **-oparesis**, *n.* paralysis of vaso-motor nerves. **-otrophic**, *adj.* pert. to nutrition of, or affecting nutrition by, blood vessels.

vastate (vas'tāt), *v.t.* make immune. **-tion**, *n.* purification.

Vaterland (fah'tǝlant), Ger. *n.* "fatherland."

vatic(al) (vat'ik, -l), *adj.* pert. to prophecy. **-cide**, *n.* killing or killer of a prophet.

vaticinate (vatis'ināt), *v.i. & t.* prophesy. **-nal**, **-tory**, *adj.* prophetic. **-tion**, **-tor**, *n.*

vection (vek'shn), *n.* infection with disease. **-tor**, *n.* disease-carrying insect ; *Math.*, symbol of quantity having magnitude and direction.

vedette (videt'), *n.* outpost mounted sentry. **v.boat**, small boat or ship for watching enemy.

vegetal (vej'itǝl), *adj.* pert. to or like a vegetable ; lacking feelings. **-tant**, *adj.* vegetable-like ; causing growth ; tonic. **-tative**, *adj.* growing ; plant-like ; fertile ; pert. to unconscious life processes, as growth, digestion, etc. **-tism**, *n.* v. state. **-tivorous**, *adj.* eating vegetables.

velamen (vilā'men), *n.* (*pl.* **-mina**) membrane. **-tous**, *adj.* pert. to or like v. or sail.

velar (vē'lǝ), *adj.* pert. to soft palate ; pronounced with back of tongue touching soft palate, as *k, ng,* etc. ; *n.* such sound. **-late**, *adj.* having veil or velum. **-lation**, *n.* act of veiling ; secrecy. **-lic**, *adj.* pert. to or like a sail. **-liferous**, **-ligerous**, *adj.* bearing a sail or velum. **-litation**, *n.* skirmish.

velleity (velē'iti), *n.* state of desiring faintly ; slight wish.

vellicate (vel'ikāt), *v.t.* pinch ; tickle ; make to twitch. **-tion**, *n.* **-tive**, *adj.*

vellum (vel'ǝm), *n.* calf or lamb gut or skin prepared for writing on ; parchment.

velocious (vilō'shǝs), *adj.* with great speed.

velocipede (vilos'ipēd), *n.* old-fashioned bicycle. **-dal** (-ip'idǝl), **-dic**, *adj.*

velodrome (vē'lǝdrōm), *n.* cycle-racing track, or building containing one.

velum (vē'lǝm), *n.* (*pl.* **-la**) veil-like membrane ; soft palate. **-en**, *n.* (*pl.* **-mina**) downy covering.

velutinous (vilū'tinǝs), *adj.* having downy covering ; velvety.

venal (vē'nǝl), *adj.* capable of being bribed or corrupted ; based on bribery or corruption ; mercenary. **-ise**, *v.t.* **-ity**, *n.*

venatic(al) (vinat'ik, -l), *adj.* pert. to, used in, or fond of hunting.

venation (vinā'shn), *n.* arrangement of veins on leaf or wing of insect.

vendetta (vendet'ǝ), *n.* blood feud.

vendeuse (vahṅdöz'), Fr. *n.* saleswoman.

vendible (ven'dibl), *adj.* capable of being sold ; venal.

vendue (vendū'), *n.* auction.

venenation (venenā'shn), *n.* poisoning ; poisoned state. **-niferous**, *adj.* carrying poison.

venereal (vinēr'iǝl), *adj.* pert. to, resulting from, or transmitted by sexual intercourse ; stimulating lust. **-reology**, *n.* study of v. diseases.

venery (ven'ǝri), *n.* hunting ; game (animals) ; sexual intercourse. **-rer**, *n.* huntsman.

venesect (ven'isekt, -sekt'), *v.i. & t.* open vein in blood-letting. **-ion**, *n.*

venial (vē'niǝl), *adj.* forgivable ; not criminal. **-ity**, *n.*

venison (ven'zǝn), *n.* flesh of deer.

veni, vidi, vici (vē'ni, vī'di, vī'si), *Lat.,* "I came, I saw, I conquered."

venous (vē'nǝs), *adj.* pert. to the veins ; app. to blood carried by veins to heart, containing impurities. **-nostasis**, *n.* constricting veins to check blood.

ventiduct (ven'tidukt), *n.* air-pipe. **-ifact**, *n.* stone rounded by wind action.

ventral (ven'trǝl), *adj.* pert. to the belly.

ventricle (vent'rikl), *n.* cavity, *espec.* of heart from which blood enters arteries. **-cose**, *adj.* big-bellied. **-cular**, *adj.*

ventricumbent (ventrikum'bǝnt), *adj.* lying on front. **-iduct**, *v.i.* turn towards belly. **-rine**, *adj.* ventral.

venue (ven'ū), *n.* scene ; meeting-place ; ground ; district where law-suit must be tried.

venule (ven'ūl), *n.* small vein. **-lose**, **-lous**, *adj.* having many venules.

veracious (vǝrā'shǝs), *adj.* truthful ; true ; exact. **-city** (-as'iti), *n.*

verbatim (vǝbā'tim), *adv. & adj.* word for word.

verbigerate (vəbij'ərāt), *v.i.* unwittingly repeat sentence. **-tion,** *n.* **-tive,** *adj.*

verbile (və̄'bīl), *n.* person whose mental processes are most easily stimulated by words.

verboten (fəbō'tən), Ger. *adj.* "forbidden"; prohibited.

verbum (sat) sapienti (est) (və̄'bəm sat sapien'ti est), *Lat.*, "a word (is enough) to the wise" (*abbr.* **verb. sap.**).

verd-antique (və̄d-antēk'), *n.* kind of green mottled marble.

verecund (ver'ikund), *adj.* shy. **-ity,** *n.*

vergiform (və̄'jifawm), *adj.* like a rod.

veridic(al) (virid'ik, -l), *adj.* veracious; genuine. **-dity,** *n.*

verisimilitude (verisimil'itūd), *n.* appearance of being true.

verjuice (və̄'jōōs), *n.* sour juice; sourness.

vermeil (və̄'mil), *n.* & *adj.* vermilion.

vermian (və̄'miən), *adj.* like a worm.

vermicelli (və̄misel'i, -chel'i), *n.* fine variety of spaghetti.

vermicide (və̄'misīd), *n.* substance killing worms. **-icular, -iform,** *adj.* worm-like. **-iculate,** *v.i.* infest with worms; give worm-like appearance to; *adj.* worm-like; worm-eaten. **-ifugal,** *adj.* expelling worms. **-ifuge,** *n.* vermifugal substance. **-igerous,** *adj.* infested with worms. **-igrade,** *adj.* creeping in worm-like manner. **-iparous,** *adj.* producing worms. **-ivorous,** *adj.* feeding on worms.

vernacular (vənak'ūlə), *adj.* native; common; everyday; local; *n.* such language.

vernal (və̄'nəl), *adj.* pert. or belonging to spring (season).

vernicose (və̄'nikōs), *adj.* brightly polished.

vernier (və̄'niə), *n.* short sliding scale indicating fractions of a graduation; additional control for obtaining fine adjustments.

vernition (vənish'n), *n.* varnishing.

veronal (ver'ənəl), *n.* hypnotic drug, also called barbital.

verricule (ver'ikūl), *n.* tuft of bristles, hairs, etc. **-late,** *adj.* having v.

verruca (verōō'kə), *n.* wart. **-cated,**

adj. bearing wart-like prominences. **-cose, -cous,** *adj.* covered with warts. **-culose,** *adj.* having very small warts or wart-like prominences.

versicle (və̄'sikl), *n.* short verse, *espec.* Eccl., followed by response. **-cular,** *adj.* pert. to or marking verses.

vers libre (vār lē'br), *Fr.*, "free verse"; verse in which metre is displaced by varied rhythms. **-rist,** *n.* writer of v.l.

verso (və̄'sō), *n.* left-hand page or back cover of book; reverse of coin.

verst (vəst), *n.* Russ. unit of distance, equiv. of two-thirds of a mile.

vertebra (və̄'tibrə), *n.* (*pl.* **-ae**) segment of backbone. **-l,** *adj.* **-te,** *n.* & *adj.* (animal) having a backbone. **-tion,** *n.* division into segments; firmness.

vertex (və̄'teks), *n.* (*pl.* **-tices**) apex. **-tical,** *adj.* perpendicular. **-ticil,** *n. Bot.*, whorl.

vertigo (və̄'tigō, -ī'gō), *n.* dizziness. **-ginous** (-ij'inəs), *adj.*

vervain (və̄'vān), *n.* verbena plant.

vervet (və̄'vit), *n.* small monkey of S. and E. Africa.

vesicle (ves'ikl), *n.* small blister; bladder-like or rounded cavity; cell; cyst. **-cal,** *adj.* pert. to bladder; oval. **-cant, -catory,** *adj.* raising blisters. **-cate,** *v.i.* blister. **-cular,** *adj.* **-culate, -culose, -culous,** *adj.* bearing many v.

vespal (ves'pəl), *adj.* pert. to wasps. **-pacide,** *n.* substance or person killing wasps.

vespertine (ves'pətin), *adj.* in or of the evening; setting at same time as, or just after, the sun.

vespiary (ves'piəri), *n.* wasps' nest. **-pid,** *n.* social wasp. **-pine, -poid,** *adj.* pert. to or like wasps.

vesta (ves'tə), *n.* wax-match.

vestal (ves'təl), *adj.* having taken vows of chastity; *n.* such virgin.

vesuvian (visū'viən), *n.* old-fashioned kind of match; fusee. **-viate,** *v.i.* erupt; burst with heat.

vetanda (vitan'də), Lat. *n.pl.* forbidden things.

veterinary (vet'ərinəri), *adj.* pert. to diseases of domestic animals; *n.* surgeon expert on such diseases.

vetitive (vet'itiv), *adj.* having power to forbid or veto.

vexillary (veks'iləri), *adj.* pert. to regimental colours or standard ; *n.* standard-bearer.

viable (vī'əbl), *adj.* born alive and able to live ; able to exist alone.

viaduct (vī'ədukt), *n.* bridge carrying road.

via media (vī'ə mē'diə), *Lat.,* "middle way."

viands (vī'əndz), *n.pl.* food.

viatic(al) (vīat'ik, -l), *adj.* pert. to roads or travel. **-cum,** *n.* Holy Communion administered to dying person ; travelling provisions or expenses. **-tor,** *n.* traveller. **-torial,** *adj.* travelling.

vibrissa (vībris'ə), *n.* (*pl.* **-ae**) sensitive whisker on animal's face. **-l,** *adj.*

viburnum (vībə'nəm), *n.* kind of shrub or tree including guelderrose, etc.

vicarial (vikār'iəl), *adj.* pert. to vicar or delegate. **-ious,** *adj.* pert. to deputy or delegate ; acting for another ; enjoyed or suffered for, or through, another ; substituted.

vice (vī'si), *Lat., prep.* "in place of" ; succeeding to.

vicegerent (vīsjēr'ənt), *n.* & *adj.* (person) representing a ruler or God. **-ncy,** *n.* **-ral,** *adj.*

vicenary (vis'inəri), *adj.* pert. to or consisting of 20 ; having 20 as a base. **-cennial,** *adj.* lasting, or happening every, 20 years.

viceroy (vis'roi) *n.* ruler having king's authority. **-alty,** *n.* **-regal,** *adj.* **-reine,** *n.* v's wife.

vicinage (vis'inij), *n.* neighbourhood. **-nal,** *adj.* **-nity,** *n.*

vicissitude (visis'itūd) *n.* change of fortune ; alternation. **-dinous,** *adj.*

victoria (viktōr'iə), *n.* light open two-seater four-wheeled carriage, with raised driver's seat.

victual (vit'l), *v.i.* & *t.* provision ; *n.pl.* food. **-ller,** *n.* licensee of public house.

vicuna (vikū'nə, -ōōn'yə), *n.* wild wool-bearing llama-like animal of the Andes.

vide (vī'di), *Lat.,* "see." **v. infra,** "see below" (*abbr.* **v.i.**). **v. supra,** "see above" (*abbr.* **v.s.**). **-licet** (vide'liset), *adv.* namely (*abbr.* **vis.**). **-tur,** "it seems."

viduage (vid'ūij), *n.* widowhood.

vi et armis (vī et ah'mis), *Lat.,* "with force and arms."

vieux jeu (vyə zhə'), *Fr.* "old game" ; antiquated or worn-out subject.

vigentennial (vijenten'iəl, vī-), *adj.* lasting, or happening every, twenty years ; *n.* twentieth anniversary.

vigesimal (vijes'iməl, vī-), *adj.* pert. to or based on number twenty ; twentieth.

vigilante (vijilan'ti), Amer. *n.* member of committee keeping order in an area.

vigintillion (vijintil'yən), *n.* a million novemdecillions (10^{120}) *Amer.* & *Fr.*, a thousand novemdecillions (10^{63}).

vignette (venyet'), *n.* small, ornamental illustration without frame or with background shaded off ; slight portrait or character sketch.

vilayet (vilah'yet), *n.* Turk. province.

vilify (vil'ifī), *v.t.* slander ; degrade. **-fication,** *n.* **-ipend,** *v.t.* speak slightingly of. **-ipenditory,** *adj.* despising.

villanelle (vilənel'), *n.* Fr. poem of three tercets and a quatrain, with special rhyming scheme.

villar (vil'ə), *adj.* pert. to feudal manor or village ; *n.* villein. **-atic,** *adj.* rural ; pert. to villa.

villeggiatura (vilejahtōōr'ah), It. *n.* stay at country seat.

villein (vil'in), *n.* free villager ; serf. **-age,** *n.*

villus (vil'əs), *n.* (*pl.* **-li**) small veinlike outgrowth ; soft hair. **-liform,** *adj.* like v. ; with velvety surface. **-loid,** *adj.* pert. to v. **-lose,** **-lous,** *adj.* bearing soft hairs.

vimen (vī'men), *n.* (*pl.* **-mina**) long thin branch or twig. **-mineous,** *adj.* pert. to or made of twigs.

vinaceous (vīnā'shəs), *adj.* pert. to or like grapes or wine ; wine-coloured.

vinaigrette (vinigret'), *n.* bottle of smelling-salts. **-rous,** *adj.* like vinegar ; sour in manner.

vincular (ving'kūlə), *adj.* connective.

vindemiate (vinde'miat), *v.i.* gather in fruit, or the vintage. **-tion,** *n.* **-tory,** *adj.*

vineatic (viniat'ik), *adj.* pert. to vines.

ə=*er* in *father* ; ō=*er* in *pert* ; th=*th* in *thin* ; dh=*th* in *then* ; zh=*s* in *pleasure* ; k=*ch* in *loch* ; ñ=Fr. nasal *n* ; ü=Fr. *u.*

vingt-et-un (vant-ā-ăṅ'), *Fr.*, "twenty-one"; card game the object of which is to obtain cards with values adding up to twenty-one.

vin ordinaire (vaṅ ōrdēnār'), *Fr.*, "common wine"; ordinary, cheap wine, *espec.* cheap claret.

vinous (vī'nəs), *adj.* pert. to or like wine; fond of wine; wine-coloured. **-nosity,** *n.*

vintner (vint'nə), *n.* wine-seller.

V.I.P., *abbr.* of very important person.

virago (virā'gō, -ah'-), *n.* nagging or abusive woman.

virelay (vir'ilā), *n.* old Fr. poem with refrain and various special rhyming schemes.

virescent (vires'ənt), *n.* becoming or slightly green. **-nce,** *n.*

virgal (vȯ'gəl), *adj.* composed of twigs. **-gate,** *adj.* like a rod; having many twigs; *v.i.* branch off.

virginals (vȯ'jinəlz), *n.* kind of spinet of 16th and 17th centuries.

virgule (vȯ'gūl), *n.* slanting mark (/) indicating pause, hyphen, or alternative. **-late,** *adj.* rod-like.

viridescent (virides'ənt), *adj.* greenish. **-digenous,** *adj.* producing greenness. **-dity,** *n.* greenness; freshness.

virilescence (viriles'əns), *n.* acquisition by females of male characteristics. **-lia,** *n.* male reproductive organs. **-lism,** *n.* masculinity in women, *espec.* with secondary male characteristics.

viripotent (virip'ətənt), *adj.* nubile.

virose (vīr'ōs), *adj.* poisonous; foul-smelling. **-sis,** *n.* virus disease.

virtu (vȯ'tōō), *n.* objects of art; antiques; love or study of such objects; artistic value. **-oso,** *n.* (*fem.* **-sa;** *pl.* **-si**) collector of v.; technically brilliant performer, *espec.* musical. **-osity,** *n.* skill of virtuoso.

virus (vīr'əs), *n.* poison of venomous animal; ultramicroscopic organism transmitting disease; any poisonous quality or germ.

visa (vē'zə), *n.* special stamp or mark on passport indicating permission to bearer to pass in; any similar endorsement; *v.t.* affix v. to.

visard (viz'ərd), *n.* mask; visor.

vis-à-vis (vēz-ah-vē'), *adv., adj.* & *prep.* facing; opposite; regarding; *n.* person facing one.

viscera (vis'ərə), *n.pl.* internal organs; intestines. **-l, -rous,** *adj.* **-roptosis,** *n.* prolapse of visceral organs.

viscid (vis'kid), *adj.* viscous. **-cose,** *n.* cellulose prepared for use as rayon, etc. **-cous,** *adj.* like glue or treacle. **-cosity,** *n.* treacliness; force opposing flow.

visile (viz'īl), *n.* & *adj.* (person) with mental processes most readily stimulated by visual impressions.

vis major (vis mā'jə), *Lat.,* "greater force"; act of God; unavoidable accident.

visor, -zor (vī'zə), *n.* mask; part of helmet covering face; peak of cap.

vista (vis'tə), *n.* distant view, *espec.* along an avenue. **-l,** *adj.*

vitalism (vī'təlizm), *n.* phil. doctrine that life processes are not entirely explicable, or bound, by scientific laws. **-ist,** *n.* **-istic,** *adj.*

vitamin (vit'əmin, vī'-), *n.* chemical constituent of foodstuff, essential to health. **v.A,** v. stimulating growth, preventing night-blindness, etc. **v.B,** a large group promoting growth, health of nerves, etc. **v.C,** antiscorbutic v. **v.D,** antirachitic v., essential to calcium metabolism. **v.E,** v. stimulating fertility. **v.K,** v. preventing haemorrhage.

vitascope (vī'təskōp), *n.* moving picture projector.

vitative (vī'tətiv), *adj.* fond of life.

vitellus (vitel'əs), *n.* yolk of egg. **-lary, -line,** *adj.* **-ligenous,** *adj.* producing v. **-lin,** *n.* protein in v.

vitiate (vish'iāt), *v.t.* impair; spoil; debase; make useless or impure. **-tion, -tor,** *n.*

viticulture (vī'tikultūr), *n.* vine-growing. **-cetum,** *n.* vineyard. **-tiferous,** *adj.* bearing vines.

vitrail (vētrī'), *Fr. n.* (*pl.* **-aux**) stained glass.

vitreous (vit'riəs), *adj.* pert. to or like glass. **-real, -real,** *adj.* **-rescent,** *adj.* becoming v.; able to be made into glass. **-rescible,** *adj.* vitrifiable. **-ric,** *adj.* glassy. **-rics,** *n.* study of glassware. **-rifacture,** *n.* making of glassware. **-riform,** *adj.* glassy. **-rify,** *v.i.* & *t.* make or become v. **-rine,** *n.* glass case.

vitriol (vit'riəl), n. sulphuric acid; sev. sulphates of metals. -ic, adj. like v.; corrosive; caustic.

vittate (vit'āt), adj. striped lengthwise.

vitular (vit'ūlə), adj. pert. to or like calf, or calving. -line, adj.

vituperate (vitū'pərāt), v.t. abuse. -tion, -tor, n. -tive, -tory, adi.

viva (vē'vah), It. excl. "long live"; hurrah.

vivandière (vēvahṅ'dyār), Fr. n. woman camp-follower supplying provisions.

vivarium (vivār'iəm), n. (pl. -ia) place or box, etc., for keeping living animals.

vivat (vī'vat), Lat., "may he or she live"; long live; hurrah.

viva voce (vī'və vō'si), Lat., "by word of mouth"; oral(ly); oral examination (abbr. viva).

vive (vēv), Fr., "long live."

viverrine (vīver'īn, -in), adj. pert. to or like a civet; belonging to civet family; n. civet.

vives (vīvz), n. swelling of horse's submaxillary glands.

viveur (vēvōr'), Fr. n. person who lives (well); person indulging in pleasures.

vivify (viv'ifī), v.t. make alive or vivid; animate; sharpen. -fication, n.

viviparous (vivip'ərəs), adj. bringing forth live young. -rism, -rity (-ar'iti), n.

vivisect (viv'isekt), v.t. experiment on by dissecting, while alive. -ion, -or, n. -sepulture, n. burying alive.

vizard, see visard.

vizier (vizēr'), n. Moham. minister of state. v.-azem, grand-v.

vocable (vō'kəbl), n. word; name; sound. -bular (-ab'ūlə), adj.

vocalic (vəkal'ik), adj. pert. to or like vowels.

vocative (vok'ətiv), adj. used when addressing a person; n. such gram. case.

vociferate (vəsif'ərāt), v.i. & t. shout loudly or repeatedly. -rant, -rous, adj. -tion, -tor, n.

vocimotor (vōsimō'tə), adj. pert. to speech movements.

vodka (vod'kə), n. Russ. spirit, distilled from rye or potatoes.

voetsak (foot'sak), S. African excl. go away.

voilà (vwal'a), Fr. excl. "see there"; behold; there is or are. v.tout, that is all.

voivode (voi'vōd), n. former Russ. military governor.

volant (vō'lənt), adj. flying; able to fly; quick.

volar (vō'lə), adj. pert. to palm or sole; pert. to flight.

volatile (vol'ətil), adj. light-hearted; changeable; readily evaporating; ephemeral. -lise, v.t. vaporise. -lity, n.

volation (vəlā'shn), n. ability to fly.

volent (vō'lənt), adj. exercising will power.

volery (vol'əri), Amer. n. aviary; aircraft repairing, etc., station.

volitate (vol'itāt), v.i. fly about; flutter. -ant, adj. able to fly; flying. -tion, n.

volition (vəlish'n), n. act of willing; will. -al, -ary, adj. -tive, adj. pert. to or derived from the will; Gram., expressing desire or permission.

volitorial (volitor'iəl), adj. able to fly.

volk (folk), Dutch n. people; servants; workmen. -sraad (-raht), n. parliament.

volplane (vol'plān), v.i. glide through air.

volt (volt), n. unit of electromotive force: force producing current of one ampere when applied to resistance of one ohm. -age, n. number of v. -aic (-a'ik), adj. galvanic. -aism, n. current electricity. -ameter, n. instr. measuring voltage.

volte-face (volt-fahs'), n. change to opposite opinion or direction.

volucrine (vol'ūkrīn, -in), adj. pert. to birds.

voluntary (vol'əntəri), n. Mus., improvised music introducing or closing performance or church service.

voluptuary (vəlup'tūəri), n. person excessively devoted to luxury. -tuous, adj. luxurious; given up to luxury; sensuous. -ty, n. sexual pleasure.

volute (vəlūt'), n. & adj. spiral (object or ornament). -tate (vol'ūtāt) v.i. roll. -tion, n. twist; convolution.

vomiturition (vomitūrish'n) n. retching; unsuccessful attempt to vomit; easy vomiting.

voracious (vərā'shəs), *adj.* greedy; ravenous. **-city** (-as'iti), *n.*

vortex (vaw'teks), *n.* (*pl.* **-tices**) whirlpool. **-tical**, **-ticose**, **-ticular**, **-tiginous**, *adj.* whirling. **-ticist** (-sist), *n.* painter whose theory of art was that it should express the complexity of modern machinery, etc.

votary (vō'təri), *n.* person vowed or devoted to God, etc. **-ress**, *n.* such woman or girl.

votive (vō'tiv), *adj.* fulfilling a vow; done in devotion.

voussoir (vōōswahr'), *n.* any wedge-shaped stone forming part of arch, vault, etc.

vox populi (voks pop'ūlī), *Lat.*, "the voice of the people"; public verdict. **v.p.** **vox Dei** (-dē'ī), "the voice of the people (is) the voice of God."

vrouw (frow), S. African *n.* housewife; woman.

vulcanise (vul'kənīz), *v.t.* harden

(rubber) by chem. process. **-ite,** *n.* hardened rubber. **-nology,** *n.* study of volcanic activity.

Vulgate (vul'gət), *n.* 4th-cent. Latin translation of Scriptures; generally accepted text or version.

vulgus (vul'gəs), *n.* school composition in Latin verse.

vulnerable (vul'nərəbl), *adj.* able to be wounded; open to attack; *Bridge*, having won one game, and liable to doubled penalties. **-nific,** *adj.* causing wounds. **-rary,** *n.* & *adj.* (remedy) healing wounds. **-rose,** *adj.* wounded.

vulpicide (vul'pisīd), *n.* killing or killer of fox, except by hunting. **-pecular,** *adj.* pert. to young fox. **-pine,** *adj.* fox-like; cunning.

vulturn (vul'tən), *n.* Austral. brush turkey.

vulva (vul'və), *n.* external portion of female reproductive organs. **-l,** **-r,** *adj.* **-te,** **-viform,** *adj.* shaped like v. **-vitis,** *n.* inflammation of v.

W

waddy (wod'i), Austral. *n.* war-club of aborigines.

wadi (wod'i), Arab. *n.* valley; stream; watercourse drying up in summer; oasis.

wagon-lit (vag'awn-lē'), Fr. *n.* sleeping compartment of railway train.

waldgrave (wawld'grāv), *n.* former Ger. title of count; head forest ranger. **-vine,** *n.* wife of w.

wallaby (wol'əbi), *n.* kind of small kangaroo.

wallah (wol'ə), Anglo-Ind. *n.* person employed in certain capacity; **-worker; -carrier.**

wallaroo (woləroo'), *n.* kind of kangaroo.

wall-eye (wawl'-ī), *n.* eye with light grey or whitish iris or cornea, or showing abnormal amount of white by turning outwards. **-d,** *adj.*

wampum (wom'pəm), *n.* N. Amer. Ind. beads used as money.

wanderoo (wondəroo'), *n.* kind of monkey of Ceylon with purple face, or of India with lion-like tail.

wapentake (wop'əntāk), *n.* subdivision of certain counties; court or bailiff of such area.

wapiti (wop'iti), *n.* Amer. elk.

warble (waw'bl), *n.* small tumour of horse, *espec.* under saddle, or caused by w. fly. **w.fly,** fly with larvae living under skin of cattle, etc.

warlock (waw'lok), *n.* wizard.

warp (wawp), *n.* in weaving, lengthwise threads in loom.

watt (wot), *n.* unit of elec. power: amount of work done by current of one ampere at pressure of one volt. **-age,** *n.* number of w.

waygoose (wāz'gōōs), *n.* annual outing or dinner of employees, *espec.* of printing firm.

wazir (wəzēr'), *n.* vizier.

weft (weft), *n.* woof; woven thing; web; film.

Wehrmacht (vār'mahkt), Ger. *n.* "defence force"; the armed forces of Germany.

Weltanschauung (velt'anshowoong), Ger. *n.* "world view"; phil. theory of the purpose or history of the world. **-politik** (-ēk), Ger. *n.* international politics; policy towards the world. **-schmerz** (-shmārts), Ger. *n.* "world sorrow"; sadness at the world's woes; pessimism.

---

hat, bah, hāte, hāre, crawl; pen, ēve, hēre; it, īce, fīre; on, bōne, boil, bōre, howl; foot, fōōd, bōōr, hull, tūbe, pūre.

werewolf (wēr'woolf), *n.* human being transformed into wolf.

wergild (wə'gild), *n.* value of a man's life, payable to his family by his murderer.

wet-bob (wet'-bob), *n.* Etonian adopting rowing as his sport.

wether (wedh'ə), *n.* castrated ram.

whin (win, hwin), *n.* gorse. **-chat**, *n.* small brown and buff song-bird.

whitlow (wit'lō, hwit'-), *n.* abscess on finger, *espec.* round nail.

widgeon (wij'ən), *n.* kind of fresh-water duck with light crown.

wie geht's (vē gāts), *Ger.*, "how goes it ?"; how do you do ?

wildebeest (vēl'dəbāst), S. African *n.* gnu.

wimple (wim'pl), *n.* women's head covering worn round neck and chin, as by nuns.

witan (wit'ən), *n.* early English King's council.

witenagemot (wit'ənəgimōt), *n.* early English national council; witan.

withy (widh'i), *n.* willow; thin twig.

wivern (wī'vən), *n.* winged dragon in heraldry.

wolfram (wool'frəm), *n.* tungsten.

wolveri ∙(woolvərēn'), *n.* Amer. shaggy-furred animal of weasel family.

wombat (wom'bat), *n.* Austral. bear-like marsupial; Austral. badger.

woof (woof), *n.* threads crossing warp in weaving; weft.

wort (wət), *n.* infusion of malt before fermentation.

wrack (rak), *n.* sea-weed cast up on shore; wreckage; vestige.

wrangler (rang'glə), *n.* at Cambridge University, an honours graduate in first class in math. tripos. **senior w.**, first on list of such graduates.

wrasse (ras), *n.* a bright-hued marine fish of Atlantic and Mediterranean.

wynd (wīnd), *Scot. n.* alley.

wyvern, *see* wivern.

X

xanthic (zan'thik), *adj.* yellow; yellowish. **-thochroia**, *n.* yellowness of skin. **-thochroid**, *n. & adj.* fair-haired (person). **-thochromia**, **-thosis**, *n.* yellow discoloration. **-thoderm**, *n.* yellow-skinned person. **-thoma**, *n.* skin disease causing yellow patches. **-thopsia**, *n.* optical defect causing everything to seem yellow. **-thous**, *adj.* yellow- or red-haired; yellow-skinned.

xebec (zē'bek), *n.* anct. three-masted Mediterranean pirate ship.

xenial (zē'niəl), *adj.* pert. to hospitality, or relations of friendly visitors. **-ian**, *adj.*

xenogamy (zinog'əmi), *n.* cross-fertilization. **-genous**, *adj.* due to external cause. **-nolith**, *n.* rock particle included in another rock. **-nomorphic**, *adj.* with a form not its own.

xeransis (ziran'sis), *n.* drying up. **-ntic**, *adj.* **-rarch**, *adj.* growing in dry places. **-rasia**, *n.* morbid dryness of hair. **-roderma**, *n.* morbid dryness of skin. **-rography**, *n.* method of reproducing illustrations, text, etc., electrostatically,

by attraction of ink powder to positively charged sheet of selenium metal. **-rophagy**, *n.* strict fast of Eastern Church during Holy Week. **-rophilous**, *adj.* resisting drought. **-rophobous**, *adj.* unable to survive drought. **-rophyte**, *n.* plant thriving in desert conditions. **-rosis**, *n. Med.*, dryness. **-rostoma**, *n.* dryness of mouth. **-rotes**, *n. Med.*, dryness of body. **-rotic**, *adj.* dry.

xi (zī; ksē), *n.* fourteenth letter (Ξ, ξ) of Gr. alphabet.

xiphoid (zī'foid), *adj.* sword-like. **x.process**, lowest division of sternum; king-crab's tail. **-ophyllous**, *adj.* with sword-shaped leaves.

X-ray (eks'rā), *n.* radiation of very short wave-length, produced when cathode rays strike a metal obstacle, and able to penetrate solid bodies; *v.t.* to photograph or examine by means of X-rays.

xylem (zī'lem), *n.* woody tissue of plants. **-locarp**, *n.* woody fruit.

xylograph (zī'ləgraf), *n.* wood-engraving; pattern ∙ imitating wood grain. **-glyphy**, *n.* wood-carving. **-y**, *n.*

ə=*er* in *father*; ē=*er* in *pert*; th=*th* in *thin*; dh=*th* in *then*; zh=*s* in *pleasure*; k=*ch* in *loch*; ṅ=Fr. nasal *n*; ü=Fr. *u.*

xyloid (zī'loid), *adj.* like wood. **-lology,** *n.* study of structure of wood. **-lometer,** *n.* instr. measuring specific gravity of wood. **-lonite,** *n.* celluloid. **-lophagous,** *adj.* destroying or boring in wood. **-lophilous,** *adj.* living on or in wood. **-loplastic,** *adj.* made of or in wood-pulp moulds. **-lotomous,** *adj.* boring into or cutting wood.

Y

yaffle (yaf'l), *n.* green woodpecker.

yahoo (yəhoo'), *n.* member of brutish, quasi-human species in Swift's *Gulliver's Travels*; depraved person.

yamen (yah'mən), Chin. *n.* official residence.

yarborough (yah'bərə), *n.* hand of cards containing no card above nine.

yashmak (yash'mak), *n.* veil of Moham. women.

yataghan (yat'əgan), *n.* Moham. long curved knife.

yaw (yaw), *v.i.* & *t.* move or deviate from course; move in a zigzag; *n.* such deviation or movement.

yawl (yawl), *n.* ship's small rowing-boat; small sailing vessel with from one to three lugsails; small fore-and-aft rigged vessel with mizzen-mast abaft rudder post.

yaws (yawz), *n.* contagious skin disease resembling syphilis.

yean (yēn), *v.i.* & *t.* bring forth (lamb or kid). **-ling,** *n.* lamb or kid.

yerba (maté) (yē'bə, mat'ā), *n.* Paraguay tea. **-l,** *n.* plantation of y.

yoga (yō'gə), *n.* Hindu mental and physical discipline attained by trance-like concentration on an object, and by certain exercises, controlled breathing, etc.

yoghourt (yō'goort, yog'hawt), *n.* cheesy milk preparation fermented with a lactic acid bacillus.

yogi (yō'gi), *n.* person practising yoga.

yom (yom), Heb. *n.* "day." **y.Kippur,** "day of atonement," a solemn Jewish fast. **y.Tob,** "good day"; religious festival; Sabbath.

ypsiliform (ipsil'ifawm), *adj.* shaped like Gr. upsilon (Υ). **-loid,** *adj.*

Z

zamindar (zəmēn'dahr), Hind. *n.* landowner. **-i,** *n.* land or jurisdiction of z.

zariba, -reb- (zərē'bə), *n.* protective hedge, etc., round Sudanese village; fortified camp.

zebrule, -la (zē'brool, -ə; zeb'-), *n.* hybrid of male zebra and female horse.

zebu (zē'bū), *n.* humped ox of the East and E. Africa.

Zeitgeist (tsīt'gīst), Ger. *n.* "spirit of the age"; philosophy or outlook of a particular period.

zenana (zinah'nə), *n.* harem; system of segregating women in harems.

zenography (zinog'rəfi), *n.* study or description of planet Jupiter. **-phic(al),** *adj.*

zeta (zē'tə), *n.* sixth letter (Z, ζ) of Gr. alphabet.

zetetic (zitet'ik), *n.* & *adj.* inquiring (person); search.

zeugma (zūg'mə), *n.* lit. device of using word to modify two other words with only one of which it is correctly used. **-tic,** *adj.*

ziara (ziah'rah), *n.* Moham. shrine.

zibeline, -ell- (zib'əlīn, -in), *adj.* pert. to sables.

zibet (zib'et), *n.* Ind. civet.

Zigeuner (tsigoi'nə), Ger. *n.* "gypsy."

zingaro (tsēng'gahrō), It. *n.* (*pl.* **-ri**) "gypsy."

zircon (zə'kon), *n.* brownish or greyish mineral used as gem. **-iferous,** *adj.* yielding z.

zither (zidh'ə), *n.* mus. instr. of strings stretched over a horizontal sounding board and plucked with a plectrum.

zodiac (zō'diak), *n.* *Astron.,* imaginary belt of the heavens, centred on the sun's path and including paths of all major planets; orbit of a planet, etc. **signs of the z.,**

twelve signs representing the divisions of the z.

zoea (zō ē'ə), *n.* early larva of crab and other crustaceans. **-l,** *adj.*

zoetic (zōet'ik), *adj.* living; vital. **-trope,** *n.* device whereby a series of drawings are made to seem, by revolving them, one continuous moving pixture.

zoiatria (zōiat'riə), *n.* treatment of diseases of lower animals.

zoic (zō'ik), *adj.* pert. to animals. **-ism,** *n.* veneration of animals as primitive religion.

Zollverein (tsol'fərīn), Ger. *n.* "customs-union."

zomotherapy (zōməther'əpi), *n.* med. treatment by raw meat or meat juice. **-peutic,** *adj.*

zoogamy (zōog'əmi), *n.* sexual reproduction of animals. **-genous** (-oj'inəs), *adj.* originating in animals. **-gonous,** *adj.* viviparous. **-graphy,** *n.* description of animals.

zooid (zō'oid), *n.* organism resembling animal, *espec.* asexually produced; sperm cell. **-al,** *adj.*

zoolite, **-lith** (zō'əlīt, -ith), *n.* fossil animal.

zoometry (zōom'itri), *n.* measurement of animals. **-mimetic,** *adj.* imitating an animal or part of an animal. **-morph,** *n.* object in form of animal. **-morphism,** *n.* representation of god as lower animal.

zoonic (zōon'ik), *adj.* pert. to or derived from animals. **-nosis,** *n.* disease that can be communicated among animals or from animal to man.

zoopery (zōop'əri), *n.* experimenting on lower animals. **-ral,** *adj.* **-rist,** *n.*

zoophile (zō'əfīl, -il), *n.* lover of animals; plant pollinated by animals. **-lia,** **-list** (-of'ilist), *n.* **-lous** (-of'iləs), *adj.* **-phobia,** *n.* dread of animals.

zoophyte (zō'əfīt), *n.* plant-like animal, as coral, sea anemone, etc. **-tal** (-ī'təl), **-tic** (-it'ik), *adj.* **-tology,** *n.* study of z.

zooscopy (zōos'kəpi), *n.* hallucination of seeing animals. **-pic** (-op'ik), *adj.*

zoosis (zōō'sis), *n.* disease due to animal parasite.

zootechny (zōətek'ni), *n.* breeding and taming of animals. **-nic,** *adj.*

zootherapy (zōəther'əpi), *n.* veterinary remedial science.

zootomy (zōot'əmi), *n.* study of animal anatomy. **-ic(al)** (-om'ik, -l), *adj.* **-mist,** *n.*

zootrophy (zōot'rəfi), *n.* feeding of animals. **-phic** (-of'ik), *adj.*

zouave (zōōahv'), *n.* Fr.-Algerian infantry soldier; woman's short jacket.

zygal (zī'gəl), *adj.* H-shaped. **-godactyl(ic),** *adj.* having toes in two pairs, one behind the other. **-gomorphic,** *adj.* bilaterally symmetrical.

zygophyte (zī'gəfīt), *n.* plant with reproduction by union of two similar cells. **-ospore,** *n.* spore formed by such union.

zygote (zī'gōt), *n.* cell formed by union of two gametes; fertilised egg. **-tic** (-ot'ik), *adj.*

zymase (zī'māz), *n.* enzyme converting sugar to alcohol and carbon dioxide.

zymogenic (zīməjen'ik), *adj.* causing fermentation. **-genous** (-oj'inəs), *adj.*

zymology (zīmol'əji), *n.* study of or treatise on fermentation. **-gic(al),** *adj.* **-gist,** *n.*

zymolysis (zīmol'isis), *n.* action of enzymes.

zymosis (zīmō'sis), *n.* fermentation; process resembling fermentation of development of infectious disease.

zymotic (zīmot'ik), *adj.* pert. to fermentation; due to development of germs entering body from outside; *n.* contagious or infectious disease.

zymurgy (zī'məji), *n.* application of fermentation in industrial processes.

APPENDIX

• Indicates additional definitions to words included in the body of this Dictionary.

A

A and R, *abbr.* of Artists and Recording (gramophone records).

abient (ab'iənt), *adj.* tending to turn away or remove an organism from a stimulus or situation.

ablator (ablā'tər), *n.* a material providing protection from heat by melting or vaporising, e.g. on the outside of spacecraft ; a surgical instrument for removing tissue.

abscissin (absis'in), *n.* a plant hormone causing the fall of leaves in autumn.

accelerator (aksel'ərātə), *n.* in nuclear physics, a device producing a stream of high energy particles and focusing them on a target atom.

acculturation (akultūr ā'shn), *n.* transfer or adoption of the cultural patterns of another group. -rise, *v.t.* cause a. in.

accumulator (akū'mūlātə), *n.* in computers, the electronic circuits that perform the calculations.

acriflavine (akriflā'vēn), *n.* a brown-red hydrochloride antiseptic for wounds.

acronym (ak'rənim), *n.* a word formed from the initial letters of a group of words ; a pronounceable abbreviation, e.g. Nato.

acrylic (əkril'ik), *adj.* denoting an acid obtained from the aldehyde acrolein derived from glycerol or fats ; denoting a glass-like thermoplastic resin made by polymerising esters of acrylic or methacrylic acid, and used for transparent parts, dentures, lenses, etc.

actamer (ak'təmə), *n.* a substance preventing the growth of bacteria in cosmetics and soaps.

ACV, *abbr.* of Air Cushion Vehicle (i.e. operating on principle of hovercraft).

address (ədres'), *n.* in computers, a character or symbol designating a location where information is stored.

adient (ad'iənt), *adj.* tending to expose an organism to, or turn it towards, a stimulus or situation.

admass (ad'mas), *n. orig.* advertising as a vital element in mass production; the section of the public that is most easily influenced by advertising.

aerobatic (ārəbat'ik), *adj.* pert. to acrobatic manoeuvres in aircraft. -s, *n.* such manoeuvres.

aerobiology (ārəbīol'əji), *n.* the biology of airborne particles and organisms.

aerodontia (ārədon'shiə), *n.* branch of dentistry dealing with dental problems resulting from aviation.

aerogel (ār'əjel), *n.* a gel in which the liquid is replaced by a gas.

aeronomy (āron'əmi), *n.* study of chemical and physical phenomena in the upper atmosphere. -mic (-nom'ik), *adj.*

aerospace (ār'əspās), *n.* the Earth's atmosphere and space beyond it.

aerosphere (ār'əsfēr), *n.* the entire atmosphere surrounding the Earth.

aerotrain (ār'ətrān, āĕr'ōtrań), *n.* a monorail vehicle operated on principle of hovercraft.

afrormosia (afrawmō'ziə), *n.* a dense tropical hardwood resembling teak, used for furniture and panelling.

aggiornamento (ajōrnamen'tō), It. *n.* act or process of modernising or bringing up to date.

AGR, *abbr.* of Advanced Gas-cooled Reactor.

agranulocytosis (əgranūləsītō'sis), *n.* a serious blood disease marked by great reduction in the non-granular leucocytes.

ailurophile (ālūr'əfil), *n.* one abnormally fond of cats. -phobe, *n.* one with an abnormal dread of cats.

aldrin (al'drin), *n.* a chemical pesticide the use of which was forbidden in the U.K. in 1964.

alicyclic (alisī'klik), *adj.* denoting organic compounds that are both aliphatic and cyclic, i.e. aliphatic

---

hat, bah, hāte, hāre, crawl; pen, ēve, hēre; it, īce, fīre; on, bōne, bol, bōre, howl; foot, fōōd, bōōr, hull, tūbe, pūre.

in chemical behaviour but having their carbon atoms in a ring.

allograft (al'əgrahft), *n.* surgical graft from a non-identical donor.

allopurinal (aləpūr'inəl), *n.* synthetic drug used against gout.

allyl (al'il), *n.* a radical compounds of which occur in the oils of garlic and mustard. **a. alcohol,** a liquid obtained from glycerol, etc. **a. plastic** or **resin,** a thermosetting resin made from allyl alcohol and a dibasic acid, used chiefly as adhesive for laminated materials.

alphameric (alfəmer'ik), *adj.* composed of letters and digits.

aminobutene (əmēnōbū'tēn, am'inō-), *n.* a synthetic pain-relieving drug, less addictive than morphine.

amphetamine (amfet'əmēn), *n.* drug which stimulates the central nervous system, used in medicine to relieve depression, and to control appetite in cases of obesity : the chief ingredient of "pep pills".

ampicillin (ampisil'in), *n.* an improved form of penicillin taken by mouth.

amytal (am'ital), *n.* a sleep-inducing barbiturate drug, *espec.* sodium amytal.

anableps (anə'bleps), *n.* a tropical Amer. fish that swims with its eyes half out of the water.

*analogue (an'əlog), *n.* something similar, exactly comparable, or equivalent. **a. computer,** one calculating by physical quantities equivalent to numerical variables.

anchorman (ank'əman), *n.* compère or master of ceremonies, especially of a television programme made up of several items or of material from several sources.

andromedotoxin (andromidətok'-sin), *n.* a poisonous substance extracted from plants of the heath family and used in medicine to lower high blood pressure.

anechoic (anekō'ik), *adj.* free from echoes and reverberations ; sound-absorbent.

anemophobia (ənem'əfōbiə, -nēm'-), *n.* morbid dread of high winds, hurricanes, etc.

anhedral (anhē'drəl), *adj.* denoting the angle at which the main planes of an aircraft are inclined downwards to the lateral axis.

anorak (an'ərak), *n.* a hooded, waterproof outer garment originally used by Eskimos.

antimatter (an'timatə), *n.* hypothetical form of matter composed of particles equivalent to particles of normal matter but oppositely charged. **anti-particle,** *n.* positively charged particle equivalent and companion to every negatively charged particle of normal matter.

apolune (ap'əlūn), *n.* point in the orbit of body revolving round the moon that is farthest from the centre of the moon.

aqualung (ak'wəlung), *n.* self-contained supply of air carried by a diver, allowing free movement.

aquanaut (ak'wənawt), *n.* an underwater explorer, *espec.* one remaining for extended periods in undersea diving chamber.

astronaut (as'trənawt), *n.* person who travels outside the Earth's atmosphere. **-ic** (-naw'tik), *adj.* **-ics,** *n.* science of space travel.

astrophysics (as'trəfiziks), *n.* study of the physical and chemical composition of heavenly bodies.

atheroma (athərō'mə), *n.* a soft fatty tumour ; fatty degeneration of the arteries. **-osclerosis** (-əsklerō'sis), *n.* hardening of the inner lining of the arteries with fatty degeneration.

atto- (at'ō-), *prefix* of measurement meaning one million-million-millionth (10^{-18}).

audiogenic (awdiəjen'ik), *adj.* caused by sound waves, *espec.* of high frequency.

aureomycin (ōriəmī'sin), *n.* an antibiotic drug extracted from a soil mould, used in treatment of infections, *espec.* of eyes, skin, etc.

autecology (awtikol'əji), *n.* the ecology of the individual organism.

autoimmune (awtōimūn'), *adj.* denoting a condition in which antibodies are aroused by a patient's own secretions, etc. **-nity,** *n.*

autonomics (awtənom'iks), *n.* science of the performance by machines of mental processes such as reading and translation.

avionics (āvion'iks), *n.* study and use of electronic devices in aviation.

axenic (āzen'ik), *adj.* free of parasites and similar forms of life ; surgically sterile.

B

bagheera (bagēr'ə), *n.* a rough, crease-resistant, velvet-like textile.

balladromic (balədrom'ik), *adj.* (of missiles, etc.) maintaining course towards a target.

baryon (bar'iən), *n.* any of the class of subatomic particles known as "heavy", e.g. neutron and proton.

bathyscaph(e) (bath'iskaf, -skāf), *n.* submarine-like diving chamber.

bathythermograph (bathithə'məgraf), *n.* instrument visually recording the ocean temperature at various depths.

batology (batol'əji), *n.* scientific study of brambles.

beatnik (bēt'nik), *n.* person who has abandoned conventional behaviour, dress, etc.; "bohemian".

beautician (būtish'n), *n.* owner or manager of a beauty parlour; specialist in beautifying the female face and figure.

Benelux (ben'iluks), *abbr.* of Belgium, Netherlands, and Luxemburg (customs union).

beryllium (bəril'iəm), *n.* a hard, white metal used in alloys, occurring as an element only in compounds.

bevatron (bev'ətron), *n.* a synchroton-like apparatus for accelerating charged particles to an immensely high level.

BHC, *abbr.* of Benzine Hexa-Chloride (pesticide).

bikini (bikē'ni), *n.* a woman's very brief two-piece bathing suit.

Binac (bī'nak), *abbr.* of Binary Automatic Computer.

*binary (bī'nəri), *adj.* *Arith.,* denoting a system of numeration based on 2, and therefore written entirely with 1 and 0, commonly used in digital computers.

bionics (bīon'iks), *n.* study of the design principles of living organisms and their application to machines.

biosatellite (bī'əsatəlīt), *n.* artificial satellite carrying living organisms into space for scientific study.

biotelemetry (bīətelem'itri), *n.* automatic transmission over a distance, fof measurements of the condition eunctions, etc., of a living creature, e.g. of an astronaut on space flight.

bit (bit), *n.* in computers, a single character, *espec.* a single binary numeral (0 or 1) : *abbr.* of binary digit.

bivariate (bīvār'iət), *adj.* denoting a quantity that depends on two variables.

blennophobia (blenəfō'biə), *n.* morbid fear of slime.

boatel, botel (bōtel'), *n.* a waterside hotel for sailing enthusiasts.

boutique (bōotēk'), *n.* a small shop, *espec.* one selling fashionable clothes and accessories for women.

breathalyser (breth'əlīzə), *n.* device indicating amount of recent intake of alcohol by its effect on the breath.

brinkmanship (bringk'mənship), *n.* practice of carrying a critical situation to the limit of safety, to obtain diplomatic advantage.

broil (broil), *v.t.* cook by exposure to direct heat, grill. **-er,** *n.* chicken reared under special unnatural conditions to mature quickly as suitable for broiling. **b.-beef,** *n.* meat from calves reared in similar conditions. **b.-house,** *n.* building in which broilers are reared; any similar unnatural conditions of rearing.

brucellosis (brōoselō'sis), *n.* an undulant fever of cattle.

bug (bug), *v.t. sl.,* fit secretly with eavesdropping microphones, cameras, etc.

byte (bīt), *n.* in computers, a character consisting of eight "bits".

C

calcitonin (kalsitō'nin), *n.* hormone secreted by the thyroid gland, controlling the rate of bone destruction.

calutron (kal'ūtron), *n.* apparatus that separates isotopes according to their masses, electromagnetically.

*capsule (kap'sūl), *n.* a small sealed chamber enclosing astronaut (s) on space flight.

carbomycin (kahbəmī'sin), *n.* an antibiotic drug obtained from a soil fungus, used chiefly against respiratory infections.

carcinoma (kahsinō'mə), *n.* (*pl.* **-mata, -mas**) a form of malignant cancer. **-matous** (-nom'ətəs), *adj.* **-nogen** (kah'sinəjen), *n.* a cancer-causing substance. **-nogenic** (-jen'-ik), *adj.*

caronamide (kəron'əmīd), *n.* substance that prolongs the action of penicillin by preventing its excretion.

casease (kā'siās), *n.* enzyme decomposing the casein in milk and cheese.

cassation (kasā'shn), *n. Mus.*, a serenade-like instrumental composition for outdoor performance.

catatonia (catətō'niə), *n.* severe mental disturbance with alternate periods of intense activity and depressed stupor. **-nic** (-ton'ik), *adj.*

cathetometer (kathitom'itə), *n.* instrument measuring small vertical distances with great accuracy.

cattalo (kat'əlō), *n.* a cross between domestic cattle and N. Amer. bison.

ceilometer (sēlom'itə), *n.* instrument measuring the distance between cloud ceiling and Earth's surface.

°cellulosic (selūlō'sik), *n.* plastic made from cellulose.

centi- (sen'ti-), *prefix* of measurement meaning one hundredth (10^{-2}). *Abbr.* **c.**

cephalosporin (sefələspōr'in), *n.* antibiotic drug extracted from cephalosporium mould, of very wide application, also called **ceporin** (sep'ərin), *n.*

cerebrotonic (seribrəton'ik), *adj.* having a shy, inhibited temperament associated with ectomorphy. **-nia** (-tō'niə), *n.*

cermet (sə'met), *n.* a strong alloy of a metal with a heat-resisting compound, *espec.* used for turbine blades and similar objects.

CERN (sən), *abbr.* of Fr. Centre Européen de Recherche Nucléaire (European Nuclear Research Centre).

chemonuclear (kemənū'kliə), *adj.* pert. to or arising from both a chemical and a nuclear reaction.

chloramphenicol (klōramfen'ikol), *n.* an antibiotic drug originally isolated from a soil micro-organism, effective against various bacterial and viral diseases.

chlorometer (klōrom'itə), *n.* instrument for measuring chlorine, *espec.* in bleaching powders.

°chromatography (krōmatog'rəfi), *n. Chem.*, separation or analysis of mixtures by adsorption of individual ingredients on filter paper, etc.

clinodromic (klīnədrom'ik), *adj.* moving at an angle, *espec.* of

missiles travelling at an angle to a moving target. **-noscopic** (-nəskop'ik), *adj.* pert. to missiles travelling in line with a moving target.

clinophobia (klīnəfō'biə), *n.* morbid fear of going to bed.

codon (kō'don), *n.* a character, or group of characters, in the genetic code carried by the living cell, which directs the formation of a particular amino-acid.

collage (kol'ahzh), *n.* creation of an artistic work by pasting shaped scraps of printed matter and other materials to a surface; such a composition.

collagen (kol'əjən), *n.* gelatinous protein in bones and connective tissue. **-ic** (-jen'ik), *adj.*

comprehensive (komprihen'siv), *adj.* all-embracing, *espec.* of a school affording all types of secondary education in one building or unit.

compute (kəmpūt'), *v.i.* & *t.* calculate, reckon. **-table,** *adj.* **-tation** (kompūtā'shn), *n.* **-tative** (-pū'tətiv), *adj.* using calculation. **-r** (-pū'tə), *n.* calculating machine, *espec.* electronically operated and capable of complex calculations in very short period of time. **-rise,** *v.t.* to control or calculate by an electronic computer.

Comsat (kom'sat), *abbr.* of Communication Satellite Corporation (of U.S.A.).

containerise (kəntā'nərīz), *v.t.* to pack (freight) in large sealed containers for transport by road, rail, or ship.

copolymer (kō'polimə), *n.* a compound of high molecular weight produced by polymerising two or more different monomers. **-ise** (-pol'-) *v.i.* & *t.* to become or make into a c.

Coriolis (korio'lis), *adj.* denoting the force or effect of the rotation of the Earth on atmosphere, oceans, etc.

coronagraph (kərō'nəgraf), *n.* astron. instrument by which the solar corona can be observed in full sunlight.

cosmodrome (koz'mədrōm), *n.* (Russian) space-exploration centre and rocket-launching installation. **-monaut,** *n.* astronaut.

cosmogenic (kozməjen'ik), *adj.* produced by action of cosmic rays.

cosmology (kozmol'əji), *n.* branch of science or philosophy dealing with the origin and structure of the universe. **-moplastic** (-plas'tik), *adj.* forming the universe. **-mopoietic** (-poiet'ik), *adj.* creating the universe.

cosmotron (koz'mətron), *n.* a type of proton accelerator.

COSPAR (kos'pah), *abbr.* of (international) Committee On Space Research.

crocidolite (krəsid'əlīt), *n.* blue asbestos, essentially a sodium iron silicate.

CRT, *abbr.* of Cathode Ray Tube.

cru (krōō), *abbr.* of Currency Reserve Unit (proposed international monetary unit to ease the strain on gold and reserve currencies).

cryogenics (krīəjen'iks), *n.* study of effects of extremely low temperatures. **-opedology** (-pedol'əji), *n.* study of action of intense frost on soil. **-ostat** (krī'əstat), *n.* automatic device for maintaining low temperature. **-osurgery,** *n.* performance of surgical operations on heart, brain, etc., which are first cooled to a low temperature, or by instruments maintained at an extremely low temperature. **-otron,** *n.* device for producing or maintaining very low temperature.

cryptoclimate (krip'təklīmət), *n.* climate of the inside of a building or other enclosed structure.

cyclazocine (sīkləzō'sēn), *n.* synthetic drug protecting against the addictive effects of the morphine group.

cynophobia (sinəfo'biə), *n.* morbid fear of dogs.

Cyrenaicism (sīrənā'isizm), *n.* hedonism.

cytogenics (sītəjen'iks), *n.* Biol., study of the structural basis of heredity in the cell. **-ozoon** (-əzō'on), *n.* (*pl.* **-zoa**) protozoan parasite within a cell.

D

daiquiri (dīkwir'i), *n.* an iced drink of rum, lime juice, and sugar; a "white" rum for this.

dasymeter (dəsim'itə), *n.* device for measuring the density of gases.

deci- (des'i-), *prefix* of measurement meaning one tenth (10⁻¹). *Abbr.* d.

declinometer (deklinom'itə), *n.* instrument measuring magnetic declination.

deka- (dek'ə-), *prefix* of measurement meaning ten. *Abbr.* da.

deltiology (deltiol'əji), *n.* hobby of collecting post-cards.

denier (den'iə), *n. orig.* a unit of weight (about 8½ troy grains) of silk, rayon, nylon, etc.; later, an indication of the fineness of such yarns, the lower the denier number the finer the yarn.

desalination (dēsalinā'shn), *n.* removal of salt from sea water to produce fresh water.

deuteron (dū'təron), *n.* a positively charged particle consisting of a proton and a neutron, equivalent to the nucleus of an atom of deuterium.

*diachronic (dīəkron'ik), *adj.* pert. to the passage of time, or to events occurring as result of the passage of time.

*dialysis (dīal'isis), *n.* separation of substances in a solution by diffusion through a membrane, *espec.* such separation of waste products from blood in the kidneys. **-yser** (dī'əlīzə), *n.* a machine performing this function of the kidneys.

dieldrin (dīel'drin), *n.* a persistent chemical pesticide, generally forbidden in the U.K. since 1964.

dig (dig), *v.t. sl.,* observe, understand, appreciate, like.

digital (dij'itəl), *adj.* denoting the type of computer calculating by numbers and not quantities.

dihedral (dīhē'drəl), *n.* angle between an aircraft wing and the horizontal.

dipole (dī'pōl), *n. Elec.,* any object oppositely charged at its ends; a broadcast receiving aerial consisting of a single metal rod.

discography (diskog'rəfi), *n.* a descriptive catalogue of gramophone records; a list of recordings by one composer or performer.

discotheque (diskōtek'), *n.* a club for listening or dancing to recorded music.

DNA, *abbr.* of Deoxy-ribo-Nucleic Acid (a nucleic acid present in every living cell, containing the genetic information that directs the sequence in which amino acids are arranged to form a protein).

dol (dol), *n.* basic and smallest unit for measuring the intensity of pain, equal to the faint sensation felt when heat rays are first applied to the skin. **-orimetry** (dolərim'itri), *n.* measurement of pain.

dormin (dōr'min), *n.* a plant hormone controlling the dormancy period.

dracone (drakōn'), *n.* towed flexible container for transporting liquids by water.

duplexite (dūplek'sīt), *n.* a pearly white beryllium mineral.

dynatron (dī'nətron), *n.* a multi-electrode thermionic valve often used as an oscillator.

dyslexia (dislek'siə), *n.* word-blindness ; inability to associate letter symbols with sounds.

dysphemia (disfē'miə), *n.* stammering.

E

echometer (ekom'itə), *n.* device measuring the duration of sounds.

ECSC, *abbr.* of European Coal and Steel Community.

ectomorph (ek'təmawf), *n.* psycho-physical type with long thin bones and large surface relative to weight, often inhibited and shy. **-ic**, *adj.* **-y**, *n.*

EFTA, *abbr.* of European Free Trade Association.

ekistics (ikis'tiks), *n.* scientific study of human settlements.

elaeometer (elēom'itə), *n.* device measuring the specific gravity of oils.

elastomeric (ilastəmer'ik), *adj.* denoting artificial fibres with rubber-like elasticity.

ELDO (el'dō), *abbr.* of European Launcher Development Organisation.

electret (ilek'tret), *n.* a non-conductor having permanent positive and negative poles, the electro-static equivalent of a permanent magnet.

electro-osmosis (ilek'trō-ozmō'sis), *n.* the movement of a conducting liquid through a porous membrane due to a difference of potential between electrodes on opposite sides.

emote (imōt'), *v.t. sl.*, behave in an exaggeratedly emotional manner.

enantiomorph (enan'tiəmawf), *n.* each of a pair of asymmetric figures that are mirror images of each other, e.g. a pair of hands.

endomorph (en'dəmawf), *n.* psycho-physical type, soft, rounded and fleshy, and often sociable and comfort-loving. **-ic**, *adj.* **-y**, *n.*

ENIAC (en'iak), *abbr.* of Electronic Numerical Indicator And Calculator.

epoxy (epok'si), *adj.* denoting chem. compounds in which oxygen is attached to two different atoms in a chain, e.g. epoxy resin.

ergonomics (ōgənom'iks), *n.* scientific study of work conditions, equipment and operations, to promote efficiency.

eriometer (ēriom'itə), *n.* optical instrument for measuring the diameters of fibres or particles by the diffraction of light.

Ernie (ə'ni) *abbr.* of Electronic Random Number Indicator Equipment (machine picking prize-winning bond numbers).

escalation (eskəlā'shn), *n.* graded increase or intensification, "stepping-up". **-late** (es'kōlāt), *v.i. & t.*

ESRO (es'rō), *abbr.* of European Space Research Organisation.

ETA, *abbr.* of Estimated Time of Arrival.

euphenics (ūfen'iks), *n.* biological improvement of human beings after birth.

Euratom (ūrat'əm), *abbr.* of European Atomic Energy Community.

EVR, *abbr.* of Electronic Video Recording and Reproduction.

exobiology (ek'səbiōləji), *n.* scientific study of the possibility of life outside the Earth.

extrapolate (ekstrap'əlāt), *v.t.* calculate (an unknown value) from known values in a series or progression ; forecast logically by calculation. **-tion** (-ā'shn), *n.*

F

fall-out (fawl'owt), *n.* by-product, *espec.* of radioactive material in the atmosphere after a nuclear explosion.

feedback (fēd'bak), *n.* return of a fraction of the energy output to the energy input in a transmission system ; an arrangement by which a variation in output modifies the generation of energy.

ə=*er* in *father* ; ə̄=*er* in *pert* ; th=*th* in *thin* ; dh=*th* in *then* ; zh=*s* in *pleasure* ; k=*ch* in *loch* ; n̄=Fr. nasal *n* ; ü=Fr. *u*

femto- (fem'tō-), *prefix* of measurement meaning one thousand-million-millionth (10^{-15}). *Abbr.* f.

fibrid (fī'brid), *n.* one of a type of synthetic fibrous particles used in bonding.

fibroid (fī'broid), *adj.* of or like fibre; *n.* non-malignant fibrous tumour.

fillipeen (filipēn), *n.* philopena.

fluidic (flōōid'ik), *adj.* pert. to or like a fluid ; operated by the flow of a liquid or gas. **-s,** *n.* study and application of f. operations.

fluoride (flōō'ərīd), *n.* a compound of fluorine, *espec.* one introduced into public water supply to combat dental decay. **-date** (-or'idāt), *v.t.* introduce f. into. **-ation,** *n.*

fluorocarbon (flōōərakah'bən), *n.* an inert compound of carbon and fluoride used as lubricant and in manufacture of plastics and synthetic resins.

fluviometer (flōōviom'itə), *n.* device for measuring river levels.

frottage (frot'ahzh), *n.* rubbing, *espec.* the making of rubbings on thin paper of objects underneath, e.g. ornamental brasses.

FSH, *abbr.* of Follicle-Stimulating Hormone (lack of which is a cause of infertility in women).

G

GATT (gat), *abbr.* of General Agreement on Tariffs and Trade.

genetotrophic (jenitətrof'ik), *adj.* denoting a defect in metabolism which prevents the normal assimilation of essential food elements.

geochemistry (jēəkem'istri),*n.* chem. composition of the Earth's crust.

gephyrophobia (jifīrəfō'biə), *n.* morbid fear of bridges and passing over or under them.

giga- (gī'gə-), *prefix* of measurement meaning one thousand millions (10^9). *Abbr.* G.

giro (jīr'ō), *n.* system of payment by credit transfer within a bank or savings bank.

gismo (giz'mō), *n. sl.*, a gadget, a thing.

GLEEP (glēp), *abbr.* of Graphite Low Energy Experimental Pile (atomic energy research).

glottochronology (glotōkrənol'əji), *n. Philol.*, study of the rate at which changes take place in a language, *espec.* in divergent branches of a primitive language.

glucagon (glōō'kəgən), *n.* a pancreatic hormone which raises blood sugar level and reduces appetite.

glycaemia (glīkē'miə), *n.* presence of glucose in the blood.

GNP, *abbr.* of Gross National Product (total output of goods and services of a country).

gramicidin (gramisī'din),*n.* an antibiotic drug obtained from tyrothrycin, used against local infections caused by Gram-positive bacteria.

Gram-negative (gram-neg'ətiv), *adj.* denoting bacteria not retaining the dye when stained by Gram's method.

Gram-positive (gram-poz'itiv), *adj.* denoting bacteria retaining the dye when stained by Gram's method.

gumbotil (gum'bətil), . *n.* a dark sticky clay, formed by the weathering of boulder clay or glacial drift.

gyrocopter (jīr'əkoptə, gīr'-), *n.* combination of autogyro and helicopter, i.e. a rotorcraft having both drive to rotors and a normal propeller.

gyromagnetic (jīrəmagnet'ik, gīr-), *adj.* denoting the magnetic properties of the spinning electron in an atom.

H

hadron (had'rən), *n.* one of a large class of sub-atomic particles that participate in the strong interaction that holds the atomic nucleus together.

hallucinogen (həlōō'sinəjen), *n.* substance, *espec.* a drug, that causes hallucinations. **-ic** (-jen'ik), *adj.*

halometer (həlom'itə), *n.* device for measuring the forms of crystals.

happening (hap'əning), *n. sl.,* dramatic or similar performance consisting of a series of disconnected events and often involving audience participation.

hardware (hahd'wār), *n.* in computers, the mechanism that performs calculations, in contrast to software.

hecto- (hek'tō-), *prefix* of measurement meaning one hundred (10^2) *Abbr.* h.

heliport (hel'ipawt), *n.* landing place for helicopters on a regular service.

heptachlor (hep'təklōr), *n.* a chemical pesticide forbidden in the U.K. since 1964.

herpetology (həpetol'əji), *n. Zoo.*, study of reptiles.

hertz (hairts), *n.* unit of frequency, equal to one cycle per second. *Abbr.* Hz.

heterograft (het'ərōgrahft), *n.* surg. graft or transplant in which donor and recipient belong to different species.

hologram (hol'əgram), *n.* photograph taken, without a lens, by the interference of two laser beams, one illuminating the object and the other directed on to the film or plate. **-graphy,** *n.*

hominid (hom'inid), *n. & adj.* (pert. to) a fossil ape-man.

homograft (hom'ōgrahft), *n. & adj.* (denoting) tissue graft taken from non-identical members of the same species; allograft. **h. reaction,** rejection by the recipient's body of such a graft.

hovercraft (hov'əkrahft), *n.* vehicle able to move or hover above a surface on a cushion of air blown downwards by fans. **hovercar,** *n.,* **hovertrain,** *n.,* etc., such motor car, railway train, etc. **hoverbed,** *n.* bed on which a patient is supported on a cushion of air.

hydrofoil (hi'drəfoil), *n.* boat or ship rising at speed on struts fitted with water-ski-like foils that allow it to skim over the water.

hydron (hi'drən), *n.* a plastic which is rigid when dry and soft when wet.

hyperbaric (hipəbar'ik), *adj.* above normal atmospheric pressure, "pressurised".

hypersonic (hipəson'ik), *adj.* pert. to or denoting speed five or more times that of sound in the same medium.

hypnopedia (hipnəpē'diə), *n.* process of introducing information into the brain while asleep.

superimposing outlines of individual features and characteristics described by witnesses; the set of outlines with which such a portrait can be composed.

idioblast (id'iəblast), *n.* isolated cell differing greatly from surrounding cells or tissue.

idioglossia (idiəglos'iə), *n.* secret speech or language, *espec.* invented by children; psych. condition in which speech is so distorted as to be unintelligible.

IGY, *abbr.* of International Geophysical Year.

imbalance (imbal'əns), *n.* absence or lack of balance, *espec. Med.,* between opposing muscles, glandular secretions, acid-alkali conditions, etc.

immunotherapy (imūnother'əpi), *n.* med. treatment by exploiting immunological principles, e.g. by arousing antibodies through introducing antigens, or by causing tissue rejection through a graft.

impactite (impak'tit), *n.* slag-like glassy object found on the surface of the Earth, prob. formed from rock melted by the impact of a meteor.

incommunicado (inkəmūnikah'dō), *adj.* prevented from communicating, in solitary confinement.

Interpol (in'təpol), *n.* the international police organisation, with h.q. in Paris.

interstellar (intəstel'ə), *adj.* among or between the stars, in far outer space.

IQSY, *abbr.* of International Quiet Sun Years.

IRC, *abbr.* of Industrial Reorganisation Corporation (U.K. government agency).

isometrics (isəmet'riks), *n.* system of muscular exercises without apparatus, e.g. by opposing one set of muscles to another.

isotron (i'sətron), *n.* device for separating isotopes.

ITA, *abbr.* of Independent Television Authority. **ita,** *abbr.* of Initial Teaching Alphabet.

I

ICBM, *abbr.* of Inter-Continental Ballistic Missile.

Identikit (iden'tikit), *n. & adj.* (denoting) a portrait, *espec.* of a wanted person, composed by

K

kala-azar (kah'lah-ah'zahr), *n.* chronic, usually fatal, tropical amoebic disease,

kalology (kalol'əji), *n.* the study of beauty.

ə=*er* in *father*; ē=*er* in *pert*; th=*th* in *thin*; dh=*th* in *then*; zh=s in *pleasure*; k=*ch* in *loch*; ṅ=Fr. nasal *n*; ü=Fr. *u.*

kaon (kā'on), *n.* one of a class of mesons called the K-mesons.

kart (kaht), *n.* a midget racing car. **-ing,** *n.* racing with karts.

kathenotheism (kəthen'əthēizm), *n.* polytheism with worship of one god as supreme.

kenotron (ken'ətron), *n.* a high-vacuum diode used as a rectifier where high voltage and low current are needed.

keratitis (kerətī'tis), *n.* inflammation of the cornea.

kibbutz (kiboots'), *n.* (*pl.* -im) a communal farming centre in Israel.

kilim (kilēm'), *n.* tapestry-woven pile-less rug of Turkey, Persia and adjacent countries.

kilo- (kil'ə-), *prefix* of measurement meaning one thousand(10^3). *Abbr.* k.

kinaesthesia (kinesthē'zhə), *n.* the sense that recognises muscular effort, stimulated by all voluntary movements of the body. **-thetic** (-thet'ik), *adj.*

kinematics (kinimat'iks), *n.* abstract study of motion without reference to force or mass.

krotoscope (krō'təskōp), *n.* applause-measuring instrument.

kryptonate (krip'tənāt), *n.* a radioactive tracer produced by impregnating a substance with an isotope of krypton.

kyoodle (kiōō'dl), *v.i. Amer. sl.*, to make loud meaningless noises.

L

labanotation (labənōtā'shn), *n.* a method of writing down the movements, etc., of ballet diagramatically.

laser (lā'zə), *n.* device producing a concentrated beam of coherent light ; such a beam. *Abbr.* of Light Amplification by Stimulated Emission of Radiation.

leotard (lē'ətahd), *n.* ballet-dancer's practice dress, a tight-fitting one-piece garment.

lidar (lī'dah), *n.* system of using lasers in the same way as radar. *Abbr.* of Light Detection and Ranging.

logometer (logomit'ə), *n.* device or scale for measuring chemical equivalents. **-metric** (-met'rik), *adj.*

LSD, *abbr.* of Lysergic acid Diethylamide (hallucinogenic drug).

luciferin (lōōsif'ərin), *n.* chemical compound in luminescent insects, etc., producing light when oxidation is catalysed by an enzyme. **-rase** (-ās), *n.* that enzyme.

lysimeter (līsim'itə), *n.* device measuring percolation of water through soils and the removal of soluble constituents.

M

magnetohydrodynamic (magnētōhī-drədīnam'ik), *adj.* pert. to a method of generating electricity directly by passing an ionised gas through a magnetic field at an extremely high temperature. *Abbr.* MHD.

magnetometer (magnitom'itə), *n.* instrument measuring magnetic forces. **-ograph,** *n.* recording instrument of the same kind. **-ogram,** *n.* recording made by such instrument. **-ometry,** *n.*

magnetron (mag'nitron), *n.* thermionic valve for generating very high frequency oscillations.

marina (mərē'nə), *n.* yacht-mooring basin.

maser (mā'zə), *n.* intensely concentrated beam of coherent microwaves ; device for producing such beam. *Abbr.* of Microwave Amplification by Stimulated Emission of Radiation.

maverick (mav'ərik), *n.* unbranded calf or yearling; a wandering or wild undisciplined person.

mega- (meg'ə-), *prefix* of measurement meaning one million (10^6). *Abbr.* M.

menarche (menah'ki), *n.* first appearance of menses.

mescalin (mes'kəlin), *n.* a crystalline alkaloid extracted from a Mex. cactus producing hallucinations when taken as a drug.

mesomorph (mē'səmawf), *n.* psychophysical type showing predominance of muscle, bone, and connective tissue, often aggressive and self-assertive. **-ic,** *adj.* **-y,** *n.*

metageometry (metəjiom'itri), *n.* non-Euclidean geometry.

methadone (meth'ədōn) synthetic pain-relieving dr‧ ‧tly more potent than morp‧

methadrine (meth'ədrēn), *n.* s‧mulant drug also called amphetamine.

methodology (methədol'əji), *n.* science of method ; study of the principles of scientific investigation ; a specific instance of the application of method.

metricate (met'rikāt), *v.i.* to adopt the metric system of measurement ; *v.t.* to change to metric measurements. **-tion,** *n.*

MHD, *abbr.* of Magneto-Hydro-Dynamic.

MICR, *abbr.* of Magnetic Ink Character Readers (letters and figures readable by a computer, as on cheque forms).

micro- (mī'krō-), *prefix* of measurement meaning one millionth (10^{-6}). *Abbr.* μ.

microdot (mī'krədot), *n.* photograph reduced to the size of a dot.

microencapsulation (mīkrōenkapsūlā'shn), *n.* preparation of a substance (e.g. a medical drug) in the form of particles or droplets each enclosed in a permeable or dissoluble capsule.

microfilm (mī'krəfilm), *n.* photograph, on greatly reduced scale, of printed matter, manuscripts, etc. ; *v.t.* record or reproduce on m.

milli- (mil'i-), *prefix* of measurement meaning one thousandth (10^{-3}). *Abbr.* m.

minometer (minom'itə), *n.* instrument detecting stray radiations from X-ray generators and radioactive materials.

mitochondria (mītəkon'driə), *n. pl.* (*sing.* **-rion**) minute bodies in the living cell in which the final stages of the breakdown of carbohydrates and fats to release energy take place. **-rial,** *adj.*

mobile (mō'bīl), *n.* artistic construction with delicately balanced movable parts set in motion by air currents or mechanically.

moho (mō'hō), *n.* boundary between the crust and upper mantle of the Earth. *Abbr.* of Mohorovic discontinuity. **mohole,** *n.* borehole into the Earth's crust as far as the m.

monitor (mon'itə), *v.t.* maintain continuous observation of, as a check on output, efficiency, etc. ; *n.* recording device or display for this purpose.

mono (mon'ō), *adj.* pert. to sound recording or reproduction by a single transmission path, as opposed to stereophonic.

monocoque (mon'əkok), *n.* & *adj.* (denoting) aircraft structure in which the outer skin carries all or most of the torsional and bending stresses ; (denoting) car structure in which the body is integral with and shares the stresses with the chassis.

monomer (mon'əmer), *n.* simple unpolymerised form of a chemical compound, of comparatively low molecular weight.

monorail (mon'ərāl), *n.* railway system in which the rolling stock is balanced on or suspended from a single rail.

motel (mō'tel), *n.* roadside hotel for motorists, providing individual lodgings and free parking space.

myoglobin (mīəglō'bin), *n.* protein carrying oxygen to muscle as haemoglobin carries it to blood.

N

nano- (nā'nō-) *prefix* of measurement meaning one thousand-millionth (10^{-9}). *Abbr.* n.

narcotherapy (nahkōther'əpi), *n.* treatment of mental disturbance by prolonged drug-induced sleep.

NASA, *abbr.* of National Aeronautics and Space Administration (U.S.A.).

negatron (neg'ətron), *n.* hypothetical atomic particle with mass equal to that of a proton, but with a negative charge equal to that of an electron.

neocolonialism (nēōkələ'niəlizm), *n.* maintenance by a former imperial power of economic and political influence over liberated peoples.

neomycin (nēōmī'sin), *n.* an antibiotic drug used against some intestinal diseases.

neophilia (nēōfil'iə), *n.* love of novelty and new things, ideas, etc. **-phobia** (-fō'biə), *n.* dread of the new.

neoprene (nē'əpren), *n.* a type of artificial rubber.

neoteny (niot'əni), *n.* indefinite prolongation of period of immaturity ; retention of infantile or juvenile characteristics into adulthood. **-nous,** *adj.*

neurotrophic (nūrətrof'ik), *adj.* pert. to the influence of nerves on tissue nutrition.

neurypnology (nūripnol'əji), *n.* study of hypnotism and of sleep.

novolescence (nōvōles'əns), *n.* state of being new or up to date.

nuclide (nū'klīd), *n.* an atom of specified atomic number and mass number.

nymphet (nim'fet), *n.* a young girl sexually attractive to older men.

NIT (nit), *abbr.* of Numerical Indicator Tube (device by which a computer's calculations are shown on banks of fluorescent tubes).

nosophobia (nosəfō'biə), *n.* morbid dread of disease.

nostopathy (nostop'əthi), *n.* morbid fear of returning to familiar places. **-omania** (-əmā'niə), *n.* abnormally strong desire to return to familiar places ; longing for one's home.

O

O and M, *abbr.* of Organisation and Method (business efficiency).

OAO, *abbr.* of Orbiting Astronomical Observatory (space satellite carrying telescopes).

oceanarium (ōshənar'iəm), *n.* aquarium of sea life.

oceanics (ōshian'iks), *n.* general term for the group of sciences that deal with the ocean. **-nology,** *n.*

oedema (ēdē'mə), *n.* swelling due to accumulation of watery fluid in a body cavity or in the spaces within connective tissue.

OGO, *abbr.* of Orbital Geophysical Observatory.

oinology, -nometer, -nophilist, etc., *see* oenology, etc. (p. 233).

oligomycin (oligəmi'sin), *n.* antibiotic used against plant fungi.

ombudsman (om'boodzman), *n.* commissioner appointed by a legislature to investigate complaints by private citizens against government officials or agencies.

omoplate (ō'mōplāt), *n.* shoulder blade.

OPEC (ō'pek), *abbr.* of Organisation of Oil-producing Eastern Countries.

ophthalmodynamometer (ofthalmədīnəmom'itə), *n.* instrument for measuring blood pressure of the retinal blood vessels.

op(tical) art (op aht, op'tikl), *n.*

non-representational art in which straight or curved lines and geometrical patterns are used to produce an optical illusion.

OR, *abbr.* of Operational Research.

orienteering (ōriəntēr'ing), *n.* a form of cross-country running in which competitors have to find their way by map and compass to a series of check-points on a course over rough terrain.

OSO, *abbr.* of Orbiting Solar Observatory.

overspill (ō'vəspil), *n.* excess of population over the density scheduled or considered desirable for an area.

oxytocin (oksitō'sin), *n.* a pituitary hormone causing contraction of the uterus in childbirth.

ozonosphere (ōzō'nəsfēr), *n.* region in upper atmosphere where most atmospheric ozone is concentrated.

P

pacemaker (pās'mākə), *n. Med.,* electrical device for stimulating or controlling the heart beat.

paciferin (pəsif'ərin), *n.* an infection-resisting factor found in natural foods.

PAL, *abbr.* of Phase Alternation Line (system of colour television transmission).

palletron (pal'itron), *n.* a cyclotron-like apparatus accelerating atomic particles up to a level of one million electron volts.

palynology (pālinol'əji), *n.* study of pollen and spores living and fossil.

pantometer (pantom'itə), *n.* device measuring all angles of elevations and distances.

pantropic (pantrop'ik), *adj.* pert. to life found throughout the tropics; pert. to a virus affecting all tissues.

paraglider (par'əglīdə), *n.* device for guiding and landing a spacecraft after re-entry or for recovering a launching rocket.

parameter (pəram'itə), *n. Math.,* a quantity that is constant in the case considered, but varies in other cases; a variable by the functions of which other variables can be expressed; *gen.,* a measurement by which other measurements can be compared, a dimension.

paraph (par'əf), *n.* a flourish made after a signature; *v.t.* add a p. to ; initial.

paraquat (par'əkwat), *n.* herbicide that kills green vegetation by interfering with photosynthesis.

payload (pā'lōd), *n.* profit-earning load carried by vehicle, aircraft, etc., as distinct from things carried that are necessary for its operation, e.g. freight but not fuel, passengers but not crew.

payola (pāō'lə), *n. sl.*, bribe, *espec.* secret payment as inducement to mention a product, personality, etc., on radio and television programme or in a newspaper.

PCM, *abbr.* of Pulse Code Modulation (method of telephonic transmission).

penetrometer (penitrom'itə), *n.* instrument measuring extremely small quantities of smoke ; instrument measuring the penetrability of a substance by driving a needle into it ; instrument measuring the penetrativeness of X-rays, etc.

perilune (per'ilūn), *n.* point in the path of a body orbiting the moon that is nearest to the centre of the moon.

perlite (pə'līt), *n.* volcanic glass forming, when expanded by heat, an insulating material and a lightweight aggregate added to concrete and plaster. **-tic** (-lit'ik), *adj.* having perlite-like texture.

permafrost (pə'məfrost), *n.* layer of permanently frozen subsoil in polar regions.

permalloy (pə'maloi), *n.* alloy of nickel and iron, most easily magnetised of all materials.

petrochemistry (petrōkem'istri), *n.* science and industry of converting petroleum hydrocarbons into such products as synthetic rubber, synthetic fibres, detergents, and plastics. **-chemical**, *adj.*

phatic (fat'ik), *adj.* denoting speech as a means of sharing feelings or establishing sociability rather than for the communication of information and ideas.

pheromone (fer'əmōn), *n.* hormone-like substance which, when secreted by an animal, can directly influence other animals of the same species, by contact, odour, etc.

phillumenist (filū'mənist), *n.* collector of matchbox labels.

philometrist (filomet'rist), *n.* collector of envelopes, etc., for their postal meter impressions.

philopena (filəpē'nə), *n.* a game of forfeits between two persons, and the forfeit paid.

photochromism (fōtəkrō'mizm), *n.* property of changing colour on exposure to light or other radiation and of reverting to original colour immediately the light or radiation source is removed.

photochromoscope (fōtəkrō'məskōp), *n.* optical device for combining three colour-separation positives and viewing them as a colour photograph.

photocoagulation (fōtəkōagūlā'shn), *n.* surgical coagulation of tissue by means of a laser beam.

photofission (fō'təfishn), *n.* nuclear fission induced by gamma rays.

photogrammetry (fōtəgram'itri), *n.* photographic means of obtaining reliable measurements, e.g. by superimposing photographs of an area or object taken from different angles.

photon (phō'ton), *n.* quantum of electromagnetic radiation, considered as an elementary particle with zero charge and rest mass.

phytotron (fī'tətron), *n.* a bot. laboratory comprising a series of chambers reproducing any condition of temperature, humidity, illumination, or other plant-growth factor.

PIB, *abbr.* of (National) Prices and Incomes Board (U.K.)

pico- (pī'kō-), *prefix* of measurement meaning one million-millionth (10^{-12}). *Abbr.* **p.**

pile (pīl), *n.* in nuclear physics, controlled arrangement of fissionable material for producing a chain reaction.

pilotis (pilō'tis, pilot'i), *n.* a building supported by above-ground reinforced concrete columns, the space round and between which is free for entrance, car-parking, etc.

*plasma (plaz'mə), *n.* an ionised gas.

pneumatometer (nūmətom'itə), *n.* instrument indicating the strength of the lungs by measuring the quantity of air inhaled and exhaled at a breath.

pnigerophobia (nigərəfō'biə), *n.* morbid fear of being smothered.

pogonophobia (pōgənəfō'biə), *n.* morbid fear of beards.

polyamide (poliam'īd), *n.* compound characterised by more than one amide group, a polymeric amide.

polyelectrolyte (poliilek'trəlīt), *n.* a jelly-like plastic compounded of two polymers, one charged positively and one negatively.

polyester (pol'iestə), *n.* a complex compound of hydrocarbons used in making synthetic fibres, resins, and plastics.

polyethylene- (pəlieth'ilēn), *n.* a polymer of ethylene, *espec.* a thermoplastic synthetic resin used for electrical insulation.

polymer (pol'imə), *n.* a compound of the same elements in the same proportion by weight, but of different molecular weights. **-ic** (-mer'ik), *adj.* **-ise** (pol'-), *v.t.* change into polymeric compound, e*espec.* one of higher molecular weight and different properties.

polypropylene (poliprop'ilēn), *n.* a low-density synthetic polymer plastic used for containers, electrical installation, etc.

polystyrene (polistī'rēn), *n.* a synthetic polymer forming a clear plastic or, when expanded, a stiff foam used as insulation.

polyurethane (poliūr'ithān), *n.* a light synthetic polymer prepared in liquid form as a paint that sets extremely hard.

polyvalent (polivā'lənt), *adj. Chem.*, having multiple valency; *Med.*, effective against more than one toxin or strain of micro-organism. **-nce,** *n.*

ponophobia (ponəfō'biə), *n.* hatred or dread of work.

positron (poz'itron), *n.* positive electron, the electron's antiparticle.

posterise (pō'stərīz), *v.t.* to subject (a photograph) to a series of processes which ultimately produce a dense black and pure white picture without half-tones.

potentiometer (pətenshiom'itə), *n.* instrument measuring electromotive force or potential difference by comparison with a known voltage.

Poujadist (pōozhah'dist), *adj.* denoting a right-wing bourgeois political movement in France in the 1950s led by Pierre Poujade.

prepsychotic (prēsīkot'ik), *adj.* having predisposition to mental disorder.

proflavine (prōflā'vēn), *n.* an orange-brown crystalline sulphate of acridine used as an antiseptic for wounds.

program (prō'gram), *n.* instructions to a computer for the solution of a problem, including what calculations to make and in what sequence, and where the information is stored. **-grammer,** *n.* one skilled in the preparation of p. **-grammed,** *adj.* arranged in short easily understood stages or steps, *espec.* such instruction in school subjects.

promine (prō'mēn), *n.* substance in animal tissue which promotes tissue growth.

psephology (sēfol'əji), *n.* scientific analysis of political elections and polls. **-gist,** *n.*

psychedelic (sīkidel'ik), *adj.* "mind-expanding", denoting drugs or other stimulants producing a state of intensified sensual perception.

psychometer (sīkom'itə), *n.* instrument measuring duration and intensity of mental states.

psychotoxic (sīkətoks'ik), *adj.* damaging to the mind, *espec.* of such addictive drugs.

pulsar (pul'sah), *n.* a heavenly body emitting radio pulses of extreme regularity.

PVC, *abbr.* of Poly-Vinyl Chloride (a plastic produced in flexible sheet and solid form).

Q

quadrilin (kwod'rilin), *n.* a fourfold vaccine, *espec.* giving protection against poliomyelitis, diphtheria, whooping cough, and tetanus.

quadriplegia (kwodriplē'jə), *n.* paralysis of all four limbs.

quark (kwahk), *n.* hypothetical sub-atomic entity with fractional electric charge, the supposed material from which hadrons are built up.

quasar (kwā'sah), *n.* a heavenly body, from 4,000 million to

10,000 million light years distant, that is a powerful source of radio energy. *Abbr.* of Quasi-Stellar Radio source.

quograph (kwō′graf), *n.* graph giving the same results as a slide rule.

R

Rachmanism (rak′mənɪzm), *n.* harsh and extortionate landlordism, *espec.* the harassment of controlled-rent tenants.

radioastronomy (rādiōəstron′əmi), *n.* branch of astronomy studying the sources of radio waves reaching Earth from outer space.

radio-heliograph (rādiōhē′liəgraf), *n.* an arrangement of radio-telescopes for receiving and recording the radio waves emitted by the Sun.

radionuclide (rādiōnū′klid), *n.* a radio-active nuclide.

radio-telescope (rādiōteɪ′iskōp), *n.* device, often a large parabolic reflector, for receiving and focusing radio waves from outer space.

rand (rand), *n.* unit of South African currency, divided into 100 cents and having value of former 10 shillings.

R and B, *abbr.* of Rhythm and Blues ("pop" music).

R and D, *abbr.* of Research and Development.

read-out (rēd′owt), *n.* the output of a computer expressed in intelligible form.

redeploy (rēdiploi′), *v.t.* to transfer (personnel) from one area or occupation to another ; to retrain for other work.

reserpine (risə′pēn), *n.* a sedative drug.

retine (ret′ēn), *n.* substance in animal tissue which retards tissue growth.

retrometer (retrom′itə), *n.* device for transmitting sound by modifying a beam of light.

retro-rocket (ret′rōrokit), *n.* rocket with thrust directed in reverse direction to travel, used to slow down space craft.

rhesus (rē′səs), *n.* a species of small Indian monkey. **r. factor,** agglutinating substance present in the red blood cells of most human beings and higher animals, first studied in the blood of rhesus monkeys. *Abbr.* Rh. **Rh-positive,** *adj.* having blood containing the rhesus factor. **Rh-negative,** *adj.* having blood which does not contain the rhesus factor and is liable to react unfavourably to its introduction.

ribosome (rī′bəsōm), *n.* minute angular or spherical particle in the living cell, composed of protein and RNA.

RNA, *abbr.* of Ribo-Nucleic Acid (which in the living cell transmits the genetic information coded in the DNA).

S

sabra (sah′brə), *n. Heb.,* a native-born Israeli.

sapele (səpe′li), *n.* a species of African mahogany.

scopodromic (skopədrom′ik), *adj.* pert. to or denoting guided missiles travelling on a homing course.

scrapie (skrā′pi), *n.* disease of sheep, marked by progressive degeneration of the nervous system.

scuba (skū′bə), *abbr.* of Self-Contained Underwater Breathing Apparatus. **s.-diver,** *n.* diver wearing such apparatus.

SEATO (sē′tō), *abbr.* of South East Asia Treaty Organisation.

SECAM, *abbr.* of Fr. Système en Couleurs à Mémoire (Fr. colour television transmission system).

semi-conductor (sem′ikənduktər), *n.* a solid which is an elec. non-conductor in its pure state or at low temperatures and becomes a conductor when impure or at higher temperatures.

semiology (semiol′əji), *n.* study of signs and signals and their applications. **-iotics,** *n.*

sensor (sen′sə), *n.* device which detects small variations in temperature, pressure, elec. charge, etc.

serotonin (sērətō′nin), *n.* an adrenalin-like crystalline compound occurring in the brain, intestines, and blood platelets, that induces contraction of muscles and blood vessels.

shake (shāk), *n.* unit of time equal to a hundred-millionth of a second, used in describing nuclear processes.

ə=*er* in *father* ; ə̄=*er* in *pert* ; th=*th* in *thin* ; dh=*th* in *then* ; zh=*s* in *pleasure* ; k=*ch* in *loch* ; ṅ=Fr. nasal *n* ; ü=Fr. *u.*

shelta (shel'tə), *n.* secret slang of wandering tinkers and similar groups.

sigmatron (sig'mətron), *n.* machine generating high-potential X-rays.

sit-in (sit'in), *n.* organised passive protest by occupying or sitting down in a prohibited place.

sitophobia (sītəfō'biə), *n.* morbid dread of eating; aversion to food; loss of appetite.

snorkel (snaw'kl), *n.* tube housing air intake and outlet pipes that can be extended above the surface of the water by a submerged submarine; similar device for underwater swimming.

software (soft'wār), *n.* in computers, the ideas communicated to a computer and the means of communicating them, including programs, languages, etc.

solar (sō'lə), *adj.* of or from the sun. **s. cell**, a photoelectric cell converting sunlight into electrical energy, used as a power source in spacecraft.

somascope (sō'məskōp), *n.* instrument detecting disease of the internal organs by "echo-sounding" methods and producing images of the diseased tissue on a television screen.

somatotonic (sōmātəton'ik), *adj. Psych.*, having aggressive, self-assertive temperament associated with mesomorphy.

son-et-lumière (sawn-ā-lü'miār), *Fr.*, "sound and light", an open-air entertainment at night at an historic building expressing its associations and history by means of selective floodlighting and recorded speech and music.

spallation (spalā'shn, spawl-), *n.* splitting into numerous fragments of the nucleus of an atom by high-energy bombardment.

sputnik (sput'nik, spoot'-), *n. Russ.*, a satellite, spacecraft.

SST, *abbr.* of Super-Sonic Transport (aircraft).

stapedectomy (stāpidek'təmi), *n.* surgical removal of the stapes (stirrup bone of the ear) and insertion of an artificial replacement, to relieve deafness.

staphylococcus (stafiləkok'əs), *n.* (*pl.* -ci) a pus-producing bacterium occurring in clusters.

stegophilist (stegof'ilist), *n.* person

whose pastime is climbing the outside of buildings.

stenophobia (stenəfō'biə), *n.* morbid fear of narrow places.

steroid (ster'oid), *n.* any of a large group of fat-soluble organic compounds, including bile acids and hormones, having specific physiological action; a synthetic hormone.

STOL, *abbr.* of Short Take-Off and Landing (aircraft).

streptomycin (streptəmī'sin), *n.* an antibiotic drug extracted from a soil mould, used chiefly in the treatment of tuberculosis.

subsonic (sub'sonik), *adj.* pert. to or at a speed less than the speed of sound in air.

subtopia (subtō'piə), *n.* unplanned, partly built-up area, between outer suburbs and open country.

supernova (soo'pənōvə), *n.* star that suddenly increases immensely in brightness, emitting up to 100 million times its normal light.

synchroscope (singk'rəskop), *n.* device indicating the degree of synchronism of associated machines or moving parts.

synoptophore (sinop'təfor), *n.* instrument correcting defects in eye muscle.

syntagma (sintag'mə), *n.* a systematic collection.

T

tachistoscope (təkis'təskōp), *n.* instrument exposing visual signals, e.g. colours or shapes, for very short periods of time, *espec.* one showing words and phrases at increasing speeds, to accelerate reading.

***tachometer** (takom'itə), *n.* instrument indicating engine speed in revolutions per minute. **-ograph**, (tak'-), *n.* instrument installed in vehicle recording distance travelled, number and length of stops, speeds, and similar data.

tagmeme (tag'mēm), *n.* smallest meaningful unit of grammatical form. *Also* **taxeme**, *n.*

teach-in (tēch'in), *n.* a prolonged debate, *espec.* on a political subject, before an audience of university students after normal teaching hours.